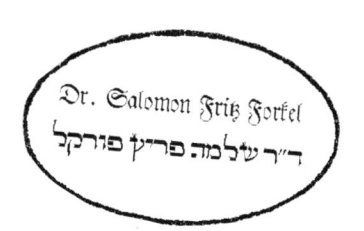

Fijian Reference Grammar

Fijian Reference Grammar

by

Albert J. Schütz

PacificVoices · Honolulu · 2014

Fijian Reference Grammar

Copyright © 2014 by Albert J. Schütz

Cover illustration: Jean Charlot, Qaravi Yaqona: *Kava Ceremony, Kei Viti* No. 2. Color lithograph. 1976, 511 x 411 mm. ©The Jean Charlot Estate, LLC. With permission.

The print depicts the preparation of *yaqona* (*Piper methysticum*), the most important ceremonial drink in Fiji. Two *buli* (cowrie shells) are tied to the *tānoa* (wooden bowl) with a cord made of *magimagi* (sennit), twisted and braided coconut fiber. With one or more *buli* at the far end, the cord points in the direction of guests of rank.

Cover design by James Rumford

For permissions, contact PacificVoices at schutz@hawaii.edu

Photographs, including chapter decorations, © 2014 by Albert J. Schütz

All rights—ink, paper, electronic—reserved.

ISBN–13 978-1499257885
     –10 1499257880

Library of Congress Control Number 2014912694

PacificVoices Press, Honolulu 2014

(PacificVoices.net)

a b c d e f g h
November 2015

DEDICATION

This book is dedicated to the people who helped to produce the first edition, *The Fijian language* (*TFL*): the staff of the Fijian Dictionary Project (FDP), and especially to Tevita R. Nawadra.

Fijian Dictionary Project Staff
Top row: Tevita Nawadra, Paul Geraghty, Albert J. Schütz, Saimone Nanovu
Bottom row: Erelia Nayacakalou, Adi Bera Kurasiga
Not present: Luisa Tuvuki
N.d., but late 1970s

CONTENTS

ACKNOWLEDGMENTS xxvi

INTRODUCTION xxviii

  Purpose xxix

  Methodology xxxi

    1. Use of previous grammars xxxi
    2. The Fijian Dictionary Project and its role in the grammar xxxi
    3. An attempt to avoid translation analysis xxxi
    4. Discourse xxxi
    5. Bibliographic sources xxxii
    6. Glosses xxxii
    7. Text material xxxii
    8. Elicited material, or material out of context xxxiii
    9. Phonology xxxiii
    10. Material from *TFL* excluded from this edition xxxiv
    11. Material added to this edition xxxiv

  Pacific collections consulted xxxv

  Abbreviations xxxv

    1. General xxxvi
    2. Language names xxxvi
    3. Symbols xxxvi
    4. Grammatical terms xxxvii
    5. Texts and other sources xxxviii
    6. Sources of personal communication xxxviii

  Geographical and other data xxxviii

  Decorations xxxviii

A SKETCH OF FIJIAN SPELLING AND PRONUNCIATION 1

1 SOUNDS AND LETTERS 3

  1.1 The alphabet and what the letters represent 4

    1.1.1 Vowels 4
      1.1.1.1 Diphthongs 5
    1.1.2 Consonants 5

  1.2 The Fijian sound system 5

    1.2.1 Syllables 5
    1.2.2 Accent units 5
    1.2.3 Longer phonological units 6

1.3 Discussion: The story behind the alphabet 6

II GRAMMAR: SENTENCES AND VERB PHRASES 9

2 SENTENCE TYPES 10

2.1 Sentence types: Meaning 11
- 2.1.1 Active sentences (VP) 11
- 2.1.2 Stative sentences (VP) 12
- 2.1.3 Existential 12
- 2.1.4 Identifying sentences 12
  - 2.1.4.1 Indefinite identifying sentences (VP) 13
  - 2.1.4.2 Definite identifying sentences (NP + NP) 13
    - 2.1.4.2.1 *A cava* and *o cei* 13

2.2 Sentence types: Form 14
- 2.2.1 VP sentences 15
  - 2.2.1.1 Components of VP sentences 16
- 2.2.2 NP sentences 16

2.3 Phrase order and intonational features 17
- 2.3.1 Intonation as a guide to grammatical structure and meaning 17

2.4 Summary 18

3 CLASSIFYING WORDS AND MORPHEMES 19

3.1 Root vs. marker 19
- 3.1.1 The gray areas of morpheme classification 21

3.2 Discussion 23
- 3.2.1 Root vs. marker 23
- 3.2.2 Noun vs. verb 23

3.3 Summary 26

4 SUBJECTS 28

4.1 Person 29

4.2 Number 29

4.3 Inclusive-exclusive 29

4.4 Forms of respect 30

4.5 Referents: Human or nonhuman? 30

4.6 Morphological analysis 31

4.7 (*K*)*o*- 32

4.8 Morphophonemic changes 32

4.9 Phonological variation 33

4.10 Discussion: Subjects and predicates? 34

- 4.10.1 The traditional analysis 34
- 4.10.2 A reanalysis of "subject" 36
  - 4.10.2.1 The traditional view 38
  - 4.10.2.2 The present view 38

5 VERB PHRASE MARKERS PRECEDING THE HEAD 40

- 5.1 Subjects 40
- 5.2 Tense 41
  - 5.2.1 Past tense (PT): *ā* 41
  - 5.2.2 Future tense (FT): *na* 42
- 5.3 Aspect (ASP) 42
  - 5.3.1 Contrast (past): *sā* 42
  - 5.3.2 Contrast (future): *se* 43
  - 5.3.3 Order change 44
- 5.4 Sequence (SEQ) 45
  - 5.4.1 Unmarked sequence: *qai* 45
    - 5.4.1.1 Order of markers 45
  - 5.4.2 Marked sequence: *mani* 46
    - 5.4.2.1 Order of markers 46
- 5.5 Iteration (ITR): *baci* 46
- 5.6 Habitual (HAB): *dau* 47
  - 5.6.1. *Dau*: Order changes 47
- 5.7 Initiation (INI): *tei* 48
- 5.8 Tentative (TEN): *bau* 48
- 5.9 Individuality (IND): *dui, yā-* 49
  - 5.9.1 *Dui* 49
    - 5.9.1.1 *Dui*: Order changes 50
  - 5.9.2 *Yā-* 50
- 5.10 Extreme, excess (EXT): *rui* 50
  - 5.10.1 *Rui*: Order changes 50
- 5.11 (5.6) *Dau* 50
- 5.12 Proximity, readiness (PRX): *vakarau* 50
- 5.13 Limits of an action/state (LIM) 51
  - 5.13.1 Origin (ORG): *tekivū* 51
  - 5.13.2 Completion (ULT): *tini* 51
- 5.14 Directional (DIR) 52
  - 5.14.1 Preverbal *mai* 52
  - 5.14.2 *Lai* 53
    - 5.14.2.1 *Lai*$_1$ 54

    5.14.2.2 *Lai₂* 54
    5.14.3 *Mai, lai*: Order changes 55
  5.15 Appearance (APR): *rairai* 55
    5.15.1 Order changes 55

6 VERB PREFIXES: *VAKA-* 56

  6.1 Causative 57
    6.1.1 S1 → S2 58
    6.1.2 S2 → A2 58
    6.1.3 S1 → A2 59
    6.1.4 Causatives with the object signaled and expressed (S1 → A2) 60
    6.1.5 A1 → A2 60
    6.1.6 A2 remains A2, but changes roles 61
    6.1.7 Some special kinds of causatives 62
    6.1.8 Causatives: A summary 62
  6.2 Frequentative / distributive / intensive 62
  6.3 Manner and time 63
    6.3.1 N < *vaka*-N 63
    6.3.2 V < *vaka*-N 63
    6.3.3 V < *vaka*-V (stative) 64
  6.4 Possessing N or characterized by N 64
  6.5 Pretend, perform as a game 65
  6.6 *Vaka-* and grammatical ambiguity 65
  6.7 Discussion: *Vaka-* 66

7 VERB PREFIXES: *VEI-* / *VĪ-* 67

  7.1 Reciprocal, mutual (active) 67
    7.1.1 Types of verbs 68
    7.1.2 Expressing an object 69
  7.2 Reciprocal, mutual (stative) 69
    7.2.1 Kin terms and other relationships 69
    7.2.2 Spatial and distance relationships 70
  7.3 General, formalized *vei-* forms 71
    7.3.1 General, formalized: Verbs of motion 71
    7.3.2 General, formalized: Other active verbs 72

8 VERB PREFIXES: *VIA-*, *VIAVIA-*,
  ***TAWA-*, AND OTHERS 74**

  8.1 Desiderative: *via-* 74
  8.2 Impression: *viavia-* 76

8.3 Negative: *tawa-*, *tabu-* 76
   8.3.1 *Tawa-* 76
   8.3.2 *Tabu-* 77

8.4 Stative prefixes 77
   8.4.1 *Lau-* 77
   8.4.2 *Ma-* 78

8.5 Artificial or created circumstances: *-tā-* 79

8.6 More *-tā-* forms 80

8.7 Stative prefix: *sa-* 80

8.8 Continuing motion: *sau-* 80

8.9 Stative suffix: *-(C)a* (with or without reduplication) 80

8.10 Distributive counter: *yā-* 81

9 VERB CLASSIFICATION 1: EXISTENTIALS 82

9.1 Existential verbs 82
   9.1.1 *Tiko, tū* 83
   9.1.2 Less common existentials 83
   9.1.3 *E* + numeral 83

9.2 Summary 84

10 VERB CLASSIFICATION 2: ACTIVES AND STATIVES (VALENCY 1) 85

10.1 The active-stative opposition 85
   10.1.1 Semantic criteria 85
   10.1.2 A functional criterion 86

10.2 Problems with the classification 86

10.3 Summary 90

11 VERB CLASSIFICATION 3: ONE- AND TWO-REFERENT VERBS (VALENCY 2) 91

11.1 One-referent verbs 92
   11.1.1 A1 verbs 92
   11.1.2 S1 verbs 94

11.2 Two-referent verbs 94
   11.2.1 A2 verbs 94
   11.2.2 S2 verbs 95

11.3 Discussion 96

11.4 Summary 97

12 VERB CLASSIFICATION 4: SEMANTICS 98

12.1 Verbs referring to motion 98
12.2 Verbs referring to emission or projection 99
12.3 Verbs referring to processes 99
12.4 Verbs referring to states of mind 99
12.5 Verbs referring to judgment 100
12.6 Verbs referring to skills 101
12.7 Miscellaneous verbs 101

13 VERB DERIVATION: HOW VERBS CHANGE CLASSES 103

13.1 The mechanics of derivation 103
13.2 Types of derivation 104
    13.2.1 Active to stative 104
        13.2.1.1 A2 → S2 104
        13.2.1.2 A2 → S2 (*lau-*) 105
    13.2.2 Stative to active 105
        13.2.2.1 S2 + -C-a → A2 105
        13.2.2.2 S2 + reduplication → A2 106
        13.2.2.3 S2 + modifier ("incorporated object") → A2 106
        13.2.2.4 *Vei-* + S2 → A2 107
        13.2.2.5 S1→A2 107
13.3 Prefixes that delete the actor 107
    13.3.1 The distinction among statives 109
13.4 A prefix that deletes the goal, producing a1 verbs 110
13.5 Discussion 111
    13.5.1 Reduplication as a means of providing contrasting forms 111
    13.5.2 Discussion: *ta-*, *ca-*, et al. 112

14 VERB REDUPLICATION 115

14.1 To indicate repetition, frequency, or prolongation 115
14.2 To allow an S2 verb to be used actively without signaling or expressing the object 117
14.3 To form S1 verbs from a variety of roots (with -C)*a*) 117
14.4 To allow certain verbs to modify nouns 117
14.5 To indicate collection, groups 118
14.6 To indicate pretense, aimlessness (with *vaka-*) 119
    14.6.1 *Vaka-*, *-tā-*, and partial reduplication 119
14.7 To modify verbs 120
14.8 To indicate discontinuous, dispersive (partial reduplication) 120
14.9 To form S1 verbs from S2 verbs 121

14.10 To indicate a partitive sense 121
14.11 To indicate aimless action 121
14.12 Miscellaneous changes through reduplication 121
    14.12.1 Semantic changes 121
    14.12.2 Ambiguity, and some efforts to avoid it 122
14.13 The formal manifestations of reduplication 122
    14.13.1 Restrictions 122
    14.13.2 Derived forms 124
    14.13.3 Compounds 126
14.14 Reduplication of markers 126
14.15 Reduplication of person-number markers, including possessives 128
14.16 Reduplication of borrowed words 128

15 COMPOUND VERBS 129

15.1 Formal classification 130
    15.1.1 Markers of transitivity following the construction 130
    15.1.2 Markers of transitivity after each root 130
    15.1.3 Markers of transitivity and other markers 131
15.2 The semantics of compound verbs 131
15.3 Discussion 132

16 TRANSITIVITY 133

16.1 The transitive suffixes 134
16.2 Different transitive suffixes with the same verb 135
16.3 The meanings of the *-Caki* forms 136
    16.3.1 General transitivizer 136
    16.3.2 Reason 138
    16.3.3 Means or accompaniment 140
    16.3.4 Intensive 142
    16.3.5 Lexical change 143
    16.3.6 Duration 144
    16.3.7 Dispersive movement: *-yaki* 145
16.4 Constructions without the transitive suffix 146
    16.4.1 The *gunu-yaqona* construction 146
    16.4.2 The *viri na polo* construction 150
        16.4.2.1 Discussion 152
        16.4.2.2 *Gunu-yaqona* type constructions: Conclusions 153
16.5 Summary 153
16.6 Transitivity: History and discussion 154
    16.6.1 Definitions of transitivity 154

16.6.2 The meaning (?) of *-C-* 156
16.6.3 Suffix or part of the stem? 157
16.6.4 *-Ca* vs. *-Ci* 158
16.6.5 The various functions of *-Caki* 158
  16.6.5.1 The independence of *vaka-* and *-taki* 158
  16.6.5.2 The meaning of the *-Caki* forms 160

17 OBJECTS 163

17.1 Person-number markers and names 163
17.2 Classification according to person 164
  17.2.1 First person, second person, and proper noun 164
  17.2.2 Third person 164
17.3 Discussion: Underlying *i* object marker? 164

18 VERB PHRASE MARKERS AFTER THE HEAD 166

18.1 Objects 166
18.2 Direction (DIR) 166
  18.2.1 *Cake* 'upward' 166
  18.2.2 *Sobu* 'downward' 167
  18.2.3 *Tani* 'away, different' 167
  18.2.4 *Laivi* 'utterly' 168
18.3 Concomitant (CNC): *vata* 168
18.4 Completive aspect (asp): *oti* 169
18.5 Potential (POT): *rawa* 169
  18.5.1 The difference between *rawa ni V* and *V rawa* 169
18.6 Limitation (LIM): *wale, bau, bulu* 170
18.7 Inclusion (INC): *kece, taucoko* 171
  18.7.1 *Kece* 'all' 171
  18.7.2 *Taucoko* 'wholly, completely' 171
  18.7.3 *Duadua* 'alone' 172
  18.7.4 *Soti/sō* (intensifier) 172
18.8 Intensive (INT): *sara* 172
18.9 Iteration (ITR): *tale* 174
18.10 Respectful address (RES): *saka* 174
18.11 Continuative aspect (CNT): *tiko, tū, koto, nō, toka, voli* 175
  18.11.1 *Tiko* 175
  18.11.2 *Tū* 176
  18.11.3 *Toka* 176
  18.11.4 *Koto* (*nō*) 177
    18.11.4.1 *Nō* 178

18.11.5 *Voli* 'roundabout' 178
 18.12 Initiation (INI): *beka*, *mada*, *bagi* 178
   18.12.1 *Beka* (moderative) 179
   18.12.2 *Mada* 179
   18.12.3 *Bagi* (expectation) 180
   18.12.4 *Gona* 'aforementioned' (AFM) 180
 18.13 Limitation (LIM): *gā*, *lā* 180
   18.13.1 *Gā* with other markers: *tale gā*, *wale gā*, and *mada gā* 181
     18.13.1.1 *Tale gā* 'also' 181
     18.13.1.2 *Wale gā* 'only' 181
     18.13.1.3 *Mada gā* 'just' 182
   18.13.2 *Lā* 182
 18.14 Direction (DIR) 182
   18.14.1 *Mai* (toward focal point) 182
   18.14.2 *Yani* (toward a point established by context) 184
   18.14.3 Discussion: The reference point for VP directional markers 186
 18.15 Affirmation/negation 186
   18.15.1 *Lī* 'really?' (AFF) 186
   18.15.2 *Nē* 'is it not?' 186
   18.15.3 *Ē* Sentence-final affirmation 186

19 THE NOUN PHRASE: SEMANTICS AND CLASSIFICATION 188

 19.1 The semantic function of the NP 188
 19.2 Noun and NP classification 191
   19.2.1 Integral and partitive nouns 191
   19.2.2 Common vs. proper 192
     19.2.2.1 Place names 192
     19.2.2.2 Personal names 193
   19.2.3 Primary vs. secondary NPs 193
 19.3 Semantic and grammatical mismatches 195
 19.4 The structure of the basic NP 195
 19.5 Interrogative nouns 196
 19.5.1 *Cava* 'what?' 196
 19.5.2 *Cei* 'who' 196

20 NP ARTICLES 197

 20.1 *O*: Proper article 197
   20.1.1 Proper nouns as part of the VP 197
   20.1.2 *I*: Proper object marker 198
   20.1.3 Proper pronouns specifying subjects 198

20.1.4 Proper pronouns specifying objects 199
20.1.5 Proper NPs in a special use beyond personal names 199

20.2 *Na*: Common/definite article 199

20.2.1 Definiteness based on sentence structure 200
20.2.2 Definiteness based on semantics 201
20.2.3 Indefinite constructions 202
20.2.4 Generalization: Dealing with the requirements of discourse 204
20.2.5 The analysis of a text with respect to definiteness, indefiniteness, and generality 206
20.2.6 *Na* vs. *a* 208
20.2.7 Optional omission of *na* before possessives 209
20.2.8 Summary 209
20.2.9 Nouns that can take either *na* or *o*, or both 209

21 NP FUNCTION MARKERS 211

21.1 Ablative NPs 212

21.1.1 Types of nouns that occur in common ablative phrases 212
21.1.1.1 Time 212
21.1.1.2 Space 212
21.1.1.3 Time and space 213
21.1.1.4 Means or instrument 214
21.1.1.5 Material, contents 215
21.1.1.6 Metaphorical space or time 215
21.1.1.7 Ambiguity 215

21.1.2 Function of ablative NPs 216
21.1.2.1 Locatives 216
21.1.2.1.1 *E* 216
21.1.2.1.2 *Mai* 216
21.1.2.1.3 Locative NPs as comment 217
21.1.2.2 Directional NPs 218
21.1.2.2.1 *I (ki)* 218
21.1.2.2.2 Ablative *mai* vs. postverbal *mai* 219
21.1.2.3 *Vei* 220
21.1.2.3.1 *Mai vei* and *ki vei* 221
21.1.2.4 Contractions of the ablative markers 221

21.1.3 Discussion: Ablative NPs 223
21.1.3.1 Are locative and directional dependent on the semantics of the verb? 223
21.1.3.2 The function of ablative NPs 224

21.2 Comitative NPs 224

21.2.1 Discussion: How many entities involved? 225
21.2.2 Contraction of *kei* + third person singular: *kaya* 225
21.2.3 Discussion 225

21.3 Proper accusative NPs 226
21.4 Vocative: i_3 226
21.5 Attributive possessive 227

22 NP GRAMMATICAL MODIFIERS 228

22.1 Discourse marker: *gona* 'aforementioned' (AFM) 228
22.2 Limitation (LIM): *wale gā* 228
22.3 Inclusion (INC) 229
    22.3.1 *Kece* 'all' 229
    22.3.2 *Taucoko* 'all, wholly, completely' 229
    22.3.3 *Soti* (*sō*) 229
22.4 Intensifier (INT): *sara* 230
22.5 Iteration (ITR): *tale, tale gā* 230
22.6 Moderative, dubitative (TEN): *beka* 230
22.7 Limitation (LIM): *gā* 231

23 NOUN AFFIXATION 232

23.1 Collective, distributive (DIS): *vei-* 232
23.2 Individuality (IND): *dui* 233
23.3 "Poetical suffixes": *-ri, -a, -ya* 233
23.4 Reduplication of noun roots 234
    23.4.1 Form 234
    23.4.2 Semantic categories 234

24 NOMINALIZATION 235

24.1 Derived nominalization: *ī-* nouns 235
    24.1.1 Reduplication of *i-* forms 236
    24.1.2 *I-* nouns from derived verbs 236
    24.1.3 *I-* nouns: A semantic view 237
        24.1.3.1 Another source for *i-* nouns? 239
24.2 Direct nominalization: Verbs used as nouns 239
    24.2.1 The function of direct nominalization 239

25 PERSONAL DEICTIC NOUNS 242

25.1 Deictic locative nouns 242
25.2 Personal locatives used as locative phrases 242
    25.2.1 *Ayā* 243
25.3 Time 243
25.4 Personal locatives in the NP + NP construction 244

25.5 The optional *o* 245
    25.5.1 *Oyā* vs. *koyā* 246

SECTION IV: OPERATIONS 247

26 SPECIFICATION 249

  26.1 Specification within the VP 250
    26.1.1 Formal manifestations 251
    26.1.2 Levels of specificity 252
      26.1.2.1 Implicit 252
      26.1.2.2 Signaled 252
      26.1.2.3 Expressed 253
    26.1.3 Proper NPs as objects 254
  26.2 Specification outside the VP: Added NPs 255
    26.2.1 NPs specifying the subject 255
    26.2.2 NPs specifying the object 256
    26.2.3 NPs specifying both the subject and the object 256
      26.2.3.1 Ambiguity in subject and object NP specification 257
      26.2.3.2 Summary of subject and object specification 259
    26.2.4 NPs specifying possessive forms 260
      26.2.4.1 Limitations on specification of possessives 260
      26.2.4.2 "Translationese" and its effect on possession specification 261
      26.2.4.3 Discussion: Specification of possessed forms 261
  26.3 NPs specifying person-number markers in secondary NPs 262
  26.4 How many referents? 264
  26.5 Multiple specification 264
  26.6 Examples of different levels of specification 265
  26.7 Summary: Specification 269

27 VERB MODIFICATION 271

  27.1 Verb + (*vaka-*) stative 271
    27.1.1 Simple adverbs 271
    27.1.2 Derived adverbs 273
      27.1.2.1 Statives 273
      27.1.2.2 Deictic locatives 273
      27.1.2.3 Numerals (including interrogative) 274
      27.1.2.4 Nouns (including interrogative) 274
  27.2 Verb + noun 275
  27.3 Verb + ablative NP 275
  27.4 Verb + subordinae VP 275

28 NOUN MODIFICATION 276

28.1 Types of semantic attribution 276

28.2 Formal types of modification 277

    28.2.1 Nouns modified by verbs or verb phrases 278

    28.2.2 Nouns modified by nouns or forms related to nouns 278

28.3 Nouns modified by verbs 278

    28.3.1 Integral noun < stative: *vale levu* 'big house' 279

    28.3.2 Partitive noun < *i* + stative: *raba-i-levu* 'wide' 279

    28.3.3 Noun < (partitive noun < stative): *tamata mata dua* 'one-eyed person' 280

    28.3.4 Noun < (partitive noun + *i* + stative of extent): *vale raba-i-levu* 'wide house' 280

    28.3.5 Noun < (S2 < N): *kā tau-ci uca* 'rained-upon thing' 280

    28.3.6 Series of modifiers: *qito kaukaua ka savasavā* 'hard and clean game' 281

    28.3.7 Noun < active verb: *waqa vuka* 'flying boat (airplane)' 281

    28.3.8 Noun <*dau*-active verb: *tamata dau gunu* 'person always drinking (drunkard)' 282

    28.3.9 Noun < VP: *kā e rai-c-a* 'thing she saw' 282

28.4 Nouns modified by nouns or related forms 284

    28.4.1 Noun < noun: *vale vatu* 'stone house' 284

    28.4.2 Noun < (integral N + S1): *vanua qele vinaka* 'good-soiled land' 285

    28.4.3 Noun < *vaka*- form: *vale vaka-Viti* 'Fijian house' 285

    28.4.4 Noun < (*ni* + Noun): *vale ni kuro* 'house for pots (kitchen)' 285

29 SUBORDINATION 286

29.1 *Ni* 286

    29.1.1 *Ni* phrases that specify 286

        29.1.1.1 Object specification 287

        29.1.1.2 Subject specification 288

            29.1.1.2.1 Subject raising and the idiomatic use of *ni* phrases 288

            29.1.1.2.1.1 Negation and *ni* phrases 289

        29.1.1.3 Layering of *ni* phrases 289

    29.1.2 *Ni* phrases that modify 289

        29.1.2.1 *Ni* phrases that indicate cause 290

        29.1.2.2 The meaning of modifying *ni* phrases 291

    29.1.3 Morphophonemic changes 292

    29.1.4 *Ka ni* 293

    29.1.5 The intonation of *ni* phrases 293

    29.1.6 Structural differences between types of *ni* phrases 294

29.2 *Me* 294

29.2.1 *Me vakā* 296
29.2.2 Morphophonemic changes 296
29.3 *Kē* 296
29.3.1 Relationships outside the sentence 297
29.3.2 *Kē* marking both phrases 297
29.3.3 *Kevakā* 298
29.3.4 Morphophonemic changes 298
29.4 *Sē* 298
29.4.1 Types of verbs in the independent phrase 299
29.4.2 The semantic relationship between *sē* and the independent VP 300
29.4.3 Question words in *sē* phrases 300
29.4.4 Morphophonemic changes 301
29.5 *Dē* 301
29.5.1 Adversative vs. subjunctive 301
29.5.2 Morphophonemic changes 302

30 POSSESSION 303

30.1 Possessive forms 304
30.1.1 Suffixes 304
30.1.2 Possessive classifiers (PC) 304
30.1.3. Phrasal markers 305
30.2 Morphological and syntactic patterns 305
30.3 Alienable vs. inalienable possession 306
30.3.1 Inalienable possession 307
30.3.1.1 Person-number markers 307
30.3.1.2 *Kē-$_2$* 308
30.3.2 Alienable possession 308
30.3.2.1 Possessive classifier prefixes 309
30.3.2.1.1 *Mē-* 309
30.3.2.1.2 *Kē-$_1$* 310
30.3.2.1.3 *Nō-* 310
30.4. Phrasal possessive modifiers 310
30.4.1 *Ni* 311
30.4.1.1 Semantic narrowing 311
30.4.1.2 Layering of attributive *ni* phrases 312
30.4.1.3 Some semantic problems 314
30.4.1.4 Nominalization with *ni* phrases 315
30.4.1.5 Attribution outside the *ni* phrase 316
30.4.1.6 *Ni* as a word-builder 316
30.4.2 *I* 317
30.4.2.1 Possessive classifiers + *i* 317

30.5 The semantics of possession 318
   30.5.1 Different relationships between the referents of the possessor and the possessed 318

30.6 Definiteness 319

30.7 Variables of the alienable-inalienable contrast 320

30.8 Semantic and formal mismatches 322

30.9 Possessives used as nouns 322
   30.9.1 Discussion 323

30.10 Reduplication of possessive forms 323

30.11 Specification and variation in possessive constructions 323

30.12 Discussion: Possession as gender? 324

31 COORDINATION, SENTENCE MODIFIERS, AND SUMMARY OF OPERATIONS 326

31.1 Coordination 326
   31.1.1 *Ka (a)* 326
   31.1.2 *Kei* 327
   31.1.3 *Sē* 327
   31.1.4 *Ia* 328

31.2 Sentence modifiers of affirmation (AFF) 328
   31.2.1 *Lī* 'isn't that so?' 328
   31.2.2 *Nē* 'is it not?' 329
   31.2.3 *Ē* Sentence-final affirmation 329

31.3 Summary of operations 329

SECTION V: PHONOLOGY 331

32 PHONOLOGICAL UNITS: A SUMMARY 332

32.1 Phonological units and their characteristics 332

32.2 Segmental phonemes 333

32.3 Syllables 334

32.4 Measures 334

32.5 Phonological phrases 334

32.6 Phonological sentences 335

33 VOWELS 336

33.1 Short vowels 336

33.2 Long vowels 337
   33.2.1 Simple long vowels 337
   33.2.2 Complex long vowels (diphthongs) 338

33.2.2.1 Defining *diphthong* 338

33.3 Vowel sequences across morpheme boundaries 341

   33.3.1 Accent determined by morpheme type 341
   33.3.2 Accent determined by position 342
   33.3.3 Accent determined by speech style 342

33.4 Vowel assimilation 342

   33.4.1 The influence of accent on vowel quality and length 343
      33.4.1.1 Stress 343
      33.4.1.2 Length 343
      33.4.1.3 Vowel position 343
      33.4.1.4 Tension 344
      33.4.1.5 Pitch 344
   33.4.2 Vowel assimilation in diphthongs 344
   33.4.3 A note on different degrees of noncontrastive vowel length 345

33.5 Vowel sequences *ao* and *oe* 345

33.6 A recent addition to the vowel inventory 346

34 CONSONANTS 347

34.1 Indigenous consonants 347

   34.1.1 /t/ [t] Voiceless apico-alveolar stop, unaspirated and lenis 347
   34.1.2 /k/ [k] Voiceless dorso-velar stop, relatively unaspirated and lenis 349
   34.1.3 /b/ [mb] Voiced prenasalized bilabial stop 349
   34.1.4 /d/ [nd] Voiced prenasalized apico-alveolar stop 349
   34.1.5 /q/ [ŋg] Voiced prenasalized dorso-velar stop 349
   34.1.6 /r/ [ř] ~ [r̃] Voiced apico-alveolar tap ~ trill 349
   34.1.7 /dr/ [nř] ~ [nr̃] Voiced prenasalized apico-alveolar tap~trill 349
   34.1.8 /s/ [s] Voiceless apico-alveolar grooved fricative 349
   34.1.9 /v/ [β] Voiced bilabial slit fricative 349
   34.1.10 /c/ [ð] Voiced apico-dental fricative 350
   34.1.11 /m/ [m] Voiced bilabial nasal 350
   34.1.12 /n/ [n] Voiced apicodental nasal 350
   34.1.13 /g/ [ŋ] Voiced back-velar nasal 350
   34.1.14 /l/ [l] Voiced apicoalveolar lateral 350
   34.1.15 /w/ [w] High back rounded glide 350
      34.1.15.1 Problems with /w/ 350
   34.1.16 /y/ [ɛ] ↔ [y] 351
      34.1.16.1 *Y*: Discussion 352

34.2 "Traditional" introduced consonants 353

   34.2.1 /p/ [p] Voiceless bilabial stop, relatively unaspirated and lenis 353
   34.2.2 /f/ [f] Voiceless labiodental slit fricative 354

34.2.3 /j/ [č] Voiceless alveo-palatal affricate 355
34.3 More recent introductions from other Fijian languages 355
    34.3.1 /z/ [nǰ] Prenasalized voiced alveo-palatal affricate 355
    34.3.2 /h/ Voiceless glottal fricative 355
      34.3.2.1 Discussion: *h* 355
    34.3.3 /ʔ/ *Gato* (glottal stop) 356
    34.3.4 /x/ Voiceless dorso-velar fricative 356
    34.3.5 /xw/ Labialized voiceless dorso-velar fricative 356
    34.3.6 /kw/ Labialized voiceless dorso-velar stop 357
    34.3.7 /qw/ Labialized voiced prenasalized dorso-velar stop 357
    34.3.6 /gw/ Labialized voiced dorso-velar nasal 357
34.4 More recent introductions from outside 357
    34.4.1 Voiced stops without a preceding nasal 357
34.5 New consonants borrowed from English 358
    34.5.1 *sh* [š] 358
34.6 Alternate forms 358
34.7 Sociolinguistic context 358

35 SYLLABLES 360

35.1 Types of syllables 360
35.2 Integrated syllables 361
35.3 Two major interpretations of Fijian syllables 362
    35.3.1 The phonetic syllable: An interpretation based on auditory impression 362
    35.3.2 The phonological syllable: An interpretation based on a possible underlying structure 362
    35.3.3 Summary of the orthodox position 363
35.4 Changes to the traditional syllable structure 364
    35.4.1 Syllable-final consonants 365
      35.4.1.1 Resultant consonant combinations 365
    35.4.2 Consonant clusters 365
      35.4.2.1 Syllable-initial clusters 366
      35.4.2.2 Syllable-final clusters 366
    35.4.3 Syllabic consonants 366
35.5 Sociolinguistic context 366
    35.5.1 Speech vs. writing 367
    35.5.2 Regional and stylistic variation 367
    35.5.3 Generational differences and Urban Fijian 367
    35.5.4 Formal vs. informal 368
    35.5.5 Innovative vs. conservative 368
    35.5.6 Urban vs. rural 368

35.5.7 Control of English 368

36 MEASURES AND ACCENT 370

36.1 Measure types 371

36.2 Diphthongization as a means of shortening bases 372

36.3 Vowel and diphthong shortening 373

    36.3.1 Shortening of simple long vowels 373

    36.3.2 Shortening of complex long vowels (diphthongs) 374

    36.3.3 Realignment of measures through vowel and diphthong shortening 375

    36.3.4 The effects of vowel and diphthong shortening 376

        36.3.4.1 Reducing the number of syllables 376

        36.3.4.2 Reducing the number of V syllables 376

        36.3.4.3 Reducing the number of measures 376

        36.3.4.4 Movement toward CVCV—the optimum measure type 377

            36.3.4.4.1 The effect of diphthongization on the number of CVCV forms 378

36.4 The relative stability of different measure shapes 379

36.5 Vowel shortening across phrase boundaries 379

36.6 The effect of one-syllable suffixes on accent 381

36.7 The phonemic status of accent 381

36.8 Is accent predictable? 382

    36.8.1 Rules based on syllable count 382

    36.8.2 The utility of loanwords as data 383

    36.8.3 Accent patterns in indigenous words and phrases 384

        36.8.3.1 Disyllables and trisyllables 384

    36.8.4 Does morphology play a role in determining measures? 386

36.9 The predictability of accent: Summary 387

36.10 The relationship between measures and morphemes? 388

    36.10.1 The study 388

    36.10.2 The results 390

36.11 Summary 390

37 PHONOLOGICAL PHRASES 391

37.1 Phrase peaks that indicate normal phrase accent 391

37.2 Phrase peaks that indicate contrast 392

37.3 Phrase terminals 393

37.4 Discussion: Phonological phrases as contrastive units 394

38 PHONOLOGICAL SENTENCES 396

38.1 Phonetic details 396

38.1.1 Portion 1 396
38.1.2 Portion 2 398
38.1.3 Portion 3. The terminal 399
38.2 Match between intonation portions and measures 399
38.3 Intonational segmentation of shorter sentences 399
38.4 Step vs. glide 400
38.5 Formal and functional classification 401
  38.5.1 Terminal phrases 401
    38.5.1.1 Falling phrases 401
      38.5.1.1.1 Special characteristics of questions with question words 401
    38.5.1.2 Rising phrases 401
      38.5.1.2.1 Vocatives 403
  38.5.2 Nonterminal phrases 403
    38.5.2.1 Series intonation 404

39 LINKS BETWEEN GRAMMAR AND PHONOLOGY 405

39.1 The relationship of accent to morphology-syntax 406
39.2 Formal and functional classification of morphemes 407
  39.2.1 Classification according to form (phonological) 407
  39.2.2 Classification according to function (grammatical) 407
39.3 Combining forms 408
  39.3.1 Particle + base 408
  39.3.2 Base + particle 409
  39.3.3 Base + particle + base 409
  39.3.4 Base + base 410
  39.3.5 Particle + particle 411
  39.3.6 Particle + base + particle 412
  39.3.7 Summary 413
39.4 The effect of complementary or opposing tendencies 413

40 INTONATION AND ITS GRAMMATICAL CORRELATES 414

40.1 Sentences consisting of two phrases 414
  40.1.1 Embedding of phonological phrases 417
40.2 Phonological sentences consisting of more than two phrases 417
  40.2.1 Hierarchical structure 417
40.3 Summary 422

41 THE LAST WORD 423

41.1 New features 424
41.2 Features that are not new, but need to be emphasized 424

      41.2.1 Phonology 424
      41.2.2 Subjects, objects, and transitivity 425
      41.2.3 Specificity 427
      41.2.4 Verb classification 428
      41.2.5 Verb derivation 428
      41.2.6 *Na*: definite N marker 428
  41.3 How suggestions from reviews are treated 429
  41.4 Summary 431

REFERENCES 433

INDEX 443

ACKNOWLEDGMENTS

The preparation of the predecessor to this work, *TFL*, was made possible in part by a grant from the Program for Research Tools and Reference Works of the National Endowment for the Humanities, an independent federal agency. Further support came from:

The American Council of Learned Societies
The American-Fijian Foundation and Raymond Burr
The Center for Asian and Pacific Studies, University of Hawai'i at Mānoa
The Research Council, University of Hawai'i at Mānoa
The Social Science Research Institute, University of Hawai'i at Mānoa

As for help with the analysis and examples, almost every chapter includes the initials of my colleagues at the Fijian Dictionary Project. Primarily, I drew on the advice of Paul Geraghty and Tevita R. Nawadra, as shown by the many references to their writings and advice. The other members of the staff who advised me were Saimone Nanovu, Adi Bera Kurasiga, Luisa Tuvuki, and Erelia Nayacakalou. David Arms, although not on the staff, was always willing to offer his insights into the language. I am grateful also to Apenisa Seduadua, of the Department of Education, who helped with the grammar when he was an MA candidate at the University of Hawai'i at Mānoa. Because there are so many "personal communication" citations from these people, I have abbreviated such references to initials (TRN, PG, SN, BK, LT, EN, DA, and AS) and the date. To all those people—*Vinaka vakalevu*!

Although he is already mentioned above, I owe special thanks to Tevita R. Nawadra, who was closely associated with the dictionary project, first as a trainee in linguistics at the University of Hawai'i at Mānoa, and next as the first Editor of the dictionary. His death deprived me not only of a valued colleague but also of a good friend.

In addition to those people mentioned earlier whose contributions are noted throughout the text, many other friends and colleagues have assisted in the development of the first edition of this grammar from a rough idea through various articles and drafts to the published version. Those who read drafts or helped otherwise with the content are:

David G. Arms, Bruce G. Biggs, B. J. Blake, Iovanna Condax, Samuel H. Elbert, Jeanne D. Gibson, Ward Goodenough, George W. Grace, Sheldon P. Harrison, Renée Heyum, Charles F. Hockett, Irwin J. Howard, Karl K. Ichida, Robert Krohn, Patricia Lee, Frank Lichtenberk, Peter C. Lincoln, Anatole Lyovin, Timothy Macnaught, Pio Manoa, George B. Milner, Paz Naylor, Andrew K. Pawley, Kenneth L. Rehg, Archibald C. Reid, Maciu Salato, Hans Schmidt, Jeff Siegel, Lawrence C. Thompson, M. Terry Thompson, Robert Tonkinson, Lindsay I. Verrier, John U. Wolff, and A. H. Wood.

I am especially grateful to James A. Tharp for his careful reading of the entire manuscript. His sharp eye for inconsistencies and typographical errors removed a number of stumbling blocks for the reader. In addition, I should like to thank the official editor, Joel Bradshaw, not only for his work, but for his patience in helping to meet a deadline.

The following people helped with the computer aspects of the project:

Sue Archibeque, Eileen Cain, Steven Egesdal, Joel Fagan, Robert Hsu, Gregory Lee, Mariana Maduell, Ann Peters, M. Terry Thompson, and Judith Wang.

Without the help, advice, and encouragement of Lawrence C. Thompson and M. Terry Thompson, I could never have completed the tedious task of printing *TFL* in the days before personal computers and laser printers.

A number of people helped in ways not directly connected with the content of the grammar, but still essential for its completion: Byron W. Bender, Fergus Clunie, Julia Hall, W. Vance Hall, Tom Hill, K. Lunde, Robert Kiste, Beatrice Parham, Helena Parham, Jemesa Robarobalevu, Robert T. Sanders, Kerry E. Stevens, Manoa Tawake, Sandra Tawake, Donald M. Topping, Stephen Uhalley, Jr., and Sara Wolf.

I should like to express my gratitude to His Excellency the Prime Minister of Fiji, Ratu Sir Kamisese Mara, for his guardianship over the dictionary project, which made a decade of research possible.

For help with the present edition, *vinaka vakalevu* to David Lagilagi Dugucanavanua, Steven Egesdal, Apolonia Tamata (of the Fijians Trust Fund Board in Suva), Larry Thomas, and Kevin Bätscher. Also, *mahalo* to Nora Lum and Jennifer Kanda (who keep the Department of Linguistics running smoothly) for their help in solving computer problems.

I am especially grateful to James Rumford for his help in navigating through the terra incognita of a new kind of publishing, for his outstanding cover design, and for his artist's eye that helped convince me that a 7 x 10 format would make for easier reading.

Finally, a special *vinaka vakalevu* to a lineage of curators of the Pacific Collection at Hamilton Library, University of Hawai'i at Mānoa for the past fifty years—Janet E. Bell, Renée Heyum, Karen M. Peacock, Stuart Dawrs, and Eleanor Kleiber—and their talented and friendly staff members, all of whom made research on Fijian both pleasurable and rewarding.

INTRODUCTION[1]

By the term Fijian language ... I mean the language of the predominant race of people resident in what have been long known as the Fiji Islands and which is fast becoming the lingua franca of the whole group.

"The Fijian language"
Beauclerc 1908–10b:65

Bau is the Athens of Fiji, the dialect there spoken has now become the classical dialect of the whole group. In it all translations and official documents are written, and it will probably soon supersede all other forms of the language, except among the lowest orders of the people.

Two years in Fiji
Forbes 1875:167–68

The most elegant of these is the dialect of Mbau, which is as much the Attic of Fiji, as those by whom it is spoken are the Athenians of the group ...

Fiji: Our new province in the South Seas
De Ricci 1875:38

BAU IN 1961. ©AJS

---

[1] The gist of this section appears in *TFL*, although some changes have been made.

In 1971, a committee of people interested in Fijian—both native speakers and visiting linguists—decided that a Fijian monolingual dictionary was needed. The Fijian representatives on the committee wrote:

> The basic outlook of the dictionary should be one of recording Fijian words for speakers of Fijian now and in the future.

It was with this philosophy that the Fijian Dictionary Project (FDP) was formed. Since that time, it moved from external to internal direction and support, reflected in its new name: Tabana Ni Vosa Kei Na iTovo Vakaviti (Institute of Fijian Language & Culture). It serves not only as a research unit but as an *académie* as well, advising on linguistic matters and helping to form language policy for education. As a matter of fact, the present grammar and its predecessor, *The Fijian Language* (*TFL*) had their origins in materials developed by the FDP for a number of workshops, designed to spur the interest of Fijian teachers in the history and structure of their own language.

In Fijian linguistic matters, the present contrasts sharply with the past. The first grammarians and compilers of dictionaries were Wesleyan missionaries from Scotland and England, who were acquiring firsthand knowledge of the language. In the 1920s and '30s, when a revised dictionary and grammar were proposed, the search for compilers was almost exclusively external. For example, it was suggested that the leading figure in Melanesian linguistics at the time, Sydney H. Ray, write the grammar, even though Ray's knowledge about Fijian was entirely secondhand. Now, most Fijian linguistic research in Fiji is carried on by native speakers.

PURPOSE

This work is not directed to a particular readership, but simply to those who want to learn more about Standard Fijian (SF). It is intended as a reference work, treating in detail such topics as verb and noun classification, transitivity, the phonological hierarchy (especially prosodic units), orthography, various types of specification, possession, subordination, and the definite article (among others). In addition, it is an attempt fit these pieces together into a unified picture of the structure of the language.

However, in the attempt to achieve such unification, I have found it difficult to treat a multidimensional topic, for after all, writing flows in only one direction. For instance, it is impossible to describe one unit on the hierarchical scale without referring to the smaller units that are its constituents and to the larger unit of which it itself is a constituent.

Within the presentation of each topic, or each unit, I have paid more than customary attention to previous works. The reason for this practice is somewhat of a missionary effort to achieve these goals:

1. to trace the development of ideas about Fijian grammar;
2. to understand the framework in which grammatical statements were made;
3. to correct mistakes (with apologies to my predecessors); and

4. to explain why my interpretations of certain features may differ from those of other linguists.

METHODOLOGY

1. Use of previous grammars

In this grammar, as in my previous works on the history of the study of Fijian, I have tried to understand the earlier descriptions according to the linguistic models of the periods in which they were written. Very few grammars are completely original; for example, David Cargill's pioneering work on Fijian drew on his experience with Tongan grammar and his previous training in the classical languages. The present work is no exception, for I have used the three major Fijian grammars—those by David Hazlewood, C. Maxwell Churchward, and George B. Milner—as starting points for many sections of this description. Where I have relied most on my predecessors, especially Milner, is in the treatment of grammatical markers, both their meaning and their order in the phrase. It would have been shortsighted to ignore Milner's valuable tables showing an order-class analysis of the "general phrase," even though he did not make the necessary distinction between the verb phrase and the noun phrase.

In addition, for topics such as transitivity, the organization of markers in the verb phrase, and others, I have used several insightful articles by David G. Arms and Aubrey L. Parke's MA thesis.

Most features of higher-level organization—e.g., the hierarchical organization of the phonology, the concept of the accent unit applied to units larger than the word, the approach to sentence construction, the forays into discourse analysis through a grammatical category called specification—are original, along with the overall form of verb classification. Underlying all these areas of the grammar is an attempt to explain as many features as possible from the differing points of view of form, function, and meaning.

Just above, I expressed my belief that it is important to trace the development of ideas about Fijian grammar. Observant readers may notice that certain parts of the analysis here are similar to those in another grammar. As flattering as it is to have had an effect on other works, it is important to set the record straight. To this end, readers should note that the first edition of the present work appeared in 1985 and that computer printouts were circulating a year or two earlier. Here are the pertinent comments from Jeff Siegel's review of Dixon 1988:

> ... [A]s the book turns out to be another grammar of Fijian in general ... it would be expected to build on previous studies. Thus, it is surprising that there are only a few references to the extensive work of Albert J. Schütz, especially his recent, definitive volume, *The Fijian Language* ... Instead of refuting or refining Schütz's original (and sometimes controversial) analyses, Dixon describes Fijian again in a mostly conventional framework.
>
> In some places where such a framework is inadequate, however, the two writers' analyses appear very similar. For example, Dixon's discussion of the mismatch between morphological units and phonological units (pp. 21–26)

seems to follow closely that of Schütz (1985a, pp. 473–484). Dixon also uses similar conventions to link and separate forms that belong to the same or different "phonological words" (analogous to Schütz's "measures"). But for some reason, Dixon does not refer to Schütz's earlier work in these areas.

I touch on this matter only because some readers of Dixon 1988 may not be familiar with *TFL*. It is important that they be aware of the relative chronology of the two works.

2. The Fijian Dictionary Project and its role in the grammar

Just as important as this grammar's forerunners is its connection with the FDP. Although the main goal of the project was the monolingual dictionary itself, it was also concerned with many other aspects of language and culture, including grammar. I developed the grammar out of the lexicographic work, especially through designing the original entry format and classifying verbs (although the details were changed and greatly expanded for the final product). As Director of the FDP from 1972–79, I had access to the dictionary files, the preliminary work with verb derivation, original text material, and—most important—the advice of the rest of the staff, already named in the Acknowledgments.

3. An attempt to avoid translation analysis

There were valid reasons that most of the previous Fijian grammars concentrated on translation: their purpose was to help those whose goal it was to translate religious work in English into Fijian (e.g., Christian missionaries), or to help people who wanted to or were required to learn to speak and read Fijian (e.g., civil servants in the Colonial Administration).

But one must take care in using English translations, especially to explain Fijian function words. For example, grammars sometimes translate the marker *mada* (which makes initiating an action more culturally acceptable) as 'just', as in *kauta mada mai* 'just bring it here'. This translation does not help to understand the function of *mada*, for in my variety of English, *just* does not indicate politeness, but rather, makes a command more abrupt, and would not be used except in exasperation.

As another example, one grammarian said that the marker *gā* had "several important functions," but failed to list them. Instead, he explained different uses of *gā* through translations. This is not what I understand by the term "function." Furthermore, the primary responsibility for defining Fijian words lies with the dictionary. Throughout the present grammar, I have tried to follow this principle: not to rely wholly on translations to explain the function and meaning of grammatical markers.

4. Discourse

This study took an important turn toward discourse analysis (albeit at an elementary level) when it became apparent that the presence of a noun phrase in a sentence could not be accounted for by looking at only the sentence itself. This is when the concept of specification began to grow and color my view of other parts of the language, from the analysis of markers to the treatment of contrastive intonation. As a result, although many examples are given out of context, analyzing a number of grammatical features depended on an environment larger than the sentence.

However, the analysis of discourse is still at an embryonic stage. I hope that it will be possible to extend the study of Fijian grammar so that it reaches beyond the sentence.

5. Bibliographic sources

The Acknowledgments, the References, and especially the section "Pacific Collections Consulted" give some indication of the libraries and archives that have provided material for the historical sections of this work. In addition to the wide geographical spread of this part of the study, it has been of long duration, beginning in 1960 and continuing through the completion of the final draft of *TFL* (with a number of extended periods of concentration), and then sporadically for another twenty-five years.

Since the first edition was published, some of its Fijian data and analysis have appeared in a number of works. Such treatments are interesting in that they often view Fijian through the lens of a particular grammatical or phonological theory, such as Optimality Theory. However, since they are mainly derivative, they contribute little to our knowledge about the language, and thus have not been added to the references.

In the first edition, the references include nearly every comment on the language—amateur or professional, brief or extensive—that I could find in the various Pacific collections listed below. (I do not claim, however, as another grammarian did, to have "consulted everything previously produced on Fijian grammar"!) Thus it is valuable as a Fijian linguistic bibliography for works up to 1985. For the sake of brevity, the present edition includes only those works referred to in the text.

6. Glosses

In a grammar of this type, the purpose of a gloss is to help the reader understand the particular feature that is being explained. It follows, then, that stylistically pleasing English is not the most important consideration.

7. Text material

Insofar as possible, I have avoided using translated material as a source of examples. Thus excluded are Bible translations (except for an occasional example of "translationese") and Fijian translations of such English classics as *The Pilgrim's progress* and *Treasure island*. In an effort to use fairly simple material, at first I concentrated on two series of Fijian primers—*The Fijian readers* and *Na Viti*—although the former seems to have based its stories on outside models, and the latter, in order to simplify, has sometimes distorted natural discourse.

In this work, the sources of most example phrases and sentences are identified so that the reader can find the contexts.

8. Elicited material, or material out of context

Some of the work on verb classification has drawn from the extensive work done by the FDP. Based on the primary classification of verbs into active and stative, Tevita R. Nawadra developed a checklist for verbs, showing forms that might occur. This list was based on the more nearly regular verb affixes; the irregular verb forms could not be dealt with in such an organized manner. For these verb roots, Saimone Nanovu checked the forms he knew.

Although the analysis of the semantics of verb affixes is based mostly on forms in context and on the advice of the FDP staff, the basic classification of verbs (CH 9–12) was very useful for certain formal matters, such as multiple transitive suffixes for some verb, and the different forms and functions of reduplication.

9. Phonology

Like some of the other parts of the grammar, the phonological description began by consulting earlier studies. The most important source for phonology and phonetics is Scott 1948. Cammack 1962 was useful for its detailed treatment of intonation, although the model he used is difficult to follow. My treatment of individual intonation types is based first on Milner's sketch (1972:147–51), although his approach was to construct analogues of pitch contours, and mine was to seek contrastive patterns. For simple sentences, I used Milner's recordings (kindly supplied by him), designed to accompany his text. In the chapters on phonology, some examples are labeled according to Milner's transcription of the records. Other recorded materials used were:

A recording of English loanwords by Saimone Nanovu
A recording made for Charles F. Hockett by Niko Bulai
Recordings made by Apenisa Seduadua during his course work at the University of Hawai'i at Mānoa
Language-learning tapes made for the University of Hawai'i at Mānoa by Paul Geraghty, Lasarusa Vusonivailala, and Pio Manoa

The statements in the sections on vowel shortening are supported by extensive acoustic phonetic research by Iovanna Condax, conducted at the University of Hawai'i at Mānoa in 1978–79.

These more formal sources were supplemented by listening to the language in context and by direct eliciting from the FDP staff members.

10. Material from *TFL* excluded from this edition

In order to keep the present edition to a manageable size, two major sections of *TFL* were cut:

Section One, chapters 1–5
Appendix: The early word lists

These sections were rewritten slightly, combined, and supplemented, and will appear as a monograph intended to provide Fijian teachers with a history of their language.

In addition, many lists of examples were shortened, and, except for topics I considered essential, a number of discussions of previous grammatical viewpoints were shortened or deleted.

11. Material added to this edition

The most significant addition to our knowledge of Fijian in the interval between the two editions of this grammar is the Fijian monolingual dictionary, which resulted mainly from the efforts of the FDP, *Na ivolavosa vakaViti* (*VV*) (2005). It was particularly important as a data source for describing additions to the alphabet and changes to syllable structure for certain styles of Fijian. This topic is discussed and exemplified in Section V: Phonology.

Some topics, such as Specification, have been expanded to cover more areas of the grammar. Others, such as the relationship between morphemes and accent measures, have been introduced. Such features, other changes, and justifications for the new edition are discussed in the last chapter of the grammar.

PACIFIC COLLECTIONS CONSULTED

Australian National Library, Canberra
Barker Library, Suva
Bernice P. Bishop Museum Library, Honolulu
Essex Institute Library, Salem (MA)
Fiji Archives, Suva
Hocken Library, University of Otago, Dunedin
Houghton Library, Harvard University, Cambridge (MA)
Library of Congress, Washington DC
Mitchell Library, Sydney
Pacific Collection, Hamilton Library, University of Hawai'i at Mānoa
Peabody Museum Library, Salem
School of Oriental and African Studies Library, University of London
Seminar für Indonesische und Südseesprachen, Universität Hamburg
Tozzer Library, Harvard University, Cambridge (MA)
Turnbull Library, Wellington
Wesleyan Methodist Missionary Society Library, London

ABBREVIATIONS

1. General

k.o.	kind of	p.c.	personal communication
s.t.	something		

2. Language names

ENG	English	MAO	Māori	TON	Tongan
FIJ	Fijian	SAM	Samoan	UF	Urban Fijian
HAW	Hawaiian	SF	Standard Fijian		

3. Symbols

[ ] in quotations: a guess, or, if empty, an undecipherable word
* proto-form, or an incorrect form
' ' gloss
" " quotation
( ) grammatical explanation, as opposed to a gloss
+ in a gloss, "+" after a noun or a verb means 'and such like'. This convention is from Geraghty 1983:10.
↓ falling intonation
↑ rising intonation
· measure division
| phonological phrase division
|| phonological sentence division
x < y   y modifies x
x > y   x modifies y

4. Grammatical terms

(A)	active	NOM	nominalizer
(A1)	one-referent active	(NP)	noun phrase
(A2)	two-referent active	NUM	numerical
ABL	ablative	ORG	origin
AFF	affirmation	P	plural
AFM	aforementioned	pl.	plural
APR	appearance	PC	possessive classifier
ASP	aspect	POS	possessive
CAU	causative	POT	potential
CNC	concomitant	PP	prepositional phrase
CNJ	conjunction	PRP	proper
CNT	continuative	PRX	proximity
D	dual	PT	past tense
DEF	definite article	PUR	purpose
DEM	demonstrative	REC	reciprocal
DES	desiderative	REL	relative marker
DIR	directional	RES	respect
DIS	distributive	S	singular
(du.)	dual	(S)	stative
EMP	emphatic	(S1)	one-referent stative
(excl.)	exclusive, exclamation	(S2)	two-referent stative
(freq.)	frequentative	SEN	sentence modifier
FT	future tense	SEQ	sequential marker
FUT	future	sg.	singular
GEN	general	STA	stative affix
HAB	habitual	SUB	subordinate marker
I	inclusive	T	paucal (trial)
INC	inclusion	TEN	tentative
IND	individuality	TR	transitive
INI	initiation	ULT	ultimate
INT	intensifier	VOC	vocative
(intens.)	intensive	(VP)	verb phrase
ITR	iteration	X	exclusive
LIM	limiter	1	first person
LOC	locative	2	second person
MAN	manner	3	third person
(no.)	number		

Grammatical terms are abbreviated with no more than three small capital letters. In an interlinear gloss, the only single capital letters that stand alone indicate proper names. Abbreviations in parentheses are not used interlinearly.

These abbreviations were compiled before the Leipzig glossing rules were published (Lehmann 1982). Since the conventions were similar, I saw no reason to change mine.

5. Texts and other sources

FMC61	conversations recorded and transcribed on Bau in 1961 by Floyd M. Cammack (with the assistance of Rusiate T. Komaitai) as part of the linguistic research leading to his PhD dissertation
FDP	Fijian Dictionary Project
FR	*The Fijian readers*, 1–6
NL	*Nai Lalakai*. Fijian language newspaper
NV	*Na Viti*, 1–4. Materials prepared by the Curriculum Development Unit of the Ministry of Education, Suva
SF	*Spoken Fijian* (Schütz and Komaitai 1971)
SR	*Siga Rarama*. Fijian language newspaper
*T*74	*Tovolea*, four stories written in Fijian, edited by Asesela Ravuvu
VG	*Na Volagauna*. Fijian language newspaper
VV	entry in *Ivolavosa VakaViti* (*VV*) and material recorded and transcribed for the FDP (The introduction to *VV* contains the spellings *vakaviti*, *Vakaviti*, and *vakaViti*.)

6. Sources of personal communication

AS	Apenisa Seduadua
BK	Adi Bera Kurasiga
DA	David Arms
EN	Erelia Nayacakalou
LT	Luisa Tuvuki
PG	Paul Geraghty
SN	Saimone Nanovu
TRN	Tevita R. Nawadra

Fuller identifications, such as "Nawadra 1982," refer to items in the References.

GEOGRAPHICAL AND OTHER DATA

Information such as the following—geographical data, maps, language affiliation, sociolinguistic data, dialects, and number of speakers—is now easily accessible on-line.

DECORATIONS

The section from a Fijian *masi* 'tapa' that introduces each chapter was scanned from a photograph of a piece that was given to me decades ago. The photographs on the pages that begin the six sections were taken by me in 1960–61, with an Argus C-3 camera.

* * * * *

SECTION I:
A SKETCH OF FIJIAN SPELLING AND PRONUNCIATION

View of Viti Levu from Bau (1961). ©AJS

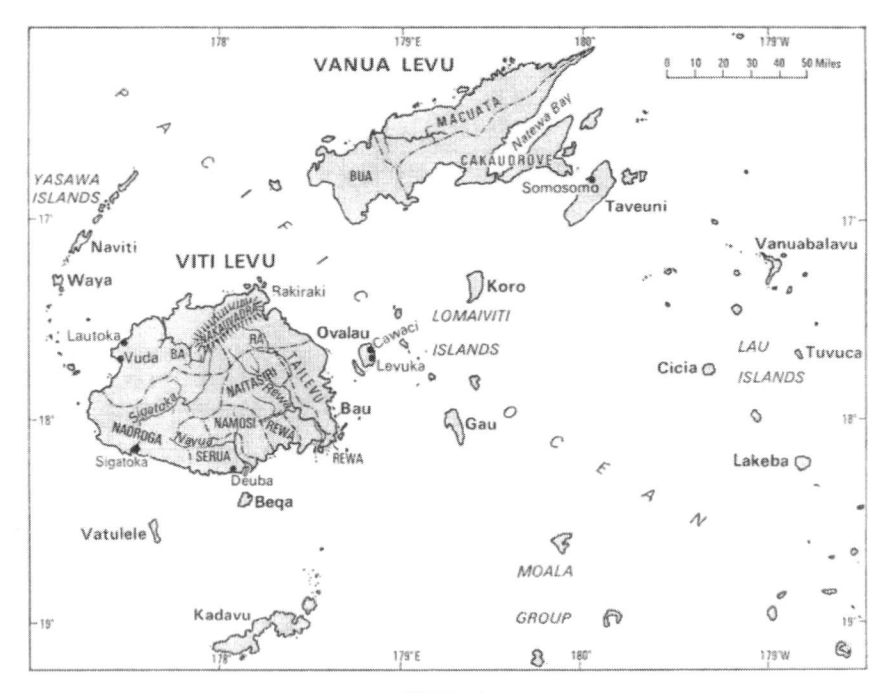

Fiji Islands

Schütz 1972a:xii

1 SOUNDS AND LETTERS

The first written samples of the Fijian language to reach the English reading public were the twelve words collected in Tonga in July, 1777 by William Anderson—physician, naturalist, and philologist on James Cook's third voyage.[1] Although Anderson did not comment on the sounds of Fijian, the spelling system he used was one that he had developed earlier and used consistently as he transcribed samples of a number of languages that he examined on Cook's second and third voyages.

It is hard to determine Anderson's own view of the relationship between sounds and letters, but writings of his contemporaries suggest that they gave more importance to the latter than to the former. In other words, rather than telling how sounds should be written, they began with letters and described how they should be pronounced. This philosophy was not made explicit, but how else can we explain such phrases as "the powers of the letters," and "*A* has three sounds"?

In contrast, Peter Duponceau, in his monograph *English phonology*, suggested that putting the letter before the sound was backwards. He wrote (1817:231):

> Instead of applying the process of analysis to the sounds themselves, independent of, and abstracted from, the signs which represent them, grammarians have looked to the signs in the first instance, and proceeded from them to the sounds which they are supposed to represent.

He went on to propose what we would now call a phonetic alphabet, his "phonology of language." Thus, Duponceau's insights represent an important advance in our understanding that sounds are primary and letters are only representations of sounds.

In this introductory chapter, however, I have temporarily reverted to the earlier approach. The reason is that the overall organization of the main part of this grammar is to proceed from larger units to smaller ones—i.e., from sentences and phrases to sounds. What lies behind this ordering is my conviction

---

[1] The sounds he transcribed suggest that his informant was either a Tongan or a Fijian using Foreigner Talk.

that to understand how the language works, we should begin with sentence types rather than phonetic and phonological details. Also, larger phonological units are linked, in part, to corresponding grammatical units. Thus, understanding morphology and syntax will help to illuminate the phonology. Finally, to someone reading a grammar, the written word, by necessity, comes first. And to readers not familiar with Fijian's unusual spelling conventions, it is important to fix these conventions in their minds. For this reason, it is necessary here first to relate letters to sounds, not vice versa.

1.1 THE ALPHABET AND WHAT THE LETTERS REPRESENT

TABLE 1.1: VOWELS

i		u
e		o
	a	

TABLE 1.2: CONSONANTS[2]

	BL	LD	AD	AA	AP	DV
STOPS	(p)		t			k
	b [mb]		d [nd]			q [ŋg]
TRILLS/FLAPS				r [ř ~ r̃]		
				dr [nř ~ nr̃]		
FRICATIVES		(f)		s		
	v [β]		c [ð]			
(AFFRICATES)					(j) [č]	
					(z) [nǰ]	
NASALS	m			n		g [ŋ]
LATERAL				l		
GLIDES	w				y [ɛ̯]	

BL = bilabial   LD = labiodental   AD = apico-dental   AA = apico-alveolar
AP = alveo-palatal   DV = dorso-velar. Parentheses mark borrowed consonants.

Note in particular the letters that are followed by phonetic symbols. These, as the symbols show, are the letters that are used differently than they are in English.

1.1.1 Vowels

The Fijian vowel system consists of five vowels, shown in table 1.1. (Vowels are treated in more detail in CH 33.) The vowels are pronounced roughly as follows:

---

[2] See §§34.3, 34.4, 34.5, and subsections for additions to this inventory through newer (and perhaps unassimilated) borrowings.

a as in f**a**ther
e as in b**ai**t, but without the [y] glide at the end.
i as in b**ea**t, but without the [y] glide at the end.
o as in b**oa**t, but without the [w] glide at the end.
u as in b**oo**t, but without the [w] glide at the end.[3]

Each vowel occurs both short and long (but not in all positions in a word; see §36.3.1), resulting in a ten-way contrast in the vowel system.

1.1.1.1 Diphthongs

Certain vowel combinations—*ai, au, ei, eu, oi, ou,* and *iu*—are classed as diphthongs not only because of their form (nucleus + offglide), but mainly because of their function—i.e., they act as units. As evidence, we can hear that no matter where these vowel clusters appear in a word, the first vowel is accented. Thus, they are FALLING DIPHTHONGS. This topic is amplified in later sections, especially §33.2.2 and subsections.

1.1.2 Consonants

The consonant letters, along with their phonetic representation, are shown in table 1.2. Consonants are treated in more detail below and in CH 34.

1.2 THE FIJIAN SOUND SYSTEM

Tables 1.1 and 1.2 show Fijian letters, which correspond to segmental phonemes. The following sections show, in summary, how they fit into a phonological hierarchy (treated in greater detail in CH 32 to 39).

1.2.1 Syllables

A Fijian syllable has this shape: (C)V, where (C) represents an optional consonant, and V represents a short vowel, a long vowel, or a diphthong.[4]

1.2.2 Accent units

Accent is predictable only in short words:

1. In words of two or three short syllables, it is always on the second-to-last syllable. In the following examples, the vowel of the accented syllable is in boldface:

| *d***u***a* | one | *m***a***ta* | eye, face |
| *t***o***lu* | three | *t***o***toka* | beautiful |

2. A syllable with a long vowel or a diphthong as its nucleus is accented, no matter what its position:

| *vā* | four | *r**ai*** | seen |
| *kilā* | know it | *mā·r**au*** | happy |

---

[3] The examples are from American broadcast-standard English.
[4] Deviations from this pattern are discussed in §35.4

From a prosodic point of view, longer words and phrases are made up of short accent units, called MEASURES.⁵ In the list just above, the word *mā·rau* is divided into two measures, and the boundary is marked by a raised period—not part of the usual writing system, but a convention that shows the location of accents in longer words. For example (in addition to *mā·rau* above):

bulu·makau	cattle	*dai·dai*	today
bā·ravi	coast	*leka·leka*	short
posi·tō·vesi	post office	*ivā·vā*	shoes

As you can see from the vowels in boldface, each diphthong, long vowel, and penultimate vowel in a measure is accented. Moreover, the last measure in a word is given slightly more emphasis, giving the impression of primary accent.

In the grammar, measures are marked only when accent is being discussed.

1.2.3 Longer phonological units

Phonological phrases and sentences are treated in CH 37 and CH 38.

1.3 DISCUSSION: THE STORY BEHIND THE ALPHABET⁶

By the time the Fijian alphabet was developed (from 1835 on), the vowel letters (and their phonetic correlates) shown in table 1.1 had already replaced the largely inconsistent "English" way of writing vowels. The pioneers in this small but significant revolution were missionary linguists describing Tahitian, Māori, and Hawaiian, who chose an Italianate or classical method of writing vowels.

In contrast to this now common way of writing vowels, the spelling of Fijian consonants is significantly different from the systems used for any of its Polynesian neighbors. When we look at these letters and their "values," we move from the expected to the unexpected.

At first glance, Fijian spelling seems strange, since it uses several familiar letters in an unfamiliar way. The consonant letters whose use seems unusual to English readers are these:

b, which represents [mb],   as in *member*.
d, which represents [nd],   as in *Monday*.
q, which represents [ŋg],   as in *finger*.
dr, which represents [n(d)r̃],   as in *Andrew*.
g, which represents [ŋ],   as in *singer*.
c, which represents [ð],   as in *father*.

Contrary to some lay opinions, these letters were not chosen through incompetence or by chance. Instead, the choices were based on sound principles of analysis through trial and error, and moreover, strengthened by the opinions of native speakers.

---

⁵ See CH 36.

⁶ For a more detailed discussion of these matters, see *The Fijian language* (*TFL*), Schütz 1972, and *Early studies of Fijian* (in preparation).

Before the final form of the alphabet was adopted, the Methodist missionaries David Cargill and William Cross devised several systems, experimenting with each by noting how Fijians reacted to them. If one plan didn't work, they discarded it and tried another. Eventually, they developed a system that was simple, regular, and very satisfying to the Fijians, who were eager to learn to read.

Why were the letter shown above chosen? When Cargill first started writing Fijian, he used the consonant combinations *mb*, *nd*, and *gk* (for [ŋg], as in *finger*). Although speakers of English hear two consonants in each case, Fijian treats each cluster as if it were a single consonant. Moreover, each consonant must be followed by a vowel. So when Cargill wrote the island name *Lakemba*, his pupils inserted a vowel after *m*, pronouncing the word *La-ke-ma-mba*. This practice led Cargill to take the next step in discovering how the system worked:

> We therefore substituted one consonant for the two, & the natives were quite delighted with the improvement, and joyfully exclaimed, "You have just now known the nature of our language; we are just now able to read the books which you have written."

Thus, Cargill relied not on an English speaker's impression that these sounds were clusters, but on the Fijians' intuitive knowledge that they were units.

No doubt *g* would have been a good choice to represent *ng+g* (as in *finger*) had it not already been used in Tongan—and then in Fijian—for [ŋ].[7] Instead, *q* was selected. So far as we know, neither Cargill nor Cross explained why they chose it. But we might guess that it was because it looks more like a *g* than does *x* or *z*, which were also possible candidates to represent the sound.

The sound that *dr* represents is really [nr̃], but an excrescent [d] is heard between the two sounds.

Historical records tell us how *c* came to represent [ð]. When Cargill began studying Fijian in Tonga, he saw that *th* was not the best way to spell the Fijian sound, since *th* is ambiguous in English, representing either [Θ] or [ð]. Drawing on his background in classical languages, Cargill asked John Hobbs, the printer, for a special symbol, a theta. This is what Hobbs wrote in his diary (Spooner and Melville 1955:23):

> I next printed a leaflet for Fiji. Mr. Cargill said, "I want you to cast me some Greek thetas." I said, "The *Th* in Fijian is flat [voiced], and I am not a type founder; take one of our spare letters and make that do." In a short time I got the thing printed giving *C* the sound of *Th*.

The name *Fiji* contains two consonants (*f* and *j*) not normally used in the language except in some of the Lauan varieties of Fijian and in loanwords. This spelling is rather like an archaeological ruin that reflects a piece of the past. Although the standard language uses *Viti* for the name of the country, Tongans—at least before the mid-1800s—called the group *Fiji* (once pronounced *Fichi*, and

---

[7] In 1943, the Tongan government changed the *g* spelling of [ŋ] back to *ng*. Thus, *Toga* became *Tonga*.

now *Fisi)* because of the palatalization of /t/ before /i/ and the regular correspondence between Tongan /f/ and Fijian /v/.

Explorers, missionaries, and traders who were in the area near the turn of the nineteenth century probably first heard the name from Tongans. Their pronunciation is preserved in the early spellings *Fejee* and *Feejee*. These orthographic relics persisted long after the spelling of other words was fixed. The double-vowel spelling may explain why in English the word *Fiji* is often mispronounced with both syllables accented, or the accent on the second syllable (it's actually *Fiji*—accented on the first syllable).

The result of Cargill's and Cross's brilliant work is a spelling system that is economical and, more important, *regular*. It is this second quality that gives readers an excellent chance of pronouncing words correctly when they read them.

SECTION II

GRAMMAR: SENTENCES AND VERB PHRASES

At night [I] began and I had a hard tug at the verbs till 20 minutes to l o'clock. This subject I feared more than any other as being so important and so difficult. But I believe the Lord helped me and I was surprised at my work when I had done it. Good or bad, it is very much better than I had anticipated. The great difficulty was in a proper arrangement. But I flatter myself that the one I have followed is the clearest and the most useful.

David Hazlewood, Journal
entry for 4 December 1850

VITI LEVU, BĀ–NADROGĀ AREA, JULY 1961. ©AJS

2 SENTENCE TYPES

The structures described in this chapter are BASIC sentence types—i.e., sentences with no subordinate, coordinate, or prepositional phrases added.[1]

A FULL SENTENCE in Fijian is a phrase (or series of phrases) that contains elements that refer to the semantic categories of TOPIC and COMMENT. The topic is the entity about which something is said; the comment is what is said about the topic.[2] For example, in the following sentence, which consists of a verb phrase (VP) alone, *era* 'they (plural)' expresses the topic, and the rest of the sentence expresses the comment.

TOPIC   COMMENT
[Era]   [ā dabe tiko.][3]   'They were sitting.'
3P   PT sit   CNT

In the next example, which consists of two noun phrases (NPs), the first phrase expresses the comment, and second, the topic.

COMMENT   TOPIC
[Na yaca ni yalewa] [o Mere.]   'The name of the woman is Mere.'
DEF name POS woman   PRP M

An ELLIPTICAL sentence contains reference to only one of these elements, the other being supplied through context. Note the following sentence:

---

[1] Variations on basic sentences are described in the chapters on NP and VP markers and in the section on OPERATIONS.

[2] Lyons (1968:335) sketched the development of definitions of topic and comment, beginning with Sapir's view (1921) of subject and predicate, and continuing to Hockett's adaptation (1958:201), which is used here.

[3] In the interlinear glosses and grammatical explanations, the glosses for content forms are in lowercase letters, and the abbreviations for grammatical explanations are in small caps. To save space, most proper nouns are glossed with initials only. Hyphens connect closely bound forms. It is difficult to label one marker with the same term consistently and still give the required grammatical information about its use in that particular example. Therefore, the description of that marker will explain its function and meaning more thoroughly than its gloss.

O   ira.   'They.'
PRP 3P

This is an elliptical sentence; it could answer the question:

O   cei   ā   dabe tiko?   'Who was sitting?'
PRP who PT sit   CNT

Both these sentence types (full and elliptical) are distinct from exclamations—such as *Sobo!* (expression of surprise) or *Isa!* (expression of emotion)—which cannot be expanded into full sentences.

In this grammar, the term "sentence" is taken to mean "full sentence" unless further qualified. In general, elliptical sentences can be analyzed only by examining the context.

There are two principal ways to classify full sentences: through MEANING and through FORM. The next two main sections, §2.1 and §2.2, follow this dichotomy. But like many such classifications, affiliations change when the criteria change. Thus, we find that some categories overlap. For example, as the examples just below show, identifying sentences can differ in form. And conversely, as we will see still later, sentences with a particular form can fall into different semantic categories.

2.1 SENTENCE TYPES: MEANING

Based on the semantic relationships among the referents of the constituents, Fijian sentences can be divided into four types:

1. Active   2. Stative   3. Existential   4. Identifying

To show that all these types are common in even the simplest discourse, note the following story, written in the style of a nineteenth-century primer. (The third column shows the sentence type.)

Raica mada!	'Look [at it] (please)!'	ACTIVE
E dua na niu oqō.	'This is a coconut.'	IDENTIFYING
A cava na kā oqō?	'What's this thing?'	IDENTIFYING[4]
E niu madū.	'It's a mature coconut.'	IDENTIFYING
E levu na niu e Viti.	'There are a lot of coconuts in Fiji.'	EXISTENTIAL
E yaga sara.	'It's very useful.'	STATIVE
Sā volitaki.	'It's been sold.'	STATIVE

The following sections describe each of these four main types.

2.1.1 Active sentences (VP)

In an active VP, the subject[5] represents the ACTOR—someone or something performing an action (in a broad sense) or causing an action to be performed. Thus, in most cases, the actor is controlling a situation. Examples are:

---

[4] Note that the "identification" here is the question phrase *a cava*.

E kana. 3S eat	'She eats.'[6]
Au vodo. 1S ride	'I ride.'
Daru sīsili. 1DI bathe	'Let's (dual inclusive) bathe.'
Era laga sere. 3P sing song	'They (plural) are singing.'
E qoli. 3S fish	'He's fishing.'

2.1.2 Stative sentences (VP)

In a stative VP, the subject represents the GOAL: someone or something being acted upon or described. The goal, in contrast to the actor, does not control the situation:

E levu. 3S big	'It's big.'
Era bulu. 3P buried	'They (plural) are buried.'
E cola-ti. 3S carry-TR	'It was carried.'
Keirau rai-ci. 1DX see-TR	'We (dual exclusive) were seen.'

2.1.3 Existential

In an existential VP, the subject represents neither the actor nor the goal, but merely something/someone whose existence is being affirmed. An existential VP also indicates that something/someone exists in a particular location or time, in a particular quantity, or in a particular posture (PG 7/82). Examples are:

E tiko. 3S stay	'There is some. / It's here.'	*E levu.*[7] 3S big	'There are a lot.'
E dua. 3S one	'There's one.'	*E sega.* 3S not	'There is none.'

2.1.4 Identifying sentences

In an identifying sentence, the referent of the subject is identified as a member of a class. Again, it is neither acting, acted upon, nor described. There are two types of identifying sentences: INDEFINITE and DEFINITE.

---

[5] The examples show my interpretation of "subject"—a marker showing person, number, and exclusitivity that precedes the verb. Most other analysts have had a different view of what the subject is in a Fijian sentence. See CH 4.

[6] The first two sentences in this list may sound strange in isolation, but not in a particular context. I have tried to give minimal examples, free of grammatical modifiers.

[7] Note that this phrase is identical in form to the one in §2.1.2. The different meanings can be determined only through context.

2.1.4.1 Indefinite identifying sentences (VP)

In this construction, which is a VP, the class is represented by a noun that serves as a verb; the individual member of the class is represented by the grammatical subject. For example, *qase-ni-vuli* 'teacher' is usually a noun, but in this construction, it serves as a verb:

E qase-ni-vuli. 3S elder-PC-learn	'He/she's a teacher.'
E siga ni lotu.[8] 3S day POS religion	'It's a day for worship.'
E vinivō totoka. 3S dress pretty	'It's a pretty dress.'
E kau yaga sara. 3S tree use INT	'It's a very useful tree.'

The following phrase is an example of an identifying VP in the negative:[9]

... ni sega ni tamata dina SUB not SUB person true	'... that he was not a real human' (*FR5*:16)

2.1.4.2 Definite identifying sentences (NP + NP)

Sentences that are composed of two NPs identify an entity by stating that a specific (definite) topic belongs to a class. In the following sentences, the NPs are joined by "+" (Note that these sentences do not contain grammatical subjects.)

Na yaca ni gone + o Tubarua. DEF name POS child PRP T	'The name of the child was T.' (*FR6*:6)
Na kā e qara-i + na totolo. DEF thing 3S need-TR DEF fast	'What is needed is speed.' (T74:52)
Na ke-na i-liuliu + na kānala. DEF PC-3S NOM-lead DEF colonel	'Its leader is a colonel.'

The following list shows the semantic structure for each example.

Comment	Topic
General class	Specific member
na yaca ni gone	*o Tubarua*
na kā e qara-i	*na totolo*
na ke-na i-liuliu	*na kānala*

2.1.4.2.1 *A cava* and *o cei*

In many NP + NP sentences, one of the phrases is *a cava* 'what?' or *o cei* 'who?'

---

[8] As in many languages, the conventions for writing compounds are erratic. Even though *qasenivuli* is written as one word, and *siga ni lotu* as three, the constructions are similar, perhaps differing only in how idiomatic they are. Also, the accent patterns are the same. Finally, since these two forms come from an introduced culture and language, perhaps the English glosses had an effect on whether the new form was interpreted as a word or a phrase: 'teacher' vs. 'day for worship'.

[9] With subordinate markers such as *ni*, the subject *e* is deleted.

Na cava + *na i-wali ni leqa?*   'What was the solution to the
DEF what   DEF NOM-anoint POS problem   problem?' (*SR* 20/4/82)

A cava beka + *na vu-na?*   'What might the reason be?'
DEF what INI   DEF reason-3S   (*NL* 13/5/82)

O cei + *oyā?*   'Who's that (over there)?'
PRP who DEM:3

The form of such questions, however, is not always NP + NP; like other nouns, *cava* can be used as a verb. In the following sentence, note that *cava* is the head of a VP, surrounded by such VP markers as *sā*, *bau*, and *mada*:

Sā bau cava mada e *tuku-n-a vei iko na no-mu vūniwai?*
ASP TEN what INI   3S tell-TR-3S ABL 2S DEF PC-2S doctor
'Just what is it that your doctor told you?' (T74:51)

Cei works similarly, but only when preceded by *o*:

Sā o cei beka o koya? 'Who's he?'
ASP PRP who TEN PRP 3S

This sentence, however, is appropriate only in certain contexts. See §5.3.1.

2.2 SENTENCE TYPES: FORM

Another way to classify sentences is by their form. Note the different structures in the following sentences, similar to the set in §2.1:

[Rai-c-a mada!]   VP
look-TR-3S INI
'Look (please)!'

[A cava] [na kā oqō?]   NP NP
DEF what   DEF thing DEM:1
'What's this thing?'

[[E dua] [na niu]] [oqō.]   [VP NP] NP
3S one   DEF coconut DEM:1
'This is a coconut.'

[E niu madū.]   VP
3S coconut mature
'It's a mature coconut.'

[[E levu] [na niu]] [e Viti.]   [VP NP] PP
3S big   DEF coconut   ABL Fiji
'There are a lot of coconuts in Fiji.'

[E yaga sara.]   VP
3S use INT
'It's very useful.'

These sentences are fairly simple; you might find them in the first few lessons of any primer. But they show that even the most elementary conversation can contain a number of different types of sentences.

Earlier, we described the four categories in a semantic classification:

1. Active   2. Stative   3. Existential   4. Identifying

However, it is impossible to keep the semantic and formal descriptions entirely separate. For example, the first three sentence types—active, stative, and existential—are centered on the VP. Identifying sentences are divided into two subtypes, one of which involves the VP, and the other, NPs. Thus, we must discuss these two structures.

2.2.1 VP sentences

Sentences that consist of a verb phrase alone may seem unusual to speakers of English, in which sentences are generally divided into SUBJECT + PREDICATE. But this type is common in Fijian, for every VP contains a MARKER that serves as the SUBJECT,[10] and some contain one that serves as the OBJECT as well. In the following sentences, the first contains only a subject, and the second, both a subject and an object:

Au gunu.	'I'm drinking.'
1S drink	
Au gunu-v-a.	'I'm drinking **it**.'
1S drink-TR-3S	

Note the following sentences (*NV1*:1–5, 15), each of which consists of a VP alone (either complex or compound):

E siga ni lotu.	'It's a day for worship.'
3S day POS religion	
E bogi ni lotu.	'It's a night for worship.'
3S night POS religion	
Au rawa ni lako.	'I can walk.'
1S able SUB go	
Au rawa ni qasi.	'I can crawl.'
1S able SUB crawl	
E katu tolu.	'It's three fathoms long.'
3S fathom three	
E vaka-somo ka vā-kula.	'It's blackened and fringed.'
3S MAN-stained CNJ MAN-fringe	

Within each VP, *e* 'he, she, it' or *au* 'I' functions as the subject. An NP would be included in the sentence only if the speaker wanted or needed to be more specific about the referent of the subject. Thus, in each of the sentences above, the subject could be SPECIFIED (see CH 26) by adding an NP. E.g.:

| *E katu tolu **na ibe**.* | '**The mat** is three fathoms long.' |
| 3S fathom three DEF mat | |

---

[10] However, third person singular *e* can be omitted. See §4.9.

2.2.1.1 Components of VP sentences

A VP consists of two obligatory items: a SUBJECT and a VERB. A SUBJECT is one of a closed set of MARKERS (function words) that indicate person, number, and exclusiveness. For the complete set of subjects, see table 4.1.

A VERB consists of a ROOT (content word; see §3.1), which may have affixes as well (such as a causative prefix or a transitive suffix + object). It follows the subject and allows the VP it functions as part of to serve as a complete utterance.

In the following examples of VPs, each of the verb roots is in boldface:

Au **lako**. 1S go	'I'm going.'
Keirau **tiko**. 1DX stay	'We (dual exclusive) are staying.'
Keitou **gunu**. 1TX drink	'We (trial exclusive) are drinking.'
Keimami sā **cala**. 1PX ASP wrong	'We (plural exclusive) are wrong.'
E **gunu**-*vi*. 3S drink-TR	'It is drinkable.'
E **gunu**-*va*. 3S drink-TR	'She drinks it.'

2.2.2 NP sentences

By referring to the semantic definition of a sentence (§2.1), one can see that most utterances consisting of a single NP are not full sentences, but elliptical ones. For example, the following short utterances were taken from transcribed conversations (FMC 61). Each relies on context to supply the missing topic or comment:

Ke-na vuaka. PC-3S pig	'His pig' (the speaker prompts the previous speaker).
Cola-i-Suva, ē? (place name) yes?	'C-i-S, right?' (the speaker provides the word when the other speaker hesitates)
Oi, mai Mokani. oh ABL M	'Oh, from M' (the speaker repeats the last phrase of the previous speaker's sentence)
Koya! DEM:3	'That's it!'
Kei cei? CNJ who?	'With (and) whom?' (a response to *Keirau sā na qai gādē* 'We (dual exclusive) will then holiday') The answer is the following:
Tū[11] *Rusi*. (title) Rusi	'(With) Tū [short for Rātū] Rusi.'

---

[11] In normal speech, this vowel usually shortens.

2 Sentence Types

One type of NP sentence—the modified NP—is complete in itself, since it contains reference to both topic and comment. Examples (FMC 61) are:

Na soli cava? DEF offering what?	'Which offering?'
Oi vanua batabatā. oh land cold	'Oh, a cold land.'
Mate cava? ill what?	'What kind of illness?'
Tamata levu? person big	'A big person?'

Although these sentences appear to be examples of ellipsis, they are instead full sentences. As the section on noun modification shows (§28.3.1), each of these examples is related to a sentence that consists of two phrases:

[A cava] [na soli?] DEF what? DEF offering	'What's the offering?'[12]	NP NP
[E batabatā] [na vanua.] 3s cold DEF land	'The land is cold.'	VP NP
[A cava] [na mate?] DEF what? DEF ill	'What's the illness?'	NP NP
[E levu] [na tamata?] 3s big DEF person	'Is the person big?'	VP NP

2.3 PHRASE ORDER AND INTONATIONAL FEATURES

In the NP + NP sentences immediately above, the intonation pattern is similar to that of VP (+ NP) sentences. This similarity matches their similarity in semantic structure: that is, the order of COMMENT + TOPIC. Many NP + NP sentences, however, contain a fronted topic—a phrase that would normally follow the comment. E.g.:

Oyā + o Mataisuva.   'That's Mataisuva.' (*FR5*:10)
DEM:3 PRP M
(from *[O Mataisuva] [oyā]*)

O yau + na luve i Radi ni Nawaitale.
PRP 1S DEF child POS R POS N
'I am the child of Radi ni Nawaitale.' (*FR5*:12)

In these sentences, the intonation of the first phrase is similar to that of other fronted phrases (see §40.1(F)).

2.3.1 Intonation as a guide to grammatical structure and meaning

An NP + NP sentence in which one of the NPs is *oqō* 'this', *oqori* 'that (by you)', or *oyā* 'that (distant)'[13] can sometimes be ambiguous in its written form. Note the following:

---

[12] As the glosses show, *cava* following a noun takes on an idiomatic meaning: 'what kind of?, which?'

Na   vosa   ni   i-Vola   Tabu   oqō.
DEF language POS NOM-write sacred DEM:1

If the peak of intonation (in boldface below) is the accented syllable of *Tabu,* the two phrases make up a full sentence, as follows:

*Na vosa ni i-Vola **Ta**bu + oqō.*
'This is the language of the Bible.'

In this sentence, *oqō* constitutes a separate phrase, and can be fronted. However, if the phrase peak is on *oqō*, the whole phrase makes up an elliptical sentence, as follows:

*Na vosa ni i-Vola Tabu o**qō**.*
'The language of this Bible.'

(See CH 40.)

2.4 SUMMARY

In this chapter we have discussed the interwoven relationships between two main types of classification of basic sentences: those based on meaning, and those based on form. The following diagram shows these relationships:

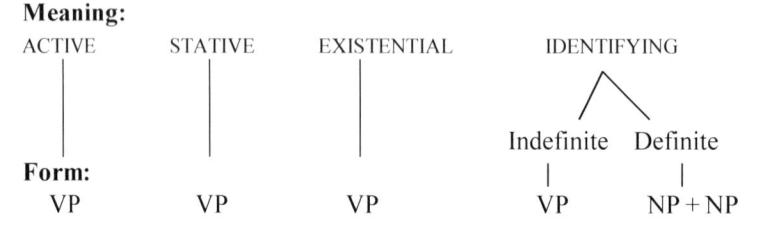

Meaning:
ACTIVE   STATIVE   EXISTENTIAL   IDENTIFYING
  | | | Indefinite   Definite
Form: | |
  VP   VP   VP   VP   NP + NP

In the following chapters, first we classify words and morphemes. Next, we deal with specific elements in basic sentences, beginning with SUBJECTS and, for constructions involving transitivity, OBJECTS.

---

[13] In normal spoken Fijian, the forms are usually *qō*, *oqori*, and *oyā*

3 CLASSIFYING WORDS AND MORPHEMES

Most part-of-speech classifications are based on the WORD. Although for Fijian, the concept "word" is difficult to define precisely, the term and others connected with it (e.g., "prefix" and "suffix") are convenient ways to refer to forms.

Since this discussion applies to prefixes and suffixes, as well as to words, all these units figure in the classification here.

3.1 ROOT VS. MARKER

In this grammar, three criteria—function, form, and meaning—are used to classify words into two main types: ROOT and MARKER (also discussed in §39.2.2). Here are some general characteristics of these two types of words or affixes.

A **root**:

1. is at least one MEASURE (accent unit) in length; see §32.4, CH 36.
2. usually serves as the peak of the phonological phrase.
3. is reduplicated much more often than a marker.
4. occurs as the head of each basic phrase.
5. usually refers to such entities as persons, actions, qualities, etc.
6. belongs to an open class: that is, new forms can enter freely.

A **marker**:

1. can be less than a measure in length—that is, a short syllable. However, it can also be a full measure in length.
2. is ambiguous in its function in the phonological phrase. Certain types of markers can serve as the peak of a phrase; others cannot.
3. is seldom reduplicated.[1]

---

[1] The qualifier in this statement refers to a few markers that can be reduplicated. They seem to be of two types: (1) Those that involve a change in meaning. E.g., *Via* 'desirous of' *viavia* 'act as if, pretend to be', as in *e viavia tūraga* 'he acts like a chief'. (2) Those that seem closer to the root, such as *Ca-* occurring with two-topic statives, which seem to be reinterpreted as part of the root when reduplicated:

ta-ta-bale-bale 'stagger' *ta-ta-gede-gede* 'shaking agitatedly up and down'

For more examples of reduplicated markers, see §14.14.

4. never occurs as the head of a basic phrase.
5. usually shows relationships among roots, changes class membership of a root, or signals grammatical categories.
6. can be a prefix or suffix that attaches to a root.
7. belongs to a relatively closed class. Markers form a nearly finite set, and new forms develop slowly.[2]

Of these criteria, those that refer to *function* are the most important. Roots function as heads of phrases; markers do not. In other words, *root vs. marker* is mainly a morphological classification.[3]

In the following sentences (*NV1*:74), words are classified as either root (R) or marker (M).

E	*dau*	*cici*	*tale*	*gā*	+	*na*	*basikeli.*	'A bicycle also runs.'
3S	HAB	run	ITR	INT		DEF	bicycle	
M	M(R)	R	M(R)	M		M	R	

In this sentence, the centers of the two grammatical phrases[4] (separated by +) are the verb *cici* and the noun *basikeli*. Both are roots and are always used as such. *E* satisfies all the conditions of a marker. Note particularly that it consists of a short syllable and is therefore accented only according to its position in the measure (see §39.3.1). *Dau* consists of a long syllable, but functions as a marker, as well as a root.[5] *Tale*, as well, has a dual function: it can be used either as a root (as in *e tale mai* 'he returned') or as a marker (as in the example sentence above).[6] *Gā* and *na* are both used exclusively as markers.

E	*rua*	*gā*	+	*na*	*yava-na.*	'It has only two feet (i.e., wheels).'
3S	two	INT		DEF	foot-3S	
M	R	M		M	R M	

The new forms in this sentence are the two roots, *rua* and *yava*, and the marker *-na*.

---

[2] Both of these conditions may have to be revised as we learn more about SF and how it changes. The following observations indicate that the system of function forms may be less rigid than previously thought. (1) As shown later, some markers seem to have developed from roots. (2) There seem to be a number of fossilized markers with very limited distributions. (3) Perhaps markers can be borrowed from other Fijian languages more easily than we had thought. Geraghty's work (especially 1977 and 1983) has revealed some of the complex relationships among the speech communities in Fiji.

[3] As opposed to base vs. particle, which is a phonological classification. See §39.2.1.

[4] The grammatical phrase is defined by structure. The relationship between grammatical phrases and phonological phrases is rather like that between the arguments in a syllogism: the end of a phonological phrase also indicates the end of a grammatical phrase, but the converse is not necessarily the case.

[5] In *dau ni X* 'expert at X' and *ke-na dau* 'expert at it', we can consider *dau* a different lexical item with limited distribution: it does not occur in constructions such as *na dau 'the expert' or *e dau 'he is an expert'.

[6] It is also possible to consider these forms as two morphemes each—that is, as separate entries in a dictionary.

Au sega ni dau vodo + e   na motokā.
1S not SUB HAB ride   ABL DEF car
M   R   M   M(R) R   M   M   R
'I don't usually ride in an automobile.'

In this sentence, there are three roots: *sega*, *vodo*, and *motokā*. The new markers are *ni*, which introduces a subordinate phrase, and a different *e*, which marks an ablative phrase.

In summary, roots include such words as the following:

bā	'fence'	*cā*	'bad'	*baba*	'side'	*vinaka*	'good'
baca	'worm'	*cabe*	'ascend'	*baka*	'banyan'	*cadra*	'rise'
bale	'fall'	*cagi*	'wind (n.)'	*cici*	'run'	*vale*	'house'

Markers include such words as:

1. Person-number indicators used as subjects and objects:

au	1st singular	*keirau*	1st dual exclusive
keitou	1st trial exclusive	*keimami*	1st plural exclusive

2. Articles

   na definite   *o* proper

3. Ablative markers

   e 'at'   *mai* 'at, from, hither'   *i* 'toward'

4. Prefixes and suffixes

   vaka- causative   *-qu* 'my'   *-C-a* transitive + 3d singular

This short list is only a sample. In addition, there are a number of other function morphemes—that is, any forms that are used (at least for the nonce) in a position other than the head of a phrase. We now discuss these forms and some difficulties in classifying them.

3.1.1 The gray areas of morpheme classification

In the discussion of the first sample sentence above, we noted that the form *tale* could serve as either root or marker. There are a number of such morphemes and/or morpheme combinations; for example:

tiko	'stay'[7]	*wale*	'worthless'	*koto*	'lie'
mai	'come'	*tū*	'stand'	*koso*	'sever'
vaka	'resemble'	*vaka-rau*	'ready'	*lai/laki*	'go to'
tekivū	'begin'	*toka*	'squat'	*voli*	'go around'

In Arms's extensive treatment of VP markers and affixes (1986:200–201), he marked the following forms as those "which may occur with related meaning in a capacity other than as markers" (those listed above have been deleted):

---

[7] The glosses given here are more appropriate when the forms are used as roots.

rairai, vakatekivū, tini, lesu, yādua, yārua, tani, laivi, cake, sobu, oti, rawa, makawa, duadua, taudua, taurua, sō, dina, saka, tale, nō, gona, lā, mai, oqō, oqoka, oqori, oyā, gona, and *vuā.*

As an example of *VV*'s treatment of this duality of function, note that *tekivū* has two main entries: one as a verb and the other as a marker preceding a verb.[8]

It might be more accurate, then, to view our two-part classification instead as a continuum, with most words belonging at either the root end or the marker end, but with a number of forms at various points closer to the middle. Figure 3.1 illustrates such a continuum (adapted from Schütz 1975:112).

FIGURE 3:1 THE CONTINUUM NATURE OF ROOT VS. MARKER[9]					
ROOT					MARKER
←					→
vale	*tiko*	*qai*	*mai*	*tī-*	*e*
totoka	*koto*				*i*
gunu					*kē*

The forms at the extremes are "purely" root or marker: *vale* 'house', *totoka* 'beautiful', and *gunu* 'drink' can be used only as roots. *E* 'at', *i* 'to', and *kē* 'if' can be used only as markers. But (moving from left to right) *tiko* 'stay' and *koto* 'lie' are used not only as roots, but also as forms with more of a grammatical function than most roots have—in this case, to indicate progressive or continuative action. *Qai*, used in Standard Fijian (SF) to show that a verb is one part of a sequence, occurs in other Fijian languages as a root, with the meaning 'go'. *Mai* 'hither', on the other hand, seems primarily a marker, but it can be used as an imperative (a contraction, perhaps, of *lako mai*) meaning 'Come!' *Tī-* rarely occurs as a root,[10] but seems fused to certain morphemes, as in *tītolo* 'pith of certain trees' (also *tīdolo*) and *tīdromu* 'sink', to indicate vertical movement or distance.

It has been suggested in a number of sources that markers develop from roots. Among others, the Nguna language (Schütz 1969), with its "verbal prepositions" (Ray 1926:218–19), offers contemporary evidence for such a hypothesis. Thus, we might envision—for a few forms—a slow left-to-right drift in figure 3:1.

---

[8] In contrast, Capell's dictionary (1941) includes only one function—that as a verb. It may be that less common forms interpreted here as markers have been analyzed as parts of compound verbs (see CH 15.

[9] Adapting the suggestion of note 6 would eliminate the continuum by assumption. For each of the forms in any position except the extremes, there would be two meanings: one as a root, and one as a marker.

[10] PG noted that *tī* is used in the context of root crops to indicate downward growth.

3.2 DISCUSSION

3.2.1 Root vs. marker

The division of forms into roots and markers[11] closely follows George B. Milner's innovative treatment (1956 [1972]). With this classification, he formed a working definition of the phrase—one obligatory root with (mostly) optional markers clustering around it (see his tables, 1972:84, 94, and 116).

Perhaps because of the relative freedom of most roots to occur in both noun phrases and verb phrases,[12] Milner did not classify roots further. In a review of Milner's work, Biggs and Nayacakalou (1958:80–82) criticized that classification for being too broad:

> The implication is that all bases can occur with both nominal and verbal particles. This is not the case for Fijian. While it is true that most Fijian bases can occur with either nominal or verbal particles, there is a large class which can occur only with nominal particles, e.g., *ose* (horse), *kolii* [*kolī*] (dog), *vale* (house). The failure to differentiate such classes impairs the value of a grammar as a set of combinatorial rules for constructing acceptable utterances in the language.

Milner (personal communication) countered this argument with examples like these:

| *keu* | *ose* | 'if I were a horse' | *keu* | *vale* | 'if I were a house' |
| SUB | horse | | SUB | house | |

in which *ose* and *vale* appear in a verb phrase. But these examples are actually indefinite identifying constructions; see §2.1.4.1 Because any noun can appear in such a construction, the argument is not useful.

Each side of the disagreement seems to show the futility of the opposite position. This is why I have chosen a more subjective criterion for classification: how forms are *usually* used.

3.2.2 Noun vs. verb

The next step in classifying words is find a pattern in the distribution of roots. Based on general knowledge of other languages and linguistic theory, we look first for a division between verb phrase and noun phrase.[13] Such a division, it turns out, is a clear-cut one. All verb phrases that can serve as independent sentences

---

[11] We use different terms here; Milner (1972) used "base" and "particle." I have reserved those terms for phonological units; see §39.2.2.

[12] Nor did he distinguish between these two phrase types, for he showed both "nominal particles" and "verbal particles" in the same table. For me, it was Buse's articles on Rarotongan (1963) that pointed out the necessity of describing noun phrases and verb phrases separately, which I did for Nguna (Schütz 1969).

[13] Milner (9/79) suggested that it be made clear here that nouns and verbs are not absolute terms. It is especially important to note that neither the use of these terms, nor the designation of noun phrases and verb phrases, assumes that the Indo-European subject-predicate relationship holds for Fijian. See Schütz and Nawadra 1972:101.

begin with a marker that indicates person and number.[14] This marker, then, serves to identify verb phrases. Phrases without such a marker are, by default, classified as noun phrases.

However, although the larger element—the grammatical phrase—can be identified formally, its principal component—the head—is not so easily labeled. In Fijian, simple roots contain no formal clues as to functional class: for instance, verbs do not consistently end in a particular vowel, begin with a particular consonant, have a special number of syllables, or have an infinitive form (as Latin does). And although including some markers closely associated with certain bases, such as *-va* in *gunu-va* 'drink it', increases the chances that a form will be used in verb phrases, it may still be used in a construction like *na no-na gunu-va* 'his drinking it', which is a NP. And conversely, there are forms that do not take such suffixes as *-va*, but still appear to be verbs.

Because of these difficulties, we end up with guidelines (rather than a definition) similar to those for distinguishing between a root and a marker: a verb is a form that occurs *most commonly* as the head of a verb phrase. In the absence of extensive statistical information about the use of words, "most commonly" is sometimes difficult to determine. However, the following examples (from *FR1*:10) show that the matter is often straightforward (verb phrases are enclosed in square brackets; the verb appears in boldface):[15]

1 *[Sā **dua** tani]*   na   katakata.   'The heat is exceptional.'
   ASP one different   DEF hot

2 *[E **katakata**] na   gone.*   'The child is hot.'
   3S hot   DEF   child

3 *[E **katakata**] na   tina   ni   gone.*   'The child's mother is hot.'
   3S hot   DEF   mother POS child

4 *[Erau sā **lako**] ki   na vūnikau na   tina   ni   gone.*
   3D   ASP go   ABL DEF tree   DEF   mother POS   child

   kei   na   gone.   'The child's mother and the child go to the tree.'
   CNJ   DEF   child

5 *[Sā **koto**] e   na   ruku   ni   vūnikau na   ibe.*
   ASP lie   ABL   DEF   under POS   tree   DEF   mat
   'A mat is lying under the tree.'

---

[14] As we treat the structure of the verb phrase in more detail, we will find that there are a number of constructions in which the verb phrase marker has been deleted. Such a deletion is common for second person singular (in imperative sentences) and for third person singular.

[15] The style of the following story does not represent normal conversation, particularly since a NP specifies most subjects. But the sentences do show a clear contrast between root and marker.

6 *[E **sega**] ni **katakata** e na ruku ni vūnikau.*[16]
   3S not SUB hot   ABL DEF under POS tree
   'It isn't hot under the tree.'

7 *[E na **dabe**] e na ruku ni vūnikau na tina ni gone.*
   3S FT sit   ABL DEF under POS tree   DEF mother POS child
   'The child's mother will sit under the tree.'

8 *[E na **davo**] e na ruku ni vūnikau na gone.*
   3S FT lie   ABL DEF under POS tree   DEF child
   'The child will lie under the tree.'

The phrases themselves are defined in this way: the beginning is marked by a person-number morpheme that serves as subject, or by certain markers with which the third person singular subject is deleted. For our purposes here, one phrase ends where another begins.

I chose this simple story, even though the style is not colloquial, because all the words used as heads of phrases turn out to occur "most commonly" in such a position. Often, such is not the case. On the first page of another primer (*NV1*), we find:

E siga ni lotu.   'It is a day of worship.'
3S day POS worship

with *siga* 'day' fulfilling one of the requirements just stated for verbs: it occurs after the person-number marker. However, *siga* with this meaning (it can also mean 'to stop raining, to dry') occurs more often in noun phrases than in verb phrases.[17] Therefore, it is not classified as a verb, but as a form *used* as a verb.

So far, most of the verbs have been easily recognizable as the element within the phrase that carries "lexical meaning." Then too, the orthography reinforces our impressions: particles indicating (for example) aspect and tense are written separately from the verb.

But as more function morphemes are added to flesh out such skeleton phrases, it becomes harder to classify them. Although the person-number marker is easily identified (from a closed list of fifteen forms), other function morphemes present a problem: should they be interpreted as affixes or as separate particles? The solution adopted is a partially functional one.

First, those markers that change the ultimate classification of the verb (with respect to the relationship between actor and goal) are considered to be derivational affixes and are written here as part of the verb.[18] Examples are:

---

[16] This sentence actually has two verb phrases; the second is introduced by a subordinate marker. See §29.1.1.2.1.

[17] The construction itself is classed as identifying—a type that regularly uses a noun in the verb phrase.

[18] The official orthography treats *via* as a separate word, *vaka-* (causative) as a prefix, and *vei* sometimes as one, sometimes as the other.

vei-vaka-mate-i	'destruction, killing'	*vaka-cici*	'make [s.t.] run'
vei-wati-ni	'[be] husband and wife'	*via-gunu*	'thirsty'[19]

In contrast, those markers that show tense, aspect, discourse relationships, respect, etc., and which do not change the classification of the verb, are treated not as affixes, but as separate markers. Examples are:

ā	(past)	*sā*	(aspect)	*qai*	(sequential)	*na*	(definite)
bau	(tentative)	*baci*	(iteration)	*mani*	(sequential)		

Next, markers occurring between such derivational affixes and the base, while not necessarily making derivational changes, are considered affixes. Examples:

vaka-tā-kilā 'reveal it'   *vaka-nā-daku*[20]   'turn the back'

Finally, because of customary orthographic conventions, the transitive marker (*-Ci* or *-Caki*; the first C may be Ø) and the third person singular object *a* are written as suffixes:

rai-c-a[21]   'see it'

When C is Ø, and the base ends in *-a*, the addition of the object *a* results in a long vowel, which is written *ā*, rather than *aa, and no orthographic separation is possible. Thus,

kila + Ø + *a* → *kilā*   'know it'

In addition, the other markers (discussed earlier) that were once considered to "change the accent" are written as suffixes.

On the other hand, the objects other than third person singular, since they are all at least a measure in length, are written separately:

rai-ci ira	'see them (plural)'	*rai-ci iko*	'see you (singular)'
rai-ci keirau	'see us (dual exclusive)'	*raici au*	'see me'

Following is a partial list of verbal markers often written as affixes:

via-	(desiderative)	*vei*	(reciprocal)
vaka-	(causative, etc.)	*ta-*, etc.	(stative)
-tā-	'pretend, play at, etc.'	*-Ci*	(transitive marker)
-Caki	(transitive marker)	*-a*	(third-person singular object)
-(C)a	(stative suffix)	*yā*	(counter)

3.3 SUMMARY

This chapter has discussed the primary division of Fijian words and morphemes into ROOTS and MARKERS, and the characteristics of each type. In some cases, the hazy line between the two categories suggests that individual membership in

---

[19] It is uncertain whether this verb is a stative or an active.

[20] PG (79) suggested that *nā* might originally have been a verb. In Lau, *vaka-nā wai* means 'channel, collect water'.

[21] The *i* is lost before the third person singular object *a*. For a historical discussion, see Geraghty 1983:263–66.

one of the two categories is dynamic, not static, and that a continuum is a more accurate model for the classification than a dichotomy.

*****

In the chapters that follow, grammatical markers and content forms are treated in the order in which they occur in the VP.

4 SUBJECTS

In this chapter, we examine the obligatory[1] element—the subject—that combines with a verb to form a basic VP.

A subject is a form that indicates the grammatical categories of PERSON, NUMBER, and the INCLUSIVE-EXCLUSIVE distinction. Its semantic referent is either an actor or a goal, depending on the type of verb it precedes: with an active verb, the subject represents the actor; with a stative verb, it represents the goal.

TABLE 4.1: SUBJECTS[2]

	First person exclusive	First person inclusive	Second person	Third person
Singular	au		o	e
Dual	keirau	(e)daru	(o)drau	(e)rau
Trial	keitou	((e)da)tou	(o)dou	(e)ratou
Plural	keimami	(e)da	(o)nī	(e)ra

(In table 4.1, TRIAL refers to three or a few. The parentheses show parts of the subject that can be omitted in casual or faster speech.[3] For example, for first person trial inclusive, one might also hear *tou*, *datou*, or *edatou*. For a discussion of the results of such

---

[1] Obligatory at least in the underlying structure. On the surface, there are a few constructions in which the subject is deleted. See these exceptions just below table 4.1.

[2] The table follows Milner 1972:54 and Geraghty 1977. The forms in parentheses are explained in §4.9.

[3] Arms (1987:104) gave an example of a whole form (e.g., *eratou*, which would normally begin the VP) being omitted: *rairai vinaka dina [o ratou* 'they'] *[na luvemu* 'your children'] 'Your children are really good-looking.' It raises at least three questions. (1) How would native speakers describe the style? (2) What was the context from which the sentence was taken? (3) Can all first-person and second-person subjects also be deleted, or only third-person forms? Note that there can be no ambiguity, since the two bracked phrases, especially the first, specify the missing subject. However, it does point the way to further research on the grammatical category of specification (see CH 26). See also the next footnote.

shortening, see §36.2.4.3. For (*o*), see §4.7.)

With the exception of third person singular,[4] which is often deleted, and imperatives, in which the subject is optional, each VP contains a subject.

4.1 PERSON

The category of PERSON deals with the relationship among three entities: SPEAKER (1st person), ADDRESSEE (2nd person), and SPOKEN-ABOUT (3rd person). However, "person" can be described by referring to only the first two components. Thus, the components of first and second person are obvious; third person can be defined negatively as [-speaker, -addressee].

4.2 NUMBER

Within its set of subjects (and objects), Fijian distinguishes among four numbers: singular, dual, trial, and plural. Only the singular and dual are as straightforward as the labels suggest. For example, a simple experiment[5] showed that even in a contrastive situation, a group of three and a group of twelve could both be referred to by *eratou*, traditionally called "trial." Some consultants suggested that groups as large as fifteen could still be referred to with the trial form; others thought that the upper limit could be much larger. Thus, there is no explicit dividing line between trial and plural. Instead, the key seems to be not absolute numbers, but *contrast*.[6]

4.3 INCLUSIVE-EXCLUSIVE

For first person [1], numbers higher than singular are different than those for second [2] and third [3] person (Lyons 1968:277). (As an English example: *we* does not equal two or more *I*'s.) Thus, first person dual, trial, and plural can consist of different combinations of persons: [+1, +2, +3], [+1, +2, -3], or [+1, -2, +3]. The inclusive-exclusive distinction hinges on whether [2] is included.

This system is not quite as orderly as it appears. The componential treatment just given shows two possibilities for [+2]: one with and one without [3]. Fijian does not distinguish between these two situations; the exact arrangement either doesn't matter, or must be ascertained through context. All second person forms greater than singular show the same ambiguity. For example:

onī   (second person plural)

can refer literally to a group of addressees, or any combination of addressees and entities other than speaker and addressee.

---

[4] PG (10/83) pointed out that actually, it is only third person that is deleted, since the singular marker is zero.

[5] On 7 July 1981, I showed consultants a series of boxes, each with a different number of circles representing people. The consultants were requested to choose a subject that could refer to specific groups of "people," as represented by the circles in both individual boxes and those grouped for comparisons.

[6] PG collected a text in which approximately thirty people are referred to variously with trial and plural.

4.4 FORMS OF RESPECT

As do many other Pacific languages, Fijian uses the number distinction within the set of subjects to show respect. In SF, terms of respect relate principally to second person forms—that is, terms of address. Thus, the respectful address is confined to the set of subjects, and is specifically *onī*, literally second person plural.

Within first person, the number does not change to show respect; e.g., a speaker referring to a chief and himself would use the dual form *keirau*, not the plural form *keimami*. Nor does second person, when one is not directly addressing a person of rank, reflect such respect: e.g., 'you (singular) and the chief' would be referred to as *odrau*, not *onī*.

PG noted (10/83), however, that first person dual inclusive can be used in a deferential way, when actually first person singular exclusive is meant. And to achieve the opposite effect, second person dual is used (when actually referring to third person singular) when making disparaging comments. DA added (10/84) that the dual also seems to be used in place of the singular when addressing a person who is in a certain relationship to the speaker.

Third person forms present some variation. TRN (7/81) reported that SF does not usually use *era* (3rd person plural) to refer to a chief. However, influence from other areas—principally Bua and Lakeba, but others as well—has resulted in instances of *era* being used in that way. But ceremonial Bauan, more conservative, still uses the singular: e.g., *vuā na tūraga* 'to the chief', not *vei ira na tūraga*. When *era* is used for respect, it is only for very high chiefs (PG 10/83).

In more "traditional" Fijian culture, it is likely that the sole recipients of such a sign of respect were persons of hereditary rank. This system remains: hereditary chiefs are still accorded such respect. But as new institutions with their own hierarchical structures have been introduced, the domain of the system has expanded. Now people with nonhereditary status—e.g., a prime minister, director, chairman, bishop, teacher, principal, spouse of an important person, even a linguist, etc.—are often addressed in the plural (LT 7/81). One might suggest that people in these positions, along with visitors, are automatically accorded honorary status.

All in all, the system is complex—depending on a number of variables. Among them are age, rank, chieftainship, status, familiarity, kin, clan, occupation, and political position.

4.5 REFERENTS: HUMAN OR NONHUMAN?

It has been suggested in a number of sources that nonsingular third person subjects refer only (or nearly so) to humans. Data do not support this observation. The criterion for nonsingular subjects seems to be not humanness, but *individuality*. Entities treated as individuals are countable. Note the following examples (VPs—without modifiers—are enclosed in brackets, subjects in boldface). Here, *eratou* refers to the types of *masi* 'tapa' named in the preceding sentence.

O iratou oqori, [*eratou raba-i-lelevu ka bababalavu.*]
PRP 3T   DEM:2   3T   width-PC-big CNJ long
'Those (just named)—they are wide and long.' (*NV2*:71)

In the following sentence, *era* refers to *soqe* 'pigeons':

[***Era** dau kune gā*] *vaka-levu e   na vei-kau loa.*
3P HAB found INT MAN-big ABL DEF forest dark
'They're found in quantity in the dense forest.' (*NV2*:63)

In the next sentence, the nonsingular form refers to 'customs':

[***Erau** i-tovo   vinaka*] *na vaka-bula kei na vaka-yadra.*
3D   NOM-custom good   DEF say-hello CNJ DEF say-good-morning
'Saying hello and good morning are two good customs.' (*NV3*:1)

In the following example, the dual subject refers to 'beauty' and 'excellence':

Oqō   e dua na salusalu totoka [*ni   **rau** lako vata*] *na totoka ni*
DEM:1 3S one DEF lei   beauty SUB 3D go   CNC DEF beauty POS

ke-na i-rairai kei na daumaka ni   kena i-boi.
PC-3S NOM-see CNJ DEF excellent POS PC-3S NOM-smell

'This is a beautiful lei because these things go together: the beauty of its appearance and the excellence of its fragrance.' (*NV3*:29)

In the following sentence, *era* refers to caterpillars:

[*E sō*] *na bānuve* [***era** drokadroka*], [*e sō   dravu*].
3S some DEF caterpillar 3P green   3S some grey
'Some caterpillars are green, some are grey.' (*NV2*:47)

At first, there seems to be a grammatical mismatch between *e* and *era*. However, the phrase *e sō* is existential (and idiomatic) and by itself means 'There are some.'[7]

The following sentence refers to three entities that are definitely nonhuman: the Lakeba, Bau, and Rewa languages:

[*Ni **ratou** rogo-ci vata*] *na vosa   ni vanua e tolu,* [*eratou duidui*
SUB 3T   hear-TR CNC DEF language POS land 3S three 3T   different

sara]. 'When the languages from these three places were compared,
INT   they were very different.' (*SR* 20/4/82)

In summary: the nonsingular forms are used when entities are being treated as individuals.

---

[7] TRN (4/82) thought that such personifying was an innovation. He preferred the nonpersonal construction using just *e*. At least in this instance, in which the category of "caterpillar" is being referred to as a whole, there is no need to specify its number.

4.6 MORPHOLOGICAL ANALYSIS

Earlier, it was indicated that subjects and objects have the components of person and number. It follows, then, that each subject can be divided into at least two morphemes. Geraghty (1977:5–6) suggested that for subjects, *e* (1st person inclusive), *o* (2nd person), and *e* (3rd person) be considered person markers, even though they are "redundant as such."[8]

If so, the residue in each subject can be considered a number marker. Thus, the person-number morphemes are:

Singular: zero
Dual: Three allomorphs, *daru*, *drau*, and *rau*
Trial: Three allomorphs, *datou*, *dou*, *ratou*
Plural: Four allomorphs, *mami*,[9] *da*, *nī*, *ra*

These allomorphs are morphologically conditioned.

One can notice immediately that this set contains a number of forms that recur, but not in an orderly pattern. In the analysis, one reaches a point of diminishing returns, resulting in a morphological solution that is more complicated than the problem.

The one remaining recurring form is *kei-*, which can be called a marker of exclusiveness. If so, the inclusive forms present a problem. Either we consider them base forms, with *kei-* added to form the exclusive; or we propose a zero morpheme for inclusiveness.

In addition to the general distinctions just discussed, we need to deal with the following matters. The first are concerned only with the set of subjects.

4.7 (*K*)*O*-

The "alternation" between *o* and *ko* has at least two dimensions: geographic and stylistic. David Cargill's manuscript grammar (1839) and early word lists show that *ko* was prominent in the Lau-Vanua Levu area, and *o* in the Bau-Rewa area. Cargill's use of *ko* may have been reinforced by his knowledge of Tongan. Therefore, *o* might have been thought to be a reduced form of *ko*. As an example of the other dimension, Hazlewood ([1850] 1872) described the following alternation: *o* "chiefly" at the beginning of a sentence, *ko* elsewhere. However, an examination of texts that are transcriptions of the spoken language (e.g., Cammack 1961) shows that this "rule" was false—at least in 1961.

Second person subjects do alternate, however, between *o-* and Ø. In informal speech, *o-* forms are seldom heard. Even the singular can be reduced to Ø in commands: e.g., *Lako mada!* 'Please go!'

4.8 MORPHOPHONEMIC CHANGES

The subjects that appear in table 4:1 represent base forms that occur in indicative[10] constructions. Certain morphophonemic changes take place in subordinate

---

[8] That is, even without them, the other forms are all distinct.

[9] Because of the historical development of the forms, Geraghty did not include the first person exclusive forms in the morphological analysis (10/83).

and imperative constructions. These changes are treated in the appropriate sections in CH 29 (e.g., after the markers *ni*, *me*, *kē*, *sē*, and *dē*).

4.9 PHONOLOGICAL VARIATION[11]

The use of parentheses around *e* in table 4:1 represents not only morphophonemic deletion, but also phonological variation. Milner (1972:17) noted:

> *E* is always written and in a formal style of speech it is pronounced, but with the exception of the singular, in colloquial speech it is hardly ever heard, there being at most only a suggestion of it.

A more colloquial writing style, however, often omits *e*. Note the following sentence:

Bāravi totoka,   ni   nuku vulavula.
beach beautiful POS sand white
'It was a beautiful beach, because of the white sand.' (Nawadra 82:1)

And note the contrast in form, but not function, in the following two sentences from the same text (Nawadra 82:1):

Erau   *dau qoli e   na nō-drau tolo   ni   bāravi.*
3D   HAB fish ABL DEF PC-3D   middle POS beach
'They (dual) always fish in their stretch of beach.'

Rau *dau segasega sara ni bau qoli tani.*
3D   HAB not   INT SUB TEN fish DIR
'They (dual) never fish away from there.'

Other writers vary their practice as well. For example, the writer of a newspaper story (*SR* 20/4/82) used *era* exclusively, but preferred *rau* and *ratou* to *erau* and *eratou*.

There are a number of factors that might figure in the variation:

1. *E* serves no function; as Geraghty pointed out (1977:6), "every pronoun form uniquely specifies its person." Thus, zero could represent third person—a common phenomenon.

2. Since *e* is dropped in many other constructions, analogy might encourage omitting it here.

3. In all the forms, *e* constitutes a syllable on its own, unsupported by a consonant. Such syllables are, under certain conditions, unstable. See §36.2.4.2.

4. In *edaru* and *erau*, *e* is unaccented, a feature that works with factor #3 to produce instability.

5. The loss of *e* in *edatou* and *eratou* allows these two-measure forms to shorten to one-measure forms (see §36.2.4.3).

---

[10] "Indicative" here refers to constructions other than subjunctive and imperative.

[11] The reason I refer to this as variation rather than "loss" of *e* is that the situation is closer to a continuum than an either-or matter. Note that Milner's phrase (just below) "a suggestion of [the *e*]" indicates that it is not always possible to determine, in faster speech, whether or not *e* has been uttered.

6. If *e* drops in *eda* and *era*, the resultant *da* and *ra* can combine with following even bases, again reducing the number of measures. See §36.2.4.3.

7. Before [n] forms (*daru, datou, da*), *e* is phonetically less distinct than it would be before other consonants. That is, in faster speech, [e] is indistinguishable from an early onset of voicing before apico-alveolar contact is made for [n].

4.10 DISCUSSION: SUBJECTS AND PREDICATES?

This analysis of the Fijian sentence differs markedly from previous ones by interpreting the so-called pronominal element that precedes the verb as the subject.[12] To understand the reason for doing so, we first review how Fijian grammarians have treated the matter.

4.10.1 The traditional analysis

Following the fashion of their era, Fiji's first grammarians discussed not the subject, but the NOMINATIVE.[13] Hale (1846:382) observed that "the nominative, if it be a pronoun preceded by *ko* or *koi*, usually follows the verb; other pronouns commonly precede. If the nominative be a noun, it generally follows the verb ..." Note that Hale used three adverbial escape words in his description: *usually, commonly,* and *generally*.

Hale did not recognize what eventually came to be the major problem in defining the subject: that one sentence often contains two words or phrases, each of which might qualify as a subject. The following sentence is a simple example (the elements that could be considered subjects are in boldface):

Erau sā dabe **na gone**. 'The two children were sitting.'
3D ASP sit DEF child

In this sentence, both *erau* 'they (dual)' and *na gone* 'the child' could fit the traditional definition of "subject." Sentences such as this, in which two phrases refer to the same entity, are the source of most of the controversy about the subject in Fijian.

Curiously, Hale did not treat any sentences with this specific structure—i.e., a NP specifying the subject, but came close to the matter when he discussed the following sentences (which actually illustrate his "*ko* or *koi*," but with modern spelling):

O yau, au sā lako. 'As for me, I go.'
PRP1S 1S ASP go

Au sā lako o yau. 'I go myself.'
1S ASP go PRP 1S

The first example, he said, was a NOMINATIVE ABSOLUTE, and the second, a

---

[12] Schütz and Nawadra (1972:101) questioned the traditional notion of "subject" in Fijian.

[13] Perhaps they were influenced by Latin grammatical terms.

REFLEXIVE. His translation of the second—'I go myself.'[14]—underscores his analysis: But in fact, the function of the *o yau* phrase is the same in each sentence. The only difference is that the first is fronted, marked in writing by a comma and in speech by a special intonation.

Hazlewood, however, did confront the problem, and he did so by treating the relationship between the two entities as one of several types of CONCORD (1872:56).[15]

Like his predecessors, Churchward (1941) did not treat syntax in detail, which makes it difficult for the reader to form a clear idea of his concept of "subject." But he seems to have interpreted the NP at the end of the sentence as the clearest example of a subject, for he noted (p. 14) that "the predicate usually precedes the subject." All his examples, however, are in the third person—what one might call an "accident of examples" that has continued to the present and contributes to the confusion. In sentences with first or second person subjects, such as:

Au   lako.   'I'm going."
1S   go

O   lako.   'You're going.'
2S   go

the subject was considered to have shifted to precede the predicate. For anything other than the third person singular person marker (*e*), it was suggested that the main function of the "pronouns" that precede the verb is to signal the number of the NP subject (p. 15):

> ... the use of a pronoun ... in apposition or concurrence with the noun, often serves to show whether one, two, a few, or many, are referred to ...

When we examine Milner's treatment, we find that he interpreted a sentence to consist of three main parts (1972:13):

1. Particle	2. Predicate	3. Subject	
Sā	*moce*	*na gone.*	'The child is sleeping.'
E[16]	*lekaleka*	*na lawa.*	'The net is short.'

However, it is difficult to find in his description a consistent use of the term "subject." The problem is the one mentioned earlier: that two very different entities appear to function as subject—the "pronominal" element preceding the verb, and the NP that refers to the same semantic referent. Milner stated (1972:19)[17] that "the pronoun only 'signals' the number and person and the subject may not come until the end of the sentence." Thus, one assumes that the NP

---

[14] In the ENG translation, *myself* does not have a reflexive function, but an emphatic one. See §20.1.3 for Milner's similar misinterpretation.

[15] Cf. the now-common use of the terms "agreement" and "agreement markers" as an attempt to account for the Fijian pattern.

[16] It wasn't until later (see §4.10.2) that grammarians interpreted *e* as a pronoun.

[17] The first edition of Milner's grammar appeared in 1956; most of the references in the present work refer to the 1972 edition.

alone is the subject. But later (p. 53), he listed "the first person verbal pronouns … in the form used when they occur before the base, that is to say as the subject of a sentence." On the next page, he renamed these "verbal pronouns" as "subjective verbal pronouns" or simply "subjective pronouns."

Floyd M. Cammack began his description of the subject (1962:80) by presenting a number of types of subjects, but did not specify which are obligatory and which are optional. But further on (p. 81), he introduced two ideas: apposition (a term that Churchward had used) and split subjects:

> If the phrases in apposition are divided between preposed and postposed subject position, we speak of a *split subject*. The preposed part is ordinarily a cardinal pronoun and may serve to specify the number not indicated by the postposed part.

Here, as did several of his predecessors, Cammack seemed to consider that one of the main functions of the person-number marker preceding the verb is to serve as an indicator of number—a task shirked by the NP.

4.10.2 A reanalysis of "subject"

The present solution hinges first on the interpretation of *e* as third person singular. The origin of such an interpretation is unclear, but Hocart (1917–18:889–90) reported the following native-speaker reaction. In the sentence:

E vinaka na kawai.   'The yam is good."

the speaker responded that "*e* merely stands for *kawai*," which Hocart footnoted "He has been taught to look upon *e* as a pronoun." However, this analysis was not widely known, and it remained for Arms (1974:34–36) and Andrew Pawley (e.g., 1973a:118) independently to propose the idea, thus removing the "irregularity" that earlier grammarians noticed in the lack of a third person singular "subject pronoun" before the verb. If we use this analysis, we can see that all VPs begin with a person-number marker (allowing for the deletion of *e* in many instances, and *e* or *o* in most imperatives).

The next stage in the analysis concerns the frequency of sentences with and without an NP "subject." It is possible that we have received our impression of a "normal" Fijian sentence from the type of linguistic questioning that was common until fairly recently. Just as some phonological misinterpretations have resulted from eliciting words in isolation, so have similar problems grown out of eliciting short sentences out of context. And just as each "word" was actually a complete phrase with respect to intonation, so was each isolated sentence (in a sense) a discourse in itself. As an example, note the following sentences (adapted from *FR1*), in each of which the NP "subject" is in boldface:

*E   dabe   tiko   o   **Jone**.*   'Jone is sitting.'
3S sit   CNT   PRP J

*E   tū   cake   tū   o   **Mere**.*   'Mere is standing up.'
3S stand DIR   CNT PRP M

4 Subjects

*Sā lako tiko i vale o **Jone**.* ASP go CNT ABL house PRP J		'Jone is going home.'
*Sā lako tiko i vale o **Mere**.* ASP go CNT ABL house PRP M		'Mere is going home.'

and the following language-learning exercises (adapted from Moore 1906:12):

*Sā vinaka **no-qu** vatu-ni-volavola.* ASP good POS-1S stone-of-writing	'My writing slate is good.'
*Sā ra-musu **na no-munī** i-sele.* ASP STA-broken DEF POS-2P knife	'Your knife is broken.'
*Sā cā **na** me-dra wai.* ASP bad DEF POS-3P water	'Their water is bad.'
*Sā lako oti **na** tamata.* ASP go ASP DEF person	'The man has come already.'
*Sā lako mai **na** gone.* ASP go DIR DEF child	'The child has come.'

Granted, the purpose of the exercises was to fix particular patterns in the minds of the learners. But some linguists have used such texts as authentic examples of the language. As a result, impressions they have formed are misleading. Following my suggestion, Geraghty (1983:391) found that in a body of transcribed tapes (Cammack 1961), only a minority of sentences followed the pattern illustrated above by including the subject NP. Thus, we see that the subject NP is not obligatory but optional, added to give more information about the semantic reference *when that information is necessary to the hearer*.[18]

Let us return to a summary of the traditional view, that of Churchward (1941:15), quoted above:

---

[18] This view is not so unorthodox. In their search for language universals, popularized in recent years, and in many of the grammatical models proposed during a much longer period, many analysts seem to have forgotten that some very well-studied languages have something rather different from an NP + VP sentence structure.

But the situation has not gone entirely unnoticed. In his argument that nouns are "the one substantive universal of syntactic theory," Lyons (1966:230) admitted that linguists in search of such universals must "account for the fact that in very many languages, the 'verbal complex' may stand as a 'one-word sentence,' independently of the occurrence of previous utterances from which nouns may be 'understood' to function as the subject or object of the sentence in question. Since the 'things' referred to in utterances are often physically present in the situations in which the utterances are spoken, there need be merely a 'pronominal' indication, or no overt indication at all, of the 'things' referred to."

Lyons's description fits one of the cornerstones of classical linguistics: Latin. For Latin, the "personal endings" of the verb show the person and number of the "subject.: Every student who has recited "*portō* 'I carry', *portās* 'you carry' ..." has in fact been uttering a set of complete—albeit strange—sentences. It was not necessary to say "*Ego portō*."

... the use of a pronoun ... in apposition or concurrence with the noun, often serves to show whether one, two, a few, or many, are referred to ... E.g., *erau sā tiko na gone* 'the two children are present' —where *erau* ... meaning 'they-two', shows that *gone* refers to two children.

Much later, Pawley wrote (1986:96): "The following sentences illustrate the use of pronouns to determine the number of subject ... subject and direct object ... and possessor."

I suggest that this approach is backwards. Instead, the "pronoun" (now called the subject) refers to the entity or entities serving as the actor or goal, and the optional NP following the VP *specifies* one of these entities if its identity cannot be determined from the context, or if it seems necessary to emphasize it. Thus, interpreting one of these person-number[19] forms as the subject not only simplifies the concept, but explains some other NP constructions as well (see CH 26). Let us look at arguments on both sides of the question.

4.10.2.1 The traditional view

The following outline summarizes and questions previous analyses of the subject.

1. If only an NP can be the subject, then:
    a. Only a sentence in the third-person has a subject.[20] This question then follows logically: Does a sentence with a first or second person "pronoun" have no subject?
    b. Even in the third person, many sentences have no subject NP at all. Are these subjects then "understood"? Must one resort to proposing underlying forms that include NPs?
2. If both person-number forms and NPs can be subjects:
    a. Sometimes the subject precedes the verb; at other times it follows.
    b. If both a person-number form and an NP are present, which is the subject? Or are they both subjects? This dilemma has prompted such terms as "split subjects," "appositives," "preverbal subject markers," "nominative absolute," "reflexive," and "pronominal agreement markers." The last term is especially inappropriate. Because NPs are not inflected for person, number, or case, it is not clear what is agreeing with what.

4.10.2.2 The present view

Interpreting the person-number forms as subjects has these advantages:

1. There is only one set of subject forms.

---

[19] First person forms also show the inclusive-exclusive distinction, but there seems to be no convenient way to include this in the label.

[20] Except for the independent pronouns (see §20.1.3 and following paragraphs) that are sometimes used for emphasis.

2. Their position is fixed: they precede the verb.
3. The presence of a NP following the VP is considered an instance of specification. Its absence merely means that for discourse purposes, it is unnecessary. In other words, no NP appears in the underlying structure; its function is to add information, to clarify, or to add emphasis.
4. The specification of subjects fits in with two other types: specification in secondary NPs (§26.2) and possessive specification (§26.3). Thus, this interpretation ties together three types of similar phenomena, never before combined into one cohesive system.

For these reasons, it is clear that the present analysis is more satisfactory than the previous ones.

5 VERB PHRASE MARKERS PRECEDING THE HEAD

This section is organized as follows: the position before the head is divided into slots that are arranged according to the order in which the markers occur.[1] Thus, two (or more) markers that are mutually exclusive fit into the same slot.

The general outline is as follows:[2]

1. Subjects
2. Tense: *ā, na*
3. Aspect: *sā, se*
4. Sequence: *qai, mani*
5. Iteration: *baci*
6. Habitual: *dau*
7. Initiation: *tei*
8. Tentative: *bau*
9. Individuality: *dui, yā-*
10. Extreme: *rui*
11. Habitual: *dau*
12. Proximity: *vakarau*
13. Limitation: *tekivū, tini*
14. Directional: *mai, lai*
15. Appearance: *rairai*

In the illustrative phrases and sentences, the particular marker being described is in boldface, and square brackets enclose the VP in question.

5.1 SUBJECTS

Subjects are treated in CH 4. See table 4.1 for an exhaustive list, and other sections of the chapter for a discussion.

David Arms (1986:2026) described the following order changes with respect to the subject and VP markers:

> The subject pronoun may invert around the first occurring marker if this be *ā, sā, se, qai* or *mani* … Where *ā, sā, ā se, sā na,* or *se na* occur, however, the first person exclusive pronouns (and only these) invert around both elements if inversion takes place. For other combinations (e.g. *se qai, sā mani),* the first person exclusive pronouns may invert around one marker only or both. All these

---

[1] The general order is based on Milner's tables (1972:84,116). As frequent quotations show, I also found the analysis in Arms 1986 very useful. Since it was not possible to note every instance in which the order of markers might be changed or another marker substituted in a particular slot, I advise a careful reading of Arms's article.

[2] The qualifier "general" is important, since this order is not absolute.

pronoun inversions are a stylistic property of more lively discourse. Inversions involving *sā* and *se* are the most common.

5.2 TENSE

Two forms mark tense: *ā* past and *na* future. Since past and future cannot (under normal conditions) be associated with the same event, we place them in mutually exclusive categories. However, the past tense marker precedes an aspect marker, and the future tense marker follows it.

E ā sā lako…   'He went (already) …'
E sā na tara vale….   'He will be house building …' (*SF* 36)

5.2.1 Past tense (PT): *ā*

[Erau ā vei-talanoa toka] ko Pita S kei Meke R. 'PS and MR were
3D   PT REC-tell   ASP   PRP PS CNJ MR   telling stories.' (T74:1)

[Ā   mai ravi tū gā]   e   tau-tuba ko Jone. 'J came and leaned
PT DIR lean ASP LIM ABL outside PRP J   outside.' (T74:1)

The past tense marker is optional; it need not be indicated grammatically once it has been established by such time phrases[3] as the following:

e   nanoa   'yesterday'   or   *e   na   vula   sā   oti*   'last month'
ABL yesterday   ABL DEF month ASP finished

The following example refers to time, but is not marked for tense. Because the time has been established by the phrase *e liu*, it is not necessary to include the past tense marker:

E   liu, [era sega ni dau vei-voli] na no-da   qase era dau
ABL ahead 3P   not SUB HAB GEN-buy DEF PC-1PI elder 3P HAB

vulagi gā.   'Before, our elders didn't engage in business/trade, they
visit   INT   practiced visit-gift-exchange.' (*NV*4:11)

PG pointed out (10/83) that both *ā* and time phrases may be omitted; speakers may choose not to be specific about tense or time.

Earlier Bible translations are an exception to this system of optional tense marking; they suggest that the translators tried to apply to Fijian the English system of obligatory tense marking. For example, of the thirty-one verses in the first chapter of Genesis, twenty-three begin with *ā*, regularly followed by *sā* (aspect). However, *ā* does occur in spontaneous, untranslated material, both with and without a phrase referring to time:

Na   gauna ni i-valu levu sā   oti   [era ā   kaci-vi kece ki-na]
DEF time POS fight big ASP finished 3P PT call-TR INC ABL-3S

na   cauravou ni Merekē me ra curu ki na   mata-i-valu.
DEF youth   POS America SUB 3P enter ABL DEF center-PC-war

---

[3] One must distinguish here between *tense*, a grammatical term, and *time*, an element of the real, extralinguistic, world.

'(At) the time of the past great war, all the young men of America were called to enlist in the Army.' (FMC 61)

[Rau ā la-ki sota sara ki-na] o rau na lewe rua oqō.
3D PT go-ABL meet INT ABL-3S PRP 3D DEF people two DEM:1
'These two people went to join.' (FMC 61)

5.2.2 Future tense (FT): *na*

Like *ā*, *na* (future) is optional, but somewhat less so. A sentence representing a proposed situation *can* be marked for future tense by *na*:

*[Au **na** lako nimataka.]*   'I'll go tomorrow.'
1S FT go tomorrow

However, if the time is indicated by a content word, it is not essential to mark the tense. For example, it is omitted in the following sentence, which contains the time word *nimataka*:

[Au lako nimataka.]   'I'll go tomorrow.'
1S go tomorrow

The following examples include *na*:

*[**Na** sega] ni rawa ni vaka-tara-i[4] [m-odou **na** lako taucoko.]*
FT not SUB able SUB CAU-get-TR SUB-2T FT go INC
'It will not be permitted for all of you to go.' (FMC 61)

*Ia [me-u **na** lai tuku-n-a vaka-cava?]*
CNJ SUB-1S FT PUR tell-TR-3S MAN-what
'But how should I tell it? (FMC61)

Na also marks an action/state that the speaker thinks should or must happen (PG 7/82):

*[O sā **na** kana oti.]*   'You should have finished eating by then / I
2S ASP FT eat ASP   presume you've already eaten.'

*[E **na** tiko beka] mai Nausori oqō.*   'It should be at N now.'
3S FT stay TEN ABL N DEM:1

5.3 ASPECT (ASP)

5.3.1 Contrast (past): *sā*

The marker *sā* indicates that an action/state contrasts with a previous one. The effect of this contrast is to focus attention on the action/state marked by *sā*. For example, the following sentence would be appropriate only if it applied to a newborn child who has just been named or to a person who changed his name frequently (PG 7/82):

---

[4] In this form, the phonological and morphological representations are at odds. Adding *-i* to the final *-a* forms a diphthong: *ai*.

[*Sā* o cei beka] o koya?   'Who's that now?'
ASP PRP who TEN PRP 3S

Contrast is especially apparent in the use of *sā* with statives that indicate a nonpermanent state:

[*Sā* bula vinaka] o Tē.   'T's well (now).'
ASP health good   PRP T

This statement implies that T had been ill, but is now well. In other words, the condition has changed.

The following two statements occur in a recorded conversation (Cammack 1962:197), just after a stretch of bawdy talk. The speakers, reflecting on what they have just said, say:

[Au *sā* galu tū gā.]   'I'm keeping quiet (now).'
1S ASP dumb CNT INT

[*Sā* qai dua na niusi rere-vaki.]   'This is a more dangerous report
ASP SEQ one DEF news fear-TR   than any before.'

Some expressions seem to include *sā* automatically. For example:

[*Sā* oti.]   'It's finished.'
ASP finished

The state *oti* 'finished' is usually in contrast to an opposing state. Thus, the meanings of the verb and the aspect marker seem to reinforce each other. However, after subordinate markers (such as *ni* 'when, because'), *oti* occurs without *sā*. (PG).

Similarly, in

[*Sā* vinaka.]   'Very well.'
ASP good

one has the impression that this expression of approval naturally contrasts with an implicit opposing state. Other verbs, as well, give that impression:

madū	'(+coconut) ripe'[5]
matua	'ready for harvesting'
qase	'old'

Sā occurs almost redundantly with certain markers as well as verbs. When *oti* 'finished' is used as a marker after the verb, *sā* is likely to occur in the same VP. See the examples in §18.4.

5.3.2 Contrast (future): *se*

Se is the opposite of *sā*: the action/state in question is contrasted with one that will or may happen. For example, in the following sentence, it is expected that T will eventually arrive:

---

[5] This convention, introduced in Geraghty 1983, means "always or usually used with the following word, or others like it."

[*Se* bera ni lako mai] o Tai.   'T hasn't come yet.'
 ASP late SUB go   DIR PRP T

With statives, *se* indicates that the state may possibly end (thus contrasting it with a future state):

[*se* koto gā] na yago-ni-mate qō
 ASP lie INT DEF body-PC-dead DEM:1S
'while the corpse was still there' (Cammack 1962:192)

e   na gauna [ā *se* bera] ni tekivū ki-na   na i-valu
ABL DEF time PT ASP late SUB begin ABL-3S DEF NOM-fight
'at the time before the war began' (FMC 61:1)

Se followed by *qai* has the meaning of 'just, as soon as' (see Milner 1972:93):

[ni *se* qai kana oti] o Bera   'as soon as B had eaten.'
 SUB ASP SEQ eat ASP PRP B

In informal SF, and perhaps in some other Fijian languages, *se* is replaced by *sa*, called "short *sa*" in some descriptions to distinguish it from *sā*. VV has entered it an alternate to *se*.

5.3.3 Order change

Milner (1972:17) noted that *sā* could occur before subjects, giving the set of third person subjects as an example. He explained the difference between, for example, *erau sā* and *sā rau* as follows:

... in *e ratou sā lako* ... it may be assumed that they have gone some time ago while in *sā ratou lako* ... that they have just gone.

In his discussion of the past tense marker (p. 33), Milner gave the same set, showing that both *ā* and *sā* could occur before the subject.

Arms (1978:1270) could find no difference in meaning[6] in such forms:

This inversion does not correlate with any real semantic difference, but is a matter of style, and occurs much more frequently in informal than in formal contexts.

He also described the extent of the change in order:

All the subject pronouns can invert in this way around *sā* and *se*; also around the past-tense marker *ā*. Where a tense marker and a tense-aspect marker occur together (that is, where *ā sā*, *ā se*, *sā na*, and *se na* occur), the pronouns invert around the first element only (e.g. *ā ra se lako*). The first person exclusive pronouns, however, prefer to come after the second element (e.g. *ā se keimami lako*, *sā na keimami lako*).

Finally, we can note that when *sā*, *se*, or *ā* comes before the subject, the shorter subject forms are used (see the list of subjects in CH 4, table 4.1).

---

[6] This is a narrow use of "meaning." A stylistic difference has meaning as well. I have no examples of the inverted order in texts, and cannot comment on the function of the change of order.

5.4 SEQUENCE (SEQ)

5.4.1 Unmarked sequence: *qai*

Qai indicates that the VP in which it appears refers to a situation that is part of a sequence of two or more. *Qai* does not necessarily mean that something is the effect of an earlier cause, but merely that one situation follows an earlier one.

Qai often appears in a description of a process. The following excerpt is from a story about washing clothes (*NV4*:2–3):

*Ni sā oti oyā, [sā **qai** tuvu-laki kece sara] na i-sulu*
SUB ASP finish DEM:3 ASP SEQ beat-TR INC INT DEF NOM-clothe

   ka ra vuso-laki yani.
   CNJ 3P foam-TR DIR
'After that was finished, the clothes were beaten thoroughly until they were sudsy.'

*[Sā **qai** vaka-wai-vinaka-tak-a kece sara] na i-sulu   ko Nau*
ASP SEQ CAU-water-good-TR-3S INC INT DEF NOM-clothe PRP N

   ka loba-ki   ira sara vaka-vinaka.
   CNJ squeeze-TR 3P INT MAN-good
'Then N soaked the clothes thoroughly and wrung them well.'

*[Sā **qai** tau-r-a   mai] na bēseni ka vaka-tawa-n-a.*
ASP SEQ take-TR-3S DIR DEF basin CNJ CAU-filled-TR-3S

   vaka-vei-māmā e na wai ka uli-a ki-na na wai-loaloa.
   MAN-REC-half ABL DEF water CNJ mix-3S ABL-3S DEF bluing
'Then she brought the basin, and filled it half full of water and poured bluing into it.'

The first example above shows a common sequence of constructions: a *ni* 'when' phrase (especially with *oti* 'finished') followed by a *qai* phrase. The meaning is 'when ... then'. Another example:

Ni sā sevu oti gā na duruka ki vuā   na tūraga,
SUB ASP given ASP INT DEF *duruka* ABL ABL-3S DEF chief

   *[sā **qai** rawa] me se-vi   me lau-kana.*
   ASP SEQ able SUB pick-TR SUB STA-eat
'After the *duruka* has been presented to the chief in the first-fruits ceremony, then it can be picked for eating.' (*NV4*:9)

PG noted (10/83) that *qai* can be used with the sequence implied, as in the following example:

*[**Qai** boko-c-a]   na cina.*   'Turn the light off (after you've finished
SEQ extinguish-TR-3S DEF light   what you're doing).'

5.4.1.1 Order of markers

The order of subject + *qai* can be reversed: *qai* + subject + verb.

5.4.2 Marked sequence: *mani*

Mani, like *qai*, is a marker that relates the situation of the VP in which it occurs to a previous one. Unlike *qai*, however, it indicates more than a sequential relationship between them. Moreover, it seems confined to two situations: that indicated by the *mani* VP is compared to another broad one. Finally, it usually refers to a situation that is the unexpected result of the preceding one—something unusual or the opposite of what might naturally have followed.

> ... ni   lako voli yani,   [e   ā   **mani** kune-a]   e   dua na   loga ni
>   SUB go   DIR DIR   3S PT SEQ   found-3S   3S one DEF plot POS
>
> teitei   levu   '... when he was wandering around, he (unexpect-
> garden   big   edly) found a large garden plot' (*FR5*:10)

> Ni   sā kana oti, [sā **mani** yaco sara]   me   bukete.
> SUB ASP eat ASP   ASP SEQ   arrive INT   SUB pregnant
> 'After eating, it unexpectedly happened that she was pregnant.' (*FR5*:11)

In addition to these definitely unexpected situations, *mani* can also indicate a situation that occurs by chance:

> Era vulagi-taki waiwai na ibe, na uvi sē dalo sē ika;
> 3P   visit-TR   oil   DEF mat   DEF yam CNJ taro CNJ fish
>
> ia   [kē **mani** vula i   vuata], era na vulagi-tak-a.
> CNJ SUB SEQ   month POS fruit   3P   FT visit-TR-3S

'They take (for ritual visiting) oil, mats, yams or taro or fish, and if it should happen to be the season for fruit, they take it. (*NV4*:11)

Note that in the following examples, *mani* is frequently used when things are found:

> Ia   [kē **mani** bera] na ua, me   ratou bau tibi kaikuku mai me i-coi
> CNJ SUB SEQ   late DEF tide SUB 3T   TEN pick shellfish DIR SUB i-coi
>
> ni   vaka-yakavi.   'Since the tide was still coming in, they might pick
> POS supper   mussels for the evening meal's *icoi*.' (*NV4*:12)

> Ka   ni   sā   dī levu tū   gā na mati, [eratou **mani** canu dairo
> CNJ SUB ASP dry big   CNT INT DEF tide   3T   SEQ   gather sea-slug
>
> tale gā mai.]   'And if the tide is very low, they (trial) can then
> ITR LIM DIR   gather sea slugs as well.'

5.4.2.1 Order of markers

Arms noted (1986:202) that *mani* may precede *qai* ...

5.5 ITERATION (ITR): *BACI*

Baci indicates that the situation represented by the VP has occurred a number of times before, and that the present one is merely one more instance:

> Oti   na katalau, [sā   **baci** kau-t-a   tū] ko   Vilive
> finish DEF breakfast ASP   ITR   carried-TR-3S ASP PRP V

5 Verb Phrase Markers Preceding the Head

  na ke-na i-vaka-siga-levu ki vale ni vuli.
  DEF PC-3S NOM-MAN-day-big ABL house POS learn
'After breakfast V once more carried his lunch to school.' (*FR3*:44)

  *[Sā **baci** vōleka tale tiko gā mai] na gauna ni tā dovu.*
  ASP ITR near ITR CNT LIM DIR DEF time POS cut sugarcane
'Once again cane cutting time is drawing near.' (*FR3*:57)

Baci often has a mildly afflictive (and noniterative) sense:

  *Sega ni dedē, [sā **baci** basi-k-a mai] na vucesā oyā.*
  not SUB long ASP ITR appear-TR-3S DIR DEF lazy DEM:3
'Before long that lazy person will appear again (*VV*)

  *[O na **baci** kana kuita.]*   'You'll be whipped.' (*VV*)
  2S FT ITR undergo whip

5.6 HABITUAL (HAB): *DAU*[7]

Dau indicates that a situation occurs regularly. For example, it is used to indicate the regularity of seasonal events:

  *Na ivi e vua-t-a ni yabaki [ka ni **dau** vua gā] vaka-dua*
  DEF *ivi* 3S bear-TR-3S POS year CNJ SUB HAB bear LIM MAN-one

    e vei-yabaki.   'The *ivi* is an annual fruit because it bears fruit
    ABL DIS-year   just once each year.'

  *[E **dau** qai matua] na ivi e na vula i nuqa lailai.*
  3S HAB SEQ mature DEF *ivi* ABL DEF month POS *nuqa* small
'Then the *ivi* (fruit) matures in December.' (*NV4*:15)

Or it indicates that something is done through custom or convention:

  *E na ke-na i-valavala dina vaka-vanua, [e **dau** sevu na ivi.]*
  ABL DEF PC-3S NOM-custom true MAN-land 3S HAB offer DEF *ivi*
'In true Fijian custom, the *ivi* is always presented as an offering.' (*NV4*:15)

PG (10/83) added the idiom *ni ... dau* 'whenever':

  *Ni-u **dau** rai-ci koya, au tagi.*   'Whenever I see her, I cry.'
  SUB-1S HAB see-TR 3S 1S cry

This marker also occurs in slot 5.11.

5.6.1. *Dau*: Order changes

Arms (1986:202 noted that *dau* could occur in different positions: "It ... may occur ahead of the preceding markers up to and including *qai* ..." However, except for the common inversions *bau dau ~ dau bau*, other changes are less common.

---

  [7] *Dau* functions in VPs and NPs. In the former, it acts as one of the so-called moveable markers in the periphery of the phrase; in the latter, as a prefix to the base. For example, in *dau-gunu* 'drunkard', *dau* precedes a verb; the whole form functions as a noun.

5.7 INITIATION (INI): *TEI*

Tei preceding a verb indicates that the action/state represented is the first of a series. When *tei* occurs, the verb is often followed by *mada* (see §18.12.2).

[*Tou **tei** sili   mada], qai kana.*   'Let's (trial) bathe first, then eat.'
 1TI INI bathe INI   SEQ eat   (*VV*)

[*Au **tei** kana mada], au qai lako.*   'Let me eat first, and I'll go.'
 1S INI eat   INI   1S SEQ go   (Capell 1941:41)

[*Me-u **tei** vaka-macala-tak-a mada] na   vu-na.*
 SUB-1S INI CAU-clear-TR-3S   INI   DEF reason-3S
'Let me first explain the reason.' (Milner 1972:107)

In his dictionary, Hazlewood suggested that *tei* might be an intensive.
    Milner (1972:107) defined the sequence *tei* ... *mada* (as well as *taumada*) as 'first of all', 'beforehand'.
    Tei also means 'quickly, first', and can occur without *mada* (PG 82):

[*Au sā tei lako.]*   'First of all, I'll go.'
 1S ASP INI go

5.8 TENTATIVE (TEN): *BAU*

The marker *bau* makes the stance of the speaker (or actor) less assertive, determined, or purposeful.[8]

[*E **bau** coko   tale gā] ki-na   e dua na   qiō.*
 3S TEN caught ITR LIM ABL-3S 3S one DEF shark
'Even a shark as well was caught in it.' (*NV2*:11)

[*ni sā **bau** mate sara] e   na liliwa e   na bogi*
 SUB ASP TEN die   INT ABL DEF cold ABL DEF night
'that he suffered extremely from the cold during the night' (*FR5*:18)

[***Bau** dua mada gā] na   luvē-daru me daru dau lasa voli ki-na*
 TEN one INI   LIM DEF child-1DI SUB 1DI HAB happy DIR ABL-3S
'Just one child would make us happy.' (*FR5*:15)

Without *bau*, each of these statements would be too abrupt.
    Bau is used in questions and imperatives for the same reason: to make them less assertive:

[*E **bau** i-vola   vinaka] ko wili-k-a   tiko oqori?*
 3S TEN NOM-write good   2S read-TR-3S CNT DEM:2
'Is that book you're reading any good?' (*FR3*:43)

[*Qai **bau** wili-k-a   tale gā?]*   'Then perhaps you should read it, too?'
 SEQ TEN read-TR-3S ITR LIM   (*FR3*:43)

---

[8] At least as reflected in speech, these qualities are not culturally desirable, but are perceived as abrupt and immodest.

*E rawa [ni-u **bau** toma-ni kemudou tū yani?]*
3S possible SUB-1S TEN accompany-TR 2T CNT DIR
'May I accompany you in that?' (*NV3*:15)

*A cava [e sā **bau** tuku-n-a] na no-na vū-ni-wai?*
DEF what 3S ASP TEN tell-TR-3S DEF PC-3S source-POS-water
'What does her doctor say? (T74:41)

VV adds a meaning of 'ever, once':

*[O sā **bau** kana gata]?*   'Have you ever eaten snake?'
2S ASP TEN eat snake

*[Au sega ni **bau** rogo-c-a] na yaca-na.* 'I've never heard his name.'
1S not SUB TEN hear-TR-3S DEF name-3S

5.9 INDIVIDUALITY (IND): *DUI, YĀ-*

5.9.1 *Dui*

Dui, which occurs with subjects greater than singular, refers to actions performed or states maintained individually.

*E duidui na tiki ni sere [eratou **dui** laga-t-a] na domo-vā.*
3S differ DEF part POS sing 3T IND sing-TR-3S DEF voice-four
'They are all different—the parts that a quartet sings.'

In the example above, the domain of *dui* is the VP itself: it refers to (and names) the individual situations. The example below shows that it can also occur in the NP (*no-dra dui vosa gā*).

The following extended example comes from a passage explaining that a number of missionaries were engaged in translating the gospels into the languages of their respective areas. The repeated use of *dui* makes it clear that each operation was a separate one. The passage also uses *dui* in an NP, and *duidui* as a verb.

*[Ratou sā **dui** volavola] ka taba i-vola na i-talatala e na*
  3T ASP IND write CNJ print NOM-write DEF NOM-tell ABL DEF

*vei-vanua [eratou ā **dui** tū] ki-na e na ke-na vosa gā. [Era sā*
DIS-land 3T PT IND CNT ABL-3S ABL DEF PC-3S talk LIM 3P ASP

***dui** vuli volavola] kei na wili-i-vola na Lotu e na*
IND learn write CNJ DEF read-NOM-write DEF religion ABL DEF

*no-dra **dui** vosa gā, ia sā tekivū votu ka vā-kila-i mai*
PC-3P IND talk LIM CNJ ASP begin appear CNJ CAU-know-TR DIR

*e dua tale na leqa, oyā ni sega ni ra mani **duidui** sara*
3S one ITR DEF trouble DEM:3 SUB not SUB 3P SEQ different INT

na vosa ni vei-vanua, ka sā na vaka-levu cakacaka gā
DEF talk POS DIS-land CNJ ASP DEF MAN-big work LIM

*[ke ra **dui** taba-ki.] Na cava na i-wali ni leqa?*
CNJ 3P IND print-TR DEF what DEF NOM-salve POS trouble

'The clergymen (individually) wrote and printed books in the various places where they stayed (individually) in the language (that is, of each place). They (those who had professed Christianity) studied (individually) writing and reading in their respective languages, but there began to appear and become known another problem—that the languages of the various places weren't after all very different, it would increase work if they were each printed. What was the solution to the problem?' (*SR*/20/4/82).

5.9.1.1 *Dui*: Order changes

Arms (1986:202) noted that *dui* could "invert around ... *mai*, *lai*, and *laki* ... with the possibility of a slight meaning difference."

5.9.2 *Yā-*

This marker is treated as an affix in §8.10. As noted there, however, it is in complementary distribution with *dui*, which is why it is included here.

5.10 EXTREME, EXCESS (EXT): *RUI*

The marker *rui* indicates an extreme or excess quality or quantity. It usually occurs with S1 verbs:

| [Sā **rui** levu.] | 'It was very/too big.' / |
| ASP EXT big | 'There were very/too many.' |

[Sā **rui** drēdrē.]   'It was very/too difficult.'
ASP EXT hard

But it can be used with other types of verbs as well:

[Au sā **rui** loma-leqe-taki   Ālisi] vaka-levu. 'I'm very worried
1S ASP EXT inside-trouble-TR A   MAN-big   about A.' (T74:41)

[Au sā **rui** loma-ni   koya] vaka-levu.   'I care for her very much.'
1S ASP EXT inside-TR 3S   MAN-big   (T74:41)

5.10.1 *Rui*: Order changes

Arms wrote (1986:202): "From its common position ... it may move ahead of any of the preceding markers up to and including *qai*. It may also follow [*dau*, *dui*, *mai*, *lai*, and *laki*]."

5.11 (5.6) *DAU*

See §5.6 for a discussion of this marker in a different position.

5.12 PROXIMITY, READINESS (PRX): *VAKARAU*

Vakarau, used as the main verb, means 'ready':

[Sā **vakarau**] na kākana.   'The food is ready.'
ASP ready   DEF food

As an auxiliary, it means 'near, ready to be, about to be':

[Eda sā   na **vakarau** galala.]   'We'll soon be free.'
1Pl ASP FT PRX   free

*E na bati ni toba [keimami **vakarau** curu-m-a.]*
ABL DEF edge POS bay 1PX PRX enter-TR-3S
'At the edge of the bay we were beginning to enter.' (*FR6*:7)

To show the order of *vakarau* and the markers closest to it, TRN supplied the following examples:

*E **vakarau** tekivū kana.*   'He was ready to begin to eat.'
3S PRX   ORG   eat

*E **vakarau** lai kana.*   'He was ready to go eat.'
3S PRX   DIR eat

The order of *vakarau* and *lai* is somewhat flexible.

5.13 LIMITS OF AN ACTION/STATE (LIM)

Two markers—*tekivū* and *tini*—are used to set the limits of an action/state.

5.13.1 Origin (ORG): *tekivū*

Tekivū, used as the head of a VP, means 'begin':

***Tekivū** mada.*   'Please begin.'
begin   INT

Preceding another verb, it serves as a marker:

*[Sā **tekivū** taba-ki] na i-Vola   Tabu e   na vosa vaka-Lakeba.*
ASP ORG   print-TR DEF NOM-write sacred ABL DEF talk MAN-L
'The Bible was begun to be printed in the Lakeba language.' (*SR* 20/4/82)

*[Me tou sā na **tekivū** tau-ri-vak-a] na i-vaka-rau   oqō.*
SUB 1TI ASP FT ORG   take-TR-TR-3S DEF NOM-CAU-fit DEM:1
'Let us begin to use these instructions.' (FDP)

When *tekivū* is used as a verb, the prefix *vaka-* adds a causative meaning. But with *tekivū* as a marker, *vaka-* does not seem to change the meaning. Note the following examples:

*[Sā qai vaka-**tekivū** soko lesu tale mai] ki Rewa.*
ASP SEQ CAU-ORG   sail return ITR DIR ABL R
'Then she started sailing back to R.' (*FR5*:11)

*[Sā vaka-**tekivū** kani-a sara] na ke-na vudi.*
ASP CAU-ORG   eat-3S INT DEF PC-3S banana
'She started eating her banana.' (*FR5*:11)

5.13.2 Completion (ULT): *tini*

Tini, used as the head of a VP, means 'to conclude':

*E **tini-a** na i-tukutuku.*   'He finished the story.' (Capell 1941)
3S finish-3S DEF NOM-tell

As a marker, *tini* indicates that the action/state referred to by the main verb is the final one in a series, or otherwise completes a cycle.⁹

*Na no-mu vaka-welewele, [e na **tini** druka] ki-na na no-mu timi.*
DEF PC-2S MAN-careless 3S FT ULT lose ABL-3S DEF PC-2S team
'Through your carelessness, your team will end up losing.'

*E na totoka ni cila ni vula, [au ā **tini** vaka-muri sala kina.]*
3S DEF beauty POS shine POS moon 1S PT ULT CAU-follow path ABL-3S

'With the beauty of the shining of the moon, I was finally able to follow the path because of it.'

5.14 DIRECTIONAL (DIR)

There are two directional markers that occur before the verb: *mai* and *lai*. The term "directional" applies loosely here; each marker can indicate metaphorical as well as literal direction.

5.14.1 Preverbal *mai*

One common meaning of *mai* before a verb is to indicate literal motion toward a reference point. For example:

*[E **mai** soko-tak-a] na no-na waqa.*   'He came to sail his canoe.'
3S DIR sail-TR-3S DEF PC-3S canoe

Note that the motion is independent of the meaning of the verb. This use of *mai* contrasts with its use after the verb:

*[E soko-tak-a **mai**] na no-na waqa.*   'He sailed his boat here.'
3S sail-TR-3S DIR DEF PC-3S canoe

In this sentence, the idea of motion is contained in the verb itself, and *mai* serves to indicate direction only.

Mai also has a less literal use.¹⁰ It shows that the action is a consequence of another action/state and that the actor is not in control—even though the grammatical form of the VP may be subject (representing the actor) + active verb. Examples require an explanation of the context:

*[M-odou **mai** rogo-c-a mada.]*   'You (trial) please hear it.'
SUB-2T DIR hear-TR-3S INI   (Milner 1972:93)

Here, the volition is not on the part of the actor, but the one who tendered the invitation. Another example is similar in that the *mai* phrase is also an imperative—and thus contrary to fact:

*M-o la-ki kaci-vi koya mada [me **mai** vuke-i iko.]*
SUB-2S DIR call-TR 3S INI SUB DIR help-TR 2S
'Please go and call him that he might help you.' (Milner 1972:93)

---

⁹ Thanks to PG for bringing this marker to my attention, and to BK for supplying the examples.
¹⁰ Thanks to TRN for helping to distinguish among the different uses of *mai*.

Here, helping would be an act performed because of an influence outside the control of the actor.

Another example, with context supplied (TRN 4/82): T skips breakfast; later in the day he feels faint and says:

*[Au sā **mai** ciba].*   'I have fainted.'
 1S ASP DIR faint

Although the subject *au* represents the actor, the actor is not responsible for the condition. Instead, it is the consequence of an external factor.

Another example shows *mai* with little to do with literal direction or motion:

*E dina [ni ra sā **mai** volā]   na   vosa era rogo-c-a.*
 3S true SUB 3P ASP DIR write-3S DEF talk   3P hear-TR-3S
'It is true that when they came to write the words they heard.' (*SR* 20/4/82)

The following example (Nawadra 1981) is an extended one. It contains four examples of preverbal *mai*. Since it is more important to understand the total context than the individual words, the text has no interlinear gloss, but the appropriate VPs are numbered. Morphemes within a word are separated by hyphens.

Na kā gā e toro sobu ka vorovoro-yate ni ā vaka-curu vosa na vūlagi vuā na i-Taukei me kilā na vosa ni tani, ia o i-Taukei (1) *[sā **mai** leca-vi koya ki-na] ka mai vaka-bō-bula-taki e na kā e sega ni no-na; ia na vuli kei na ke-na tabacakacaka e liga ni vei-vaka-bō-bula-taki, ka* (2) *[sā **mai** bō-bula tū ki-na oqō] na i-Taukei e na vei-kā tani e vuqa. Na vuli, e dodonu me sala ni vei-sere-ki, vei-vaka-rārama-taki, kei na vei-vaka-dei-taki. Oqō* (3) *[sā **mai** vaka-sau-rārātaka] me be-c-a na no-na vosa, ka* (4) *[sā **mai** rawa-i] me sā dokā duadua gā na vosa vaka-Peritania ka kai-naki vuā ni oqō na vosa duadua gā ni kila-kā, ni vuli kei na gauna vou.*

'The humiliating and discouraging thing about it all is that the foreigner has influenced the Fijian to acquire foreign tongues, so much so that (1) [he has come to lose his identity] and is thus being enslaved by what is totally foreign to him. Education and its relevant department have been the means of this enslavement, and the Fijian (2) [has been enslaved] in many foreign things when, in fact, they ought to be the source of freedom, enlightenment, and security in one's own standing. As it is, (3) [this has forced the Fijian to look down on] his own language, and (4) [has persuaded him] to respect the English language alone. He is being led to think that the latter is the only language of knowledge, education, and of the modern age.'[11]

5.14.2 *Lai*

Lai, as well as *mai*, has literal and metaphorical uses. But because the meanings are more distinct, and because there is a formal difference of sorts, it is divided (albeit tentatively) into two markers.

---

[11] Thanks to SN for polishing the translation.

5.14.2.1 *Lai*$_1$

In written material, this marker is usually spelled *laki* or *la'ki*. *Lai*$_1$ preceding the verb signifies literal movement with intention or purpose:

    ka   [**laki** *rai-ci* *taci-na*]   'and went to see her sister' (T74:41)
    CNJ DIR see-TR sibling-3S

    [*me-u* **laki** *rai-c-a* *mada*] *na* *no-qu cakacaka* *sa* *vō*   *tū*
     SUB-1S DIR see-TR-3S INI   DEF PC-1S work   ASP remain CNT
    'so I might go and attend to my unfinished work' (T74:59)

Although *lai*$_1$ is treated as a marker, it might be analyzed as the main verb *lako* 'go' plus the marker *i*, described principally as ablative, but also indicating purpose. For example, the first sentence above can be considered a shortened form of:

    ka **lako i**   *rai-ci* *taci-na*
    CNJ go ABL see-TR sibling-3S

This *i*, described in §21.1.2.2.1, is used with other verbs as well. For example:

    ka *yau*   *yani ki sisili*   'and disperse (in numbers) to bathe'
    CNJ disperse DIR ABL bathe   (*NV3*:23)

    Lako mada i   *kana.*   'Go and eat.'
    go   INI ABL eat

5.14.2.2 *Lai*$_2$

This marker indicates that an action happened by chance, not by intention. It is not a contraction of *lako i*. Examples are:

    [*E ā* **lai** *nanu-m-a tale mai*] *na kā*   *e tuku-n-a vuā.*
     3S PT DIR think-TR-3S ITR DIR DEF thing 3S tell-TR-3S ABL-3S
    'She happened to recall what he had told her.' (T74:49)

    Au ā tovolea me-u *yadra tiko, ia* [*au* **lai** *moce gā.*]
    1S PT try   SUB-1S wake CNT CNJ 1S DIR sleep LIM
    'I tried to stay awake, but I just went to sleep.'

The following examples are ambiguous:

    [*Sā qai* **lai** *tuku-n-a*] *o*   *gone-tagane vei* *tama-na.*
     ASP SEQ DIR tell-TR-3S PRP child-male ABL father-3S (*VV* text)

This sentence can mean either of the following:

    'Then the boy went to tell his father', or
    'Then the boy happened to tell his father.'

    E ā tū   *cake ka* [**lai** *iro sara.*]
    3S PT stand DIR CNJ DIR look INT

The VP in question here can mean either:

    'and she got up and went to look', or
    'and she got up and happened to look' (T74:44)

5.14.3 *Mai, lai*: Order changes

Arms (1986:203) noted that *lai* and *mai* may invert around *via*, with a resultant meaning difference.

5.15 APPEARANCE (APR): *RAIRAI*

As can many other markers described in this chapter, *rairai* can function as the head of a VP, meaning 'look' (in a passive sense), 'appear':

*[E **rairai** vinaka] na no-mu sote.*   'Your shirt looks nice.'
3S appear good   DEF PC-2S   shirt

*[E **rairai**] ni vakā ki-na.*   'It looks that way.' (T74:59)
3S appear SUB like-3S ABL-3S

As a marker, it indicates that the action/state referred to by the main verb is only probable or apparent:

*[Sā **rairai** lako.]*   'She appears to have gone.'
ASP APR go

*[E na **rairai** tuku-n-a beka] me na kau ki vale ni bula.*
3S FT APR tell-TR-3S TEN SUB DEF carried ABL house POS health
'He'd probably say that she should be taken to hospital.' (T74:52)

*E **rairai** dau lako i na Garrick.*   'He probably frequents the
3S APR HAB go DIR DEF G   Garrick [bar].'

5.15.1 Order changes

Arms (1986:202) wrote:

> [R]*airai* ... may also occur after *qai* or *mani* ... It may even occur after *baci* or *bau* ... but this is not common.

6 VERB PREFIXES: *VAKA-*

In CH 6–8, we discuss the meaning and function of verb prefixes. Here, we begin with *vaka-* (and its alternate form *vā-*, which occurs before velars).

Whether through inheritance[1] independent development, or both, *vaka-* in SF now has a number of separate meanings/functions. Although the lines of distinction are not always clear-cut, these functions fall into five separate categories:[2]

1. Causative. E.g., **vaka**-*totolo-tak-a* 'make it fast', from *totolo* 'fast'.

2. Actives that indicate frequentative/distributive/intensive. E.g., **vaka**-*muri-a* 'follow it in detail, persistently', from *muri-a* 'follow it'.

3. Statives that indicate manner, duration, frequency. E.g., **vaka**-*veitālia* 'haphazardly, carelessly', from *veitālia* 'never mind'.

4. 'Provide(d) with, in possession of'. E.g., **vaka**-*wati* 'married', from *wati* 'spouse'.

---

[1] PG (10/78) noted that related forms in Tongan suggests multiple origins for Fijian *vaka-*: in addition to *faka-* there is *fa'a-*, and there are a number of examples of contrast between the two.

[2] For some constructions it is difficult to decide whether *vaka* is a root or a marker. One such construction is illustrated in the following examples:

*E **vaka**-bula vei au.*	'He said "Bula" to me.'
*Sā qai **vaka**-ō vei au.*	'And he called "Ō" back to me.'
*E **vaka**-mōmō vei au.*	'He calls me "Mōmō".'

This last construction is used with kin terms or titles, but there is some disagreement about its use with proper names (PG 9/83).

But note that *vaka* can be used as a full verb, complete with object (realized as the long vowel in the following example):

*E **vakā** o koya, "Tuba."*   'He said, "Get out."'

This form of *vaka* leads us to interpret the construction exemplified in *vaka-bula* and *vaka-ō* as examples of verb plus modifier—that is, the *gunu-yaqona* type. As with that type, *vaka-bula* can be related to a whole phrase that includes the specified object:

*E **vakā** vei au, "Bula."*   'He said to me, "Bula."'

5. 'Pretend, perform as a game or out of the ordinary surroundings'. E.g., ***vaka**-lomaloma-n-a* 'pretend to be sorry for her', from *loma-n-a* 'have compassion for her'. This function of *vaka-* is only cross-listed in this section; it is discussed in the section on reduplication.

6.1 CAUSATIVE

Verbs can be classified according to four different kinds of actions or states (see further discussion in CH 9, 10, and 11):

SITUATION	EXAMPLES	
A1: X acts	*E gutuwā.*	'He fled.'
A2: X acts-on Y	*E kani.*	'He ate.'
S1: Y is in a state	*E katakata.*	'It is hot.'
S2: Y is in a state caused by X	*E bulu.*	'She was buried.'

The causative construction introduces an actor from the outside: Z, who is removed from the situation, but causes it to take place:

SITUATION
Z CAUSES
X to act
Y to be in a state

In the semantics of the causative construction, Z is now the actor, and X and Y are goals—but they can be expressed only one at a time. Translating the descriptions into sentences produces the following:

	SITUATION
*E **vā**-gutuwā-tak-a.*[3]	'He (Z) caused it to flee.'
*E **vā** –kani-a.*	'He (Z) fed it.'
*E **vaka**-laila-tak-a*	'He (Z) made it small.'

The reason that only two participants can occur with the causative is that S2 verbs and the causative construction are incompatible, or, more accurately, redundant. This redundancy arises because S2 verbs automatically become *semantically* causative when the transitive marker and object are added:

E bulu.   'It is buried.'
E bulu-t-a.   'He buried it (that is, caused it to be in a buried state).'

---

[3] *Vaka-* changes to *vā-* before velars (see, e.g., Hazlewood 1872:58). *Vaka-* in other positions can also be shortened in fast speech. In AS's reading of *FR2*:4–5, he shortened ***vaka**-dike-v-a* to *vā-dike-v-a*. Note that this long vowel can then shorten, leaving two "ideal" measures: ***vadi·keva**.*

One *can* express the idea that someone causes someone else to bury something (i.e., three participants), but it cannot be done within the formal area of transitivity. Instead, a verb meaning, for example, 'force' or 'request' is used in an additional phrase.

The causative *vaka-* does not always change a stative into active, nor does it always add a referent. But it does have the effect of bringing the actor into play or into a more prominent role.

6.1.1 S1 → S2

Note the following example:

(Me) ***vaka****-lailai mada na retiō.*
SUB CAU-small INI DEF radio

At first, this sentence seems to be an active imperative: 'Turn the radio down!' But *na retiō* is not the specified object, but the specified subject instead, since there is no grammatical object and no transitive marker. Thus, a translation that is grammatically closer[4] to the Fijian is 'Let the radio be turned down!'—still an imperative, but in the third person rather than second person, and stative rather than active. Thus, *vaka-* changes an S1 verb to an S2 verb:

lailai S1   vs.   ***vaka****-lailai* S2

For the state indicated by *lailai* there is no actor at all. For *vaka-lailai*, the actor enters the picture, but remains implicit. Still, the construction indicates that the state (decreased volume) is caused by someone.

Other examples are:

(Me) ***vaka****-levu na vaivo.*	'Let (the flow in) the pipe be increased.'
(Me) ***vaka****-totolo na cakacaka.*	'Let the work be speeded up.'
E ***vaka****-sīnai vei au.*	'It's being filled for me.'[5]

The basis of the S2 classification is (as usual) the role of the subject—in these examples, a deleted *e* (third person singular), representing the goal.

6.1.2 S2 → A2

A form more common than those above is *vaka-rau* 'made ready, prepared'. Although **e rau* 'it is sufficient (?)' does not occur, the form *vaka-vaka-rau* 'getting ready' suggests that *rau* is an S2 verb (PG 9/83). More-over, the use of *vaka-rau* as S2 and of *rau-t-a* 'suffice for it' as A2 indicates that *rau* might fit with a small class of statives such as *oti* 'finished' (made A2 in *oti-v-a* 'finish it') and *cā* 'bad' (made A2 in *ca-ta* 'hate it').

As with other S2 verbs (such as *caka* 'made', *biu* 'left', and *dola* '(to be) open'), these forms become A2 with the addition of the transitive marker and object:

E ***vaka****-lailai-tak-a.*	'She made it small.'
E ***vaka****-levu-tak-a.*	'She made it big.'
E ***vaka****-totolo-tak-a.*	'She made it fast.'

---

[4] That is, one that reflects the grammatical structure as well as the meaning.
[5] Example from PG.

6.1.3 S1 → A2

This change is common. Examples are:

E levu.	'It is big.'
*E **vaka**-levu-tak-a*	'He made it big.'
E katakata.	'It's hot.'
E vā-katakata-ra.	'She made it hot.'
E cā.	'It is bad.'
*E **vaka**-cācā-na na cagi laba.*	'The hurricane destroyed it.'

Note here the change in the role of the subject. With *vaka-*, the subject is now the actor. In other words, *vaka-* has again brought the actor into the picture, but in these examples, it is represented by the subject.

Although examples of verbs in this "bare" state are somewhat rare, they are more common in other constructions, such as the following. In this construction (treated at length in §16.4.1), there is no grammatical object present, although the goal is represented by the modifier.

***vaka**-bula i-lavo*	'saving money'
***vaka**-mate vuaka*	'killing pigs'
***vaka**-oti gauna*	'wasting time'
***vaka**-dewa i-vola*[6]	'translating books'
***vaka**-dewa vosa*	'translating language'

Another construction in which the causative appears without a transitive marker and expressed object is in nominalizations (Milner 1972:105):

*na i-**vaka**-yadra*	'awakener, alarm clock'
*na i-**vaka**-bula*	'savior'
*na i-**vaka**-sala*	'advice'
*na i-**vaka**-macala*	'explanation'

Note that the hierarchical structure is as follows:

(*na* (*i* (***vaka**-bula*)))

Some roots, however—for various reasons—require that the transitive marker be included in this construction. For example,

*na i-**vaka**-nanu-mi*	'memorial, souvenir'

There are two possible explanations for this form. First, *nanu* 'think' does not occur alone as a root—that is, the verb phrase *e *nanu* does not occur. However, it does occur with *vaka-*:

nanu-m-a	'remember it, think of it'
vaka-nanu-m-a	'ponder on it'

In the second example, *vaka-* seems to indicate duration, frequency, or intensity, rather than causative. This suggests that *-mi* as a transitive marker distinguishes the form from other possible meanings. Another example, with *rai* 'see/seen':

*na i-**vaka**-rai-taki*	'token, exhibit (that is, something to be seen)'

---

[6] Examples from Milner 1972:82.

Here, ***vaka**-rai* would present the following ambiguity:

***vaka**-rai* ⟨ -ci   'watch over'
         -taki   'cause to be seen'

Thus, *-taki* adds "lexical meaning" (from an English point of view, at any rate) to the form to distinguish it from the meaning 'watch over'.

6.1.4 Causatives with the object signaled and expressed (S1 → A2)

The following examples show a more common causative construction:

E mate.   'He (A) is dead.'
*E **vaka**-mate-a.*   'He (B) killed him (A).'[7]

The example just given shows no consonant in the transitive marker. Further examples are:

cala	'wrong'	***vaka**-calā*	'deem it wrong'
lialia	'foolish'	***vaka**-lialiā*	'make him appear foolish'
bula	'alive'	***vaka**-bulā*	'save her'
oti	'finished'	***vaka**-oti-a*	'finish it'
gata	'sharp'	***vā**-gatā*	'sharpen it'

However, there are also forms in which the consonant does appear:

| *sīnai* | 'full' | ***vaka**-sīnai-t-a* | 'fill it' |
| *yadra* | 'awake' | ***vaka**-yadra-t-a* | 'wake her' |

All the preceding forms are unusual in one respect: they signal the goal with a one-syllable transitive marker. Since they are all very common words, it is tempting to consider them remnants of a period when a one-syllable suffix as transitive marker was the norm. Such is no longer the case; not only newly borrowed words, but also *most* S1 verbs take *-taki* as the transitive marker in the causative construction. For example:

levu	'big'	***vaka**-levu-tak-a*	'make it big'
mārau	'happy'	***vaka**-mārau-tak-a*	'make her happy'
mamaca	'dry'	***vaka**-mamaca-tak-a*	'dry it'
viqi	'pink'	***vaka**-viqi-tak-a*	'make it pink'
rauni	'round'	***vaka**-rauni-tak-a*	'make it round'

As a matter of fact, this construction is so common that *vaka ... taka* has sometimes been analyzed as an "envelope" into which to insert statives, or—in other terms—as a discontinuous morpheme. Such an interpretation is discussed (and dismissed) in §16.6.5.1.

6.1.5 A1 → A2

Verb roots that are active also enter into the causative construction. With such constructions, the new actor does not bring about a state, but he/she causes someone or something else to do something.

---

[7] This relationship between A and B assumes that the phrases occur together in context.

E gutuwā.   'He fled.'
E vā-gutuwā-taka   'He caused her to flee.

With the examples above, the goal remains implicit, since it is neither signaled nor expressed. The goal can be made more specific by signaling it with *-taki* and expressing it with the object *-a*:

E vā-gutuwā-tak-a   'She caused him to flee.'

As with S1 verbs, adding *vaka-* to these verbs changes the roles played by the referents. That is, in normal conversation, the participants would be identified as follows:

E gutuwā.   'He (X) fled.'
E vā-gutuwā-taka.   'She (Z) caused him (X) to flee.'

6.1.6 A2 remains A2, but changes roles

In this type of causative construction, both the underived and the derived forms belong to the A2 class, but certain roles are changed:

E kani-a.   'He (X) ate it (Y).'
E vā-kani koya.   'She (Z) fed him (X) / (Z) caused (X) to eat.'

As indicated in the introduction to this section, (Z) is acting as an outside agent, causing the situation in the sentence *e kani-a* to happen:

(Z) causes → *e kani-a*

For another example of this construction, we use *davo* 'lie':

E davo.   'He (X) lay.'
E davo-r-a.   'He (X) lay-on it (Y).'
E vaka-davo-r-a.   'She (Z) made him (X) lie down.'

Note that, as mentioned before, although in the examples above there are three referents—(X), (Y), and (Z)—only two of these at a time can be expressed in the transitive-causative construction itself. A third referent can be expressed, not by the causative-transitive construction, but as follows:

*E vā-kani koya **e na dalo**.*   'She fed him taro.'
*E vaka-davo-r-a **e na ibe**.*   'She (Z) made him (X) lie on the mat (Y).'

In these sentences, the Fijian equivalents of *taro* and *mat* are each indicated by a prepositional phrase (in boldface).

Another way to include a third referent in the construction is first to qualify the verb with it:

kana dalo   'taro eating'

and then to use this phrase as the head of the causative-transitive construction:

E vā-kana-dalo-taki koya.   'She taro-fed him.'

The following example shows this head-modifier construction used without the transitive marker:

*E **vaka**-cici-ose.*   'He makes horses run.'

The hierarchical structure of the verb is:

(**vaka** (*cici-ose*))

6.1.7 Some special kinds of causatives

The following examples show functions of *vaka-* different from the main types.

1. Concerning verbs of judgment

E lasu.	'It is false.'
*E **vaka**-lasu-y-a.*	'She judged it to be false.'
E tabu.	'It is taboo.'
*E **vaka**-tabu-y-a.*	'He declared it to be taboo.'
E dina.	'It is true.'
*E **vaka**-dina-t-a.*	'She recognized it as true.'

For each of these states—*lasu*, *tabu*, and *dina*—its existence depends upon external judgment. Therefore, judging something to be false is, in a sense, *making* it false. Hence, we can interpret this construction as a causative. (See also §12.5.)

2. Concerning greetings

Sā yadra.	'Good morning.'
*E **vaka**-yadra-tak-a.*	'She bade him "good morning."'
Sā bula.	'Greetings.'
*E **vaka**-bula-tak-a.*	'He greeted her.'

Although these constructions can be translated by 'say [ ]', the meaning of 'say' seems to lie more in the root than in *vaka-* (see note 2).

6.1.8 Causatives: A summary

With both kinds of active verbs, causation can be compared to a puppet show. When a puppet does something, he is the actor, but with respect only to the situation that the spectators see. Judy may hit Punch; hence, Judy is the actor, Punch is the goal. But behind the scenes, the puppeteer is the actor, and in that larger context, the puppets are goals—no matter who is doing what to whom.

6.2 FREQUENTATIVE / DISTRIBUTIVE / INTENSIVE

Vaka- with active verbs "modifies" the action to give the meanings listed in the heading. For example:

E rai-c-a.	'He saw / looked-at it.'
*E **vaka**-rai-c-a.*	'He searched-for it (repeatedly or more thoroughly)'
E gunu.	'He drank.'
*E **vā**-gunugunu.*	'He drank repeatedly / in small sips'
E muri-a.	'He followed it.'
*E **vaka**-muri-a.*	'He followed it in detail, persistently, more closely.'
E dike-v-a.	'He scrutinized it.'
*E **vaka**-dike-v-a.*	'He researched it.'

Note that the specific meaning of *vaka-* varies according to the semantics of the

root. For example, one could not drink the same liquid repeatedly.
Other examples are:

E bubura.	'She looked for places to pierce for turtle eggs or eels.'
*E **vaka**-bubura.*	'She pierced repeatedly / distributively.'
E bari.	'She nibbled.'
*E **vaka**-babari.*	'She nibbled repeatedly / distributively.'

In our sample, other verb stems in this class are:[8]

caqe	'kick'	*dara*	'wear'	*belu*	'bent'
digo	'inspect'	*dolo*	'broken'	*dike*	'scrutinize'
iro	'peep'	*bili*	'push'	*bolo*	'pelt'
kalu	'whistle'	*kaci*	'call'	*iri*	'fan'
kere	'beg'	*garo*	'lust for'	*digi*	'choose'
dusi	'point'	*drami*	'lick'	*cai*	'copulate'

For some verbs in this class, the meaning of the *vaka-* forms varies, dependent on some semantic features of the root itself. Consider, for example, the difference in the processes of *dolo* 'break off/in two' and *bulu* 'buried'. Forms with *vaka-* have the following meanings:

*E **vaka**-dolo-k-a.*	'He broke it a number of times / he broke a number of things in two.'
*E **vaka**-bulu-t-a.*	'He buried it slowly / carefully / according to custom.'

6.3 MANNER AND TIME

The statives that are formed from *vaka-* refer to manner, frequency, and duration—but not to absolute time. That is, such concepts as "yesterday" and "next month" are handled by phrases, not by forms with this prefix.

There are two main types of *vaka-* constructions in this category, and one of them can be further divided into two types: occurring with nouns, and occurring with verbs.

6.3.1 N < *vaka*-N

Vaka- shows a particular relationship between two nouns. The first noun is qualified by the *vaka-* form, which here means 'in the manner of', or 'X-style' (arrows indicate the direction of the attribution):

na vosa	<	***vaka**-Viti*	'Fijian language' (*Viti* 'Fiji')
na i-tovo	<	***vaka**-vanua*	'local customs' (*vanua* 'land')
na i-sulu	<	***vaka**-Toga*	'Tongan-style sarong' (*Toga* 'Tonga')
na kā	<	***vaka**-tamata*	's.t. human-like' (*tamata* 'person')
na i-valavala	<	***vaka**-Saimone*	'an act characteristic of S'

6.3.2 V < *vaka*-N

In this construction, a verb is modified by a *vaka-* construction:

Sā votā	<	***vaka**-mataqali.*	'It was shared according to the *mataqali*.'

---

[8] Some of these verbs belong to the S2 category, although this is not always reflected in the gloss.

Sā kilā	< ***vaka**-cava?*	'How did he know it?'
E caka-va	< ***vā**-qori.*⁹	'He did it like that.'
E lako mai	< ***vā**-gauna.*	'She comes from time to time.'
E mārau	< ***vā**-gauna*	'She's happy from time to time.'

As the last two examples show, statives derived from *vaka-* can modify both active and stative verbs.

6.3.3 V < *vaka*-V (stative)

Examples of this change are as follows:

Sā vinaka	< ***vaka**-levu.*	'It was very good / thank you very much.'
E vosa	< ***vaka**-vuqa.*	'He spoke many times.'
E sau-mi	< ***vaka**-vula.*	'She was paid monthly.'
E gādē	< ***vaka**-yabaki.*	'She took a holiday annually.'
E tiko	< ***vaka**-vuni.*	'He stayed secretly.'

In most of these examples, the head of the *vaka-* construction is a stative itself, but the whole construction in turn serves as a stative to modify a verb (either active or stative).

Some of these forms can be used as verbs:

*Rau dau **vaka**-totolo ki vale ni lotu.* 'They always hurry to church.'
3D HAB MAN-fast LOC house POS religion (*FR*3:3)

but such a usage might be considered a short form of *lako vaka-totolo* 'go fast'.

For some common roots, the *vaka-* is omitted in this construction. Note the following examples (*FR*3:3):

Rau dau seruseru vinaka. 'They always comb (their hair) well.'
3D HAB comb good

*Rau dau **vaka**-rorogo vinaka.* 'They always mind well.'
3D HAB listen good

but:

*Rau dau kana **vaka**-mālua.* 'They always eat slowly.'
3D HAB eat MAN-slow

When the transitive marker and object are added, these stative forms become active (like S2 roots: *caka* vs. *caka-va*) and have the meaning 'provide him / her / it with [noun]'. The following examples are from Cammack 1962:108:

i-tikotiko	'place'	***vaka**-i-tikotiko-tak-a*	'provide a place for her'
i-cili	'guest house'	***vaka**-i-cili-tak-a*	'provide a guest house for her'
i-lavo	'money'	***vaka**-i-lavo-tak-a*	'provide money for him'
i-sele	'knife'	***vaka**-i-sele-tak-a*	'provide a knife for her'

---

⁹ See the previous note.

6.4 POSSESSING N OR CHARACTERIZED BY N

Vaka- forms of this type are used as statives, both as full verbs and as modifiers:

    *na kove **vaka**-suka*   'coffee with sugar'

Here, the coffee is "sugared,"—that is, characterized by having sugar in it. The construction is such (stative) that the emphasis is not on the coffee "having" or "possessing" sugar, but being distinguished from other kinds of coffee by having that feature.

Other examples of this construction:

*E **vaka**-wati.*	'She's married.'
*E **vaka**-sucu.*	'It has milk in it.'
*E **vaka**-vale.*[10]	'He has a house.'
*E **vaka**-moli ka vaka-rōkete.*	'It has lemon and chili peppers.'

Because this is a stative construction, the principal function of the *vaka-* form is to describe the subject, not to emphasize that the subject possesses something. For example, *vaka-i-sulu* in the following sentence serves to describe *yalewa*, not to emphasize that the woman owns or has clothes.

    *na yalewa **vaka**-i-sulu*   'the clothed woman'
    DEF woman MAN-clothing

6.5 PRETEND, PERFORM AS A GAME

This function of *vaka-* is discussed in CH 14.

6.6 *VAKA-* AND GRAMMATICAL AMBIGUITY

With at least five distinct functions of *vaka-*, one might well expect to find instances of grammatical ambiguity. We now examine each of the constructions with respect to its constituents and its function to see if such ambiguity exists.

Causative and frequentative both occur with a verb root, as heads of verb phrases, and in both active and stative constructions.

The "manner" construction usually occurs as the modifier of a noun, but seldom as the head of a verb phrase.

The "provided-with" construction has a noun as its head and is stative.

The "pretend" construction is set off from the others by the affix *-tā-*.

Since "manner" and "provided-with" are similar, sometimes they look similar and are paired off semantically:

*na i-sulu **vaka**-Toga*	'Tongan-style sarong'
*na i-sulu **vaka**-taga*	'sarong with pockets'

But the same root would rarely occur in both constructions in the same context.

There is, however, free ambiguity between causative and frequentative. Note the following examples:

---

[10] Idiomatic, as well as literal. This can also mean 'having a spouse and family'.

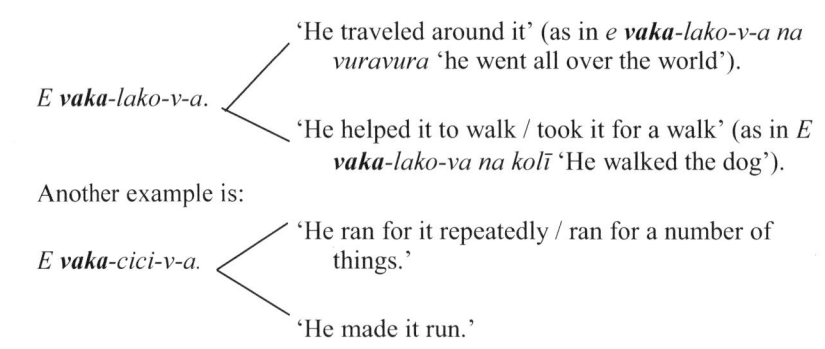

*E **vaka**-lako-v-a.*
- 'He traveled around it' (as in *e **vaka**-lako-v-a na vuravura* 'he went all over the world').
- 'He helped it to walk / took it for a walk' (as in *E **vaka**-lako-va na kolī* 'He walked the dog').

Another example is:

*E **vaka**-cici-v-a.*
- 'He ran for it repeatedly / ran for a number of things.'
- 'He made it run.'

6.7 DISCUSSION: *VAKA-*

Ask students of Oceanic languages to name a prefix that typifies those languages, and chances are they'll say *vaka-* (or *faka-* or *faʻa-* or *hoʻo-* ...). In Pawley's grammatical comparison of Eastern Oceanic languages (1972:45), this verbal prefix is the first listed, and of the 31 languages compared, all but one show some reflex of the form. As an example of its visibility in dictionaries of Oceanic languages, Churchward's Tongan dictionary (1959) has 112 pages of *faka-* forms.[11]

For Fijian, it is part of the first expressions an outsider learns: ***vaka**-Viti* 'Fijian'; *vinaka **vaka**-levu* 'thank you very much'. As an example of its frequency in a text, it occurs in 12 out of 73 content words in one paragraph from the text of an address (Rabukawaqa to Workshop, August 1978).[12]

Along with its widespread occurrence in most Eastern Oceanic languages is a widespread multiplicity of function. Pawley (1972:45) listed causative as a general description of the proto-form **paka-*, and noted that SF has in addition the functions of multiplicative and simulative. Grammars and dictionaries of related languages use similar terms: for Hawaiian (Pukui and Elbert 1986): "causative/simulative;" for Tongan (Churchward 1959): "likeness, causation (causing or allowing), supplying, etc."; for Samoan (Milner 1966): "1. Cause ... 2. Characteristic or, proper to belonging to ... 3. Like, in the manner of, of the same kind ... 4. Give, provide [someone or something] with ..."

---

[11] The number of *faka-* forms was, of course, partially dependent on the lexicographer's decision to include such derivations as separate entries, even those that were not idioms.

[12] Its frequency is lower in more informal texts.

7 VERB PREFIXES: *VEI-* / *VĪ-*

The prefix *vei-*[1] with verbs serves two main functions:

1. Reciprocal, mutual 〈 Active
                      Stative

2. General, formalized 〈 motion (no goal, or changed goal)
                         other active verbs (no goal)

7.1 RECIPROCAL, MUTUAL (ACTIVE)

The verbal prefix *vei-* has usually been called RECIPROCAL (e.g., Hazlewood 1872:42, Churchward 1941:20, Milner 1972:111–13). In the strictest sense, this term (as applied to verbs) implies a mutual relationship or activity between or among two or more parties. Such a definition carries with it certain conditions.

First, it is apparent that a true reciprocal relationship is confined to certain kinds of participants—generally to animate beings, thus allowing the actor-goal relationship to work both ways. For example, a verb commonly used as an illustration for the reciprocal is *vei-loma-ni* 'love one another', as in

*Erau sā **vei**-loma-ni.*   'They (dual) love each other.'

We can consider that each of these phrases is derived from two[2] underlying ones, identical in structure, but with the roles of the referents reversed:

E loma-ni koya.   'He (A) loves her (B).'
E loma-ni koya.   'She (B) loves him (A).'

Similar examples are:

Erau vei-	*tautau-ri.*	'They (dual)	held on to each other.'
	taratara-i.		got close to each other.'
	kaci-vi.		called each other.'
	vosa-ki.		spoke to each other.'

---

[1] *Vī-* is a nonstandard form. It is heard in casual conversation in SF, but is the only form in many of the other Fijian languages.

[2] When the subject is trial or plural, more underlying phrases are assumed, sufficient to cover each pair within the total number of participants.

At first glance, it seems that the participants in the situations represented by these examples should be human. However, they could also be certain animals that Fijians might anthropomorphize. Actually, some such limits are built into the verbs themselves, even without a reciprocal affix. *Loma-ni*, for example (*loma* isn't used as a verb without the transitive marker), involves compassion, pity, humanity—emotions that humans feel for each other (or for a pet), but not generally for inanimate objects.[3] Certainly, when one of the referents is clearly inanimate, a reciprocal relationship cannot exist. For example, the referents in the following sentence are unlikely to appear in a reciprocal construction:

E dabe-c-a na vatu. 'He sat on a rock.'

for the rock cannot "sit on him."

7.1.1 Types of verbs

Some verbs have a degree of reciprocity built into them. For example, vosa-k-a 'talk to him' is said to be rare; vei-vosa-ki 'converse' is common. In other words, it is part of the nature of discourse that A speaks to B, and B speaks to A. In fact, one might consider that unless there is reciprocal action, the nature of the verb is changed. Other examples of semantically reciprocal verbs are:[4]

valu	'wage war'	*bō*	'take hold'
cai	'copulate'	*qito*	'play'
mau	'play (game)'	*bā*	'dispute, deny'
regu	'kiss'	*sau*	'retaliate, exchange'

Because of the reciprocal nature of these verbs, for some of them, there is not much difference between the root alone and *vei-* + root:

1. *Erau vala.* 'They (dual) fought.'
2. *Erau **vei**-vala.* 'They (dual) fought.'[5]

Although (1) can mean that they are both engaged in fighting (on the same side), it first gives the impression that two people are fighting each other—even without the reciprocal prefix.

A different kind of example is *leti* 'argue'. Although the Fijian-English dictionary lists *leti-tak-a* 'argue about it', some speakers say that they have heard only ***vei**-leti-tak-a*. Such a discrepancy might be due to the influence of semantics on the grammatical paradigms of some verb roots.

On the other hand, some verbs that refer to actions requiring at least two participants can occur without the reciprocal prefix:

E valu-t-a. 'It made war on it/ he fought him.'
E cai-t-a. 'He copulated-with her.'
E sōlevu. 'It (one participant) did its part in the ceremonial exchange.'

---

[3] TRN (11/79) said that the verb can be used with such notions as "country" or "church" as a goal, but with a somewhat different meaning of 'feel concern for'.

[4] PG (19/83) noted that *sau*, *bō*, and *mau* cannot occur without *vei-*.

[5] Examples such as these should be studied further. There may be subtle differences in meaning, although the translations are identical.

Compare these with ***vei**-valu*, ***vei**-cai*, and ***vei**-sōlevu*.

One verb that seems inherently reciprocal in its semantics has neither a reciprocal nor a transitive form:

lūlulu[6]   'shake hands'

7.1.2 Expressing an object

With *vei-* forms, the goal can more explicit by signaling and expressing[7] it. In the following examples (from Milner 1972:113), the general transitivizer *-taki* is used:

***vei**-sau*	'change'	***vei**-tāqa-vi*	'layered'
***vei**-sau-takā*	'change it'	***vei**-tāqa-vi-tak-a*	'lie-on-top-of it'
***vei**-vosa-ki*	'converse'		
***vei**-vosa-ki-tak-a*	'converse-about it'		

The *vei ... yaki* forms, already including a transitive suffix, can also include an object (example from Milner 1972:113):

***vei**-soli-yak-a*   'distribute it'

Strictly speaking, each of the forms ***vei**-vosa-ki-tak-a* and ***vei**-taqa-vi-tak-a* has two transitive markers—but only formally. These derived active verbs seem to treat what precedes *-taki* as an idiomatic unit rather than as a sum of the component parts. ***Vei**-vosa-ki-taki* illustrates this point: ***vei**-vosa-ki* means literally that A speaks to B and B speaks to A. But *-taka* (*taki* + *a*) introduces a different kind of goal, and what precedes it can be reinterpreted as 'discuss'. (I realize that we are in danger of analyzing by translation, but I suggest that the Fijian concept of ***vei**-vosa-ki* is an idiomatic one, treating it more like one morpheme than like a derived reciprocal.)

7.2 RECIPROCAL, MUTUAL (STATIVE)

7.2.1 Kin terms and other relationships

Vei- forms are used to designate relationships, even those that seem (to the outside observer) to be unequal. To illustrate this type, we will begin with one that seems equal, and show how we can analyze it (as we did above) as the result of two underlying phrases that are structurally similar:

*Erau **vei**-wati-ni.*   'They (dual) are husband and wife.'

For the next example, the underlying sentences are not formally transitive, but possessive:

E wati-na.   'He (A) is her (B's) spouse.'
E wati-na.   'She (B) is his (A's) spouse'

But most kin relationships are not so evenly balanced. Consider the following:

*Erau **vei**-taci-ni.*   'They (dual) are siblings.'

---

[6] I suspect that this word was introduced from Tongan by the missionaries. Tongan has *lulu* 'shake'.

[7] For an extensive discussion of the term "signal" and "express," see CH 26.

Perhaps the relationship is not exactly mutual or balanced, since *taci-na* means 'his/her younger sibling'. Therefore, A has a different relationship to B than B has to A. The same supposed inequity holds for the following examples:

*Erau **vei**-tama-ni.*   'They (dual) are father-and-child.'
*Erau **vei**-vasu-ti.*   'They (dual) have the *vasu* relationship to each other.'
*Erau **vei**-vaka-vuli-ci.*   'They (dual) share a teacher-student relationship.'

One analysis of these last examples is that the meaning of the root prohibits a literal A-to-B, B-to-A equality. For example, one sibling must be older than the other. A similar relationship holds for the other forms above: two people cannot be father to each other, or both have the same role in the *vasu* relationship. With the roots *vuli* and *bula*, however, the relationship could be literally reciprocal: two people teaching each other or nursing each other.

But even with such roots as *tama*, *taci*, and *vasu*, if we interpret these kinship and other terms as referring primarily to *the sharing of a relationship,* with each participant acting his role in the culturally or biologically defined way, we can look on all these *vei-* forms as semantically, as well as grammatically, reciprocal.

Perhaps kin terms that refer to a negative relationship could be considered a special subset:

*Erau **vei**-biu tū.*   'They (dual) are separated.'

Note that with *vei-*, these forms refer to states without a cause, although the roots are classified as S2. These forms are different from those composed of *vei* + kin term, which are derived from possessed nouns. The absence of the transitive markers *-ti* and *-ki* fits such an interpretation, since those affixes would signal an actor, or cause of the state.[8]

7.2.2 Spatial and distance relationships

Vei- forms are used to indicate the position of two or more items with reference to each other:

*Erau **vei**-bāsa-i.*[9]   'They (dual) are opposite each other.'
   yawa-ki   far apart.'
   taratara-i   adjacent.'
   voleka-ti.[10]   near each other.'
   dōnu-i.   opposite each other.'

---

[8] The transitive suffix does occur in this construction:

*E **vei**-sere-ki na tūraga ni lewā.* 'The magistrate granted the divorce (i.e. he "divorced").

Here, *vei-sere-ki* refers to the general act of divorcing.

[9] Showing the morphological divisions of this form obscures the measure divisions: vei·bā·sai.

[10] This form also occurs tentatively in the reciprocal active category, which points out that we are unsure of its basic classification.

7.3 GENERAL, FORMALIZED *VEI-* FORMS

To illustrate that many *vei-* forms are not remotely reciprocal, note the contrast between the following two examples:

    kakase[11]   'slander'   ***vei****-kase-ti*   'gossip'

For this *vei-* form, the action is seldom reciprocal or mutual, for the essence of gossip is that it is not about mutual parties but someone else instead. ***Vei****-kase-ti*, then, illustrates not the reciprocal, but the GENERAL use of *vei-*.

For this category, the examples all appear to be active. The reason may be that S1 verbs (either simple or derived) are already general, in the sense that they refer to general states and not specific instances. To illustrate:

    E levu.   'It is big.'   *E kila-i*   'It is known.'

S2 verbs, on the other hand, need a means of indicating that a general action, not a state, is being referred to. Thus, although *bulu* on its own refers to the state of being buried, the *vei-* form has the following meaning:

    *Era **vei**-bulu tiko.*   'They were burying (general activity).'

The general, formalized category is divided into two subtypes: verbs of motion, and other active verbs (including S2 verbs that have become active).

7.3.1 General, formalized: Verbs of motion

Since their goals are usually locations, verbs of motion do not normally enter into a true reciprocal relationship. That is, in the following sentence:

    E qalo-v-a.   'She swam toward it.'

one does not expect a corresponding sentence reversing the grammatical roles of actor and goal (unless the goal happens to be human). Such verbs do, however, take the *vei-* prefix, with a special suffix *-yaki*. The derived forms convey a sense of motion without a goal: that is, to and fro, or random. The standard texts contain abundant examples:

*E **vei**-cavu-yaki.*	'She tacked (in sailing).'
*E **vei**-lako-yaki.*	'She toured around.'
*Era **vei**-suka-yaki.*	'They (plural) dispersed severally.'
*Era **vei**-cici-yaki.*	'They (plural) ran in all directions.'
*E **vei**-voce-yaki.*	'She paddled back and forth.'

If these verbs do take an object, it no longer refers to location, for the essential meaning of this construction is that any kind of locative goal is scattered, random, or alternating. Instead, the grammatical object now refers to a different kind of goal:

*Era **vei**-butu-yak-a.*	'They (plural) trampled it all over.'
*Era **vei**-bini-yak-a.*	'They (plural) piled it in several places.'
*Era **vei**-kau-yak-a.*	'They (plural) carried it to several places.'

---

[11] Incidently, *kase* by itself cannot be classified as either active or stative, but only as a two-referent verb.

One can tell from the examples above that in this construction, a singular subject is required to perform an oscillating kind of action, whereas with a plural subject, each individual can proceed in one direction, but the action as a whole has to be one of dispersal in several directions.

7.3.2 General, formalized: Other active verbs

Vei- is used with active verbs (other than verbs of motion) to refer to general, formalized action, rather than to a specific instance. Note the following contrast:

E vuke-i au.	'He helped me (on a specific occasion).'
*E dau **vei**-vuke.*	'He helps.'
*E sega ni **vei**-kati.*	'It doesn't bite (people).'

The last sentence is from a discussion of sharks that swim up the Sigatoka River. Using *kati* with an object would refer to a specific instance:

E ā kati-a.   'It bit it.'

Note that these forms do not signal or express a goal. For example, in:

*E **vei**-caqe.*   'He's playing football / kicking a football around.'

the *vei-* form focuses on the activity. The only way that the semantic entity "ball" enters the picture is that it is an implicit part of the activity.

Vei-caqe is formally classified as active because it cannot serve alone to modify a noun, but only with *dau* (habitual):

*E tamata dau **vei**-caqe.*   'He's a person who plays football.'

which corresponds to:

E tamata dau gunu.   'He's a drinker.'

Vei-caqe is an example of a semantic subset with a number of members: games. Although one might suggest that games are examples of reciprocal activity, the *vei-caqe* example shows that reciprocity is not essential. The common feature of the set seems instead to be formalized, ritualized activity. The following are further examples; they all refer to games, but many are difficult to gloss:

***vei**-ciu*	'cat's cradle'	*vei-tiqa*
***vei**-ladekanace*	'hop, skip, jump'	*vei-bona*
***vei**-lawavuevue*		*vei-moli*
***vei**-mau*	'cards'	*vei-yama*
***vei**-tara*		*vei-bō*

The *vei-* prefix is by no means confined to indigenous words; *vei-māpolo* 'play marbles' shows that it can be used with borrowings.

Some forms are ambiguous, overlapping with reciprocal action:

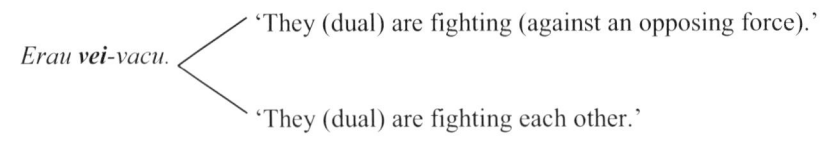

*Erau **vei**-vacu.*
- 'They (dual) are fighting (against an opposing force).'
- 'They (dual) are fighting each other.'

In addition to this ambiguity, other evidence suggests that this formalized meaning of *vei-* developed from the reciprocal meaning. For example, many ceremonies do involve reciprocity:

vei-*sōlevu-ti*   'fête each other with *sōlevu*'
vei-*sau gone*   'child barter'

Moreover, there is one type of game, with many examples, that does not always include *vei-* in its names: string figures. Although this activity certainly involves ritual, complete with *meke* chorus in some instances, we might conclude that *vei-* is missing because forming the figure itself does not necessarily involve more than one participant (Hornell 1927).

PG noted (7/82) that some *vei-* forms contrast with reduplicated forms (another means of focusing on the activity rather than the goal):

vei-*koti*	'hair-cutting'	*kotikoti*	'cutting'
vei-*sele*	'(surgical) operation'	*selesele*	'cutting'
vei-*cula*	'vaccination'	*culacula*	'sewing'

Like some other morphological processes (especially reduplication), perhaps the main function of *vei-* here is to provide a new meaning within the same broad semantic area.

In the examples noted so far, the *vei-* forms are connected with animate beings.

8 VERB PREFIXES: *VIA-*, *VIAVIA-*, *TAWA-*, AND OTHERS[1]

8.1 DESIDERATIVE: *VIA-*

Via- is a marker that directly precedes the verb, indicating a desire for, nearness to, or attempt at the state or action represented by the verb. All these conditions are contrary to fact (in the traditional grammatical terms): in a *via-* phrase, the state or action has not yet been achieved or perhaps never will be.

Since desire is a human (sometimes animal) condition, phrases with this meaning are confined to animate actors:

*E **via**-gunu.*	'She wishes to drink (i.e., is thirsty).'
*E **via**-kana na vusi.*	'The cat wants to eat (i.e., is hungry).'

Many such *via-* forms can be qualified:

*E **via**-gunu-yaqona.*	'He is thirsty for kava.'
*E **via**-kana-ika.*	'She is hungry for fish.'

The constituent structure of this construction is as follows:

(***via*** (*kana ika*))

Another type of modifier:

*E **via**-kana vaka-levu.*   'She was very hungry.'

can produce a different constituent structure:

((***via**-kana*) *vaka-levu*)

The alternate structure:

(***via*** (*kana vaka-levu*))

would mean, structurally at least,[2] that she wanted to eat a large quantity.

---

[1] David Arms noted (10/84) that some elements can occur between *via* and the verb. Such may also be the case for the other markers treated here; thus their classification as "affixes" is tenuous. At any rate, the distinction between affixes and separate markers seems neither clear nor important for Fijian—except for spelling.

[2] It would take a special context for it to be interpreted this way.

8 Verb Prefixes: *Via-*, *viavia-*, *tawa-*, and others

Via- forms can also occur with the transitive suffix and object (with or without a noun phrase specifying the object):

*E **via**-gunu-v-a (na kove).*	'She wanted to drink it (the coffee).'
*E **via**-kani-a (na tavioka).*	'She wanted to eat it (the manioc).'

Fitting in with the general description of "contrary to fact," *via-* also has the meaning of 'attempt to':

*E **via**-vacu-k-a na kena i-sā.*	'He tried (in vain) to punch his opponent.'

Via- can be used with A1 verbs:

*E **via**-cibi.*	'He wants to do the *cibi* dance.'
*E **via**-colovu.*	'She nearly tripped.'

and with borrowings as well:

*E **via**-dānisi.*	'She wants to dance.'
*O **via**-sunuka?*	'Do you want to play snooker?'

The following are examples of *via-* with S1 verbs:

*E **via**-balavu o koya.*	'He'd like to be tall.'
*E sā sau-ni ni **via**-rairai vinaka.*	'She's made up because she wants to look nice.'

With S2 verbs, the meaning changes somewhat to indicate need. Since the subjects of most S2 verbs in their root form refer to non-human goals, the "wish, desire" comes from outside. In the glosses for the following sentences, I have used an idiomatic expression,[3] which just happens to fit grammatically:

*Era **via**-kau na i-dabedabe oqō.*	'These chairs want (need) carrying.'
*Sā **via**-bulu na benu oqō.*	'This garbage needs burying.'
*Sā **via**-loba na bulumakau.*	'The cow needs milking.'

When S2 verbs are used with a transitive suffix and an object, *via-* can be used, just as with A1 verbs:

*E **via**-kau-t-a na i-dabedabe oqō.*	'He wants to carry these chairs.'
*E **via**-bulu-t-a na benu oqō.*	'He wants to bury this garbage.'
*E **via**-loba-k-a na bulumakau.*	'She wants to milk the cow.'

In all the previous examples, it is difficult to decide whether the referent of the subject is acting or is in a state. Although semantically the examples appear to be more stative, they do not enter into the usual stative pattern, i.e., following a noun as an attribute. Instead, they are required to be preceded by *e* or *dau*, after the pattern of active constructions:

*na tamata dau **via**-gunu-tī.*	'the person who craves tea'
*na tamata e **via**-gunu-tī*	

---

[3] *Want* with this meaning is somewhat outside most dialects of American English, but I recognize it.

In general, with inanimate subjects, *via-* has the meaning of 'disposed to', 'inclined to', 'off-' (as in 'off-white'), or—as Hazlewood pointed out—'nearly', 'not quite':

E **via**-damudamu.	'It is brown (reddish, nearly red).'
E **via**-karakarawa na ika oyā.	'That fish is blue-greenish.'
Sā **via**-mate mai na i-soqosoqo.	'This organization is on its last legs (about to die).'

8.2 IMPRESSION: *VIAVIA-*

A situation represented by a *viavia-* construction, while also "contrary to fact," usually involves an element of deception or pretense that is missing from *via-*. It means 'try to be', 'act as if', 'give the impression that':

E **viavia**-vuku o koya.	"He tries to act intelligent.'
E **viavia**-levu.	'She acts as if she's important.'
E **viavia**-tūraga.	'He acts like a chief (but isn't).'
E **viavia**-yalewa.	'He acts like a women / dresses as a woman.'

Note that the very failure to deceive is inherent in the meaning, since *viavia-* calls attention to it. PG noted (10/83) that this use of *viavia-* is not productive. However, the form can also mean 'nearly', or 'about to be', with no pejorative meaning:

Sā bau **viavia**-yaco-v-a toka mai.	'It's close to happening now.'
Sā qai **viavia**-vinaka toka mai.	'It's going to be better now.'

8.3 NEGATIVE: *TAWA-, TABU-*

8.3.1 *Tawa-*

Tawa- is a negative prefix that occurs before some stative verbs.[4] For example:

tawa-yaga	'useless'	**tawa**-mudu	'endless'
tawa-macala	'unclear'	**tawa**-kilikili	'inappropriate'
tawa-kila-i	'unknown'		

The last example above shows that *tawa* can be used with S2, as well as S1, forms.[5]

Cargill (1839) defined *tawa* thus: "a negative particle much used in composition. It is placed almost at will before adjectives & verbs; it is of [the] same signification & use as the English 'un-'" Although Cargill was writing about the Lakeba language, Hazlewood (1872) repeated his statement (almost verbatim) for SF. Milner (1972:117, 117n), however, identifying *tawa* as a Lauan word, wrote that it "is only found before a limited number of bases." As examples of forms that cannot take *tawa-*, BK (7/82) supplied the following:

lasa	'contented'	*levu*	'large'
tītobu	'deep'	*mārau*	'happy'

---

[4] Examples from Hazlewood, Churchward, Milner, and BK.
[5] Not S2 roots, but derived verbs that function as two-referent statives.

8.3.2 *Tabu-*

Tabu- as a prefix means avoiding a certain state or action. If that state or action is desirable, then the *tabu-* form has a pejorative meaning:

tabu-*sili*   'unwashed'   **tabu**-*teve* 'uncircumcised'
tabu-*lotu*   'irreligious'

Thus, the pejorative meaning is a product of the whole form, rather than of the prefix. Note the following:

tabu-*siga*   'practice of keeping betrothed women out of the sun to lighten their skin (lit., avoiding sun)'
tabu-*magimagi* 'kind of adze not tied with sennet (lit., without sennet)'

In these examples, *tabu-* seems to have no pejorative sense.

8.4 STATIVE PREFIXES

8.4.1 *Lau-*

One common prefix not discussed in the sections on the derivational effects of ta-, ca_1, ka-, ra-, and ca-$_2$ (see §13.52) is *lau-*. As Arms (1974:54–55) noted, it differs from the first four in that it occurs with both actives and statives (however, with only the two-referent variety of each):[6]

*E **lau**-kana.*   (from an A1 verb)   'It was eaten/edible.'
*E **lau**-musu.*   (from an S2 verb)   'It was cut.'

Lau- is not regular in its distribution. In a list of 728 verb stems[7] it occurs with 108.[8] There seems to be no pattern to its occurrence, except—as Hazlewood noticed—an attraction for verbs with the "idea of wounding or injuring." PG suggested (10/83) that *lau-* is definitely adversative in meaning, giving the following contrasting pairs as evidence:

Vako-ti na kau.   'The wood was nailed.'
nail-TR   DEF wood

***Lau**-vako o Jisu.*   'Jesus was nailed.'
STA-nail   PRP J

Tā na buka.   'The firewood was cut.'
cut DEF firewood

***Lau**-tā na liga-na.* 'His hand was cut.'
sta-cut DEF hand-3S

However, perhaps the adversative meaning occurs only with human referents, for not all *lau-* forms have it.

---

[6] This stands to reason, since *lau* - forms, although all stative, still include an implicit actor—unlike forms with *ta-*, ca_1, et al.

[7] Compiled by Saimone Nanovu in 1979. It was not a representative sample of all verbs, but appropriate for *lau-*, since it concentrated on two-referent verbs.

[8] It should be remembered that the sample used was by no means complete.

Of these 108 forms mentioned above, there is a preference for A2 verbs, with a total of 67, whereas there are only 41 examples of *lau-* with S2 verbs.

With active verbs, there is no problem stating the function of *lau-*; it changes them to statives. But with S2 verbs, the crucial question is this: What is the difference in meaning between the root form and the *lau-* form? To complicate matters, some S2 verbs can occur with one of several stative prefixes. For example:

E musu.	'It is cut.'
*E **ra**-musu.*	'It is cut.'
*E **lau**-musu.*	'It is cut.'

Within this trio, the *ra-* form is easiest to account for, since the actor has been deleted (or, in traditional terms, the word is the spontaneous form).

It remains to find a difference between *musu* and ***lau**-musu*, which—according to native speakers—is not a simple matter. The following analysis has been proposed:[9] the *lau-* form concentrates more on the goal than does the root form alone. The actor is not eliminated altogether, but it is relegated more to the background. However, a more complete answer to the question awaits further research.

With one verb, *lau-* forms a contrast between goals:

E sui na sēnikau.	'The flowers are watered.'
*E **lau**-sui o Pita.*	'P was spilled on.'

But according to TRN (11/79), this example may be the only one of its kind.

Lau- forms are also discussed in §14.13.3.

8.4.2 *Ma-*

As the various counts (those above and those made by Arms) show, there is considerable diversity in the frequency of the different verb prefixes. For example, if there are only five examples of *ra-* (pending more careful examination of *VV*), should it really be discussed along with *ta-* or *lau-*, with some twenty-fold that number? Arms grouped them together for good reason: except for *lau-*, they seem to be the only prefixes with what he called the spontaneous meaning (1974:76).

If we apply the same kind of elementary statistics to another such prefix, *ma-*, we find that we may have been misled by previous grammatical statements. For example, Capell's entry for *ma* (1941) suggests that examples abound. He explained the form as "a particle compounded with many words, forming adjs of state or condition." However, combing through words beginning with *ma-* for possible derivatives does not bear this out. For example, is *macē* 'having a soft husk, very ripe, of *ivi*' formed from *ma-* + *cē* 'weak, not able to accomplish one's purpose'? Unlikely, although greater sins of analysis have been commit-

---

[9] By AS.

ted. Is *mākudru* 'to sound as voices at a distance' from *mā-* + *kudru* 'to groan, to grumble'?

As a matter of fact, among twelve possibilities from Capell's dictionary, only two seem clearly to reflect the defined function of *ma-*: **ma**-*lele* 'bending down, of the branches of a tree; stative of *lele-ca* ('to bend down a long branch ... ') and **mā**-*vuru* 'crumbled' (from *vuru* 'crush or crumbled in the hands').[10] PG (11/79) added **ma**-*tosi* 'scratched' (from *tosi* 'score, scratch').

We must infer, then, that labeling *ma-* as "semi-productive," for Fijian, in spite of the relative productivity of cognate forms in some other Austronesian languages, is a result of misplaced faith in the grammatical explanations that appear in Capell 1941.[11]

8.5 ARTIFICIAL OR CREATED CIRCUMSTANCES: -*TĀ*-[12]

As the convention of writing *-tā-* indicates, this affix must always be preceded as well as followed by another form: it is preceded by *vaka-* and followed by the verb root. It is difficult to find a common meaning for it in all its various occurrences, but perhaps the label in the heading can be justified. In its use in the causative construction, *-tā-* conveys the impression that a special situation has been set up to bring about the result of the verb root. Note this example:

*vaka-**tā**-vuli-c-a*   'teach it/her (make her learn)'

Explaining the "artificial" label requires a cultural excursus of a conjectural nature. If one imagines a society without a structured segment called "teachers" (as opposed to those segments that did exist, such as the *bete* 'priests', *mata-ni-vanua* 'heralds', and others), then the principal meaning of *vuli* was not 'teach' but 'learn', and it was something accomplished not in a structured situation, but through observation and then participation—the method, for example, of learning the *meke*, the traditional dance-chant. "Teaching" the *meke*, or the language, or any other kind of skill, involves setting up an artificial situation, indicated in the label by the *-tā-* affix.[13]

Milner (1972:104) gave three examples of *-tā-* forms that have been nominalized:[14]

*na i-vaka-**tā**-kila-kila*   'sign, symbol'
*na i-vaka-**tā**-gede-gede*   'level, stage, grade'
*na i-vaka-**tā**-kara-kara*   'statue, figure'

---

[10] This definition has been modified to fit the S2 nature of *vuru*; the dictionary treats it as an active.

[11] The entry in *VV* says (in translation) "added to only a few roots, its meaning is not clear." Eight examples are given, including those in the preceding paragraph.

[12] Perhaps *-dē-* has a similar meaning. See *vakadēkamikamica* in Capell's dictionary. Another example is *E vaka-dē-milamila*. 'It wants to be scratched.'

[13] This point of view was developed through discussions with TRN.

[14] I have altered his glosses somewhat.

For these meanings, too, a sense of artificiality prevails—at least in the sense that these things are representations of reality.

8.6 MORE -TĀ- FORMS[15]

-Tā- also occurs in a number of forms, preceded by *sau*, and referring to kinds of continuing motion:

sau-tā-gelegele	'jump around, roll'	*sau-tā-kurekure*	'vibrating'
sau-tā-legelege	'kicking in pain'	*sau-tā-ribariba*	'flopping about'
sau-tā-wiriwiri	'feeling dizzy'		

These forms seem to mean the same as *sau-* + reduplicated root (see §8.8 and CH 14).

8.7 STATIVE PREFIX: *SA-*

In a limited number of examples, *sa-* appears as a prefix, possibly like the set of stative prefixes:

qoqo	'shrivelled'	***sa**-qoqo*	'shrivelled'	*lobi*	'folded'
balibali	'awkward'	***sa**-balia*	'foolish, clumsy'	*sa-lobi*	'folded'

8.8 CONTINUING MOTION: *SAU-*

Sau-, followed by *-tā-* (§8.5, 8.6), occurs in a number of forms that refer to kinds of continuing motion. See the examples in §8.6.

The following examples show *sau-* without *-tā-*:

***sau**-mama*	'noise of chewing (from *mamā* 'chew')'
***sau**-rī*	'suddenly (from *rī* 'quick')'

8.9 STATIVE SUFFIX: *-(C)A* (WITH OR WITHOUT REDUPLICATION)

As examples of this suffix, note the following (from *VV*): *boro-a*, *soro-a*, *tubu-a*—all with the general meaning of 'crowded'. The two following examples illustrate this meaning well:

tubu	'grow, spring up'	*tubu-a*	'overgrown with grass and weeds'
vuti	'body hair'	*vutivuti-a*	'having much body hair'

Other examples are:

dreke	'cavity'	*dreke-a*	'(liquid) nearly empty'
weli	'saliva'	*weliweli-a*	'smeared with saliva'
voto	'thorn'	*votovoto-a*	'thorny'
qaro-t-a	'prick it'	*qaroqaro-a*	'prickly'
vere	'plot'	*verevere-a*	'intricate'

The following examples show *-Ca* (*VV* notes these possibilities for *C*: *c*, *l*, *n*, *r*, *s*, *w*):

---

[15] Some speakers pronounce it with a short vowel.

drega	'gum'	*dregadrega-**ta***	'sticky'
cagi	'wind'	*cagi-**na***	'ventilated'
		*cagicagi-**na***	'much blown about'
qili	'twist'	*qiliqili-**ca***	'twisted'
sosoko	'thick (liquid)'	*sokosoko-**ta***	'thick (liquid)'
cō	'grass'	*cōco-**na***	'overgrown with weeds'

This process is very common, particularly with *-a*. Many common S1 verbs have this form, even though the root may not exist on its own. Examples are:

*karakara-**wa***	'blue, green'	*batabatā* (*a* + *-a*)	'cold'
*kamikami-**ca***	'sweet'	*dromodromo-**a***	'yellow'

8.10 DISTRIBUTIVE COUNTER: *YĀ-*

The prefix *yā-* before numerals indicates an even distribution. The derived form can be used as the main verb:

*E **yā**-dua na i-vola.*   'There was one book each.'
*E **yā**-lima na dola na ke-na i-sau.*   'Five dollars each is the price.'

Note that the verb has an existential meaning in these sentences, occurring after *e* (third person singular). With nonsingular subjects, the elements in the sentence refer to a different kind of situation: entities are apportioned in a way that is often reflected semantically as possession:

*Eratou **yā**-rua na vale.*   'They have two houses each.' (Milner 1972:83)
*E vinaka me ratou **yā**-rua*   'It is good that they (plural) have two books
   na i-vola.   each.' (Churchward 1941:44)

Yā- can also be preceded by *tau-* (Churchward 1941:44), which—according to Milner (1972:83)— "adds emphasis."

Yā- forms can also be used as modifiers:

*na tamata **yā**-dua*   'each of the persons' (Milner 1972:83)
*na katu **yā**-lima*   'five fathoms each (Churchward 1941:44)
*lako **yā**-dudua*   'go one at a time (Churchward 1941:45)
*vei keda **yā**-dua*   'to each of us (inclusive plural) (Churchward 1941:45)

PG noted (7/79) that *yā-* is in complementary distribution with another distributive marker, *dui*—the former occurring only with numerals, and the latter with other roots. Thus, perhaps *dui* should also be treated as an affix. However, because of its wider distribution, it is now treated in §5.9.

9 VERB CLASSIFICATION 1: EXISTENTIALS

This chapter and those that follow concentrate on verbs, describing such matters as verb classification and the relationship of affixation to derivation.

The major classification of a verb follows the classification of the VP in which it occurs—or can occur.[1] It, in turn, is based on the semantic relationship between the entity and the action/state that the subject and verb refer to, respectively. To provide a test frame, we use the following pattern, with the subject represented by *e* 'he', 'she', or 'it':

SUBJECT	VERB
E	____ .

Next, we ask a series of questions, based on the meaning of the verb in this frame:

1. Does the verb assert the existence of something, or the existence of a certain quantity?
2. Does the verb represent an action?
3. Does the verb represent a state?

Thus, verb types are based on the types of VPs discussed in CH 6, with this exception: because the head of an indefinite identifying VP[2] is a noun serving as a verb, it cannot be classified. This leaves three main types of verbs to be treated: existential, active, and stative. Existential verbs are described in this chapter, active and stative verbs in the following two chapters.

9.1 EXISTENTIAL VERBS

Existential verbs, introduced in §2.1.3, indicate either that (1) an entity does or does not exist, or (2) a particular number or quantity exist(s).

---

[1] Compare with Hockett's "privileges of occurrence" (1958:162).
[2] E.g., *E vale.* 'It's a house.'

9.1.1 *Tiko, tū*

The most common verb in the first category is *tiko*, which in some contexts means 'stay, reside'. However, in its existential use it can be considered a separate lexical item, meaning that there exists or is available (at a particular time) an unspecified number or quantity of some entity. Thus, *tiko* has taken on a special meaning in this use. For example, one might ask a storekeeper:

Q: *E **tiko** e sō na raisi?*   'Is there any rice?'
     3s exist 3s some DEF rice

A: *Io, e **tiko**.*   'Yes, there is.'
     yes 3s exist

According to TRN (2/82), *tiko* refers to entities that are moveable, not fixed in a place. Note that this meaning corresponds to the meaning of 'temporary continuance' that *tiko* has as a marker (§18.11.1).

An alternate answer to the question above illustrates another common member of this category: *sega*, a negative existential, meaning 'there is none':

A: *E **sega** (na raisi).*[3]   'There isn't any (rice).'

Following are other, less common members of this class.

Tū. The nonexistential meaning of this word is 'to be upright'. However, it is also used as an existential similar to *tiko*, but indicating more permanent existence, and hence, not confined to the situation at hand.

E tū.   'There's some (somewhere); there's a general quantity available.'

9.1.2 Less common existentials

There are other members of this class, but they are more restricted in their use. For example, *dodo* is used to assert the existence of something stretched out horizontally, such as a road or a rope. *Tawa* refers to the existence of the contents of a container:

*E **tawa** e na tavaya.*   'There's some in the bottle.'

Taqa means 'to exist in layers'; *tō*, 'to be filled (with liquid)'. Others, such as *koto* and *nō*, seem derived from other dialects, and are now used in literary Fijian as synonyms of *tiko*.[4]

9.1.3 *E* + numeral

The construction *e* + numeral means 'there are (so many)'. In addition to numbers, the category "numeral" includes the following:

---

[3] This construction contrasts with one that looks similar but is actually different:

E sega ni raisi.   'It isn't rice.'

Here, *sega* negates what is asserted by the subordinate verb phrase, introduced by ni. The basic verb phrase underlying this subordinate phrase is the identifying construction:

E raisi.   'It is rice.'

[4] I am grateful to PG and TRN for the examples of less common existentials.

sō	'some'	*vica*	'few'	*vuqa*	'many'	*levu*	'many'
lailai	'few'	*vica?*	'how many?'	*bini*	'plentiful		

These numerals occur with a number of restrictions. For example, *levu* and *lailai* mean 'many' and 'few' when used as existential verbs, but mean 'big' and 'small' when used as statives. They are also different from other numerals in that they do not occur as modifiers after nouns (except with their stative meaning).

Although a specific number (preceded by *e*) may modify a noun:

    *na vale e **tolu***   'three houses'

the general numeral may not:

    *na vale e levu   'a lot of houses'

Fijian linguists do not accept the use of *vuqa* as a numeral meaning 'many', noting that it is "missionary Fijian" (TRN 7/81) in such contexts as:

    *Sā **vuqa** na tiki-na e na vale ne-i Tama-qu.*
    ASP many DEF part-3S ABL DEF house PC-POS father-1S
    'In my Father's house are many mansions.' (John 14:2)

In its undisputed use, it occurs after *lewe*, referring to numbers of people:

    *e lewe **vuqa***   'there are many (people)' (Milner 1972:36)

Other numerals are limited in certain constructions (PG). SF does not use the following:

    *E bini na vale.   'There are lots of houses.'
    *E lailai na vale.   'There are few houses.'

9.2 SUMMARY

Existential verbs indicate either that (1) an entity does or does not exist, or (2) a particular number or quantity exist(s). This category differs from those described in the following chapters in that it is relatively closed—ie., confined to the examples listed here (discounting omissions) and not likely to be added to by borrowings.

10 VERB CLASSIFICATION 2: ACTIVES AND STATIVES (VALENCY 1)

10.1 THE ACTIVE-STATIVE OPPOSITION

This classification can also be called Valency 1—that is, a grammatical category that refers to types of referents (arguments).[1] Valency 2, treated in the next chapter, refers to the number of entities involved. Thus, both oppositions can be united as types of one phenomenon.

10.1.1 Semantic criteria

To classify a verb as active or stative, we examine it in the context described earlier—the basic VP. Again, we place it in the frame:

SUBJECT	VERB
E	____.

and we ask the following questions (introduced in §2.1.1 and §2.1.2):

1. Does the subject represent the **actor**? If so, the verb is ACTIVE (A).
2. Does the subject represent the **goal**—that is, something or someone being acted upon or described? If so, the verb is STATIVE (S).

The following examples show the difference between these two categories (tense is not specified; each translation could be either present or past):

STATIVE		ACTIVE	
E mate.	'It is dead.'	*E cawī*	'It flew fast.'
E levu.	'It is big.'	*E kedru.*	'It snored.'
E totolo.	'It is fast.'	*E kaka.*	'He stuttered.'
E kau.	'It is carried.'	*E lāmawa.*	'She yawned.'
E caka.	'It is done'	*E lako.*	'She goes.'

For each item in the left-hand column, we find that the referent of the subject is not acting, but is being described. Thus, these verbs are stative. In contrast, for those sentences in the right-hand column, the referent of the subject is acting. Thus, these verbs are active.

---

[1] Following a suggestion by William O'Grady in 2007.

Almost any verb can be classified using this frame. For example, *mate* 'dead' is classified as a stative. Also, any morphologically complex construction can be classified according to how it is used in the frame. Thus, although *mate* is a stative, *vaka-mate-a* 'kill it' is identified as an active, because in

    E vaka-mate-a.   'He killed it.'

the subject *e* represents the actor.[2]

10.1.2 A functional criterion

So far, the criterion for classification has been semantic. It is also possible to propose a functional criterion for identifying statives. Although all verbs occur in the frame above, generally only statives occur in the following frame:[3]

    NOUN   +   STATIVE

The components of this construction are HEAD + ATTRIBUTE. Examples are:

kalavo mate	'dead rat'	*manumanu yaga*	'useful animal'
kā levu	'big thing'	*gauna makawa*	'olden times'
draki cā	'bad weather'	*vale levu*	'large house'

In general, active verbs do not fit into this frame, unless through idiomatic usage (as in *manumanu vuka* 'bird [lit., flying animal]').[4] Thus, we do not usually find such constructions as the following:

| **tamata gādē* | 'strolling person' |
| **gone qalo* | 'swimming child' |

A functional characteristic of active verbs not shared by stative verbs is their occurrence as imperatives.[5] Note the following:

| *M-o lako!* | 'Go!' |
| *M-o vosa!* | 'Speak!' |

10.2 PROBLEMS WITH THE CLASSIFICATION

As with most systems of classification, the one just proposed does not explain all the data as neatly as we might wish. There are at least three hazy areas, each connected with the active-stative distinction.

---

[2] See CH 2.

[3] That is, opposed to actives. Some nouns also occur in this position, e.g., *vale vatu* 'stone house'.

[4] Such modifiers might be from a VP: *manumanu e vuka* 'animal that flies'.

[5] Biggs (1975:493) proposed the imperative test for actives. His requirement that *mo* (*me + o*) [subjunctive plus second person singular] be included is especially useful, for in purely formal terms, one-referent statives can also occur as one-word utterances. They cannot, however, have the imperative meaning with second-person subjects.

Two-referent statives can occur with the subjunctive particle, with the meaning 'let it be done'. Note the following context (AS): In the process of preparing a *lovo*, someone suggests that the work be interrupted for, say, swimming. A possible reply is *me bulu mada* 'let it (the *lovo*) be buried (that is, covered) first'.

10 Verb Classification 2: Actives and Statives (Valency 1)

1. Some verbs do not occur in the test frame *E [   ]*. *Kila* 'know' ('known') is an example. *E kilā* 'She knows it' is common; **E kila* does not occur. Therefore, how can we know whether the base *kila* is active or stative? *Kila* does occur in other constructions, however; for example, *kila kā* 'intelligent (lit., knowing things)'. But this use alone does not solve the problem, for both active and stative verbs enter into such a construction:

caka kākana	'food preparation'	(*caka* is stative)
gunu wai	'water drinking'	(*gunu* is active)

No doubt, semantics plays an important role here. Just as some verbs occur more often with only one referent expressed (e.g., *lako* 'go' occurs with the actor alone expressed more often than with the goal also expressed), so others—perhaps because of their meanings—more often express both actor and goal. For example, it might be unusual to speak of "knowing" in a general sense, without a goal expressed; "eating," on the other hand, is often discussed as a general activity, without referring to the goal.

Thus, the behavior of some bases requires us to classify them not according to the active-stative opposition, but rather, only to the number of referents implicit in their meaning. But this matter should be treated in a dictionary rather than in a grammar.

Sometimes the presence of other forms provides a clue as to how the base might be classified, even if it doesn't occur in the frame *E [   ]*. Following a suggestion by Arms (1974), we begin with a root that we can classify: e.g., *caka* 'done, made'. We know that if the transitive marker and an object are added, *e* will switch to express not the goal, but the actor. But suppose we want to suggest that the actor is engaged in an activity, while keeping the goal implicit. The phrase *E caka-vi* will not suffice, for *e* still represents the goal. There is no choice but to alter the root morpheme in a way that lies outside the grammatical area of transitivity, but in such a way that keeps its morphological identify. Reduplication is such a change (see CH 14).

If a root does not occur in the frame *E [   ]*, but the rest of its behavior matches that of *caka*, we could guess that it might be classified as two-referent (see the next chapter). Consider *wā* 'wait' as an example. **E wā* does not occur. But table 10:1 shows how its various derivatives compare with those of *caka* (A2 = two-referent active; S2 = two-referent stative). Based on its similarity to *caka*, we might suggest that *wā* be classified as an S2. The FDP took a more cautious approach and classified such forms simply as two-referent verbs, omitting the active-stative distinction.

2. For some bases, even when they do occur in the frame *E [   ]*, it is difficult to decide whether the subject is the actor or the goal. Consider *vuce* 'swell, swollen':

Sā	*vuce*	*tū*	*na*	*vacu-mu*	*i-matau*.	'Your right eyebrow is swollen.'
ASP	swell	CNT	DEF	eyebrow-2S	ABL-right	(*FR3*:40)

TABLE 10:1: *WĀ* AND *CAKA* COMPARED

wā 'wait'	*caka* 'done'	Classification
	e caka 'it is done'	S2
wā-raka 'wait for it'	*caka-va* 'do it'	A2; goal signaled and expressed[6]
e wāwā 'she waits'	*e cakacaka* 'he is working'	A2, goal implicit

In the sentence above, part of the meaning reflected in the English translation by the participial form of the verb is due to the presence of the aspect markers *sā* and *tū* (see Schütz and Nawadra 1972:102). So the question remains: is the subject acting or being described? If the verb is active, it is an A1, since there is no way to express a goal. If it is stative, it is S1, since there is no way to express an actor.

Other examples are *moce* 'sleep, asleep', *yadra* 'wake, awake', *mate* 'die, dead'. In *e moce*, *e yadra*, or *e mate*, does the subject *e* represent the actor or the goal? Or, in the following example, is the subject acting or in a state?

| *E bue na wai.* | 'The water boils.' |

The solution to this problem lies in function, rather than semantics. We mentioned earlier a functional criterion for identifying a stative: its occurrence as an attribute after a noun. By applying that test here, we find that the two verbs are stative, as illustrated by the following phrases:

| *na mata vuce* | 'swollen eye' |
| *na wai bue* | 'boiling water' |

Lasu 'false, tell a lie' is a root that is similarly ambiguous. But *lasu* differs from the verbs just discussed: when it is active, the subject represents a human actor:

| *E lasu.* | 'She is lying.' |

With the stative meaning, however, the goal that the subject represents is non-human and inanimate:

| *E lasu.* | 'It is false.' |

As with some other verbs, one might divide *lasu* into two separate roots: one active, and one stative.

PG (81) pointed out a small class of verbs that strain the classification. Examples are *mātai* 'skilled', *vōraki* 'reluctant', and *māqusa* 'excited'. In the frame *e [ ]*, each behaves as a stative. But unlike stative verbs, two NPs can follow the VP:

E mātai sara o koya na qoli. 'He's skilled at fishing.'
3s skilled INT PRP 3s DEF fish

---

[6] See CH 26 for a formal definition of these terms.

E vōraki o koya na laga sere.   'He's reluctant to sing.'
3S reluctant PRP 3S   DEF sing song

Sā māqusa ... na vaka-rau i-voli.   'It was excited ... about
ASP excited   DEF prepare selling   preparing goods.' (*NV4:*12)

In each of these examples, its classification is uncertain because of the doubtful function of the last noun phrase. Clearly, the *e* in each refers to the goal: "he" or "it" is being described. One would expect, then, that the last phrase would be "prepositional": e.g., *e na qoli* 'at fishing'. On the other hand, if we consider that *mātai* means "skilled at," it should be capable of occurring with the markings of transitivity, such as a transitive suffix and an object.

Historically, it seems that the former possibility was correct. PG noted (7/82) that when the last NP is fronted, the contraction *ki-na* is added to the VP. *Ki-na* normally substitutes for a fronted ablative phrase under those conditions:

Na qoli, e mātai ki-na.   'As for fishing, he's skilled at it.'
DEF fish 3S skilled ABL-3S

Thus, it is likely that the underlying sentence is:

*E mātai e na qoli.
3S skilled ABL DEF fish

The following example represents a somewhat different situation:

E gū na vuli.   'He's keen on studying.'
3S eager DEF learn

One might have expected sentences with *gū* to behave like those with *rawa* 'able' or *sega* 'not'—that is, to introduce the second verb with a subordinate marker. But the following sentences, each with an appropriate subordinate marker, are unacceptable:

*E gū ni vuli.   'He's eager to study.'
3S eager SUB learn

*E gū me-u lako.   'She's eager for me to go.' (PG)
3S eager SUB-1S go

3. Some recently borrowed words seem to function as either active or stative, depending on the context, rather than on formal differences (such as reduplication; see §13.3.2), to make the contrast. Apolonia Tamata found and discussed these examples, among others (2003:217–19):[7]

---

[7] I have changed some of the morpheme labels to fit in with the terminology used in the present work, and have also added a macron on *lālaga* 'wall'. For a discussion of the innovative syllable patterns, see CH 35.

Sentence	Gloss	Classification
E skrab o Ana. 3S scrub PRP A	'Ana scrubs.'	A2
E skrab na lālaga. 3S scrub DEF wall	'The wall is scrubbed.'	S2
E skrab-tak-a na lālaga o Ana. 3S scrub-TR-3S DEF wall PRP A	'Ana scrubbed the wall.'	A2
E miks o Jo. 3S mix PRP J	'Jo mixes.'	A2
Sā miks tū na yaqona. ASP mix CNT DEF kava	'The kava is already mixed.'	S2
E miks-tak-a o Jo na yaqona. 3S mix-TR-3S PRP J DEF kava	'Jo mixed the kava.'	A2

10.3 SUMMARY

In spite of a few examples that strain the classification somewhat, most verbs (both morphologically simple and complex) can be classified according to the criteria discussed above. Of the three classes treated, the existential class is relatively static, for its members do not enter into derivation. The most significant classes are active and stative, which figure prominently in the derivational changes brought about by affixation.

11 VERB CLASSIFICATION 3: ONE- AND TWO-REFERENT VERBS (VALENCY 2)[1]

In this chapter, we treat Valency 2—the number of referents (arguments) indicated in the verb.

In our first test for active vs. stative, we asked if the subject represented the actor or goal. So that we can refer to these entities, which are semantic rather than grammatical, we use the term REFERENTS. Throughout this discussion it is important to keep such semantic entities distinct from grammatical entities, such as subject and object. The following example illustrates the difference.

E regu-ci rau ruarua.   'He kissed them both.' (*FR3*:4)
3S kiss-TR 3D INC

The ACTOR in the event that the story relates is Peni,[2] which has been established in the preceding context. The GOAL is his two children, Rejieli and Apisai, also identified in the context. Thus, the terms "actor" and "goal" are defined in terms of the event itself.

SUBJECT and OBJECT, on the other hand, are elements in the sentence: *e* is the subject; *rau* is the object. We say that in this construction, the subject *e* REPRESENTS the actor, and the object *rau* REPRESENTS the goal.

"Referent" then, is a general term that includes both actor and goal. When we classify verbs, we will treat only these two referents that enter into the meaning of the verb. That is, actor and goal can be manifested in the basic VP only by the subject and the object.

Since this classification is semantic, the actor and goal are not necessarily referred to explicitly in the verb phrase. Thus the basis of the classification is IMPLICIT reference to either actor or goal, or both. "Implicit" in this sense means expressible, but not necessarily expressed grammatically. Here, "implicit" is a technical term. As an example of the difference between these two levels, note the following:

---

[1] This chapter deals with the classification of roots. Derived forms are treated in CH 13.

[2] Here, and in later sections, I deliberately use English as a metalanguage—a means of describing the situation referred to by the sentence being discussed.

> *E   kaba   tiko.*   'He's climbing.
> 3S climb CNT

In this sentence, only one referent is expressed grammatically: *e* 'he', which refers to the actor. However, *kaba* is the type of verb that contains an implicit goal, for in semantic terms, one has to climb something. This goal may remain implicit, as in the sentence above, or it may be expressed by a grammatical marker, as in:

> *E   kaba-t-a.*   'He climbed it.'
> 3S climb-TR-3S

Thus, *kaba* 'climb' is a two-referent verb. With respect to voice, the subject refers to the actor, so it is also an active verb. Its complete label, then, is A2.

However, verbs such as *cawī* 'fly fast' operate differently. In the frame:

> *E   cawī.*   'It flew fast.'
> 3S fly-fast

the subject represents the actor. But there is no goal implicit in the meaning of the verb.[3] In a sentence with *cawī*, a goal cannot be expressed as an object or a subject, but only as the object of a prepositional phrase. Therefore, *cawī* is classified as a one-referent active verb (A1).

11.1 ONE-REFERENT VERBS

When only one referent is expressed (i.e., indicated grammatically), it is always as the subject, and not as the object. The subject of a one-referent verb can represent either the actor or the goal. When it represents the former, it is classified as one-referent active (A1); when it represents the latter, it is classified as one-referent stative (S1).

11.1.1 A1 verbs

In the sentence

> *E gādē.*   'She strolled.'

e, the subject, represents the actor. There is no goal, either implicit or formally expressed.[4] In fact, it is not possible to express a goal formally:[5] one does not *gādē* to a place or for a purpose. In this respect, it differs from the common verb *lako* 'go', which does imply a goal.

---

[3] Of course, the meaning of the verb and its range of uses are closely bound, for it is the latter that lets us determine the former. Thus, we are, in a sense, using grammatical criteria to help determine whether a verb has one referent or two, for we look for its occurrence with the formal markers that objects condition. That is, we look for *cawī* with a transitive marker and an object: *cawī-C-a or *cawī-Cak-a

[4] For some speakers, *gādē* is an A2 verb. No doubt, some speakers will disagree about the classification of other verbs as well.

[5] That is, not within the framework of verbs, transitive markers, and objects. Goals can be indicated formally by ablative NPs, but these lie outside the scope of the classification.

11 One- and Two-referent Verbs (Valency 2)

VV reflects this difference in its definitions and classifications. *Lako* is classified as a transitive verb, and examples include its transitive form, *lako-v-a*. *Gādē*, in contrast, is classified simply as a verb (the unmarked label seems to mean "intransitive"), its definition could be translated as 'to go with no purpose or intention', and there are no transitive forms within the entry.

Examples of other verbs of motion in the A1 category are:

caqu	'hasten'	*ceba*	'swerve'
cōlovu	'fall headfirst'	*vāniqa*	'go about stealthily'
drī	'rebound'	*kutuāvenuvenu*	'wriggle about'
boleseu	'leap up'	*qera*	'fall heavily'

For the verbs of motion listed above, it is the manner, rather than the goal, that seems important. For the following set of verbs of motion describing natural phenomena, a goal is either obvious or nonexistent:

E cadra.	'It (+sun, moon) rose.'
E mudre.	'It (+wind) blew gently.'
E dromu.	'It (+sun, moon) set.'[6]

Another set of A1 verbs refers to actions confined to a particular body part:

bobo (perhaps both A and S)[7]	'close eyes, have eyes closed'
lāmawa	'yawn'
māue	'be noisy'

Still another set refers to nonverbal noises that the actor makes. Thus, there is no goal implicit in their meanings. Examples are:

E kedru.	'She snorted.'	*E vutugū.*	'He groaned.'
E samila.	'He lisped.'	*E tavidi.*	'It made a slight noise.'
E kaka.	'She stuttered.'	*E vadugu.*	'It (+reef) rumbled.'
E tata.	'He stammered.'	*E cevu.*	'It exploded.'

But not all verbs with similar meanings are A1. Note the following A2 verbs:

E kodro-v-a	'It barked-at her.'	*E dredre-vak-a.*	'He laughed-at it.'
E ci-t-a.	'She farted-at it.'	*E tagi-c-a.*	'She cried-for it.'

We have given only a sampling of A1 verbs. Some others that do not fit into semantic sets are:

E būrau.	'He prepared (kava) without proper means.'[8]
E cū.	'He turned-buttocks (as insult).'
E tatalai.	'She warmed-before-fire.'

Most of the forms we have just dealt with have been either simple roots (such as *caqu*) or dubious compounds (such as *bole-seu* or *ceguoca*).

---

[6] *Dromu*, with the meaning 'push under water', occurs with *-c-a* (and is hence classified as a two-referent verb), but not with "sun" or "moon" as a subject.

[7] PG noted that *mata bobo* 'wink' suggests A rather than S.

[8] Here, again, the emphasis seems to be on the manner, rather than the goal.

Some grammarians have claimed that A1 verbs are rarities or exceptions. For a discussion, see §11.3.

11.1.2 S1 verbs

For verbs in the S1 class, the subject expresses the goal or that which is being described. Although traditionally called adjectives, these forms have more recently been classified as statives—a subclass of verbs, since their use in many constructions is parallel to that of active verbs. In the present treatment, their further subclassification into S1 verbs points out the special nature of the state indicated: that it is without actor or cause. In other words, it is viewed as having come into being of its own accord.

The verbs in the following examples are classified as S1 because the subject expresses the goal rather than the actor (as in the previous section):

E maleka.	'It's pleasant.'	*E levu.*	'It's large.'
E balavu.	'It's long.'	*E damudamu.*	'It's red.'
E liliwa.	'It's cold.'	*E bera.*	'It's late.'

11.2 TWO-REFERENT VERBS

When two referents—both actor and goal—are implicit in the meaning of the verb, we refer to the grammatical manifestation of the relationship between the two as TRANSITIVITY. In the etymological sense of the term, the verb acts as a connection between the actor and the goal.

11.2.1 A2 verbs

Verbs in this class express the actor as the subject, and the goal as the object. Note the following phrases. First:

E rai.   'She sees.'

In this phrase, one referent—the actor—is both implicit in the meaning and expressed grammatically by the subject *e*. Another referent—the goal—is also implicit in the meaning. And although it is not always necessary, or even desirable, to be explicit about the goal, it still exists in the meaning of the verb. In other words, verbs of this type have the notion of actor and goal built into them. Next:

E rai-c-a.   'She sees it.'

In this phrase, the actor is again both implicit and expressed by the subject *e* (as in the previous phrase). But the phrase differs from the preceding one in that here the goal is not only implicit, but is also indicated formally in two ways:

1. It is signaled[9] by the suffix *-ci* (contracted here to *-c-*).
2. It is expressed[10] grammatically by the object *-a* 'it'.

---

[9] See CH 26 for an explanation.
[10] See CH 26 for an explanation.

Earlier, we noted that the verb *gādē* 'stroll' was classified as A1 because no goal was implicit, and that it contrasted with a word with a similar meaning, *lako* 'go', which can express a goal:

E lako-v-a.   He went-for/went-on it.[11]

A more detailed discussion of this class appears in CH 16, in which we examine transitivity.

11.2.2 S2 verbs

There is a large class of verbs that in most constructions appear to belong to the A2 verb class just described.[12] However, in their underived form, they are stative (with an expressed goal), with an implicit actor as well. Hence, they are classified as S2. A common example is:

bulu   'buried'

This form, without affixes or other roots joined, is stative. A paradigm with subjects would be translated as follows:

Au bulu.[13]   'I am buried.'
O bulu.   'You are buried.'
E bulu.   'She is buried.'   (and so on)

In each of these phrases, the subject expresses not the actor, but the goal—which is the definition of "stative." However, verbs like *bulu* differ from verbs like *vinaka* 'good' in this way: for the former, the state has been caused by something or someone. Thus, a second referent—the actor—is implicit in the meaning.

These verbs have sometimes been called inherently PASSIVE. And certainly, if we define a passive verb as one that focuses on the goal, rather than the actor, the label is appropriate. (But it should be remembered that a sentence with an S2 verb, whether simple or derived, cannot express the actor within the forms of transitivity.)

So long as an S2 verb stays in its simple form, only the goal, and not the actor, can be expressed. In two other common constructions, however, the actor is here expressed by the subject. In the first type, the goal is expressed by the object:

*E bulu-t-**a**.*   'He buried it.'
*E vavi-**a**.*   'She baked it.'
*E basu-k-**a**.*   'She broke it open.'

In the second type, no markings of transitivity are present, and a noun that refers to the goal now functions as a modifier:[14]

---

[11] *Lako-v-a* is seldom used with this second meaning.

[12] In spite of the number of S2 words in Fijian, it is my impression that it has not been increased by borrowings. That is, words have been borrowed from English as A2, not S2. However, this assumption needs to be tested.

[13] The use of this verb with first person seems unlikely, but could occur with a legend, for example, or the future tense.

[14] This common construction is discussed at length in §16.4.

E caka were.	'He was garden-making.'
E kau yalewa.	'He courted (lit., 'woman carried').'
E tali magimagi.	'She was sennit-plaiting.'
E canu kaikoso.	'She was collecting shellfish.'
me qiso lovo.	'to level hot stones in oven'

In the constructions above, these verbs are now classified as A2 verbs. That is, the following constructions are parallel:

Au rai-c-a. (*rai* is A2)	'I saw it.'
Au bulu-t-a. (*bulu* is S2)	'I buried it.'
E gunu bia. (*gunu* is A2)	'He was beer-drinking.'
E tā sala. (*tā* is S2)	'He was cutting road.'

This falling together of the two types explains the convergence at the bottom of figure 11:1.

11.3 DISCUSSION

In *TFL*:115, footnote 3, I wrote: "For some speakers, *gādē* is an A2 verb. No doubt, speakers will disagree about the classification of other verbs as well." However, I did not expect that other grammarians would dispute the very existence of the A1 category, or question its extent. For example, see Dixon 1988:201. In this treatment, the writer referred to the difference in the respective sizes of our sets of data, suggesting that "[i]t is doubtful that these discrepancies are due just to dialect differences between [SF] and [Boumaa]." (Readers are left to fill in the blanks, as it were, in this comment.) Finally, the writer treated us to a mini-lecture on elicitation techniques, based on his six months in the field.

This criticism can be easily countered. First, my data on this topic were obtained mainly by native speakers combing through the FDP files. Naturally, a different set of researchers might produce a slightly different set of forms. And indeed, after comparing 31 examples in *TFL* with entries in *VV*, I found that the latter included formal transitive forms for two words on the list, which were then deleted. (Three words in my data set did not appear as entries in *VV*.)

Next, the existence of prefixes that can delete the goal also justifies the A1 category and the symmetry of the classification. See §13.4, which gives a number of examples of forms with the prefix *ca-*. All these words have one feature in common: there is no implicit goal. Thus, they are derived A1 forms.

11.4 SUMMARY

The relationships among these four types and verbs in general are shown in figure 11:1.

FIGURE 11:1: VERB VALENCY

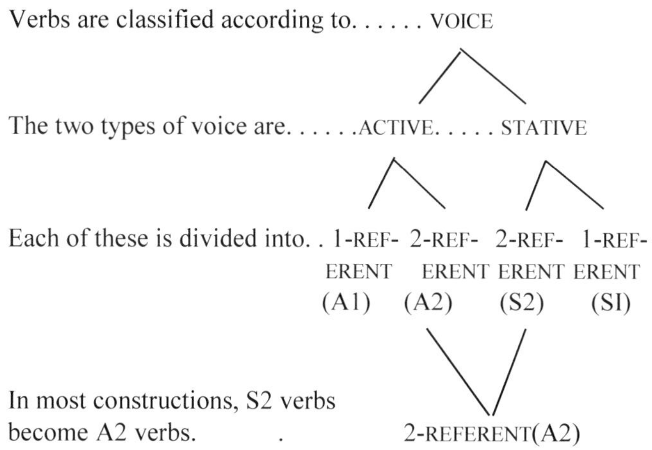

Verbs are classified according to...... VOICE

The two types of voice are...... ACTIVE..... STATIVE

Each of these is divided into.. 1-REF- 2-REF- 2-REF- 1-REF-
                                            ERENT ERENT ERENT ERENT
                                            (A1) (A2) (S2) (S1)

In most constructions, S2 verbs become A2 verbs.   2-REFERENT(A2)

12 VERB CLASSIFICATION 4: SEMANTICS

In the two previous dimensions of verb classification, the term "semantics" referred primarily to the manifestations of various relationships among *actor*, *action/state*, and *goal*. Even so, we noted some tendencies toward semantic unity within certain classes. For example, A1 verbs were shown to include (1) verbs referring to *motion*, with an emphasis on *manner* rather than destination; (2) verbs referring to *natural phenomena*; (3) verbs referring to certain *sounds*. S1 verbs might be characterized as referring to the *qualities* that an entity has. Finally, S2 verbs have often been described as referring to *processes*.

In this chapter, we classify verbs in terms of their internal semantic components, rather than external (referent) components, focusing on some distinct types of verbs in both subtypes of the large two-referent class (A2, S2). For the most part, the classification is not based on meaning alone, but a combination of meaning and behavior.

The following list of subclasses is not exhaustive; the whole set of verbs (from the files of the FDP) has not yet been studied comprehensively:

1 Motion 2 Emission or projection 3 Processes 4 States of mind
5 Judgment 6 Skills 7 Miscellaneous

12.1 VERBS REFERRING TO MOTION

A2 verbs that involve motion constitute a large subclass. The special behavior of these verbs is that they can often indicate two different kinds of goals, but only one at a time. These goals are often the destination and an accompanying entity. Examples are:

lako-v-a	'go-for it'	*lako-vak-a*	'go-with it'
voce-r-a	'row-to it'	*voce-tak-a*	'row it (boat+)'

CH 16 contains more examples of such contrasts.

12.2 VERBS REFERRING TO EMISSION OR PROJECTION

With verbs referring to emission or projection, the actor causes something to move to a destination. These verbs, too, allow two different kinds of goals to be expressed: the projectile, and the target. Examples are:

kaci-v-a	'call her'	*kaci-vak-a*	'call it (call+)'
talā	'send her'	*tala-vak-a*	'send it (message+)'

12.3 VERBS REFERRING TO PROCESSES

This semantic classification involves mainly S2 verbs. In looking at S2 verbs from this point of view, we examine the nature of the state referred to. Following Chafe 1970:99–101, William A. Foley (1976:159–61) labeled verbs in the S2 category PROCESS VERBS.[1] For such verbs, the state of the goal (expressed by the subject with the simplest form of the verb) is changed, often irreversibly, by the process indicated by the verb. Note that the feature of change applies to most of the following examples, as does the feature of irreversibility.

E bali.	'It was kneaded.'	*E bili.*	'It was divided'
E bena.	'It was dyed (hair).'	*E bola.*	'It was cloven.'
E beti.	'It was plucked.'	*E bono.*	'It was blocked

Note also the contrast with A2 verbs, which usually do not change the goal by means of the action. For example, verbs of motion, such as:

E cabe-t-a.	'He ascended it.'	*E cici-v-a.*	'She ran-for it.'
E cabe-tak-a.	'He ascended-with it.'	*E cici-vak-a.*	'She ran-with it.'

Here, the goals are unchanged or largely unaffected by what has happened to them except for a change in location.

12.4 VERBS REFERRING TO STATES OF MIND

Another subset of S2 verbs consists of verbs that indicate a state of mind, or an emotion. In the usual frame, they are indistinguishable from S1 verbs:

S1:	*E levu.*	'She's big.'	**S2**: *E cudru.*	'He's angry.'
	E lila.	'She's thin.'	*E mārau.*	'He's happy.'

The S2 verbs differ, however, in that they can indicate, through the formal markings of transitivity, the cause of the state—that is, the actor:

E lasa-v-a na cocoka	'He enjoys spearing.'
Au cudru-vak-a no-qu kolī.	'I'm angry because of my dog (e.g., someone harmed it).'
Au cudru-v-a.	'I'm angry at it.'
Au mārau-tak-a na no-qu sote vou.	'I'm happy about my new shirt.[2]

Although translation-analysis might tempt one to analyze these verbs as active, with subject and object representing actor and goal, the semantics of the situation lead to this interpretation instead: the grammatical object refers to the

---

[1] This use of "process" is somewhat different from that of Lyons (1968:366), apparently based on work of M.A.K. Halliday (no reference).

[2] This last sentence can also be an example of *-taki* (reason).

cause of the state of mind or emotion. In that sense, the construction can be considered a transformation of a causative construction.[3] For example:

E vaka-lasā na soqo.	'It amuses the crowd.'
E vaka-cudru-i au.	'She makes me angry.'
E vaka-mārau-taki au na no-qu voli-a na sote vou.	'My buying a new shirt makes me happy.'

Some other verbs that fit into this class are:

oca	'tired'	*nini*	'angry'	*ririko*	'anxious'
kidacala	'startled'	*reki*	'joyful'	*māduā*	'ashamed'
taqayā	'worried'	*gū*	'earnest'	*kurabui*	'surprised'

Another difference between this set and S1 verbs is the way in which they are possessed. Since S1 verbs refer to qualities without an agent (actor), we can consider these qualities to be innate. Thus, possessing these qualities sets up a relationship that the possessor does not control: she/he neither initiates nor terminates it. Such a relationship is marked by a *kē-* possessive:

na ke-na lila[4] 'its thinness'   *na ke-na tītobu* 'its depth'

The verbs in the state-of-mind class, however, are possessed with *nō-* possessives, perhaps reflecting the ephemeral nature of emotions or states of mind (confined to human possession):

na no-na lasa[5] 'his delight'   *na no-na mārau* 'her happiness'

This construction is similar in both semantics and form to the reason construction (discussed in §16.3.2):

E vosa-tak-a na loma-na.   'He spoke (it) because of his feelings.'[6]

In this sentence, one might interpret the function of *na loma-na* 'his feelings' as cause: 'his feelings caused him to speak'. Compare this interpretation with the analysis above: in both, the object represents the cause of the state.

12.5 VERBS REFERRING TO JUDGMENT

Another class of S2 verbs refers to states that are not absolute, but exist only as the result of someone's judgment. Consider, for example, the stative *yaga* 'useful'. Can something be intrinsically useful? Or is usefulness always a matter of judgment? The behavior of verbs in this class suggests the latter. Examples are:

E yaga.	'It is useful.'
E yaga-n-a.	'He deems it useful.'
E dina.	'It is true.'
E dina-t-a.	'She deems it true.'

---

[3] The causative constructions seem to indicate specific instances, whereas the stative constructions indicate general conditions.

[4] These are all nominalizations, not merely verbs "used as" nouns. See Geraghty 1983:246–49.

[5] *Ke-na lasa* means 'its capability of causing delight'.

[6] This construction seldom has this meaning.

12 Verb Classification 4: Semantics

E drēdrē.   'It is difficult.'
E drēdre-t-a.   'He deems it impossible.'

Note that in each pair, the role of the subject switches from goal to actor; when the object enters the construction, it then expresses the goal—the usual behavior for S2 verbs.

For one of the verbs at least, some of the causative forms reflect the idea that the state exists mainly through judging it as such. Thus:

E vaka-dinadina.   'He confirmed, witnessed.'
E vaka-dinadina-tak-a.   'He ratified it.'
na i-vaka-dinadina.   'the witness'

12.6 VERBS REFERRING TO SKILLS

Some stative verbs referring to skills occur with a transitive marker and object, with the object referring to the activity at which the person is skilled. Examples are:

E maqosa.   'She's clever, skilled.
E maqosa-tak-a.   'She's clever at it.'
E maqosa-tak-a na tali magimagi.   'She's clever at plaiting sennit.'
E vuku.   'She's wise, learned.'
E vuku-tak-a.   'She's wise about it.'
E vuku-tak-a na vuli.   'She's wise about learning.'

12.7 MISCELLANEOUS VERBS

This section cannot be a complete catalog; it is only a sketchy treatment of stative verbs that take a transitive marker and show a somewhat different relationship among actor, verb, and goal. Therefore, the patterns are less obvious than those in the previous sections. For example, in:

E wele.   'He's careless.'
E wele-tak-a.   'He neglected it.'

it stretches the imagination somewhat to propose that the object—the thing neglected—can be interpreted as the actor, or cause of the state.

With *lasu* 'untrue', the possibility of a homophonous root arises. Note that the root itself seems ambiguous as to classification as active or stative:

E lasu.   'It's untrue / he's lying.'
E lasu-tak-a.   'He lied-to him / he lied-about him.'

For this verb, the stative use of *lasu* seems to be secondary; the form with the transitive marker and object shows the usual relationships that A2 verbs show.

The following verbs show similar (but not identical) patterns:

E bī.   'It is heavily laden.'
E bi-t-a.   'It lies heavily on it.'
E bī-tak-a.   'It lies heavily on it.'

Sā oti.	'It's finished.'
Sā oti-v-a.	'He finished it off.'
E vaka-oti-a.	'He completed it.'

Note that the translations for the last two forms attempt to keep them distinct. The distinction, however, is not clear: *oti-v-a* seems just as causative as *vaka-oti-a*. SN suggested that *oti-v-a* emphasizes the process. For instance, it could be used with the meaning of seeing an area completely (for example, to tour New Zealand completely and see all there was to see), whereas *vaka-oti-a* would not have that meaning. The latter form, according to SN, emphasizes the end result. But it is also likely that the presence of the aspect marker *sā* contributes to the difference in meaning (see §5.3.1).

13 VERB DERIVATION: HOW VERBS CHANGE CLASSES

In CH 10 and 11, a verb root was classified first by its valency—i.e., according to the semantic role of its expressed subject (does it refer to the actor or to the goal?). The next criterion was its ability to express either one or two of these referents.

Changes in valency are brought about by DERIVATION. For the time being, we shall treat derivation at the sentence or phrase level, describing (1) the specific changes that operate on verbs, and (2) the forms that manifest those changes.

13.1 THE MECHANICS OF DERIVATION

The 2 x 2 system of classification described in the earlier chapters developed from a lexicographic point of view, for it labels VERB ROOTS—the forms that usually comprise (for verbs) the main entries in the dictionary. However, the criteria for classification—the role of the grammatical subject, and the number of referents implicit in the meaning of the form—hold for any verb, even if it consists of more than just a simple root. Thus, if we put the following root *gunu* 'drink' in the frame *E* _____ :

E gunu.   'He drinks.'

we find that it is **active**. We can also classify it as a **two-referent verb** by taking account of its meaning and the other constructions it occurs in.

Similarly, we can also classify a form that consists of more than just a bare root by putting it in the same frame:

E gunu-vi.   'It is drunk.'

Here again we note the relationship between subject and verb, finding that the subject is not acting, but is being described. Thus, the form is **stative**. And again, by noting the semantics and privileges of occurrence, we find that **two referents** are involved: that which is drunk, and the actor who has caused the state to occur.

When a root is changed so that the resultant verb has a different classification, we speak of this change as derivation. Because of the nature of our system of classification, there are main four types of changes possible, arranged in three main sets:

1. Active → stative, stative → active
2. Number of referents
3. Both 1 and 2

Derivation involves at least one of these changes. If there are two changes, it follows logically that they must be from different sets.

13.2 TYPES OF DERIVATION

13.2.1 Active to stative

13.2.1.1 A2 → S2

A2 verbs become S2 (or passive; see below) when *-Ci* or *-Caki* is added and no object follows:

E drē.	'He pulled.'	*E dre-**ti**.*[1]	'It was pulled.'
E gunu.	'She drank.'	*E gunu-**vi**.*	'It was drunk.'
E masu.	'He prayed.'	*E masu-**laki**.*	'It was prayed-for.'
E cabe.	'He ascended.'	*E cabe-**ti**.*	'It was ascended.'
E tagi.	'She cried.'	*E tagi-**ci**.*	'It was cried-for.'

Since the subject of a stative verb represents the goal rather than the actor, this particular derivational process has the effect of bringing the goal into the verb phrase and rendering the actor less prominent. Note that in the examples above, the forms with *-Ci* or *-Caki* indicate that the state (represented by the verb) was caused by someone or something. But the grammatical form does not make this actor (or agent) specific.

Forms in the second column have traditionally been called PASSIVE, along with S2 verbs with no suffixation, such as *bulu* 'buried'. Both these types of verbs satisfy one of the usual criteria in the definition of *passive*—that the goal, not the actor, is in focus. However, both types are NONAGENTIVE—that is, without an actor expressed overtly. In other words, it is impossible to translate an English sentence of the form *The kava was drunk by the visitor* into Fijian without changing the sentence to active voice.

Thus, there is no simple answer to the question: Does Fijian have a passive construction? If "passive" means simply "goal-focused," the answer is yes. If one insists that a passive sentence contain reference to the actor, the answer is no.

Perhaps it would be useful to ask, for each S2 construction (whether simple or derived) if the entity obliquely referred to:

1. Is it undergoing a process? Or, 2. Is it in a state?

It is likely that the answers to these questions lie outside the grammatical category of transitivity, in the surrounding discourse and perhaps in the aspectu-

---

[1] Note that the forms in the second column are identical with those that precede proper objects. Thus, the following contrast is possible:

*E rai-**ci**.*	'She was seen.' (stative)
*E rai-**ci** koya.*	'He saw her.' (active)

al markers connected with the VP. For example, the following two sentences clearly show processes:

Ni sā oti oyā,   *[sā **qai** tuvu-laki kece sara] na i-sulu*
SUB ASP finish DEM:3   ASP SEQ beat-TR INC INT DEF NOM-clothe

ka ra vuso-laki yani. 'After that was finished, the clothes were beaten
CNJ 3P foam-TR DIR   thoroughly until they were sudsy.' (*NV4*:2–3)

*[Sā **tekivū** taba-ki] na i-Vola   Tabu e   na vosa vaka-Lakeba.*
ASP ORG   print-TR DEF NOM-write sacred ABL DEF talk MAN-L
'The Bible was begun to be printed in the Lakeba language.' (*SR* 20/4/82)

And it may be that the markers *qai* and *tekivū*, indicating sequence and origin, emphasize the processes.

As an example of a derived S2 verb indicating a state rather than a process, consider the word *vinakati* (*vinaka-ti*) 'wanted', seen on a poster under a picture of an escaped prisoner.

Finally, rather than to argue endlessly whether these constructions are or are not passives, it is more useful to examine the subtle shades of differences in the way that the actor is indirectly referred to. This is the topic of CH 26, which treats the matter as an instance of SPECIFICATION, reaching beyond transitivity into the beginnings of discourse analysis.

13.2.1.2 A2 → S2 (*lau-*)

Some A2 verb are also made stative by adding the prefix *lau-*.[2] See the discussion of *lau-*, §8.4.1.

13.2.2 Stative to active

Stative verbs are made active in several ways:

13.2.2.1 S2 + *-C-a* → A2

Most S2 verbs (the "irregular passives" of earlier descriptions) become A2 by adding the transitive marker and the grammatical object:

STATIVE		ACTIVE	
E musu.	'It is cut.'	*E musu-k-a.*	'He cut it.'
E sogo.	'It is shut.'	*E sogo-t-a.*	'She shut it.'
E dola.	'It is open.'	*E dola-v-a.*	'She opened it.'

---

[2] The patterning of *lau-* is not as simple as these examples indicate, since the word also occurs with statives. For example,

*E **lau**-tā.*   'It's been chopped.'

It can also occur with derived statives:

*E **lau**-gunu-vi.*   'It's drunk/drinkable.'

So far, it has not been possible to determine any difference between these constructions and those without *lau-*:

E tā.   'It's been chopped.'
E gunu-vi.   'It's been drunk.'

It should be pointed out here that any morpheme in this class appearing with the transitive suffix and an object can also appear with the transitive suffix alone:

E musu-ki.	'It is cut.'	*E kau-ti.*	'It is carried.'
E sogo-ti.	'It is closed.'	*E biu-ti.*	'It is left.'
E dola-vi.	'It is opened.'	*E kau-ti.*	'It is carried.'

This process, however, is not treated as derivation, since no change in classification has taken place. That is, both *sogo* and *sogo-ti* are S2 verbs. The difference between them is in *sogo-ti* the actor is more SPECIFIC—a concept treated in CH 26.

13.2.2.2 S2 + reduplication → A2

Some S2 verbs become active through reduplication. Consistent with the general nature of reduplication, the process used for this type of derivation is irregular. As an example, consider *caka* 'done, made'. In its underived form, it is classified as an S2:

E caka.   'It was done.'

However, an expressed object changes its status, for then the subject represents the actor, and the object represents the goal:

E caka-v-a.   'He did it.'

The reduplicated form allows the subject to represent the actor without SIGNALING, EXPRESSING, or SPECIFYING the goal:[3]

E cakacaka.   'He's doing (something), working.'

This form, in turn, can also take the transitive suffix and an object:

E cakacaka-tak-a.   'He worked-with it (+tool).'

In a way, then, reduplication is used to provide a form to fill a desired function.[4] As Arms (1974:79) explained it:

> This means that reduplication is filling out a gap in the paradigm of Patient verbs, providing them with an Agent-oriented intransitive form comparable in many respects[5] to the simple intransitive form of Agent verbs.

13.2.2.3 S2 + modifier ("incorporated object") → A2

S2 verbs can become active by adding a modifier, sometimes (but mistakenly) interpreted as an INCORPORATED OBJECT, but usually without a transitive marker and always without the definite article before the noun (see §16.4.1):

E caka.	'It is done.' (S2)
E caka kākana.	'She is food-making.' (A2)
E moku.	'It is struck.' (S2)
E moku siga.	'She is wasting time (lit., day-killing).' (A2)

---

[3] See CH 26 for definitions of these terms.

[4] See the discussion section. Also, this function of reduplication was referred to briefly in the section on verb classification.

[5] I think Arms was being too cautious here. In what respects would this form differ?

E cā.   'It is carried.' (S2)
E cā buka.   'She is gathering firewood.' (A2)

13.2.2.4 *Vei-* + S2 → A2

The following examples were suggested by PG (9/83).

qara-vi	'served'	***vei***-*qara-vi*	'serve'
cula	'pierced, innoculated'	***vei***-*cula*	'administer an injection'
sele	'operated on'	***vei***-*sele*	'perform an operation'
koti	'clipped'	***vei***-*koti*	'cut hair'

13.2.2.5 S1→A2

S1 verbs become A2 by adding the causative *vaka-* (see §6.1):

E katakata.   'It is hot.'   *E vā-katakata.*   'It heats.'

Vaka- also occurs with A2 verbs, but it does not change their class. In an example such as

*E **vaka**-cici basi.*   'He runs buses.'

the subject expresses the actor, just as in the following form without *vaka-*:

E cici.   'He runs.'

However, in the *vaka-* form, the cast of characters (so to speak) has been realigned, even if there has not been "true" derivation.

Since the verbs of judgment discussed in §12.5 appear with *-Ci* or *-Caki* markers plus objects (as *dina, dina-t-a*), they can also occur with the transitive marker alone (without the object), meaning that the subject represents the goal:

*E dina-**ti**.*   'She is believed.'   *E vinaka-**ti**.*   'She was wanted.'

In this respect, the forms are similar to those verbs in another subcategory, the process verbs:

E dola.   'It is open / it is opened.'
*E dola-**vi**.*   'It was opened (not by itself, but by an unexpressed actor).'

But the relationships do not seem identical, for *dola* and *dola-vi* seem closer to each other than do *vinaka* and *vinaka-ti*. Consider the example cited above—the "wanted" poster picturing an escaped criminal. Is this verb the same, then, as *vinaka* 'good', except that the agent has been made more explicit? Does the same relationship hold for *cā* 'bad' and *ca-ti* 'hated'? It seems unlikely. What is more likely is that for some pairs of words, the *-Ci* functions more to keep meanings separate, or to produce idioms, than to indicate derivation.

13.3 PREFIXES THAT DELETE THE ACTOR

The derivational changes discussed so far can be divided into two types: those that change the role of subject, and those that add a referent. The derivation effected by four prefixes (*ta-*,[6] *ca-₁*, *ka-*, and *ra-*) falls into neither of these types, for it deletes the actor. With *sere*, for example, the two stative forms we have discussed so far indicate two different levels of specificity: In the phrase

---

[6] AS reported that some speakers say *tā-*. PG considered it extremely rare.

  E sere.   'It is untied.'

e, as subject, EXPRESSES the goal. The actor remains implicit, but still a participant. In the phrase

  *E sere-**ki***   'It is untied.'

the actor is SIGNALED by the suffix *-ki*. Although it cannot be further specified, it is made one degree more explicit than in the preceding phrase. However, in

  *E **ta**-sere.*   'It is untied.'

"it" has become untied by itself. The following example shows an actual context for the forms.[7] As a woman was stepping through a door that was swinging shut, it closed on her dress ties (rather like apron strings), untying them. Her comment was *E ta-sere*.

  Viewing the situation from outside the language, we might propose that the door was actually the actor, but that is not the view from within the language. For although in English we can speak of the wind closing the door, or the door pulling the ties loose, Fijian does not allow an inanimate subject for such verbs (especially, it seems, for these "process" verbs), unless the item is being anthropomorphized. Thus, the following sentence

  **E sere-k-a na i-oro na i-sogo ni kātuba.*
  3S untied-TR-3S DEF waistband DEF door POS doorway
  'The door untied the waistband.'

would be allowed only if we were to ascribe human characteristics to the door.

  As another example, AS reported that his daughter misjudged the weight of a cup as she put it in the sink for washing up; as a result, the handle was chipped. Her comment was:

  *E **ta**-beti.*[8]   'It's chipped.'

thus removing the actor from the process.

  Note a (linguistically) similar situation in the following sentences from a written text:

  *E na gauna oqō, sā ladelade tiko na bulumakau ka **ta**-sova*
  ABL DEF time DEM:1 ASP jump CNT DEF cow CNJ spilled

   ki-na na sucu. 'Now the cow was jumping and (in its
   ABL-3S DEF milk doing so) the milk was spilled.' (FR3:51)

Two sentences later:

  *Ni **ta**-luva gā na dali qai cē-murī Apisai.*
  SUB untied LIM DEF rope SEQ pursue A
  'When the rope became untied, then it [the cow] charged A.'

  For the states referred to in these last two sentences as well, one could (from an outside point of view) posit an actor: the cow spilled the milk, then caused the rope to become untied by pulling on it. However, the states do not seem to

---

  [7] I observed the incident on 20 July 1979.

  [8] The dictionaries give *bete* for 'chipped'. *Beti* may be a trace of the speaker's Kadavu language.

be interpreted as direct or deliberate results of actions, but are incidental to them.

In other words, the actor has been eliminated, and the derived form *ta-sere* (for example) is an S1 verb, with only the goal indicated. Thus, similar to *balavu* 'long' and *levu* 'big', *ta-sere* refers to a state that was not caused by an actor.[9]

Examples of the other prefixes are:[10]

***ka**-basu*	'torn open'	***ka**-voro*	'broken (something brittle)'
***ka**-sova*[11]	'spilled, emptied'	***ka**-musu*	'cut/broken in two'
***ca**-bola*	'cleft (with axe)'	***ca**-lidi*	'cracked, popped'
***ra**-gutu*	'severed'	***ra**-musu*	'broken in two'

Of the four prefixes, *ta-* is the most frequent. Hazlewood's dictionary includes over 40 forms with this prefix. In Arms's (1974:269–74) useful lists,[12] we can make the following count: *ta-*: 101; *ka-*: 46; *ca-*: 21; *ra-*: 5.

Although the prefixes are not usually interchangeable, they overlap somewhat. For example, Hazlewood described *ca-bola* and *ka-bola* as "nearly syn." Capell added *ta-bola*. As another example, *gutu* can occur with *ca-* as well as *ra-*.[13]

Since Arms listed only 173 forms that take these prefixes, we are left with a large number of S2 verbs that do not occur with any of them. A common example is *caka* 'made'. Perhaps the semantics of such terms prohibit their use with a "spontaneous" prefix—one that deletes the actor.

At any rate, on the basis of inclusiveness, the prefixes are not productive, for there are many verbs in this category that do not occur with them. Another test for productivity—use with new borrowings—is problematic. Note the examples in §10.2, which can be either A or S.

13.3.1 The distinction among statives

The existence of *-Ci* forms for nearly all S2 verbs[14] and *ta-* forms for many of them, produces a set of three statives that must be distinguished. For example:

---

[9] Some verbs are semantically incompatible with this meaning: e.g., *kana* 'eat', *gunu* 'drink'.

[10] Examples are from Arms 1974:270–72. In its entry for *ta-*, *VV* lists also *ca-*, *ka-*, and *ra-*.

[11] Note the alternate form, *ta-sova*, in the example sentence.

[12] It is necessary to add a caveat here: the forms in Arms's list must be examined carefully, for a number of them probably should not be there. In his discussion of the "spontaneous form," Arms began, "The spontaneous form of a verb consists of the base plus one of the spontaneous prefixes *ca-*, *ka-*, *ra-*, and *ta-*." Thus, we must be able to apply with some assurance standard morphological principles to the forms he listed. We are not always able to do so. For example, if *ca-wī* 'fly very fast' is to be included, there must be a verb *wī* with a related meaning. There is none.

[13] AS suggested that such variation might be due to the influence of other speech communities on the standard language. A similar situation exists for the transitive markers for some forms.

bulu   *bulu-ti*   *ta-bulu*

are all statives meaning 'buried'. The distinctions are as follows:

Bulu: a continuing state that is uncommitted as to actor, which remains at the implicit level. This form is opposed to both of the following:

Bulu-ti: a state definitely caused by someone (but who cannot be further specified), brought about at a particular time.

Ta-bulu: a state without a human actor; therefore interpreted grammatically as being without any actor.

In discussing these three options, TRN suggested this potential situation to show the distinctions. A body was found buried (*bulu*). The conditions were such that it could not be decided whether a person had done it (*bulu-ti*), or whether it was done by a landslide—and therefore by no one (*ta-bulu*).

13.4 A PREFIX THAT DELETES THE GOAL, PRODUCING A1 VERBS

In scanning the pages of *ca-* entries in Capell's dictionary, or the appendices to Arms's treatment (1974:269–74), one finds a number of exceptions to the label "passive prefix" (Capell) or "spontaneous prefix" (Arms 1974:72) for *ca-*. First, it is not always clear whether *ca-* is actually a prefix and not part of the base itself. But regularity of function and meaning provides evidence that in most cases it is a prefix. This regularity sets it apart from the *ca-* just discussed. Note the following examples:

cacali	'to talk or sing about'[15]
caqou	'make the sound of a club hitting the body'
caquru	'make the sound of crunching'
caroba	'make the sound of flapping wings'
carotu	'make the sound of a speared fish'
caroka	'make a rustling sound'
carubi	'make the sound of beating fans in a meke'
cavo	'fish with a rod'
cawadru	'slip through the fingers, as a line with a fish'
cagutu	'make a snapping sound'

All these forms have one feature in common: there is no implicit goal. Thus, they are classified as A1. Next, most of them refer to sounds or special types of activities—those that concentrate on the manner of doing something, rather than on the goal of the activity. Finally, some forms are clearly made up of two morphemes, allowing us to demonstrate the goal-deleting function of *ca-*:

E gutu-v-a.	'He (A) cut through or snapped it (B).'
E ca-gutu.	'It (B) made a snapping sound.'

---

[14] Arms (1974:42) mentioned a few S2 verbs lacking a corresponding transitive form.

[15] This gloss suggests that it takes a goal, but the goal is manifested by a *vei* phrase, not with a transitive marker and an object.

Although in the second phrase, B is now the subject, it does not express the goal, but the actor. In other words, B is now doing something, not being acted on. Further examples are:

E roba-k-a.	'It flapped it (its wings).'
E ca-roba.	'It made the sound of flapping wings.'
E qou-t-a.	'He hit it (with his knuckles).'
E ca-qou.	'It made the sound of hitting/being hit.'
E wadru-c-a.	'He stripped it.'
E ca-wadru.	'It slipped through the fingers.'
E rubi-c-a.	'He beat it.'
E ca-rubi.	'It made a beating sound.'
E bolo-g-a.	'He pelted it.'
E ca-bolo.	'It exploded.'

13.5 DISCUSSION

13.5.1 Reduplication as a means of providing contrasting forms

From a theoretical point of view, the proposal that one of the functions of reduplication is simply to provide a contrasting form or fill a hole in a pattern is interesting, since it reduces the morphological regularity of reduplication. That is, suppose language learners know the meaning of a root and also its classification. When they first encounter the reduplicated form, what are their chances of predicting its classification?

For example, let us return to *caka* 'made'. If we know that the verb in *e caka* 'it is made' is an S2, but in *e caka-v-a* 'he/she made it' it is an A2, is there any way we can predict the classification of the verb in *e cakacaka* 'he/she is working'? We might make a prediction from a statistical point of view, but we could never achieve total accuracy.

How, then, can we describe reduplication? One way is to look not for total uniformity, but for tendencies, such as the following ones.

When the subject of a reduplicated form continues to refer to the goal, the reduplication generally carries an added meaning of repetition or continuation. For some verbs—e.g., *vavi* 'baked', *tavu* 'broiled', and *qaqi* 'crushed'—the active and stative forms are kept distinct by using partial reduplication for the actives: *vāvavi*, *tatavu*, and *qāqaqi*. For others—e.g., *bulu*, *kau*, *sogo*, *sele*, *kola*, and *moku*—the reduplicated forms are examples of grammatical homophony.

This pattern points to two conclusions. First, it shows that derivation has a demarcative function that is seldom discussed. That is, some verbs have a potential for many derivatives, and sometimes affixes seem to be used not as part of a paradigm, *but merely to maintain an opposition between meanings.* Such is especially the case for reduplication and for the various forms of the transitive marker.

Second, it shows that a language can tolerate a limited amount of grammatical homophony, so long as the hearer can disambiguate it through context.

13.5.2 Discussion: *ta-*, *ca-*, et al.

Although the affixes just described eventually came to be known as passive prefixes (e.g., Churchward 1941:20), they did not have that label at first. In his sketch of Lakeba grammar (1839), Cargill stated flatly that there was no passive ("though it is sometimes indicated by a participle or adjective," p. 46), listed no *-Ci* or *-Caki* forms, and described the following verb form as a participle (p. 42):

> *Sā ta-dola a kātuba.*   'The door is opened.'

Hazlewood (1872)—after setting up an extensive class of passives to deal with those *-Ci* and *-Caki* forms, among others—wavered between a passive and an adjective label for the forms with prefixes. He began by showing how the more extensive class of passives, such as *rere-vaki* 'fearful' could be "used as adjectives." Then he added to that class

> verbs with the prefixes ka, *ta*, and *ra*, as kavoro, broken; tamusu, cut in pieces; ramusu, broken. See under Ta and Ka in the Dictionary. Perhaps these are more properly *passive forms of the verb*.

The last sentence underscores his indecision about the classification of *ta-* and other forms. If we follow his instructions and look under *Ta* in his dictionary, we find the following:

> Ta, like Ka, is prefixed to the intr. or pass. forms of many verbs, and changes them into adj. or pass. part. as, Tadola, open, from Dola-va, to open. Words thus formed differ from adj. and pass. verbs generally in this respect, that they imply that the thing has become so *of itself*. But it appears to be used also when they *do not wish to mention*, or when they *do not know* the agent by whom the thing has come into the state expressed by this form of the verb, or by this kind of adj. They might be called impersonal passive verbs, as they are never used but in third pers. sing.[16] I have generally called them a. or v. pass. The prefixes *ka* and *ra* appear to be used in the same manner.

Hazlewood's label for "impersonal" is open to question. We tend to interpret "impersonal" as not relating to human referents. The statement holds for such verbs as *dola* 'open', or *cavu* 'pulled up', for in normal discourse, a human would not serve as the goal. And it follows, then, that first and second person subjects (representing the goal) would not normally be used:

> **Keirau ta-dola*   ***'We (dual exclusive) are open.'

But what of *lau-rai* 'visible', *lau-coka* 'pierced', or *ka-love* 'bent'? These statives, as well as many others, could apply to human goals. It appears that Hazlewood's restriction was a semantic one, not a grammatical one, and a generalization too hastily formed.

---

[16] Hazlewood seems to have meant here that third person subjects with a number greater than singular (that is, *erau*, *eratou*, and *era*) cannot used to refer to nonhumans. If the statement was accurate at the time he made it, the language has changed; it is still a somewhat controversial matter, but many speakers use the subjects above for nonhuman referents (see §4.5).

13 Verb Derivation: How Verbs Change Classes

However, Hazlewood's grammatical explanations in the dictionary differ somewhat from those in the grammar (later scholars have tended to use only the latter; using both sources gives a fuller picture). Whereas these derivatives hover between passive and adjective in the dictionary explanation, they seem to have fallen toward "passive" in the grammar (1872:44):

> Passives of some verbs are formed by prefixes, or by the passive form of some other verb, as by *lau*, *ka*, *ra*, *ta*, and perhaps some other particles. They are all prefixed to the short passive form of the verb.

(By "the passive form of some other verb," he meant *lau*, which he considered to stem from *lau* 'hurt, injured'. Accordingly, his examples all convey this "afflictive" sense, and he omitted the examples that do not fit this hypothesis, such as *lau-rai* 'visible', *lau-kana* 'edible', *lau-koda* ('capable of being) eaten raw', or *lau-gunu* 'drinkable, drunk'.)

Churchward (1941:20) labeled *ta-* (and other) forms as passives rather than as adjectives. He also discussed the *lau-* forms and was careful to express some doubt about the relationship of the prefix to the verb *lau,* including such apparent anomalies as those examples given above.

Milner also called this set of affixes "passive prefixes," but did not distinguish the meaning of the forms from that of the other "passives," except by claiming that "the majority denote violent and/or disruptive processes" (1972:113). It may be that such a meaning is derived from the meanings of the verbs, rather than a meaning intrinsic in the prefixes.

Choosing to follow Cargill's interpretation, Schütz and Nawadra (1972:105–6), in their argument against passives in Fijian, classified the forms in question as participial prefixes. (It now seems likely, however, that that position was too extreme. See the discussion of "passive" in §13.2.1.1.)

Through all the treatments just discussed (with the exception of Milner's) run two common themes: (1) that the states indicated by the derived forms do not have an external cause, and (2) that the verb roots appearing with these prefixes (except *lau-*) are themselves stative[17] (or passive). For example, Hazlewood pointed out both in the dictionary entry for *ta-* and in his more general discussion in the grammar that "the thing has come into that state *of itself.*" Moore (1906:46) used terminology more familiar to modern linguists: "when the thing has happened without any direct cause or *agent* [emphasis added] ..." Capell, in his entry for *ta-* (but for none of the other prefixes), used the term "spontaneity."

It is this last term that served as a theme for Arms's careful and thorough treatment (1974:72–76, 121–23, 269–74). Calling the set "spontaneous forms," Arms developed the two themes just mentioned, especially the first: "Spontaneous forms indicate that the state or process is being viewed independent of any Agency" (p. 73). In addition, he emphasized that "states, not passive actions" were involved.

---

[17] Schütz and Nawadra did not mention this second theme.

I think that the advantage of the present treatment is that it clarifies the "agentless" notion by fitting it into our more comprehensive verb classification: the two oppositions of active/stative and one-referent/two-referent. It accomplishes this by viewing such forms as *ta-dola* as being not merely without an actor, but as the result of a process that has operated on a verb that is classified as two-referent (here, *dola* '(to be) open') and has, through derivation, deleted the actor. Thus, *ta*- and the other prefixes in this limited set[18] fit in with other affixes of derivation—that is, those that change a verb's classification.

---

[18] PG (9/83) suggested that *ca*-, *ka*-, and *ra*- convey an adversative meaning.

14 VERB REDUPLICATION

If we examine the **form** of reduplicated words, we find that certain parts of the base words can be repeated:

Type		Example
1	one syllable	*levu* → *le-levu*
2	two syllables	*levu* → *levu-levu*
3	portions of a form that are no longer phonological syllables, but which function as "grammatical syllables"	*vou* → *vovou*
4	combinations of these types.	*ta-basu* → *ta-ta-basu-basu*

As for functions, reduplication produces grammatical variations of a word without introducing a separate new affix, or—less frequently—it allows semantic variation within the same general meaning. The following grammatical and semantic functions have been noted:[1]

1. To indicate repetition, frequency, or prolongation.
2. To allow an S2 verb to be used actively, but still without signaling or expressing the object.
3. To form S1 verbs from a variety of roots (sometimes with *-(C)a*).
4. To form modifiers that can follow nouns (from verbs that would not normally do so).
5. To form collectives for S1 verbs (rare).
6. To indicate feigning, pretense (with *vaka-*).
7. To form modifiers that can follow verbs (from verbs that would not normally do so).
8. To indicate discontinuous or dispersive action.
9. To form S1 from S2 verbs.
10. To indicate a partitive meaning: 'nearly, partially'.
11. To indicate aimless action (perhaps related to 8).

The first two types are by far the most frequent. Semantic changes are discussed in a separate section.

---

[1] This is not a closed list.

14.1 TO INDICATE REPETITION, FREQUENCY, OR PROLONGATION

Some verbs are semantically more compatible than others with the meanings of repetition, frequency, and prolongation—especially those referring to physical actions (including verbal ones). Therefore, we find such pairs as the following in our sample:

boso-k-a	'mix it'	*boso-boso-k-a*	'mix it intensely or often'
buku-t-a	'fasten it'	*buku-buku-t-a*	'fasten it often'
buki-a	'fasten it'	*buki-buki-a*	'fasten it often'
bura$_1$	'oozing'	*bura-bura*	'ooze often'
bura$_2$	'pierced'	*bura-bura*	'prolonged piercing'

These modifications may also apply to an identical operation on a number of referents of the subject.

Some other verbs in this sample that behave similarly are:

vau-c-a	'tie it up'	*bari-a*	'nibble at it'
bulu-t-a	'bury it'	*bete-k-a*	'break it'
yalo	'wave'	*bisi-a*	'pitch it'
bali-a	'knead it'	*basi-a*	'spread it'
basu-k-a	'break it'	*benā*	'daub it'

Note that this function of reduplication is similar to that of *vaka-$_2$*.

With some S1 verbs, the reduplicated forms add an intensive meaning:

E sīnai.	'It's full.'	*E sī-sīnai*	'It's full to the brim.'
E balavu.	'It's long.'	*E bala-balavu.*	'It's very long (as compared to width, as *na dali bala-balavu* 'long rope')'

The lowest numerals (which can also be stative verbs) are reduplicated, with these meanings:

dua-dua 'one alone'[2]   *rua-rua* 'both'   *tolu-tolu* 'all three'

These reduplicated numerals also function as post-verbal markers. See §20.7.3.

Churchward observed (1941:44) that in the compound numerals, only these same morphemes are reduplicated; for example, *tolu-tolu-sagavulu* 'all thirty'.

Note the following contrasts between the simple and reduplicated forms:

E sega ni tau-vi-mate ...	'He isn't ill ...'
ka sega ni tau-tau-vi-mate	'and doesn't get sick very often.' (*FR3*:44)
E butako-ca.	'He stole it.'
E buta-butako-ca.	'He kept stealing it.' (*FR5*:7)

---

[2] Also the extended meaning of 'exceptional, most'. Milner (1972:47) considered this a special category of 'superlative, excessive'.

14.2 TO ALLOW AN S2 VERB TO BE USED ACTIVELY WITHOUT SIGNALING OR EXPRESSING THE OBJECT

As we saw in §10.2, S2 verbs such as *caka* 'made' are stative in the frame *e [ ]*. They become active with the addition of (1) the transitive marker and object, or (2) a noun modifier. For example (as shown before), *caka* 'done, made' is an S2 verb in:

    E caka.   'It was made.'

but the following derivatives belong to the A2 class:

    E caka-v-a.   'She made it.'
    E caka-were.   'She made-garden.'

Reduplication allows S2 verbs to be active but with the semantic goal implicit. In the form:

    E caka-caka.   'She worked.'

the subject *e* now represents the actor, and the goal is implicit. As another example:

    Keimami dau laki voli-voli ki-na. 'We go shopping (buying) there.' (*FR3*:6)

Some examples above show a number of S2 verbs in their reduplicated form; the following list contains further examples:

E buta.	'It was taken out.	*E buta-buta.*	'She was taking-out.'
E bulu.	'It was buried.'	*E bulu-bulu.*	'He was burying.'
E bini.	'It was piled.'	*E bini-bini.*	'He was piling.'
E biri.	'It was set (snare).'	*E biri-biri.*	'He was setting (snare).'
E boko.	'It was extinguished.	*E boko-boko.*	'He was extinguishing.'

14.3 TO FORM S1 VERBS FROM A VARIETY OF ROOTS (WITH -(C)A)

Many statives are formed by reduplicating a root and adding *-(C)a* (see §17.8). For some, as in the following list, the roots are still identifiable:

qili	'twist, rub'	*qili-qili-a*	'rough, unkempt (hair)'
cō	'grass'	*cō-co-na*	'overgrown with weeds'
dravu	'ashes'	*dravu-dravu-a*	'covered in ashes'
drega	'gum, sap'	*drega-drega-ta*	'sticky'
tui	'salt (water)'	*tui-tui-na*	'salty'

For others, as in the following examples, the root no longer occurs in its underived form.

caba-cabā	'unkempt (hair)'	*bure-bure-a*	'muddy (water)'
dravi-dravi-a	'slippery'	*droga-drogā*	'hoarse'
dromo-dromo-a	'yellow'	*drugu-drugu-a*	'stinking, moldy'
dugu-dugu-a	'dirty, old, smoked'	*saka-sakā*	'clumsy'

14.4 TO ALLOW CERTAIN VERBS TO MODIFY NOUNS

Generally, active verbs do not modify nouns. But some can in their reduplicated forms:

rere	'fear'	*na tamata rē-rere*	'fearful person'
nini	'tremble'	*na tamata nī-nini*	'trembling person'
garo	'lust-for'	*na tamata garo-garo*	'lustful person'
saga	'strive'	*na tamata sa-saga*	'striving person'

14.5 TO INDICATE COLLECTION, GROUPS[3]

A small number of statives (only seven in our collection so far) change their function through reduplication or through changes to forms that are already reduplicated. As Richard B. Lyth stated (Hazlewood 1872:25), most of them are "adjectives of size" (and as such, seem to arrange themselves into semantic oppositions). In the following examples, the forms on the right are used to indicate collections of items:

lai-lai	'small'	*la-lai*	*leka-leka*	'short'	*le-leka*
levu	'large'	*le-levu*	*balavu*	'long'	*ba-balavu*

For example:

gone lai-lai   'small child'   *gone la-lai*   'small children'

One pair shows an opposition of "quality":

vinaka	'good'	*vi-vinaka*[4]
cā	'bad'	*ca-cā*

and one form has no semantically opposing form:

vou   'new'   *vo-vou*

PG noted (10/83) that the reduplication of *vinaka*, *cā*, and *vou* with nonsingular referents is not obligatory. These derived forms are used only as noun modifiers, as in the following construction:

na vale le-levu   'lots of big buildings'

That is, they do not occur in the following construction:

*E le-levu na gone.   ***'There are a lot of children.'

Nor do they indicate plural, in the sense of 'two or more'. When low numbers are specifically stated, the forms in question are seldom used:

e rua na gone levu   'two large children'

---

[3] It may be that this category functions to distinguish statives from the existential use of (at least) *levu* and *lailai*, and tells us, for example, whether the meaning is 'a large X' or 'lots of X'.

[4] Some consultants suggest *vī-vinaka*. Since the putative long vowel is in the position that allows shortening, it is difficult to decide whether the underlying form is long or short. However, it is more reasonable to posit a long element that shortens than the opposite situation, which is unattested.

Five of the seven forms are reduplicated one step further to indicate 'extremely'; the construction is not common:

la-la-lai	'extremely small'
le-le-levu	'a very great number'
ba-ba-balavu	'extremely long'
le-le-leka	'extremely short'
vi-vi-vinaka	'extremely good'

14.6 TO INDICATE PRETENSE, AIMLESSNESS (WITH *VAKA*-)

Full reduplication, preceded by *vaka-*, conveys the notion of pretending to do something, or feigning. Examples are:[5]

vaka-moku-moku-t-a	'pretend to kill him'
vaka-mate-mate-a	'pretend to die'
vaka-loma-loma-n-a	'pretend to be sorry'
vaka-leve-leve-a	'pretend to hit him'
vaka-tosi-tosi-a	'pretend to scratch it'

Other examples can be formed from the following:

teke	'kick'	*lave*	'lift'	*muri*	'follow'	*musu*	'broken'
keve	'carry'	*qiri*	'ring'	*kari*	'scraped'	*galu*	'silent'

This construction can be used with a modifier ("incorporated object"):

E vaka-belu-belu kava. 'He's pretending to bend metal. / He's bending metal aimlessly.

With the partially reduplicated form, a slightly different meaning is conveyed (according to TRN):

E vaka-be-belu kava. 'He appears to be bending metal (but since he's taking so long, he must be fooling around).

PG (2/82) questioned this interpretation, suggesting that the principal semantic feature in some examples found so far seemed to be "slow, deliberate action."

14.6.1 *Vaka-*, *-tā-*, and partial reduplication

The partially reduplicated form of the verb, preceded by *vaka-* and followed by *-tā-*, is used to refer to an action performed in an artificial situation—that is, away from the usual environment, using something different from the usual components, or because of different stimuli. Examples are:

kana	'eat'
vaka-tā-ka-kana	'(to) picnic (eat away from the usual environment)'
lovo	'make an oven'
vaka-tā-lo-lovo,	'make a small *lovo*, as children would do, with small
vaka-tā-lovolovo	bits of food to bake'

---

[5] Examples from TRN.

riri   'cook by boiling'
vaka-tā-ri-riri   'cook small things in small pans, as children do in play'
vuli   'learn'
vaka-tā-vu-vuli   'practice'

Since it is difficult to tell whether the meaning of pretense is conveyed by reduplication, by *vaka-*, or by both, this construction is cross-listed in the section on *vaka-*.

14.7 TO MODIFY VERBS

As we saw in the section on *vaka-*, that prefix allows one verb to modify another, as in *cici vaka-totolo* 'run fast'. Full reduplication is another way (for certain verbs). Examples are:

bati 'tooth'   +   *digi* 'choose'
bati-digi-digi 'eat discriminately, choosing carefully'

siwa 'fish with line'   +   *kolo* 'throw'
siwa kolo-kolo 'fish with thrown line'

lako-v-a 'fetch it'   +   *qasi* 'crawl'
lako-v-a qasiqasi 'fetch it crawling'

boi 'smell'   +   *beta* 'be ripe'
boi beta-beta 'smell of ripe fruit'

Not all verb + verb modification follows this pattern. Some forms seem constructed in order to provide semantic variation. Note the following:

yā   'be in motion (a group of things)'
yā vala   'moving'
yā va-vala   'unsteady'
yā vala-vala   'fidgety, nervous'

These forms are interesting, since *vala* exists in SF only in such constructions and in *i-vala-vala* 'habitual act, conduct', which may be a loan from Lauan (PG, 10/83). Lauan Fijian still has, however, *vala-t-a* 'do it, make it' (TRN, and Hale 1846:419).

14.8 TO INDICATE DISCONTINUOUS, DISPERSIVE (PARTIAL REDUPLICATION)

For some verbs, the partially reduplicated form indicates that the action is performed a bit at a time, or here and there. Examples are:

ka-kana   'peck at food, eat small bits'
cī-cici   'run in short bursts, chase and spear fish on reef'
ba-bari   'nibble a bit at a time'
ba-bale   'fall down here and there'
to-toki   'peck here and there'
qe-qera   'fall down (fruit+) here and there'

14.9 TO FORM S1 VERBS FROM S2 VERBS

S2 verbs, by definition, contain semantically a cause of the state (an actor). We have seen elsewhere (§13.5) that certain prefixes, such as *ta-*, can add the meaning that the state has been achieved by itself.

Some verbs attain a similar meaning through reduplication. *Bī*, for example, means 'heavily laden' (by something), and the actor comes into play in the form:

    bi-ta   'press down on it (with weight)'

However, the reduplicated form *bībī* 'heavy, important' seems to indicate a state without an actor at all, not one that has "come about" (even by itself), but one like *levu* 'large' or *balavu* 'long'.

14.10 TO INDICATE A PARTITIVE SENSE

Reduplication can convey a partitive or inchoative sense:

    bota 'ripe'   *bo-bota* 'beginning to be ripe'

14.11 TO INDICATE AIMLESS ACTION[6]

A reduplicated verb can show that an action was performed aimlessly, without purpose or goal:

    E dabe. 'He sat.'   *E dā-dabe.* 'He sat here and there.'
    E kaba. 'He climbed.'   *E kā-kaba.* 'He climbed without purpose.'

14.12 MISCELLANEOUS CHANGES THROUGH REDUPLICATION

This section treats changes brought about by reduplication, but not easily classified into the categories discussed in the previous chapter. Generally, these changes are semantic ones.

14.12.1 Semantic changes

Semantic changes are sometimes difficult to distinguish from grammatical ones. *Rai* and *rairai* constitute a case in point. The former is usually glossed as 'see', the latter as 'appear':

    E rai. 'She looks/sees.   *E rai-rai [ ]* 'She looks/appears [ ]

Thus, grammatically, the subject of *rai* represents the actor; that of *rairai*, a goal. One might interpret the difference this way: our appearance is how others see us. But this interpretation poses the question: Is the difference between *rai* and *rairai* semantic or grammatical? Here, it seems to be both.

In general, I use the following criteria to distinguish between the two types. A grammatical change has an effect on the classification of a verb—with respect to the active-stative opposition, or to the roles played by topics. Such a change can also be connected with other grammatical categories—such as tense, aspect, person, or number—that are generally manifested by markers less closely connected with the verb than those we consider affixes.

---

[6] Perhaps the same as §14.8.

A semantic change, then, can be defined negatively: a change in meaning not included in the various types of grammatical change. For example, some reduplicated forms of verbs do not seem related to the root in any grammatical way so far described, but still the two forms seem related in meaning:

E kilā. 'She knows, thinks, believes it.'
E kila-kilā. 'She guesses it.'
E drēdrē. 'It is difficult.'
E drē-dre-t-a. 'She considered it difficult.'

To show that there is no grammatical difference between the members of the following pair, note that each can modify a noun. The difference seems to lie in the lexical meaning:

na tamata oga 'a person with many appointments or duties'
na tamata oga-oga 'a busy person (perhaps just for the time being)'

Other miscellaneous pairs are:

sama-k-a	'rub it (with hands)'	*sa-sama-k-a*	'sweep, clean it'
bula	'alive'	*bula-bula*	'healthy'
droka	'uncooked'	*droka-droka*	'green (leaf, wood)'
qase	'old person'	*qase-qase*	'cunning'
donu	'straight, level'	*do-donu*	'correct'

14.12.2 Ambiguity, and some efforts to avoid it

It may have been noticed that there are more functions than there are formal types of reduplication. For some of the functions, there is no chance of ambiguity, for they are manifested in different grammatical constructions. But the two most common functions—frequentative, and stative-to-active—could be confused, for each can occur as the head of a verb phrase. For example, an S2 verb can be reduplicated, so that the subject now represents the actor, e.g.:

E bulu. 'It's buried.'
E bulu-bulu. 'He's burying.'

How is this construction kept distinct from frequentative? In this instance, it isn't; *e bulu-bulu* is ambiguous, for it also can mean 'It's been repeatedly buried.' However, some of the forms are kept distinct by using partial reduplication as a contrast:

E vavi. 'It's baked.'
E vavi-vavi. 'It's baked for a long time.'
E vā-vavi. 'She's baking.'

14.13 THE FORMAL MANIFESTATIONS OF REDUPLICATION

14.13.1 Restrictions

Krupa (1966), Geraghty (1973), Arms 1974:130–36), and Milner (1982) have discussed various associative and dissociative characteristics of the consonants

14 Verb Reduplication

in CVCV roots. Such forms as *babe, *biba, *beba, *biba, and *buba⁷ are disallowed, while baba, bebe, bibi, bobo, and bubu are allowed.

However, even these allowed forms cannot be fully reduplicated; only partial reduplication is allowed. Thus, one does not find such forms as

*baba-baba, *bebe-bebe, etc.

Following are examples of CVCV verbs with only one syllable reduplicated.⁸ In some cases, the first syllable is lengthened,⁹ although vowel length in that position is suspicious; there is much variation among speakers.

dede	'opened (hand)'	*dē-dede*	'open continually'
drudru	'skinned'	*dru-drudru*	'skin continually'

The restriction also holds in forms that are first derived, then reduplicated:

ta-cece 'separated (layers)' *ta-ta-ce-cece* 'shivering, trembling'

When trisyllables consisting of only one morpheme are reduplicated, only the first, or first two syllables are repeated:

bolomo	'steeped (food)'	*bo-bolomo*	'steep continually'
cobutu	'covered (with hand or under a pot)'	*co-cobutu*	'cover continually'

Some forms have more than one option:

cēmurī 'drive away, pursue' *cemu-cēmurī, cē-cēmurī*¹⁰

Since most roots are made up of two syllables (which we can symbolize as CVCV, CVV,¹¹ or VCV), most of the examples of reduplication dealt with so far involve the repetition of one or both of these syllables.

---

⁷ There are some exceptions: *qaqi, qaqo, qiqō* (however, perhaps forms with long final vowels are excluded from the restriction), and *vavi*.

⁸ There are at least two possible explanations for this long vowel, and others—such as in *vā-vava, vā-vavi,* and *qā-qaqi*. First, there might be an underlying long vowel in the root, such as **dēde*. It would regularly shorten in penultimate position. But *vava* doesn't seem to work this way, for when an object is added, the form is *vavā* and not *vāvā*. Thus the second possibility: that some forms with Ca syllables are borrowed from languages in western Fiji, which lengthen *a* syllables in antepenultimate position (Geraghty 1983:68).

⁹ Thanks to BK for helping with the definitions for many of the reduplicated forms.

¹⁰ These two forms are not quite as erratic as they look. In the sections on phonology we discuss the difficulty with the vowel-shortening rule in positions other than penultimate. Here, even the form on the left varies: the vowel is somewhat long in citation form, but not as long as it would be if followed by an accented vowel. In the first reduplicated form, both *ce* syllables are perceived by speakers as being short, although the underlying vowels are long. In the second reduplicated form, the *cē* syllable is perceived as long, because it is phonetically longer due to its position before an accented syllable.

¹¹ This abbreviation refers to those forms that clearly sound like two syllables—that is, with vowel sequence of high to low, or *ui*. Other vowel sequences are classified as potential diphthongs.

However, there is another type of root that can be reduplicated: that which consists of a long syllable, either simple or complex. An examination of how these syllables are reduplicated leads one to suspect that the grammatical behavior of such forms points toward a different analysis than does their phonological behavior.

In the first of these subtypes (CV̄), there are 74 potential forms: 14 x 5 for the "normal" consonants, plus 3 *w* syllables, plus 1 *y* syllable. Of these potential forms, only 5 are reduplicated:[12]

ca-cā	'bad (collective)'	*so-sō*	'assemble (for a meeting)'
dra-drā	'spotted with blood'	*wa-wā*	'tired out'
dri-drī	'flying off (chips)'		

Complex long syllables (those consisting of an optional consonant plus one of the vowel sequences *ai au oi ou ei eu iu*) bring the total to 115: 14 x 7, plus 5 *w*-syllables, plus 2 *y*- syllables. From these, we find the following reduplicated forms:

ra-rai	(in *vaka-ra-rai* 'watch')
la-lau	'pricked (many places or many goals)'
sa-sai	'skinny (from *sai* 'runt')'
va-vau	'bundled (many items or bundles)'
bo-boi	'smelled (many items or people)'
ce-ceu	'carved (many items)'
dre-dreu	'ripened (many fruit)'
se-seu	'scratched (as a hen)'
vo-vou	'new (collective)'

Although the vowels in these long syllables now operate phonologically as units, it seems more convenient to consider them as vowel sequences—indeed, as separate syllables—when we are describing reduplication. From this point of view, *lai* and *cā* (for example) could each be considered two "grammatical" syllables. Thus, *lai-lai* and *cā-cā* could be classified as examples of full reduplication; *la-lai* and *ca-cā* partial reduplication.

14.13.2 Derived forms

When verbs derived with prefixes that consist of one short syllable are reduplicated, they take the following form:

CV + root → CV + CV + root + root [13]

The following examples show three common prefixes: *ta-*, *ca-*, and *ka-*. With each of the reduplicated forms, the meaning is 'frequentative':

---

[12] Based on a small sample of questioning. Other speakers may have other such items that are reduplicated.

[13] See Tippett 1953–54 for an interesting discussion of this pattern of reduplication.

14 Verb Reduplication

ta-basu	'broken (by itself)'	*ta-ta-basu-basu*	frequentative
ta-bili	'go in (great no.)'	*ta-ta-bili-bili*	freq.
ta-bola	'split in two'	*ta-ta-bola-bola*	freq.
ca-bura	'(boil+) burst'	*ca-ca-bura-bura*	freq.
ca-druti	'broken (rope+)'	*ca-ca-druti-druti*	freq.
ka-belu	'bent, folded'	*ka-ka-belu-belu*	freq.
ka-bola	'split in two'	*ka-ka-bola-bola*	freq.

These three prefixes frequently co-occur with reduplication. More examples:

ka-dolo	*ka-ka-dolo-dolo*	*ta-cece*	*ta-ta-ce-cece*
ta-cega	*ta-ta-cega-cega*	*ta-cere*	*ta-ta-cere-cere*
ta-cila	*ta-ta-cila-cila*	*ta-coca*	*ta-ta-coca-coca*
ca-riba	*ca-ca-riba-riba*	*ca-roba*	*ca-ca-roba-roba*
ca-drī	*ca-ca-drī-dr ī*	*ka-bete*	*ka-ka-bete-bete.*

Less common than the affixes above are the following, no longer productive:

1. *So-*

    kidi   'crinkled, creased'
    so-kidi   'crinkled, water- dappled'
    so-so-kidi-kidi   (intens.) cf. *so-ro-kidi-kidi* 'light playing on surface'

2. *Kaca* (see Capell 1941:76: *kaca-roka-roka* 'burst of thunder')

3. *Sa-*. The status of *sa-* as a prefix is uncertain. Since it is a short syllable, it has the form of a particle, but it is difficult to attach a meaning to it. The following forms use *sa-* + reduplication:

    sa-sa-kure-kure   'vibrating'
    sa-sa-lobi-lobi   'wrinkled'
    sa-sa-bila-bila   'moving up and down'

4. *Ma-*

    ma-ma-cedru-cedru   'hiccough continually'

5. *Ka-*

ka-dresu	'rent, torn (clothes)'	*ka-ka-dresu-dresu*	freq.
ka-droso	'producing hollow sound'	*ka-ka-droso*	freq.
ka-isi	'torn (cloth), split (wood)'	*ka-ka-isi-isi*	freq.

6. *Tava-*. In some examples, the *tava-* derivatives have the same meaning as those with *ta-ta-*

    tava-liso-liso (S1)   'black and shiny'
    ta-ta-liso-liso

    tava-qasi-qasi (A1)   'not keeping still, esp. making sound of
    ta-ta-qasi-qasi   things creeping on dry leaves'

    tava-yalu-yalu (S1)   'emotionally unstable'
    ta-ta-yalu-yalu

Other examples of *tava-* forms, with a meaning different from *ta-ta-*forms:

tava-kere-kere (A1)	'make the sound of boiling water'
tava-reki-reki (S1)	'joyful'
tava-laqu-laqu (S1)	'undecided'

14.13.3 Compounds

As opposed to derivatives, compounds reduplicate only the first element:

$$ROOT_1 + ROOT_2 \rightarrow ROOT_1 + ROOT_1 + ROOT_2$$

tā-bisa	'cut branches and block roadway'	*tātā-bisa*	freq.
tabu-siga	'keep out of sun'	*tabu-tabu-siga*	freq.
tā-caqe	'stumble'	*tā-tā-caqe*	freq
tā-cagu-cagu	'go quickly'	*tā-tā-cagu-cagu*[14]	freq.
laga-sere	'sing'	*laga-laga-sere*	freq.

Forms with the stative prefix *lau-* behave as compounds:

lau-caqe	*lau-lau-caqe*
lau-vacu	*lau-lau-vacu*[15]

as do some with *vaka-*:

vaka-sobu	*vaka-vaka-sobu*	'many disembarking'
vaka-drē	*vaka-vaka-drē*	'tighten very firmly'[16]

Note that these are forms that are first compounded, then reduplicated. They differ from compounds such as

yā-kure-kure   'move in shaking fashion'

In this form, *kure* 'shake' is reduplicated to modify *yā* 'move' (see §14.4).

The reason for this particular pattern of reduplication may be that *lau-*, as a long syllable, and *vaka-*, as a disyllable, are phonologically more like roots than markers. On the other hand, these forms may serve as evidence that the *lau-* forms are compounds, rather than derivatives.

Note that these compounds reduplicate differently from modified forms.

14.14 REDUPLICATION OF MARKERS

Although reduplication is a process generally confined to roots,[17] some markers are also reduplicated. The process can be divided into two types: (1) reduplication of an affix, usually with the root reduplicated as well; and (2) reduplication of a separate marker independent of the root.

In the previous section on formal manifestations, there are many examples of the first type:

---

[14] There is also *ta-ta-caqu-caqu* (in the fashion of the derived forms, but TRN says it "looks suspicious."

[15] Examples from Cammack 1962:106.

[16] Examples from Cammack 1962:107.

[17] Earlier this feature served as a criterion for identifying roots.

14 Verb Reduplication

ta-basu   *ta-ta-basu-basu*
ta-bili   *ta-ta-bili-bili*
etc.

Some forms reduplicate one syllable of the root along with the affix:

lidi   'burst or strike, as sound of explosion'
ca-lidi, cali-calidi   'burst or strike, but with no sparks'

Other forms reduplicate only the affix:

caqe   'kick'
lau-caqe   'kicked (stative)'
lau-lau-caqe   freq.

The following word represents an extreme example of reduplication combined with other types of affixation:

vei-vaka-ta-ta-cavu-cavu-taki   'caused to be pulled up repeatedly'

Although such a pattern of reduplication is productive, its productivity is confined mainly to a special set of words—those that take the prefixes *ta-, ca-, ka-* (and some others less frequent), and that belong to a rather specialized semantic set: sounds, bursting-like actions, and special types of movement (see Arms's discussion of such types, 1974:72–76). For some very common prefixes, such as *vei-*, reduplication in rare but possible:

Sā dau vei-vei-sau   vaka-totolo na   no-na nanu-m-a.
ASP HAB REC-REC-change MAN-fast   DEF PC-3S think-TR-3S
'Her thoughts always change rapidly.' (T74:42)

e vei-vei-gauna   'at different times'

Vaka- can be reduplicated as well:

Era vaka-vaka-tawa gā.   'They kept continuous watch.' (*FR5*:7)
i-vaka-vaka-cau   'solicitation from a *kalou*'

For a few verbs, a different type of reduplication includes the object as well as the verb:

se-a   'split it'
sea-sea   'tear many things in two'
dre-t-a   'pull it'
dreta-dre-t-a 'pull it continuously'

The reduplication of *via* to *via-via* indicates more of a semantic change than a grammatical one, for these two forms could well be interpreted as different prefixes. However, even though there are a number of differences in their meanings, the two forms do share a common meaning: 'contrary to fact, not quite achieved'.

A reduplication of a different kind of marker was shown by Churchward (1941:45). The distributive counter *yā-*, discussed in §17.10, is reduplicated in the examples

lako yā-yā-rua	'go two at a time'
lako yā-yā drau	'go a hundred at a time'

In each instance, the form is an alternate of that with the main verb reduplicated.

14.15 REDUPLICATION OF PERSON-NUMBER MARKERS, INCLUDING POSSESSIVES[18]

The following person-number markers can be reduplicated. In the list, the markers are mixed: some are subjects, some are possessives; others are proper noun phrases.

nō-nōdrau	'always theirs (dual)'
Sā noqu-noqu tū.	'It's always mine.'
Sā koya-koya.	'It's always like that.'
Yau-yau.	'It's always me.'
Sā nona-nona tū gā.	'It's still in his possession.' (Capell 1941)

14.16 REDUPLICATION OF BORROWED WORDS

Borrowed words can be reduplicated, showing that the process is an active one:

tera	'formidable (from 'terror')'	*vaka-tera-tera*	'trying to look tough'
sovu	'soap'	*sovu-sovu-t-a*	'apply soap thoroughly to it'[19]
boela	'boil'	*boe-boela*	'boil for a long time' (*VV*)

---

[18] Data from SN, who supplied these examples when questioned about *koyakoya* (from Capell 1941).

[19] Examples from PG (10/83).

15 COMPOUND VERBS

A compound verb is a sequence of two verb roots, each of which has the same relationship to the subject and to the object (if any). In other words, in a VP of the shape *e* X Y, the roots could also be joined by a conjunction: *e* X *ka* Y. In the following examples the roots are in boldface.

*ā **sika bote**-a   tale mai ki-na ...*   'there appeared again there ...'
PT appear-break-into it ITR DIR ABL-3S   (*SR* 20/4/82)

If the compound verb is divided into two VPs, we find the following:

*ā **sika** ka **bote**-a ...*   'it appeared and broke into it ...'
PT appear CNJ break-into-it

However, the two verbs are not quite parallel, for the transitive suffix has to serve for the whole compound. The immediate constituent structure is as follows:

*ā (**sika** ka **bote**)-a*

As examples of sequences of roots that do not satisfy the condition above, note the following:

*E sā **veve makawa** tū gā.*   'It was bent from of old.' (*FR*5:27)
3S ASP bent old   CNT LIM

If we insert *ka*, as in:

E sā veve ka makawa tū gā
3S ASP bent CNJ old   CNT LIM

the meaning changes, for in the basic underlying phrases

E sā veve.   'It was bent.'
E sā makawa.   'It was old.'

the subjects do not refer to the same entity: it is the state of being bent that is old. Thus, this sequence of roots is not a compound, but instead a verb + underived adverb (see §31.1.1). The same relationship holds for the following:

E cagi donu na no-dra soko.   lit., 'Their sailing blew straight.'
3S wind straight DEF POS-3P sail   (*FR*5:26)

Here, the subjects in

E cagi.	'It is a wind.'
E donu.	'It is straight.'

refer to different entities. Thus, the structure is verb + underived adverb.

The following examples, also of verb + adverb, show not only these different semantic relationships, but also a formal reason for not interpreting the sequence as a compound: the markers of transitivity come between the roots:

... *ka na qai laki tuku-n-a mālua na kā   e vinaka-t-a.*
    CNJ FT SEQ DIR tell-TR-3S slow DEF thing 3S want-TR-3S
'... and will then go tell later the thing he wants.' (*FR5*:20)

...*ka vaka-rai-ci koya matua.*   'And stare at him. (*FR5*:12)
   CNJ CAU-see-TR 3S   firm

The following sections show compound verbs in various constructions.

15.1 FORMAL CLASSIFICATION

15.1.1 Markers of transitivity following the construction

Note the following words, phrases, and sentences:

***rogo kivi**-t-a*	'hear it inaccurately'

In this construction, the verbs are:

rogo	'(be) heard'
kivi	'turn head suddenly'

*E ā **kila kā-sami**-tak-a   sara ni   butako-ci.*
3S PT know-consider-TR-TR-3S INT SUB steal-TR
'He strongly suspected that they were stolen.' (*FR5*:11)

The compound in this example is from the verbs:

kila	'know'
kā-sami	'suspect'

Further examples are:

***sele-druti**-a*	'cut it off'
sele	'cut'
druti	'torn off'
***cula bāsika**-t-a*	'pierce through it'
cula	'pierced'
bāsika	'passed through it'
***butu-voro**-k-a*	'tread on it and break it'
butu	'tread'
voro	'break'

15.1.2 Markers of transitivity after each root

***kati**-a **cavu**-k-a*	'bite it off (thread)'
kati	'bite'
cavu	'(string+) snapped'

In the sentence:

... *me rawa ni dau **kati**-a **voro**-k-a ki-na na ke-na vua-ni-kau*
   SUB able SUB HAB bite-3S smash-TR-3S LOC-3S DEF POS-3S fruit
... to make it possible for it to bite-break its fruit with it (*NV3*:21)

the meanings of the components of the compound verb are:

kati   'bite'
voro   'smashed'

In the following example:

*Ā **vosa**-k-a vaka-**macala**-tak-a taumada.*
PT talk-TR 3S CAU-clear-TR 3S   INC
'First of all, he talk-explained it.'

the verbs roots are:

vosa   'talk'
macala   'clear'

Finally, the following sentence:

*E **kani**-a **oti**-v-a e dua na lovo.*   'He ate-finished one oven.'
3S eat-3S finish-TR-3S 3S one DEF oven   (*FR5*:16)

uses the roots:

kani   'eaten'
oti   'finished'

15.1.3 Markers of transitivity and other markers

Note the following example:

*vaka-**lutulutu-dromu**-taki koya*   'drown him' (*FR5*:16)

Here, the roots are *lutu* 'fall' and *dromu* 'sink'; they are preceded by the causative prefix and followed by a transitive suffix and object.

15.2 THE SEMANTICS OF COMPOUND VERBS

One of the problems with considering the grammatical relationship between the constituents of a compound verb is that the language has another common mechanism for indicating serial actions: to join two VPs together with the conjunction *ka*. Thus one is led to suggest that verb compounding is a lexical matter—a means of forming a new verb of a type similar to a kenning in Old English, but somewhat less metaphoric.

From such a point of view, some of the compounds above are clarified:

kani-a oti-v-a   'finish it, consume it by eating'

Here, explaining the form by calling it a "serial verb" ('eat' and 'finish') seems less appropriate than considering the action referred to by *kania otiva* to be one continuous process, and the verb itself a separate lexical item.

Similarly, does *katia votoka* 'bite-smash it' in the sentence above refer to a serial action? It seems closer to the semantics of the situation to consider the whole compound a new lexical item, and thus, compounding a means of enlarging the lexicon.

15.3 DISCUSSION

Verb compounding made an early appearance in Fijian grammatical descriptions. In the preface to his dictionary (1872:5), Hazlewood wrote:

> The natives frequently, by compounding verbs, express themselves with astonishing clearness, brevity, and force; which cannot be imitated in English. We have generally to express the sense by two verbs with a preposition or conjunction between them, or by a verb and an adverb, as, sa qasilutu ki nai keli na gone, the child has crept and fallen into the pit; me varomusuka, to saw in pieces, or asunder; me tamusuka, to chop asunder; me vosacudrucudruya, to speak angrily; me sovabiuta, to pour out and throw away; me tayabiuta, to chop off and throw away: but the English does not well express the native idea ...

This present study of compounding is far from complete. But now that *VV* is in print, it should provide examples to draw from for a more detailed description.

16 TRANSITIVITY

Two-referent verbs (A2 and S2) are key players in a grammatical system that shows the relationship among the SEMANTIC entities of actor, action/state, and goal. This system is called TRANSITIVITY, which is manifested formally in the VP—and not beyond the VP—by the grammatical items shown in table 16.1, in the order given.

Many previous definitions of Fijian transitivity have concentrated on its formal manifestations (see §16.6.1 for examples). In the treatment here, form and meaning weave in and out of the discussion.

Another important innovation in the present description hinges on the departure from convention in its definitions of subject (CH 4) and object (CH 17), relegating NPs to the category of optional, not obligatory, features of transitivity. Thus, there are no NPs in the categories in table 16.1.

TABLE 16.1: ELEMENTS IN THE TRANSITIVE CONSTRUCTION

	SUB.	VERB	(TR. SUF.)	(OBJECT)	GLOSS
1.	*E*	*rai*	*-ci*	*-ira.*	'She saw them (pl.).'
2.	*Au*	*rere*	*-vak-*	*-a.*	'I feared it.'
3.	*Keirau*	*gunu*	*-v-*	*-a.*	'We (du. excl.) drank it.'
4.	*O*	*kila*	Ø	*-a.*	'You (sg.) know it.'

The subject in each of the sentences above represents the actor, and the object represents the goal.

These sentences show a common morphophonemic change. With the third person singular object *-a*, as in (2), (3), and (4), the transitive suffix, which has the underlying shape *-Ci* or *-Caki*, loses its final vowel. Thus:

   -Ci + *-a* → *-Ca*   *-Caki* + *-a* → *-Caka*

In (4), the consonant in the transitive suffix is Ø. The sequence of two like vowels /a/ + /a/ forms a long vowel, /ā/.

When the transitive suffix is not followed by the object (*a*), the subject represents the goal. Note the glosses in table 16.2.

Although the actor is expressed (by the subject) in the sentences in table 16.1, it is not, and cannot be, expressed in those in table 16.2. Even so, the actor is not entirely ignored, for the form of the sentence tells us that the state (such as "seen" or "feared") did not come about by itself, but was caused by an actor. These examples show that Fijian transitivity is not an either-or matter, but instead, divided into degrees of SPECIFICITY, a topic treated as a grammatical category in CH 26.

TABLE 16.2: TRANSITIVE CONSTRUCTIONS WITHOUT OBJECTS

	SUB.	VERB	(TR. SUF.)		GLOSS
1.	Era	rai	-ci	Ø.	'They (pl.) were seen.'
2.	E	rere	-vaki	Ø.	'It was feared.'
3.	E	gunu	-vi	Ø.	'It was drunk.'
4.	E	kila	-i	Ø.	'It was known.'

Specificity also links transitivity with NPs that occur outside the VP. The formal manifestations of transitivity, then, lie within the VP, but the system is tied to forms that occur at the level of the sentence, and ultimately, at the level of discourse. In this chapter, however, we treat only those manifestations of transitivity that occur in the VP, discussing the following topics:

1. The transitive suffixes
2. Different transitive suffixes with the same verb
3. The meanings of some suffixes that seem to pattern regularly
4. Constructions that seem semantically transitive without a transitive suffix

16.1 THE TRANSITIVE SUFFIXES

Whether they are simple or derived, verbs with two referents can SIGNAL[1] a second referent grammatically with a suffix of the shape -Ci or -Caki. Note that we do not call this suffix an object marker, although it might be interpreted as one in many constructions. But in some, such as:

Era tuku-ni. 'They (plural) were told.'

there is no object to be marked, and the suffix indicates (signals) an actor that is implicit in the meaning but not further specified.

Table 16.3 (adapted from Milner 1972:27, 89) shows the consonants that occur (1) in monosyllabic and (2) in disyllabic transitive markers.

PG has suggested (see note 2) that forms with Ø and *y* are allomorphs. (The distribution of the "dispersive" suffix *-yaki* supports this proposal; see the discussion of *y* in the phonology section.) If we follow this analysis, the only differences between the two sets are the absence of *g* in the disyllables and the absence of *l* in the monosyllables. The former can be explained by examining the limitations on the distribution of consonants: sequences of *$gVkV$ or *$kVgV$ are prohibited. This leaves us with *l*; its absence in the set of monosyllables is unexplained (see Milner 1982, 1985).

---

[1] "Signal" is used here as a technical term; later (CH 26) it is described as a particular level of specificity.

Other prohibitions on sequences of consonants have a direct bearing on which transitive suffixes can occur with which roots (see Arms 1974, Geraghty 1983, and Milner 1982, 1989).

TABLE 16.3: CONSONANTS THAT OCCUR IN TRANSITIVE MARKERS

In monosyllables	Ø[2]	c	g	k		m	n	r	t	v	y[3]
In disyllables		c		k	l	m	n	r	t	v	y

16.2 DIFFERENT TRANSITIVE SUFFIXES WITH THE SAME VERB

For some verbs, context plays an important role in sorting out what seem to be (from an English viewpoint) rather divergent meanings when coupled with different kinds of goal referents. For example, when the goal of *lako* 'go' is an object that can be carried, *e lako-v-a* means 'he went-for it, he fetched it'. When the goal is a route, such as a path, the same sentence means 'he went on it'.[4] Thus, different sorts of goals are signaled by the same transitive marker, *-vi*, when used with *lako*, and the hearer depends on context to resolve the ambiguity.

But a great many verbs—particularly those involving motion—indicate grammatically various sorts of goals with different transitive markers. Formally, they differentiate the markers in two ways:

1. Different consonants in the transitive marker. As examples, note the contrast between the members of the following pairs:

E gole-a.   'He turned it (head+).'
E gole-v-a   'He turned-toward it.'

---

[2] The symbol "Ø" is merely a descriptive device to indicate that no consonant occurs before the object. I am not proposing it as a unit. PG suggested (7/82) that Ø and *y* might be considered allomorphs, with this distribution: Ø after *a*, *e*, and *i*; *y* after *o*, *u*. See the discussion of *y* in the next note.

[3] Historically, the *y* in this list represents no consonant (see §34.20.1.1), since it is an *i* that has lost its syllabicity by joining with a preceding *a* to form a diphthong *ai*, which in turn shortens in the penultimate position in the measure. In *kaya* 'say it' (which we might interpret as /kaia/ (with *ka* accented), the *i* is part of the root, as shown by another transitive form, *kai-nak-a*. For *taya* 'chop it', it may be that the *i* is retained to keep the form that includes the object distinct from the base, since /tā/ + /a/ can yield only /tā/, there being no three-way vowel-length contrast in the language. As an afterthought: *ta-ya* is the only CV̄ type of verb that has retained the *i*; most others use a disyllabic suffix; those with monosyllabic suffixes are *ca-t-a* and *va-c-a*. However, *tuya* 'tow it' (/tu/ + /i/ + /a/?) has also retained the /i/.

PG suggested (7/82) that *tā* is an irregular verb, since some areas near Bau have *ta-taya* and *tataka*, rather than *taya*.

[4] *Lako-v-a* seldom has this meaning.

E dabe-c-a. 'He sat-on it (mat+).'
E dabe-r-a. 'He put it down.'⁵

2. A contrast between monosyllabic and disyllabic transitive markers:

E cabe-t-a. 'She ascended it.
E cabe-tak-a. 'She ascended-with it.
E iri-v-a. 'She fanned him.
E iri-tak-a. 'She fanned-with it.

Note that the translations using *with* are ambiguous. In the first set, the goal indicated by *-Caki* is concomitant, whereas in the second, it serves an instrumental function.

16.3 THE MEANINGS OF THE *-CAKI* FORMS

The four *-Caki* examples above all involve performing some action directly by means of an instrument, or carrying something while performing another action. But these are by no means the only, or even the most common, meanings of the *-Caki* form. The following sections treat these meanings:

1. General transitivizer
2. Reason
3. Means or accompaniment
4. Intensive
5. Lexical change
6. Duration
7. Dispersive movement

16.3.1 General transitivizer

For words that have not inherited a *-Ci* form, *-taki* is used as a general transitivizer. This meaning of *-taki* occurs in the following types of forms:

1. Words that are not used primarily in verb phrases. Their use with *-taki* allows a subject and an object to be stated grammatically, thus clarifying the semantic role of the subject. Take, for example, *gato* 'glottal stop'. In this form, the morpheme is usually used in noun phrases, although it can, of course, occur in the existential construction. With *-taki* (and *-a*, the object), however, it becomes an A2 verb:

*E gato-**tak-a.*** 'He spoke it in one of the dialects that is characterized by glottal stop.'

Other examples are:

bai 'fence (n.)'
*bai-**tak-a*** 'put a fence around it'

---

⁵ PG proposed (7/82) that there are two *dabe* roots: the one that takes *-ci* is A2; the one that takes *-ri* is S2.

2. Loanwords. Words borrowed from English[6] obviously do not include their own special transitive marker. But some can be used transitively, with the object signaled by what seems to be the all-purpose transitive marker, -*taki*. An example from *VV* is:

*haya-**tak**-a*   'hire him/her'

Note also the following:[7]

*na no-na   ā parofisai-**tak**-a e   na yabaki sā   oti*
DEF POS-3S PT prophesy-TR-3S ABL DEF year   ASP finished
'his having prophesied it last year'

*no-na   i-tavi   na rejisitā-**tak**-a   na i-Soqosoqo Cokovata*
POS-3S custom DEF register-TR-3S DEF assembly   joint
   ni   Vei-voli   'its custom of registering the Cooper Society
   POS commerce   for Commerce'

*sē taipa-**tak**-a   me vei-yawa-ki   na ke-na   i-yatu*
CNJ type-TR-3S   SUB REC-far-TR   DEF POS-3S row
'or type it double-spaced'

*ni   ke-na   mākete-**taki** na jinijā ki   vanua tani*
SUB POS-3S market-TR   DEF ginger   LOC land   other
'for the foreign marketing of ginger'

*E   pasi-**tak**-a   na polo.*
3S pass-TR-3S   DEF ball
'He passed the ball.'

bom-taka/bomu-tak-a 'bomb it' (*VV*)

Interestingly, some one-syllable suffixes are used with loanwords:

bata-r-a[8]	'butter it (bread+)'
bomu-t-a	'bomb it (place)'
loka-t-a	'lock it (building+)'
pamu-t-a[9]	'pump it (liquid)'
sovu-t-a	'wash it with soap'
kala-t-a	'color it'
jili-a na i-mau	'shuffle the cards (from *deal*)'
ki-v-a (Lauan)	'lock it (from *key*)'

Some of these borrowed roots enter into other transitive constructions:

*loka-**taki** koya*	'lock him'
*sovu-**lak**-a vā-kaukaua*	'wash it vigorously'

---

[6] PG supplied the following examples of loans from other languages: *joro-tak-a* 'steal it' and *talaki-tak-a* 'search him', from Fiji Hindi; *talanoa-taka* 'story-tell it', from Tongan. See also Tamata 2003.

[7] These examples come from *VG* and *NL*.

[8] These forms were supplied by AS from a list of about 800 loanwords (Schütz 1978b).

[9] These first four examples are disputed. They seem rather innovative to some speakers.

3. The suffix *-taki* also has a special (but not exclusive) relationship with *vaka-* (causative) (see §6.1), directly related to its use as a general transitivizer. Once a verb is made causative with *vaka-*, the object can be included grammatically if preceded by the usual transitive marker for that root. But because many causatives are formed from words that do not usually occur with the transitive marker, *-taki* is the form most often used to mark the object. Examples are:

*vaka-dinadina-**tak**-a*	'confirm it'
*vaka-yaga-**tak**-a*	'use it'
*vaka-levu-**tak**-a*	'increase it'
*vaka-rau-**tak**-a*	'prepare it'
*vaka-mārau-**tak**-a*	'make it happy'

16.3.2 Reason

One construction involving the transitive marker *-taki*[10] provides the most nearly regular form-meaning correspondence of the set. This form, with the meaning 'reason for, because of' occurs most often in a question, with the goal specified by the interrogative NP *a cava* 'what?'.

*A cava e gole-**tak**-a?*	'What is he turning for?'
*E gole-**tak**-a na kā.*	'He's turning because of something or other'
*A cava e gutuwā-**tak**-a?*	'What is she fleeing for?'
*E gutuā-**tak**-a na kā.*	'She's fleeing because of something or other.'

As some indication of the extent of its use, 41 of a sample of 50 verbs[11] could occur in the *a cava e [ ] -taki* construction in their simple form, and another 7 in their reduplicated form. And although the English loanwords in our data include few words that can be classified as primarily verbal, the following, as a sample, can be used as verbs with *-taki* in the "reason" construction:

dānisi	'dance'	*fika*	'figure'	*tuisi*	'(dance the) twist'
inisua	'insure'	*draiva*	'drive'	*kati*	'(play) cards'
drili	'drill'	*loka*	'lock'	*ota*	'order'
pasi	'pass'	*pamu*	'pump'	*sikinala*	'signal'

In addition to verbs that are made up of either simple or reduplicated roots, another type of verb can also be used with "reason" *-taki*. It is based on an un-

---

[10] Foley (1976:270) claimed that *-Caki* is rare with P[rocess]-verbs (S2). He seems to have made the statement without considering the extent of *-taki* (reason) and *-laki* and *-raki* (intensive). The following are some are some examples of S2 verbs that occur with one or more of these suffixes:

bura	'pierced' :	*-laki*	*-taki*	
bete	'broken' :	*-laki*		
belu	'bent' :	*-laki*		
dolo	'broken' :	*-laki*		
bolo	'pelted' :	*-laki*	*-taki*	
gudu	'cut off' :	*-raki*	*-taki*	

[11] These verbs were elicited directly, not found in context.

derlying relationship between action and goal, but grammatically, its form is verb plus modifier.[12] Some examples are:

gunu-yaqona	'kava-drinking', as in:
A cava e gunu-yaqona-tak-a?	'Why is he kava-drinking?'
rai-koro	'village-inspecting', as in:
A cava e rai-koro-tak-a?	'Why is he village-inspecting?'

In the frame sentence, the NP *a cava* 'what?' is the specified object. Thus, all the verbs in this construction specify the object with an NP and indicate the subject grammatically. It follows, then, that *-taki* has the effect of adding a second referent to A1 verbs, such as *kedru* 'snore'. Thus, *kedru-taki*, in this construction, can be translated as 'snore-for', but with its goal always confined to the meaning of "reason."

To show that *-taki*, and not *a cava*, carries the meaning of "reason," note the following examples:

Q:	*A cava e rai-**tak**-a?*	'Why is he able to see?/what causes him to look? / Why is he looking?'
A:	*(E rai-**tak**-a) ni sā via-kana.*	'(He's looking) because he's hungry.'

or

*(E rai-**tak**-a) na no-na via-kana.*	'(He's looking) because-of his hunger.'

The first alternative provides no proof, since the meaning 'because' is built into *ni*. But in the second answer, *na no-na via-kana* 'his hunger' is not marked in any way for "because" or "reason," so that meaning must lie in *e rai-tak-a*.

For some verbs, "reason" is also built into another construction—the basic transitive form—but not as the central meaning. For example:

E lako-v-a na i-vola.   'He went-for the book.'

could be interpreted as 'He went for the purpose of getting the book.' But this meaning is conveyed more directly by the form:

*E lako-**tak**-a na i-vola.*

For other verbs, *-taki* is the principal (and for some, the only) transitive marker. The following are some examples:

bā 'deny' *nui* 'hope' *liu* 'precede' *bai* 'fence' *basori* 'stop up' *bei* 'accuse' *baece* 'extend (ramparts)'

Theoretically, then, *-taki* forms with such roots could be ambiguous. However, it has been suggested (PG 7/82) that the ambiguity does not exist, because "reason" *-taki* is added only to verbs with which it does not indicate a goal. For example,

wā-tak-a*, but *wāwā-tak**-a*	'wait because of it'
leti-tak-a*, but *veileti-tak**-a*	'dispute over it'
kere-tak-a*, but *kerekere-tak**-a*	'request leave of it'

---

[12] Remember that *-Cak-a* represents two morphemes: the transitive marker *-Caki* fused with the third person singular object *-a*.

In each of these examples, the stem of the verb has been rendered "intransitive," either by reduplication or the addition of *vei-*.

For some verbs that take only *-taki*, the semantics of the root are such that the goal and reason can be the same sort of referent. *Nui* 'hope' is one of these:

*A cava e nui-**tak**-a?*   'What did he hope-for?/what is the reason he is hoping?'

For each of the readings, the answer could be:

Na i-loloma.   'A gift.'

Rai 'see', cited earlier, may be the same kind of verb, for one could argue that the object of seeing is the reason for seeing. But with *rai*, the two meanings are made distinct with the suffixes *-ci* vs. *-taki*, so there is a difference in form between 'what did he see?' and 'why is he looking?'.

Another kind of ambiguity exists for *gutuā-taki*:

*A cava e gutuā-**tak**-a?*   'What is he fleeing-for? / What is he fleeing-with?'

Here, the form can be interpreted as involving either "reason" or "accompaniment."

Semantically, many of the verbs that take only *-taki* are different from, say, verbs of motion, in that fewer topics and fewer modifications of the action are normally involved. (Take *liu* 'precede', for example. Perhaps it is awkward to imagine speaking of preceding something while carrying an object or preceding something with intensity. If the need arose to express these meanings, the speaker could express them as modifying phrases.)

Some verbs use not *-taki*, but a transitive marker with a different consonant to indicate a meaning similar to that of the reason construction. An example is:

*E oso-**vak**-a na no-na via-kana.* 'He's barking because of his hunger.'

With *oso* 'bark', different transitive markers, *-vi* and *-vaki*, maintain a contrast between 'bark-at' and 'bark-because-of'. But, as in some of the previous examples, the semantic difference can become rather hazy:

*E oso-**vak**-a na vulagi.*   'He's barking because of the visitor.'
*E oso-**v**-a na vulagi.*   'He's barking at the visitor.'

In summary: The *-taki* construction, indicating "reason" as a goal, although not mentioned in Fijian grammars before *TFL*, is a construction of high frequency. However, as some of the preceding examples show, "reason" is only one possible meaning of the construction (see Arms 1987:111).

16.3.3 Means or accompaniment

When describing the function of the disyllabic transitive marker, analysts have often focused on "means" or "accompaniment." This function usually occurs with verbs that refer to motion.

For verbs of motion such as the following, the subject refers to something or someone moving toward a destination (marked by *-Ci*), by means of or accompanied by something (marked by *-Caki*). This accompanying object (in both senses) never refers to another actor,[13] but to something that can be carried.

lako-v-a	'go-for it'	*lako-vak-a*	'go-with it'
qalo-v-a	'swim-to it'	*qalo-vak-a*	'swim-with it'
sobu-t-a	'descend-for it'	*sobu-tak-a*	'descend-with it'
dromu-c-a	'sink-under it'	*dromu-cak-a*	'sink-with it'
soko-t-a	'sail-to it'	*soko-tak-a*	'sail it (canoe+)'

Some verb roots show a similar contrast in goals not with *-Ci* vs. *-Caki*, but with a different contrast in transitive markers. (In the following examples, the transitive marker is Ø in the first column:)

uli-a	'steer it'	*uli-v-a*	'steer-toward it'
kele-a	'anchor it'	*kele-v-a*	'anchor-at it'
voce-a	'paddle it'	*voce-r-a*	'paddle-to it'

At least one A2 verb takes only the suffix referring to accompaniment:

E cāroba.	'He fell face-down.'
E cāroba-tak-a na i-vola.	'He fell face-down with the book.'

The following verbs of emitting or projecting are similar to verbs of motion, but here the actor himself does not move to the destination (marked by *-Ci*), but causes something else (indicated by *-Caki*) to do so:

kaci-v-a	'call him'	*kaci-vak-a*	'call it (the call+)'
kalu-v-a	'whistle-at him'	*kalu-vak-a*	'whistle-it (whistle or tune)'
kāsivi-t-a	'spit-on it'	*kāsivi-tak-a*	'spit it (saliva or blood+)'
vanā	'shoot-at it'	*vana-tak-a*	'shoot-with it'
viri-k-a	'throw-at it'	*viri-tak-a*	'throw it'
ula-k-a	'throw-at it'	*ula-tak-a*	'throw it (club+)'
kolo-v-a	'throw-at it'	*kolo-tak-a*	'throw it'
cokā	'pierce (spear) it'	*coka-tak-a*	'spear-with it' (spear+)
rabo-k-a	'sling-at it'	*rabo-tak-a*	'sling it'
dia-k-a	'throw-at it'	*dia-tak-a*	'throw it' [also "reason"]
mi-c-a	'urinate-on it'	*mī-cak-a*	'urinate it (urine)'
talā	'send him'	*tala-vak-a*	'send it (message+)'

The following verbs may fit into the category above, but for these, the *-Caki* form has often been described as instrumental. It is not clear, however, that these goals are any more instrumental than, say, spit is for spitting, or a spear is for spearing.

ta-y-a	'chop it'	*tā-tak-a*	'chop-with it'
iri-v-a	'fan it'	*iri-vak-a*	'fan-with it'
kaki-a	'scrape it'	*kaki-tak-a*	'scrape-with it'
ko-r-a	'gargle it (throat)'	*kō-rak-a*	'gargle-with it (liquid)'
uso-r-a	'poke it (oven)'	*uso-rak-a*	'poke-with it (stick+)'

---

[13] Another actor could be included in the subject—for example, a singular subject would change to dual.

And where do the following forms fit?

*masu-**t**-a* 'pray-to it'   *masu-**lak**-a* 'pray-for it'
*soro-**v**-a* 'atone-to him'   *soro-**vak**-a* 'atone-for it'

The function, then, of the disyllabic transitive suffix to indicate means or accompaniment is fairly common among two-referent verbs. The label of "instrument," however, is too limited to serve for this category.

16.3.4 Intensive

Two transitive markers, *-laki* and *-raki*, occur with a large number of roots to add an intensive meaning to the action. "Intensive" here is a general label that covers meanings such as "repeatedly," "thoroughly," "multiple," and "violent," depending on the various meanings of the roots. For example, *gude* 'shake (container of liquid+)' already involves rather vigorous, repeated action. Thus, *e gude-rak-a* is glossed 'he shook it violently'. A similar relationship exists for *yamo* 'massage, grope' and *yamo-lak-a*, *yamo-rak-a*. For bases with which both the *l* and *r* forms occur, the *r* form is more intensive.

As for the frequency of these indicators, in a sample of 57 roots, 27 took *-laki*, 2 took *-raki*, 3 took both, and 25 took neither.[14] The semantics of the various roots account partially for this distribution. Examples of roots that take *l* are:

tuki	'pound'	*dusi*	'point'	*drē*	'pull'	*kana*	'eat'
domo	'desire'	*cai*	'copulate'	*dia*	'throw'	*bete*	'broken'
bolo	'pelted'	*bura*	'pierced'	*bila*	'lie-on'	*bari*	'nibble'
kati	'bite'	*ceru*	'sip'	*kara*	'scold'	*caqe*	'kick'
kere	'beg'	*belu*	'bent'	*dolo*	'broken-in-two'		

The two that take only *r* are:

bili 'push'   *gude* 'shake'

Those that take both *l* and *r* are:

yamo 'massage'   *dabe* 'set, place'   *bika* 'press'

Finally, the following are a sample of the roots that take neither:

bei	'blame'	*iri*	'fan'	*gādē*[15]	'stroll'
garo	'lust'	*katariva*	'blink'	*gudu*	'cut (vine, rope+)'
katalau	'breakfast'	*digi*	'choose'	*bole*	'challenge'
bā	'deny'	*taro*	'ask'	*yadra*	'wake, awake'
gunu	'drink'	*cabe*	'climb'	*dike*	'investigate'
iro	'peep'	*dara*	'put on'	*kalu*	'whistle'
digo	'inspect'	*kaci*	'call'		

For many of these verbs, intensifying the action does not seem likely. This is not, however, a claim for complete predictability of *-laki* or *-raki* on semantic (or any other) grounds. To see how the meaning of one root allows the *-laki* and *-raki* forms, while that of another does not, compare the following forms:

---

[14] Different speakers would probably produce different results.

[15] Note that some of these examples are A1 verbs.

16 Transitivity

    cavu   'pull up'   *cavu-**lak**-a*   'pull it up vigorously'
    cavu-t-a   'pull it up'   *cavu-**rak**-a*   'pull it up vigorously'

but only the following for its homophonous form:

    cavu   'pronounce'   *cavu-t-a*   'pronounce it'

16.3.5 Lexical change

For a number of verbs, the contrast between *-Ci* and *-Caki* marks an important semantic distinction in the root itself. For example,

    *sau-**m**-a*   'answer, repay it'
    *sau-**mak**-a*   'reverse it'
    voli-a   'buy it'[16]
    *voli-**tak**-a*   'sell it'
    sili   'bathe'
    vei-sili   'bathing (general)'
    *sili-**m**-a*   'plunge-for it'
    *vei-**sili**-mi*   'diving (general)'

Several different roots have the form *tau*, but they occur with different transitive suffixes. For example, *tau* '(rain) fall on' takes *-ci*:

    *E tau-**ci** au na uca.*   'The rain falls on me.

Tau 'infect' (be infected?) takes *-vi*:

    *E tau-**vi** mate o koya.*   'She's ill (infected by illness).

Tau 'hold, take' takes *-ri*:

    *E tau-**r**-a.*   'He took it.'

This form, in turn, can enter into further derivation:

    *E tau-**ri**-**vak**-a.*   'He used it.

    *na vosa e sō ka sā tau-**ri**-**vaki** rāraba tū*
    DEF talk 3S some REL ASP take-TR-TR wide CNT
    'some words that are widely used' (*SR* 20/4/82)

It has been suggested (PG 7/82) that we could interpret *tauri* 'use' here as a separate root, since its connection with *tau-ri* is tenuous. The same suggestion has been made with respect to the various meanings of *sau* above. From this point of view, then, the whole matter of the transitive suffixes as "lexicalizers" is complex. From a lexicographic stance (to which this grammar is closely connected), we are faced with a choice: does the difference in meaning of such

---

[16] G. B. Milner suggested (9/79) that attaching the glosses 'buy' and 'sell' to these forms might be an attempt to make them match English usage. He proposed that *voli* originally referred to barter, and that from each participant's point of view, the operation was the same, but with different transitive markers to indicate either *acquiring* a commodity or *disposing* of it.

Currently, with a cash economy, the transaction might not be viewed primarily as an exchange, since one of the commodities is now required to be cash.

morphologically complex forms come from the transitive suffix, or does the language contain a large number of homophonous roots?

The complexity of the situation is an argument against the simplistic treatment of -*Ci* and -*Caki* as different case endings (see, for example, Foley 1976:166–67).

16.3.6 Duration

A special use of -*Caki* appears with two common words that refer to specific stretches of time: *siga* 'day' and *bogi* 'night'. The constructions do not lend themselves easily to parsing, and might be considered idioms:

*E siga-**lak**-a na no-dra yadra.* 'They were up until dawn (lit.,
3S day-TR-3S DEF POS-3P wake their wakefulness lasted until day)'

*E bogi-**vak**-a na bose.* 'The meeting lasted until night.'
3S night-TR-3S DEF meeting

*Sā kama siga-**vak**-a.* 'It burned until morning.'
ASP burn day-TR-3S

*E Siga-Tabu-**vak**-a na soqo.* 'The meeting lasted until Sunday.'
3S day-sacred-TR-3S DEF meeting

VV lists under *bogi* 'night' the following forms with transitive markers: -*caki*, -*laki*, -*taki*, -*vaki*. All the forms are defined as 'last from daylight to dark'. Examples in sentences are:

*E bogi-**cak**-a na nei-tou teitei: e tekivū mai e na*
3S night-TR-3S DEF POS-1TX planting 3S begin DIR ABL DEF

  siga ka yaco-v-a na bogi na nei-touteitei.
  day CNJ arrive-TR-3S DEF night DEF POS-1TX planting

'Our (trial exclusive) planting lasted all day: it started in the daylight, and lasted until dark—our planting.'

*E bogi-**cak**-a na nei-tou sara qito: e yaco-v-a na bogi*
3S night-TR-3S DEF POS-1TX look play 3S arrive-TR-3S DEF night

  na neitou sara qito.
  DEF POS-1TX look play

'Our (trial exclusive) game-watching lasted all day: it lasted until dark—our game-watching.'

*A cava o bogi-**tak**-a mai? A cava na vū ni no-mu*
DEF what 2S night-TR-3S DIR DEF what DEF source POS POS-2S

  qai yaco bogi tū mai?
  SEQ arrive night CNT DIR

'Why are you continuing until dark? What is the reason for your continuing until dark?'

*Ratou siwa ka bogi-**vak**-a: ratou tekivū siwa ni se siga ka*
3T fish CNJ night-TR-3S 3T begin fish SUB ASP day CNJ

  yaco-v-a na bogi.
  arrive-TR-3S DEF night

'They (trial) fished until night: they began fishing before it was light and continued until dark.'

In the first two examples, the meaning seems to be that the activity (expressed by the subject *e* and specified by the NP) lasted until the beginning of the period represented by the verb root. (Note that we refer here to *siga* and *bogi* as verb roots. They are not usually used as such, but their use with a transitive marker gives them at least temporary status as such.)

These constructions are hard to analyze, because it is not clear what the object *-a* refers to. Unlike other *-Caki* constructions, they seem to have the notion of "object" built into the verb root itself.

In the third example, the *-Caki* construction is used as an attribute.

The following construction (Capell 1941) is somewhat different:

*Sā butō-**lak**-a na vula.*   'The moon does not rise until late at night.'[17]

16.3.7 Dispersive movement: *-yaki*

The transitive suffix *-yaki*,[18] used with *vei-* + root, shows that the action is dispersed or unfocused. Some examples showing literal movement are:

lako	'go'	*vei-lako-yaki*	'go around'
suka	'disperse (after meeting)'	*vei-suka-yaki*	'disperse (in separate directions)'

The following examples include verbs that do not refer to literal movement but are still active:

*E ā   vei-leca-**yaki** na i-tovo ni vā-kāsama ne-i Mārica.*
3S PT GEN-forget-TR DEF manner POS CAU-think POS M
'M's way of thinking was confused.' (T74:41)

*E levu na kā e vei-nanu-**yak**-a ko Mārica.*
3S big DEF thing 3S GEN-think-TR-3S PRP M
'There were a number of things M was thinking about (jumping from one topic to another).' (T74:41)

*E ā vei-rai-**yaki** toka ko Mārica.*
3S PT GEN-see-TR CNT PRP M
'M was looking all around.' (T74:43)

Arms noted (1974:95) that *-yaki* differs from the other two-syllable transitive suffixes in that it takes the major stress (that is, in the present analysis, the phrase accent). This intonational feature is evidence for interpreting *-yaki* differently from the other transitive suffixes: in terms of its function at the phrase level, *-yaki* is more like an attribute than a grammatical marker.

---

[17] AS did not recognize the construction. *Butō* differs from *siga* and *bogi* in that it refers to a state ('darkness'), rather than a period of time. But it could figuratively mean a period of darkness, i.e., night.

[18] Milner's treatment (1972:113) does not clarify the distinction between *-yaka* and *-yaki*. Note the contrast illustrated by the last three examples above. Only the second expresses the object (*-a*) and specifies it (with the NP *na kā*).

16.4 CONSTRUCTIONS WITHOUT THE TRANSITIVE SUFFIX

A definition of transitivity based solely on form (that is, on the presence of the transitive marker) is strained by two constructions—one argued about since Hazlewood's time, the other generally unnoticed by grammarians.

16.4.1 The *gunu-yaqona* construction

Let us take Arms's definition of transitivity (1973:503) as a prototype of the strictly formal approach:

> ... an intransitive verb ... is made transitive by the addition of a transitive suffix.

According to this definition, how should the construction illustrated by the following phrases be interpreted (Hazlewood 1872:36–37)?

me caka were	'to work garden'	*me vau waqa*	'to fasten canoe'
me tara vale	'to build house'	*me vavi vuaka*	'to bake pig'
me wili ivola	'to read book'	*me voli kā*[19]	'to buy things'

Most of the examples here are simple ones. The construction can, however, be more complex:

*ka **cola** i-sū mata-ni-dalo tiko*
CNJ carried bundle taro-stems CNT
'and was carrying bundles of taro stems' (*NV*2:4)

Here, *cola* is the verb, and the constituent directly following is *i-sū mata-ni-dalo*. Note that the continuative marker *tiko* occurs outside this whole construction: *ka (cola (i-sū (mata-(ni-dalo))) tiko)*

Nor is the element that follows the verb confined to forms that are obviously nouns:

*na gauna ni dui **caka no-na** e na vosa*
DEF time POS DIS done POS-3S ABL DEF talk
'the time of doing one's own thing with respect to (writing) the language.'
(*SR* 20/4/82)

In this construction, the noun-like element is *no-na* 'its'. Hazlewood, who was not bound by a formal definition of transitivity, classified these items as "indefinite transitives" (1872:31):

> These are the shortest form of the verb, or the simple root; which is *immediately* followed by the noun which is its object. It does not admit of an article or any other word to intervene between it and the noun which it takes as its object. And it expresses an action in a general and indefinite manner.

---

[19] Incidentally, the modifying element is not always a single noun, but can be a phrase (*FR3*:23):
*Erau voli **ke-drau pīnati**, ka gunu loli tale gā.*
3D buy POS-3D peanut CNJ drink lolly ITR INT
'They (dual) bought their peanuts, and had lollies, too.'

Note also that this construction involves only third person singular (i.e., general) "objects." This by itself sets it off from the formal transitives.

16 Transitivity

If we deal with only Hazlewood's data, there are two formal characteristics of this construction: (1) the verb is used without the transitive markers -*Ci* or -*Caki*; (2) the noun (or nominal) is used without an article.

However, Churchward enlarged on Hazlewood's treatment and showed that the first formal characteristic was not necessary: that the transitive marker can, in fact, occur in this construction—as in:

masu-laki[20] *kā*   'pray for things'
pray-TR   thing

Thus, the second characteristic—lack of an article before the noun—is the main defining feature. (Note, however, that the transitive suffix -*laki* still lacks the object *a* [PG 7/82].)

Churchward retained Hazlewood's "indefinite" label, using it in the following contrast:

tali-a   na   magimagi   (DEFINITE)   'plait the sennit'
plaited-3S DEF   sennit

tali   magimagi   (INDEFINITE)   'sennit plaiting'
plaited sennit

(But do the terms DEFINITE and INDEFINITE apply to the noun or the verb?)

Most later linguists, particularly those who were discussing transitivity in general rather than describing Fijian in particular, followed Hazlewood's and Churchward's analysis, sometimes changing the terminology. Clark (1973:564), for example, called the noun in this construction a "generic object ... incorporated[21] into the VP."[22]

---

[20] The function of -*laki* is discussed below.

[21] The term "incorporation" refers to including a noun in the VP. It is often used for two separate constructions in Fijian: the one discussed here, and one that includes a proper noun (that is, a noun that in other constructions in the same discourse would be preceded by *o*). Examples of the second type are:

E rai-ci koya.   'He saw her.'
E rai-ci Erelia.   'She saw Erelia.'

It should be emphasized that the similarity between the two constructions seems to be a historical accident, and that their functions are quite distinct.

[22] A note here might serve to illustrate the pitfalls connected with the casual and superficial use of grammatical descriptions for comparative work. Clark's insistence that "the [transitive] suffix does *not* appear" is odd, in light of his reference to Churchward's treatment and examples. Churchward (1941:19) wrote: "A transitive verb which has an indefinite object is *usually* [emphasis mine] a simple root word, the verb's transitive suffix (as well as the article before the noun) being dispensed with." In the next paragraph (and characterized by the word "frequently"), he mentioned the "indefinite-transitive" construction occurring with both one-syllable and two-syllable suffixes.

Clark seems to have missed those examples. However, he (apparently) added this note to the original version (1973:599): "For the record, Pawley (p.c.) says that in Bauan Fijian some verbs bear the -*Ci* suffix even before generic objects." Note, however, that this is only half a correction, since it fails to mention the two-syllable suffixes.

These later interpretations had the disadvantage of being based largely on sentences out of context. As a contrast, Milner's analysis (1972:26) was based on his knowledge of the language in discourse. His solution is markedly different from the others: he did not interpret the construction as transitive, but as attributive.

Wolff (1976:3) characterized both the *gunu-yaqona* type and the *kumu-ni i-lavo* type (to be discussed later) as having within the predicate "a noun phrase which refers to the goal." But he distinguished between them by referring to the verb in the former as intransitive, that in the latter as transitive. The inconsistency of this analysis comes to light in one of the main points of the article (p. 5):

> ... the transitive verb focuses on the object of the action; the intransitive, on the action itself.

Thus, according to Wolff's proposal on "focus," *gunu-yaqona* and *kumu-ni i-lavo* have quite different functions within the sentence. But in fact, their functions are identical, as I will show below. This view shows the disadvantage of a formal definition of transitivity that forces the analyst to make a distinction that doesn't exist.

I think each of these views is accurate in some respects. Hazlewood's has merit because it recognizes that transitivity depends not only on grammatical particles, but on meaning as well. In addition, his definite-indefinite distinction is a step in the right direction.

Milner's analysis, in spite of the intransitive label, is appealing because his explanation of one base qualifying another is closer to an accurate description of the function of the noun with respect to the verb.

Next, a transitive suffix can occur in this construction only if it marks a lexical distinction. For example, note the following two phrases:

voli yaqona   'kava buying'
*voli-**taki** yaqona*   'kava selling'

Here, the function of *-taki* is obvious: it lexicalizes—that is, it expands the meaning of the root.

Consider the root *masu* 'pray' in the example below. Its two transitive markers distinguish between two types of goals:

*E masu-**t**-a.*   'She beseeched him.'
*E masu-**lak**-a.*   'She prayed-for it.'

Now, if *masu* is to enter into the *gunu yaqona* construction, perhaps the form

*masu [noun]

is avoided to bypass the ambiguity of whether something is being prayed *to* or *for*. Thus, for the meaning 'say grace' (in the sense of praying before eating), the *-laki* form is used:

masu-laki kākana   'say grace, pray-for food'

This form avoids the ambiguity that **masu kākana* would produce.

Another example, very similar, is *viri-taki polo* 'ball throwing'. *Viri* can take either of two transitive markers:

viri-k-a 'throw-at it'
viri-tak-a 'throw it'

Therefore, in the construction *viri-taki polo*, the function of *-taki* might be to resolve the ambiguity that *viri polo would produce.

We can see, then, that the function of the transitive suffix in this construction is no longer to index the referents, but rather to keep meanings apart.

Finally, although the meaning of the construction is loosely related to a definite-indefinite opposition, I think that this distinction operates *not on the noun, but on the verb*. One of the reasons for assigning the distinction to the noun has been the pairing of the wrong constructions for contrast. For example, Hazlewood (1872:40–41) presented a list of thirty-seven verb roots in three construction types, arranged and labeled as in table 16:4.

TABLE 16:4: HAZLEWOOD'S TRANSITIVE CONSTRUCTION TYPES

[1]	[2]	[3]
Indef. trans.	Def. trans.	Act. intrans.
caka were	*caka-v-a na were*	*cakacaka*
bulu ivi	*bulu-t-a na ivi*	*bulubulu*
tavu uvi	*tavu-n-a na uvi*	*tatavu, tavutavu*
...		

[The meanings of the roots are: *caka* 'made', *bulu* 'buried', *tavu* 'broiled', *were* 'garden', *ivi* 'chestnut', *uvi* 'yam'.]

Possibly because of the neat contrast of labels on columns 1 and 2, Churchward chose to use those pairs to illustrate the contrastive meaning of the construction in question:

1. *E tali magimagi.* 'She was sennit plaiting.'
2. *E tali-a na magimagi.* 'She plaited the sennit.'

I suggest that another significant contrast is between columns 3 and 1:

3. *E talitali.* 'She was plaiting.'
1. *E tali magimagi.* 'She was plaiting sennit.'

Talitali refers to a broad range of plaiting. For example, one can plait *i-dreke* 'carrying cord', *ibe* 'mat', *wā* 'string, yarn', *i-sū* 'basket', or *ketekete* 'basket'. But note especially that *tali wā*, *tali ibe*, and *tali magimagi* refer to distinct activities, as reflected (only incidentally, of course) by their English translations: 'knit', 'weave', and 'plait'. So whereas *talitali* refers to the general activity, *tali magimagi* refers to a particular type of that activity. Thus, one function of this construction is to make a general activity more specific.[23]

---

[23] Note that with respect to discourse, the construction does not introduce a theme into the conversation or story. It is different, then, from other specified referents.

The construction can also be described in terms of its function in discourse, for it allows an entity to be introduced into a discourse without calling attention to it. Note the following:

ni   da ... vaka-rogo i-vunau   'when we listen to a sermon'
SUB 1PI CAU-hear sermon   (*SR* 20/4/82)

Here, in "listening to a sermon," the entity "sermon" is brought up only as an example, and has no further use in the discourse. Using "sermon" in a construction such as

vaka-rogo-c-a   na vunau   'listen to the sermon'
CAU-hear-TR-3S DEF sermon

would give the entity importance in the discourse.[24] This contrast is also discussed in CH 20 with reference to *na* (definite article).

16.4.2 The *viri na polo* construction

Another construction,[25] closely related in form to that just described, is made up of an A2 verb[26] without a transitive marker or object, followed by a noun phrase, this time marked with *na*. Note the following examples:

E ā viri   na polo vei Jone.   'He threw the ball to Jone.'
3S PT throw DEF ball ABL J

ni sā dreke   ko Taraivini na kato kaikoso ki   no-dratou   vale
SUB ASP carried PRP T   DEF basket shellfish ABL POS-3T   house
'when Taraivini carried the basket of shellfish to their house'

E dau cola   na buka.   'It (regularly) carries firewood.'
3S HAB carried DEF firewood

Era dau drē   na i-siviyara.   'They (regularly) pull a plow.'
3P HAB pull DEF plow

E cici sara ki vuli, ka roqo toka na niu.
3S run INT ABL learn CNJ carry CNT DEF coconut
'He ran to school and carried the coconut (*FR4*:4)

For each of the verbs in the sentences above, there is a form consisting of a root + transitive marker + object:

viri-tak-a   dreke-t-a   cola-t-a   dre-t-a

I should emphasize that in general terms, my analysis (at least the most important part of it) follows Milner's (1972:26).

[24] Ignoring the discourse function of this construction is a serious fault of studies that treat it simply as one of several kinds of objects—e.g., Aranovich 2013.

[25] PG (1/79) first drew my attention to this construction.

[26] Sometimes an S2 verb occurs in this construction, although it is then ambiguous, as we show later in the discussion.

16 Transitivity

Further examples (elicited, not taken from texts) are:

E ciqo na polo.	'He caught the ball.'
E caqe na polo.	'He kicked the ball.'
E pasi na polo.	'He passed the ball.'
E dara na sote.	'He put on the shirt.'
E laga na sere.	'She sang the song.'
E yavi na siwa.	'She hauled in the line.'

These verbs, as well, have forms with a transitive marker and an object:

ciqo-m-a   caqe-t-a   pasi-tak-a   dara-mak-a   laga-t-a   yavi-a

The difference between *e caqe-t-a na polo* and *e caqe na polo* cannot be explained through glosses, but only through context. Moreover, as with the construction discussed earlier, the significant opposition is among such phrases as the following:

E laga.	'She sang.'
E laga sere.	'She sang-songs.'
E laga na sere.	'She sang the song.'
E laga-t-a na sere.	'She sang the song.'

Obviously our task is to explain the last two examples, which have identical glosses.

When we examined the *laga sere* type of construction in the preceding section, we found that there is not one specific goal in the semantic structure, but a general one. Note the following examples:

tali magimagi	'sennit plaiting'
laga sere	'song singing'
sara qito	'watching sports'
sara yaloyalo	'watching cinema'
canu kaikoso	'picking up shellfish'
kana cō	'eating grass'
sili sici	'diving for trochus shell'
basu tubu	'breaking off new growth'
loba sucu	'milking'

However, in the *laga na sere* type, the underlying semantic goal is a specific one. The sentence:

E laga sere.   'She was singing.'

refers to the general activity of singing songs—but not one particular song. The sentence:

E laga na sere.   'She was singing the song.'

still concentrates on the activity, but now one specific song is involved.

Both these constructions, then, consist of:

HEAD + MODIFIER

and contrast with:

E laga-t-a.	'She sang it.'
E laga-t-a na sere.	'She sang the song.

The last two examples draw attention to the goal (signaled by *-ti* and expressed by the object *-a*, and, in the second example, further specified by the noun phrase).

16.4.2.1 Discussion

1. The construction just described (*viri na polo*) cannot occur with all verbs; for example, *gunu* 'drink', *masi* 'rubbed', *sava* 'washed', *keli* '(been) dug' cannot be used in this construction.

2. With S2 verbs, the construction (when it is possible) presents an ambiguity unless the subject is specified. For example, of the sentences given earlier, the one repeated here is ambiguous:

E yavi na siwa.   'She hauled in the line / the line was hauled in.'

The following examples are also ambiguous:[27]

E tavo na waqa.	'He drew the canoe / the canoe was drawn.'
E talo na yaqona.	'He poured the kava / the kava was poured.'
E tabe na i-kovu vonu.	'She carried the turtle-bundle / the turtle-bundle was carried.'
E vue na lawa.	'He lifted up the net / the net was lifted up.'
E yau na i-yaya.	'She carried the goods / the goods were carried.'
E yaku na sosō.	'She removed (with fingers) the dirt / the dirt was removed.'
E yara na vuaka.	'He dragged the pig / the pig was dragged.'
E yavi na i-kelekele.	'He hauled up the anchor / the anchor was hauled up.'

3. In one respect, however, the *laga na sere* construction differs from the *laga sere* one: in the placement of postverbal particles. The shorter construction is treated as a unit, and particles such as *tiko gā* and *mada* occur after it, just as they do with a simple verb, a verb with a transitive marker and an object, or a verb with a proper object:

*Gunu **mada**.*	'Go ahead and drink.'
*E gunu yaqona **tiko gā**.*	'He's drinking kava.'
*Gunu-va **mada**.*	'Go ahead and drink it.'
*Rai-ci koya **mada**.*	'Just look at him.'

But with *laga na sere*, such particles precede the noun phrase modifier:

*Laga **mada** na sere.*	'Go ahead and sing the song.'
*E laga **tiko gā** na sere.*	'He was singing the song.'

Thus, structurally this feature allies the construction more closely to *laga-t-a na sere* or *gunu-v-a na yaqona*, even though semantically it is closer to *laga sere* or *gunu yaqona*.

---

[27] SN compiled the list.

16.4.2.2 *Gunu-yaqona* type constructions: Conclusions

One reason that these types of constructions have been difficult to classify is that they include two main oppositions: definite vs. indefinite, and transitive vs. intransitive. I suggest the following analysis.

1. They are semantically transitive—i.e., they refer to two referents.
2. They are formally intransitive, since they lack an object.[28]

In terms of context (all-important for this construction), both transitivity and definiteness are significant. It is the "intransitive" label that takes precedence, for the lack of an object removes the referent of the noun from the "thread of discourse." For example, consider the following two sentences:

E ā gunu-v-a na bia. 'He/she drank the beer.'   (transitive, definite)
E ā gunu bia tiko.   'He/she was beer-drinking' (intransitive, indefinite)

Even though these sentences refer to the same event, they have quite different discourse functions. Moreover, *bia* is definite in the first sentence, but indefinite in the second, illustrating the two oppositions mentioned above. Rephrasing Wolff's statement above (1976:5):

> ... the transitive verb, strengthened by a definite NP, focuses on the goal of the action; the intransitive, with an indefinite/general N, on the action itself.

16.5 SUMMARY

A superficial view of the grammar of Fijian transitivity is that each verb occurs with one transitive marker. As an example of a verb that can take several of the suffixes discussed above, we use *coka* 'head-long movement toward, thrust':

E cokā na ika.	'He speared the fish.'
E coka-v-a.	'He lunged-toward, dived-toward it.'
E coka-t-a.	'He tackled him.'
E coka-tak-a na moto.	'He speared with the spear.'
E coka-tak-a na no-na cudru.	'He speared because of his anger.'
E coka-rak-a na vuaka.	'He speared (intensively) the pig.'
E coka-lak-a na vuaka.	'He speared (repeatedly) the pig.'

We can see, then, that in addition to its primary use, an important function of the transitive marker is to expand the meaning of the root—to allow a number of variations on a theme.

This chapter discussed the form of the transitive suffixes (*-Ci*, *-Caki*) and some general differences between these two major types. It was shown that the specific consonant for *C* was nearly the same in the two types, except for three fewer consonants in the disyllabic forms (table 16.1). These two types of variables (monosyllabic vs. disyllabic; different consonants as the onset of the first syllable) are shown to produce a number of derived forms for any root.

---

[28] Note that this construction includes both types that Wolff referred to above (i.e., the *gunu-yaqona* type and the *kumu-ni i-lavo* type)

As we saw in §16.3, the functions/meanings of the different transitive suffix fall into the following categories:

1. General transitivizer
2. Reason
3. Means or accompaniment
4. Intensive
5. Lexical change
6. Duration
7. Dispersive movement

Of these, "reason" is perhaps the most interesting, since it has not been noted before.[29]

Finally, constructions that are "transitive" in meaning, but without the formal trappings of transitivity, were discussed from the point of view of generality vs. specificity.

16.6 TRANSITIVITY: HISTORY AND DISCUSSION[30]

16.6.1 Definitions of transitivity

Hazlewood (1872:34) considered that the

> distinctions into *Intransitive*, *Transitive*, and *Passive* are much more important in Feejeean than in English, on account of the variety of forms assumed by the Feejeean verb to express these distinctions.

His criteria for determining the differences among these types are a mixture of semantic and formal. The first definition is from "the grammars":

> Intransitives "are those in which the thing (action) expressed is confined to the actor, and does not pass on to an object. They include the class usually termed neuter verbs, as well as those which, though active, are intransitive."

As examples of active-intransitive, he gave (among others):

Au cakacaka. 'I work.'
Era sā vavavi. 'They [pl.] bake.'

As neuter-intransitives:

Au sā moce. 'I sleep.'
Era sā tū. 'They [pl.] stand.'

The members of this second class, he noted, could become active-transitives with the addition of a "transitive termination":

moce-r-a[31] 'sleep upon [it]'
tu-r-a[32] 'stand upon [it]'

---

[29] That is, before *TFL*.

[30] For the most part, in this version of the grammar I've deleted the long discussions of grammatical topics that *TFL* included. But transitivity has long been a controversial topic, so here I have included the earlier discussion and have added to it.

[31] Not used now in this sense. *Moce-r-a* is used to mean 'sleep with him/her'—with a sexual connotation.

He defined transitives as follows (1872:31):

> Transitive, or active verbs are those in which the action expressed by the verb passes on to, or affects, some object; as, Au sa loma-ni koya, I love him; eratou a kauta na waqa, they took the canoe.
>
> The *object* of a transitive verb must be expressed or clearly understood.

Hazlewood's two criteria are emphasized by the following statement: "There are two kinds of transitive verbs in Feejeean which are clearly distinct both in their *senses* and *forms*." He labeled them *Indefinite* and *Definite*. We discussed the indefinite type, called the *gunu-yaqona* construction, in §16.4.1.

Hazlewood's classification, complete with the indefinite-definite transitive contrast, survived for slightly over a century. Then Milner made the move toward a totally formal definition that most analysts have since followed. As indicated earlier, Milner analyzed transitive and intransitive in very simple terms: a transitive form is defined as "a base followed by a transitive particle"; intransitive is defined negatively.

In his extensive treatment of Fijian transitivity, Arms (1974:17–18) based his definition on form, but in rather vague terms:

> Decisions about transitivity depend a good deal on surface form. Of the various possible noun phrases in a clause, one or two typically enter into an especially close relationship with the verb and with each other. This close relationship may consist of physical proximity to the verb, special ordering requirements, loss of specific case marking, phonological prominence, or some other feature or combination of features. The construction where two noun phrases[33] exhibit these properties is regarded as a "transitive" construction.
>
> Another factor in determining transitivity is the ways in which the cases of agent and patient[34] (cf. Chafe 1970) are typically realized in a language. The typical structure employed when these two cases occur together is the transitive structure of the language—a structure that may also be used, however, by other cases.

The main problem with Arms's definition of transitivity is that it hinges on the function of NPs, which play no part in the VP itself and are optional in the sentence. In other words, there are a great many sentences that exhibit transitivity but have no NPs at all.

In his second paragraph, Arms brought up the crucial matter of the semantic relationship between the entities that the subject and object refer to (in relation to the verb). His reference in passing, however, to "other cases" that may be manifested by transitivity is a controversial point. The issue is whether "other

---

[32] *Tu-r-a* is not used now with this meaning. Instead, *vaka-tu-r-a* 'make it stand (somewhere)' it used. The latter also means 'to propose it (law, motion+)'.

[33] Note the dependence, in this definition, on noun phrases, which I consider optional elements in the sentence. See CH 26.

[34] Here, actor and goal.

cases," such as instrumental and comitative, lie in the structure of Fijian or in the minds of the analysts. If there is an answer to this question, more research is needed before we find it.

As he was plowing new semantic ground (so to speak) for Fijian, Arms occasionally confused semantic and formal matters. He was careful to begin with a purely formal definition of subject and object (1974:19): "In this work, 'subject' and 'object' will be used to designate certain elements of Fijian surface structure." The confusion arises in the next sentence: "The subject is the referent of the pronoun occurring before the verb in the verb phrase, the object the referent of the pronoun or proper noun occurring after the verb in the verb phrase ... " Referents, of course, cannot be forms in a sentence; instead, they are entities that exist in the real—or extralinguistic—world, and that are *denoted by* a form.

The other problem with this definition is that it implicitly confines "subject" and "object" to NPs, which often do not appear in unelicited sentences.

Several other studies of transitivity in general followed that of Arms, drawing on his ample and generally accurate[35] supply of data. They also followed a strictly formal definition of transitivity. For example:

> Foley (1976:3): "Transitive clauses in Fijian are those in which the verb is marked with a transitive suffix."

> Wolff (1976:3): "Fijian ... has transitive and intransitive verbs. The transitive verbs are marked by the presence of the transitivizing suffix, a morph shaped -i (or zero in Bauan if the third-person singular object marking suffix -a is present)."

> Naylor (1978:25): "It is clear from the literature that the term "transitive" is generally used to refer to form rather than to meaning. If a verb has a transitive suffix, it is ipso facto transitive. For example, Fijian gunuva 'drink-it' is transitive but gunu 'drink' is intransitive."

16.6.2 The meaning (?) of -*C*-

The possibility that the consonant that introduces the transitive marker carries meaning began with Hazlewood (1872:37–40), who could not, with certainty, predict which ending a verb might take, but still suggested that the choice was not entirely arbitrary.

First, he noted that "verbs formed from nouns without prefixing vaka" take -*na*, and related that -*na* to the third person singular pronoun (evidently comparing it with the possessive form). Next, he proposed a semantic connection for -*va*, listing twenty verbs of motion that take that suffix, while admitting that some verbs outside this category also occur with that suffix. Then he noted that two-syllable suffixes often "have either a *more intensive sense* or *take a different object*." He singled out -*laka* and -*raka* for their use as intensives.

---

[35] Unfortunately, every user of Capell's dictionary is hindered by its errors and omissions.

As a summary, Hazlewood proposed that "most probably the terminations ... were originally distinct words, and that in their present use they retain more or less of the original sense." After this speculation, he returned to the business at hand with: "But this may be a subject for further investigation. It is not of essential importance."

This idea lay dormant for well over a century. Then the further investigation that Hazlewood proposed was carried out in detail by Arms (1973, 1974), who examined some 1100 different morphemes, occurring as formal transitives in 1680 forms. He suggested meanings for the nine[36] one-syllable suffixes and eight two-syllable suffixes, arriving at an average of 60 percent "semantic fit".

On the whole, the exercise was a useful one, for Hazlewood's suggestion should indeed have been acted upon. But for a number of reasons, it is safer to use the study as an indication of tendencies rather than as conclusive findings. Its major weakness is the semantic framework that is assumed. Although some of the categories, such as Motion, support the argument, others are so vague as to discourage any exceptions. For instance, Pliancy; Gentle Contact; Bodily Experience (also singled out in their general criticism by Geraghty (1979:253) and Clark (1977:10–11)), and which includes *bika* 'press down', *boi* 'smell', and *kuvu* 'puff into smoke'); Use of Limb or Instrument; Moderate Force; Performative (which includes *bora* 'speak angrily to', *cā* 'hate', and *kaba* 'climb'). This example shows that one might achieve perfect "semantic fit" if one makes the categories general enough. For a detailed criticism, see Milner 1982, 1985.

Finally, there is a chicken-and-egg quality about the whole problem. One might just as well suggest that the *v* in *lako-v-a* 'go for it' or *cici-v-a* 'run for it' means Motion Toward simply because the semantic quality of motion is inherent in the root. Once the most common verbs of motion (such as *lako*) are firmly established with -*v*- as a transitive marker, analogy might play an important role in enlarging the class to include more and more verbs of motion.[37] One has only to note the current disagreement among speakers over certain forms (for example, Cammack 1962:94–97 and discussions with the staff of the FDP, August 1978) to suggest that there is competition among consonants for some forms. It follows that the status of SF as a second language for the majority of the population makes the choice of consonant rather a moot point for more obscure words.

16.6.3 Suffix or part of the stem?

Both Arms's position and the variation just mentioned play parts in another, though minor, grammatical controversy: should words like *lakova* be divided morphologically as (1) *lako-va*, (2) *lakov-a*, or (3) *lako-v-a*?

---

[36] Arms deleted *y* from the list.
[37] As an example, I have cited *gādē* 'stroll' to illustrate A1 verbs (as Arms did to illustrate "true" verbs without a transitive suffix). However, as noted elsewhere in this work, some speakers do use it with the transitive marker -*vi*.

Solution (1) seems to have been considered standard until fairly recently. The first appearance of the second solution that I am aware of is an exercise in Hockett 1958:469–70, in which the reader is given a number of pairs of words (intransitive and transitive, in the traditional use of these terms) and asked, first, to propose a base form that will allow one to predict both forms, and, second, to infer the form of verbs in "Pre-Fijian." For both these requirements, we assume that the correct answer is a list of verbs ending in a consonant.

Cammack (1962:91) followed the practice of writing verbs with a final -C-, describing this consonant as a "connective element between the base and the suffix which we take to be part of the stem, and which we shall call a *thematic consonant*."

This interpretation is directly opposed to that of Arms, which assumes a meaning for each consonant. The merit of Hockett's analysis is that it allows one to predict either form from a hypothetical base. Of course, citing only the longer form would have the same effect, but the device was born during a period when economy of description was more important than the reactions of native readers.

Also, both these analysts overestimated the reliability of Capell's dictionary and underestimated the amount of variation that exists. As we find more verbs with multiple "thematic consonants," the efficiency of such a system dwindles.

In the present study, I follow the third interpretation, based mainly on the work of Pawley and Arms, who reinterpreted the -*Ca* suffix as the morphophonemic result of -*Ci* + -*a*.

16.6.4 -*Ca* vs. -*Ci*

It is now generally accepted that in SF, the final -*a* of the syllable -*Ca* and disyllable -*Caka* is not part of the transitive marker, but instead the third person singular object. Thus, the transitive suffixes themselves are -*Ci* and -*Caki*.

I cite the -*C-a* and -*Cak-a* forms frequently, for I consider it important to include and identify the object while discussing the verb. Thus, *raica*, for example, will regularly be glossed not as 'see' but as 'see it'.

16.6.5 The various functions of -*Caki*

16.6.5.1 The independence of *vaka-* and -*taki*

Although Hazlewood (1872:46) discussed the causative function of *vaka-* without saying or implying that -*taki* was connected with it, Churchward (1941:21) expanded the earlier statement, beginning a misconception that some other analysts have adopted. Churchward's statement gives the impression that the causative in Fijian is formed by a kind of envelope—that verbs are surrounded by a prefix and a suffix to make them causative. He wrote:

> Causative verbs are formed by means of the prefix *vaka-* and a transitive suffix.

However, he noted correctly that with verbs derived from other types of roots, the suffix was not always -*taka*, giving examples of roots inherently verbal, with their own monosyllabic transitive marker: *vaka-tu-r-a* 'cause to stand', *vaka-bale-a* 'cause to fall over', *vaka-yaco-r-a* 'cause to happen'. Still, he mistakenly considered the transitive marker as an integral part of causatives.

Milner (1972:67) avoided confusing the causative and the transitive, albeit defining causative rather idiosyncratically:

> Often a form with *vaka-* has a "more decided," "more active" or "more thorough" meaning than one without. For that reason *vaka-* has sometimes been called a "causative" particle. It may be compared to a specialised use of the prefixes *per-* and *for-* in English:
> e.g.
> form and perform
> swear and forswear
> annual and perennial

All his Fijian examples, however, have a causative meaning:

vaka-mate-a	'cause him to die'
vaka-sucu-ma	'cause him to be born'
vaka-bulā	'cause him to live'

One statement, perhaps related to the causative (1972:88), is in error: "-*taka* is the only two-syllable suffix that can be used with the *vaka-* prefix." Note the following exceptions (a sample):

vaka-roba-lak-a	'slap him repeatedly'
vaka-butu-rak-a	'charge, mob him'
vaka-bali-lak-a	'knead it repeatedly'
vaka-bari-lak-a	'scrape it (with teeth) repeatedly
vaka-basi-lak-a	'split it repeatedly, randomly'
vaka-vesivesi-lak-a	'break it off (more and more)'
vaka-basu-rak-a	'tear it into bits'

Milner may have had in mind the causative use of *vaka-*; these examples show its frequentative, distributive use. They have this structure:

(((*vaka-roba*) *lak*) *a*)

To show that the prefix and the suffix occur in different layers of the hierarchy, note the following construction:

E vaka-roba gone.   'She was (repeatedly) child-slapping.'

In the previous example, -*laki* indicates an intensification of the action; -*a* is the object.

Although Cammack (1962:90) listed a "causative -*Cak-* suffix," he kept the functions of causative and transitive separate in his discussion (one example: *vaka-yadra* 'wake someone up'; his use of "someone" in the examples signifies a goal that is not expressed grammatically). In addition, his list of "combinations of prefixes, suffixes, and stems" (pp. 104–13) is a conveniently organized treatment of some of the most common "word-forming" processes in Fijian.

Arms's statement about causatives (1973:517) is a swing back to the Churchwardian view:

> The ending *-tak* is used regularly with the prefix *vaka-* to form causatives.

The errors in this statement are the assumptions that the suffix is part of the causative, and that *-tak* occurs "regularly" with *vaka-*. In statements like this, it is difficult to decide whether "regularly" represents a statistical or an impressionistic judgment. Perhaps it is the latter, because Arms contradicted the statement in the same paragraph:

> Causative forms in *vaka-* and Ø are also common.

Through several of these treatments, then, runs a common thread of misanalysis: that the transitive indicators are an inseparable part of the causative construction.

16.6.5.2 The meaning of the *-Caki* forms

Grammarians from Hazlewood through Cammack were properly general about a meaning for the *-Caki* forms. Hazlewood, for example, noted for suffixes other than *-laka* and *-raka* a general use (1872:33–34): "different terminations affect different objects; or the same object in a different manner … " After listing a number of examples, he concluded:

> The above examples will be sufficient to show that many verbs take different objects when they take a different termination; or if they affect the same object, it is in a very different manner; as, me vanataka nadakai, is to shoot *with* a gun; me vaná na dakai, to shoot a gun. It is not to be supposed that the nouns given above express *only* objects which either of the terminations take.

But Pawley (1972:46), possibly from comparative data, attached the label of "dative, instrumental" to a list of cognate suffixes from thirty-one Eastern Oceanic languages, including SF. In the introduction to his article on the transitive endings, Arms (1973:503) adopted this label:

> the dative-instrumental suffix *-ak-* (cf. Pawley 1972:46), e.g., *cici-vi* 'run to', *cici-vaki* 'run with'.

Whatever the situation in the other thirty languages examined by Pawley, the label "dative, instrumental" is clearly too narrow for SF. First, a true instrumental use is relatively rare. Some examples, such as the following, do show an instrumental meaning:

E t ā-tak-a.   'She chopped-with it.'
E kaki-tak-a.   'She scraped-with it.'

but the examples usually quoted (for example, *cici-vak-a* above) might lead us to assume that English "with" always implies instrument. In *cici-vak-a*, and most of the other verbs of motion, the object does not refer to an instrument of the action, but simply something carried along.

16 Transitivity

Next, underlying the argument for "dative, instrumental" is the assumption that -*Caki* and -*Ci* refer to different goals. However, one of the most frequent uses of -*Caki* is in intensive (-*laki*, -*raki*), for which the object refers to the same goal as does that for the -*Ci* form.

In summary, the "dative, instrumental" label seems to have been based on a few, often repeated examples, rather than on a comprehensive study of a large number of verbs.

Wolff (1980:158–59) labeled the difference between -*Ci* and -*Caki* as "close transitive" and "remote transitive". His examples:

Close transitive: *dreti* 'pull something'
Remote transitive: *dretaki* [*drētaki*] 'pull on'

He explained the difference as follows:

> In Fijian the close transitive is marked by -*i* and the remote by -*aki* ... The close transitive verb focuses on a goal which is directly affected by the action or (in the case of verbs of movement or posture) refers to the place gone to, on, or at, or the thing gone to fetch. The remote transitive form focuses on the instrument, cause, concomitant, or the thing conveyed. Some oft-quoted pairs from Fijian: *kabati* 'climb[ed] upon', *kaba-taki* 'climb bringing'; *kacivi* 'call (a person)', *kacivaki* 'announce'; *curumi* 'enter a place', *curutaki* 'place inside ...'; *murii* 'follow', *muritaki* 'escort'.[38]

These labels are as over-generalized as most of the others, although the more detailed description is accurate in some respects. Of course, it gives the impression that most verbs that are marked for transitive allow such a two-way contrast. It is not at all clear that such is the case.

As another example, note the following verbs:

kaci 'call'   *kalu* 'whistle'   *kāsivi* 'spit'   *viri* 'throw'
ula 'throw'   *kolo* 'throw'   *rabo* 'sling'   *vosa* 'talk'

For these actions, the goal is often not made formal in any way. Still, it occurs semantically. Which suffix is likely to be used if the goal is given formally? Those indicated by a one-syllable suffix are generally semantically optional; those indicated by a two-syllable form ("remote") are essential. For example, one cannot spit without material to do it with; one cannot throw without an object to use. But one can certainly spit without spitting *at* something, or throw without throwing *at* something. And as an anonymous colleague has noted, it is often the case that one breaks wind without doing it *at* someone.

Foley's treatment (1976:167) of -*Caki* is a slight an improvement; he recognized not just one case relation for the marker, but a list of them: "Instrument/Comitative, Source and Benefactive." In particular, comitative is treated accurately: "[a] sub-role of Instrument when it is not efficacious to the action, but merely accessory."

---

[38] Wolff may have been using these -*i* forms as base forms. Otherwise, they are S2 words, as I indicated by adding -*ed* to *climb*. The glosses for the verbs that follow could be similarly corrected.

But even though Foley's label for -*Caki* is not so narrow as to call the suffix "instrument" alone, it still operates within a framework that will not work except in a very general way. To understand why, one has only to return to some previous examples:

E voli-a.　　　　　　'She bought it.'
E voli-tak-a.　　　　'She sold it.'

Can this difference be explained by a case label? And what is the difference, with respect to case, between the following:

E gunu yaqona.　　　　'He drank kava.'
E masu-laki kākana.　　'He said grace.'

It has already been shown (§16.4.1) that the transitive marker in *masu-laki kākana* is used to avoid ambiguity, and that the function of the form of the last two examples—one without and one with a transitive marker—is exactly the same. Thus, the use of the marker is not regular.

One should not like to claim, however, that patterns do not exist in this area of Fijian grammar; certainly the earlier discussion shows that there are some uses of particular transitive markers that form fairly regular sets. But an attempt to fit the markers into neatly organized pigeonholes ignores a very important function of their diversity: *it provides an additional way of distinguishing among different meanings.*

17 OBJECTS

Like a subject, an object is a morphologically complex form that includes the grammatical categories of PERSON, NUMBER, and the INCLUSIVE-EXCLUSIVE distinction.[1] Its semantic referent is a goal.[2]

TABLE 17.1: OBJECTS

	First person exclusive	First person inclusive	Second person	Third person
Singular	au		iko	a
Dual	keirau	kēdaru	kemudrau	rau
Trial	keitou	kedatou	kemudou	iratou
Plural	keimami	keda	kemunī	ira

Objects occur under the conditions described in the chapters on verb classification (9–12), transitivity (16), and specification (26). In summary: objects occur with two-referent verbs when the goal is specified to a degree beyond implicit and signaled—in other words, at the "expressed" level of specificity (see §26.1.2).

For a discussion of person, number, inclusive-exclusive, forms of respect, human vs. nonhuman referents, and a morphological analysis, see CH 4.

17.1 PERSON-NUMBER MARKERS AND NAMES

In addition to the objects listed in table 17.1, there is another type. This second type is used to represent a single entity with a name, such as a person or place. When such a form occurs outside the VP as an NP, it is introduced by the proper marker *o*. Examples are:

o Tēvita	'Tēvita' (person's name)
o Eta	'Eta' (person's name)
o Verata	'Verata' (place name)
o koya	'he, she, it'

---

[1] See the definitions of these terms in CH 4.

[2] Although every object refers to a goal, not every goal is represented by an object. See the discussion of statives (CH 10).

These constructions are independent proper NPs, and their function is to specify a grammatical marker, such as subject, object, or possessor.

But when such a noun or pronoun occurs within the VP,[3] it does so without the proper marker *o*. For example:

*Rai-ci **Tēvita** mada.*	'Look at **T** (if you will).'
*Rai-ci **keirau** mada.*	'Look at **us** (if you will).'

This set consists of all proper nouns, plus *koya* (third person singular).

17.2 CLASSIFICATION ACCORDING TO PERSON

Another way to classify objects is as follows:

17.2.1 First person, second person, and proper noun

For example:

*E ā rai-ci **au**.*	'He saw **me**.'
*E ā rai-ci **iko**.*	'He saw **you**.'
*E ā rai-ci **Lala**.*	'He saw **L**.'

In such phrases as these, the referent is clear. Therefore, it need not be specified. But when it is, the purpose seems to be to emphasize or to clarify unknown participants in the nonsingulars. For example, although the terms *keirau, keitou,* and *keimami* (first person exclusive dual, trial, and plural) include the first person (which, of course, does not have to be identified), they may include entities that may need to be further specified for the hearer.

17.2.2 Third person

As opposed to first and second person, the referent(s) of third person is/are unclear, unless explained in the context, or apparent through gesture, etc. For example:

E ā rai-c-a.	'He saw it.'
E ā rai-c-i irau.	'He saw the two of them.'
E ā rai-c-i iratou.	'He saw the few of them.'
E ā rai-c-i koya.	'He saw her/him'

How each of these referents can be further specified is explained in CH 26.

17.3 DISCUSSION: UNDERLYING *I* OBJECT MARKER?

There are several factors that suggest an underlying *i* that marks objects:

1. The occasionally heard proper accusative marker i_2 (21.3).

2. The influence of independent personal NPs on grammatical objects (see Geraghty 1977).

---

[3] Such objects, along with the nouns in *rai koro* 'village inspection' and *gunu yaqona* 'kava drinking', have often been called incorporated objects. As §16.4.1 shows, *koro* and *yaqona* are not objects at all, and there is no reason why the word "incorporated" should be used for names.

3. The existence of an optional *i* before a number of personal nouns (see CH 24, note 2).

4. The current forms of both sets—grammatical objects and personal nouns.

It is interesting to examine the set of personal nouns with respect to the occurrence of the so-called optional *i*. Although Milner's statement (1972:100) gives the impression that *i* is optional in all the forms, it is not. Instead, some forms always occur with *i*: *iau*, (which results in *yau*), *iko*, and *ira*; some forms often do: *irau* and *iratou*; and the remaining forms never do.[4]

The basic principles of morphological analysis suggest this hypothesis: that *i* is a separate morpheme. What, then, might be the conditions that make it obligatory in some forms and optional in others? The phonology suggests some answers.

1. Content[5] forms beginning with /a-/ are relatively rare. Some forms that have /a-/ historically have added a nonphonemic glide, now written as *y*.

2. Content morphemes are never less than a measure in length. Thus, *o ko and *o ra may be disfavored, since the accent would be on the proper marker *o* and not the person-number form. Keeping *i* in these forms might be a way to make a new form that can be accented. Note that *o-ratou* (*ora·tou*) is permitted (TRN 6/82). Here, although one accent is on /o/, the major phrase accent is on /tou/. Thus, some part of the content form is accented.

The suggestion of an *i* object marker is made tentatively, for the analysis is clouded by an extremely complex history of development for these forms (Geraghty 1977), including the influence on SF from the other Fijian languages.

---

[4] Except in what PG calls "Old High Fijian."

[5] Classifying these forms as content morphemes is rather a departure from the usual definition, but I suggest that these (historically) bundles of morphemes now function as a special type of content form.

18 VERB PHRASE MARKERS AFTER THE HEAD

This chapter is organized as follows:[1]

1. Objects
2. Direction: *cake, sobu, tani, laivi*
3. Concomitant: *vata*
4. Aspect: *oti*
5. Potential: *rawa*
6. Limitation: *wale, bau, bulu*
7. Inclusion: *kece, taucoko*
8. Intensive: *sara*
9. Iteration: *tale*
10. Respectful address: *saka*
11. Aspect: *tiko, tū, toka, koto (nō), voli*
12. Initiation: *beka, mada, bagi, gona*
13. Limitation: *gā, lā*
14. Direction: *mai, yani, soti/ sō*
15. Affirmation/negation: *lī, nē, ē*

18.1 OBJECTS

Objects are treated in CH 17.

18.2 DIRECTION (DIR)

Two directional markers (*cake* 'up' and *sobu*[2] 'down') are used as heads of locative NPs, as in:

[E   tiko e   cake.]   'It's up there.'
 3S stay ABL DIR

However, they, as well as two other forms, also occur in the VP as markers.

18.2.1 *Cake* 'upward'

Cake can be used to refer literally to upward direction:

---

[1] The general order is based on Milner's table (1972:94). Changes are based on my own observations and those of PG and TRN. This chapter has also benefitted from Arms's paper (1984, 1986) on surface order in the VP, which is especially valuable for its discussion of subtle differences of meaning that occur when certain markers change order. I also consulted Parke 1981. As with the markers before the head, the order is approximate.

[2] PG noted that *sobu* cannot be the head of a locative (ablative) phrase as *cake* can. Instead, *rā* serves that function.

[Ā tū **cake**] ko Mārica, dola-v-a   e dua na droa
PT stand DIR   PRP M   open-TR-3S 3S one DEF drawer
[ā tau-r-a **cake** mai] na i-vola.
PT take-TR-3S DIR DIR DEF letter
'M stood up, opened a drawer, took (toward her) a letter.' (T74:41)

[Ā tau-r-a **cake**] na talikaramu.   'She picked up the telegram.'
PT take-TR 3S DIR   DEF telegram   (T74:41)

Cake can also be used after statives in a more figurative sense of a comparative:

[E vinaka **cake**.]   'It's better.'
3S good   DIR

[... ni vinaka **cake**] me ra ...   'that it would be better if they ...'
SUB good   DIR   SUB 3P   (*FR5*:35)

However, this construction may be tainted by translation.[3] Certainly, comparison is not a grammatical category for Fijian. Usually, it can be implied by context. For example, *levu* 'big' may imply a comparison with *lailai* 'small'. In this respect, Fijian statives are not unusual; implicit comparison may be a semantic feature of similar pairs of statives in any language.

18.2.2 *Sobu* 'downward'

This marker, like *cake*, has both literal and figurative uses. In the former, it refers to downward movement:

[Au ā mani kau-t-a   **sobu**] na nei-tou bēseni levu.
1S PT SEQ carried-TR-3S DIR   DEF PC-1TX basin big
'Then I carried down our (trial exclusive) big basin.' (*NV4*:2)

[sā qai drodro **sobu** yani]   'then it flows down' (*FR5*:10)
ASP SEQ flow   DIR DIR

In urban areas (more subject to advertising), *sobu* appears frequently in the idiom *lutu sobu*, literally 'fall down', but now meaning a 'sale' (i.e., the prices have fallen).

The figurative use of *sobu* is to qualify a stative. Thus, it means 'lesser':

[Sega ni lailai **sobu**] na no-drau kidroā.   'Their (dual) surprise was
not SUB small DIR   DEF PC-3D   surprise   not any less.' (*FR5*:18)

18.2.3 *Tani* 'away, different'

This marker can refer to literal distant location:

E tiko **tani**.   'She's staying in a different place.' (*VV*)
3S stay DIR

Sā vaka-wati   **tani**.   'He's married outside his area.'
ASP MAN-spouse DIR

---

[3] Of course, even if it is the result of translations, it should be treated here so long as it is in the current idiom.

Tani also has a more figurative use as 'different':

E dua ***tani***.   'It's a different one.'
3S one DIR

PG suggested (7/82) that although *tani* fits semantically with the directional markers *mai* and *yani* (§18.14), it is structurally mutually exclusive with *sobu* and *cake*. He also noted that another marker, *laivi* (see the next section), has the same function as *tani*.

Unlike *yani*, *tani* is context-oriented only in the sense that it refers to motion away from a reference point. We might construct this metaphor to compare *yani* with *tani*. Because *yani* refers to a place fixed by context, movement to that place is like a line with one end fixed at that point, but originating from an unspecified direction and an unspecified distance—unless the context specifies each. With *tani*, the line is fixed at the locus of discourse, and the movement is merely outward, with the direction and distance unspecified.

18.2.4 *Laivi* 'utterly'

Capell (under *lai*) described *laivi* as the passive form of *lai* 'leave, permit' and noted that it was used in certain compounds: *biuta laivi* 'reject, abandon', *taya laivi* 'cut off and discard', *musilaka laivi* 'break off and discard'. See also Churchward 1941:49. On the other hand, *VV* glosses it *tani* 'elsewhere, different'—but also indicating emphasis, with example phrases *lako laivi*, *biu laivi*, *viritaki laivi*.

18.3 CONCOMITANT (CNC): *VATA*

Vata after a verb shows that the action/state had more than one participant, and that they performed an action or existed in a state together. Examples are:

*[Keirau ā qase-ni-vuli   **vata**] mai Kadavu.*
1DX   PT elder-PC-learn CNC   ABL K
'We (dual exclusive) were teachers together on K.' (*VV:ā*)

*Ia [ni ratou rogo-ci **vata**] na vosa ni vanua e tolu*
CNJ SUB 3T hear-TR CNC DEF talk POS land 3S three   'But when the languages from these three places were heard together' (*SR* 20/4/82)

Vata is often used with the NP marker *kei* to translate 'with'. To show that they are separate markers belonging to separate phrases, note the following examples (both the VP and the NP in question are bracketed). In the first, *vata* and *kei* are separated by *gā*:

*Ia [sā toka **vata** gā] [**kei** na ke-na i-colacola.]*
CNJ ASP stay CNC LIM CNJ DEF PC-3S NOM-carry
'But there's a burden that goes along with it.' (*NV4*:2)

In the next example, *vata* and *kei* belong to separate phrases as well, but only the intonation contours show this separation:

*Sā qai bulu   na   lovo [ka sā bulu **vata**] [**kei** Ulumalaidua.]*
ASP SEQ buried DEF oven CNJ ASP buried CNC   CNJ U
'Then the oven was covered and buried along with it was U.' (*FR5*:16)

In some instances, however, *vata kei* has been reinterpreted as a compound marker. In the following example, the phrases are bracketed to show that here, *vata* cannot be interpreted as part of the VP. When the sentence is read, the intonation shows that *vata kei* is a unit within one phonological phrase:

[Eratou lako mai] [na   tagane] [vata kei iratou] [na   yalewa.]
  3T   go   DIR DEF male   CNC CNJ 3T   DEF female
'The men are coming together with the women.' (Milner 1972:82)

18.4 COMPLETIVE ASPECT (ASP): *OTI*

Oti as a root is an irregular[4] S1 verb meaning 'finished'. As a marker, it follows another verb to show completion of its action or state:

*na vei-i-vola [sā vola-i   **oti**]*   'the books that were already
DEF DIS-book ASP write-TR ASP   written' (*SR* 20/4/82)

*[Ni   sā kana **oti**] sā mani yaco sara me bukete.*
 SUB ASP eat ASP ASP SEQ arrive INT SUB pregnant
'After eating, it then happened that she was pregnant.' (*FR5*:11)

*[ni   sā cabo   **oti**] na no-na i-kaukau*
 SUB ASP presented ASP DEF PC-3S gifts
'after his gifts had been presented' (*FR5*:20)

18.5 POTENTIAL (POT): *RAWA*

Rawa is a verb that means 'able to'. Following a verb it indicates an ability to perform the action referred to:

*[ni   ra sā wili-k-a   **rawa**] na no-dra vosa*
 SUB 3P ASP read-TR-3S POT   DEF PC-3P talk
'when they were able to read their language' (*SR* 20/4/82)

*ni   sā sega [ni   sau-m-a   **rawa**] no-na dīnau*
SUB ASP not SUB pay-TR-3S POT   PC-3S debt
'when he isn't able to repay his debt' (*VV*)

18.5.1 The difference between *rawa ni V* and *V rawa*[5]

One difference between these two constructions is that in *rawa ni V*, *rawa* is a verb, and the next phrase is subordinate. In *V rawa*, *rawa* is a marker. At one

---

[4] *Oti* might be considered irregular if we group it with a small number of S1 verbs that take a transitive suffix. On the other hand, we might classify it as a "process" verb (see §12.3).
[5] Thanks to TRN (4/82) for explaining the difference.

level, the meaning of the two constructions is the same: able to perform the action referred to by the verb. At another level, however, they are different.

E rawa ni V refers simply to the ability. It implies that such a situation has always existed; it does not contrast it with an opposing situation. For example:

E **rawa ni** cegu na tamata e vanua, ia e sega ni **rawa ni**
3S able SUB breathe DEF person ABL land CNJ 3S not SUB able SUB

   cegu e loma ni wai. 'Man can breathe on land, but
   breathe ABL inside POS water he can't breathe in [under] water.'

V rawa, however, adds something to the basic meaning: that the ability was not always present. For example:

[E cegu **rawa**.]   'He's able to breathe (now—perhaps
3S breathe POT   after a seizure).'

[Au ā rai-c-a **rawa**] e sō na taga.   'I was able to see some
1S PT see-TR-3S POT 3S some DEF bag   bags.' (*NV2*:46)

In these two examples, the ability is not innate, but acquired—often, recently acquired. Related to this last meaning is one added by PG (10/83): 'already':

Sā sau-mi **rawa**.   'It's already been paid.'
ASP pay-TR POT

yaqona tu-ki **rawa**   'kava already pounded'
kava pound-TR POT

18.6 LIMITATION (LIM): *WALE, BAU, BULU*

The marker *wale* after a verb signifies, first, a fruitless effort:

[E oga **wale**] na kōmiti.   'The committee was busy (to no
3S busy LIM DEF committee   effect).'

[E oca **wale**.]   'He tired himself without success.'
3S tired LIM

Wale also means 'free, idle':

[E curu **wale**.]   'She entered without paying.'
3S enter LIM

All these meanings seem somewhat adverbial in function.[6] *Wale* seems more like a marker in its use with another limiter, *gā*. The combination limits or restricts the meaning of the VP:

[E tolu **wale** gā.]   'There were only three.'
3S three LIM LIM

Bau (*gā*), less common than *wale gā*, seems to have the same meaning:

[E dua **bau**.]   'There was only one.'
3S one LIM

---

[6] This indeterminancy is another example of the hazy dividing line between verb and marker, verb and underived adverb, and compound verbs.

>   [E dua **bau** gā.]   'There was only one.'
>   3S one   LIM   LIM

Its use seems restricted to these expressions; *VV* lists *dua bau* as an idiom. *Bau* also occurs before the head; see §5.8.

Bulu has a similar meaning and distribution:

>   E vica   na i-sau [e dua **bulu**] na maile?   'What's the cost for
>   3S how-many DEF cost   3S one LIM   DEF mile   just one mile?'

>   Era kilā   tale gā ni sega [ni dua **bulu** gā] na vosa e   Viti.
>   3P know-it ITR LIM SUB not   SUB one LIM LIM DEF talk ABL Fiji
>   'They also knew that there wasn't just one language in Fiji.' (*SR* 20/4/82)

18.7 INCLUSION (INC): *KECE, TAUCOKO*

The markers in this category are more closely allied semantically with entities rather than actions/states. Thus, one would expect them to occur in the NP, rather than the VP. However, they do occur in the VP.

18.7.1 *Kece* 'all'

Kece indicates that all the referents of the subject or object participate in the action/state. Examples are:

>   ka [cabe **kece**] ki   vanua   'and all go up to the shore' (*NV*2:20)
>   CNJ climb INC   ABL land

>   Eda sega [ni   rawa-t-a   **kece**] na cakacaka.
>   1PI not SUB   able-TR-3S INC   DEF work
>   'We can't all do the work.' (*NL* 13/5/82)

When both subject and object are included, and both are greater than singular, *kece* could refer to either of them. For example, the following sentence is ambiguous:

>   [Era rai-ci   ira **kece**.]   'They all saw them/they saw them all.'
>   3P see-TR 3P INC

18.7.2 *Taucoko* 'wholly, completely'

Taucoko is similar to *kece* in meaning, but sometimes refers to the completeness of an entity rather than to each and every individual. For example:

>   [Damudamu **taucoko**] na   yago-na.   'Its body is completely red.'
>   red   INC   DEF body-3S   (*VV*:bō)

But *taucoko* can also be used like *kece*:

>   Na sega ni rawa ni vaka-tara-i   [m-odou na lako **taucoko**.]
>   FT not SUB able SUB CAU-hold-TR   SUB-2T FT go   INC
>   'It won't be possible to get it unless you all go.' (FMC61)

Taucoko can also be used as a verb:

>   Ia   ā sega [ni   mani **taucoko** sara] na ke-na vaka-dike-vi
>   CNJ PT not   SUB SEQ complete   INT   DEF PC-3S CAU-look-TR

sē vosa cava me vola-i.   'But choosing which language was to be
SUB talk what SUB write-TR   written wasn't completed.' (*SR* 20/4/82)

Usually, however, *taucoko* and *kece* are synonyms.

18.7.3 *Duadua* 'alone'

This reduplicated form of *dua* occupies a tentative place in this section of markers, for it might be classified as an underived adverb. But it does operate like the other members of this class:

*E ā lako **duadua**.*   'She went alone.'

Other reduplicated numerals (generally up to ten) can also be used in this position: for example, *ruarua* 'both', etc.

18.7.4 *Soti/sō* (intensifier)

Soti and its alternate, *sō*, have a somewhat limited distribution among VPs: they are used mainly with negatives.[7] Examples are:

*[E sega **soti**] ni vuli lēsoni vaka-dedē ko Vilive.*
3S not INT SUB learn lesson MAN-long PRP V
Vilive didn't study his lessons long at all (*FR3*:42)

*[E sega **sō**] ni kele yarayara na lori.*   'The truck didn't make
3S not INT SUB stop drag DEF truck   many stops.' (*NV4*:70)

The following examples show that *soti* can be used in sentences other than negative ones. Note, however, that it is used in NPs:

*[O cei **soti**] oyā?*   'Who in the world are they over
PRP who INT DEM:3   there?' (*FR3*:55)

*[A cavacava **sō**?]*   'What in the world is that?'
DEF what INT

Some of these forms are also treated as NP grammatical markers (CH 22).

18.8 INTENSIVE (INT): *SARA*

When *sara* follows an S1 verb, it serves as an intensifier:

*[E drēdrē **sara**.]*   'It's very difficult.'
3S hard INT

With an active verb, *sara* conveys the sense of immediate or purposeful action:

*[Ā talatala **sara** mai] o Tui Cakau.* 'Tui C sent (someone)
PT send INT DIR PRP *Tui* C   immediately.' (*SR* 4/20/82)

*Sava oti [sā tekivū lobaloba **sara**.]*
wash ASP ASP LIM squeeze INT
'After washing he immediately started milking.' (FR3:51)

---

[7] The actual use of *soti* belies Capell's explanation that it is a "particle modifying a negative."

With verbs referring to quotation, *sara* is used to show that the quotation given is exact, literal:

[Sā vakā **sara** nē][8]   'And said exactly the following'
ASP say-3s INT EMP   (Nawadra 1981:1)

ka [taro **sara**]   'and asked (explicitly, followed by
CNJ ask INT   direct quotation)' (Nawadra 81:2)

Sara has a similar meaning when used with *vei* 'where':[9]

[E   vei   **sara**?]   'Where, exactly?'
3S where INT

With *vaka* 'resemble', *sara* also has the meaning of 'exactly, very much':

Na dari [e vakā   **sara**] na i-bulibuli ni bēseni.
DEF *dari* 3S resemble-3S INT DEF NOM-form POS basin
The *dari* (pot) is very much like the shape of a basin.' (*NV3*:24)

It is used similarly in the following construction—an identifying VP:

Ka [ke-na dau **sara** tale gā.]   'And he is also quite an expert at it.'
CNJ PC-3S skill INT ITR LIM   (*NV3*:18)

When used with a series of verbs, the actions/states to which *sara* refers are not always discrete. That is, it is not clear that one is finished and another begins immediately. For example:

[Sā tubu **sara** na lovo] ia ni sā waqa ka caudre vinaka
ASP heated INT DEF oven CNJ SUB ASP burn CNJ ablaze good

   [sā coro-gi **sara**] na vuaka.
   ASP singe-TR INT DEF pig

'The oven is being heated, and when it's burning and well ablaze, the pig is hair-singed (*NV3*:31)

Note that these are all, in a sense, processes. The relationship among them is different from that which would use *qai*, for they are not in a sequence. Instead, the states or actions are concurrent, or at least overlapping. Another example:

Ni sā bulu oti na lovo, [eratou ā laki vei-sili-mi **sara**.]
SUB ASP buried ASP DEF oven 3T PT DIR GEN-bathe-TR INT
'When the *lovo* is covered, they go bathing (in a group).' (*NV3*:31)

[Ā ceka-t-a **sara**] na ke-na o Tui ka [vakā **sara**.]
PT untie-TR-3S INT DEF PC-3S PRP T CNJ say-3S INT
'T unwrapped his and said' (*NV4*:71)

Sara is also treated as an NP grammatical marker (CH 22).

---

[8] See §18.15.2 for a discussion of *nē*.

[9] *Vei* is usually described as a locative noun, not a verb. However, the phrase *e vei* often seems to function as a VP; for example, it can be preceded by the aspect marker *sā*.

18.9 ITERATION (ITR): *TALE*

Tale following a verb indicates that the action or similar circumstances are repeated:

*[E sā curu **tale**] e rua na mata-ni-i-vola vou.*
3S ASP enter ITR 3S two DEF letter new
'Two more new letters have been added (have entered).' (Geraghty 1982:5)

*[Ā wili-k-a **tale**] vaka-vica na talikaramu ko Mārica.*
PT read-TR-3S ITR MAN-how-many DEF telegram PRP M
'M read the telegram for the nth time.' (T74:41)

E ā volavola mada yani m-o lako mai, oti,
3S PT write INI DIR SUB-2S go DIR finish

  *[sā qai talikaramu **tale** yani] [m-o sā kua **tale**.]*
  ASP SEQ telegram ITR DIR SUB-2S ASP don't ITR
'She wrote there for you to come, then, after having done that, she
  telegrammed there for you not (in turn) to come.' (T74:42)

In this last example, note that *tale* is referring to actions that are not—strictly speaking—repeated. Instead, the *tale* emphasizes the irony of the contrasting circumstances.[10] Such a use of *tale* for contrast is common (PG 9/82):

*[Sā dramudranu **tale**]*   'He's being obnoxious (while
ASP insipid ITR   intending to be funny).'

Tale (and *tale gā*) are also treated as an NP grammatical marker (CH 22). For *tale gā*, see §18.13.1.

18.10 RESPECTFUL ADDRESS (RES): *SAKA*

Saka is a polite or chiefly vocative (direct address) not easily classified as either a marker or a root with restricted occurrence. We treat it with the VP markers because principally, it functions as part of the VP. Its position within the VP is definitely after the verb, but it does not have one fixed position. Milner (1972: 109) placed it "usually ... after *tū* and *tiko*,[11] but before *mada*." The qualifier "usually" is necessary; one of the following examples shows it before *tiko*. Some speakers say they always put it before *tū/tiko*.

The two examples that follow have been selected to show its repeated use in some direct quotations.[12] (Since *saka* is used to address persons of either sex. 'Sir' is used here merely as a convenient translation.)

*[Sā vinaka **saka**], [me ra kau-ti au **saka**] e sō na tūraga*
ASP good RES SUB 3P carried-TR 1S RES 3S some DEF chief

---

[10] TRN (5/82) pointed out that in one sense, *tale* is still referring to repeated actions, since telegramming is a form of *volavola* 'writing'.

[11] That is, *tū* and *tiko* as markers, not as main verbs.

[12] As a vocative, it cannot be used other than in direct quotation; it refers directly to the addressee.

ni mataka. [Au kune-a **saka** tiko] e dua na vū   ni   vesi levu
SUB morning 1S find-3S RES CNT 3S one DEF origin POS vesi big

   [e na rau-t-a   vaka-vinaka **saka**] me mai vatavata vaka-tūraga.
   3S FT suffice-TR-3S MAN-good   RES SUB DIR canoe   MAN-chief
'It would be good, sir, if some chiefs would take me tomorrow. I find, sir, a large *vesi* tree; it will serve well, sir, for a chiefly canoe (*FR5*:25)

[Au sa (se) bau talanoa **saka** mada yani] vei kemunī Ratū Na Mata
1S ASP   TEN tell   RES INI   DIR ABL 2P   Ratū Na Mata

sā vakā **saka** oqō:— [Keimami tiko **saka**] oqō   e Niu Kini
ASP like-3S RES DEM:1   1PX   stay RES DEM:1 ABL New Guinea

e   na vuku ni lotu. [Ia, keimami tiko vata **saka** gā] kei na
ABL DEF sake POS worship CNJ 1PX   stay CNC RES LIM CNJ DEF

no-da Matanitū   kaukaua Vaka-peritania ka [kemami sā dui   gū
PC-1PI government   strong British   CNJ 1PX   ASP IND eager

saka gā] e   na cakacaka keimami tiko ki-na me vinaka cake mai
RES   LIM ABL DEF work   1PX   stay ABL-3S SUB good   DIR DIR

na vanua oqō.
DEF land DEM:1

'I should like to tell a story, sir, to you, Ratū *Na Mata* (addressing the editor of the publication), to wit: We (plural exclusive) are staying, sir, here in New Guinea for the sake of Christianity. But we are staying sir, with our (plural inclusive) powerful British government, and we are all eager, sir, in the work we are doing to better this land.' (*FR6*:4)[13]

Saka is not confined to the VP. Note its use in an NP + NP sentence:

[Oqō **saka**] na niu   ni Toga.   'Here, sir, is the Tongan
DEM:1 RES   DEF coconut POS Tonga   coconut.' (*FR5*:14)

Saka is also used in the formal salutation in a letter, preceded by *i*—perhaps the accusative marker:

   Isaka.   'Dear Sir/Madam.'

18.11 CONTINUATIVE ASPECT (CNT): *TIKO, TŪ, KOTO, NŌ, TOKA, VOLI*

A number of markers after the verb are aspectual, in that they indicate the duration of the action/state. The most common of these are *tiko* and *tū*; *toka*, *koto* (and its synonym *nō*), and *voli* are rare.

18.11.1 *Tiko*

This marker is used to indicate temporary duration (see Milner 1972:29; confirmed by TRN):

---

[13] Each instance of *saka* was translated as 'sir' only to show the frequency of this marker in a particular kind of discourse.

```
E    na vei-sau         sā    na rawa [ni   yaco    tiko] e   na vosa
ABL  DEF REC-respond    ASP   FT able      SUB happen CNT   ABL DEF talk
```
'in the changes that will keep happening to the language' (*SR* 20/4/82)

```
[E    lako tiko] i    Suva.          'He's going to S.' (SR 20/4/82)
 3S   go   CNT  ABL   S
```

```
[Sā   vei-vuke  sara tale tiko gā]   vaka-levu na  matanitū
ASP   REC-help  INT  ITR  CNT  LIM   MAN-big   DEF government

   ki   na  rārā  ni   waqa-vuka mai Nadi.
   ABL  DEF field POS  airplane  ABL N
```
'The government has also greatly helped (and continues to do so) the airport at N.' (*NL* 13/5/82)

Note that none of these action/states is permanent; each is subject to change.

18.11.2 *Tū*

An action/state followed by the marker *tū* is more permanent:

```
[Sā   vaka-mata-ni-saisai tū]    na  sasaga.
ASP   spread              CNT    DEF strive
```
'The efforts were spread out in too many directions.' (*SR* 20/4/82)

```
Era dui vaka-yaga-tak-a gā   na   i-vola      [sā   vola-i   tū.]
3P  IND CAU-use-TR-3S   LIM  DEF  NOM-write   ASP   write-TR CNT
```
'They (individually) used the books that were written.' (*SR* 20/4/82)

```
ka   laki rai-ci  taci-na      [ni   sā   tau-vi-mate  levu  tū]
CNJ  DIR  see-TR  sibling-3S    SUB  ASP  infect-TR-ill big   CNT
```
'and go see her sister because she's very ill' (T74:41)

```
kē   ā   sega beka  [ni   tau-vi-mate  bībī   tū]   'if perhaps she hadn't been
SUB  PT  not  TEN    SUB  infect-TR-ill heavy  CNT  very ill' (T74:42)
```

Note particularly the last two examples, in which the seriousness of the disease is indicated by *tū*—that is, there are evidently no signs of improvement. This unchanging status is underscored by a sentence later in the discourse:

```
A    cava  [e   sā   bau tuku-n-a    tū]   na   no-na  vū-ni-wai?
DEF  what   3S  ASP  TEN tell-TR-3S  CNT   DEF  PC-3S  doctor
```
'What does her doctor say?' (T74:43)

This difference between *tiko* and *tū* can be illustrated by the following minimal pairs (supplied by PG, 7/82):

*tau-vi-mate **tiko***   'temporary illness'   *voli-taki **tiko***   'for sale at the moment'
*tau-vi-mate **tū***   'long illness'   *voli-taki **tū***   'always for sale'

18.11.3 *Toka*

Toka indicates a provisional, rather unfixed, approximate duration of an action or uncertain quality of a state. As examples of unfixed or uncertain duration:

Ratou vei-lewā -tak-a **toka***] ka masumasu-tak-a me tau mai*
3T REC-discuss-TR-3S CNT CNJ pray-TR-3S SUB fall DIR

na lewā vā-kalou.
DEF judgment MAN-god

'They "discussed around" (for an indeterminate length of time) and prayed that a heavenly decision would come.' (*SR* 20/4/82)

As an example of "approximate":

[*rau-t-a vitu* **toka***]* 'about seven' (*NV4*:69)
suffice-TR-3S seven CNT

However, note that *rauta* also conveys that meaning.

Milner (1972:91) and Churchward (1941:70) both gave examples of *toka* used with statives, with *toka* serving in an "adverbial" sense, meaning 'fairly':

[*Sā vinaka* **toka**.] 'It is fairly good.'

Thus, we can establish a three-way contrast among this marker and the previous two:[14]

Sā vinaka **tū**. 'It's definitely good (on a permanent basis).'
Sā vinaka **tiko**. 'It's good (for the time being).'

Toka can be used with suitable verbs of motion (PG 5/82):

E yabe **toka**. 'She was strolling along.'
E qiqi **toka**. 'It's rolling slowly.'

PG added that *toka* sometimes seems to imply that an action was done "easily, quietly, casually, or without strain." Because of this tone, the marker is often used in polite commands:

Kana **toka**. 'Carry on eating at your leisure.'

Often, the marker *toka* is associated with verbs that match the meaning of the root *toka*: 'hunker, squat'. For example, Milner (1972:91) noted its use with verbs related to sitting, such as *dabe* 'sit' and *kana* 'eat'. The following is an example:

[*ni ratou sā katalau* **toka***] e na mataka ni siga ka tara-v-a*
SUB 3T ASP breakfast CNT ABL DEF morning POS day REL follow-TR-3S

'When they were having breakfast on the morning of the next day' (*FR3*:43)

18.11.4 *Koto (nō)*

As described by Churchward and Milner, *koto* is used to indicate a continuing state that is related to the meaning of *koto* as a verb: 'lie down'. Thus, its use as a marker is "more or less coloured by [its] primary significance" (Churchward 1941:17):

ni dua [e tau-vi mate **koto***] mai na no-na vale*
SUB one 3S infect-TR ill CNT ABL DEF PC-3S house

'when one is at home ill' (*NV3*:13)

---

[14] Confirmed by TRN (5/82).

Milner (1972:91) noted an additional function: to indicate that something has come to a conclusion:

*Kē vakā [me de-i **koto** gā] na yavu   ni i-Taukei, ia me de-i*
SUB like-it SUB fix-TR CNT LIM DEF foundation POS owners CNJ SUB fix-TR

na ke-na vosa. 'If a foundation for the Fijians is to be firmly fixed,
DEF PC-3S talk   their language must be firmly fixed.' (*SR* 20/4/82)

Note here that the state itself has not come to an end, but the process of 'fixing the foundation' has ended with its completion.

18.11.4.1 *Nō*

Nō functions as a synonym of *koto*. It is used as a marker in SF (TRN 5/82) only after *koto*, when *koto* is used as a main verb meaning 'lie down':[15]

*[E koto **nō**.]*   'She was lying down.'
3S lie CNT

PG noted (5/82) that even *koto* is not widely used as a marker in Colloquial Fijian, although more formal and written Fijian uses it.

18.11.5 *Voli* 'roundabout'

The marker *voli* after a verb indicates that the activity took place here and there, or counter to the actor's original purpose.[16]

*[E gādē **voli**] o koya ni mai cakacaka.*
3S stroll CNT PRP 3S SUB DIR work
'He took a holiday when he had actually come to work.'

*[tiko **voli** e vale]*   'staying at home (without purpose)' (*FR3*:51)
stay CNT ABL house

*Sā dedē na no-dratou [tiko **voli**] na vei-luve-ni   oqō.*
ASP long DEF PC-3T   stay CNT DEF REC-offspring-TR DEM:1
'The family stayed around for a long time (FR3:55)

*[E tiko **voli** e vale.]*   'She's staying about the house (going from
3S stay CNT ABL house   place to place within the house).' (PG)

PG added (10/83) that a second function of *voli* is continuative, when the head of the VP is *tiko*. Thus *tiko voli* could also mean 'staying temporarily'.

---

[15] PG noted that the reason for using *nō* here might be to avoid the construction *koto koto, similar to avoiding *kina kina. See Geraghty 1976:516n.

[16] Thanks to TRN for the explanation. The term "continuative" is not quite satisfactory for the meaning of *voli*, but the marker seems to fit with the others in this class in terms of its position.

18.12 INITIATION (INI): *BEKA, MADA, BAGI*

These markers are labeled as "initiation" to reflect their function of making permissible such culturally disapproved acts as initiating an action, stating a fact flatly, or making an abrupt suggestion.

18.12.1 *Beka* (moderative)

Beka (moderative[17]) is used to avoid making a flat statement of fact or asking an abrupt question. It changes such a statement or question into a suggestion or proposal, subject to the hearer's approval. It can also add an element of doubt. The *VV* uses the descriptive phrases "something that is uncertain," "to lighten (soften) a question." Examples are:

> *[E   na qai vā-gasagasa-taki tale **beka**] na bula e   na cava?*
> ABL DEF SEQ CAU-enrich-TR   ITR INI   DEF life ABL DEF what
> 'Then what could life possibly be enriched with?' (*SR* 20/4/82)

> *[A   cava **beka**] na vu-na?*   'What might the reason be?'
> DEF what INI   DEF reason-3S   (*NL* 13/5/82)

When used with numerals, *beka* adds the meaning of 'approximate':

> *[e   na tini **beka**] na kaloko*   'about ten o'clock'
> ABL DEF ten INI   DEF clock

> *[e   rua-saga-vulu **beka**] na yabaki* 'about twenty years'
> ABL twenty   INI   DEF year

18.12.2 *Mada*

When used with imperatives (i.e., second person), *mada* adds an element of politeness, rather like the English *please*:

> *[M-o   kau-t-a   **mada** mai.]*   'Please bring it here.'
> SUB-2S carried-TR-3S INI   DIR

> *[Sogo-t-a   **mada**] na kātuba.* 'Please close the door.'
> closed-TR-3S   INI   DEF door

With a first person subject, *mada* as a marker is closer to its use (in some areas) as a root meaning 'precede, ahead'. Here, one might suggest that using *mada* is an apology for a culturally awkward action: setting oneself apart from the group by taking the initiative or making the first move. Thus, *mada* is often used in expressions of taking leave:

> *[Au se lako **mada**.]*   'I'm going (if you please).'
> 1S ASP go   INI

> *[Au se vaka-cegu **mada**.]*   'I'll excuse myself (if you please).'
> 1S ASP retire   INI

---

[17] This term is from Churchward 1941:52. Jeff Siegel pointed out (9/83) the dubitative and tentative meaning of *beka*.

Using *mada* with third person is rarer because of the semantic properties just described. But it can be used with the subjunctive:

*Wāwā. [Me bulu **mada**.]*   'Wait. Let it (the earth oven) be
wait   SUB buried INI   buried first.'

*ka vaka-masu-ti koya [me lako **mada** yani]* 'and pleaded with her to go
CNJ CAU-plead-TR 3S SUB go INI DIR   there' (T74:41)

The combination of the negative existential *sega* and *mada* has the idiomatic meaning of 'not even':

*Ka lē   levu [era sega **mada**] ni kilā   na vosa vaka-Viti.*
CNJ NUM big 3P not INI   SUB know-3S DEF talk MAN-Fiji
'And many of them didn't even know Fijian.' (Geraghty 1982:4)

PG (5/82) added a further meaning for *mada*: that it is also used when one says something that is contrary to the hearer's expectations.

18.12.3 *Bagi* (expectation)

Bagi, quaintly translated as 'forsooth' by Hazlewood and Capell, is used in both VPs and NPs. It reflects a desire on the part of the speaker to seek confirmation. For example, the context for the following sentence is that the addressee was expected to have gone to a wedding:

*[Ko ā sega **bagi**] ni lako yani e   na nō-drau vaka-mau.*
 2S PT not INI   SUB go   DIR ABL DEF PC-3D   wedding
'So you didn't go there to their wedding.' (T74:62)

*[O ā sega **bagi**] ni tiko ki-na.*   'You didn't stay there after all.'
 2S PT not INI   SUB stay ABL-3S

In comparison with most other markers, *bagi* seems rarely used. Therefore, it is difficult to fix its position exactly. But it does seem to be mutually exclusive with *beka* and *mada*; it occurs after *sara* and before *mai* and *yani*.

Bagi seems to be a conversational device—a tool used to return to old information, expressing interest or mild doubt, or asking for confirmation.

18.12.4 *Gona* 'aforementioned' (AFM)

Gona is another example of a conversational device. It refers to one particular instance of the general category just mentioned, and—in that sense—functions as a type of deixis. It is found in both VPs and NPs (see §22.1).

*[Dua **gona**] na siga, sā tuku-n-a   o   koya ...*
 one AFM   DEF day   ASP tell-TR-3S PRP 3S
'One (particular) day, he said ...' (Schütz and Komaitai 1971:111)

*[Sega tiko **gona**] ni macala vei au.*   'It still isn't clear to me.'
 not CNT AFM   SUB clear ABL 1S   (FMC61:51)

18.13 LIMITATION (LIM): *GĀ, LĀ*

The function of *gā* is to limit the extent of a general action/state to that of the verb involved. Thus, *gā* tends to focus attention on that particular action/state.

*[E kalougata **gā**] ni totolo na nei-tou coki i-sulu.*
  3S lucky   LIM SUB fast   DEF PC-1TX take-in clothes
'It was just lucky that our taking the clothes in was fast.' (*NV4*:3)

*[Ni oti **gā**] na katalau e na mataka ni siga Vakarauwai*
  SUB finish LIM DEF breakfast ABL DEF morning POS day Saturday
Just after breakfast on Saturday morning' (*NV4*:9)

In the last example, by focusing on *oti* 'finished', *gā* has the meaning 'just, immediately'.

*Ia [e sega **gā**] ni o koya sara.*   'But it wasn't exactly that'
CNJ 3S not LIM SUB PRP 3S   INT   (*SR* 20/4/82)

Here, *gā* focuses on the negative, *sega*.

*Ka [sā na vaka-levu cakacaka **gā**] kē ra dui taba-ki.*
CNJ ASP FT CAU-big   work   LIM SUB 3P IND print-TR
'But it would only increase the work if they were printed individually.' (*SR* 20/4/82)

18.13.1 *Gā* with other markers: *tale gā*, *wale gā*, and *mada gā*

Gā in combination with the markers *tale*, *wale*, and *mada* forms idioms that must be treated separately.

18.13.1.1 *Tale gā* 'also'

The compound marker *tale gā* is not equal to the sum of its parts. Note the following change of meaning:

*E lako **tale**.*   'He went again.'
*E lako **tale gā**.*   'He also went.'

If *tale gā* were not idiomatic, the *gā* in the second sentence would merely emphasize *lako tale*, or focus on it.

These two markers do not have to be contiguous. In the following examples, they are separated by another marker, *tū* (continuous), but still with the idiomatic meaning of "also":

*[ka tau-r-a **tale** tū **gā**] e dua na taga o Pita.*
  CNJ carry-TR-3S ITR CNT LIM 3S one DEF bag PRP P
'And P also carried a bag.' (*NV4*:70)

*[E ā kau-t-a cake **tale** tiko **gā**] e dua na me-na i-olo wai.*
  3S PT carry-TR-3S DIR ITR CNT LIM 3S one DEF PC-3S parcel water
'He was also carrying up there his parcel of water.' (*FR5*:23)

18.13.1.2 *Wale gā* 'only'

The phrase *wale gā* is idiomatic as well. *Wale*, described in §18.6, is more like an adverb than a grammatical marker. With *gā*, the construction functions as a limiter, translated as 'only, just':

*[se qai vula tini **wale-gā**]* 'who was just 10 months old'
ASP SEQ month ten LIM (*FR6*:5)

*[e dua **wale-gā**] na kā* 'just one thing' (T74:59)
3S one LIM DEF thing

As with *tale gā*, the two words need not be contiguous:

*[ni kau-t-a **wale** tiko **gā** yani]*
SUB carry-TR-3S LIM CNT LIM DIR
'that he was only carrying there' (*FR5*:20)

*ka ni ra kurabui-tak-a ni [cola-t-a **wale** tū **gā** yani]*
CNJ SUB 3P surprise-TR-3S SUB carry-TR-3S LIM CNT LIM DIR
'because they were surprised that he had only carried there' (*FR5*:21)

18.13.1.3 *Mada gā* 'just'

*[Me tou sā lako **mada gā**.]* 'Let's just go.'
SUB 1TI ASP go INI LIM

*[Eratou sā kana oti **mada gā**.]* 'They've just finished eating.'
3T ASP eat ASP INI LIM

18.13.2 *Lā*

This marker is an alternate to *gā*.

*[Au se qai kana oti **lā**.]* 'I've just finished eating.'
1S ASP SEQ eat ASP LIM

Speakers questioned thought *lā* was the same as *gā*; PG (7/82) agreed, but thought there were occasions on which one was more appropriate than the other. For example, he has never heard **tale lā* or **wale lā* (confirming, as Jeff Siegel (8/83) pointed out, the idiomatic status of *tale gā* and *wale gā*). Moreover, he noted that although *lā* is used fairly often in SF, it never is in Colloquial Fijian.

18.14 DIRECTION (DIR)

18.14.1 *Mai* (toward focal point)

The marker *mai* indicates literal or figurative movement toward a focal point, which is established by context, and which often changes within a discourse. For example, the focal point of the following sentence is the speaker:

*[Lako mada **mai**.]* 'Please come here (toward me).'
go INI DIR

In many contexts, however, the reference point shifts along with the narrative, particularly in the common narrative situation that includes only third person. In such a context, *mai* no longer centers on the speaker, but instead, on the *locus of the context*. Note the following examples:

18 Verb Phrase Markers after the Head

> *Erau lako tiko ki na i-teitei me na lau tale e sō na*
> 3D go CNT ABL DEF garden SUB DEF planted ITR 3S some DEF
>
> *mata ni dalo. [Erau na lesu tale **mai**] ni sā yakavi.*
> stem POS taro 3D FT return ITR DIR SUB ASP evening
>
> 'They're going to the garden so that the taro stems might be planted. They'll return in the afternoon-evening (literally, when it becomes evening).' (*NV2*:5)

Here, *mai* refers to a reference point that is vaguely established by the context: the point from which they set out. It is not connected at all with the speaker, who is entirely removed from this context.

> *[Era kaila-vak-a **mai**] e na vei-yasa ni koro ni sā laba*
> 3P shout-TR-3S DIR ABL DEF DIS-part POS village SUB ASP strike
>
> *na cagi [ka ni sā toro cake tiko gā **mai**] na ke-na kaukaua.*
> DEF wind CNJ SUB ASP move DIR CNT LIM DIR DEF PC-3S strength
>
> 'They shout it (hither) in all parts of the village that the storm is striking and that its strength is moving up.' (*NV2*:51)

In this context, neither *mai* is directed toward the narrator, but instead toward the village in general.

> *[ka votu **mai**] na yabaki vou*   'and the new year appears' (*NV3*:22)
> CNJ appear DIR DEF year new

In the following examples, *mai* represents figurative movement:

> *[Sā vaka-tū-loaloa **mai**] na vanua.*   'The land is darkening.' (*NV3*:22)
> ASP CAU-stand-dark DIR DEF land

> *Oqō e dau caka gā me bale-t-a [ni da sā galala **mai**] e na*
> DEM:1 3S HAB done LIM SUB because SUB 1PI ASP free DIR ABL DEF
>
> *no-da cakacaka e na siga.*   'This is done (visiting in the evening)
> PC-1PI work ABL DEF day   because we become free from our
>   day's work.' (*NV3*:14)

Here, *mai* seems to give the idea of becoming free—rather like a state that approaches gradually.

> *[E kau **mai**] [na yaca-na e na rorogo ni domo ni no-na tagi.*
> 3S carried DIR DEF name-3S ABL DEF sound POS voice POS PC-3S cry
>
> 'It gets its name (is carried hither) from the sound of its cry.' (*NV3*:21)

With some verbs, the motion implied by *mai* is not concurrent with that of the main verb, but takes place before or after it:

> *[M-o voli-a **mai**.]*   'Buy it (and bring it back).'
> SUB-2S buy-3S DIR

[E ā kele **mai**] ki Suva e na mācawa sā oti e dua
3S PT anchor DIR ABL Suva ABL DEF week ASP finished 3S one

na melisitima levu. 'There came to anchor at Suva last week a large
DEF ship big ocean liner.' (*NV2*:45)

With a stative, the meaning of postverbal *mai* is even further removed from the sense of literal movement:

[Au sā oca **mai**], au sā via lesu tale ki vale.
1S ASP tired DIR 1S ASP DES return ITR ABL house
'I've become tired; I want to go home.' (*NV3*:41)

Here, the meaning that *mai* imparts is that the state has been reached. The phrase could be translated: "I've become tired."

Sā urouro [ka levulevu **mai**] na geti. 'The pig has become fat
ASP fat CNJ big DIR DEF pig and big.' (*NV3*:37)

Mai, like other markers occurring after the verb, comes after the modifier in the *gunu-yaqona* construction (see §12.4):

E ā tala-i au ko Nānā [me-u laki cavu tavioka **mai**.]
3S PT send-TR 1S PRP Mother SUB-1S DIR pull tapioka DIR
'Mother sent me to go pull up tavioka (and bring it back).' (*NV2*:29)

and also after proper objects:

[Eratou na biu-ti Ositerelia **mai**] e na i-ka-lima.
3T FT left-TR Australia DIR ABL DEF fifth
'They (trial) will leave Australia (and come here) on the fifth.' (Milner 1972:60)

In the following sentences, note the juxtaposition of *mai* and *ki*:

ka ra sā vōleka [ni uru **mai**] ki vanua.
CNJ 3P ASP near SUB arrive DIR ABL land
'and they are nearly approaching land' (*NV2*:62)

[E ā kele **mai**] ki Suva. 'It came to anchor at Suva.' (*NV2*:45)
3S PT anchor DIR ABL Suva

18.14.2 *Yani* (toward a point established by context)

The marker *yani* establishes literal or figurative movement toward a point that has been mentioned, or is otherwise known to both speaker and hearer. In the following example (*NV3*: 13–14), note how the reference point for *yani* (and *mai* as well) shifts as the locus of the story changes:

Ni dua e tauvi-mate koto mai na no-na vale, [era dau kau kākana
SUB one 3S ill CNT ABL DEF PC-3S house 3P HAB carried food

yani] ko ira era laki vei-siko. 'When a person is at home ill, those people
DIR PRP 3P 3P DIR REC-visit who go "ritual visiting" take food there.'

Here, the locus of context for *yani* is the place that has just been mentioned.[18]
Further examples are:

*E rawa [ni-u   bau toma-ni   kemudou tū   **yani**?]*
3S able SUB-1S TEN accompany-TR 2T   CNT DIR
'May I go with the three of you there?' (*NV3*:15)

*Na no-dra qele na vei-mataqali   vakā-oqō,   [e sā sukā   **yani**] me*
DEF POS   land DEF DIS-(kin unit) MAN-DEM:1 3S ASP disperse-3S DIR SUB

   māroro-y-a na   matanitū.   'The land of such a mataqali reverts
   care-TR-3S DEF government   to the government's keeping.' (*NV3*:22)

In its figurative use, *yani* is often used in the sense of 'returning' answers to questions:

*[Erau sau-m-a   sara **yani**] na vei-tavaleni.* 'The two cousins answered
   3D answer-TR-3S INT DIR   DEF REC-cousin   back.' (*NV3*:15)

Here, the locus of *yani* is the previous question. In fact, *yani* is often used repeatedly in reporting conversations. Note the following:

"E na mārau beka o Ālisi ni-u   sā lako mai?" [ā   taro yani] ko Mārica.
 3S FT happy INI PRP A   SUB-1S ASP go DIR   PT ask DIR   PRP M

*"O! io! Na cava sara mada [e volā   **yani**?]" [E ā sau-m-a*
 oh yes DEF what INT INI   3S write-3S DIR   3S PT answer-TR-3S

***yani**] ko Leone. "O! e ā talikaramu gā yani me-u kua ni   lako mai,"*
 DIR   PRP L   oh 3S PT telegram LIM DIR SUB-1S not SUB go DIR

*[ā kaya **yani**] ko   Mārica.*
 PT say DIR   PRP M

"Will A be pleased that I've come?" asked M. "Oh, yes. Just what exactly
   did she write you?" L answered back. "Oh, she wired me not to come,"
   M said back.

One example, however, of *yani* without a reference point established by context is the opening line in a story:

*[Ni   drodro **yani**] na uciwai.*   'When the river flows forth' (*FR5*:22)
 SUB flow   DIR   DEF river

But we might argue that it is known that the destination of all rivers is the sea. This kind of reference point is one that is established by general knowledge. A sentence further on in the first paragraph strengthens such an argument:

Ni sā oti   na cegu ni wai   e   na tobu koyā sā qai drodro
SUB ASP finish DEF rest POS water ABL DEF pool DEM:3 ASP SEQ flow

   *sobu **yani** e   na ke-na i-drodrodro.*
   DIR DIR   ABL DEF PC-3S course
'After the water rests in that pool, it then flows down in its course.'
(*FR5*:22)

---

[18] The *mai* in this sentence does not belong to the VP but to the following NP.

18.14.3 Discussion: The reference point for VP directional markers

Mai and *yani* have traditionally been described as speaker-oriented.[19] One is tempted to label such a statement as translation analysis—moreover, translation out of context. In the following examples (Milner 1972:29), the translations show a simple opposition: toward the speaker and away from the speaker:

| *Erau lako **mai**.* | 'They (dual) come.' |
| *Erau lako **yani**.* | 'They (dual) go.' |

However, the second statement makes no sense out of context, for *yani*—as the discussion above shows—refers to a specific place.

18.15 AFFIRMATION/NEGATION[20]

18.15.1 *Lī* 'really?' (AFF)

Cammack (1962:66) noted that *lī* "often implies expectation of a negative answer."

*E dina **lī** ni ko ā naki-t-a mo vaka-mate-i tamamu?*
3S true AFF SUB 2S PT intend-TR-3S SUB-2S CAU-die-TR father-2S
'Is it really true that you did mean to kill your father?'

*A cava **lī** ko ā sega ki-na ni tuku-n-a vei au?*
DEF what AFF 2S PT not ABL-2S SUB tell-TR-3S ABL 1S
'Why really, did you not tell me?'

| *E lasu **lī**?* | 'Is it really false?' |
| 3S lie AFF | |

| *E sā sava oti **lī**?* | 'Has it really been washed?' |
| 3S ASP clean ASP AFF | |

18.15.2 *Nē* 'is it not?'

This marker anticipates a 'yes' answer.

| *O na lako **nē**?* | 'You'll go, won't you?' (Capell 1941:153) |
| 2S FUT go AFF | |

Cammack (1962:66) referred to *nē* as "quotative" as well, noting that it occurred in the set phrase *vakā oqō nē* 'to speak thus':

*e ā vakā oqō **nē** na kā e kaya ko Rusiate, "...*
3S PT say-it DEM:1 AFF DEF thing 3S say PRP R
'Rusiate said something to this effect, " ..."'

18.15.3 *Ē* Sentence-final affirmation

| *O na lako tale gā i Nausori, **ē**?* | 'You're also going to Nausori, |
| 2S FUT go ITR INT DIR N AFF | aren't you?' (Cammack 1962:67) |

---

[19] For example, Churchward 1941:53: "*mai*: towards the speaker ... *yani*: away from the speaker or towards the person spoken to ..." Milner (1972:29: "*Mai* and *yani* are used from the point of view of the speaker."

[20] These markers are also treated in CH 31 as sentence modifiers.

Section III: NOUN PHRASES

Nouns have three properties, viz: Gender, Number and Case ...

A grammar of the Feejeean language
David Cargill, 1839

Nouns, which are names of all natural objects, celestial and terrestrial, as the names of the heavenly bodies, trees, animals, and natural productions generally, are mostly primitive or underived words. As, a tamata, a man; a waqa, a canoe ...

But the verbs are the most fruitful source of nouns in the Fijian. Almost all nouns which express *actions*, *agents*, *and instruments*, are derived from verbs. . .

To nouns belong the properties of *genders*, *numbers*, and *cases*.

A compendious grammar of the Feejeean language ...
David Hazlewood, 1872

INTERIOR, VITI LEVU, JULY 1961. ©AJS

19 THE NOUN PHRASE: SEMANTICS AND CLASSIFICATION

19.1 THE SEMANTIC FUNCTION OF THE NP

At the beginning of CH 2, it was pointed out that many Fijian sentences consist of a VP alone.[1] The reason they can do so is that a VP contains elements that refer not only to an action/state, but also to the actor and/or goal related to it (i.e., the subject and the object). For example, in the VP

Au ā kaba.   'I climbed.'
1S PT climb

au refers to the actor, and *kaba* refers to the action/state. In grammatical terms, *au* functions as the subject, and *kaba* as the verb.

Note that the sentence *Au ā kaba* is complete in itself, for it is clear that *au* refers to the speaker and no one else. Therefore, no further clarification is necessary. Such is usually the case when the subject refers to the speaker or the addressee alone (in grammatical terms, first person singular or second person singular). However, when the subject refers to an entity or entities other than those just mentioned, the sentence is grammatically complete, but not semantically so—at least, not on its own. Note the following sentence, similar to the one above:

E ā kaba.   'He/she/it climbed.'
3S PT climb

Although this sentence is grammatically complete in itself, it seems to have been taken out of a context that might have clarified the referent of *e*. Such clarification can take place within the sentence itself with a reference to a specific entity (indicated by boldface and brackets):

E ā kaba [na gone].   'The child climbed.'
3S PT climb DEF child

In this example, the subject refers to the actor. As previous chapters showed, subjects with S1 or S2 verbs, simple or derived, refer to the goal.

---

[1] This stricture automatically excludes sentences that are composed of juxtaposed NPs. Sentences that are VPs of the identifying type should also be excluded, unless we can— for the nonce—consider that identification is an action/state.

In a transitive construction, a simple VP can refer to two entities: the actor and the goal. Expanding the original VP produces this sentence:

E ā kaba-t-a.   'He/she/it climbed it.'
3S PT climb-TR-3S

Again, although this sentence is grammatically complete, it seems to have been taken out of a context that might have clarified the referent of *-a*. And as before, the situation can be clarified within the sentence by adding a reference to a specific entity:

E ā kaba-t-a [na vuniniu] [na gone].
3S PT climb-TR-3S DEF coconut tree DEF child
'The child climbed the coconut tree.'

In the examples above, the NPs add information about the referent of the object and the subject, respectively.

An NP can also clarify other grammatical markers. For example:

E lako ki-na.   'He went there.'
3S go ABL-3S

I vei?   'Where?'
ABL where

*I **na Bose ni Yasana**.*   'To the Provincial Council.'
ABL DEF meeting POS province

In this short discourse, *na Bose ni Yasana* gives more information about *-na* (third person singular).

TABLE 19.1 SEMANTIC FUNCTIONS OF NPs[2]

1	ACTOR	who or what is performing the action
2	CAUSE	an actor who or which causes another actor to perform an action
3	DIRECT GOAL	the entity directly affected by the action/state
4	INDIRECT GOAL	the recipient of an entity given, sent, etc.
5	LOCATION 1	destination for an entity in motion
6	LOCATION 2	area (time or space) for action/state
7	INSTRUMENT	entity (other than actor) that facilitates an action
8	ACCOMPANIMENT	something or someone present, but not participating in the action/state
9	REASON	motivating force behind the action/state

---

[2] It should be emphasized that these are semantic, not grammatical, terms. Nor is the list meant to be closed. It was compiled after examining the semantic role of the grammatical subject, of different grammatical objects (distinguished by the varying transitive suffixes), and of unmarked and marked NPs.

From a semantic point of view, then, an NP adds information about such entities, and others, that are involved in the situation that is being discussed. Such entities can be classified according to how they relate to the action/state that the verb refers to. Table 19:1 above shows some semantic functions that an NP can fulfill with respect to the verb.

The following examples illustrate the types of entities listed in the table (the NPs are in boldface and any element in the sentence that it specifies is underlined):

1. ACTOR

*Eratou moce tiko **na gone**.* 'The children were sleeping (lit., the few
3T sleep CNT DEF child   of them were sleeping–the children).'

2. CAUSE

E̲ vā-kani-a o Tai. 'T fed it (lit., she caused it to eat–T).'
3S CAU-EAT-3S PRP T

3. DIRECT GOAL

*Au kaba-t-a̲ **na vū-ni-niu**.* 'I climbed the coconut tree (lit., I
1S climb-TR-3S DEF coconut-tree   climbed it–the coconut tree).'

4. INDIRECT GOAL

*E soli-a **vei Pita**.* 'He gave it to P.'
3S give-3S ABL P

5. LOCATION 1

*Erau soko **i cakau**.* 'The two of them sailed toward the reef.'
3D sail ABL reef

6. LOCATION 2

*E tiko **mai Bā**.* 'She stays in B.'
3S stay ABL B

7. INSTRUMENT

*E caka e **na kau**.* 'It's made of wood.'
3S made ABL DEF wood

8. ACCOMPANIMENT

*E kaba-tak-a̲ **na matau**.* 'He climbed with the axe.'
3S climb-TR-3S DEF axe

9. REASON

*E rarawa-tak-a̲ **na no-na via-kana**.* 'She's sad because of her hunger.'
3S sad-TR-3S   DEF PC-3S DES-eat

Although only one example is given for each type, a particular semantic role is not always realized grammatically in the same way. For example, reason is sometimes expressed by the grammatical object, at other times by an oblique NP.

19.2 NOUN AND NP CLASSIFICATION

A noun can be classified as either:

    INTEGRAL or PARTITIVE

An NP can be classified according to two oppositions—as either:

    COMMON or PROPER   PRIMARY or SECONDARY

19.2.1 Integral and partitive nouns

An integral noun is one whose referent does not depend on a relationship with another entity for its existence. Examples are *vale* 'house', *tamata* 'person', *ika* 'fish', and *Seru* (personal name).

In contrast, a PARTITIVE noun refers to an entity that exists only as a part of a larger entity. For example, *tina-* 'mother' exists only as a part of the mother-offspring relationship. *Liga-* 'hand' exists only as a part of the body. *Dela-* 'top' also exists only as a part of something. These three examples illustrate three major semantic categories of partitive nouns: kin terms, body parts, and parts of a whole.

Most partitive nouns take suffix or a *ni* or *i* phrase in their relational use. Thus, one would not say:

**E yaco mai na tama.*	*'The father arrived.'

but instead:

*E yaco mai na tama-**na**.*	'His father arrived.'
*E yaco mai na tama **ni** gone.*	'The child's father arrived.'
*E yaco mai na tama **i** Seru.*	'S's father arrived.'

The following context (with the picture, adapted from *NV1*:9) shows the two types of nouns referring to the same entity:

Oqō na tagane.	'This is a man.'
E taci i tama-qu.	'He's my father's younger brother.'

Here, *tagane* 'male' is an integral noun—that is, it can stand alone. But both *taci* and *tama* are partitive nouns. In each case, the larger entity (here, a kin relationship) must be referred to. First, *taci* is related to the other participant in the younger-older brother relationship by the marker *i*. Next, *tama* is related to the other participant in the father-offspring relationship by the possessive person-number suffix *-qu*.

19.2.2 Common vs. proper

A common noun is a word that refers to an entity; a proper noun is the given name of a person or place. For example, *gone* 'child' is usually a common noun; *Apenisa*, the child's name, is usually a proper noun.[3]

In order to examine the semantics of naming, we need to make a basic assertion: the name of something differs from the word for it. For people and places, the word is often obscure or not specific enough. Thus, naming is a way to be specific about people and places.[4]

19.2.2.1 Place names

In Fijian, the common nouns that are used in phrases referring to location are relative, not specific. For example, with the vertical dimension, the following nouns, among others, are used:

cake	'up (from point of reference)'
rā	'down (from point of reference)'
dela-na	'its top'
ruku-na	'space under it'

Similarly, the common nouns referring to horizontal space are ranged around a reference point:

e liu 'ahead'

imawī 'left' —REFERENCE POINT— *imatau* 'right'

e muri 'behind'

With respect to motion, *mai* and *yani* are toward and away from a reference point; *cake* and *rā* are toward generally opposite points on an island (PG, 3/82).

Points along the vertical dimension seem to have remained unnamed, but naming places positioned in a horizontal plane[5] is the most convenient way to refer to specific locations or areas on the globe's surface without using quantita-

---

[3] Charles F. Hockett (1958:232) considered that the categories of "common" and "proper" in Fijian constituted a gender system. However, because his knowledge of the language was limited to written grammars, this classification violated his main condition for a gender system (stated elsewhere)—that it "must be exhaustive and must not involve extensive intersection: that is, every noun must belong to one of the classes, and very few can belong to more than one." (E.g., a number of personal names in Fijian honor notable events at the time of a child's birth.) Later (§40.11), we will see a similar mistake—Milner's characterization of certain elements in the possessive system as reflecting gender.

[4] The entity "person" and the entity "place" each consist of an extremely large number of individual members. The ones that are important to the speakers of a language are individually named. Sometimes other entities are given the same special attention: individual animals that are important to people are often given names.

[5] Usually *on* the earth's surface, but *o Bulu* is the name of a subterranean mythological location. *Lomālagi* refers to 'Heaven'.

tive means.[6] Place names cover a range from general to specific. They can be as general as

o Viti   'Fiji'

but also more specific as well, using names from the hierarchy of administrative divisions or that of kin units:[7]

o Lau   'the Lau group of islands'
na yasana o Bā   'Bā Province'
na tikina o Tavua   'Tavua *Tikina*'

19.2.2.2 Personal names

There are two types of personal names in Fijian. The first is semantically specific only with respect to person and number, and the inclusive-exclusive distinction. The term "pronoun" is usually used for this class. Examples are:

o yau   'I'
o ira   'they (plural)'

The second type is semantically specific, at least to the extent that one's full name is usually unique in a community, even if one's given name or family name isn't. Examples are:

o Jone   'Jone'
o Joeli Bulu 'Joeli Bulu'
o Bera   'Bera'

If there is still some ambiguity as to the referent, these names can be specified by giving further information—such as location, family ties, occupation, characteristic features, etc.

19.2.3 Primary vs. secondary NPs

A primary NP is one that is limited to certain functions. For example, the NP *na gone* 'the child' may serve as one of the following:

1. A specified subject, object, or possessor (see CH 26)

*Sā moce **na gone**.*   'He is asleep (now)—the child.'
*E rai-c-a **na gone**.*   'She saw him—the child.'
*na no-dra qito **na gone***   'their (plural) playing—the children'

2. The interior of a secondary phrase

(*mai* (***na vale***))   'from the house'

---

[6] Using latitudinal and longitudinal figures would be a quantitative way to refer to location, rather like temperature readings for *hot* vs. *cold*, or hertz figures for high vs. low pitch.

[7] At the smaller levels, such as *yavusa*, *tikina*, *itokatoka*, and *mataqali*, the terms are primarily names for groups of people. However, in a society with strong kin ties and relatively permanent residences, a particular group of people is often associated with a particular place.

Note that the functions of these primary NPs cannot be determined out of context.

A SECONDARY NP is one marked for functions beyond those just listed.[8] For example, note the following phrases:

mai na vale	(ablative)	'from the house'
i na koro	(ablative)	'to the village'
kei Jone	(comitative)	'with J'
i Tē	(vocative)	'oh, T'

For these NPs, their function is identified by the form of the phrase itself—specifically, by the markers that begin each phrase.

Thus, the functions of a primary NP are of two main types: to specify certain grammatical forms that are identified as to person and number, but no further, and to serve as the interior of a layered phrase that is marked for an ablative or other function.

To show the interrelationships between primary and secondary NPs, we move to a more complicated example. In this example, NPs are underlined, the multiple lines showing layering of NPs.

'The three were playing in the shade of a banyan tree—Wati, Marama, and Ratava.' (*NV2*:91)

> The three were playing
> *Eratou ā vakatatalo tiko*
>
> in the shade of a banyan   Wati, Marama, and Ratava
> *e na ruku ni vū ni baka   ko Wati, Marama, kei Ratava*
> 1_____   5_____
>   2_____   6___
>   3_____
>   4_____

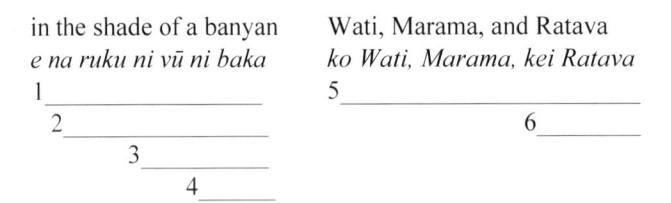

The NPs are as follows (P = primary; S = secondary):

1. S. An ablative phrase. Its function is to modify the verb.
2. P. This phrase serves as the interior of #1.
3. S. An attributive phrase. Its function is to modify *ruku*.
4. S. An attributive phrase. Its function is to modify *vū*.
5. P. This phrase specifies the subject *eratou*.
6. S. A comitative phrase. Its function is to show an accompanying entity: *Ratava*.

(PG noted (11/83) that each of these names would normally be preceded by *o* (rather than *ko*, which appears only in a more formal written style), and that marking the last with *kei* was optional.)

---

[8] These phrases could also be called OBLIQUE.

19.3 SEMANTIC AND GRAMMATICAL MISMATCHES

In other sections of this grammar, we have seen that semantic classes and grammatical classes do not always coincide. Proper nouns (a grammatical term) and names (a semantic term) constitute another instance of such a mismatch. The area in question is personal names vs. place names. They pattern alike in their occurrence after *o*; they pattern differently in how they occur after locative markers. Specifically, only common nouns or place names occur after *e*, *mai*, and *i*.

Note also a slight difference in "number." The nonsingular members of the set of proper nouns, such as *o ira*, *o iratou*, etc., refer more often to people than to places, but places are not totally excluded.

Similar semantic and grammatical mismatches hold for the integral-partitive opposition. For example, there are a number of terms for body parts that do not take suffixed possessive markers. For example, *vicovico* 'navel', *itaukuku* 'fingernail'. Geraghty has noted (1983) that such terms as *itau* 'friend' as well do not take the expected suffixes.

19.4 THE STRUCTURE OF THE BASIC NP

A BASIC NP is defined in terms of three items:

1. An obligatory phrase head, preceded by
2. an optional function marker and/or an article, and/or followed by
3. optional grammatical modifiers, indicating limitation, exclusion, etc.

The phrase head is either a noun or a form used as a noun. The criteria used to determine such a part-of-speech classification are somewhat loose.

A noun is a form that occurs *most often* after an article or one of the secondary function markers, and *least often* in a VP.[9] Semantically, it refers to an entity rather than an action/state. Formally, it occurs in certain morphological environments, such as with the prefixes *i-*, *vei-*, *dui-*; or before the suffixes *-qu*, *-mu*, etc.[10]

An article is a marker that simply identifies an NP as definite-common or proper. It does not designate the function of an NP. There are only two articles in Fijian; both are illustrated above: *na* and *o*.

A function marker, on the other hand, labels the syntactic function of an NP. The function markers in the phrases above are *vei*, *i*, and *mai*. A complete list appears in CH 21.

A grammatical modifier limits or expands the extent of the referent. Examples are *kece* 'all', *wale* 'only', and *gā* (limiter).

Affixes, treated in CH 23 and 24, are treated as part of the noun itself and not as part of its periphery.

---

[9] However, indefinite identifying sentences (§2.1.4.1) are common.

[10] For a more detailed discussion of word classification—particularly semantic, formal, and functional criteria—see Schütz 1975.

Any other element within an NP, such as an attribute, is treated as the result of an OPERATION (section 4). Therefore, it lies outside the basic phrase.

Examples of basic NPs are:

1. *na waqa*	'the boat'	6. *mai na waqa*	'on the boat'
2. *na vale*	'the house'	7. *i vale*	'homeward'
3. *o Esiteri*	'E'	8. *mai waqa*	'on board'
4. *vei Esiteri*	'to E'	9. *na motokā tale gā*	'the car as well'
5. *i na vale*	'to the house'		

The examples above illustrate the rather complex relationship between articles and function markers: one of them must be present in an NP.[11] That is, in normal speech there are no NPs like *vale* or *waqa*.

The examples also show that layering is possible. For example, *na vale* can serve not only as an NP itself, but also as the interior of a marked phrase: *i na vale*.

19.5 INTERROGATIVE NOUNS

19.5.1 *Cava* 'what?'

Cava 'what' occurs after the definite noun marker *(n)a*:

*A **cava** qō?*   'What's this (by me)?'

It can also occur after a noun it modifies:

*Na mataqali vūnikau **cava** beka oqo?*   'What kind of tree is this, please?'

19.5.2 *Cei* 'who?'

Parallel to the distribution of *cava*, *cei* occurs after the proper noun marker *o*:

*O **cei** beka na yacamunī?*   'What is your name, please?'
*O **cei** oyā?*   'Who's that (over there)?'

Note that in its use as a proper noun substitute, it can also refer to a place:

*O **cei** nomu koro?*   'What (lit., who) is your village('s name)? (*VV*)

---

[11] An apparent exception is a proper noun that serves as an object. However, there are two ways to treat this exception. First, an implicit solution is to include such nouns in the set of grammatical objects. Next, there is evidence for a suppressed *i* accusative marker before such nouns in that position. Thus, in the deeper structure, a proper noun in that position would also be marked for function.

20 NP ARTICLES

Nouns are generally preceded by one (or both) of two kinds of markers: (1) ARTICLES, which mark the distinctions PROPER and COMMON / DEFINITE; and (2) FUNCTION markers. This chapter deals with only the first type: articles.

20.1 *O*: PROPER ARTICLE

In the previous chapter, we discussed the semantic category called NAMES.[1] Names are represented in the grammar by PROPER NPs, which are marked by the article *o*.[2]

There are two classes of proper NPs:

1. The name of a specific person or place. E.g.:

o Mere	'Mere (personal name)'
o Semesa	'Semesa (personal name)'
o Suva	'Suva (place name)'
o Navitilevu	'Navitilevu (place name)'

Note that although certain nouns—such as *tamata* 'person', *yalewa* 'female', *tagane* 'male', *itau* 'friend', and *gone* 'child'—refer to people, they are not *names* of people. Therefore, they are not proper nouns.

2. A combination of morphemes indicating person and number, and—with *o*—constituting a separate phrase. See table 20.1

20.1.1 Proper nouns as part of the VP

When a proper NP specifies a grammatical subject, it appears in its full form—that is, with *o*:

---

[1] This simple definition has to be expanded somewhat to include things other than persons and places. (1) Some entities outside this category, such as pets and organizations. The latter must be investigated further, but it is my impression that organizations, in spite of the conventions of English capitalization adopted into Fijian, are definite. For example, *na* Fiji Times, etc. (2) Others are counted as individual entities in the grammatical organization of the VP, like nonhuman concepts that are referred to by nonsingular subjects or objects.

[2] An alternate *ko* often appears in written material.

*Sā vaka-yakavi tiko o **Jone**.*   'J is having supper.' (*FR1*:12)³
ASP MAN-evening CNT PRP J

The NP in this form can be fronted for emphasis:

***O Jone**, sā vaka-yakavi tiko.*   'As for J, he's having supper.'

However, when a proper noun specifies the object, the NP occurs without the proper article and fits in with the set of grammatical objects:

*E ā rai-ci **Paula**.*   'She saw P.'
3S PT see-TR P

*E ā rai-ci **au**.*   'She saw me.'

Thus, *-a*, the usual third person singular object, does not occur in addition to the proper NP.

As evidence that the proper NP is an integral part of the VP when it specifies the object, note that postverbal markers follow it, rather than the verb:

*Rai-ci **Jone** tiko.*   'Keep looking at J.'
see-TR J   CNT

*Rai-ci **Jone** mada*   'Look at J (please).'
see-TR J   INI

When a feature, such as fronting, disrupts this contiguous placement of verb and proper noun, the proper article is used and either the third person singular object *-a* reappears:

***O Jone**, au rai-c-a.*   'As for J, I saw him.'
PRP J   1S see-TR-3S

or the proper pronominal form *koya* serves as the object:

***O Jone**, au rai-ci koya.*   'As for J, I saw him.'
PRP J   1S see-TR 3S

20.1.2 *I*: Proper object marker

The *o* phrases above appear in this general section on unmarked NPs because their function is not indicated. But related to the section immediately above is i_2, a proper object marker that seems to be a relic of an earlier system. This is an example:

I cei mada yā?   'Who was it?'
PRP who INI DEM:3

However, since an *i* phrase *is* marked for function, it is treated in §21.3.

20.1.3 Proper pronouns specifying subjects

Table 1 shows the set of proper pronoun NPs that specify a subject. Note that they are nearly identical to grammatical subjects (CH 4, table 4.1). As specified subjects (or objects), they do not add any semantic information, but their func-

---

³ *Ko* has been replaced by *o*.

tion could be vaguely labeled as emphasis. Milner (1972:99) noted that this set corresponded to English reflexives, giving this example:

*Au sā cakava **ko iau**.* 'I did it myself.'

However, for this particular gloss, 'myself' is not a reflexive; the function could better be described as emphasis.

TABLE 20.1: PROPER PRONOUNS

	First person exclusive	First person inclusive	Second person	Third person
Singular	*o yau*	—	*o iko*	*o koya*
Dual	*o keirau*[4]	*o kēdaru*	*o kemudrau*	*o rau*
Trial	*o keitou*	*o kedatou*	*o kemudou*	*o iratou*
Plural	*o keimami*	*o keda*	*o kemunī*	*o ira*

20.1.4 Proper pronouns specifying objects

As noted in §20.1.1, in this construction, the pronominal NP appears as the grammatical object itself, without the *o* marker. Therefore, the set of NPs nearly corresponds to object pronouns (CH 17).[5]

20.1.5 Proper NPs in a special use beyond personal names

As the discussion in §4.5 showed, although a person-number marker used as a subject or an object generally refer to a person, it sometimes refers to another entity when there is a need to treat it as an individual. The same situation holds for proper NPs. In the following example, both the specified subject NP and the subject—in that order—appear in boldface:

O	***iratou***	*oqori,*	***eratou***	*raba-i-lelevu.*	'Those (just listed) are wide.'
PRP	3T	DEM:2	3T	wide	(*NV2*:71)

The larger context shows that *o iratou* refers to the different types of *masi* 'tapa' listed in the preceding sentence. Evidently, this nonhuman entity is given proper NP status here because there is a need to draw attention to a specific number of types.

20.2 *NA*: COMMON/DEFINITE ARTICLE

In Fijian, definiteness is a grammatical category that operates on common NPs.[6] Formally, it is manifested by the article *na* before the noun, as *na vale* 'house' or *na ulu ni vanua* 'mountain (lit., head of land)'. Thus, the presence of *na* is the formal criterion for definiteness.

---

[4] Milner's table (1972:99) shows an optional *i* before the head in all the nonsingular forms in first and second person. He noted (p. 100) that not all speakers use it.

[5] The first and third person singular forms differ in the two sets.

[6] As opposed to a proper NP, which is already semantically definite in that it refers to a specific person or place.

Semantically, one can relate the occurrence of *na* to the notion of old information vs. new information: that is, what the hearer knows or doesn't know about the topic of conversation.

From this point of view, there are two types of definiteness that are—in a sense—automatic, for in certain constructions, NPs are always definite. These types are based on (1) sentence structure, and (2) semantics.

We now discuss the two types in detail.

20.2.1 Definiteness based on sentence structure

Although this type of definiteness depends on one of the distinguishing features of Fijian grammar, it has not been discussed before from this point of view. The analysis here depends on the reinterpretation of two elements within the VP, often called "pronouns," or "subject marker" and "object marker" (see ch 4, 17). For example, in the following VP,

E rai-c-a.   'He sees it.'
3S see-TR-it

e is the subject and *-a* is the object.[7] Optional NPs added to this VP *specify* the subject and the object—that is, they narrow the semantic reference. For example:

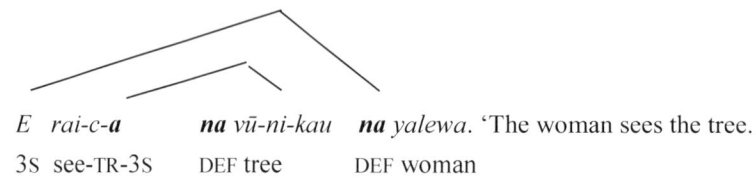

E rai-c-a   na vū-ni-kau   na yalewa. 'The woman sees the tree.'
3S see-TR-3S   DEF tree   DEF woman

There is no question about the interpretation of this sentence: it refers to a particular woman and a particular tree.

This reanalysis of *na* rests on this premise: If we take the concepts of old and new information literally, when a specifying NP appears, it is already old information, since the subject and the object (if there is one) have already been expressed in the VP. For example, in the sentence above, "tree" and "woman" are old information (since they have already been referred to by the subject *e* and the object *-a*), and in any such sentence, we consider that the NPs that "echo" the subject and the object relay old information and therefore require the definite marker.[8]

---

[7] This interpretation is based on that of Arms (1974) and Pawley (1973b).

[8] Strictly speaking, this analysis holds only when the VP precedes the NP, which is the unmarked order of phrases. Other orders are marked by special intonation. J. D. Gibson pointed out (11/82) that one should be careful not to imply cause and effect in this analysis, since similar conditions in other languages do not always produce similar effects.

20.2.2 Definiteness based on semantics

The second type of definiteness can be further divided into two subtypes. The first is related to further specification of the referent of the noun, effected by any of several kinds of modifiers:

1. Personal-spatial demonstratives. Examples are *oqō* 'this (near me)', *oqori* 'that (near you)', *oyā* 'that (near neither)'. In the following sentence, the use of one of these demonstratives coincides with the use of *na* in the NP:

Au dau vaka-tā-vovoce e **na** *bāvelo oyā.*
1S HAB play-paddling ABL DEF dugout-canoe DEM:3
'I play at paddling in that dugout canoe.'

Even though "dugout canoe" has not been introduced previously, it takes on definiteness through the use of the demonstrative. Had *oyā* not been used, the hearer would know that "boat" must have been referred to earlier. Moreover, it is in the nature of the demonstratives that they refer to things literally or metaphorically at hand; thus those things are immediately old information.

2. Possessives. A noun qualified by a possessive is automatically definite. For example, *no-qu vale* 'my house' refers to a semantically definite item.[9]

3. Relative phrases. This type of attribution makes old information out of a referent immediately after it is introduced. Thus, the hearers know, as it were, that the concept is going to be explained to them. As an example, note the following sentence:

Oqō **na** *vale.*   'This is the house.'
DEM:1 DEF house

Unless one is using "house" in a generic sense (see below), the sentence above leaves the hearers dissatisfied. However, if "house" is qualified by a relative phrase:

Oqō **na** *vale e moce tū ki-na.* 'This is the house he slept in.'
DEM:1 DEF house 3S sleep CNT ABL-3S

the sentence needs no further context to clarify it.

4. Miscellaneous limiting markers. In this category belong such forms as *kece* 'all' and *yā-dua* 'each'.

The second type of semantic definiteness is the GENERIC category. In this construction, the referent of the noun is not viewed as an individual member of a class (on which the opposition DEFINITE/INDEFINITE could operate), but as a class itself. We find sentences such as the following:

E kau yaga sara **na** *niu.*   'The coconut is a very useful tree.'
3S tree useful INT DEF coconut   (*NV1*:66)

Here, it is not a particular coconut that is referred to, but instead, the whole class.

---

[9] See Lyons 1968:391.

20.2.3 Indefinite constructions

The previous section showed constructions that are automatically definite. We now treat constructions that allow a contrast between definite and indefinite.[10] Note the following pairs:

    e   koro-ni-vuli   'in schools'
    ABL school

    e   **na**   koro-ni-vuli   'in the school, in school'
    ABL DEF school

    e   vale   'at home, indoors'
    ABL house

    e   **na**   vale   'in the house (a particular one)'
    ABL DEF house

These examples show that NPs with and without *na* form a grammatical opposition. Those with *na* are definite; those without *na* are indefinite.[11]

However, in ablative phrases, a number of semantic restrictions come into play. Note that in the examples above, some of the nouns represent abstractions. Some nouns that often appear in ablative phrases without *na* are abstract to begin with; for example:

    ruku 'underneath'   *dela* 'top'   *rā* 'down'   *cake* 'up'

Note two of these nouns in context:

    E dabe e   ruku ni   vū -ni-kau.   'She sat underneath the tree.'
    3S sit   ABL under POS tree

    E tiko e   dela ni   tēveli.   'It's on top of the table.'
    3S stay ABL top   POS table

When we do find an example of one of these forms with *na*, close examination shows that a kind of transformation has taken place. With *ruku* as a sample, we note that it *can* appear with *na*:

    e   na   ruku ni   tēveli oqō   'underneath this table'
    ABL DEF under POS table DEM:1

but here, a specific part of the space beneath the table has not been singled out. Instead, *na* occurs before *ruku* to convey the notion of the definiteness of 'table', since the following is prohibited:

    *ni   na   tēveli
    POS DEF table

---

[10] All these NPs are "prepositional" or "marked." Note that an indefinite NP cannot occur without a marker.

[11] We need to point out here that "indefinite" for Fijian does not necessarily mean that the NP in question would be translated into English with the indefinite article *a*. In particular, it does not mean 'one'. Instead, it refers to the *general*, rather than the *specific*.

If *ruku* and other such nouns refer to entities that are intrinsically general, there are even more examples of noun that are intrinsically specific, and therefore cannot occur in the locative construction without *na*. Take *vū-ni-kau*, for example. One can run toward a specific tree:

E cici i **na** *vū-ni-kau.*   'She runs to the tree,'
3S run ABL DEF tree

but not "tree" as an abstraction or generality:

*E cici i vū -ni-kau.

Some such nouns, however, can be made general with the prefix *vei-* (see §23.1), and thus can be used in an ablative phrase with or without *na*:

E cici i **vei**-*kau.*   'He ran inland.'
3S run ABL GEN-bush

E cici i na **vei**-*kau.*   'He ran toward the bush.'
3S run ABL DEF GEN-bush

Time phrases, as well, are definite:

e **na** *yakavi*   'in the evening'
ABL DEF evening

e **na** *siga Vakarauwai*   'on Saturday'
ABL DEF day Saturday

Such words indicating time do not occur without *na*:

*e yakavi   'evenings'
ABL evening

*e Vakarauwai   'Saturdays'

As in some previous examples, a kind of semantic generality is achieved by the use of the prefix *vei-*, which, as a generalizer, refers to a collection or a group rather than to a specific entity. Thus:

E cici i na **vei**-*kau.*   'He ran to the bush.'
3S run ABL DEF GEN-tree

e **vei**-*mataka*   'mornings'
3S GEN-morning

e **vei**-*Vakarauwai*   'Saturdays'
3S GEN-Saturday

In this last phrase, "morning" can be made definite with *na*:

e **na** *vei-mataka*   'every morning'
3S DEF GEN-morning

e na vei-Vakarauwai   'each Saturday'
3S DEF GEN-Saturday

20.2.4 Generalization: Dealing with the requirements of discourse

The preceding sections show that in a common sentence type in Fijian, NPs specifying the subject and the object are always definite, as are certain types of modified NPs. And some constructions allow a contrast between definite and indefinite. How does this complex situation relate to constructions larger than the sentence—that is, to the structure of discourse?

In a discourse, the first two types of NPs just listed remain definite, even when they are first introduced into a discourse. A text might begin:

Daru lako i   na no-qu koro.   'Let's go to my village.'
1DI   go   ABL DEF PC-1S village

Even though "my village" is new information, with *noqu* 'my', it is semantically definite. However, in those constructions that allow the definite-indefinite contrast, this contrast is conditioned by the old-vs.-new information criterion. For example, a text could begin:

E cici i   bāravi o Pita.   'P ran "beach-wards."'
3S run ABL beach PRP P

Any further mention of "beach" could use the definite phrase *na bāravi*. However, as mentioned earlier, not many nouns can appear in such constructions. Those that can occur in such locative phrases as:

| *i vale* | '(to) home' | *i vanua* | 'toward land' |
| *i wai* | 'toward the sea' | *e cakau* | 'at the reef' |

In these phrases, the words seem to have taken on the properties of such locative nouns as *cake* 'up', *rā* 'down', and *ruku* 'under'.

However, for the NPs whose definiteness is the result of sentence structure, a very different situation exists. It is here that the language engages in a tug-of-war between definite and general. If we choose to view it as a paradox, this statement might suffice: The structure of the sentence requires NPs that specify the subject or the object to be definite. But the structure of discourse requires, for this construction, that a referent be general when it is introduced.

For this construction, the dilemma is resolved not by *removing definiteness* for the purposes of discourse, but by *adding generality*, effected through numerical bases used in the existential construction. The following bases, literally numerical or numerical by extension, are examples:

dua 'one'   *vica* 'few'   *sō* 'some'   *levu* 'many'   *vuqa* 'many'

The next examples show how a specified subject and object (respectively), definite because of sentence structure, are made contextually general:

*E yaco mai e **dua**[12] na vūlagi.*   'A visitor arrived.'
3S arrive DIR 3S one DEF visitor

Because of the sentence structure, *vūlagi* must be marked with *na*. But since this is its first appearance in the discourse, it is made general with *e dua*.

*E ā mai dola-v-a e **dua** na soqo.*   'He opened a meeting.'
3S PT DIR open-TR-it 3S one DEF meeting

In this sentence, a similar situation holds for "meeting": it is grammatically definite, but general with respect to the discourse.

In each sentence, the NP that has been more general is derived from an existential VP. Thus, embedded in the sentences above are the following:

E dua na vūlagi.   'There was a visitor.'
3S one DEF visitor

E dua na soqo.   'There was a meeting.'
3S one DEF meeting

When a semantic plural is called for, *sō* and *vica* perform the same function:

*Era yaco mai e **sō** na vūlagi.*   'Some visitors arrived.'
3S arrive DIR 3S some DEF visitor

*E ā mai dola-v-a e **sō** na soqo.*   'He opened some meetings.'
3S PT DIR open-TR-3S 3S some DEF meeting

Embedded in these sentences are the following existentials:

e sō na vūlagi   'there were some visitors'
e sō na soqo   'there were some meetings'

To underscore the function of this construction as a discourse tool used to introduce new information, note the following opening sentences:

*E **na dua** na siga e ā vua toka e **na dua** na vū-ni-niu*
ABL DEF one DEF day 3S PT fruit CNT 3S DEF one DEF coconut-tree

   e dua na vua-na.   'One day a coconut tree bore one fruit.' (*FR4*:4)
   3S one DEF fruit-3S

E dua na vū-ni-maqo e bula voleka-t-a toka e dua na vū -ni-uto.
3S one DEF mango-tree 3S live near-TR-3S CNT 3S one DEF breadfruit-tree
'A mango tree was growing near a breadfruit tree.'

---

[12] Grammatically, *e dua* is an existential VP, meaning 'there is one (of something).' Even in its use as a generalizer of NPs, *e dua* still behaves as a VP. Note the following:
E qai nanu-m-a ni sega ni dua na i-coi ni kākana e vaka-rau -tak-a.
3S SEQ think-TR-3S SUB not SUB one DEF i-coi POS food 3S CAU-ready-TR-3S
'Then he remembered that he hadn't prepared any *i-coi*.' (*FR5*:19)

An NP after *sega* would be introduced by *na*, not *ni*.

20.2.5 The analysis of a text with respect to definiteness, indefiniteness, and generality

The following short text (*NV2*:87–90)[13] shows the interplay among sentence- and discourse-level definiteness, indefiniteness, and generality. All common NPs appear in brackets. Multiple bracketing indicates hierarchical structure. After each sentence in which common NPs occur, I discuss the status of the phrases.

1. *Eratou ā vavavi   o   Seru, Tui kei Tawake.*
   3T   PT oven-cook PRP S   T CNJ T
   'S, T, and T cooked-in-earth-oven.'

2. *Eratou carā sara [na no-dratou lovo] [e [na dua [na ruku]*
   3T   clear INT DEF PC-3T   oven ABL DEF one DEF under

   ni   vū-ni-uto]]   'They prepared the area immediately for
   POS breadfruit-tree   their oven under a breadfruit tree.'

Na no-dratou lovo. Here, the phrase is definite because it is limited by the possessive *no-dratou*. Such a phrase is not general even though it introduces a theme in the discourse.

Na dua na ruku ni vū-ni-uto. In this complex phrase, a number of processes are at work. With respect to the discourse, "breadfruit tree" is being introduced. However, since *ni* phrases are never definite, any concessions to sentence structure or discourse will have to take place in the outer layers of the larger phrase. Thus, *na*, required by the ablative phrase, marks *ruku* rather than *vū-ni-uto*. On the other hand, the concept is being introduced into the discourse and thus required to be general. Therefore, it is preceded by *e dua*. Finally, because *e* 'in' and *e* (third person singular) are homophonous, *na* precedes *dua* to establish that the *e* phrase is an ablative NP, not a VP.

3. *Eratou ā vavi-a [e sō   na dalo] kei [na tolu] [na kumala]*
   3T   PT cook-3S 3S some DEF taro CNJ DEF three DEF sweet-potato

   me ke-dratou i-lutua.
   SUB PC-3T   choice-pieces
   'They baked some taro and three sweet potatoes to serve as their own
       special portions.'

E sō na dalo; na tolu; na kumala. Here, the NPs specify the object, represented by *-a*; thus *dalo* and *kumala* both occur with *na*. However, since they are being introduced into the discourse, they are generalized by the numerals *sō* and *tolu*.

Although *ke-dratou i-lutua* appears to be a NP, it occurs after the verbal particle *me*. Thus, it functions as a verb in this construction, and cannot be marked for definiteness.

---

[13] I have respelled certain forms, added macrons for long vowels, and changed the punctuation where necessary.

4. *E **cara lovo** o   Seru, e **cā   buka**   ka **vaka-tubu lovo** o   Tui*
      3S clear oven PRP S   3S carry firewood CNJ CAU-light oven PRP T

   *ka **tā i-tūtū-ni-lovo** ka **soi dalo** o Tawake.*
      CNJ cut covering-leaves CNJ cut taro PRP T
   'S cleared the oven, T gathered firewood and lit the fire, and T cut
      the leaves to cover and pared the taro.'

Even though semantically the nouns *lovo*, *buka*, *i-tūtū-ni-lovo* and *dalo* represent goals, they are used as attributes in this sentence, since this construction focuses on the activity, not the goal.[14] Thus, none of them is part of an NP.

5. *Ā vavi   kulikuli gā [na kumala].*
      PT baked   skin   LIM DEF sweet-potato
   'The sweet potato was baked with its skin on.'

Na kumala. With certain tense and aspect markers, the third person singular subject *e* is deleted. I propose that it exists in an underlying form, still signaling the occurrence of *na* before *kumala*. Note that "sweet potato" is now old information with respect to the discourse, and thus does not have to be generalized.

6 *Ā tala-i   tiko gā o Seru ka ni   gone duadua.*
      PT send-TR CNT LIM PRP S   CNJ SUB child alone
   'S served as a helper because he was the youngest.'

7. *Ni sā dravu gā [na lovo] sā qiso sara, biu   yani*
      SUB ASP ash   LIM DEF oven ASP stir   INT   placed DIR

   [na lewe   ni lovo] kei [na i-tūtū]   ka bulu sara.
      DEF contents POS oven CNJ   DEF covering-leaves CNJ buried INT
   'When the wood had burned to ash in the oven and the burning bits had
      been removed the contents of the oven and the cover put in place,
      then it was immediately covered.'

Na lovo; na lewe ni lovo; na i-tūtū. Similar to its behavior in #5, *e* drops after the subordinate marker *ni*, but a third person singular subject is still implied. Therefore, these NPs are all definite.

8. *Eratou qai qe-v-a   [na no-dratou lovo] ni   sā yakavi.*
      3T   SEQ dig-TR-3S DEF PC-3T   oven SUB ASP evening
   'Then they dug out the contents of their oven when evening came.'

Na no-dratou lovo. Here, there are two reasons why "oven" is definite: it is preceded by the object *-a* (and is therefore old information), and is limited by the possessive *no-dratou*.

9. *E buta   vinaka sara [na lewe   ni lovo].*
      3S cooked good   INT   DEF contents POS oven
   'The contents of the oven were cooked thoroughly.'

---

[14] In so doing, it shows that "oven," "firewood," and "taro" do not refer to specific entities.

Na lewe ni lovo. This definite NP is anticipated by the subject *e*. It also repeats an earlier phrase.

10. *E [na levu ni   no-dratou mārau] e   ā   mani loma-dratou tale*
    ABL DEF big POS PC-3T   happy 3S PT SEQ desire-3T   ITR

    ki-na   me ratou vavavi e   [na siga] ka   tara-v-a.
    ABL-3S SUB 3T   cook   ABL DEF day REL follow-TR-3S

    'Because they were so happy, they then decided as a consequence that they would make an oven again the next day.'

Na levu; na siga. Both these NPs (constituents of larger prepositional phrases) are limited by following attributes, and therefore semantically definite.

20.2.6 *Na* vs. *a*

Cargill (1839) described a grammatical complementary distribution for *na* and *a* in the Lakeba language:

> In the Lakeba dialect, the article *na* occurs only in the oblique cases of *a*: — or after the conjunction *ka* (and), when that conjunction couples nouns or the clauses of sentences. It is used in this manner both in the nominative and accusative cases; as, *E vinaka a matau ka na kuro*, —the axe and pot are good: and *Kautamai ki ei a tagane ka na lewa*, —bring hither the man and woman.

For SF, Hazlewood (1872:5–6) described a less fixed distribution: *a* "generally (but not always) used at the beginning of a sentence." He noted a preference for *a* over *na* in this position, except "when the vocative case begins a sentence."

Churchward (1941:11) continued with this theme:

> Sometimes, especially at the beginning of a sentence, *a* is used instead of *na*, as in *a cava oqō?* what is this (literally, the what is this?), which is more usual than *na cava oqō?*

Milner (1972:11) noted the same distribution.

In the first fifty pages of FMC61, I found *a* used only with the interrogative *cava* or in constructions linked to *cava*. For example:

A   cava mada a   no-mu cakacaka?   'What was your work?' (p. 1)
DEF what INI DEF PC-2S work

A   cava mada o dredre-vak-a tiko? 'What are you laughing at?' (p. 19)
DEF what INI 2S laugh-TR-3S CNT

The only example of *na cava* was the following:

*sē   tei   ki-na   na āpolo sē   tei   tale ki-na   **na** **cava***
CNJ plant ABL-3S DEF apple CNJ plant ITR ABL-3S DEF what

'or there were apples planted there or other things planted there' (p. 4)

On the other hand, other fronted NPs used *na*:

Na ke-na siro   sobu yā,   qai sisi ki-na   na yago ni mate.
DEF PC-3S descend DIR DEM:3 SEQ slip ABL-3S DEF body POS dead

'Its descent caused the dead body to slide down.' (p. 26)

More statistical analysis of texts is needed, but it appears that *a* is somewhat idiomatically fused with *cava*, except where it would produce a disfavored vowel sequence.

20.2.7 Optional omission of *na* before possessives

Because of the semantic definiteness of possessives (see §20.2.2), *NA* might be considered redundant in possessive constructions. Thus, one can find such sentences as:

Tuku-n-a tale no-mu i-talanoa ni kāveti.
tell-TR-3S ITR PC-2S story POS cabbage
'Tell your cabbage story again.' (FMC61:1)

E dau vā-kani ira no-na manumanu.
3S HAB CAU-feed 3P PC-3S animal
'He always feeds his animals.'

In neither of these sentences does *na* occur before the possessive (*nomu, nona*), although it could.

This construction is an alternate form, not an example of a contrast between definite and indefinite.

20.2.8 Summary

In this reanalysis of the article *na*, I have shown that the presence of *na* defines definiteness formally, and its absence defines indefiniteness. The construction *e dua na*,[15] often interpreted as indefinite, is instead a means of making a definite phrase more general when the structure of discourse demands it. In short:

1. *Na* is not only a common noun marker, but a definite marker as well.

2. In its function as a definite marker, *na* forms a grammatical opposition not to the construction *e dua na*, but to the absence of a marker.

3. *E dua na* is one of several ways of generalizing a construction once it has been made grammatically definite. This process of *generalization* is separate from the definite-indefinite distinction, and is dependent on discourse.

20.2.9 Nouns that can take either *na* or *o*, or both

Some nouns, especially kin terms, alternate between common and proper. For example, one finds both

na tama-qu 'my father' and *o tama-qu* 'my father'
DEF father-1S   PRP father-1S

In addition, one can occasionally find both articles used with one noun:

o na marama 'the lady'[16]

---

[15] "Construction" is not exactly the right word, because these three morphemes never form a constituent on their own.

[16] *O na marama* is still not explained, because I have no examples in context. I would expect *na* to be functioning in its usual way here, marking definiteness—hence, old information. The person would have been mentioned before in the discourse.

The following, in spite of its surface structure, is also an example of *o na*:

*Gole-vi **na makubu-na** gā o B sā vakā sara nē*
turn-TR DEF grandchild-3S LIM PRP B ASP say-3S INT AFF
'B turned to her grandchild and said the following.' (Nawadra 1981:1)

As §20.1.3 shows, the expected form of a proper after a transitive suffix would be the proper NP with no article; e.g.:

*gole-vi **makubu-na***

And if the verb had a common object, the grammatical object *-a* would appear; e.g.:

*gole-v-a **na makubu-na***

Thus, the form of the construction forces this interpretation: that in this instance, the full phrase is *o na makubu-na*.

The next example shows *o* followed by something other than a kin term. Here, we find the proper marker with *i-tau* 'friend', which would usually be considered common rather than proper:

*Kai-nak-a sara vāqō   o   **no-na** i-tau.*   'His friend said this ...'
say-TR-3S INT   MAN-DEM:1 PRP PC-3S   friend   (FMC61:2)

The data point toward this simple interpretation: *o* phrases are *names*, not just *words*. With respect to a term with an inanimate referent, such as *vuravura* 'world' or *lomālagi* 'sky', using *o* makes it a place name. As for kin terms and other terms referring to humans, an *o* phrase is like the person's name.

21 NP FUNCTION MARKERS

A SECONDARY NP is a phrase whose function is indicated by its form. For example, the phrase *mai Suva* is marked for function: *mai* indicates that the phrase is ablative. The following outline shows the functions and their specific markers. It is followed by a more detailed treatment of each of the function markers.

1. Ablative[1]

   Locative
      e
      mai
   Directional
      i_1
      mai
   Proper (both locative and directional)
      vei
   Contractions
      ki-na
      vuā

2. Comitative

      kei_1
   Contraction
      kaya

3. Proper accusative

      i_2

4. Vocative

      i_3

5. Attributive (possessive)

ni	*me-i*
i_4	$ke\text{-}i_2$
ne-i	$ke\text{-}i_3$

---

[1] The markers in this category have a wide range of grammatical meanings, depending partially on the meaning of the head of the phrase.

21.1 ABLATIVE NPS

Although the main function of an ablative NP is to refer to location or direction in space and time, its additional functions require a label that is broader than locative or directional. "Ablative" is used as a label because it is appropriately broad in scope, covering (in its traditional use) a "range of locative or instrumental meanings" (Crystal 1980:7).

Ablative NPs can be classified according to whether their heads are common or proper. It is in common phrases that we find the most variation. The following section shows different types of nouns that occur in these phrases and affect their function.

21.1.1 Types of nouns that occur in common ablative phrases

21.1.1.1 Time

The following list (not exhaustive) shows nouns that are used in time phrases. Many are preceded by *na*:

Days of the week: *Siga Tabu* 'Sunday', *Mōniti* 'Monday', etc.
Months: *Janueri* 'January', *Feperuari* 'February', etc.
Numerals (including *vica* 'how many'), when they refer to time of day. E.g.:

*e na **dua** na kaloko* 'at one o'clock'   *e na **vica*** 'what time?'

Miscellaneous:

daidai[2]	'today'	*mataka*[3]	'morning (approx. 6:00–10:00 a.m.)
yabaki	'year'	*siga*	'day'
bogi	'night'	*vula*	'month'
gauna	'time'	*aua*	'hour'
nanoa	'yesterday'	*siga-levu*	(approx. 10:00 a.m. to 3:00 p.m.)
naica	'when?'		

21.1.1.2 Space

Most roots that refer to space are DEICTIC—that is, oriented relative to the place of utterance or another reference point indicated by the utterance. Examples are:

General referential directions:

dela	'above'	*ruku*	'beneath'
cake	'up'	*rā*	'down'
loma	'inside'	*tuba, tautuba*	'outside'

Referential directions on a horizontal plane:

liu	'ahead'	*muri*	'behind'

---

[2] *Nikua* is heard more often than *e daidai*, in spite of attempts to force the use of the latter. The use of *ni* as a time marker seems restricted to a few fused forms. See the next note. However, as Arms has pointed out (10/84), *ni* forms are actually VPs.

[3] The root *mataka* is also used in the expression *nimataka* 'tomorrow'. This idiomatic form constitutes a phrase in itself, and is not used with ablative markers.

matau	'right'	*mawī*	'left'
māliwa	'between'	*baba*	'side'

Nouns that can be used as generalized directions or locations:

vale	'home'	*vanua*	'land'
bāravi	'coast'	*matāsawa*	'beach'
cakau	'reef'	*vei-cō*	'uncultivated land'

Fixed locations—that is, place names—also fit into this category:

i Labasa	'to Labasa'	*i Taveuni*	'to Taveuni'
i Niusiladi	'to New Zealand'		

Note that with respect to ablative markers, place names are not proper, but common. Another interpretation (Arms 10/84) is simply that these ablative markers are not used with proper place names.

21.1.1.3 Time and space

Two roots—*liu* 'ahead, before' and *muri* 'behind'—are used for both time and space. For example:

*na tamata e **liu***   'the person ahead'
DEF person ABL lead

*na gauna e **liu***   'the past (literally, time ahead)'

It is tempting to imagine the Fijian concept of time as a straight line stretching ahead of and behind a person. The past is the time ahead, which is visible—and thus, known. The future is the time behind, which is not visible—and thus, unknown. Relative location along this line is important for both time and space. Sequence is indicated by the word *tara-v-a* 'be immediately next to it, follow it':

*e   na   siga ka   tara-v-a   e   **liu***   'the day before'
LOC DEF day REL follow-TR-3S ABL lead

*e na siga ka tara-v-a e **muri***   'the next day'

Constructions of this type can be diagrammed simply, as in figure 21:1.

FIGURE 21.1: *LIU, MURI,* AND A REFERENCE POINT

```
            e liu
                    e na siga ka tara-v-a e liu
                    e na siga e liu
    REFERENCE POINT
                    e na siga e muri
                    e na siga ka tara-v-a e muri
            e muri
```

It should be emphasized that the "reference point" is not necessarily the time that the utterance is spoken, nor does it necessarily refer to the speaker (and hence, place of speaking).

Some words referring to time and space can be qualified with markers that occur elsewhere.[4] Note the following progression:

> *i muri*   'to the rear'
> *i muri tale*   'further back'
> *i muri sara*   'even further back'

21.1.1.4 Means or instrument

Examples of this function are in boldface in the following examples.

*Sā oca o Filipe **e na** sausau-mi taro.*   'F was tired of/from
ASP tired PRP F   ABL DEF answer-TR question   answering questions.'

*Au vana-i koya **e na** dakai.*   'I shot him with the gun.'
1S shoot-TR 3S ABL DEF gun

*Ni sā[5] moce tū o Vilive, e oga gā **e na** culacula o tina-na.*
SUB ASP sleep CNT PRP V 3S busy LIM ABL DEF sew PRP mother-3S
'While V was asleep, his mother was busy at sewing.' (*FR3*:43)

*Keimami sā dau lasa dina **e na** neimami koro-ni-vuli.*
1PX   ASP HAB happy true ABL DEF PC-1PX   school
'We're truly happy in/with our school.' (*FR3*:6)

*Sā lade **e na** levu ni no-na reki.*
ASP jump ABL DEF big POS PC-3S joy
'He jumped with great joy (lit., in the greatness of his joy).'

*E sokonū na yago i Mārica **e na** kā e qai rogo-c-a.*
3S shudder DEF body POS M   ABL DEF thing 3S SEQ hear-TR-3S
'M's body shuddered at the thing she heard then.' (*T74*:51)

*ā sau-m-a yani o Leone **e na** mata luluvu.*
PT answer-TR-3S DIR PRP L ABL DEF face sad
'answered L with a sad face.' (*T74*:42)

*E ā mata sarasara o Mārica **e na** vei-kā vovou sā qai rai-c-a.*
3S PT eye look   PRP M ABL DEF DIS-thing new ASP SEQ see-TR-3S
'M looked excitedly at all the new things she saw.' (*T74*:42)

These last sentences produced some disagreement among speakers: several thought them ungrammatical; others said "We say it." TRN (2/79) thought that the structure was limited to sentences in which the head of the dominant phrase is a word like *sīnai* 'full'.

---

[4] PG pointed out this construction.

[5] What is written as *sa* here is probably a hypercorrection of *se* (see §5.3.2), but could also be *sā*, with a different meaning (Arms 10/84).

The grammatical source of the problem is that in a sentence whose main verb is passive (S2), an instrument[6] can be indicated by a marked phrase, but an agent cannot. Most recent grammars note that a sentence like "The house was built by the carpenter" cannot be translated into Fijian using a passive form of the verb and indicating the agent with a marked NP:

*E tara-i   na vale   *e*   **na mātaisau**.
3S build-TR DEF house ABL DEF carpenter

In the sentences in question, the semantic role of the referent of the noun in the marked NP comes rather close to agent. If we look at the English versions, we note that a rephrasing of 'The cup is filled with tea' makes "tea" look like an agent: 'The tea filled the cup.'

Still, semantically "tea" is not an agent; it is the material that comprises the quantity referred to, rather like the material that a house is built of:

na   bilo   tī   'the cup of tea'
DEF cup tea

na   vale   kau   'the wooden house'
DEF house wooden

21.1.1.5 Material, contents[7]

Examples are:

*E vati   e   **na gasau**.*   'It's lashed together with reeds.' (*NV2*:10)
3S lashed ABL DEF reed

*Sā caka   e   **na kau**.*   'It's made of wood.' (Geraghty 1976a)
ASP made ABL DEF wood

*Sā sīnai na   bilo   e   **na tī**.*   'The cup is filled with tea.'
ASP full DEF cup ABL DEF tea

21.1.1.6 Metaphorical space or time

Some *e* NPs refer to an activity, with a verb as the head of the phrase. We might consider that these activities represent metaphorical space or time. Examples:

*E   na   vuke-i   Nānā   o   tama-qu   **e   na   loba   niu**.*
3S DEF help-TR Mother PRP father-1S ABL DEF squeeze coconut
'Father will help Mother with the coconut-squeezing.' (*NV2*:17)

21.1.1.7 Ambiguity

With some combinations of nouns, it is difficult to decide whether the secondary NP serves an instrumental or a locative function. For example:

---

[6] Here, I use "instrument" and "agent" strictly in a semantic sense; I do not propose that Fijian has a formal case system.

[7] *Mai* also used for this function: VV entry: "botoboto: m[ataqali] kākana caka mai na kawai …"

Era sā sala na qā ni uvi, ka ra sā kaba **e** **na gasau**.
3P ASP climb DEF stem POS yam CNJ 3P ASP climb ABL DEF reed
'The stems of the yam climb, and they climb on reeds.' (*NV2*:15)

Here, because of the nature of climbing plants and their supports, "reeds" could serve as an instrument or location for the climbing.

21.1.2 Function of ablative NPs

21.1.2.1 Locatives

21.1.2.1.1 *E*

The primary function of an *e* phrase is to indicate a static location in time or space. There is no formal difference between time and space phrases; the meaning depends on the meaning of the root that serves as head of the phrase. For example:

Au tau-vi-mate **e** **na vula** *o Tīseba.*   'I was ill in December.'
1s ill   ABL DEF month PRP December

Au tau-vi-mate **e** **na vale-ni-kana**.   'I was ill in the restaurant.'
1s ill   ABL DEF restaurant

Most of the illustrative sentences in §21.1.1 show further examples of *e*.

21.1.2.1.2 *Mai*

Mai indicates direction away from the focus indicated by the head of the phrase, and toward another focus.

ka   sō   era tala-i **mai na nodra vei-vale**
CNJ some 3P send-TR ABL DEF PC-3P DIS-vale
'and some have been sent from their homes' (*NV3*:23)

O kilā   na gauna datou ā kele mai ki-na **mai Moturiki**?
2S know-3S DEF time 1TI PT land DIR ABL-3S ABL M
'Do you remember the time we landed here from M?' (FMC61:39)

In its locative use, *mai* refers to general or distant location:

E tiko **mai Vanua Levu**.   'She lives on VL.'
3S stay ABL VL

In what Geraghty (1976:507) called "the conventional analysis," *mai* contrasts with *e*: the former refers to a location far from the speaker, and the latter, to a location close to the speaker (cf. Milner 1972:19). Geraghty gave the following contrasting pair to illustrate this conventional analysis (p. 514):

Sā tiko **e** **waqa** *na kato.*   'The box is on the boat.'
ASP stay ABL boat DEF box   (speaker is on the boat)

Sā tiko **mai waqa** *na kato.*   'The box is on the boat.'
ASP stay ABL boat DEF box   (speaker is not on the boat)

However, he found that under certain circumstances, *e* is used, even though the speaker is not on board. He concluded that although the features "close" and "remote" still figure in the contrast, "precise" and "approximate" location count as well.

I think that Geraghty's conclusions can be restated slightly: When used in the same context, *mai* refers to a general location, and *e* narrows it down within the area referred to. In other words, a location marked by *e* may not be "precise," but it is more specific than a location marked by *mai*. Note the following sequence, an expansion of Geraghty's examples (pp. 514–15):

1. *E tiko **mai vei** o Pate?*	'Where does P live?'
2. ***Mai** Āwai.*	'In Hawai'i.
3. *E vei **mai** Āwai?*	'Where (more specifically) in Hawai'i?'
4. ***Mai** Oahu.*	'On O'ahu.'
5. *E vei **mai** Oahu?*	'Where on O'ahu?'
6. ***Mai** Onolulu.*	'In Honolulu'
7. *E vei **mai** Onolulu?*	'Where in Honolulu?'
8. ***Mai** Mānoa Valley.*	'In Mānoa Valley.'
9. *E vei **mai** na Mānoa Valley?*	'Where in Mānoa Valley?'
10. ***Mai** H Drive.*	'On H Drive.'
11. *E vei **mai** na H Drive?*	'Where on H Drive?'
12. *E na (vale) naba xxxx.*	'At (house) number xxxx.'

The *mai* in (2) establishes the location as distant, but in successive questions (3, 5, 7, 9, 11), the *e*—*mai* contrast is a matter of degree of specificity.

We might diagram this progressive interplay between *mai* and *e* as a series of boxes within boxes. Taking any box and the one next smaller in size, the larger one is comparable to a *mai* location, and the smaller one to an *e* location. Figure 21:2 shows such a relationship.

FIGURE 21.2: *MAI* AND *E*

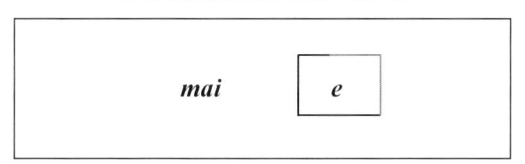

21.1.2.1.3 Locative NPs as comment

An ablative (locative) NP frequently serves as comment when the head of the phrase is *vei* 'where?' A number of examples are in the list above; further examples are:

E vei *o koya?*	'Where is she?'
ABL where PRP 3s	
Mai vei *o Tē?*	'Where's Te from?'
ABL where PRP T	

PG (6/82) supplied the following examples with phrase heads other than *vei*:

*O   yau **mai** Lau.*   'I'm from Lau.'
PRP 1s ABL L

PG also gave the example of a time root (always preceded by *ni*) that functions similarly:

Ni-mataka *na soqo*.   'The assembly will be tomorrow.'

BK added other time phrases—*e nanoa* 'yesterday', *nikua* 'today', *e na mācawa sā oti* 'last week'—all of which can be used in such constructions.

21.1.2.2 Directional NPs

The difference between ablative (in its locative sense) and directional has been compared by Lyons (1968:300) to that between static and dynamic. If we try to explain the difference through translation, we can say that *e* and *mai* are used with actions or states that take place *in* or *at* a place; *i* and *vei* are used with literal or figurative movement *to* or *toward* a place or person. Thus, the principal difference between the two types of phrases lies in the types of verbs they are used with: directional NPs are used with *verbs of motion* (again, either literal or figurative).

21.1.2.2.1 *I (ki)*

I marks a directional phrase that has a common noun as its head. The first examples show verbs referring to literal movement. In the examples, the marker is often written as *ki*; this form is explained later.

Erau lako tiko **ki** *na i-teitei*.	'They (dual) are going to the garden.'
3D go CNT ABL DEF garden	(*NV2*:5)
Era sā gole sobu **ki** *matāsawa*.	'They headed down to the beach.'
3P ASP turn DIR ABL beach	(*NV2*:8)
ka ra sā la-ki qoli **ki** *cakau*.	'and they went fishing to the reef.'
CNJ 3P ASP DIR fish ABL reef	(*NV2*:21)

An *i* phrase can also use a deictic marker as its head. Here, the deixis centers on person.

i kē	'hither (to first person)'
i keri	'toward you'
i keā	'thither (to third person)'

I is also used with locative nouns:

i rā	'downward'
i cake	'upward'

Fixed locations—that is, place names—also fit into this category:

i Labasa   'to Labasa'

Note that with respect to directional markers, place names pattern not with propers, but with commons.

As Geraghty noted (1976:517), *i* is used with verbs that do not signify motion, but location. In such a construction, the *i* phrase refers to general direction, location, or nearness.

*Tiko gā yani **ki na motokā**.*   'Just stay around the car.'
stay LIM DIR ABL DEF car   (Geraghty 1976a:517)

*Era dau tuvā toka na no-dra i-rara vakā **ki loqi**.*
3P HAB arrange CNT DEF PC-3P hearth like-3S ABL *loqi*
'They arranged (positioned) their fireplaces toward the *loqi*.' (*NV2*:73)

*E ā kele mai [**ki Suva**] e na mācawa sā oti*
3S PT anchored DIR ABL S ABL DEF week ASP finish

    e dua na melisitima levu.   'There anchored at Suva last week
    3S one DEF ship   big   a large ocean liner.'

In this example, one might think of *kele* as referring to a fixed state, but perhaps it could also be viewed as 'coming to anchor'—a process that was completed at Suva.

I phrases can also be used with verbs signifying figurative, not literal, motion.

*Era sā dui usu-mak-a na ulu-dra **ki na i-vola**.*
3P ASP IND thrust-TR-3S DEF head-3P ABL DEF book
'They each thrust their heads into books.'

*Na vei-kā era tūdai-tak-a, e vaka-tau **ki na vei-mataqali***
DEF DIS-thing 3P trap-TR-3S 3S depend ABL DEF DIS-type

    ***manumanu kila** ka ra tū e na no-dra dui vanua.*
    animal   wild REL 3P stay ABL DEF PC-3P IND land
'What they trap depends on the kind of wild animals that live in their
    respective areas.' (*NV3*:2)

Ia ā se sega mada ni ciqo-m-a na Lotu na tūraga
CNJ PT ASP not INI SUB accept-TR-3S DEF religion DEF chief

    *na Vūniivalu ka vā-qole-i **i Rewa**.*
    DEF high-chief CNJ CAU-turn-TR ABL R
'But the chief, the Vuniivalu, didn't take hold of Christianity, so it was
    turned/directed toward Rewa.' (*SR* 20/4/82)

Some grammars have treated *ki* as a base form, and *i*—if they have mentioned it at all—as an alternate. PG has suggested (7/81) that *ki* is an invention for SF, dependent on factors that influenced the missionaries to propose the proper noun marker *ko* and second person subjects with *k-*, particularly the widespread use of *ki* in Polynesia. His research on language variation shows that in the area that includes Bau, Rewa, Verata, and Gau, only Moturiki uses *ki* for a directional.

21.1.2.2.2. Ablative *mai* vs. postverbal *mai*[8]

In their written forms, the following two sentences look identical in structure:

*E lako **mai** Levuka.*   'She comes from Levuka.'
*E lako **mai** na gone.*   'The child came.'

However, phonologically they are different, as the following notation shows. (Boldface indicates the syllable that serves as phrase peak; the phrases are bracketed.)

*[E **la**ko] [mai Le**vu**ka].*[9]
*[E lako **mai**] [na **go**ne].*

In addition to the different phrase division, the intonation shows different relationships between the phrases.

Added to the phonological evidence, the principles of immediate constituent analysis (substitutability and freedom of occurrence) confirm that the grammatical phrase division is the same as the phonological phrase division above.

Another example is:

*[Era cavutū]   [mai na vei-vanua **ta**ni].*
3P   go-together   ABL DEF DIS-land different
'They have just visited different countries.' (*NV2*:45)

21.1.2.3 *Vei*

This ablative marker, used with a proper noun head, serves both locative and directional functions. Here, "proper" includes:

1. Names of people, including kin terms, and other words for humans
2. Person-number markers (pronouns)

Note that place names are excluded, since they occur in *e*, *mai*, and *i* phrases.

Examples of the first type are:

*Ā   sega gā   ni   rawa **vei** Mārica me tuku-n-a vuā.*
PT not LIM SUB able ABL   M   SUB tell-TR-3S ABL-3S
'It just wasn't possible for M to tell her.' (T74:42)

*E   ā   vaka-tabataba gā **vei** Mārica ko   Leone.*
3S PT CAU-silence   LIM ABL   M   PRP   L
'L signaled silence (to) M.' (T74:53)

Examples of the second type are:

*ka na cā vaka-levu **vei** au*   'and I dislike it very much' (T74:43)
CNJ DEF bad MAN-big   ABL   1S

---

[8] In a convincing argument, Geraghty proposed (1976:515–16) that two *mai*s underlie such sentences—one the postverbal directional, the other the ablative marker. He pointed out that there are other such restrictions against two homophonous words together.

[9] The phonological phrasing represented by this marking would occur only in slow, precise speech. In more normal speech, ablative NPs combine with the main VP to form one phonological phrase.

*O   iko m-o   tuku-n-a   **vei** ira.*   'You (singular) tell them (plural).'
PRP 2S SUB-2S tell-TR-3S ABL 3P   (*NL* 10/6/82)

*Sā bau cava mada e tuku-n-a   **vei** iko?* 'Just what did he tell you?'
ASP TEN what INI 3S tell-TR-3S ABL 2S   (T74:51)

21.1.2.3.1 *Mai vei* and *ki vei*

Sometimes read, but seldom heard in normal speech, are the redundant constructions *mai vei* and *ki vei* 'from' and 'to', respectively. For example:

*E   rai   tau-mada sara gā   **ki vei** rau na yanuyanu.*
3S look first   INT LIM ABL ABL 3D DEF island
'He looked first of all to those islands.' (*FR5*:24)

Geraghty (1976:518–19) suggested that *mai vei* and *ki vei* "are innovations coined by those non-Fijians—mostly missionaries—who were responsible for the production of formal Fijian in the nineteenth century." He then showed that when the sequence *mai* + *vei* does occur in natural speech, the two markers belong to separate phrases. For example:

*[Au tau-r-a   **mai**] [**vei** Samu]*   'I took it from S.'
 1S take-TR-3S DIR   ABL S

As confirmation, the following sentence, with *mai* + *vei* clearly within one phrase:

*[a   cava ko tau-r-a   ki-na]   [mai vei Samu]?
  DEF what 2S take-TR-3S ABL-3S   ABL ABL S
'Why did you take it from S?'

elicited the following reaction from several speakers: they themselves would not say it, but it might be heard in a sermon or on the radio.

Geraghty then proposed that *ki vei* for 'to' was formed on the analogy of *mai vei* for 'from', concluding that both "are part of a particular formal style of Fijian which originated among non-Fijians in their quest for one Fijian word to translate one English word."

21.1.2.4 Contractions of the ablative markers[10]

When any of the ablative markers *e*, *mai* (either locative or directional), or *i* is used with the third person singular rather than a noun as head of the phrase, a contraction is formed. With those markers used with common nouns, the contraction is *ki-na*.

*E   na gauna oyā,   sā   tekivū **ki-na**   na   osooso ne-i   Naisulu.*
ABL DEF time   DEM:3 ASP begin   ABL-3S DEF crowded PC-POS N
'At that time, there began (in it) N's busy-ness.'

---

[10] The analysis here is based largely on Geraghty 1976, which is the major work on Fijian "prepositions" as a class. Previous treatments of *kina* are inconsistent. For example, although Milner (1972:69) analyzed *vuā* as *vei* + *koya*, he didn't analyze *kina*, but discussed only its position and its various translations.

*Sā vaka-rau-tak-a **ki-na** na nō-drau i-yāyā na luve-na.*
ASP prepare-TR-3S ABL-3S DEF PC-3D baggage DEF child-3S
'She prepared (in it) her children's baggage.' (*FR3*:57)

In this example, both instances of *ki-na* refer back to the secondary NP *e na gauna oyā*. As the translation 'then' shows, the function of *ki-na* is tied directly to that of the coreferential phrase preceding it.

Such fronted time NPs as that in the previous example are commonly referred to later in the sentence by *ki-na*:

*E na vula o Nōveba, e dau cabe **ki-na** na balolo.*
ABL DEF month PRP November 3S HAB rise ABL-3S DEF *balolo*
'In the month of November, the *balolo* always rise (in it).'

*dau loba **ki-na** na yaqona sē niu*
HAB squeezed ABL-3S DEF kava CNJ coconut
'kava or coconut is squeezed with it' (*VV:i-bō*)

*Sā ladelade tiko na bulumakau, ka ta-sova sara **ki-na** na sucu.*
ASP jump CNT DEF cow CNJ spilled INT ABL-3S DEF milk
'The cow was jumping around, and because of it, the milk was spilled.' (*FR3*:51)

The functions of *ki-na* echo those of the underlying markers. For example, some of the sentences above show time, instrument, and reason.

Because of the position of a modifying VP relative to its head, *ki-na* is often used in such constructions. That is, the NP appears, and a coreferential *ki-na* appears in a following VP, much like the other examples of *ki-na* above. Examples are:

*kā vaka-loma-na e talo-ci sē gunu-vi **ki-na** na wai*
thing hollow 3S pour-TR CNJ drink-TR ABL-3S DEF water
'a hollow thing water is poured in or drunk from' (*VV:bilo*)

*ko ira ka ra jiko **ki-na***   'those who stay there'
PRP 3P REL 3P stay ABL-3S   (Lau language) (*FR5*:9)

The proper ablative marker *vei* plus third person singular takes the form *vuā*. It is different from *ki-na* in that it is not coreferential with a preceding NP, but can be specified by a following NP.

The following examples show *vuā* without a specifying NP:

*Drau via-vosa **vuā**?*   'Do you (dual) want to talk to him?'
2D DES-talk ABL-3S

*na no-qu loloma **vuā***   'my love for her' (T74:43)
DEF PC-1S love ABL-3S

*E ā tuku-n-a tale gā **vuā**.*   'She also told her. (T74:43)
3S PT tell-TR-3S ITR LIM ABL-3S

*Tou mai kau-t-a **vuā**.*   'Let's (trial) take it to her.'
1TI DIR carry-TR-3S ABL-3S   (*FR3*:44)

The following sentence shows *vuā* with a specifying NP:

*Era ā cabe i Vale Levu **vuā** na Gone Tūraga na Kōvana levu.*
3P PT climb ABL house big ABL-3S DEF child chief DEF governor big
'They went up to Government House to him—the chief, the Governor
  General.' (*SR* 20/4/82)

This last example has been corrected to make it more idiomatic. The original used *ki vuā*, which is a form of *ki vei*, discussed in §21.1.2.3.1.

21.1.3 Discussion: Ablative NPs

21.1.3.1 Are locative and directional dependent on the semantics of the verb?

In the analysis here, I have chosen to separate the locative and directional functions of the markers. However, there are a number of arguments for uniting them, resulting in only two common ablative markers: *mai* and *i*. The first is the absence of a distinction between locative and directional for the proper ablative marker: *vei*, whose directional or locative meaning is dependent on the meaning of the verb in the VP it is associated with.

It is possible to extend this analysis to *mai* by suggesting as well that location vs. direction lies in the verb. Thus, a *mai* phrase with a verb of motion (such as *lako* 'go') refers to direction; with a static verb (such as *tiko* 'stay'), to location.

Geraghty's treatment (1976) of *mai* lends support to this analysis, for he concluded that there is no "motion-from" *mai*. As evidence, he showed that in the following sentence:

*E lako **mai** na vale ko koya.*   'He is coming from the house.'

mai 'from' is actually the postverbal directional marker, not the "preposition." His argument (p. 515) for this particular sentence is that since in certain constructions, both *mai*s occurred:

*na siga e lako **mai** ki-na **mai** na vale*   'the day he came from the house'

the first sentence has an underlying preposition *mai* in addition to the directional. This second *mai*, one assumes, is his "remote locative," and the directional sense is from the VP: *lako mai* 'come'.

However, as the second example shows, that second *mai* has to be accounted for. I have shown (§21.1.2.2.2.1) that in terms of the intonation, in the sentence

*E lako **mai na vale**.*   'He is coming from the house.

mai na vale constitutes one phrase. Thus, the phonological evidence suggests that in this instance, *mai* does refer to "direction from," not "remote location." If one chooses a noun whose referent can be either static or moveable, it is possible to make a minimal pair, separated only by the intonational clues that mark phrase boundaries:

*[E lako **mai**] [na basi].*   'The bus is coming.'
*[E lako] [**mai** na basi].*   'He's coming from the bus.'

Thus, the question remains: is there one *mai* or two?

The hazy borders between different styles of Fijian produce a similar situation for *i*, although for different reasons. Geraghty (1984:36 proposed locative *i* vs. *e* as one of the distinguishing criteria between Colloquial Fijian and SF. If *ki* (directional marker) is indeed mainly a feature of formal Literary Fijian, then the locative and directional fall together. Thus, what is usually written as

e Suva   'at Suva'
ki Suva   'to Suva'

is spoken as

i Suva   'at Suva, to Suva'

Here again, the distinction between locative and directional would depend on the type of verb used.

21.1.3.2 The function of ablative NPs

Are ablative phrases always adverbial? In most of the examples encountered so far, ablative NPs are more closely related to a verb than to a noun. Of course, their basic reference to location and direction is usually associated with an action/state. However, there are some examples of an ablative NP attributive to a noun or pronoun. Note the following:

*Era dau vaka-yaga-tak-a na bilibili ko ira **mai na ulu-ni-wai**.*
3P HAB CAU-use-TR-3S DEF raft PRP 3P ABL DEF head-POS-water
'Those up-river always use bamboo rafts.'

In this example, the ablative phrase modifies the preceding *ko ira*. One might propose that such an example of attribution is derived from an underlying existential—e.g., 'those who *stay* up-river', and thus confine ablative NPs to adverbial usage.

21.2 COMITATIVE[11] NPS

A comitative NP is marked by *kei₁*, which has two similar functions. The first is to link NPs. E.g.:

*Erau ā lako voli yani ko Rā Kadi **kei Rā Qasikālōlō**.*
3D PT go ASP DIR PRP Rā K CNC Rā Q
'They (dual) went around—Rā K & Rā Q.' (*NV3*:14)

Note that in this example, the two NPs specify the subject *erau*.

In its second function, a *kei₁* phrase immediately follows the VP and is attributive to it:

*Erau mani sota **kei Rā I-Sua**.*   'They (dual) met with RIS.' (*NV3*:14)
3D SEQ meet CNC Rā I-S

---

[11] I have used the abbreviation CNC (concomitant) to match that used for the verb marker *vata*.

21.2.1 Discussion: How many entities involved?

The construction just described is ambiguous as to the number of entities referred to. For example,

Drau lako kei Samu.

literally, 'you (dual) go with S', could involve either two or three persons. If the former, the *kei* phrase specifies[12] the person other than the addressee referred to by *drau* 'you two'.

21.2.2 Contraction of *kei* + third person singular: *kaya*

This form is a contraction of kei_1 + third person singular. For example:

*Au ā sota **kaya**.*	'I met with her.'
1S PT meet CNC-3S	
*Au ā vei-vosa-ki **kaya**.*	'I talked with her.'
1S PT DIS-talk-TR CNC-3S	

21.2.3 Discussion

The phrases immediately above, together with their translations, would not likely be questioned by native speakers. But one particular use of *kaya*—with nonsingular subjects—does cause disagreement among speakers. Churchward (1941:42) gave the following phrase and its translation:

*Keirau ā vei-vosa-ki **kaya**.*	'I had a talk with him.'
1D PT DIS-talk-TR CNC-3S	

echoed by Milner (1972:68):

*Keirau na lako **kaya** ni-mataka.*	'He and I will go tomorrow.'
1D FT go CNC-3S tomorrow	

The bone of contention here is the number of people involved. Some speakers accept the translation; others do not. The source of the disagreement (PG 6/82) is a confusion between *kaya* and *vata*, for the opinion was expressed by some speakers that the two markers meant the same thing. Careful speakers, however, keep them separate (TRN 6/82), and maintain the following distinction:

*Keirau ā lako **kaya**.*	'We (dual exclusive) went with him (three people involved).'
*Keirau ā lako **vata**.*	'We (dual exclusive) went together (two people involved).'

PG added that *sota kaya* 'meet with him' functioned idiomatically, rather as a verb and its object.

---

[12] See CH 26 on specification.

21.3 PROPER ACCUSATIVE NPS[13]

The proper accusative marker i_2 may be underlying a number of constructions involving objects,[14] but it is heard only under special circumstances. The following two segments of discourse were reported by PG (10/80); note that *i* occurs when the phrase specifying the object occurs in isolation:

1. *Au rai-ci Jone.*   'I saw J.'
   1S see-TR J

   I   cei?   'Who?'
   PRP who

   I   Jone.   'J.'
   PRP J

2. *Au rai-c-a.*   'I saw him.'
   1S see-TR-3S

   I cei mada yā?   'Who was it?'
   PRP who INI   DEM:3

   I   Jone.   'J.'
   PRP J

Still, this construction is fairly rare: some speakers would not say *i cei*, but *o cei* instead. See *VV* (**i** 4).

21.4 VOCATIVE: I_3[15]

The vocative marker *i* precedes a personal name, and is used in a phrase preceding the main part of the sentence, set off intonationally. (A vocative is unmarked when it appears at the end of a sentence.) In each of the following examples, this intonational pattern is indicated by a comma:

*I **Filipe**, na vei-vale cava gā?*   'Oh, F, which house?' (*FR2*:11)
VOC F   DEF DIS-house what LIM

*I **Tama-qu**.*   'Oh, Father.' (*FR5*:15)
VOC father-1S

*I **Ulumalaidua**.*   'Oh, U.' (*FR5*:16)
VOC U

A vocative phrase can also be used alone to get the addressee's attention:

I Sai!   'Oh, S!'

I regularly occurs with *saka* (polite address) as the salutation in a formal letter:

I Saka,   'Dear sir, Dear madam,'

---

[13] Here, "proper" includes all proper nouns and all grammatical objects except third person singular -*a*.

[14] This marker was brought to my attention by PG.

[15] Perhaps this form is related to i_2.

l, like some other markers, may be stylistically lengthened, but the length is not phonemic; it remains unaccented.

21.5 ATTRIBUTIVE POSSESSIVE

The form and function of attributive possessive NPs are treated in CH 30.

22 NP GRAMMATICAL MODIFIERS

This chapter deals with markers other than articles and function markers. They are referred to as "grammatical modifiers" to distinguish them from other markers and from modifying elements that come from outside the phrase, i.e., adjectives.

22.1 DISCOURSE MARKER: *GONA* 'AFOREMENTIONED' (AFM)

Gona is used principally in NPs (but also in VPs; see §22.12.4), singling out a particular entity that has already been mentioned, and directing the line of discourse toward this entity.

<blockquote>

E dau siga ni savasava ne-i Nau na siga Vakarauwai. E na siga
3S HAB day POS clean POS Mother DEF day Saturday ABL DEF day

*Vakarauwai **gona** sā oti*
Saturday AFM ASP finish

'Saturday is always Mother's washing day. Last Saturday (a particular one: the one past)' (*NV4*:2)

*E kākana ni yabaki na duruka ka sā i koya **gona** oqō e sā*
3S food POS year DEF *duruka* CNJ ASP PRP 3S AFM DEM:1 3S ASP

dau nama-ki.   'Duruka is an annual food product, and because of that
HAB think-TR   (aforementioned), it is always kept in mind when its
                  time is approaching.' (*NV4*:8)

</blockquote>

22.2 LIMITATION (LIM): *WALE GĀ*

The marker *wale*, in combination with *gā*, limits the semantic field to the entity referred to by the noun. Examples are:

<blockquote>

*E kilā na vosa vaka-Nadrogā **wale gā**.*   'She knows only the
3S know-3S DEF talk man-N LIM LIM   Nadrogā language.'

*M-o tau-r-a mada na suka **wale gā**.*   'Please take only the
SUB-2S take-TR-3S INI DEF sugar LIM LIM   sugar.'

*Sā gunu-v-a na yaqona ni Viti **wale gā**.*   'He drank only kava.'
ASP drink-TR-3S DEF kava POS Fiji LIM LIM

</blockquote>

As in a VP, the markers *wale* and *gā* in an NP need not be contiguous:

> O koya **wale** sara **gā** oqori.   'That's certainly only him there.' (*VV*)
> PRP 3S   LIM   INT   LIM   DEM:2

22.3 INCLUSION (INC)

22.3.1 *Kece* 'all'

Kece indicates that the noun it is associated with refers to all the entities involved. Examples are:

> me vola-i   na   vei-i-vola **kece** sara vaka-Viti
> SUB write-TR DEF DIS-book   INC   INT   MAN-Fiji
> 'that all the books be written in Fijian.' (*SR* 20/4/82)

Note that *kece* and *sara* appear before the modifier.

> e   na   vei-gauna **kece**   'at all times' (*SR* 20/4/82)
> ABL DEF DIS-time   INC

> ia   na   vei-kā   **kece** oqori   'but all those things' (*NL* 13/5/82)
> CNJ DEF DIS-thing INC   DEM:2

> sā   laki kani-a   na   dawa **kece**   'and went to eat all the *dawa*'
> CNJ DIR eat-3S DEF *dawa* INC   (*FR*5:7)

22.3.2 *Taucoko* 'all, wholly, completely'

In some instances, *taucoko* seems to contrast somewhat with *kece*, meaning 'all of an entity' rather than 'all the entities':

> a   ke-dra   i-wiliwili **taucoko**   'their total count' (*NL* 13/5/82)
> DEF PC-3P count   INC

> e   na   bāravi **taucoko**   'on the entire beach' (*FR*5:22)
> ABL DEF beach   INC

It is also used as a synonym for *kece*:

> na   vosa vaka-Viti **taucoko** sara   'all the Fijian languages'
> DEF talk MAN-Fiji   INC   INT   (*SR* 20/4/82)

> e   na   vei-yasa i   Viti **taucoko**   'in all parts of Fiji'
> ABL DEF DIS-part POS Fiji INC   (*NL* 13/5/82)

22.3.3 *Soti* (*sō*)[1]

Soti (*sō*) is used as a marker of inclusion with *cei* and *cava*. *Kece* is not used with these roots.[2]

---

[1] This marker was noted by PG.

[2] There seems to be a restriction against *kece* in most NP + NP sentences. E.g.:

> *[O   ira] [na   tūraga **kece**.]   'All of them are chiefs.'
> PRP 3P   DEF chief   INC

> *[O   ira] [**kece** na   tūraga.]   'All of them are chiefs.'
> PRP 3P   INC   DEF chief

O cei **soti** *na nasi?* PRP who INC DEF nurse	'Who are all the nurses?'
A cava **soti** *na leqa?* DEF what INC DEF trouble	'What are all the troubles?'

22.4 INTENSIFIER (INT): *SARA*

The marker *sara* in a NP, used in the VP as well (§18.8), draws attention to or emphasizes an entity. Examples are:

i matāsawa **sara** ABL beach INT	'to the beach itself' (*FR5*:21)
na kā **sara** *gā au nanu-m-a* DEF thing INT LIM 1S think-TR-3S	'the very thing I thought' (T74:52)
ka ke-na dau **sara** *tale gā* CNJ PC-3S skill INT ITR LIM	'and another of his skills indeed'

22.5 ITERATION (ITR): *TALE, TALE GĀ*

The marker *tale*, which occurs in the VP as well (§18.9), has the sense of "other" in an NP. Examples are:

ka ke-na i-kuri na vosa vaka-Viti **tale** *e sō kei na vosa*
CNJ PC-3S supplement DEF talk MAN-Fiji ITR 3S some CNJ DEF talk

   vaka-Vāvālagi   'and its supplement, some other Fijian languages
   MAN-European   and English' (*SR* 20/4/82)

ka vinaka-ti tiko me mata-ni-i-vola ni gato e na vosa
CNJ want-TR CNT SUB letter POS glottal-stop ABL DEF TALK

   vaka-Viti **tale** *e sō* 'and is needed as a letter for the glottal
   MAN-European ITR 3S some   stop in some other Fijian languages'
                          (Geraghty 1982:5)

Tale occurs with the marker *gā* (not necessarily contiguously): the combination means 'also':

Na "ko i" **tale** *gā e dodonu me "o."* DEF *ko i* ITR LIM 3S right SUB *o*	'Also, *ko i* should be *o*.' (Geraghty 1982:2)

22.6 MODERATIVE, DUBITATIVE (TEN): *BEKA*

The marker *beka* indicates a tentative status, or a suggestion. As with VPs (§18.12), it is often used in questions or commands to avoid being abrupt. For example:

A cava **beka** *na vu-na?* DEF what TEN DEF reason-3S	'What (perhaps) is the reason?'
Na tī **beka**? DEF tea TEN	'Tea, perhaps?'

22.7 LIMITATION (LIM): *GĀ*

Gā after a noun has much the same function as it has after a verb (see §18.13): it focuses the attention on the content word. In the following sentence, note that the common translations of 'just' or 'only' cannot be used:

Ratou sā dui volavola ka taba i-vola na i-talatala e na vei-vanua
3T ASP IND write CNJ print book DEF minister ABL DEF DIS-place

eratou ā dui tū ki-na e na ke-na vosa gā.
3T PT IND stay ABL-3S ABL DEF POS-3S talk LIM

'The ministers (individually) wrote and printed books in the places where they (individually) stayed in each language.' (*SR* 20/4/82)

Here, the *gā* draws attention to each language having its own translation and printing.

*Na taci i Leone **gā**.* DEF sibling POS L LIM	'It's L's brother, in fact.' (T74:51)
*Sega, o Jona **gā**.* no PRP J LIM	'No, just J.' (T74:51)
*Na kā sara **gā** au nanu-m-a.* DEF thing INT LIM 1S think-TR-3S	'Just what I thought.' (T74:52)

23 NOUN AFFIXATION

This chapter treats a limited number of noun affixes and includes reduplication as a type of affixation.

23.1 COLLECTIVE, DISTRIBUTIVE (DIS): *VEI-*

The construction *vei-* + N, although sometimes interpreted as a plural, refers to a collection of entities, or each entity treated individually. (Al- though it is labeled as a reciprocal (REC) in VPs, it is labeled as a distributive (DIS) in NPs).

> *na **vei**-bogi*   'every night'
> DEF DIS-night

> *taba-ki e na **vei**-siga Tūsiti kei na Vakaraubuka*
> print-TR ABL DEF DIS-day Tuesday CNJ DEF Friday
> 'printed every Tuesday and Friday' (*VG* calendar, 1961)

In the second example, *vei-* applies to both the following days of the week.

In its discourse function, *vei-* prefixed to a noun generalizes it—i.e., removes its definiteness, although the definite marker often remains. In the following examples, some of the NPs with *vei-* are grammatically definite, some indefinite. But they are all general.

> *E dau vuka e **vei**-cō.*   'It always flies in the grassy areas' (*NV1*:28)
> 3S HAB fly ABL DIS-grass

> *E dau vuka e **vei**-taba-ni-kau.*   'It always flies in tree branches.'
> 3S HAB fly ABL DIS-branch-POS-tree   (*NV1*:29)

> *E tū na lali e na noda **vei**-koro kece.*
> 3S exist DEF drum ABL DEF POS-1PI DIS-village INC
> 'There's a *lali* in all our (plural inclusive) villages.' (*NV2*:37)

> *Ka tiko e na dreke ni **vei**-dalo ne-i tama-qu*
> REL exist ABL DEF bottom POS DIS-taro POS father-1S
> 'that stands in the bottom of my father's taro patch' (NV2:39)

> *Era cavatū mai na **vei**-vanua tani.*   'They (plural) come from foreign
> 3P stem ABL DEF DIS-land different   lands' (*NV2*:45)

*E serau vinaka tale gā   na **vei**-kalokalo.* 'The stars also shine.'
3S shine good   ITR LIM DEF DIS-star

The function of generalizing is particularly apparent in the last example. Since "stars" are not entities normally treated as individuals, the subject is singular (see §4.5). Thus, generalizing with *vei-* is one way to show that the topic is not a particular star. Note a similar function of *vei-* in the next sentence (from the same context). Here, the previous sentence referred to counting stars, so the subject is plural. But the concept of "evening" is kept general; it is not a particular evening on which the stars appear:

*e   na gauna era sā   qai vovotu mai ki-na   e   na **vei**-yakavi*
ABL DEF time   3P ASP SEQ appear DIR ABL-3S ABL DEF DIS-evening
'at the time they appear in the evening'

In all these examples of generalization, note the similarity in function of *vei-* used in an NP to one of the functions of the same prefix in a VP (§7.3).

23.2 INDIVIDUALITY (IND): *DUI*

A noun prefixed by *dui-* refers to an entity treated as an individual:

*ka ratou **dui** vodo sara e   na   no-dratou **dui** lori*
CNJ 3T   IND board INT ABL DEF PC-3T   IND bus
'and they immediately boarded (individually) their respective buses' (*NV4*:69)

Note that in the sentence above, *dui* appears in both the VP and the NP.[1]

23.3 "POETICAL SUFFIXES": *-RI, -A, -YA*

Churchward (1941:82) wrote:

> The suffixes **-ri** and **-a** are sometimes used in native poetry at the end of a line, for the sake of providing an extra syllable and securing assonance. Thus:
>
> *Sā sega ni bece*
> *Na nona vale**ri** [vale-ri]* 'His house [*vale*] is not despised.'

Further examples, also for a poetic match, are:

*Lomaiviti-**a*** (from the place name *Lomaiviti*)
*kina-**ya*** (from *kina*)
*Matanitū-**ya*** (from *Matanitū* 'Government')

Churchward continued (p. 83):

> These poetical suffixes do not affect the meaning in any way at all. But they do, of course, affect the accent. Thus: vale becomes valéri; Lomaiviti becomes Lomaivitía; kina becomes kináya ...

These forms join the set of suffixes that consist of a short syllable, thus conditioning a shift in accent (see §36.3).

---

[1] PG suggested (11/83) that the first *dui* is redundant, adding that if the second were deleted, the sentence could mean that they board the same bus at different times.

23.4 REDUPLICATION OF NOUN ROOTS

Reduplication of nouns is as varied and unpredictable as that of verbs (CH 14). The following discussion shows general tendencies; the list of meanings is open-ended.

23.4.1 Form

Formally, reduplication can be divided into *full* and *partial* (see §14.13; Milner 1972:47). The former seems more common than the latter, as most of the examples below show. However, the following zoological names may illustrate partial reduplication (with lengthening of the vowel in the first syllable):

dā-dakulaci	'striped water snake'	*dā-darikai*	'freshwater eel'
dā-dakuvonu	'beetle with wings like the back of a turtle)		

Semantically, reduplication is a way to narrow the scope of a particular root, keeping a formal resemblance to mirror a semantic resemblance. For example:

beka	(general name for 'bat')	*wai*	'water'
beka-beka	(specific type of *beka*)	*wai-wai*	'oil'
yasi	'sandalwood'	*via*	'large kind of taro'
yasi-yasi	'tree resembling *yasi*'	*via-via*	'noncultivated wild lily'

However, many plant and animal names are, in form, a reduplicated root for which no single-root counterpart exists—at least not in the same semantic range:

soki-soki	'balloonfish'	*dabu-dabu*	(kind of tree)
dobu-dobu	(kind of shellfish)	*doce-doce*	(kind of shrub)

Some words that refer to body parts are reduplicated forms without corresponding single roots:

gale-gale	'teeth (molars)'	*vico-vico*	'navel'

Others have a dubious relationship to single roots:

buku	'(fruit, root) pointed end; gun butt'
buku-buku ni liga	'elbow'
kiri	'tickle under the arm'
kiri-kiriwa	'armpit'

23.4.2 Semantic categories

1. Diminutive. Churchward (1941:81) discussed this class, listing some of the forms in the examples above:[2] *via-via, yasi-yasi*.

2. Greater numbers. Churchward (p. 81) gave two examples in this category:

vei-vanua 'various countries'   *vei-vei-vanua* 'larger number of countries'
vei-gauna 'times, all the time'   *vei-vei-gauna* 'times, ages'

Note that in these examples, it is the prefix—not the root—that is reduplicated.

---

[2] However, he included also "otherwise different from the genuine thing," which can be a fairly open-ended category.

24 NOMINALIZATION

This chapter treats two different kinds of nominalization. The first, DERIVED NOMINALIZATION, is marked formally by *i-*. It creates a new lexical item: a noun formed from a verb. E.g.:

sele   'cut'   *i-sele*   'knife'

The second, DIRECT NOMINALIZATION, involves no formal change. It does not create a new lexical item, but it is merely an instance of a verb being *used* as a noun:

E lako.   'She goes.'   *na lako*   'going'
E vinaka.   'It is good.'   *na vinaka*   'goodness'

24.1 DERIVED NOMINALIZATION: *I-* NOUNS

A noun derived from a verb by prefixing *i-* shows a formal link between the referent of an action/state and that of an entity connected with it. For example:

E culacula.   'She's sewing.'

A derived noun can be made from the root *cula* by prefixing *i-*; its meaning is not predictable, but it is related in some way to the general meaning of the root, 'to sew' in that it refers to an entity that is part of the activity or state referred to by the verb. In this case:

i-cula   'needle'

Here, the noun refers to an instrument that is essential for the act of sewing.

I- nouns are somewhat more restricted than verbs *used* as nouns. Roots are confined to A1, A2, and S2 verbs; thus, an S1 verb such as *totoka* 'beautiful' cannot be made into a noun by prefixing *i-*. Moreover, even in those verb types that allow such prefixing, the process is irregular. That is, a corresponding *i-*noun does not exist for every verb in the allowable categories.

PG noted (12/83) that A2 roots may be reduplicated in their *i-*derived form, whereas S2 roots may not.

There are many examples of derived nouns that refer to literal instruments for performing an action:

E seru-t-a.   'She combed it.'   *na i-seru*   'the comb'
E voce-tak-a.   'She paddled it.'   *na i-voce*   'the paddle'

E ubi-a.	'She covered it.'	*na i-ubi*	'the cover'
E kele-a.	'She anchored it.'	*na i-kelekele*	'the anchor'
E kaba-t-a.	'He climbed it.'	*na i-kabakaba*	'the ladder'

Not all instruments are manufactured:

E taqi.	'He cried.'	*na i-taqitaqi*	'the larynx'
E tilo-m-a.	'She swallowed it.'	*na i-tilotilo*	'the throat'

Moreover, not all *i-* nouns are literal instruments—i.e., tools. Some are instruments in a metaphorical sense—entities that are either an essential or an integral part of the action. For example, another meaning of *i-kelekele* ('anchor' above) is 'anchorage'. Interestingly, *kele* 'to anchor' takes two principal (one-syllable) transitive suffixes. One is given above; the other is:

E kele-v-a.   'He anchored-at it.'

Note the relationship of this particular VP to *i-kelekele* 'anchorage'; *i-kelekele* is what the object refers to.

More examples of metaphorical instruments are:

E saba-k-a.	'She slapped him.'	*na i-saba*	'the slap'
E lako-v-a.	'He went-for/-on it.'	*na i-lakolako*	'the going, path, manner'

24.1.1 Reduplication of *i-* forms

As with most types of reduplication, its use with *i-* forms is irregular. Some *i*-VV forms seem to exist merely to provide a contrast with *i*-V forms. For example:

na i-sele	'the knife'	*na i-selesele*	'the piece cut off'
E sole-g-a.	'She wrapped it up.'	*na i-sole*	'the wrapper, shroud'
na i-solesole	'the bundle'		

However, PG (12/83) considered such relationships to be regular, with the nonreduplicated derivatives representing "instruments," and the reduplicated derivatives representing "results."

One use of the reduplicated *i-* form seems more nearly regular than the others: it indicates the manner of performing the action. Examples are:

na i-kelekele	'the manner of anchoring'[1]		
E caka-v-a.	'He did it.'	*na ke-na i-cakacaka*	'the way it was done'
E buli-a.	'He formed it.'	*na ke-na i-bulibuli*	'the way it was formed'

Other forms refer to the result of the action:

E volā.	'She wrote it.'	*na i-vola*	'the book, letter'
E bini-a	'She heaped it up.'	*na i-binibini*	'the heap'

---

[1] Note that there are now three separate meanings for this one form.

24.1.2 *I-* nouns from derived verbs

The examples so far have shown nouns formed from a verb root or a reduplicated root. Derived forms can also enter into this construction:

E macala.	'It's clear.'
E vaka-macala.	'She made (something) clear.'
na i-vaka-macala	'the explanation'
E tagi.	'It cries.'
E vaka-tagi-c-a.	'It made her cry.'
E vaka-tagi-tak-a	'She played it (musical instrument).'
na i-vaka-tagi	'the musical instrument'
E bula.	'She's alive, she lives.'
E vaka-bula.	'She's giving/saving life.'
na i-vaka-bula	'the savior'

Some forms include the transitive suffix:

*E tuku-**n**-a.*	'He told it.'
na i-tukutuku	'the news, report'
*na i-tuku-**ni***	'the story, tradition'

What is the function of the transitive suffix *-ni* in the last form? Is it merely to provide a contrasting form, or does it emphasize that the story is *told*?

24.1.3 *I-* nouns: A semantic view

Some *i-* nouns refer to entities that have no existence outside the action of the verb they are derived from. As an example, note the following two sentences:

*E ā qai dreke-t-a   muri yani ko koya na **i-sulu duka**... Sā tau^2 sara*
3S PT SEQ carry-TR-3S back DIR PRP 3S   DEF clothes dirty   ASP place INT

   *na bēseni kei na **i-drekedreke**.*
   DEF basin CNJ DEF burden

'Then she carried the dirty clothes away ... She put down the basin and the burden.' (*NV4*:2)

In the first sentence, the entity that is being carried (*dreke*) is referred to explicitly (*na i-sulu duka*). However, in the second sentence, it is referred to only as *na i-drekedreke*, which means 'a burden carried in the *dreke* fashion'—that is, like a backpack. Note the following *i-* nouns, similar in formation:

kau	'carried'	*i-kaukau*	'burden'
cola	'carried (on shoulders)'	*i-colacola*	'burden'
tube	'held by handle'	*i-tubetube*	'handle'
tabe	'carry resting on palms'	*i-tabe*	'tray'

One way of viewing the referents of *i-drekedreke* and these similar *i*-nouns is to

---

[2] See §16.4 for a discussion of verbs without transitive marking and an object, but with a specified object serving as an attribute.

propose that they exist only within the context of the particular action/state referred to by the verb.

As another example, consider *i-tuki(tuki)* 'hammer', from *tuki-a* 'hammer it'. A piece of wood (*kau*) or a stone (*vatu*) can be used to hammer something; in that action, it is *na i-tuki(tuki)*. Outside that context, it is simply *na kau* or *na vatu*.

That same stone, if used as an anchor, can be referred to as *na i-kelekele*, from *kele-a* 'anchor it'.

Other examples are:

ravi-t-a	'lean-on it'
i-raviravi	'something to lean on—a wall, a tree, etc. (Outside the context of leaning, the entity is no longer *na i-raviravi*.)
seru-ta	'comb it'
i-seru	'(a) comb, even the hands used as a comb'
iri-v-a	'fan it'
i-iri	'(a) fan; anything used to fan'

In most of the preceding examples, certain entities have been referred to with *i-* nouns only when they are literally in the context of the action of the verb from which the noun is derived. However, the last two examples, *i-seru* 'comb' and *i-iri* 'fan' refer to entities (functionally, they are "instruments") that are used for a specific purpose.

Although traditional Fijian society certainly had such instruments with a specific purpose, many such words now refer to introduced tools. Consider *i-sulu* 'clothing'. It is derived from *sulu-m-a* 'clothe him' and refers to something that is worn, or anything that covers or adorns something. Therefore, originally (one might propose) its existence depended on the act of clothing or adorning someone or something.

Now, however, *i-sulu* has taken on a more specific meaning, referring usually to garments made of woven cloth—articles expressly for the purpose of wearing. Other examples are:

i-sele	'knife'. Originally, sharpened bamboo or other sharp material. *I-sele* now used principally for a metal knife.
i-koti	'scissors'. Originally a shell or shark's tooth to shave with (Hazlewood 1872).

Each of these instruments, unlike the stone used variously as an anchor or a hammer (and assuming a different name in each function), has a fixed name and purpose. Morphology binds the name and purpose together.

Some *i-* forms derived from reduplicated roots refer to location. For example, *i-kelekele* 'anchorage', *i-dabedabe* 'place for sitting', *i-sotasota* 'meeting place' (PG 12/83).

24.1.3.1 Another source for *i*- nouns?

There are many *i*- nouns for which no corresponding verb occurs. Some of these, such as:

i-tau   'friend'

may simply be instances of a verb root ceasing to be used, while the derived noun remains. However, there is at least one more possibility. Geraghty (1979:245–46) has pointed out that "many non-instrumental *i*-prefixed nouns are semantically inalienable ... " ("partitive," in my terminology; see §19.2.1). Some of his examples are:

i-matau   'right side'   *i-mawī*   'left side'
i-coi   '(meal) meat or fish, accompanying *dalo*, etc.'

This explanation seems to fit well with that above: that some *i*-nouns have no existence outside the context of the action/state they are associated with. Similarly, each of the examples above is part of a relationship.

Geraghty noted that his explanation pointed to another historical source for such *i*- nouns. However, one might also propose that the roots of such forms as those above were once used as verbs. Unfortunately, there seems to be little firm evidence to support either explanation.

24.2 DIRECT NOMINALIZATION: VERBS USED AS NOUNS[3]

As the preceding section showed, the referent of a noun derived with the prefix *i*- is *associated* in some way with the action/state that the verb represents. When a verb is *used* as a noun, it refers *directly* to that action/state. For example,

E caka.   'It is done.'
na i-cakacaka   'the manner in which it was done'

vs.

na cakacaka   'the work (i.e., the doing)'

24.2.1 The function of direct nominalization

From the point of view of discourse, direct nominalization is the ultimate way to suppress the actor and/or goal. For example, note the simple discourse that follows (*NV2*:14):

1. *E na lako mai na vū-ni-i-valu.*   'The paramount chief will arrive.'
2. *E tūraga bale ko koya.*   'He's a very important chief.'
3. *Era na wā-rak-a na qase.*   'The elders will wait for him.'
4. *E na caka **na   gunu   yaqona** kei **na   kana magiti**.*
   3S FT done DEF drink   kava   CNJ DEF eat feast
   'Kava-drinking and feasting (lit., feast-eating) will take place (lit., 'be done').'

There are a number of ways that the ideas contained in sentence (4) could have been expressed, but in the one chosen, it is the *activities* of kava-drinking

---

[3] Milner (1971:410–11) referred to "deverbal nouns."

and feasting that are important, not the performers of these actions. Incidentally, note that in this example, the nominalization takes place not on simple verbs, but on the constructions *gunu yaqona* and *kana magiti*. Further examples are:

*E na vuke-i Nana ko tama-qu e **na loba niu**.*
3S FT help-TR Mother PRP father-1S ABL DEF squeeze coconut
'Father will help Mother in squeezing coconut milk.' (*NV2*:17)

*E levu sara **na katakata**.* 'There was a lot of heat.' (*NV2*:24)
3S big INT DEF hot

*ni sā suka **na vuli*** 'when school let out' (*NV2*:39)
SUB ASP disperse DEF learn

na tagi ni vanua '(lit.) crying of the land' (*NV2*:62)
DEF cry POS land

*E totolo sara **na vuka ni manumanu oqō**.* 'This bird's flying
3S fast INT DEF fly POS bird DEM:1 is very fast.' (*NV2*:63)

*me caka e dua **na cakacaka*** 'work to be done (*NV2*:61)
SUB done 3S one DEF work

na wili kalokalo 'counting stars. (*NV2*:59)
DEF count star

One way to include the actor in this construction is to do so in the form of a possessive. In the following examples, the ultimate referent of the possessive is the actor. In the first set of constructions below—those with *active* verbs, and the actor referring to an animate being (Geraghty 1983:246–47), the *nō-* form of the possessive is used.

na no-na cakacaka 'his work'
DEF PC-3S work

*E dau **no-dra cakacaka** na yalewa **na samusamu** kei **na kesakesa**.*
3S HAB PC-3P work DEF woman DEF beating CNJ DEF dyeing
'Beating and dyeing are the women's work.' (*NV2*:69)

*E ā vaka-yaco-ri **na no-dra qito coko-vata** na cauravou.*
3S PT CAU-happen-TR DEF PC-3P play joined DEF youth
'(Lit.) it came to pass—the youths' playing together.' (*NV2*:27)

*E ā kolo-tak-a gā **na no-na siwa** ko Waqa.*
3S PT throw-TR-3S LIM DEF PC-3S fish PRP W
'W just threw his line.' (*NV2*:43)

*E sā dua-tani na **no-dra kaikaila**. E lasa sara **na no-dra***
3S ASP exceptional DEF PC-3P shouting 3S happy INT DEF PC-3P

***vei-tara tiko**.* 'Their shouting was great; their playing tag was
tag-playing CNT fun.' (*NV2*:19)

In the example just above, the second nominalized verb is modified by the possessive *no-dra* and the continuative marker *tiko*. The presence of the latter shows that not only verbs, but VPs, can be nominalized. A similar example is:

24 Nominalization

na no-na sā yadra mai DEF PC-3S ASP awake DIR	'its awakening' (*NV2*:48)

Note the presence of the aspect marker *sā* and the directional *mai*. These markers show that the whole "noun" refers not to the state of being awake, but to the process of awakening—as opposed to a previous state.

As a contrast, when a stative verb—simple or derived—appears in the NP, it is usually possessed by a *kē-* form. This behavior is consistent with the general difference between *nō-* and *kē-* forms, discussed in CH 30.

na ke-na kaukaua DEF PC-3S strong	'its strength' (*NV2*:50)
na ke-na levu DEF PC-3S big	lit., 'its size (indicating the end of a speech)'
na ke-dra kesa-vi tiko DEF PC-3P dye-TR CNT	'their being dyed' (*NV2*:71)
e **na ke-dra sā rui yawa** ABL DEF PC-3P ASP EXT far	'in their great distance' (*NV2*:58)

The last example above shows the nominalized form in a secondary NP. Other examples are:

E dau **no-dra** *cakacaka na gone tagane* **na siwa** *e na gauna* 3S HAB PC-3P work DEF child male DEF fish ABL DEF time **ni sere-ki**. POS disperse-TR	'Line fishing is always the work of boys during school holidays.' (*NV2*:42)
wā **ni vosavosa** string POS talk	'telephone line' (lit., string of talking)

Note that in this construction, the NP need not be definite.

In the following example, both NPs use verbs as their head. It is the second that illustrates a secondary NP:

na dedē ni moce *oqō* DEF long POS sleep DEM:1	'the length of this sleep'

PG noted (12/83) that a common use of such phrases was to indicate time, rather like sentence-initial adverbial phrases in English. E.g.:

no-na curu gā yani PC-3S enter LIM DIR	'just as he entered'
na neitou tiko mai keā DEF PC-1TX stay DIR LOC:3	'while we were there'

25 PERSONAL DEICTIC NOUNS

From an etymological point of view, deictic elements in a language are those that "show" or "point out."

25.1 DEICTIC LOCATIVE NOUNS

Three deictic elements—*kē*, *keri*, and *keā*—serve as the heads of common NPs. They refer to locations near first, second, and third person, respectively. These nouns are introduced by the three common locative markers—*e*, *mai*, and *(k)i*[1]. Examples are:

> *Au ā rai-c-a tale gā mai na dua na sitoa e **keā**.*
> 1S PT see-TR-3S ITR LIM DIR DEF one DEF store ABL LOC:3
> 'I also saw (it) in a store there.' (T74:58)

> *E tolu dina na maile na ke-na yawa **mai kē**.*
> 3S three true DEF mile DEF PC-3S far ABL LOC:3
> 'The distance is actually three miles from here.' (T74:55)

> *Au marau tale gā ni-u mai curu e **kē**.*
> 1S happy ITR LIM SUB-1S DIR enter ABL LOC:1
> 'I'm also glad that I came in here.' (FR3:8)

> *Tou qai la-ki vaka-toka tī gā **ki keā**.*
> 1TI SEQ go-ABL put tea LIM ABL LOC:3
> 'Then we'll go put the kettle on for tea there.' (FR3:53)

> *dua tale **mai keri***   'another one over there (by you)' (FMC61:9)
> one ITR ABL LOC:2

25.2 PERSONAL LOCATIVES USED AS LOCATIVE PHRASES

The demonstratives *(o)qō*, *(o)qori*, *(o)yā* are similar to *kē*, *keri*, and *keā* in their reference to location near first, second, and third person. They differ, however, in a number of ways.

The main formal difference is that each of the markers *oqō*, *oqori*, and *oyā* can function as a complete phrase. That is, it does not occur with locative markers:

> *E tiko e kē.*   'It's here (by me).'
> *E tiko oqō.*   'It's here (by me).'

The following examples show the personal locatives in their literal use:

Ia, mada me keirau rai-c-a   na kā   e cori-vaki tū   e   na
CNJ INI SUB IDX see-TR-3S DEF thing 3S tie-TR   CNT ABL DEF

i-sū ***qori*.*   'OK, let's (dual exclusive) see the things you have
basket DEM:2   tied up in your basket.' (*NV4*:71)

*na i-olo madrai vaka-uto-na **qō***   'this sandwich' (NV4:71)
DEF parcel bread filled   DEM:1

*Sā sīnai tū   na tamata e   na wavu **koyā**.*
ASP full CNT DEF person ABL DEF wharf DEM:3
'The people were crowded on that wharf.' (*FR6*:3)

Note that in their literal use, the forms *oqō* and *oqori* ('by me', 'by you') are limited to conversations or a special kind of narrative in which first and second persons are involved.

25.2.1 *Ayā*

Ayā is an alternate of *oyā*:

Ayā *ni sā rui nanu-m-a vaka-levu na gone*
DEM:3 SUB ASP EXT think-TR-3S man-big   DEF child
'that is that she is thinking of her child all the time' (T74:43)

TRN stated (5/82) that he could see no difference between *oyā* and *ayā*. Viewing substitutability from the other direction, Arms (10/84) noted that *ayā* also means 'namely' or 'that is', and that *oyā* cannot be substituted for it with this meaning.

25.3 TIME

In some contexts, demonstratives can refer to time as well as place. For example, the sentence in §25.2:

*E tiko **oqō**.*   'It's here (by me).'

can also mean 'It's here (right now).' But the meaning is usually much more dependent on context than previous descriptions suggest.[1] Note the following:

Ni   da ka-y-a   ni   da laki keli daira, eda laki tūdai vuaka ni vei-kau.
SUB 1PI say-TR-3S SUB 1PI DIR dig snare 1PI DIR trap pig POS DIS-tree

Oqō *eda na keli-a e dua na qara levu.*
DEM:1 1PI FT dig-3S 3S one DEF hole big
'When we say we're going to *keli daira*, we're going to trap wild pigs. Now (here), we'll dig a large pit.' (*FR3*:3)

Obviously, *oqō* 'here' does not mean the present, but instead, refers to the context of this particular activity.

---

[1] For example, see Milner 1972:19–20. The statements "... *oqō* is used for the present," "*oqori* is used for the recent past," and "*oyā* is used for the distant past" are oversimplified.

In written Fijian at least, most instances of *oqō*, *oqori*, and *oyā* have a similar contextual reference. But the relationship among the three is maintained. For example, *oqō* often refers to a point that is about to be brought up, or one that has just been presented:

o   ira **oqō**   'these (referring to the entities just mentioned)' (*SR* 20/4/82)
PRP 3P DEM:1

For reference to entities immediately preceding the sentence in question, the distinction between *oqō* and *oqori* is not clear. Sometimes the latter is used:

O   iratou **oqori**, *eratou   raba-i-levu.*   'As for those, they are wide.'
PRP 3T   DEM:2   3T   wide   (*NV2*:71)

Here, *oqori* is used because the topic (different types of *masi*) has just been presented to the reader. But more often, *oqori* refers to something in the preceding discourse, but not immediately preceding:

e   na   no-dra vei-vosa-ki   ka vei-soli   vā-kāsama tiko **oqori**
ABL DEF PC-3P DIS-converse-TR CNJ DIS-exchange consider CNT DEM:2
'in their conversation and exchange-consideration there' (*SR* 20/4/82)

In the following example, *oyā* refers to the distant past (in literal time), but not in context:

Sā digi-taki   oti na yavu me vola-i   ki-na   na vosa vaka-Viti, **oyā**
ASP choose-TR ASP DEF base SUB write-TR ABL-3S DEF talk MAN-Fiji DEM:3
na   vosa vaka-Bau.   'The foundation on which the Fijian language is
DEF talk MAN-Bau   written has already been chosen; that is the
                         Bauan language.' (*SR* 20/4/82)

In the next examples, *oyā* refers to an action that was completed in the narrative immediately preceding the sentence in question.

Oti **oyā**, *keimami sā   qai lako kece.*   'After that, we all then went.'
finish DEM:3 1PX   ASP SEQ go INC   (*FR6*:2)

In this particular text, there are four examples of this construction on one page. The position of the narrator is rather removed from the events, however, for the story is in the form of a letter written some time after the events happened.

Oyā does not always refer to the past. In some contexts, it can refer to the future as well: the phrase

e   na gauna **oyā**   'that time'
ABL DEF time   DEM:3

can refer to some time in the future that has already referred to.

The essence of the personal locatives is that they are deictic—referring not to absolute places or absolute times, but to the "situation of the utterance" (Lyons 1968:275): the speaker, the addressee, and the context of the discourse itself.

25.4 PERSONAL LOCATIVES IN THE NP + NP CONSTRUCTION

Forms in the *oqō* set are often used in NP + NP constructions (see §2.1.4.2):

Oyā + *na no-qu koro*. DEM:3 DEF PC-1S village	'That's my village.'

Here, *oyā* serves as a NP unmarked for any ablative functions, such as indicating time or place. Instead, it is one of the principal constituents in the sentence.

Arms pointed out (10/84) that members of the set can also specify the subject of a VP, as in:

*E vinaka **oqō***.	'This is good.'

In addition, these forms can serve as specified objects:

*Au na sara-v-a **oqō**.* 1S FUT look-TR-3S DEM:1	'I'll look at this.'[2]

These forms can also occur with other NP markers:

***Oqori** sara gā na vu-na.* DEM:2 INT LIM DEF base-3S	'That indeed is the reason.' (*NV4*:15)

25.5 THE OPTIONAL *O*

In the opening sentence of §25.2, the three forms are written with *o* in parentheses. This notation indicates that the forms *qō*, *qori*, and *yā* are also used. These shortened forms are more common in speech (especially faster speech) than they are in writing. Examples are:

*Sā rui mani kāveti levu sara **qori**.* ASP EXT SEQ cabbage big INT DEM:2	'That was a very large cabbage indeed there.' (FMC61:40)
*e na koro **qori*** ABL DEF pot DEM:2	'in that (by you) pot' (FMC61:40)
*kā **qō*** thing DEM:1	'this thing'
*e na dua na gauna **yā*** ABL DEF one DEF time DEM:3	'one time then (long ago)'

The shorter forms are not usually found in formal written Fijian, but do occur in works that try to represent casual conversation. For example:

*Sega soti na bete-na na kā **qori**.*[3] not INT DEF use-3S DEF thing DEM:2	'That's of no use' (T74:51)
*e na vuravura **qō*** ABL DEF world DEM:3	'In this world' (T74:59)

When the *o* drops, the prefix *vaka-* takes its *vā-* form (before velars):

vaka-oqō	'in this manner'
vā-qō	'in this manner'

---

[2] As Arms noted (10/84), this sentence (at least as written) can also mean 'I'll look at it here' or 'I'll look at it now'.

[3] Some writers use an apostrophe in these shortened forms: *'qo*, *'qori*, and *'yā*.

25.5.1 *Oyā* vs. *koyā*. In previous grammars, *koyā* has been treated as the primary form (Churchward 1941:29), or as an alternate to *oyā* (Milner 1972:20). Here, we treat *oyā* as the primary form. The conditions for the occurrence of *koyā* are similar to those for *ko* (proper marker), discussed in §20.1.

SECTION IV: OPERATIONS

TAKEN FROM THE *DEGEI*, OFF THE COAST OF VANUA LEVU, APRIL 1961. ©AJS

The preceding sections described the structure of the two principal building blocks of Fijian grammar—the VP and the NP. In addition to statements about the *forms* of these two units, there have been a number of references to their respective *functions*. For example, the basic VP has been referred to as the foundation of all sentences of a particular type. This point of view has an important effect on the rest of the grammatical description: it means that the VP and the NP are not complementary elements of a sentence as they are in some languages. Thus, the usual relationship of "subject" to "predicate," often taken as axiomatic in grammatical descriptions, does not hold for Fijian.

The aim of this section is to explain Fijian syntax (that is, relationships of elements beyond the basic VP and NP) in terms of OPERATIONS that combine phrases or add to their basic structure.

In semantic terms, most[1] of these operations narrow or SPECIFY reference. For example, SPECIFICATION narrows down the references of person-number markers in several syntactic functions. ATTRIBUTION narrows semantic reference by adding descriptive features. SUBORDINATION can be considered a type of attribution, as well as a process that shows the relationship between two action/states. POSSESSION is a special kind of attribution, indicating a particular relationship between two entities.

---

[1] Except coordination.

If we consider the order of these operations, specification must precede NP attribution, for it is specification that accounts for the presence of an NP in most sentences. This section treats these processes in this order:

Specification	Possession
Attribution	Coordination
Subordination	

The order still involves difficulties, however; for example, one type of specification assumes the reader's knowledge of possession. Therefore, the reader must supplement the usual linear order of reading with some selective skipping and rereading.

Based on the morphological similarities of the English words on the list just above, one might expect NEGATION to be another type of operation. However, since negation is largely lexical, based on the verb *sega*, it is not treated as a separate category. See §29.1.1.2.1.1 (VP negation) and §9.1.1 (negative existential).

26 SPECIFICATION

SPECIFICATION is a grammatical category that ranks the degree to which grammatical and lexical elements are explicit in their reference to participants in the action or state represented in the sentence. These participants, in the form of person-number markers and NPs, include the actor, the goal, the possessor, and also the referents of the heads of oblique phrases.

By recognizing specification as a grammatical category, we can answer the following questions and find connections among them (and others):

1. What is the function of "passive" suffixes on roots that already focus on the goal?
2. What is the function of NPs when "pronominal" subjects and objects are present in the VP?
3. What is the actual nature of a construction sometimes called the "Fijian genitive"?
4. How does apposition fit into the system?

Overall, specification can be divided into two main types:

1. Specification within the VP. This type, which applies only to the subject and/or the object, deals with three levels: IMPLICIT, SIGNALED, and EXPRESSED.
2. Specification outside the VP. This type deals with the following categories:

   The fourth level, SPECIFIED, which refers to NPs that specify the subject and/or the object
   Specification in possessive constructions
   Specification in secondary NPs

The following terms (some of which have already been discussed) and their interrelationships are important for understanding specificity:

SEMANTIC TERMS

THEME — Something in the external world (i.e., outside language) that people are talking about. Thus, it is an entity in a discourse, but whose role for a specific situation (i.e., actor or goal) cannot yet be determined. When a theme has a particular relationship to an action or a state, we call it a:

REFERENT	A theme that is an actor or goal with respect to an action or a state.
ACTOR	The initiator of an action—the performer, the one who acts.
GOAL	The recipient of an action—the person or thing affected, described, or in a state.
ACTION/ STATE	The activity or condition connected with the actor, goal, or both.

GRAMMATICAL TERMS

SUBJECT	The grammatical representation within a sentence of either the actor or the goal. Formally, it is a morpheme (or combination of morphemes) containing the features of person, number, and exclusivity. It precedes the verb.
OBJECT	With a two-referent active verb, the grammatical representation of the goal. Similar in form to the subject. It follows the verb.
VERB	The representation within a sentence of either the action or the state. It is the nucleus of the VP, following the subject and preceding the object, if there is one.

26.1 SPECIFICATION WITHIN THE VP

The realization that there are different levels of specification within the Fijian VP grew out of what Biggs (1974:425) called an "apparent anomaly" in the forms of goal-selecting (S2) verbs. Among his examples illustrating verb classes in Fijian are the following two sentences with the same gloss:

*Ā **tobo** na vuaka.* 'The pig was trapped.'[1]
*Ā **tobo-ki** na vuaka.* 'The pig was trapped.'

Biggs stated that there was "no apparent difference in meaning" between the two constructions. He added:

> -(*C*)*i* has no effect upon the classification of verbs which are already goal-subject selecting [S2] though it is freely suffixed to them. We have already observed that this apparent anomaly was noted by both Hazlewood and Milner …

These examples, and Biggs's interpretation of them, served as flashing red lights, as it were, for grammatical analysis. First (and most important), it was suspicious that a difference in form should produce no corresponding difference in meaning.[2] Next, it was not suggested that context (not given) might be responsible for a subtle difference in meaning not reflected in the translation.

---

[1] Macrons, missing in the original, have been added to the past tense marker.
[2] An obvious caveat is that one should look beyond translations for meanings. But perhaps Biggs's choice of an example was unfortunate, since there is no way to show the difference between *tobo* and *toboki* in an English translation. In the examples used below, *dola* 'open' and *dola-vi* 'opened', the difference *is* reflected in the translation.

26 Specification

It turns out that there is indeed a difference in meaning: the degree to which the actor is suggested.[3] In the first sentence, there is no hint that the state, *tobo*, had a cause—i.e., an actor. In the second, the presence of *-ki* suggests that there was an actor involved, but the structure of Fijian does not allow it to be named specifically in this construction.[4]

The following discussion shows that these formal features within the VP are not random, but instead, fit into a system.

26.1.1 Formal manifestations

In CH 16 it was shown that the basis of transitivity is primarily semantic. Therefore, the formal trappings, which were once thought to be the defining features of transitivity itself, must have some other function. In other words, we are left with a residue of formal material to explain. Within the VP, this formal material includes the following:

1. Subjects
2. Objects
3. Transitive markers

In short, we must account for the formal differences among the members of the following set:

1. *Lade!*   'Jump!'
   jump
2. *E lade.*   'She jumps.'
   3S jump
3. *E lade-v-a.*   'She jumps-to it.'
   3S jump-TR-3S
4. *E lade-vi.*   'It is jumped-to.'
   3S jump-TR
5. *E dola.*   'It is open.'
   3S open
6. *E dola-vi.*   'It is opened.'
   3S open-TR

I suggest that since all these forms contain two semantic referents, the differences among the sentences can be explained by setting up a hierarchy of SPECIFICITY. (The words in small caps represent technical terms, explained in the following sections. To highlight their status, they appear in boldface after the following paragraph.)

For example, the difference between (1) and (2) is that in (2), one referent has been made more specific by EXPRESSING it with the subject *e*.[5] In both sen-

---

[3] This difference was pointed out by TRN.

[4] See, for example, §26.1.2.2.

[5] Examples of a verb being used with neither actor nor goal being made more specific are, first, the imperative, and second, its use in a noun phrase, as *na lade* 'the jumping'.

tences, the goal remains IMPLICIT. In (3), both the actor and the goal are made more specific: each is expressed (the actor by the subject *e* and the goal by the object -*a*), and in addition, the goal is SIGNALED by the transitive suffix -*vi* (shortened to -*v* before the object -*a*).

Note the differences between (1, 2, 3) and (4):

    4. *E lade-vi.*   'It is jumped-to.'

In (4), because of the derivational effect of -*vi* on *lade*, the subject *e* **expresses** the goal, not the actor, which is referred to more subtly. It is **signaled** by the transitive suffix -*vi*. But note that the actor is not highlighted to the extent that the goal is.

As for sentences (5) and (6), whose verbs are analogous to *tobo* and *toboki* (see above), S2 verbs provide a striking example of such a subtle reference to the actor. With a verb such as *dola* '(be) open', for example, both the actor and the goal are **implicit** in the meaning. In the text frame

    E dola.   'It is open.'

the subject *e* refers to the goal. The actor remains at the **implicit** level—that is, it is not **expressed** in any way, but we know that *dola* refers to the kind of state that is different from, say, that indicated by *levu* 'big'. The state indicated by *dola* has been caused by someone or something; that indicated by *levu* has not.

With the transitive suffix added:

    E dola-vi.   'It is open / it has been opened.'

the actor enters the picture, but not directly; it is **signaled**, but not **expressed**.[6]

We now arrange these observations into a hierarchy of specification.

26.1.2 Levels of specificity

The preceding section named three levels of specificity: implicit, signaled, and expressed. Now they are explained in more detail

26.1.2.1 Implicit

An implicit referent, as stated earlier, is one that is inherent in the meaning of the verb. Every verb must have at least one referent implicit in its meaning (which is manifested at some level by the subject); many have two (the second of which is manifested by the object). See CH 11.

These implicit referents, waiting as performers in the wings (so to speak), are brought on stage in the higher levels of specificity.

26.1.2.2 Signaled

We repeat examples (5) and (6) above, with the function markers in boldface:

    5. *E dola.*   'It is open.'
    6. *E dola-**vi**.*   'It is opened.'

---

[6] In this construction, of course, the actor cannot be specified any further.

The difference between them is shown in the following two tables:

TABLE 26.1: ACTOR IMPLICIT
E dola. 'It is open.'

	Implicit	Signaled	Expressed
Actor	+		
Goal	+		+

In the second sentence, the actor is brought onto the stage, although only alluded to, i.e., signaled (table 26.2).

TABLE 26.2: ACTOR IMPLICIT AND SIGNALED
E dola-vi. 'It is opened.'

	Implicit	Signaled	Expressed
Actor	+	+	
Goal	+		+

In other words, the actor is still less specifically identified than the goal, but indicated at more than an implicit level. As confirmation that the *-Ci* suffix does give this impression, note the following example:

Era sukasuka kece mai ni sā yakavi na vanua. Era mai
3P disperse INC DIR SUB ASP evening DEF land 3P DIR

sosoqo-ni *vata toka ka yau yani ki sisili.*
assemble-TR CNC CNT CNJ disperse DIR ABL bathe

'They all come home when evening comes. They are assembled together and then disperse (there) to bathe' (*NV3*:23).

The argument inspired by this example is a negative one: TRN (5/82) criticized the form of the verb, because *sosoqo-ni* gives the impression that someone had assembled the people. He suggested that *soqo* alone (which is an S2 verb) would be better used in the phrase, giving no impression that an actor had been involved in the state.

As a matter of fact, in constructions such as this, the actor cannot be made any more specific, either within the VP or by an ablative NP. The only way to express or specify the actor is to change the form of the VP so that the transitive suffix signals the object, and the subject represents the actor, as in:

E gunu-v-a.   'He drank it.'

In other words, one cannot translate into Fijian 'It was drunk by him' without changing from passive voice to active.

26.1.2.3 Expressed

A VP in which a referent is *expressed* is one that includes a person-number form as the grammatical subject and/or grammatical object. The following sentences show both:

*E vinaka-t-**a**.*   'She wanted it.'
*E gunu-v-**a**.*   'She drank it.'

These forms produce a pattern different from the previous ones (see table 26.3). The difference stems from two factors. First, for the two constructions

E vinaka-ti.   'It is wanted.'
E vinaka-t-a.   'She wants it.'

the relationship between actor-goal and subject-(object) is reversed. That is, the first phrase shows a stative construction in which the subject represents the goal; the second, an active one in which the subject represents the actor.

TABLE 26.3: ACTOR AND GOAL EXPRESSED
E vinaka-t-a. 'She wants it.'

	Implicit	Signaled	Expressed
Actor	+		+
Goal	+	+	+

Next, only one goal can ever be signaled: the one that is not expressed as the subject. Thus, the transitive suffix in the following sentence signals the actor:

*E   vinaka-**ti**.*   'It is wanted.'
3S   want-TR

In the following sentence, it signals the goal:

*E   vinaka-**t**-a.*   'She wants it.'
3S   want-TR-3S

With an S2 verb, *bulu* 'buried' in the following example, the relationships are the same:

*E bulu-**ti***   'It was buried (by someone)'
*E bulu-**t**-a*   'She buried it.'

26.1.3 Proper NPs as objects

One common transitive construction (discussed in §17.2) seems to operate outside the system described above. When a third person singular goal is specified by a proper NP, the NP is interpreted as part of the set of grammatical objects. In the following two examples:

E rai-ci au.   'She saw me.'
E rai-ci Semesa.   'She saw Semesa.'

note that the specifying proper NP (*Semesa*) is without the proper marker *o*. Thus, there is a formal contrast with a common NP in the same position:

E   voleka-t-a   na   koro.   'It's near the village.'
3S   near-TR-3S   DEF   village

E   voleka-ti   Nukui.   'It's near Nukui.'
3S   near-TR   N

If we look at only the surface form of these two sentences, we might expect them to represent different degrees of specificity. However, it is likely that the only difference lies in the opposition of *na* versus *o*,[7] and that otherwise, the constructions indicate the same degree of specificity.

The following arguments contribute to that conclusion:

1. For the other constructions, specificity is mostly cumulative: that is, the existence of a specified actor or goal (see the next section) implies the existence of the lower levels. In a sense, then, the formal manifestations of the lower levels are redundant, unless they serve a function in addition to specificity.

2. Limited investigation of discourse so far shows no difference in the discourse environments of the two sentences above.

3. Inserting a particle immediately after the verb produces the missing elements—the object and the proper marker:

E voleka-t-a beka o Nukui.   'Perhaps it's near Nukui.'[8]

It is likely, then, that the omission of the grammatical object and proper noun marker, whatever its origin,[9] serves no function within the grammatical category of specification.

26.2 SPECIFICATION OUTSIDE THE VP: ADDED NPS

In the highest degree of specification, an NP[10] is added outside the VP. It relates to a person-number marker in one of several different functions, described in the following sections.

26.2.1 NPs specifying the subject

The following examples continue the list begun in §26.1.1. In each, the specifying NP is in boldface and bracketed. In the first example, the arrows point to the words or phrases with the same referent.

---

[7] The difference between common and proper is linked to the general area of specificity, since one of the semantic features of "proper" is "specific."

[8] Arms (10/84) noted that this sentence can also mean 'Perhaps Nukui is near it.' However, if *o Nukui* specifies the subject, it is a separate phonological phrase, at least in slower speech. See §26.2.3.1 for a discussion of ambiguity.

[9] If we propose an underlying structure for the second sentence above, it might be **E vōleka-ta o Nukui*, producing a disfavored vowel sequence *ao* (see Geraghty and Pawley 1981 for an interesting discussion of *ae* and *ao*). But perhaps phonological grounds alone are not sufficient to explain the present situation.

[10] Or more than one. See §26.5 on multiple specification.

   ↓   ↓
E lade-vi [na vatu].   'The **rock** was jumped-to.'
3S jump-TR DEF rock

E lade-v-a [na cauravou]. 'The **youth** jumped-to it.'[11]
3S jump-TR-3S DEF youth

E vinaka-t-a [o Sala].   '**Sala** likes it.'
3S want-TR-3S PRP S

E dabe tiko [ko Jone].   '**J** is sitting.' (*FR1*:4)
3S sit CNT PRP J

E davo koto e na ibe [na gone]. '**The child** is lying on the mat.'
3S lie CNT ABL DEF mat DEF child (*FR1*:9)

26.2.2 NPs specifying the object

Except for proper phrases (see §26.1.3), there is no formal difference between NPs specifying subjects and those specifying objects:

E vinaka-t-a [na dalo].   'She likes **taro**.'
3S want-TR-3S DEF taro

E lade-v-a [na vatu].   'He jumped-to **the rock**.'
3S jump-TR-3S DEF rock

E ā moku-t-a [na yava-na].   'He cut **his leg**.' (*SF* 107)
3S cut-TR-3S DEF leg-3S

Au ā rai-c-a [na waqa].   'I saw **the canoe**.' (*SF* 107)
1S PT see-TR-3S DEF canoe

Context and semantics, then, must play major roles if we are to parse the sentences correctly. In the sentences above, the opposition of animate vs. inanimate is important: Under normal circumstances, taro does not like something, a rock does not jump, a leg does not cut, and a canoe does not see. In terms of structure alone, however, the sentences are ambiguous.

26.2.3 NPs specifying both the subject and the object

The following sentences show both subject and object specification. They illustrate the default order of NPs: that which specifies the object precedes that which specifies the subject.

E lade-v-a [na vatu] [na cauravou]. 'The **youth** jumped-to the **rock**.'
3S jump-TR-3S DEF rock DEF youth

E vinaka-t-a [na dalo] [o Sala]. '**Sala** likes **taro**.'
3S want-TR-3S DEF taro PRP S

Table 26.4 shows the pattern of this fullest degree of specification.

---

[11] This sentence can also mean 'He jumped to the youth.' See §26.2.3.1 on ambiguity.

TABLE 26.4: FULLY SPECIFIED

	Implicit	Signaled	Expressed	Specified
Actor	+		+	+
Goal	+	+	+	+

The term "default pattern" was used above to refer to the common (but not exclusive) order of the specified object preceding the specified subject. However, that order is not fixed. The ambiguity that can result is discussed in the following section.

26.2.3.1 Ambiguity in subject and object NP specification

When both subject and object are in the third person and are specified by a common NP, how are they kept distinct? The previous section mentioned the default order of specified object NP followed by specific subject NP. However, as pointed out elsewhere, treating the pattern that includes both NPs as obligatory may be useful for some teaching materials and grammatical examples, but it does not represent Fijian in context.

As an example of how we can be misled by grammatical statements, consider the following statement from Priscillien 1950:13:

> The order of construction in Fijian is normally as follows: First comes the verb, then the adverb modifying it, then the object preceded by its article and followed by its qualifying adjective, finally comes the subject preceded by its article, and followed by the adjective.
>
> EXAMPLE: Sa vola vakaca na i vola balavu na tamata lekaleka.
>
> Lit. Wrote badly the letter long, the man little
> The little man wrote the long letter badly.

This description gives the impression that all these elements are essential in the sentence.

Sentences containing both NPs, especially those used as sample sentences in grammatical studies, usually show the order illustrated in the examples just above, leading those interested in universals, to draw the conclusion that Fijian is a V[erb] O[bject] S[subject] language. This statement is often made by linguists (usually not specialists in Fijian grammar) working with elicited sentences rather than larger contexts. The following quotation, from *Wikipedia* shows that the methodology persists:[12]

> The normal word order [for Fijian] is VOS (Verb Object Subject):
> E rai-c-a (1) na no-na (2) vale (3) na gone (4)
> 3-sg.-sub. see-trans.-3-sg.-obj. (1) the 3-sg.-poss. (2) house (3) the child (4)
> (The child sees his house.)[13]

---

[12] Retrieved 10 July 2007; the 16 May 2013 version shows no changes.

[13] Because of the nature of *Wikipedia*, entries change from time to time. When I first found this statement, some of the morphemes were incorrectly identified. I made the corrections (which still stand), and also contradicted the VOS classification. That correc-

Over a century and a half ago, Hazlewood had a better grasp of the situation. The following remarks (1872 [1850]:36) are about object NPs, but could apply to subject NPs as well:

> The object of a transitive verb must be expressed or clearly understood. In fact it must be somewhere expressed in a speech, otherwise the speech will be unintelligible; but being once expressed **it is seldom repeated in the same speech** [emphasis added] by good native speakers, how frequently soever the transitive forms of the same, or of other verbs referring to it, may recur. The observance of this rule is very important to the understanding of native discourse.

As statistical confirmation of Hazlewood's remarks, Geraghty (1983a:391) found in a sample from transcribed texts that in ninety-seven verbal sentences, only seven specified both subject and object, and more than a third specified neither.

Next, although in sentences in which the subject and object are both specified by NPs, there is a tendency for the specified object to follow the VP, with the specified subject in turn following it, it is not at all uncommon for the phrases to occur in different orders. For example, Geraghty (1983a) found the following orders (O = NP specifying the object, V = VP, S = NP specifying the subject):

SVO OVS VOS

But so far, in observing phrase order, little attention has been paid to the structure of discourse. For example, those who have tried to attach some typological importance to the ordering of S, V, and O have not noticed for Fijian that sometimes the specified object phrase comes first. Such an order is indeed possible (see Geraghty's observations above), and it seems likely that is it conditioned by discourse. Note how the specified object (in boldface) in the first sentence marks the theme of the following short monologue (*FR3*:40):

(1) *Ā sau-m-a   ko Vilive ka ka-y-a   "Nana, e [dua na qito*
    PT answer-TR-3S PRP V   CNJ say-TR-3S Mother 3S one DEF game

levu] keimami ā kī-tak-a; (2) *keimami ā   rakavī"*
big   1PX   PT do-TR-3S   1PX   PT   rugby

'V answered and said, "Mother, it's a big game we played; we played rugby."'

Here, the NP that specifies the object—*e dua na qito levu*—is fronted to precede the VP *keimami ā kī-tak-a*.

In the following short discourse, the specified object phrase at the beginning of each of two sentences (2, 3) serves to highlight a theme and emphasize a contrast—one basket versus the other:

---

tion had a short life; VOS soon returned. But note that in the interlinear gloss, *e* is identified as the subject, *-a* as the object ... but *vale* and *na gone*, although translated, are unlabeled. This is just one example of the inconsistency of "the analysis that will not go away."

(1) Sā mai tali sara yani e   rua *[na ketekete]* me tawa ki-na   na
    ASP DIR plait INT DIR 3S two DEF basket   SUB put-in ABL-3S DEF

manā (2) *[E dua]* e tali-a ko Ateca. (3)*[E dua]* e tali-a ko
crab   3S one   3S plait-3S PRP A   3S one   3S plait-3S PRP

Mariana.   'Two baskets were plaited to put crab in. One Ateca plaited,
M   and one Mariana plaited.' (*FR3*:35)

Here, in sentences (2) and (3), *e dua* 'one' serves as an NP specifying the object.

However, the missing element in these examples, and in those in Geraghty's study as well, is intonation. Many—perhaps most—elements that are fronted are set off by a special intonation. In text transcriptions, such elements are sometimes marked with commas. But a thorough study of phrase order needs to begin with spoken, not written, language.

Finally, the meanings of the phrases themselves play an important role in the hearer's ability to deduce the proper meaning. Aside from such manufactured sentences for elicitation purposes as "The bear killed the man. The man killed the bear," the proper assignment of the NPs according to the cultural or natural roles of the referents they represent is not so much of a problem. For example, the following sentence:

E lesa-v-a na tūraga. 〈 'He scolded the chief.'
                           'The chief scolded him.'

is more likely to have the second meaning than the first, because *lesa* implies a person of authority scolding a social inferior (not that chiefs are *always* the persons with the highest authority; they just usually are). At any rate, the context is likely to give the proper assignment of roles.

A less culturally specific example is:

E lako-v-a [na buka]   [na gone].
3S go-TR-3S DEF firewood DEF child

Here, in addition to the preference for VP—Object NP—Subject NP (when all items occur), because of the inanimate nature of firewood (suggested also in §26.2.2), the meaning is more likely 'The child fetched the firewood' than 'The firewood fetched the child.'

In short, even when both subject and object are specified with NPs (and the grammatical subject and object are of the same person and number), ambiguity is rare.

26.2.3.2 Summary of subject and object specification

A description of word/phrase order depends on identifying and defining the components of a sentence. Although identifying the verb is noncontroversial, identifying the subject and the object is a different matter. The following discussion summarizes some problem areas and my suggested solutions.

1. If "subject (S)" and "object (O)" refer to content words, then VOS is the default order if all these element occur and none of them has been fronted for emphasis. But as we saw above, sentences containing both types of NPs are in a minority, and many contain neither. Logically, then, is there no word order in a sentence without a subject NP and an object NP?

2. If we identify the (largely) obligatory person-number markers as S and O, the order is SVO. This is constant; NPs are not necessary for the statement.

3. Treating NPs as the result of specifications eliminates the necessity for such terms as "agreement," "split-subjects," and others, used in some previous studies.

4. This analysis also ties together subject and object specification with other types, treated in the following sections.

26.2.4 NPs specifying possessive forms

In the treatment of possessive attribution (CH 30), it is shown that there are two major formal types of possession:

1. Constructions in which the possessor is a possessive classifier (PC) + a person-number marker. E.g., *no-qu vale* 'my house'

2. Constructions in which the possessor is a noun. E.g., *na vale nei Pita* 'P's house'; *vale ni lotu* 'house for worship'.

Specification applies to only the first of these.

In the following examples, the person-number marker is in boldface, and the specifying NP is enclosed in brackets.

*Sā   dedē na no-**dratou** tiko voli [na vei-luve-ni   oqō].*
ASP long DEF PC-3T   CNT ASP DEF REC-child-TR DEM:1
'It was long time—their (trial) staying around—these offspring.' (*FR3*:55)

As with the NPs in other types of specification, the NP here is optional. That is, the rest of the sentence could stand alone if it were not necessary to specify the referent of *-dratou*. Note, incidentally, that the possessive itself is part of a NP (*na no-dratou tiko voli*), which specifies the subject (a deleted *e*).

*na rua na i-sulu vaka-taga   vulavula, me no-**na** [na gone oqō]*
DEF two DEF *isulu* MAN-pocket white   SUB PC-3S   DEF child DEM:1
'the two white *isulu* with pockets, to be his—this child's' (*FR3*:56)

*Sā vaka-rau-tak-a   ki-na   na nō-**drau** i-yāyā [na luve-na].*
ASP CAU-ready-TR-3S ABL-3S DEF PC-3D   luggage DEF child-3S
'She prepared then their (dual) luggage—her offspring.' (*FR3*:57)

26.2.4.1 Limitations on specification of possessives

As Milner observed (1972:23, 23n), in a construction such as the following:

na no-na vale 'his/her house'

the person-number marker cannot be specified by a proper noun. Hence, the other major type of possessive construction is used:

na vale ne-i Erelia   'E's house'

However, for the nonsingular numbers, proper noun specification is permitted.

26.2.4.2 "Translationese" and its effect on possession specification

Churchward's grammar, which was in part intended to help speakers of English learn Fijian, presents a number of topics from the point of view of translation. One of these, quoted in §26.2.4.3, mentions English possessive constructions that use the word *of*. Churchward did not attempt a word-for-word translation of such constructions, but not all translators have been so careful. Thus, one can occasionally hear and read an odd variation on the possessive specification construction involving the marker *ni*, which is often used to translate English *of*. In the following phrase, found in a translation, the portion in boldface is an example:

*na ke-**na** vaka-dewa-taki ka   taba-ki vaka-Viti **ni i-vola** oqō*
DEF PC-3S   translation   CNJ printing MAN-Fiji POS book   DEM:1
'the Fijian translation and printing of this book'

Acceptable Fijian would use the phrase *na i-vola oqō*, since that phrase specifies the person-number possessive marker *-na*.

PG reported (6/82) that the *ni* construction was acceptable in a few areas of Fiji. Its existence, however limited, plus the tendency for translators (especially on the radio) to use a word-for-word approach, may have a reinforcing influence on each other.

26.2.4.3 Discussion: Specification of possessed forms

Some previous descriptions have treated such sequences as

*[na no-**dratou** waqa] [**na cauravou**]* 'the young men's canoe'

as a single unit, interpreting the second NP as (apparently) obligatory. Hazlewood (1872:13) declined nouns through their various "cases," treating such constructions as the following as examples of the possessive case:

a   no-na   na   tamata   'the man's'
DEF PC-3S DEF person

a   no-drau na   tamata   'the two men's'
DEF PC-2D   DEF person

Milner (1972:22) called the first construction above "the Fijian genitive." Pawley (1972:35), for Proto Eastern Oceanic, but obviously based on the Fijian system, followed this analysis, treating this proto-form as one construction type:

**na ka   na ntalo na tamwane*   'the man's taro'
ART POSS. his taro ART man

Churchward's approach, the one that I have adopted here, was different. In his numerous examples (1941:32–33), he included only the simple possessive phrase, and for simplicity of illustration, confined the forms to third person singular. For example, his treatment begins with:

na no-na vale	'his house'
na no-na vanua	'his land'
na no-na i-lavo	'his money'

As for the longer construction that specifies the possessor, he wrote the following astute description (p. 37):

> Quite frequently, where English uses either the preposition "of" or the sign of the possessive case ('s or s'), Fijian prefers to use a possessive pronoun, then the noun that is to be qualified, **and then another noun explaining the possessive pronoun** (emphasis added): e.g., *na nona vale na turaga*, the chief's house (literally, his house the chief), instead of *na vale ni turaga*.

Cammack (1962:62–63) used the same approach, beginning with constructions in which a proper noun refers to the possessor:

> If the possessor is plural, and two or more names are used, the phrase contains a preposed possessive pronoun which agrees in number with the possessors, which are specified thereafter:
>
> *na nodrau waqa ko Jone kei Joo*[14] 'their (dual) canoe John and Joe'
>
> A similar construction occurs when the possessor is indicated by a common phrase:
>
> *na nodrau waqa na cauravou* 'their (dual) canoe the young men'

26.3 NPS SPECIFYING PERSON-NUMBER MARKERS IN SECONDARY NPS

Just as person-number markers serve as grammatical subjects and objects in the VP, they also serve as the heads of some secondary NPs. These markers, as well as subjects and objects, can be specified. However, the system is not so pervasive as subject and object specification, for only certain kinds of secondary phrases can be specified. Note the following examples, in which specification is not necessary:

i	*na*	*sitoa*	'to the store'
ABL	DEF	store	

e	*bāravi*	'at the shore'
ABL	shore	

mai	*vale*	'at home'
ABL	house	

Because *i*, *e*, and *mai* phrases include the noun, they are not usually specified.[15]

As for secondary phrases that do allow specification, most of them are proper phrases, often beginning with *vei*. Note the following example (boldface marks the pronoun and the specifying NP):

---

[14] In this work, double vowels represent long vowels.

[15] *I*, *e*, and *mai* phrases with a third person singular head are realized as *ki-na*. The relationship of *ki-na* to its coreferential NP is somewhat different from the specification relationships, since the NP often precedes *ki-na*. See §21.1.2.4.

[vei ira] [na vei-vosa vaka-Viti]   'to them—the Fijian languages'
ABL 3P   DEF DIS-talk MAN-Fiji

In this area of the grammar, place names pattern with common nouns, leaving the category of proper confined to personal names and certain kin relationships—but referring nearly always to humans. The example above is an exception; here *ira* refers to a nonhuman entity that needs to be especially marked for number.

Other examples of specification in secondary NPs are:

[vei ira] [na sā lesu oti yani ki-na]   'to those who had returned
ABL 3P   DEF ASP return ASP DIR ABL-3S   'there' (*FR*5:20)

(Note that in the sentence above, the NP is a nominalized VP.)

[vei ira] [na vō ni i-Taukei rāraba] [kei ira] [na no-dra tūraga]
ABL 3P   DEF left POS Fijians   wide   CNJ 3P   DEF PC-3P chief
'to those—remaining of all the Fijians, and those—their chiefs' (*NL* 10/6/82)

In the sentence just given, two person-number markers are specified.

[vuā]   [na vei-kā   vaka-polotiki]
ABL-3S DEF DIS-thing MAN-politics
'to it—all political things' (*NL* 10/6/82)

[ki vuā]   [na no-da Gone Tūraga] [na Kā-levu].
ABL ABL-3S DEF PC-1PI child chief DEF thing-big
to him—our chief the K (NL 10/6/82)

This last example shows multiple specification, discussed in §26.5. It also illustrates *vuā* as an irregular combination of *vei* + third person singular, as in the following example:

Au na tuku-n-a vuā   'I'll tell him.'
1S FUT tell-TR-3S ABL-3S

If the referent of the third person singular in *vuā* is unclear, it can be specified with an NP, as in the following examples:

Au na tukuna [vuā] [na italatala].   'I'll tell him (the minister).'
                DEF minister

Era ā cabe i   Vale Levu [vuā]   [na Gone Tūraga]
3P PT climb ABL house big   ABL-3S DEF child chief

[*na Kōvana levu.*]¹⁶   'They went up to Government House to him—
 DEF governor big   the chief, the Governor General.' (*SR* 20/4/82)

Finally, a different kind of specification involves clarifying the referents in a nonsingular subject by adding a *kei* phrase. As we saw in §21.2.1, in the following ambiguous sentence:

Drau lako kei Samu.

---

[16] Note that this is an example of multiple specification. See §26.5.

the *kei* phrase might specify the person other than the addressee referred to by *drau* 'you two'.

For subordinate phrases that specify subjects and objects, see §29.1.1, 29.1.2.

26.4 HOW MANY REFERENTS?

Even though Fijian can use different transitive suffixes to indicate different goals, a sentence can indicate only one goal at a time within the area of formal transitivity. For example:

E qalo-v-a na waqa.   'He swam-to the canoe.'
E qalo-vak-a na savumarini.   'He swam-with the goggles.'

Thus, to translate 'He swam with the thing to the canoe', the locative goal has to be indicated by an ablative phrase:

E qalo-vak-a na kā i waqa.
3S swim-TR-3S DEF thing ABL canoe

With a verb that involves what is usually called an indirect object, that type of goal is indicated by an ablative phrase or contracted pronominal phrase (see Geraghty 1976), such as in the following sentence:

*Au vaka-rai-tak-a **vuā** na vale.*
1S CAU-see-TR-3S ABL-3S DEF house
'I showed him the house.'

26.5 MULTIPLE SPECIFICATION

Up to this point, we have viewed specification in a binary way: either a person-number marker was specified by an NP, or it was not. A series of NPs can extend this type of specification is, each further clarifying the referent for the hearer.

There are a number of common types of multiple specification:

(1) Although *koya* 'he, she, it' is grammatically a proper NP, semantically it refers only to person and number. Thus, it is often necessary to specify it further. In the following examples, the bracketed NPs specify the entity represented by the boldface form:

E *na lako mai [o **koya**] [na tūraga]*
3S FT go DIR PRP 3S DEF chief
'He will come—he—the chief.'

(2) Similar to *koya* are other proper NPs that refer only to person and number:

Eratou *dau lako vata tū gā kei tama-dratou ki na i-teitei*
3D HAB go CNT ASP LIM CNT father-3T ABL DEF field
[ko irau] [na tagane].
PRP 3D DEF male
'They (dual) always go with their father to the garden plot—they (dual)—the boys.' (*FR*3:55)

It is not clear just what the function of *ko irau* is, unless it is to emphasize by this repetition that there are two boys.

26 Specification

The following sentence is similar, except that it contains four references to the semantic actors:

Eratou lako ki cakacaka, ki   na   no-***dratou*** loga ni   dovu, *[ko   iratou]*
3T   go ABL work   ABL DEF PC-3T   plot POS cane PRP 3T

    [na   tagane]. 'They (trial) go to work, to their (trial) sugarcane plot
    DEF male   —they (trial)—the boys.' (*FR3*:57)

(3) Another kind of semantic specificity is brought about by a progression from common NP to proper NP—in other words, giving a proper name to a common NP:

ni drōdrō yani [na   uciwai] [na   Wainimala].
SUB flow   DIR DEF river   DEF W

'when it flows forth—the river—the Wainimala' (*FR5*:10)

me vakā ni   da yaco-v-a   mai oqō na i-ka-24 ni yabaki
SUB like-3S SUB 1PI arrive-TR-3S DIR DEM:1 DEF 24th POS year

  *ni no-**dra** takali [na gone tūraga] [na Tui Lau sā bale]*
  POS PC-3P   loss   DEF child chief   DEF Tui L   ASP die

  [ko Rātū Sir Lala Sukuna]
  PRP Rātū Sir L   S

'because we have come to the 24th anniversary of the loss of the Chief, the Tui Lau who died, Rātū Sir Lala Sukuna' (*NL* 27/5/82)

*e   na dua na gauna makawa, e   na **koro** [ko Udu], e   na*
ABL DEF one DEF time old   ABL DEF village PRP U   ABL DEF

  yanuyanu [ko Kabara], e   na yasana [ko Lau]
  island   PRP K   ABL DEF province PRP L

'once, a long time ago, in the village of Udu, on the island of Kabara, in the Province of Lau' (*FR5*:7)

*Sā   qai tuku-n-a   na marama vei **ira** [na lewe*
ASP SEQ tell-TR-3S DEF lady   ABL 3P   DEF inhabitant

  ni yanuyanu qō]   [o   ira] [na ke-na vō]
  POS island   DEM:1 PRP 3P   DEF PC-3S left

'then she told it—the lady—to those—the inhabitants of this island—those—the remaining of it' (*VV*:Verata texts II)

Perhaps related to multiple specification is the pattern of specifying *vula* 'month' with a proper NP:

e   na vula   [ko Tīseba]   'in the month of December' (*FR2*:4)
ABL DEF month PRP December

However, here the NP is specifying another NP, not a person-number marker.

26.6 EXAMPLES OF DIFFERENT LEVELS OF SPECIFICATION

Table 26.5 summarizes the various levels of specification.

TABLE 26.5: SUMMARY OF LEVELS OF SPECIFICATION

A: Actor G: Goal I: Implicit S: Signaled E: Expressed Sp: Specified

		I	S	E	Sp	
A1 1 Gādē!	A G	+				Stroll!
2 E gādē	A G	+		+		She strolled.
3 E gādē o S.	A G	+		+	+	S. strolled.
A2 4 Lako!	A G	+ +				Go!
5 E lako.	A G	+ +		+		She goes.
6 E lako na tūraga.	A G	+ +		+	+	The chief goes.
7 Lako-v-a!	A G	+ +	 +	 +		Go for it!
8 E lako-v-a.	A G	+ +	 +	+ +		He goes for it.
9 E lako-v-a na i-sele.	A G	+ +	 +	+ +	 +	He goes for the knife.
10 Lako-v-a na i-sele!	A G	+ +	 +	 +	 +	Go for the knife!
11 E lako-vi.	A G	+ +	+	 +		It is gone for.
12 E lako-vi na i-sele	A G	+ +	 +	+ +	 +	The knife is gone for.
13 E lako-v-a o J.	A G	+ +	 +	+ +	 +	J goes for it.
14 E lako-v-a na i-sele o J.	A G	+ +	 +	+ +	+ +	J goes for the knife.
S1 15 Totoka!	A G	+				Beautiful!
16 E totoka.	A G	 +		 +		It's beautiful.
17 E totoka o M.	A G	 +		 +	 +	M is beautiful.

S2		I	S	E	Sp	
18 E tobo.	A	+				It is trapped.
	G	+		+		
19 E tobo-ki.	A	+	+			It is trapped.
	G	+		+		
20 E tobo na vuaka.	A	+				The pig is trapped.
	G	+		+	+	
21 E tobo-ki na vuaka.	A	+	+			The pig is trapped.
	G	+		+	+	
22 E tobo-k-a na vuaka na gone.	A	+		+	+	The child trapped the pig.
	G	+	+	+	+	

We will now examine each of the different constructions.

1. *Gādē!* is an example of an A1 verb, with the actor implicit in its meaning, and no goal indicated in any way. Here, the verb is used as an imperative; the actor is referred to only implicitly.

2. *E gādē* differs from (1) in that it expresses the subject. It also contrasts with (2), for in *e totoka*, the subject *e* expresses the goal. Finally, it contrasts with (8) in that *e lako* includes an implicit goal.

3. In this sentence, an NP specifies the actor. Thus, the actor is represented by three degrees of specificity: implicit, expressed, and specified (3).

4. *Lako!* is an imperative, but unlike *gādē*, it involves both an implicit actor and an implicit goal. In this form, neither is specified to any higher level; when the actor is expressed by the subject, it is one of the four possible second person forms.

5. *E lako* expresses the actor by the third person singular *e*, which serves as subject. The goal remains implicit.

6. *E lako na tūraga* goes one step further than (5) by specifying the actor with the NP *na tūraga*.

7. *Lako-v-a!* is the first imperative we have dealt with that includes a goal other than in the implicit role (as in (4)). Here, also for the first time, we note the transitive suffix *-vi* (which has coalesced with the object to form *-v-a*). Its appearance manifests the signaled degree of specificity.[17]

8. *E lako-v-a* adds one degree of specificity to (7) by expressing the actor as *e*, the subject.

---

[17] This example shows that the language uses these levels more cumulatively than individually. That is, in most constructions a higher level of specificity does not replace a lower level. In particular, none of the formal levels can replace Implicit, which is inherent in the meaning of the verb. Nor can an actor or goal be specified without being expressed (except as a proper object).

9. This sentence in turn adds the highest degree of specificity to the goal in (8) by specifying it with the NP *na i-sele*.

10. This sentence contrasts with (9) by specifying the goal with an NP. As is often the case with imperatives, the subject remains implicit.

11. *E lako-vi* is the first sentence in the table to show the transitive suffix used solely to signal a level of specificity that does not refer to the goal. This construction shows that the goal, expressed by *e*, is in a particular state, and it suggests that the state was caused by an actor. In this construction there is no way to specify the actor further: it can be neither expressed nor specified by a NP. The only possible way to express or specify the actor is to change the form of the sentence from passive to active, so that the subject represents the actor.

12. This sentence is related to the preceding one, contrasting only by specifying the goal (expressed by the subject) with a NP, *na i-sele*.

13. *E lako-v-a o Jone* is most closely related to (8), from which it differs by specifying the subject with the NP *o Jone*.

14. This sentence illustrates the fullest degree of specification possible within the framework of transitivity, for both the actor and the goal are specified by NPs. The table shows one unfilled slot, since there is no signal for subjects that corresponds to the transitive suffix *-Ci* or *-Caki*.

15. Phrases such as *Totoka!* can occur as spontaneous exclamations. They are, in a sense, the stative equivalent of the active imperative construction. Because the verb is S1, it is only the goal that plays a role. Thus it contrasts with the imperative, which must have an implicit actor (as in 1), and may also have an implicit goal, with the potential of indicating and expressing it formally. Another difference is that for imperatives, the implicit actor that would be expressed by a subject is second person; for *totoka!*, the implicit goal seems usually to be second person or third person, usually the latter.

16. *E totoka* differs from (15) in that the goal is expressed in the form of the subject *e*. The subject could, however, be any of the set of fifteen potential ones shown in CH 4.

17. *E totoka o Mere* specifies the goal to the fullest extent possible within this system by adding a noun phrase. The goal, then, is represented on three levels: it is implicit (in the meaning of *totoka*), expressed (by the subject *e*), and specified (by the NP *o Mere*).

18. *E tobo* simply affirms that something is in the state of being trapped. There is an agent implicit in the meaning, but it is not referred to in any way.

19. This sentence refers to the same condition as (18)—i.e., being trapped—but *-ki* signals that an agent was involved.

20. This sentence is similar in structure to (18), but the goal is specified by the NP *na vuaka*.

21. Similarly, this sentence specifies the actor that is only signaled in (18).

22. This sentence specifies both the actor and goal in the only way possible: it changes from passive to active voice. Therefore, it has the same pattern as (14). Similarly, any other form with *tobo-k-a* would pattern with the corresponding form with *lako-v-a*.

It should be emphasized here that specification is not a derivational process, but a grammatical category. One part of the system, however, overlaps with derivation: the addition of *-Ci* or *-Caki* to both active and stative roots:

E lako.	'She went.'	*E bulu.*	'It is buried.'
E lako-vi.	'She was fetched.'	*E bulu-t-a.*	'He buried it.'

In the first pair, the *-vi* signals a change in the role of the subject, and thus a change in the classification of the form: the verb is now an S2. In the second pair, no derivational change is effected by the addition of *-ti* alone, for both *bulu* and *bulu-ti* are S2 verbs. The change is, however, brought about by the combination of *-ti* + *-a* (producing *-ta*), which changes the role of the subject to that of actor.

26.7 SUMMARY: SPECIFICATION

The system of specificationy described in this chapter allows a more thorough identification of elements within a sentence. For example, the boldface portions of the following sentences need no longer be confused:

*E moce tiko **na gone**.*   'The child is sleeping.'

In this sentence, *e* is now identified as the subject, and *na gone* as the specified subject.

Similarly, in the following sentence:

*Au kani-a na **tavioka**.*   'I ate the tavioka.'

a is the object, and *na tavioka* is the specified object.

Moreover, the concept of specification is a way to link several seemingly unrelated features of the grammar, such as NPs specifying actors and goals, and those specifying possessors.

Returning to the example that inspired this analysis, specificity explains the difference between the following sentences, even if the glosses are the same:

Ā tobo na vuaka.   'The pig was trapped.'
Ā tobo-ki na vuaka.   'The pig was trapped.'

The difference is that, in the second of the pair, the actor is suggested more strongly than in the first.

For such examples, it is important to remember that the distinction in meaning represents a difference in the way the actor is subtly referred to, and that although the glosses obscure this difference, it can be observed by investigating discourse.

Moving beyond subjects and objects, we also saw that specification also operates within the area of possession—clarifying the referents of possessive suffixes such as *-na* (hers, his, its) when necessary.

Moreover, person-number markers in secondary NPs can also be specified by NPs.

Finally, subordinate phrases (see §29.1.1.1 and §29.1.1.2) can also be viewed as specifying subjects and objects.

In summary: In the area of discourse analysis, we can view specificity as a system that takes into account what the speaker knows about what the hearer knows. In the simplest terms, once a referent is clarified for the hearer, it need not be specified again until a potential ambiguity arises or unless there is a reason to emphasize it.

27 VERB MODIFICATION

In this chapter, we treat four[1] different kinds of verb modification. In the examples, the modifiers are in boldface:

1. Verb + (*vaka-*) stative

    *E rogo **vinaka**.* 'It sounds good.'
    *E cici **vaka-totolo**.* 'She runs fast.'

2. Verb + noun

    *E gunu **yaqona**.* 'He was kava-drinking.'

3. Verb + ablative NP

    *E tiko **mai na koro**.* 'She stays in the village.'

4. Verb + subordinate VP

    *Era suka **ni sā oti na bose**.* 'They dispersed when the meeting finished.'

Only the first type is described in detail; the other types are described elsewhere.

27.1 VERB + (*VAKA-*) STATIVE

A stative that occurs after another verb and modifies that verb is an ADVERB. There are two types of adverbs: SIMPLE (UNDERIVED) and DERIVED.

27.1.1 Simple adverbs

Adverbs without affixes are verb roots that can usually occur themselves as heads of phrases, and are usually statives.[2] For example:

*Au sā kila-i Leone **vinaka**.* 'I know L well.' (T74:60)
1S ASP know-TR L good

Here, *vinaka*, an S1 verb, serves as an adverb.

---

[1] It might be possible to treat subordinate VPs as adverbial phrases. However, I decided to deal with subordination separately in spite of the "adverbial" relationship between the phrases that sometimes holds.

[2] Some of the examples that follow will show why these conditions need to be qualified with "usually."

As the example just given shows, the position of the simple adverb is directly after the VP head and any markings of transitivity that may occur, including a proper object. Additional VP markers follow the underived adverb:

ka ni sā na rogo-c-a **vinaka** sara gā
CNJ SUB ASP DEF hear-TR-3S good INT LIM
'because one will hear very well indeed' (T74:44)

ā vosa **drēdredre** yani   'spoke thither harshly' (T74:4)
PT talk hard DIR

ka ni lala **vinaka** tū gā   'because it will be well deserted'
CNJ SUB empty good CNT LIM   (T74:60)

Although the combination of two verbs looks formally like a verb compound (CH 15), the relationship among the elements in the phrase is different. For example, if each of the verbs in a compound is expanded into a VP, the subject refers to the same entity. The compound in

ka **vuka lesu** tale   'and fly back again' (FR5:23)

can be considered derived from the following two VPs:

E vuka.   'It flies.'
E lesu.   'It returns.'

Here, the subject *e* in the two sentences refers to the same entity.

On the other hand, if each of the two verbs of a modified construction is expanded into a VP, the subjects refer to different entities:

ni **gani-ti** iko **vinaka**.   'That suits you well.' (T74:58)
SUB suit-TR 2S good

The two expanded into VPs:

E **gani-ti** iko.   'It suits you.'
3S suit-TR 2S

E **vinaka**.   'It is good,'
3S good

Here, the subjects in the first and second phrase refer to different entities: in the first, to an article of clothing; in the second, to "suiting."

The following examples show stative verbs often used as simple adverbs:

me bula **totolo**   'to get well quickly'
SUB health fast

wili **sese**   'miscount' (Capell 1941)
count wrong

na i-vosavosa kila-i **levu**   'a proverb widely known' (FR5:28)
DEF proverb know-TR big

E ā lako **wāsomā**.   'She went frequently.'
3S PT go frequent

me kau-t-a **lai-vi** na manā   'to take the crab away' (FR3:36)
SUB carry-TR-3S utterly DEF crab

Some of these underived adverbs are also used with the derivative prefix: *vaka-totolo* 'swiftly', *vaka-vinaka* 'well', *vaka-mālua* 'slowly', *vaka-levu* 'greatly', *vaka-matua* 'strongly' *vaka-wāsomā* 'often'.

Others are not: *lō* 'silently' *donu* 'directly', *makawa* 'of old'

27.1.2 Derived adverbs

Adverbs can be derived by prefixing *vaka-* to one of a number of roots. In glosses below, the prefix is labeled MAN (manner):

27.1.2.1 Statives

*Bau vosa **vaka-vinaka** vuā.*   'Please speak nicely to her.' (T74:60)
TEN talk MAN-good ABL-3S

*me rarawa **vaka-levu** tiko*   'that she's very sad' (T74:60)
SUB sad   MAN-big   CNT

*Ā vaka-rai-c-a **vaka-totolo**.*   'He looked at it quickly.' (T74:41)
PT CAU-see-TR-3S MAN-fast

*ka vā-kāsama-tak-a   **vaka-bībī***   'and considered it seriously'
CNJ CAU-consider-TR-3S MAN-heavy   (T74:55)

We can also include among the statives certain reciprocal relationships, derived with *vei-*:

*ni drau wase **vaka-vei-māmā tū*** 'that you (dual) divide in half' (T74:47)
SUB 2D divide MAN-half   CNT

*Erau ā sarasara wāvoki **vaka-vei-taci-ni**.*
3D   PT look   around   MAN-REC- siblings
'They (dual) went around sightseeing like sisters.' (T74:62)

27.1.2.2 Deictic locatives

The deictic nouns *oqō*, *oqori*, and *oyā* are also used with *vaka-* to form derived adverbs:

*ni-u biu-ti iko tū **vā-qō*** 'that I leave you like this' (T74:56)
SUB-1S left-TR 2S CNT MAN-DEM:1

*E caka-v-a **vā-qori**.*   'She does it like that (by you).'
3S done-TR-3S MAN-DEM:2

*E na sega ni rawa ni-u biu-ti iko tū **vā-qori**.*
3S FT not SUB able SUB-1S leave-TR 2S CNT MAN-DEM:1
I won't be able to leave you like this.' (T74:56)

*Sā dau tau **vā-qō** na uca.* 'The rain always falls like this.'
ASP HAB fall MAN-DEM:1 DEF rain (FMC61:40)

Note that in all these examples, the deictic nouns appear without *o-*. These forms are more indicative of conversational Fijian than the longer forms are. Since the shorter forms begin with velars, the *vā-* alternate of the prefix *vaka-* is used.

27.1.2.3 Numerals (including interrogative)

Numerals (including vica 'how many?') with the *vaka-* prefix form a derived adverb that indicates the number of times an action was performed:

*E dau cula-i au **vaka-rua** e na dua na mācawa.*
3S HAB pierce-TR 1S MAN-two ABL DEF one DEF week
'He always gives me an injection twice a week.' (T74:51)

*Nanu-mi koya tale **vaka-vica**?*   'How many times has he thought
think-TR 3S ITR MAN-how-many?   that?' (T74:59)

The form *vaka-dua* 'once' can also be used in an idiomatic sense, as the following example shows:

*E ā sega ni bau vinaka-t-a **vaka-dua**.* 'He's never wanted that at all.'
3S PT not SUB TEN want-TR-3S MAN-one   (T74: 57)

27.1.2.4 Nouns (including interrogative)

Vaka- with a noun means 'in the manner of [the noun]':

*E kana tiko **vaka-vuaka**.*   'He's eating like a pig.'
3S eat CNT MAN-pig

*E vala **vaka-Sāmoa**.*   'He fights like a Samoan.'
3S fight MAN-Sāmoa

*E vosa **vaka-tūraga**.*   'He speaks like a chief.'
3S talk MAN-chief

The placement of a derived adverb within the VP is variable, except—as with the underived adverb—it must occur after any markers of transitivity. In the following example, it occurs after the object as well:

*E loma-ni Pita **vaka-levu**.*   'She loves P very much.'
3S love-TR P MAN-big

Its relationship to other postverbal markers, however, depends on context. For example, the marker *gā* focuses attention on one root. Adding an adverb to the VP gives another option for the placement of *gā*. In the following short discourse, there is a contrast between "stroll" and "play"; in the last sentence, *gā* emphasizes the one chosen:

O bau via-gādē sē qito tēnisi?   'Would you like to stroll or play
2S TEN DES-stroll CNJ play tennis   tennis?'

Daru qito mada.   'Let's play.'
1DI play INI

*Erau ā qito gā **vaka-lailai**.*   'They (dual) played a little.'
3D PT play LIM MAN-small

In the next two sentences, however, a different contrast is brought out:

*Erau via-qito **vaka-dedē**.*   'They wanted to play for a long
3D DES-play MAN-long   time.'

*Ia, ni rau qito **vaka-lailai gā**, erau sā oca sara.*
CNJ SUB 3D play MAN-small LIM 3D ASP tired INT
'But when they had played for just a short time, they became very tired.'

Here, *gā* occurs after the adverb; its purpose is to focus on "little" rather than on "play."

However, PG noted (3/83) a tendency for markers within the VP to move closer to the verb, even though the semantics of the situation might suggest a different placement. I have already discussed the placement of *kece* within the VP, contrary to its "logical" position in the NP (§18.7.1). PG found examples pertinent to this discussion of adverbs:

*caka-v-a sara **vaka-mālua***   'do it very slowly'
do-TR-3S INT   MAN-slow

whereas we might expect:

*caka-v-a **vaka-mālua** sara*

with *sara* placed in a position so that it modifies the adverb. This attraction to the verb reduces the opportunity for contrast.

The following example shows the adverb coming at the end of a fairly long VP; thus, a number of markers separate the verb and the adverb:

*ka na draki cā sara tiko **vaka-levu** na vanua*
CNJ DEF weather bad INT CNT MAN-big DEF land
'because there was very bad weather indeed' (*FR5*:19)

27.2 VERB + NOUN

The common construction exemplified by *gunu yaqona* 'kava drinking' has long been a topic of discussion. In §16.4.1, I give reasons for following Milner's analysis of the second element as a modifier.

27.3 VERB + ABLATIVE NP

Nearly all the examples of ablative NPs given in CH 25 indicate location, time, direction, manner, and other functions that are traditionally treated as verb modification.

27.4 VERB + SUBORDINATE VP[3]

Often, a subordinate VP functions as a verb modifier. Because this construction consists of two VPs, the relationship between the two phrases is often sequential or cause-and-effect. Examples are:

*Au na lako **kē kune e sō na baca**.*   'I'll go if some bait is found.'
1S FT go   SUB found 3S some DEF bait

Like possession, subordination is an extensive process, and is treated separately (CH 29).

---

[3] Or the reverse order.

28 NOUN MODIFICATION

Noun MODIFICATION is a grammatical process that reflects semantic ATTRIBUTION—the narrowing of the semantic range of an entity by referring to its ATTRIBUTES or QUALITIES. Thus, modification is an extension of SPECIFICATION (see CH 26), which also narrows or limits the range of an entity. In the following sentences, note how the goal is made progressively more explicit.

Specification

E gunu.   'He drank.' [goal implicit]
3S drink

E gunu-v-a.   'He drank it.' [goal signaled by the transitive
3S drink-TR-3S   suffix and expressed by the object]

E gunu-v-a na wai. 'He drank the water.' [object specified by the NP]
3S drink-TR-3S DEF water

Once an NP appears, its semantic range can be further narrowed by:

Modification

*E gunu-v-a na wai **batabatā**.*   'He drank the cold water.'
3S drink-TR-3S DEF water cold

Note that this discussion does not treat a construction such as:

*E **batabatā** na wai.*   'The water is cold.'
3S cold   DEF water

In this sentence, *batabatā* is a stative verb and does not function grammatically as a modifier, in spite of the meaning of the sentence.

As the examples show, the modifier follows the noun it modifies.

28.1 TYPES OF SEMANTIC ATTRIBUTION

Semantically, entities are qualified by adding the following types of information (not an exhaustive listing):

1. Fixed qualities of an entity

*vinivō **damudamu***   'red dress'
dress red

*vale **balavu***   'long house'
house long

2. Speaker's judgment[1]
    *vale **vinaka***   'nice house'
    house good

    *i-valavala **dodonu***   'proper conduct'
    habit   right

3. Materials comprising an entity
    *vale **vatu***   'stone house'
    house stone

    *peni **kau***   'pencil (literally, wood pen)'
    pen wood

4. Purpose
    *bilo **ni** tī*   'teacup (lit, cup for tea)'
    cup POS tea
    *vale **ni** lotu*   'house of (for) worship'
    house POS religion

5. Entity's relationship to actions
    *kātuba **dola***   'open door'
    door   open
    *kātuba **dola-vi***   'opened door'
    door   open-TR
    *vale **ka-u** sucu **ki-na***   'house I was born in'
    house REL-1S born ABL-3S

6. Entity's position in discourse
    *vale **oqō***   'this house'
    house DEM:1S

7. Entity's relationship to persons
    ***no-qu** vale*   'my house'
    PC-1S   house

Note that in (4) and (7), *ni* and *-qu* are labeled as possessive markers. Classifying possession as a type of modification presents a problem in description, since it is an extensive enough grammatical category to treat separately (CH 30). In order to understand possession, then, the reader must refer to both its separate treatment and its treatment as a type of modification.

In the next section, we will see that some, but not all, of these types are reflected in the formal classification.

---

[1] This category can overlap with some attributes from category (1). For example, it might be a matter for debate whether a dress is *karakarawa* or *drokadroka* (each somewhere on the blue-to-green scale), or whether a house is *levu* 'big' or *balavu* 'long'.

28.2 FORMAL TYPES OF MODIFICATION

In its grammatical manifestation, modification can be classified formally. This classification is based on two criteria: the type of head, and the type of modifier.

28.2.1 Nouns modified by verbs or verb phrases

In this category, exemplified by examples (1–9) below, the referent of the noun is associated with an action, a state, or a quality that narrows its range of meaning.

1. vale **levu** — 'large house'
2. raba-**i-levu** — 'width'
3. tamata **mata dua** — 'one-eyed person'
4. vale **raba-i-levu** — 'wide house'
5. kā **tau-ci uca** — 'thing rained-upon'
6. qito **kaukaua** ka **savasavā** — 'hard and clean game'
7. waqa **vuka** — 'airplane (lit., flying boat)'
8. tamata **dau-gunu** — 'drunkard (lit., person always drinking)'
9. kā e **rai-c-a** — 'thing she saw'

28.2.2 Nouns modified by nouns or forms related to nouns

In this category, exemplified by examples (10–16) below, the referent of the head of the construction is associated with another entity, rather than an action, state, or quality.

10. vale **vatu** — 'stone house'
11. vanua **qele vinaka** — 'good-soiled land'
12. vale **vaka-Viti** — 'Fijian house'
13. vale **ni kuro** — 'cooking house (lit., house assoc. with pots)'
14. **no-na** vale — 'her house'
15. tama-**na** — 'her father'
16. vale **oqō** — 'this house'

Although most of these constructions show the same order of constituents: HEAD + MODIFIER, the relationship between the two constituents is different in each case, either because of the class of noun serving as head, or the class of the modifier. I have chosen the latter feature—the class of the modifier—as the basis for a classification of noun modification into two main types. The following sections deal with these types in detail.

28.3 NOUNS MODIFIED BY VERBS

The categories of noun modification by verbs follow the basic division of verbs into ACTIVE and STATIVE. Of these two, the second is far more common in modification; most of the following patterns involve statives as modifiers.

28.3.1 Integral noun[2] < stative: *vale **levu*** 'big house'

Because of the relationship between the following two constructions:

E **levu** na vale.		'The house is big.'
3S big DEF house		
vale **levu**		'big house'

we interpret the noun-modifier construction as a transformation of the VP + NP sentence. The modifier is a simple root that is an S1 verb.

S2 verbs (both simple and derived[3]) also occur in this construction; each of the following can be related to a VP + NP sentence:

kātuba **dola**	'open door'
kātuba **dola-vi**	'opened door'
wai **lau-gunu**	'potable water'
i-sulu **ka-dresu**	'torn clothes'

28.3.2 Partitive noun[4] < *i* + stative: *raba-i-levu* 'wide'

Some partitive nouns are modified in a special way:

raba[5]	'width'
width	
raba-i-levu	'extensive width'
width-*i*-big	
yava-	'foot, leg'
leg	
yava-i-vā	'four-legged'
leg-*i*-four	

This construction is limited in three ways. First, partitive nouns comprise a closed set. Next, not all statives can occur as the second root: all the examples found so far use statives of "extent," i.e., measurement or counting. In other words, statives of "quality", such as *vinaka* 'good', are not used. Finally, the *i*-construction modifies nouns that refer to nonhuman entities. Compare the following examples with those in the next section.

domo-i-levu	'loud (noise)'
liga-i-balavu	'long-handed (clock)'
mata-i-dua	'one-eyed (wink)'

The following list shows some partitive nouns that are used with *i* and statives of extent.

---

[2] For the distinction between integral and partitive nouns, see §19.2.1.

[3] A2 verb roots with certain affixes are derived S2 verbs. In the examples, *gunu* is an A2 verb root that functions as S2 with the affixes shown.

[4] See note 2.

[5] *Raba* is not now a partitive noun (that is, grammatically) in SF.

loma-	'interior'	*yava-*	'leg'	*tolo-*	'trunk'	*liga-*	'arm'
gau-	'waist'	*ulu-*	'head'	*boto-*	'bottom'	*mata-*	'eye, face'
gusu-	'mouth'	*yasa-*	'side'	*taba-*	'arm, limb'		

28.3.3 Noun < (partitive noun < stative): *tamata mata dua* 'one-eyed person'

This type of modification is similar to the preceding type, but the head of the construction refers to an entity that is human.

*qase **mata dua***   'one-eyed old person'
elder eye one

*tagane **liga balavu***   'long-armed man'
man   arm long

28.3.4 Noun < (partitive noun + *i* + stative of extent): *vale raba-i-levu* 'wide house'

The constructions described in the previous two sections can be used as attributes themselves:

*manumanu **yava-i-vā***   'four-legged animal'
animal   leg-*i*-four

*kaloko **liga-i-balavu*** 'clock with long hands'
clock hand-*i*-long

with this hierarchical structure:

(*manumanu* (*yava* (*i vā*)))

28.3.5 Noun < (S2 < N): *kā tau-ci uca* 'rained-upon thing'

This construction consists of the passive form of the verb, plus the noun that refers to the agent. For example, the common expression *tau-vi mate* 'ill' is a construction of this type; it means literally 'infected by sickness/death'. Other examples are:

*vanua **qasi-vi   kalavo***   'land crawled-upon by rats'
land   crawl-TR rat

*koro **cila-vi siga***   'village shone-upon by the sun'
village shine-TR sun

Note that the verbs here are derived S2 verbs. For example, the root *qasi* 'crawl' is an A2 verb, but the form *qasi-vi* is S2. S2 roots as well occur in this construction:

*vono **taku***   'inlaid with tortoise shell'
joined tortoise shell

*lau   **moto***   'spear-wounded'
pierced spear

With the derived S2 verbs, note their relationship to these constructions (in the examples above):

E qasi-v-a na kalavo. 3S crawl-TR-3S DEF rat	'Rats crawled-on it.'
E cila-v-a na siga. 3S shine-TR-3S DEF day	'The sun shone-on it.'

In many of the examples above, the modifier is a construction in itself, with the whole unit modifying the head. In the following type, the constituents of the modifier have an equal relationship to the head, producing a different hierarchical structure.

28.3.6 Series of modifiers: *qito kaukaua ka savasavā* 'hard and clean game'

Fijian does not string modifiers together after the head. Instead, any modifier after the first is treated as a VP and connected by the marker *ka*. Examples from texts are rare:

*qito **kaukaua** ka **savasavā*** play strong CNJ clean	'hard and clean game' (*FR3*:40)
*Oqō e dua na bilibili **levu** ka **balavu**.* DEM:1 3S one DEF raft big CNJ long	'This is a big and long bamboo raft.' (*NV2*:13)

Note that the translations could also be 'hard game that is clean', or 'big bamboo raft that is long'. There seems to be no way to distinguish between the following hierarchical structures:

(*qito* (*kaukaua ka savasavā*))   (*qito kaukaua*) (*ka savasavā*)

Thus, the construction may be analyzed as either coordinate or relative (see §28.3.9).

28.3.7 Noun < active verb: *waqa vuka* 'flying boat (airplane)'

Generally, active verbs do not serve as modifiers. In fact, the frame NOUN + MODIFIER is one of the tests used to classify verbs. However, there are a few exceptions to this pattern:

*waqa **vuka***	'airplane (lit., flying boat)'
*ika **vuka***	'flying fish'

Some similar constructions are difficult to classify, because of the various roles that verbs can play. In the following phrase, for example, it is difficult to know how to classify *kana vinaka*, for although *kana* is primarily an A2 verb, it is descriptive in the phrase *kana vinaka*:

*E uvi **kana vinaka** na vurai.* 3S yam eat good DEF *vurai*	'The *vurai* is a tasty yam.' (*NV2*:15)

As the example above shows, active verbs serve as modifiers only when they are part of larger constructions. The following section shows one of these.

28.3.8 Noun < *dau*-active verb: *tamata dau gunu* 'person always drinking (drunkard)'

The prefix *dau-*, indicating habitual action, allows an active verb to be used as a modifier. For example:

*tamata **dau-gunu***	'drunkard (literally, person who habitually drinks)'
person HAB-drink	
*gone **dau-vosa***	'child who habitually talks'
child HAB-talk	
*tagane **dau-teitei***	'man who is a farmer'
male HAB-plant	

28.3.9 Noun < VP: *kā e rai-c-a* 'thing she saw'

A noun can be modified by not only a simple verb, but also by a complete VP. In this construction, the head can include the following types of noun or form serving as a noun (the head is in small caps, the VP in boldface). The abbreviation "REL" reflects the traditional analysis of this construction as a RELATIVE:

1. A common noun:

na DAWA kece **ka ra dau lutu e na bogi**
DEF *dawa* INC REL 3P HAB fall ABL DEF night
'all the *dawa* that fall at night (*FR5*:7)

2. A proper noun:

kei IRA **era ā sā liu**   'and those who had gone ahead' (*FR5*:37)
CNJ 3P   3P PT ASP ahead

3. A possessive serving as a noun:

na KENA **era sā dreu**   'those of it that were ripe' (*FR5*:10)
DEF PC-3S 3S ASP ripe

Formally, there are two kinds of modifying VPs:

1. UNMARKED. An unmarked modifying VP is not distinguishable from a main VP, except by position. The relative VPs in examples (2) and (3) above are unmarked.

2. MARKED. In written Fijian, a modifying VP can be marked by *ka*, as in example (1). Occasionally, *a* is heard.

As do most other modifiers, the modifying VP directly follows the phrase that contains the word it modifies.

Within each modifying VP, there is an element that corresponds to N (i.e., refers to the same entity). The following list shows various relationships among this entity, the type of VP itself, and N.

1. N corresponds to the subject of an active VP

SIGA **ka tara-v-a**   'day that follows (i.e., next day)' (*FR5*:20)
day REL follow-TR-3S

ko IRA **ka ra jiko ki-na**	'those who stay there' (*FR5*:9) (Lauan)
PRP 3P REL 3P stay ABL-3S	

Sai   KOYA **ka vaka-tawa-n-a**   *tiko na vū-ni-niu.*
ASP 3S   REL CAU-filled-TR-3S CNT DEF tree-POS-coconut
'It's he who inhabits the coconut tree.' (*FR5*:12)

vei rau na YANUYANU **ka rau tiko** *e   na tokilau*
ABL 3D DEF island   REL 3D lie   ABL DEF northeast
'to those islands that lay to the northeast' (*FR5*:24)

2. N corresponds to the subject of a stative modifying VP

TAMATA **era mate koto e   sala**   'persons who were dead on the road'
person 3P dead CNT ABL road   (*FR5*:36)

BĀRAVI ... **ka vaka-toka-i**   *na Sabata*   'beach that was called S'
beach   REL CAU-proclaim-TR DEF S   (*FR5*:20)

YAQONA *e* **lau-gunu** *ni se bera gā na cavu-tū*
kava   3S STA-drunk SUB ASP late LIM DEF departure
'kava that is drunk just before departure' (*VV:i bili ni mua*)

na I-VAKA-SALA **ka tuku-ni mai vuā**   'the advice that was told her'
DEF advice   REL tell-TR ABL ABL-3S   (*FR5*:12)

3. N corresponds to the object of an active modifying VP

UVI ... **ka kau-t-a**   *tiko yani ki Ravuka*
yam   REL carried-TR-3S CNT DIR ABL R
'yams ... that he carried there to R' (*FR5*:21)

E levu sara na NIU   **erau kari-a.**   'It's a lot of coconut that
3S big INT DEF coconut 3D   grate-3S   they're grating.' (*NV2*:17)

muri-a   sē lako-v-a na KĀ *e* **boi-c-a** *tiko*
follow-3S CNJ go-TR-3S DEF thing 3S smell-TR-3S CNT
'follow or fetch something that smells' (*VV:boideru*)

na KĀ **ka lako-v-a tiko yani ko Moro**   'the thing that M sought
DEF thing REL go-TR-3S CNT DIR PRP M   there' (*FR5*:21)

e   na vuku ni KĀ **ka caka-v-a oqō**   *vei rau na kakā oqō*
ABL DEF aid POS thing REL done-TR-3S DEM:1S ABL 3D DEF parrot DEM:1S
'because of the thing that this parrot had done to them' (*FR5*:28)

4. N corresponds to the ablative or other such relation

VATU **erau ā dabe toko ki-na**   'stone they were sitting on' (*FR5*:28)
stone 3D PT sit CNT ABL-3S

5. N corresponds to the possessor

na QARA **ka ke-na i-tau-kei**   *tiko e dua na gata levu*
DEF cave REL PC-3S NOM-owner   CNT 3S one DEF snake big
'a cave, the owner-inhabitant of which is a large snake' (*FR5*:12)

28.4 NOUNS MODIFIED BY NOUNS OR RELATED FORMS

In this section we treat modifying constructions that reflect a relationship between two entities.

28.4.1 Noun < noun: *vale vatu* 'stone house'

This construction indicates a close relationship between head and modifier. There are many examples of the modifier referring to the material that constitutes the referent of the head:

*vale **bitu***	'house made of plaited split bamboo'
*vale **kau***	'wooden house'
*mata **kau***	'carved wooden image (literal wooden face)'
*veleti **veva***	'paper plate'
*yatu **vosa***	'sentence (literally, row of words)'

For some examples, the relationship is not quite so obvious. For the following, the modifier represents what comprises the collection, quantity, or type indicated by the head:

*i-binibini **dawa***	'heap of *dawa* fruit'
*i-vutu **sē-ni-kau***	'bunch of flowers'
*mataqali **ika***	'kind of fish'

Another example, *bilo tī* 'cup of tea', provides an interesting contrast with another modifying construction: *bilo ni tī* 'teacup'. In the former, *bilo* represents a quantity (in much the same fashion as *i-binibini* 'heap' and *i-vutu* 'bunch'), not a physical object, as it does in the latter.

For a few examples, this analysis does not fit very well. One of these is *ibe laca*[6] 'mat used as a sail'. Such a relationship between modifier and head is usually realized by modification type (4); thus, one would expect **ibe ni laca*. However, *laca ibe* is also used, and this construction fits reasonably well into the present category, since *ibe* could be considered a type of material.

The following examples also strain the analysis:

*gone **yalewa***	'girl (lit., female child)'
*gone **tagane***	'boy (lit., male child)'
*kolī **yalewa***	'bitch (lit., female dog)'

The title *Tui* is followed by a place name signifying the person's domain:

*Tui **Bau***   'sovereign of Bau'

But perhaps this construction is from **Tui i Bau*, with a sequence unaccented *i* + *i* reduced to a single *i*. The following examples might be due to such a phonological reduction:

| *kai Viti* | 'Fijian' | *kai Merekē* | 'American' |
| *kai Toga* | 'Tongan' | *kai-sī* | 'person without property' |

---

[6] Perhaps the construction *ibe laca* is similar to *yatu vosa*.

28.4.2 Noun < (Integral N + S1): *vanua qele vinaka* 'good-soiled land'

*vanua **qele vinaka*** land soil good	'good-soiled land'
*gone **vaka-i-sulu** vinaka* child CAU-NOM-clothe good	'well-clothed child'
*koro **vale vinaka*** village house good	'village with good houses'

28.4.3 Noun < *vaka-* form: *vale vaka-Viti* 'Fijian house'

The *vaka-* form in this construction is discussed in §6.4. The modifier here means 'in the fashion of', 'concerned with'. Examples are:

*vosa **vaka-Peritania***	'English language'
*kā **vaka-lotu***	'ecclesiastical matters'
*kā **vaka-bose***	'matters pertaining to the council'
*rumu **vaka-vonovono***	'paneled room'
*i-valavala **vaka-Paula***	'act characteristic of P'

28.4.4 Noun < (*ni* + Noun): *vale ni kuro* 'house for pots (kitchen)'

A *ni* phrase (which is itself an NP) modifies a noun by indicating a relationship between the two nouns. Although a general gloss can be constructed—something on the order of 'N1 associated with N2'—there are a number of slightly different relationships. This construction is one of several that are part of the grammatical category POSSESSION. Thus, it is treated in CH 30.

29 SUBORDINATION

A SUBORDINATE VP has a special relationship with another VP, which we call here INDEPENDENT. The specific kinds of relationships—such as specification, "if-then," and "cause-effect"—are discussed individually under section headings for specific markers. As the label suggests, a subordinate VP does not occur as an independent sentence;[1] in other words, it is not a basic VP.

As for the semantic relationship of subordinate and independent sentences to their context, Fijian presents a situation somewhat different from some other languages. Lyons (1968:307) noted that independent sentences "express simple statements of fact, unqualified with respect to the attitude of the speaker towards what he is saying." However, in Fijian, basic VPs can include such internal markers as *mani*, which *do* indicate the speaker's attitude towards what he is saying. Therefore, our grammatical classification of Fijian sentences cannot follow these guidelines exactly, and we must rely more on the form of such VPs for the present classification.

Formally, subordinate verb phrases are marked by one of a set of markers: *ni*, *me*, *kē*, *sē*, and *dē*. These markers fuse with certain subjects, and these contractions are discussed in the treatment of individual markers.

29.1 *NI*

There are two types of *ni* phrases: (1) those that specify a subject or object, and (2) those that indicate time or reason.

29.1.1 *Ni* phrases that specify

A *ni* phrase shows that a VP, not an NP, specifies an object or subject within the independent VP. Table 29.1 gives an example of object specification. The mood is indicative, and the attitude of the speaker is neutral. In sentences of this type, the order of the phrases is fixed.

---

[1] Except for the imperative. Lyons (1968:307) noted that establishing categories of mood is often difficult, because of the special behavior of imperatives, which seem to comprise a class by themselves.

29 Subordination

TABLE 29.1: OBJECT SPECIFICATION WITH *NI*

INDEPENDENT	SUBORDINATE
*Au nanu-m-**a***	***ni** sā yali.*
'I think (it)	that it's lost.'
	SPECIFIED OBJECT

Table 29.2 shows subject specification. The phrase order is also fixed.

TABLE 29.2: SUBJECT SPECIFICATION WITH *NI*

INDEPENDENT	SUBORDINATE
E rawa	***ni** sā yali.*
'It's possible	that it's lost.'
	SPECIFIED SUBJECT

The following sections discuss object and subject specification in more detail.

29.1.1.1 Object specification

The following examples show *ni* phrases that specify a preceding object, third person singular *-a* (boldfaced).

INDEPENDENT VP	SUBORDINATE VP	
*Au nanu-m-**a***	***ni** sā oti na dalo.*	'I think that there's no
1S think-TR-3S	SUB ASP finished DEF taro	more taro.'
Au kilā [2]	***ni**-o rawa ni vodo ose.*	'I know that you can
1S know-3S	SUB-2S able SUB ride horse	ride horseback.'
Au kilā	***ni** sā lako.*	'I know that she went.'
1S know-3S	SUB ASP go	

This construction has certain semantic and grammatical limitations. First, since an action/state is naturally singular, inanimate, nonhuman, and non-first or non-second person, the object that represents it is confined to third person singular.

Second, the head of the independent verb phrase is usually a member of a class whose common semantic feature is perception (such as *rai* 'see') or reporting (such as *kai* 'say'). Such phrases are often translated as 'I know that ...', 'I see that ...', 'I said that ...'

The following verbs are a sample of those that operate similarly:

vaka-beka-taki	'doubt'	*vaka-vuli-ci*	'advise'
rogo-ci	'hear'	*vā-kāsama-taki*	'consider'
vaka-donui	'permit'	*taro-gi*	'ask-about'
nui-taki	'hope-for'	*caca-vaki*	'express'
bese-taki	'refuse'	*caki-taki*	'deny'

---

[2] This word has the underlying form *kila* + *a*.

kune-i	'find'	*cau-raki*	'report'
volai	'write'	*vuli-ci*	'learn'
bole-i	'boast-about'	*talanoa-taki*	'tell'
lai-vi	'permit'	*cavu-ti*	'pronounce'
bā-taki	'deny'	*kere-i*	'request'
tadra	'dream'	*tuku-ni*	'tell'
reki-taki	'rejoice-at'	*masu-laki*	'pray-for'

In general, whenever the semantics of a verb allows an action/state (rather than an entity) to be a goal, this action/state is represented in the sentence as a subordinate VP, usually as a *ni* phrase. (A *me* phrase can also specify the object under these circumstances, but with an added subjunctive meaning. See §29.2.)

29.1.1.2 Subject specification

Verbs that allow the subject to be specified by a *ni* phrase are often verbs of judgment (*dodonu* 'correct'), existence (*sega* 'is not'), or potential (*rawa* 'able'). For example:

INDEPENDENT VP	SUBORDINATE VP	
E dodonu	*ni ra soro.*	'It is fitting that they
3s right	SUB 3P atone	made atonement.'
E dodonu	*ni lako.*	'She should go (literally,
3s right	SUB go	it's right that she go).'

In the sentence just above, the *ni* phrase specifies the subject *e*.

29.1.1.2.1 Subject raising and the idiomatic use of *ni* phrases

In some common sentences, an analysis of the relationship between independent and subordinate VPs produces unexpected results. For example, although the following sets of sentences look structurally similar, they are not:

*Au sega **ni** kilā.*	'I don't know.'
*Au rawa **ni** lako.*	'I can go.'
*E vinaka **ni** sā yaco mai.*	'It's good that she came.'
*E cala **ni**-u lako.*	'It's wrong that I went.'

If, in the first set, we try to find a grammatical function for the *ni* VP, we fail. For example, the independent VP for the first is

*au sega

which—if it had meaning at all—would mean something like ***'I am none' or ***'I am not.' And what function does *ni kilā* have? It cannot specify the subject (for it is in third person), and there is no object to specify.

A similar situation holds for the second sentence. Here, the independent sentence *Au rawa* is grammatical, meaning 'I am able'. But the *ni* phrase cannot specify the subject, and there is no object.

It appears, then, that the surface forms of these sentences are GRAMMATICAL IDIOMS, based on the following underlying sentences:

E sega ni-u kilā.   lit., 'It does not exist that I know.'
E rawa ni-u lako.   lit., 'It is possible that I go.'

Both of these sentences are grammatical possibilities, but they are less common than the idiomatic forms. In other words, in the first sentence, *e* is semantically the subject of *kilā*, but grammatically raised to be the subject of *sega*.

The following common construction is also idiomatic:

*Au bese **ni** [verb]*   'I refuse to [verb].'

Here, the idiom seems unanalyzable, even in terms of an underlying sentence. Semantically, it is the first person who is the actor. What role does the *ni* phrase play then? In terms of meaning, it should function as a specified object. But *bese* has no formal signs of transitivity.

By treating these constructions as idioms, I suggest that they are whole units that are not analyzable in terms of the function of their constituents.

29.1.1.2.1.1 Negation and *ni* phrases

As in many related languages, the Fijian negative is a verb. (*Sega* 'not' as a negative existential—i.e., with an NP—is treated in §9.1.1.) The following sentence shows the common way to negate a verb:

*Au sega **ni** kilā.*   'I don't know.'
1S not SUB know-3S

29.1.1.3 Layering of *ni* phrases

With certain verbs, a series of *ni* phrases is possible, with a hierarchical, rather than linear, structure. For example:

*Au nanu-m-a **ni** o kilā **ni** rau butako-c-a.*
1S think-TR-3S SUB 2S know-3S SUB 3D steal-TR-3S
'I think that you know they (dual) stole it.'

The hierarchical structure is as follows:

(*Au nanuma* (***ni*** *o kilā* (***ni*** *rau butakoca*)))

Another (hypothetical) example is:

*Au kilā **ni** sā sega **ni** rawa ni kay-a **ni** rau kilā **ni** ...*
1S know-TR SUB ASP not SUB able SUB say-3S SUB 3D know-3S SUB
'I know that it's not possible to say that they (dual) know that ...'

29.1.2 *Ni* phrases that modify

Table 29.3 shows a *ni* phrase that modifies the independent phrase. (In this example, the phrase is fronted.)

29.1.1.2.1.1a Prohibition is expressed with *kua* or *kākua*

Kua *ni baci lasu-taki au!*
'Don't lie to me!'

Kākua *ni lako de-o na oca wale gā!*
'Don't go, because you'll just get tired!'

*Me-u **kākua** ni caka-v-a de-u na bera wale gā.*
'I shouldn't do that, or I'll be late.'

*M-o **kua** mada ni lako!*
'Please don't go!'

TABLE 29.3: *NI* PHRASE MODIFYING AN INDEPENDENT PHRASE

SUBORDINATE	INDEPENDENT
Ni oti gā	*sā lako sara.* 'When it was finished, he left.'
ATTRIBUTE	HEAD

The underlying phrases are two independent ones:

INDEPENDENT VP: *Sā oti gā.* 'It was finished.'
INDEPENDENT VP: *Sā lako sara.* 'He left.'

Changing the first phrase to a subordinate one links the two and shows the modifying relationship. Another example:

INDEPENDENT VP: *Era suka.* 'They disperse.'
INDEPENDENT VP: *E oti na yaqona.* 'The kava was finished.'

These phrases can be linked with *ni*:

Ni   oti   na yaqona, era suka.   'When the kava was finished, they
SUB finish DEF kava   3P disperse   dispersed.'

An alternate meaning for this sentence is: 'They dispersed because the kava was finished.' The following sentence (with the *ni* phrase in its normal position) shows a similar ambiguity:

*E caka-v-a **ni** sā levu na no-na via-kana.*
3S do-TR-3S SUB ASP big DEF PC-3S DES-eat
'He did it because his hunger was great.' / 'He did it when his hunger became great.'

The following sentence shows the *ni* phrase in fronted position:

Ni sā levu na no-na via-kana, e caka-v-a.

29.1.2.1 *Ni* phrases that indicate cause

When added to a VP with an S1 verb, such as:

E vinaka.   'It's good.'

the nominalized *ni* phrase refers to the agent, which can be interpreted as reason or consequence. For example:

*E vinaka **ni** lako mai.*   'It's good that she came.'
3S good   SUB come DIR

Here, the *ni* phrase seems to be on the functional border between specifying the subject and modifying the independent VP. That is (in terms of the meaning), the *ni* phrase can elaborate on the subject *e*, or serve in an adverbial function.

Even closer to a modifying function is a *ni* phrase that occurs after verbs of emotion, such as *mārau* 'happy', which involve a human experiencer. Things or conditions are not *mārau* or *rarawa* 'sad', *reki* 'joyful', *cudru* 'angry', *rere* 'afraid', *ninini* 'excited'; however, beings with feeling are. When such statives are used in the main VP, the following *ni* phrase indicates the reason or agent of the state.

*Au mārau **ni** lako o koya.* 'I'm glad that he went.'
1S happy SUB go PRP 3S

This sentence could be interpreted as 'The reason I am glad is that he went', or 'I am glad as a consequence of his going.'

As a matter of fact, a variation on this sentence, with very little change in meaning, uses a causative construction:

E vaka-mārau-taki au na no-na lako. 'His going made me happy.'
3S CAU-happy-TR 1S DEF PC-3S go

Here, the main VP is *e vaka-mārau-taki au*; *na no-na lako* is the specified subject.

Another example is:

*E kidacala **ni**-u lutu.* 'He was surprised that I fell.'
3S surprised SUB-1S fall

For this sentence, the *ni* phrase cannot be considered as the specified subject, since the subject is animate and can be specified only by an NP referring to an animate being:

*E kidacala **ni**-u lutu o Saimone.* 'S was surprised that I fell.'

These *ni* phrases seem different from other modifying *ni* phrases in that fronting the phrase would change the meaning somewhat. For example, fronting the *ni* phrase in the example produces:

***Ni**-u lutu, e kidacala o Saimone.* 'When I fell, S was surprised.'
SUB-1S fall 3S surprised PRP S

29.1.2.2 The meaning of modifying *ni* phrases

When a subordinating *ni* phrase precedes the main phrase, it conveys the sense of both time and consequence.

***Ni** oti gā, sā lako sara.* 'Just when it was finished,
SUB finish LIM ASP go INT   he left.'

In constructions such as this, it is difficult to separate time from consequence, since the second action both follows the first chronologically, and is—in a sense—the result of the first.

***Ni** dua e tau-vi-mate koto mai na no-na vale, era dau kau*
SUB one 3S ill CNT DIR DEF POS-3S house 3P HAB carry

  kākana yani ko ira era laki vei-siko.
  food DIR PRP 3P 3P DIR REC-visit

'When/because someone is ill at home, they carry food there—those who engage in ritual visiting (*NV3*:6)'

Ni dau oti   gā na   vei-qara-vi, *era sā na tatau tale na mai vei-siko.*
SUB HAB finish LIM DEF reception   3P ASP FT depart ITR DEF DIR REC-visit
'When/because the reception had finished, those who were visiting took
   leave again.' (*NV3*:6)

Ni   sā sivi gā   na Siga-ni-Sucu, *eda sā   na yaco-v-a   yani na*
SUB ASP over LIM DEF Christmas   1PI ASP FT arrive-TR-3S DIR DEF

Vakatawase.   'When/because Christmas is over, we will come to
New-Year   New Year's.' (*NV3*:17)

Ni sā rai-c-a   na   leqa levu oqō   ko Rā R., sā dua-tani
SUB ASP see-TR-3S DEF trouble big DEM:1 PRP Mr. R. ASP another

sara na no-na domo-bula. 'When/because Mr. R. saw this big difficulty
INT DEF PC-3S fear   his fear was extraordinary.' (*NV5*:1)

In all these sentences, the action/state indicated by the main VP could not
have taken place if that in the *ni* phrase had not preceded it.

In the sentences indicating time or reason, the order of the phrases may be reversed[3] with no change of meaning; there is no chance that the *ni* phrase might be thought to specify the object (if there is any). For instance, in the second example above, there is no grammatical object, but *kau*—as a two referent verb—already has a noun modifier: *kākana*. And even if the main VP were:

era dau   kau-t-a   'they (plural) carry it'
3P HAB carry-TR-3S

the nature of the verb itself precludes interpreting the *ni* phrase as a specified object. In other words, one might *know* that so-and-so happened, or *tell* it, but one could not *carry* it.

In some instances, the *ni* phrase could be interpreted as both indicating time and consequence, and specifying the subject as well:

E dau vaka-malumu-tak-a tale gā na yago-dratou **ni**   **tunu-mak-a na**
3S HAB CAU-weak-TR-3S ITR LIM DEF body-3T   SUB warm-TR-3S DEF

draki.   'When/because the weather is close, it also weakens their bod-
weather   ies / that the weather is close also weakens their bodies.'

The different grammatical forms of the possible translations illustrate two separate grammatical interpretations. For the former, the *ni* phrase represents time and consequence: the state of the weather both precedes and causes the condition indicated by the main verb phrase. For the latter, the *ni* phrase is interpreted as a nominalization that functions to specify the grammatical subject *e*. I prefer this interpretation, because otherwise there would be nothing in the sentence or the context to explain what the subject *e* refers to.

29.1.3 Morphophonemic changes

There are certain changes connected with *ni* phrases. First, for all third person and first person inclusive subjects, the *e* is deleted. Thus:

---

[3] With a change in intonation contours.

| *ni* e lako | → | **ni** lako | 'that/when he goes' |
| *ni* eratou lako | → | **ni** ratou lako | 'that/when they (trial) go' |

And so on for the remainder of these sets.

Next, when *ni* is used with first person singular subject, the *u* allomorph is used rather than *au*: *ni-u*.[4] Table 29:4 and subsequent tables for the other subordinate markers show the phonological results of different combinations of marker + subject. Raised periods indicate measure divisions (see §32.4, CH 36).

TABLE 29.4: *NI* + SUBJECTS

ni + *u*	→	*niu*			
ni + *keirau*	→	*nikei·rau*	*ni* + *edaru*	→	*nidaru*
ni + *keitou*	→	*nikei·tou*	*ni* + *edatou*	→	*nida·tou*
ni + *keimami*	→	*nikei·mami*	*ni* + *eda*	→	*nida*
ni + *o*	→	*nio*	*ni* + *e*	→	*ni*
ni + *odrau*	→	*nidrau*.	*ni* + *erau*	→	*nirau*
ni + *odou*	→	*nidou*	*ni* + *eratou*	→	*nira·tou*
ni + *onī*	→	*nio·nī*	*ni* + *era*	→	*nira*

29.1.4 *Ka ni*

In the literary style of Fijian, the combination *ka ni* is sometimes used in the sense of 'because'. An example is:

Era dau rarawa-tak-a sara na tina-da   na   dukaveluvelu ni
3P HAB sad-TR-3S   INT DEF mother-1PI DEF dirty   POS

*no-da i-sulu **ka ni** dau drēdrē na ke-na   sava-ti.*
PC-1PI clothes CNJ SUB HAB hard   DEF PC-3S clean-TR

'Our mothers are always saddened by our dirty clothes because getting them clean is difficult.' (*NV4*:2)

Ka ni is also treated in §31.1.1.

29.1.5 The intonation of *ni* phrases

Similar to NPs that specify the subject or the object, specifying *ni* phrases are rather tightly phonologically bound to the preceding VP. For example, shorter sentences with verbs such as *sega* 'no', *rawa* 'able', or *bese* 'refuse' in the main VP are usually included in one phonological phrase:

---

[4] On the basis of evidence from other Fijian languages, Geraghty (1977, 1979) suggested that *au* is an innovation and that earlier, first person singular was indicated by *u*. A synchronic view of the situation is that first person singular has two allomorphs—*au* and *u*—and that the latter occurs after subordinate markers. From this point of view, no vowel has been dropped; *niu* is simply the result of *ni* + *u*.

*Au bese **ni** lako.*		'I refuse to go.'
1S refuse SUB go		
*E sega **ni** lako.*		'She didn't go.'
3S not SUB go		

In contrast, modifying *ni* phrases are less tightly bound, and the individual phrase peaks are distinctly marked.

29.1.6 Structural differences between types of *ni* phrases

PG (2/79) noted a structural constraint that separates specifying and modifying *ni* phrases: the former can begin with a fronted NP, as in:

*Au kilā **ni** gone oyā e tauvi-mate gā.*
1S know-3S SUB child DEM:3 3S ill LIM
'I know that that child is ill.'

This sentence is a variant of:

*Au kilā **ni** tauvi mate gā na gone oyā.*

However, one cannot front *gone* in a time, consequence phrase:

***ni** gone e tauvi-mate, au lako-v-a na wai-ni-mate.*
SUB child 3S ill 1S go-TR-3S DEF medicine
'(When/because the child was ill, I went for some medicine.)

29.2 ME

Me marks a VP that serves in a SUBJUNCTIVE relationship to the independent VP. Thus, the VP in which it is used represents a situation that does not yet exist—in relation to the independent VP.

TABLE 29.5: INDEPENDENT PHRASE + *ME* PHRASE

INDEPENDENT	SUBORDINATE
Sā rawa	***me** dua na magiti*
'It's possible	for there to be a feast.'

Me phrases have a wider range of functions and meanings than those for the other markers. The following examples show *me* phrases functioning to show purpose:

*Sā keli-a oti tū ko tama-qu na i-vākatā **me** drōdrō ki-na*
ASP dig-3S ASP CNT PRP father-1S DEF ditch SUB flow ABL-3S
na wai ni uca. 'Father has finished digging a ditch for the
DEF water POS rain rainwater to flow in.' (*NV2*:16)

*E dau tā na bitu ka viri **me** bilibili.*
3S HAB cut DEF bamboo CNJ tied SUB raft
'Bamboo is cut and lashed together to serve as a raft.' (*NV2*:12)

*Keirau ā lau-t-a   na dalo **me** ke-na i-yavoi.*
1DX PT cut-TR-3S DEF taro SUB PC-3S *i-yavoi*
'We (dual exclusive) cut the taro for its *i-yavoi*. (*NV2*:16)

Note that in each of the last two examples above, the *me* phrase is an identifying VP—one that uses a noun.

Along with the sense of "serving as" something, *me* is used in the sense of "changing into" something:

*Ni dua gā e butu-k-a   sā vuki **me** yalewa.*
SUB one LIM 3S step-TR-3S ASP turn SUB woman
'When one of them steps on it, he turns into a woman.' (*VV*:Verata text)

Note here that it is an identifying VP used with a subordinate marker. Another example from the same text:

*ia na vu-na   rau sā sega ni vuki ki-na   **me** rau yalewa*
CNJ DEF cause-3S 3D ASP not SUB turn ABL-3S SUB 3D woman
'but the reason whereby they (dual) were not turned into women'

Me is also used to propose or suggest, fitting with a notion put forth elsewhere that elocutionary acts in Fijian must be accompanied by the culturally appropriate grammatical trappings. For example:

*Io, **me** sā dua na no-qu i-talanoa.*   'Well, here's my story (if I may).'
yes SUB ASP one DEF PC-1S story   (*VV*:Naweni text)

The most common use of *me* for this purpose is with imperatives, which can occur with both second and third person. For example, with second person:

***Mo** nī lako mada.*   'You (plural or polite) go please.'
SUB 2P go INI

And third person:

***Me** vaka-lailai mada na retiō.*   '(lit.) Let the radio be turned down.'
SUB CAU-small INI DEF radio

In some uses, *me* seems indistinguishable from *ni*. Note the following:

*Oyā e qai i-matai ni gauna **me** ra rai-c-a   kina na tagane*
DEM:3 3S SEQ first   POS time SUB 3P see-TR-3S ABL-3S DEF male
   mai Burotukula.   'As for that, it was the first time that they had
   ABL B   seen (there) men at B.' (*VV*:Verata text)

The important difference between *me* and *ni* is the subjunctive meaning of *me*: referring to something that is definitely contrary to fact. Note the following minimal pair:

*Au nanu-m-a **ni** lako.*   'I think he has gone.'
1S think-TR-3S SUB go

*Au nanu-m-a **me** lako.*   'I think he should / might go.'

Milner (1972:62) illustrated the difference between the two markers with the following minimal pair:

*E rawa **ni** rau lako.*		'They can go (if they so wish).'
*E rawa **me** rau lako.*		'They have permission to go.'

This particular contrast can be illustrated in English by the pair *can* vs. *may*: *e rawa ni* means 'can'; *e rawa me* means 'may'.

From a list of verbs that take *ni* phrases, SN (2/79) suggested that the following would take *me*:

lewā	'command'	*tatau-nak-a*	'recommend'

29.2.1 *Me vakā*

The marker *me* often occurs after the verb *vakā* 'resemble it'. Here, the whole construction has the sense of 'such as', 'like', 'for instance':

*E dina ni bula e loma ni wasawasa na tavuto **me vakā** na ika*
3S true SUB live ABL inside POS ocean DEF whale SUB like-3S DEF fish

ia e sega gā ni ika. 'It's true that the sperm whale lives in the ocean
CNJ 3S not LIM SUB fish   like a fish, but it isn't a fish at all.' (*NV*5:14)

29.2.2 Morphophonemic changes

Me is somewhat different from the other subordinate markers in its morphophonemic behavior with subjects. Note, in table 29:6, the phonological result of combining *me* with second person subjects.

TABLE 29.6: *ME* + SUBJECTS

me + u	→	*meu*			
me + keirau	→	*mekei·rau*	*me + edaru*	→	*medaru*
me + keitou	→	*mekei·tou*	*me + edatou*	→	*meda·tou*
me + keimami	→	*mekei·mami*	*me + eda*	→	*meda*
me + o	→	*mo*	*me + e*	→	*me*
me + odrau	→	*modrau*	*me + erau*	→	*merau*
me + odou	→	*modou*	*me + eratou*	→	*mera·tou*
me + onī	→	*monī*	*me + era*	→	*mera*

29.3 *KĒ*

A *kē* phrase represents a potential cause, and an independent phrase represents the effect:

TABLE 29.7: INDEPENDENT PHRASE + *KĒ* PHRASE

INDEPENDENT	SUBORDINATE
Au na lako	*kē kune e sō na baca.*
'I'll go	if some bait is found.'
EFFECT	CAUSE

Note that in each of the following examples, the situation referred to by the *kē* VP is a conditioning factor for the situation referred to by the independent VP.

*Keirau na lako **kē** rawa.*
1DX FT go SUB able
'We (dual exclusive) will go if possible.' (*SF* 67)

*Daru na laki siwa **kē** galala na waqa.*
1DI FT DIR fish SUB free DEF boat
'We (dual inclusive) will go fishing if there's a boat free.' (*SF* 67)

*E vinaka **kē** daru na mai sota tale ekē.*
3S good SUB 1DI FT DIR meet ITR LOC:1
'It would be good if we (dual inclusive) could meet here again.' (*SF* 67)

29.3.1 Relationships outside the sentence

The summary description of *kē* shows the potential cause-and-effect situations represented by VPs within the same sentence. However, the situations may also be represented, within a discourse, by different sentences:

O na lako?	'Are you going to go?'
*Io, **kē** sā oti na no-qu cakacaka.*	'Yes, if my work is finished.'
O na lai siwa?	'Are you going line-fishing?'
*Io, **kē** rawa.*	Yes, if it's possible.'
E rawa niu lako tale gā?	'May I go too?'
***Kē** galala na waqa.*	'If there's room in the boat.'

In each of the pairs above, the *kē* phrase could be interpreted as one part of a truncated sentence. For example:

*Io, au na lako **kē** rawa.*   'Yes, I'll go if it's possible.'

29.3.2 *Kē* marking both phrases

Grammarians have noted[5] that both VPs can be marked with *kē*:

***Kē** ā kilā na tūraga, **kē** ā sega ni lako mai.*
SUB PT know-3S DEF chief SUB PT not SUB go DIR
'Had the chief known it, he would not have come.' (Milner 1972:68)

***Kē** bula ko koya, **kē** vinaka.*   'If he is alive, it is well.'
SUB live PRP 3S SUB good   (Churchward 1941:23)

One way to look at this construction is to consider that both VPs represent situations that are hypothetical. In each of these examples, since the verb phrases are not distinguished, phrase order must identify the first phrase as potential cause, and the second as potential effect. This situation is often reflected by 'if ... then' in the English translation.

---

[5] E.g., Churchward 1941:23; Milner 1972:68. Capell's dictionary contains a classic comment on this pattern: "Often used twice in a Fijian sentence where once is sufficient in English."

29.3.3 *Kevakā*[6]

The use of *kē* with *vakā* might be considered an idiomatic alternate to *kē* alone. However, there are some differences between the two constructions. Strictly speaking, this form is a subordinate VP in itself; the main verb is *vakā* 'be like it'. The following VP specifies the object, but it itself is not marked for subordination:

Ke-vakā   *au via-gunu, au na gunu-v-a*   *na wai-ni-moli.*
SUB-be-like-3S 1S DES-drink 1S FT drink-TR-3S DEF lemonade
'If I'm thirsty, I'll drink the lemonade.'

Arms (1985:15) noted an important feature of *kevakā*: that it may introduce a clause beginning with *me*:

ke-vakā   *me lako mai*   'if he should come'
SUB-be-like-3S SUB go DIR

29.3.4 Morphophonemic changes

Table 29.8 shows the changes that take place when *kē* is combined with a following subject. Other changes can be summarized by the following rules:

1. *Kē* + *e* → *kē*
2. *Kē* keeps its length when followed by an accented syllable, but shortens before an unaccented syllable.

For example, *kē* + *era* → **kēra* → *kera*.

TABLE 29.8: *KĒ* + SUBJECTS

kē + *u* →	*keu*		
kē + *keirau* →	*kē·kei·rau*	*kē* + *edaru* →	*kē·daru*
kē + *keitou* →	*kēkei·tou*	*kē* + *edatou* →	*kēda·tou*
kē + *keimami* →	*kē·kei·mami*	*kē* + *eda* →	*keda*
kē + *o* →	*keo*	*kē* + *e* →	*kē*
kē + *odrau* →	*keo·daru.*	*kē* + *erau* →	*kē·rau*
kē + *odou* →	*keo·dou*	*kē* + *eratou* →	*kera·tou*
kē + *onī* →	*keo·nī*	*kē* + *era* →	*kera*

29.4 *SĒ*

Phrases marked by *sē* often occur in pairs, indicating different or contradictory potential situations. If only one *sē* phrase occurs, the opposing situation is implicit. Grammatically, the phrases specify subjects or objects. An example is:

Au sega ni kilā ***se-u*** *na lako* ***sē*** *sega.*
1S not SUB know-3S SUB-1S FT go SUB not
'I don't know whether I'll go or not.' (*SF*:201)

---

[6] The underlying form of *kevakā* is most likely *kēvakā*, with *kē* shortening before an unaccented syllable. See §36.3.1.

Table 29.9 shows the structure of this construction.

TABLE 29.9: INDEPENDENT PHRASE + *SĒ* PHRASES

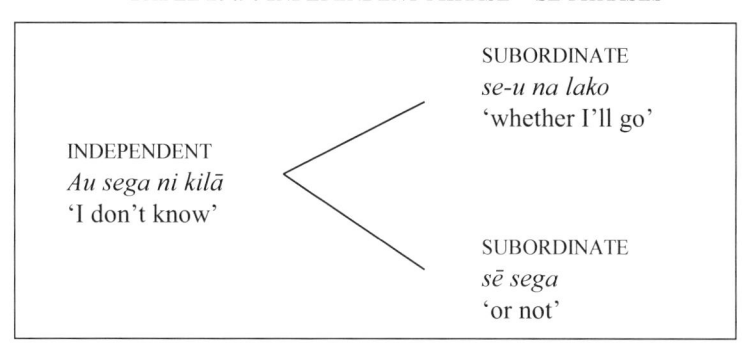

```
                                    SUBORDINATE
                                    se-u na lako
                                    'whether I'll go'
    INDEPENDENT
    Au sega ni kilā
    'I don't know'
                                    SUBORDINATE
                                    sē sega
                                    'or not'
```

29.4.1 Types of verbs in the independent phrase

It was noted earlier that *sē* phrases functioned as specified subjects or objects. We now give additional examples:

Au sega ni kilā   se-u   na lesu mai nikua sē   nimataka.
1S not SUB know-3S SUB-1S FT return DIR today SUB tomorrow
'I don't know whether I'll return today or tomorrow.'

Note that the second phrase is truncated. The following underlying structure might be proposed:

TABLE 29.10: INDEPENDENT PHRASE + *SĒ* PHRASES

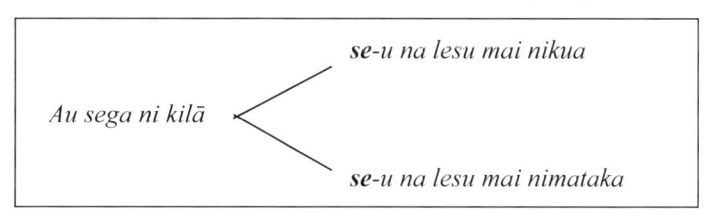

```
                        se-u na lesu mai nikua
    Au sega ni kilā
                        se-u na lesu mai nimataka
```

Both these subordinate phrases serve as the specified objects of *kilā* 'know it'.

Many of the examples collected are variants of this particular pattern, using [ ] *sega ni kilā* as the independent phrase. The contrast between two (or more) different possible situations need not be made explicit. In the following example, it is implicit.

Au sega ni kilā   se-u   na lesu   mai nikua.
1S not SUB know-3S SUB-1S FT return DIR today
'I don't know if I'll return today.'

Another common example of *sē* phrases used as specified objects involves imperatives with speech-act implications. Note the following:

M-onī tuku-n-a mada sē   yaco mai sē   sega.
SUB-2P tell-TR-3S INI SUB arrive DIR SUB not
'Tell me whether he arrived or not.'

Other possible verbs in this semantic category are *ka-y-a* 'say it', *sau-m-a* 'answer it', and *taro-g-a* 'ask it'.

Sē marking phrases as specified subjects very often occurs in a subordinate relationship to the following dominant phrase:

E sega ni macala.   'It is not clear.'
3S not SUB clear

For example,

*E sega ni macala **se**-u na lesu mai nikua.*
3S not SUB clear SUB-1S FT return DIR today
'It's not clear whether I'll return today.'

This construction is like the previous construction specifying an object in that it can state alternatives explicitly, or state only one, leaving the other(s) implicit.

29.4.2 The semantic relationship between *sē* and the independent VP

The frequency of occurrence of *sē* phrases with such examples as those above— X *sega ni kilā* 'X doesn't know it' and *e sega ni macala* 'it's not clear'— underscores an important semantic feature of *sē*: it refers to a situation that is, respectively, unknown or uncertain. This semantic property is highlighted even further in the use of *sē* phrases with two different verbs in the dominant phrase, *dei-tak-a* 'confirm it' and *tuku-n-a* 'tell it. Since their meanings are the antithesis of uncertainty, such verbs dominate *sē* phrases only when the former are set in the negative or the future. For example:

*Sā na dei-tak-a **sē** rawa **sē** sega.*
ASP FT confirm-TR-3S SUB able SUB not
'He'll confirm whether it's possible or not.'

*Sā na tuku-n-a **sē** dodonu **sē** cala.*
ASP FT tell-TR-3S SUB right SUB wrong
'She'll tell whether it's right or wrong.'

If a *sē* construction were not set in the negative or future, it would not make sense, for without those restrictions, the uncertainty would vanish. Under such circumstances, a *ni* phrase is used instead:

*Era sā dei-tak-a **ni** sega ni rawa.*
3P ASP confirm-TR-3S SUB not SUB able
'They (plural) confirmed that it wasn't possible.'

29.4.3 Question words in *sē* phrases

Consistent with the UNKNOWN or UN-CERTAIN semantic characteristics of a *sē* phrase is its use with the interrogative roots *cei* 'who?', *naica* 'when?', *vei* 'where?', and *vica* 'how many'. Examples (supplied by BK) are:

*Au sega ni kilā **sē** o cei e tiko ki-na.*
1S not SUB know-3S SUB PRP who 3S stay ABL-3S
'I don't know who's staying there.'

E sega ni macala sē ne-i cei na i-vola oqō.
3S not SUB clear SUB PC-POS who DEF book DEM:1
'It's not clear whose book this is.'

Au via-kilā se-o na lako ki-na ni naica.
1S DES-know-3S SUB-2S DEF go ABL-3S SUB when
'I want to know when you're going to go there'

Era via-rogo-c-a sē cava o ka-y-a tiko.
3P DES-hear-TR-3S SUB what 2S say-TR-3S CNT
They (plural) want to hear what you are saying.'

Me taro-gi mada sē vica me lako ki-na.
SUB ask-TR INI SUB how-many SUB go ABL-3S
'Someone please ask when (at what time) he went.'

E na gauna ka taro-gi ki-na sē cava na no-na nanu-m-a.
ABL DEF time REL ask-TR ABL-3S SUB what DEF PC-3S think-TR-3S
'at the time at which he was asked what his thoughts were' (*NL* 16/7/81)

29.4.4 Morphophonemic changes

Table 29.11 shows *sē* in combination with following subjects (see Milner 1972:55). Changes in form are similar to those described in §29.3.4 for *kē:*.

1. *Sē + e → sē*
2. *Sē* keeps its length when followed by an accented syllable, but shortens before an unaccented syllable. For example, *sē + era → *sēra → sera*.

TABLE 29.11: *SĒ* + SUBJECTS

sē + u	→	*seu*		
sē + keirau	→	*sē·kei·rau*	*sē + edaru*	→	*sē·daru*
sē + keitou	→	*sē·kei·tou*	*sē + edatou*	→	*seda·tou*
sē + keimami	→	*sē·kei·mami*	*sē + eda*	→	*seda*
sē + o	→	*seo*	*sē + e*	→	*sē*
sē + odrau	→	*seo·drau.*	*sē + erau*	→	*sē·rau*
sē + odou	→	*seo·dou*	*sē + eratou*	→	*sera·tou*
sē + onī	→	*seo·nī*	*sē + era*	→	*sera*

29.5 *DĒ*

A phrase marked by *dē* represents the effect of a cause, which in turn is represented by the dominant phrase. Such a construction differs from the one with *kē* in that the *dē* phrase reflects the speaker's opinion that the effect would be undesirable. Table 29.12 (below) illustrates the relationship.

29.5.1 Adversative vs. subjunctive

Many sentences with *dē* reflect the attitude of the speaker that (a) one should avoid a particular situation because the outcome would be undesirable, or (b) steps have been or should be taken to insure that the undesirable outcome does not occur.

TABLE 29.12: DOMINANT PHRASE + *DĒ* PHRASE

DOMINANT	SUBORDINATE
Kua ni draiva vaka-tololo	*de-o na qai coqa.*
'Don't drive fast	lest you run into something.'
CAUSE	EFFECT

The first type often involves the use of *kua* or *kākua* (prohibitive):

*Me-u   kākua ni   caka-v-a   **de-u**   na   bera wale gā.*
SUB-1S don't SUB done-TR-3S SUB-1S FT late LIM LIM
'I shouldn't do that, or I'll be late.' (*SF*)

An examples of the second type:

*E sō   era dau lade ki   wai   **dē**   cumu-ti   ira na ose.*
3S some 3P HAB jump ABL water SUB butt-TR 3P DEF horse
'Some of them would jump into the water lest the horse butt them.'
(*FR3*:34)

In both these subtypes, the relationship between the dominant and the subordinate phrases is roughly (in traditional terms) ADVERBIAL. That is, the subordinate phrase serves as a special kind of ATTRIBUTE.

However, in the second principal type of *dē* construction, the subordinate clause specifies a subject or object. For example:

*Au nanu-m-a   sara gā   **dē**   ko na sega ni   mai wāraki au.*
1S think-TR-3S INT LIM SUB 2S FT not SUB DIR wait-TR 1S
'I thought that you might not wait for me.' (*FR3*:48)

In the first of the two examples immediately above, there seems to be no afflictive meaning to the situation represented by the *dē* phrase. Instead, it seems to be merely subjunctive: the situation *might* occur.

Arms (10/84) pointed out that *dē* can also be used to introduce principal clauses, with the meaning of "perhaps."

29.5.2 Morphophonemic changes

Combining *dē* with subjects results in the forms shown in table 29.13.

TABLE 29.13: *DĒ* + SUBJECTS

dē + u	→	*deu*		
dē + keirau	→	*dē·kei·rau*	*dē + edaru*	→	*dē·daru*
dē + keitou	→	*dē·kei·tou*	*dē + edatou*	→	*deda·tou*
dē + keimami	→	*dē·kei·mami*	*dē + eda*	→	*deda*
dē + o	→	*deo*	*dē + e*	→	*dē*
dē + odrau	→	*deo·drau.*	*dē + erau*	→	*dē·rau*
dē + odou	→	*deo·dou*	*dē + eratou*	→	*dera·tou*
dē + onī	→	*deo·nī*	*dē + era*	→	*dera*

Other changes are similar to those described in §29.3.4 for *kē*.

30 POSSESSION

> The disuse of that suffixing is a decline in ful[l]ness and power[,] which Mr. Fison will no doubt tell you, begins as soon as people begin to talk to Europeans —that you know always impoverishes ... I am persuaded that he will say that the Fiji people corrupted by Europeans will say noqu liga as miserably as a Polynesian.[1]
>
> R. H. Codrington
> Letter to the Rev. George Brown, 1883

> The best way for the student to facilitate his progress through this tedious part of the grammar is, —first to make himself tolerably well acquainted with the pronouns qou and qu, —in all their numbers and cases; and then, proceed to those dual & plural pronouns[2] which are peculiar in their signification; as kei rau, kei tou, and kei mami. When he has made himself master of these, he will be able to investigate the use of qau, kemu and memu with ease and confidence. Difficulties will vanish before the light which he has obtained, and his knowledge of this otherwise perplexing subject will be accurate and gratifying.
>
> David Cargill
> Lakeba grammar (1839:30)

Possession is a common type of attribution, showing that two entities are related in a special way. The most obvious relation involves ownership, but there are other connections as well. In this chapter, we discuss both the formal features and the semantics of possession.

Because many topics overlap, it is hard to describe the categories of possession in a linear order. For example, the following oppositions must be treated:

1. Alienable vs. inalienable
2. Common vs. proper
3. Neutral vs. edible vs. drinkable (categories of classification)
4. Morphological vs. phrasal
5. Integral vs. partitive nouns

---

[1] Codrington's comment refers to the different ways that Fijian and Polynesian languages express inalienable possession.

[2] In his ms. grammar (1839:16), Cargill treated only singular, dual, and plural—but for the last category, recognized a special class that was "expressive of a small number"—i.e., trial.

We can add to this list the complexities of personal suffixes, which show the same distinctions as subjects and objects:

6. Inclusive vs. exclusive
7. First vs. second vs. third person
8. Singular vs. dual vs. trial vs. plural

Still, we use this general outline:

1. Markers (morphological forms)
2. Mechanics (morphological and syntactic patterns)

As a thread that runs through this labyrinth of oppositions, the semantics of the constructions will also be discussed.

We begin with form: a list of the morphemes that enter into possessive constructions. (Later sections treat these morphemes in more detail.)

30.1 POSSESSIVE FORMS

Every possessive construction includes one of a closed set of function morphemes. They can be divided into the following three categories: suffixes, possessive classifiers, and phrasal markers.

30.1.1 Suffixes

Possessive suffixes show the distinctions also present in grammatical subjects and objects (see CH 4 and CH 17), and—except for singulars—are also similar in form. The fifteen forms in this set show the following features:

Person (first, second, and third)
Number (singular, dual, trial, and plural)
Inclusive vs. exclusive (confined to first person)

These forms are suffixed to:

(1) the possessive classifier prefixes listed below in §30.1.2. E.g., *no-qu* 'my', which occurs with nouns in the neutral category. This type of possession is ALIENABLE.[3]

(2) partitive nouns, which represent mainly body parts, parts of a whole, and kinship relationships. E.g., *ulu-qu*[4] 'my head'. This type of possession is INALIENABLE.

30.1.2 Possessive classifiers (PC)

The following prefixes combine with the suffixes mentioned above to form independent words that precede the head of the possessive phrase.

nō-, kē-$_1$, kē-$_2$, mē-

These forms also combine with the proper possessive marker *i*, listed below.

---

[3] This is just one example of the intersecting oppositions in the area of Fijian possession.

[4] Hyphenated forms show the morphological structure and are not part of standard spelling.

30.1.3. Phrasal markers

Three types of markers occur in possessive phrases. They are represented by the following:

1 *ni*
2 *i*
3 *nei, kei, mei*

The difference between (1) and (2) hinges mainly on the common-proper opposition. The differences among the forms in (3) reflect those among the possessive classifier prefixes, discussed in §30.3.1.2 and §30.3.2 and subsections.

30.2 MORPHOLOGICAL AND SYNTACTIC PATTERNS

§30.1 and subsections list the three main types of possessives morphemes. Here we show how they combine with each other and with other elements. There are a limited number of morphological and syntactic ways to form possessives:

1. Adding a personal suffix to a classifier prefix.

    no-qu *vale* 'my house' (alienable). Table 30.1 shows the entire set.

TABLE 30.1: PERSONAL SUFFIXES

1st person exclusive		1st person inclusive	
1	*-qu*	1	——
2	*-irau*	2	*-daru*
3	*-itou*	3	*-datou*
p	*-imami*	p	*-da*
2nd person		3rd person	
1	*-mu*	1	*-na*
2	*-mudrau*	2	*-drau*
3	*-mudou*	3	*-dratou*
p	*-munī*	p	*-dra*

2. Adding *i* to a classifier prefix.

    na moli ***me-i*** *Pita* 'P's citrus' (alienable)

3. Adding a personal suffix to a partitive noun (inalienable).

    *Tama-**qu*** 'my father'. (inalienable)

4. Adding a phrase after the noun to represent a possessor or something related to the head of the construction.

    *vale **ni** bula* 'hospital; lit., house associated with health/life' (Alienable).
    *tama **i** Jone* 'J's father' (inalienable)

Note that the possessive in (1) occurs before the head of the construction, and in (2), (3), and (4), after the head.

Another way to view the constructions is to consider the semantic qualities of the entities involved. Possessive constructions refer to the POSSESSOR and the POSSESSED. Each can be represented, directly or indirectly, by a noun (including a word used as a noun), a pronoun, or a grammatical marker that contains reference to person, number, and the inclusive-exclusive opposition. These entities can be linked in various ways, as illustrated in the following constructions:

1. N – marker – N   *vale **ni** kana* 'restaurant (lit., house for eating)'
   *vale **ne-i** Manasa* 'M's house'
   *vula **i** balolo* 'ca. November (lit, month associated with *balolo*)'

These constructions differ according to the grammatical class of the possessor. In the first example above, *kana* 'eating' is a verb used as a common noun; in the second, *Manasa* is a proper noun. As for the third example, according to Churchward (1941:35), *vula* 'month' is the only common noun followed by *i*, but it might be more efficient to consider *vula* a proper noun in this construction.

2. Possessive classifier + suffix – N   *no-**qu** vale* 'my (neutral) house'
3. Partitive N + personal suffix   *mata-**qu*** 'my face'

A starting point for the following discussion is arbitrary. Still, we begin with a category that has a wider range than the others: ALIENABLE VS. INALIENABLE.

30.3 ALIENABLE VS. INALIENABLE POSSESSION

Consider what possessing an entity means in the following two examples:

no-mu vale   'your house'   *liga-mu*   'your hand'

Whereas 'house' is a commodity that one can dispose of at will, 'hand' is an integral part of one's body. We refer to the first relationship as ALIENABLE, and to the second as INALIENABLE. Entities in the alienable category are mainly physical objects; those in the inalienable category consist mainly of body parts, kin terms, and parts of a whole.[5] As Lyons (1968:301) stated it, something that is inalienably possessed is "necessarily associated with the 'possessor.'"[6]

The terms have often been misunderstood. Occasionally it is assumed that if one "inalienably possesses" an entity, one cannot cease to have it. In other words, this view assumes that the term is based on the entities themselves. On the contrary, it is not the entity that is permanent, but instead, the *relationship*.[7] For example, one can cut a lock from one's hair and burn it, but the relationship remains. Similarly, kin relationships live on, even after parties of the relationship no longer do so. Thus the terms alienable and inalienable apply to the relationship, not the individual entities.

---

[5] The first two may be considered specific categories of the third.

[6] Here, Lyons is using the term "possessor" to refer to someone/something in the real world, not a grammatical form.

[7] For what might be the first published account of this important refinement of the alienable-inalienable dichotomy, which applies not only to Fijian but also to most Polynesian languages, see Schütz and Nawadra 1972:99.

Closely tied to the concept of alienable-inalienable is another feature: CONTROL (see Lynch 1973:95). Again, the control is not over an entity, but over the relationship. In an inalienable relationship, the referent of the possessor has no control over initiating or terminating the relationship. In addition to straightforward relationships that link two entities (such as *tama-qu* 'my father'), the concept of control also applies to possessive constructions in which the possessed is a nominalized sentence and hence, ultimately connected with the relationship between the actor and the goal (see §30.5.1).

The categories of alienable and inalienable are reflected by certain formal differences. Exceptions will be pointed out in the following sections.

30.3.1 Inalienable possession

The inalienable possession construction can be classified by focusing on the class membership of the constituents.

The illustrative forms below contain examples from the markers of inalienable possession:

1. The person-number markers that are suffixed to partitive nouns, and *i*
2. The classifier *kē-$_2$*

HEAD	POSSESSOR
partitive noun	**person-number marker**
tama-	*-qu*
*tama***qu** 'my father'	
partitive noun	***i* + proper noun**
ulu	*i Jone*
*ulu **i** Jone* 'J's head'	
stative verb	***kē$_2$* + *i* + proper noun**
vinaka	*ke$_2$-i* + *Jone*
*vinaka **kei** Jone* 'J's goodness'	

The following construction shows the opposite order:

POSSESSOR	HEAD
***kē$_2$* + person-number marker**	**stative verb**
ke-na	*vinaka*
***kena** vinaka* 'its goodness'	

30.3.1.1 Person-number markers

The person-number markers that appear as suffixes are the set listed in table 30.1, with three exceptions. The nonsingular first person exclusive forms are (here, suffixed to *tama* 'father'):

*tama-**ikeirau***	'our (dual exclusive) father'
*tama-**ikeitou***	'our (trial exclusive) father'
*tama-**ikeimami***	'our (plural exclusive) father'

30.3.1.2 Kē-₂.

The marker *kē-*, marks a type of possession in which the possessor is not in control of the relationship. Examples are of two main types. First, possessed forms refer to innate qualities of the referent of the possessor:

 *na **ke-na** levu*   'its length'

As with *nō-* and *mē-*, *kē-* combines with *i* when the possessor is a proper noun. (See §30.3.1, Milner 1972:23, 23n, and Geraghty 1983:229–34 for a discussion of the restriction against specifying the possessor in the phrases immediately above with a proper noun.) The following examples show the resultant marker *kei*:

 *na levu **ke-i** Pita*   'P's size'

Next, *kē-* marks other kinds of general relationships in which the referent of the possessor is not in control:

 *na **ke-na** i-tukutuku* 'his news (i.e., news about him)'
 *na **ke-na** nanu-mi tiko na gone* 'the child's being remembered' (Milner 1972: 411)

In all the situations referred to above, the referent of the possessor is serving in a role other than that of actor, which is why we assume that he is not in control of the relationship. In the last example, the underlying situation is that someone remembers the child. The surface form—with *-Ci*—sometimes prompted the label "passive" for this kind of possession.

Analysts have sometimes been uncomfortable about the two kinds of *kē-* possession: edible, and inalienable. The former has often been related to the verb *kana* 'eat'. Geraghty has suggested (1983:249 that the second type may be related to another *kana*, with the little-known meaning of 'suffer'. Since this use of 'suffer' is somewhat archaic, I suggest 'undergo' as a more appropriate gloss. Thus, this type of *kē-* possession might be tied to situations in which the referent of the possessor is undergoing (or suffering) a process or action—a passive-like situation. The passive label emphasizes that the relationship between the referents of the possessor and the possessed is not an active one.

30.3.2 Alienable possession

Alienable possession can be divided into the following two formal categories, based on the morphological arrangements of the possessor and the possessed. What the two types have in common is three alienable possessive classifiers (*mē-*, *kē-₁*, and *nō-*), which combine with suffixes in two distinct ways.

1. In the first type, the possessive form is composed of two morphemes. The first indicates the type of possession; the second indicates the person, number, and exclusivity of the possessor. This form precedes the noun that serves as the head of the construction. Examples are:

 no-qu *vale* 'my house' **me-na** *tī* 'his tea'
 PC-1S house   PC-3S tea

In these examples, *nō-*[8] and *mē-* mark the possession type, and *-qu* and *-na* mark the person, number, and exclusivity[9] of the possessor.

2. In the second type, the possessive form—a combination of the possessive classifier and *i*—precedes an NP, a proper noun. Examples are:

vale	***ne-i***	*Erelia*	'E's house'	*tī*	***me-i***	*Paula* 'P's tea'
house	PC-POS	E		tea	PC-POS	P

A phonological change affects all the prefixes. Each is a long syllable that remains long when it is followed by an accented syllable. In the first example that follows, *mē* is followed by an accented syllable; thus the vowel remains long (a raised period separates measures; see CH 36):

mē-*daru*   mē·daru   (first person dual inclusive drinkable possessive)

However, *mē-* shortens when it is followed by an unaccented syllable:

me-*na*   mena   (third person singular drinkable possessive)
me-*qu*   mequ   (first person singular drinkable possessive)'

This vowel shortening, described in §40.2, is regular throughout SF. However, among the various Fijian languages, there is some variation in the length of the antepenultimate syllable of a word. Since a speaker's SF is often affected by his first language, one sometimes hears a short syllable in this position (Scott 1948: 745): *no-daru*. It is also likely that the long vowels shorten in faster, more casual speech. On the other hand, Milner (1972) wrote short vowels in all the forms.

30.3.2.1 Possessive classifier prefixes

SF distinguishes among three main types of alienable possession by using separate classifier prefixes. Formally, they are distinguished by the initial consonants *m-*, *k-*, and *n-*. The semantic distinctions among the three are discussed in the following sections.

30.3.2.1.1 *Mē-*

The marker *mē-* shows that the possessed entity is DRINKABLE. For example:

na ***me-na*** *tī*   'his/her tea'
na ***mē-daru*** *yaqona*   'our (first person dual inclusive) kava'

As other grammarians have noted, the category of drinkable is culturally defined, including some of what speakers of English would classify as soft foods as well as liquids. Thus, it is not clear whether or not the grammarian (in this instance, viewing the language from outside the culture) should provide a list of entities that take an unexpected (to us) possessive marker. For example, *tavako* 'tobacco' takes *kē-*; *ota* 'edible fern' and *moli* 'citrus' take *mē-*. (PG suggested that such matters should be handled in the dictionary definitions of *kana* 'eat' and *gunu* 'drink'.)

---

[8] See the explanation of vowel shortening (just below) for the three classifiers.
[9] Confined to first person.

The vowel shortening described above also applies to *mē-*. (Note the contrast in the vowel length of the initial syllables in *mena* and *mēdaru*, above.)

30.3.2.1.2 *Kē-*₁

The marker *kē-*₁ shows that the possessed entity is EDIBLE. For example:

na **ke-na** uvi	'her yam'
na **ke-na** raisi	'her rice'

As these examples show, the vowel shortening described above also applies to *kē-*.

A different kind of change affects the first person singular form of the possessive: SF uses *qau* rather than the expected **ke-qu*.

As with the drinkable category, some forms that occur with *kē-*₁ are culturally determined, even for post-contact borrowings: for example, *tavako* 'tobacco' is possessed with *kē-*, not *nō-*. This classification is echoed in the translation of 'smoking' as *kana tavako*, lit., 'tobacco-eating'.

30.3.2.1.3 *Nō-*

The marker *nō-* can be defined in negatively: it marks possession that refers to an entity that is intended to be neither eaten nor drunk. In Milner's terms, it is NEUTRAL.

na **no-na** waqa	'his canoe'	na **no-na** motokā	'his car'

As do the other prefixes, *nō-* shortens under the conditions described above. Another variation occurs as well. In the paradigm of possessive markers and person-number markers, there are three irregularities: forms with *ne-* rather than the expected *nō-*, shown in table 30.3. These are perhaps vestiges of a more widespread use of *ne-* (or *nē*?); earlier, *nequ*, *nemu*, and *nena* alternated with *noqu*, *nomu*, and *nona*; Churchward noted that the former were "seldom used" at the time of writing (1941:77), and Capell (1941) described *ne-* as "now practically obs[olete]." See Geraghty 1983:236 for a discussion of this phenomenon.

TABLE 30.2: *NŌ* + FIRST PERSON SUFFIXES

	First person	
	Morphological division	Accent measures
Dual	ne-irau	nei·rau
Trial	ne-itou	nei·tou
Plural	ne-imami	nei·mami.

30.4 PHRASAL POSSESSIVE MODIFIERS

Formally, a third type of possessive construction consists of a phrase (indicating the possessor) following the head (indicating the possessed).

As listed in §30.1.3, the following markers occur in possessive phrases:

1 *ni*   2 *i*   3 *nei, kei, mei*

For the most part, a *ni* phrase indicates an alienable relationship, and an *i* phrase, an inalienable relationship. Of these two types, an *i* phrase is closer in meaning to literal possession, especially in the forms *mei / kei / nei*.[10] In contrast, the meaning of a *ni* phrase is closer to 'associated with, characterizing'.

30.4.1 *Ni*

A *ni* phrase is itself an NP. It modifies a noun by indicating a relationship between the two nouns. Although a general gloss can be constructed—something on the order of 'N1 associated with N2'—there are a number of slightly different relationships.

It should be noted here that all *ni* phrases are grammatically indefinite, since they do not contain the definite marker *na*. Here, the semantic and grammatical match is close; in the examples, for instance, in *vale ni kana* 'restaurant', *kana* does not refer to a specific act of eating, nor in *vale ni lotu* 'house of worship' does *lotu* refer to a specific act of worship.

30.4.1.1 Semantic narrowing

With some nouns, the *ni* phrase indicates purpose or function, qualities that are not generally conveyed by stative attributes—those that specify material, or those that indicate style or manner. For example, this construction can mark a house for a specific purpose:

*vale **ni** kana*	'restaurant (house for eating)'
*vale **ni** lotu*	'church building (house for religion)'
*vale **ni** vei-vesu*	'prison (house for imprisonment)'
*vale **ni** bula*	'hospital (house for health)'
*vale **ni** mate*	'hospital (house for sickness)'

Other examples are:

*lotu **ni** kana*	'table grace (religion for eating)'
*i-coi **ni** lovo*	'noncarbohydrate food to accompany root crops baked in the oven'[11]

Note that all the forms above except the last are words for introduced concepts.

With some other nouns, the *ni* phrase also narrows the meaning, but with the sense of relating the head noun to a semantic field different from its usual one. The following examples show nouns that we assume to mean *primarily* body parts, but are now used in a different sense, perhaps closer to 'belonging to':

*ucu **ni** vanua*	'point (nose of land)'
*gusu **ni** wai*	'mouth (mouth of water)'

---

[10] The possessor is represented by a proper noun, often referring to a human—capable of literal possession.

[11] Fijian dichotomizes food in this way: *kākana dina*, which refers to taro, yam, or other root crops; and *i-coi*, the accompanying protein, such as fish, meat, or taro-leaf dishes. There are no accurate English glosses for these terms.

*yame **ni** i-sele*	'blade (tongue of knife)'
*bati **ni** wai*	'well edge (tooth of water)'[12]
*duruduru **ni** liga*	'elbow (knee of arm)'

On the other hand, one might suggest that the head nouns themselves, such as *ucu*, *gusu*, etc., have a broader meaning than just body parts, and that the attributive phrases merely specify or narrow that meaning.

Other examples, similar to those with body parts, are:

*yaloka **ni** mata*	'eyeball (egg of the eye)'
*tina **ni** viritālawalawa*	'spider (mother related to web)'
*tina **ni** vuaka*	'sow (mother related to pig)'

Most of the examples given so far show that the construction was a common way of forming new lexical items in pre-contact Fiji. With the coming of the Europeans, there was also a great influx of new ideas and items. In particular, those referred to in the Bible had to be translated into Fijian. For some, the English word was borrowed directly into the language, assuming the shape required by the phonological patterns of the language (see Schütz 1978b, 2004). But the Bible translators themselves preferred to modify existing words when possible. Many of these modifications take the form of *ni* phrases:

*qase **ni** vuli*	'teacher (elder for learning)'
*i-tūtū **ni** cina* (Rev 1:12)	'candlestick (stand for lamp)'
*i-keli **n**i waini* (Rev 14:19)	'winepress (hole for wine)'
*qiqi **ni** tamata* (Rev 18:13)	'chariot (rolling thing for persons)'

At the same time, terms for secular items were being coined, and many of these as well include *ni* phrases:

*i-vakarau **ni** cagi*	'barometer (measurer for wind)'
*yaqona **ni** vāvālagi*	'alcoholic beverage (foreign kava)'

One construction of this type uses a mid-nineteenth-century borrowing—*sitima* 'steamer'—and then qualifies it with a *ni* phrase for a later innovation:

*sitima **ni** vanua*   'train (land steamer)'

30.4.1.2 Layering of attributive *ni* phrases

The following example from the English-Fijian section of Capell's dictionary shows layers of *ni* phrases:

*sala (**ni** (sitima (**ni** vanua)))*   'railway (path of land steamer)'

Such layering is not confined to neologisms; it occurs freely with indigenous items:

na	loma	**ni**	mata	**ni**	wai	'inside the spring'
DEF	inside	POS	eye	POS	water	

---

[12] The extended meaning of *bati* is 'edge'.

*na meke **ni** dola **ni** basā **ni** koro-**ni**-vuli*
DEF *meke* POS open POS bazaar POS village-POS-learn
'*meke* for the opening of the school bazaar' (*NV2*:7)

The immediate constituent structure of the last example is as follows:

meke (***ni*** (*dola* (***ni*** (*basā* (***ni*** (*koro* (***ni*** *vuli*)))))))

The meaning of this construction seems close to that of the *vaka*-construction, but there are examples of contrast:

vosa vaka-Viti	'Fijian language'
*vosa **ni** Viti*	'languages of Fiji'

The former refers specifically to SF; the latter rather loosely to languages that are associated with or spoken in Fiji, including regional variations, English, Hindi, Cantonese, and a number of other languages spoken by the heterogeneous population.

In the following pair, the former refers to a specific style of canoe (double hulled, outrigger, etc.); the latter to any boat affiliated with Fiji, including both *waqa vaka-Viti* and foreign styles:

waqa vaka-Viti	'Fijian-style canoe'
*waqa **ni** Viti*	'boat from or connected with Fiji'

In the next pair, the former refers to a particular style of sarong: not tailored, belted, or with pockets; the latter could be either variety.[13]

i-sulu vaka-Toga	'Tongan-style sarong'
*i-sulu **ni** Toga*	'sarong from Tonga'

Other examples are:

*vuaka **ni** Viti*	'Fijian hog'
*gone **ni** Viti*	'Fijian (person)'
*tawala **ni** Toga*	'Tongan mat'
*meke **ni** Sāmoa*	'Samoan-style dance'
*agilosi **ni** Lomālagi*	'heavenly angels'

Ni constructions also contrast with the first attributive construction discussed in CH 28: N + Stative. Our view is that the *ni* phrase as an attribute keeps a proper distance, so to speak, between a head and an attribute referring to a quality that is not semantically compatible. It is often used with *kā* 'thing' when the meaning associated with the N +Stative construction is confined to nouns referring to humans. Thus:

tamata mārau	'happy person'

but:

*kā **ni** mārau*	'thing connected with happiness'

Other examples are:

---

[13] Thanks to AS for verifying these suppositions.

kā **ni** kurabui	'surprising thing'
kā **ni** māduā	'shameful thing'
kā **ni** rarawa	'sad thing'
kā **ni** rere	'fearful thing'

Because the word following *ni* in these last constructions is a stative verb, one might analyze the phrase as subordinate, with *ni* the subordinate marker, not the possessive one. If that were so, however, the constructions would be grammatically idiomatic, for the expressions would not parse. Besides, it would be more appropriate to use the relative construction. It seems more accurate to analyze this *ni* as the possessive, and the form following the marker as a stative verb serving as a noun.

30.4.1.3 Some semantic problems

It should be emphasized that the *ni* construction merely shows a relationship between two entities. The types of relationship vary. For example, note how the literal translation of the construction as 'X of Y' often assumes that anything translated by 'of' belongs to semantic possession. The following examples show a reanalysis of a number of constructions that have been thought to indicate some notion of semantic ownership:

drau **ni** ulu	'hair (excluding facial and body hair)' (*ulu* 'head')
drau **ni** kau	'leaf' (*kau* 'tree, plant')
drau **ni** veva	'sheet of paper' (*veva* 'paper')

First, it is difficult to gloss *drau*. We analyze *drau ni ulu* not as *drau* belonging to the head, but as a special kind of *drau*, this specificity indicated by the attribute *ni ulu*. The construction thus sets up an opposition among this and all the other kinds of *drau*, which are in turn indicated by other *ni* phrases.

Drau can also occur with a suffixed attribute:

drau-**na**	'its leaf (or 'hair', etc.)'

In this construction, the information that *ni ulu* or *ni kau* provides has to be gleaned from the context. For example, the following short discourse illustrates that there is no difficulty in establishing what kind of *drau* is being referred to:

E yaga vaka-levu na niu.	'The coconut is very useful.'
Na drau-**na**, e vaka-yaga-taki me tara vale.	'As for its leaves, they're used for house building.'

In a sense, *drau* is one of a number of forms that do not often occur alone, but usually with a modifier or suffix that gives each one a specific meaning. Although not all such concepts are confined to the *ni* construction, many are. Often they refer to parts of a whole (including body parts), locations, and kin terms. The following are examples in these several categories:

sē	'blossom'
sē **ni** bua	'plumeria flower'
sē **ni** kau	'flower' (*kau* 'plant, wood')
sē **ni** toa	'hibiscus flower'

vū	'source'
*vū **ni** kau*	'tree'
*vū **ni** vola*	'scribe' (*vola* 'write')
*vū **ni** wai*	'doctor' (*wai* 'medicine')
tina	'mother'
*tina **ni** gone*	'mother of the child'
tina-qu	'my mother'

As shown earlier, kin terms share with locatives and body parts the quality of postposed possessive marking:

Locative:	*loma-**na***	'its interior'
Body part:	*ucu-**na***	'his nose/its point (of land)'
Kin:	*tina-**na***	'her mother'

When these roots are linked to common nouns (which do not refer to specific people or places), *ni* is used:

*tina **ni** bulumakau*	'cow (mother of cattle)'
*luve **ni** wai*	'water spirit (water child)'
*luve **ni** sala*	'bastard (road child)'

30.4.1.4 Nominalization with *ni* phrases

One way to nominalize a verb phrase with a specified subject is to use the verb (with no derivational changes) as a head noun and change the specified subject to a *ni* phrase.[14] Thus:

E balavu na dali.	'The rope is long.'
3S long DEF rope	
*na balavu **ni** dali*	'the length of the rope'
*E rarawa na yalo-**na**.*	'Her spirit is sad.'
3S sad DEF spirit-3S	
*na rarawa **ni** yalo-**na***	'the sadness of her spirit'

The nominalized phrases have the following structure:

na > (*balavu* < (***ni*** *dali*))

One of the most common examples of this type is *mata*, which in addition to its meaning 'eye, face' also means 'source, front, center'. Many *ni* constructions with *mata* are idiomatic:[15]

*mata **ni** siga*	'sun (eye of the day)'
*mata **ni** vanua*	'herald (eye of the land)'
*mata **ni** wai*	'spring (source of water)'

---

[14] Note the variations possible if the verb is a stative:

E balavu na dali.	'The rope is long.'
*na balavu **ni** dali.*	'the length of the rope'
na dali balavu	'the long rope'
*na **kena** balavu*	'its length'

[15] *VV* has fifty-four *mata-ni-___* entries.

The spacial meaning of *mata* links it to a number of other nouns (PARTITIVE NOUNS) that refer to general locations. These, too, are made more specific by *ni* phrases:

dela	'top, surface'
*dela **ni** vale*	'top of the house'
loma	'inside'
*loma **ni** koro*	'in the village (idiomatic?)'
mua	'front, tip'
*mua **ni** cakau*	'end of the reef'
tebe	'edge'
*tebe **ni** gusu*	'lips (edge of mouth)'
ruku	'underneath'
*ruku **ni** kau*	'under a tree'

30.4.1.5 Attribution outside the *ni* phrase

In a series of *ni* phrases, the domain of a final modifier is uncertain. For example,

*vale **ni** kana vou*
house POS eat new

refers to a new restaurant, not to *nouvelle cuisine*. The structure is:

((*vale* < ***ni** kana*) < *vou*)

However, one can find *ni* phrases with the modifier appearing internally:

*na sere vou **ni** Mata-ni-tū*   'the new national anthem' (Geraghty 1976)
DEF sing new POS government

In this example, putting *vou* after *Mata-ni-tū* would change the meaning, resulting in 'song of the new government'. The same situation holds for:

*waqa lailai **ni** vāvālagi*   'small introduced canoe' (*VV:boto*)
canoe small POS European

30.4.1.6 *Ni* as a word-builder

Investigating two types of *VV* forms built on *vale* 'house' yields interesting data on word-building. In all, there are 91 entries. Seventeen of these are compounds: that is, *vale* + modifier. Some examples are:

valebola   'thatched house'   *valevatu*   'stone house'

But the majority of the examples are *vale* + *ni* phrase.

Although the construction N + *ni* phrase is by no means limited to naming post-contact items or concepts, there are enough examples to suggest that this process is productive and a common word-building mechanism. The following examples from *VV* show that it is in competition (if that is the appropriate term) with straightforward borrowing:

*vale **ni** iyāyā māroroi* ~ *miusiem* 'museum'
*vale **ni** ivola māroroi* ~ *akaiv* 'archive'
*Vale**ni**bula levu* ~ *sīdabliuem* (CWM—Colonial Memorial Hospital)

30.4.2 *I*

This marker is different from the possessive markers previously described in that:

1. It marks the possessor, rather than the possessed; and
2. It marks only proper nouns.

The following examples show that *i* links a partitive noun to a proper noun in an inalienable relationship:

na	*tama*	***i***	*Mele*	'M's father'
DEF	father	POS	M	

*na tina **i** Tē*   'T's mother'
*na ulu **i** Bera*   'B's head'
*na wati **i** Manasa*   'M's spouse'

In the last example above, the two *i* vowels combine to form *ī*, and the accent shifts from *wa* to *tī*.[16] As for the example *tina* + *i* above, *a* + *i* is a potential diphthong, and it is likely that in faster (i.e., normal) speech, it is accented as such. Such a shift in accent would verify Churchward's suggestion (1941:34–35) that *i* corresponds "to some extent" to the suffixed forms used for inalienables.

I can also occur with integral nouns, but it still marks a proper noun. In the following example, the relationship is alienable:

*Na vale **i** cei?*   'Whose house?' (*VV*, **i** 6)

Further examples of *i* are from Churchward 1941:36:

*na ulu **i** Wiliame*   'William's head'
*na luve **i** Cakobau*   'Thakombau's son [child]'
*e na vuku **i** Viti*   'for the sake of Fiji'

I also occurs in some constructions somewhat different from those described above, i.e., not obviously possessive. For example:

*domo-**i**-levu*   'loud'
*raba-**i**-levu*   'wide'

What these forms have in common is that each of the nouns that serves as head of the construction is partitive—that is, can take a possessive suffix.

30.4.2.1 Possessive classifiers + *i*

I can be suffixed to a possessive classifier to allow a proper noun to serve as possessor. For example, *mē-* combines with *i* to form a marker *me-i*:

*na tī **me-i** Paula*   'P's tea'

---

[16] Pointed out by Apolonia Tamata and confirmed by Tevita Dugucanavanua.

Kē- combines with *i* to form *ke-i*:

na dalo **ke-i** Tōmasi	'T's taro'
na uvi **ke-i** Mārika	'M's yam'

Similar to *mē-*, *nō-* combines with *i*. But the resultant form is *ne-i*:

na vale **ne-i** Pita	'P's house'
na motokā **ne-i** Nia	'Nia's car'

30.5 THE SEMANTICS OF POSSESSION

As noted in the introduction, in this treatment, the term "possession" is used both semantically and grammatically; in the discussion the context should make it clear which domain the examples refer to. Because of the nature of possession, two entities are always involved, either directly or indirectly. Grammatically, "possessor" refers to that element in the sentence that is the possessive attribute; "possessed" refers to the head of the construction. To clarify these relationships, table 30:3 shows possessive phrases that are classified according to the function of their constituents—from both an attributive and possessive point of view.

30.5.1 Different relationships between the referents of the possessor and the possessed

TABLE 30.3: RELATIONSHIPS BETWEEN POSSESSOR AND POSSESSED

ATTRIBUTE POSSESSOR	HEAD POSSESSED	ATTRIBUTE POSSESSOR	
no-na	vale		her house
ke-na	uvi		his yam
ke-na	vinaka		its goodness
me-na	moli		his citrus
	ulu	i Jone	J's head
	dalo	ke-i Bera	B's taro
	vale	ni kana	restaurant (lit., house for eating)
	tama-	-na	her father
	ulu-	-na	his head

As the examples in table 30.3 show, there are a number of different relationships that may hold between the referents of the possessor and the possessed. It should be pointed out first that the meaning of this construction is broader than just legal ownership (Lyons 1968:296–97).

However, legal ownership is not excluded. In the examples in table 30.3, the first phrase could imply such a relationship:

na **no-na** vale	'his house'	na **me-na** moli	'his citrus'
na dalo **ke-i** Bera	'B's taro'		

30 Possession

Still, there are other kinds of relationships between the members of the pairs of entities. The list explaining table 30.3 is not complete, but it contains some of the major types. In this classification, A represents the possessed, and B the possessor. Grammatically, the representation of A is the head of the construction.

1. A is owned by or associated with B, which is animate.

*na **no-na** vale*   'his house'   *na **no-na** tūraga*   'his chief'

The second example shows possession that is different from legal ownership. "Associated with" is an uncomfortably general term, but perhaps the term *must* be general. For example, *na no-na tūraga* indicates a relationship pertinent to Fijian social structure; *na no-na i-tau* 'his friend' is not restricted in the same way.

2. A is the focus of a kin relationship with B. Both A and B are animate.

*na tama-**na***   'her father'   *na luve-**na***   'her offspring'

3. A is a part of the whole, which is B. B is animate. Thus, A represents body parts and certain personal qualifications, such as "spirit."

*na ulu-**na***   'his head'   *na yalo-**mu***   'your (1) spirit'

4. A is a part of the whole, which is B. B is inanimate.

*na dela-**na***   'its top'   *na boto-**na***   'its bottom

5. A is associated with B, which is inanimate.

*na **ke-na** i tukutuku*   'the news of it'
*na **ke-na** i-tekivū*   'its beginning'

The last examples above verge on a second major class of relationships[17] that result in possessive attribution: that between an action/state and one of the entities involved in it. Grammatically, the head of the construction is a verb used as a noun; the possessive modifier refers to the actor or the goal. For example, ultimately the phrases in (5) can be semantically related to the following VPs, respectively:

E tuku-n-a.   'He told it.'   *E tekivū-tak-a.*   'He began it.'

However, *i-tukutuku* and *i-tekivū* are derivatives; the possessive attributive construction often uses as its head a verb that is not derived, but simply used as a noun.

30.6 DEFINITENESS

When a broad concept (such as "house" or "taro") is narrowed with a possessive to indicate a specific one (such as "*his* house" or "*her* taro"), it is automatically made definite (see §20.2.2).

---

[17] This dichotomy is based on Lyons 1968:297.

Possibly for this reason, *na* (definite) is sometimes omitted without any apparent change of meaning (brackets show the position of the deleted *na*):[18]

*Tuku-n-a tale [ ] **no-mu** i-talanoa ni kāveti.*
tell-TR-3S ITR   PC-2S story   POS cabbage
'Tell again your story about the cabbage.' (FMC61:1)

*E dau vā-kani ira [ ] **no-na** manumanu.*   'He always feeds his animals.'
3S HAB CAU-eat 3P   PC-3S   animal   (*FR3*:50)

30.7 VARIABLES OF THE ALIENABLE-INALIENABLE CONTRAST

Table 30.4, adapted from Geraghty 1983:242–49, summarizes the variables of the alienable-inalienable contrast.

TABLE 30:4: ALIENABLE-INALIENABLE CONTRAST

Underlying sentence. The portion representing the possessor is in boldface	Grammatical role of possessor	Semantic role of possessor	Possessed form
E levu. 'He is large.'	subject	animate	**no-na** levu 'his size'
E levu. 'It is large.	subject	inanimate	**ke-na** levu 'its size'
E talanoa-tak-a. 'He told it.'	subject	animate	**no-na** i-talanoa 'his story'
*E talanoa-taka baleti **koya**.* 'He told it about him.'	oblique	animate	**ke-na** i-talanoa 'his story'

Note that in the table, the contrast between *nō-* and *kē-* is matched to that between animate and inanimate. However, one can also find examples of such contrast in which the referents of both subjects are animate. Geraghty noted that the form *ke-na levu*, with an animate possessor, is also possible. He demonstrated a grammatical distinction between the two forms by showing that with *nō-*possessives, the head of the construction could include aspect and other VP markers. Thus, he concluded that one form is derived from the VP *e levu*, whereas in the other, *levu* is a separate lexical item, a noun meaning 'size'. Similar examples are:

ke-na *vinaka*   'his goodness (as distinct from *vinaka*, an S1 verb meaning 'good')'
ke-na *balavu*   'his height (as distinct from *balavu*, an S1 verb meaning 'long')'

---

[18] As Geraghty (1983:252) pointed out, *na* is not omitted when the possessive form itself serves as the head of a phrase, as in *na nona* 'his'. Arms added (10/84) that it is only before the *n-* possessives that *na* is omitted.

The following minimal pair is from Churchward 1941:33:

*na **kena** mate*   'his sickness'   *na **nona** mate*   'his death'

However, a strictly grammatical explanation for such an opposition is rather different from the general semantic explanation for the other examples. Because of this problem, I suggest that the choice between *nō-* and *kē-* is not based on one set of criteria alone, but on a set of sometimes conflicting oppositions:

1 actor   vs. goal
2 animate   vs. inanimate
3 control   vs. controlled
4 alienable vs. inalienable

This situation sets up a conflict with our classification of verbs according to the active/stative opposition, introducing another level that has to be observed. (In the following examples, I shall be basing the discussion on Geraghty 1983: 246–48.) This level concerns CONTROL, and sometimes coincides with, sometimes conflicts with, the active/stative dichotomy. For example, strictly speaking, in the following sentence, the subject *e* represents the actor—'the bus':

E cici tiko na basi.   'The bus is running.'

But at some semantic level, even if the bus is running, it is not in control of the situation. Thus, the possessive construction reflecting this situation is:

***ke-na** cici*   'its running'

However, in the following sentence, the subject *e* represents 'the child', which *is* in control of the situation:

E cici tiko na gone.   'The child is running.'

Thus, the possessive construction of this situation is

***no-na** cici*

This is a slight (but perhaps important) restatement of Geraghty's explanation. His operates on the grammatical situation alone, except for some confusing terms such as "underlying subject" and "inanimate subject."

Now, let us see if this approach will take care of his other example—using *nō-* vs. *kē-* for subjects that represent the goal. A straightforward example is:

***no-mu** i-vacu*   'your punch (you give)'
***ke-mu** i-vacu*   'your punch (you receive)'

Here, obviously, the actor-vs.-goal explanation works well. But with descriptive terms, such as *levu* 'large' or *vinaka* 'good', we should then expect only *kē-* forms. Such is not the case. Geraghty gave the following example:

***nomu** sā levu tiko mai*   'your getting bigger'

This example illustrates the different levels between the actor/goal opposition. Since the aspect marker *sā* changes the state into a process, even though the underlying subject represents the goal, the goal seems to be in control of the situation.

How can we unite the grammatical and semantic statements? I suggest that we expand on the animate-versus-inanimate dichotomy to say that this opposition nearly overlaps with + or – control, but the latter opposition is the more powerful one.

30.8 SEMANTIC AND FORMAL MISMATCHES

In a discussion of Fijian possession, it is especially important to keep semantic and grammatical terms separate. The literature has noted, for example, that a number of irregularities—that is, mismatches between semantics and form—occur. Churchward, for example, listed the following types of "exceptions" for the semantic category of body parts (1941:33–34):

1. Anatomical terms that begin with an *i-* prefix, such as *i-tilotilo* 'gullet' and *i-tagitagi* 'larynx', take *no-na*, etc. Geraghty (1983:259) proposed that "many non-instrumental *i-* prefixed nouns are semantically inalienable, and that *i-* prefixation and suffixed (direct) possession are in complementary distribution."

2. Other anatomical terms, such as *drā* 'blood', *mona* 'brains', and *ivi* 'kidneys', take the *nō-* forms.

As an example of mismatches in other areas, Geraghty (1983:249) suggested that in the area of passive possession, some items "may well be lexically determined." He noted the following apparent irregularities:

no-mu *i-tau* 'your friend', but **ke-mu** *meca* 'your enemy'[19]
wati-qu 'my spouse', but **no-qu** *kābani* 'my companion' and **qau** *i-sau* 'my partner'

30.9 POSSESSIVES USED AS NOUNS

There are several constructions that use a possessive as the head of a phrase. Although on the surface, the possessive may assume different roles, its basic function is as a noun. Examples are:

*Sā **no-na**.*   'It's hers.'

In this simple sentence, although the basic role of *no-na* is as a possessive, it changes its function to serve as the head of a NP. Some grammatical theories would suggest that the noun had been deleted; I prefer to analyze the construction differently. *No-na* is serving as a noun; reference to the actual entity that it is related to would have to be determined through the context, which is missing in this example. Passing from that function, it finally serves as the head of a VP in this identifying construction (see §2.1.4 *et seq.*).

In the following sentence, *me-na* goes through similar functional changes:

---

[19] Does control over the relationship explain the difference?

*Ka sā   loma-na sara me sā   laki kau-t-a   mai me **me-na**.*
CNJ ASP wish-3S   INT   SUB ASP DIR bring-TR-3S   DIR SUB PC-3S
'And he wanted very much to go get one for his own (drinkable).' (*FR5*:23)

The difference here is that in its ultimate (surface) function, *me-na* is serving as the head of a subordinate VP.

The following example shows fewer functional changes:

*Au vinaka-t-a me dua gā   na **no-qu**.*
1S want-TR-3S SUB one LIM DEF PC-1S
'I want one of my own (I want it—that there be *one*—mine).'

In this example, the surface function of *no-qu* is as the head of an NP.

The following construction is different, but it shares the feature of the previous ones in that a possessive form is serving a function that a noun usually serves:

*Oyā   na gauna ni   dui caka-**no-na**   e   na vosa.*
DEM:3 DEF time   POS IND done-PC-3S   ABL DEF talk
'That was a time of doing one's own thing with respect to (writing) the language.' (*SR* 20/4/82)

Here, *no-na* takes the place of the noun (which actually functions as a modifier) in the *gunu-yaqona* construction (see §16.4.1). That is, it fits with the following paradigm:

gunu-yaqona 'kava-drinking' *kana-ika* 'fish-eating' *laga-sere* 'song-singing'

30.9.1 Discussion

The section above is nearly unchanged from that in *TFL*, whose table of contents includes "The use of possessives as nouns." An article on the topic (Palmer and Brown 2007:208) curiously gave the impression that this construction had not been noted in Fijian grammars. Predating the treatment in *TFL*, Churchward (1941:38), under the heading "The Use of Possessive Prepositions Without a Preceding Noun," gave the following examples:

Kauta mai a nei Joni.	'Bring J's'
Kauta mai a nona/kena/mena.	'Bring his.'
Sā nei Joni.	'It is J's.'
Sā nona.	'It is his.'

30.10 REDUPLICATION OF POSSESSIVE FORMS

Some possessive forms can be reduplicated. For example:

*Sā **nomu-nomu** tū.*   'It's always yours.'

For further examples and discussion, see §14.15.

30.11 SPECIFICATION AND VARIATION IN POSSESSIVE CONSTRUCTIONS

For some possessive constructions, variations in form show no apparent differences in meaning. The following examples, only a small sample, were supplied by AT, 10 Dec. 2012. (Perhaps by coincidence, three of the phrases are examples of specification.)

Nona vale na tūraga yā	'That chief's house'
Na vale nei koya na tūraga yā[20]	'That chief's house'

In the first phrase, the NP *na tūraga yā* specifies *-na*. In the second, it specifies the proper pronoun *koya*.

Na vale nei Alipate	'A's house'
Nona vale o Alipate[21]	'A's house'

In the first example, *nei Alipate* is simply a possessive phrase (see §30.4.2). In the second, *o Alipate* specifies *-na*. It is possible that a fuller context would reveal subtle differences in meaning.

The following examples are from Churchward 1941:36:

na i tukutuku ni vanua oqō	'the story of this country'
na ke<u>na</u> i tukutuku <u>na</u> <u>vanua</u> <u>oqō</u>	″

In explaining the difference in meaning between the two, Churchward wrote that the second phrase would be "more specific." It is not certain what he meant, but his choice of words is interesting, since it matches the term used in this work to explain the function of the NP *na vanua oqō*.

30.12 DISCUSSION: POSSESSION AS GENDER?

The origin of the idea that Fijian has grammatical gender seems to be Milner's treatment (1956:64–65).[22] He explained at some length that the distinction among words that behaved differently with respect to the choice of possessive marker was one of GENDER. (Cammack (1962:56–63) adopted this approach; Schütz (1972:36) used the term as well.)

Milner divided nouns into four classes: **neutral, edible, drinkable,** and **familiar**. Two of these terms need some explanation. "Edible," marked by *kē-*, includes what I have here called *kē-$_1$* and *kē-$_2$*. "Familiar" applies to those kin terms and anatomical terms that take suffixed possessives.

Milner's short discussion (p. 66) of "Bases belonging to more than one class of gender" provides the best argument *against* relating this grammatical category to gender in—for instance—German. One of the essential characteristics of a gender system is that there is little or no movement among classes (Hockett 1958:231). Fijian violates this restriction in a degree greater than one would suspect from reading Milner's discussion. In Fijian, words do not *belong* to a gender category. Instead, the "needs of the situation" (Milner 1972:66) dictate

---

[20] Grammatically, this is an example of specification of the pronoun (proper noun) *koya*.

[21] Churchward (1941:37) noted that this construction was "contrary to native usage … Thus, it is incorrect to say *na nona vale ko Joni* for 'John's house' …" It acceptance in 2012 shows a change in what native speakers consider grammatical.

[22] In this work, most references to Milner's grammar are to the 1972 edition. Here, to show the chronology of the idea, I give the page numbers in the original (1956) edition.

the choice of the possessive marker. For example, any food or drink can be considered a commodity for trade, rather than for immediate consumption (by eating or drinking) within the context of a particular discourse. Thus, the choice of possessive marker is conditioned by context, not by word class. Unless the term "gender" is used in a very special way, applying it to this situation obscures, rather than clarifies our view of the language.

31 COORDINATION, SENTENCE MODI-FIERS, AND SUMMARY OF OPERATIONS

In this chapter, we will deal mainly with the coordination of VPs, since coordinate NPs are treated in §21.2. The marker *sē*, however, described below, is used for both NPs and NPs.

31.1 COORDINATION[1]

A coordinate relationship between VPs implies that the actions/states referred to have no cause-effect or other subordinate relationship. The actions/states may be concurrent, or, if they are in sequence, the sequential arrangement is not emphasized (see the treatments of *qai* and *mani*).

31.1.1 *Ka (a)*[2]

Ka links VPs, as in the following examples:

E vaka-yaga-taki me kākana, ***ka*** *siga-ni me voli-taki.*
3S CAU-use-TR SUB food CNJ dry-TR SUB buy-TR
'It's used for food and dried to be sold.' (*SF*:90)

Curu ki tuba ***ka*** *kākua tale ni lesu mai.*
go-through DIR outside CNJ don't ITR SUB return DIR
'Go outside and don't come back again.' (*SF*:96)

Era kana gā, ***ka*** *ra moce sara.*   'They just ate and went to sleep
3P eat LIM CNJ 3P sleep INT   immediately.' (*VV*)

Note in the example just above that *ka* has the same effect on subjects as the subordinate markers. For those subjects beginning in *e-* (e.g., *era*), *ka* replaces that sound. With the first person singular subject, the *u* allomorph is used, once thought to be a shortened form of *au* and separated from *ka* by an apostrophe:

ka'u *kilā* 'and I know' (Churchward 1941:30)

---

[1] This treatment of the coordinating markers is based almost entirely on the work of my grammatical predecessors.

[2] Churchward (1941:23) described the alternation: "At the beginning of a clause or sentence, *ka* is sometimes contracted to *a*." PG (2/83) described *a* as much more common in informal, spoken Fijian, and considered *ka* as "almost pedantic."

Geraghty 1976a showed that this is a false etymology. In current spelling practice, the apostrophe is not used.

Milner (1972:18) noted that in sentences such as the third example above, the repetition of the subject is optional. For example, a variation of that sentence is:

*Era kana gā **ka** moce sara.*

The following example shows *ka* linking modifiers (i.e., S1 + S1, etc.):

e	*dua*	*na*	*gone*	*vuku*	***ka***	*maqosa*	'a wise and clever child' (VV)
3S	one	DEF	child	wise	CNJ	clever	

Churchward (1941:22) gave this example to show *ka* linking adverbs:

Era	*sā*	*vosa*	*vaka-dedē*	***ka***	*vaka-domo-i-levu.*	'They spoke long and
3P	ASP	speak	MAN-long	CNJ	MAN-loud	loudly.'

Ka is also used in numbers larger than ten to link units with tens:

*tini **ka** dua*	'eleven'	*tolu-saga-vulu **ka** ono*	'thirty-six'
ten CNJ one		thirty CNJ six	

Morphemes for higher numbers are: *sagavulu* 'tens', *drau* '100', *udolu* 'thousand'.

e dua na udolu, e ciwa na drau, ciwasagavulu ka ciwa '1999'

VV notes that *mani* and *ka mani* are used for the same purpose:

*tini **mani** dua*   'eleven'   *tini **ka mani** dua*   'eleven'

Churchward (1941:23) remarked on the use of *ka ni* for *ni*: "Occasionally *ka ni* appears to be used in place of the simple *ni*, in this sense of 'for' or 'because'."

As Milner noted (1972:76), *ka* is used with the markers *ni* and *dē*. His examples (in my notation) are as follows:

E	*ā*	*mani*	*sega*	*ni*	*via*	*vukei*	*koya,*	***ka***	***ni***	*kilā*	*na*	*kena*	*i-naki.*
3S	PT	SEQ	not	SUB	DES	help	3S	CNJ	SUB	know-3S	DEF	POS-3S	intention

'He didn't want to help him because he knew the intention (behind it).'

Sā	*dua*	*tani*	*na*	*no-qu*	*via*	*kana,*	***ka***	***ni***	*sā*	*siga*	*dua*	*taucoko*
ASP	one	different	DEF	POS-1S	DES	eat	CNJ	SUB	ASP	day	one	INC

au	*sega*	*ni*	*kana.*	'I was very hungry because I had not eaten
1S	not	SUB	eat	for a whole day.'

Au	*sā*	*sega*	*ni*	*via*	*tuku-n-a,*	***ka***	***dē***	*rogo-c-a*	*na*	*luve-qu*	*lailai.*
1S	ASP	not	SUB	DES	tell-TR-3S	CNJ	SUB	hear-TR-3S	DEF	child-1S	small

'I don't want to say it, in case my small child should hear it.'

VV describes *ka ni* as the same as *ni*. See §31.1.1 for another example of *ka ni*.

31.1.2 *Kei*

See §21.2 for *kei* as a linker of NPs.

31.1.3 *Sē*

In addition to its use as a subordinate marker (§33.4), *sē* is used as a conjunction. For example:

O sā na lako, **sē** *sega?* 2S ASP FT go CNJ not	'Will you go, or not?'

Sē can link NPs as well:

ka ke-na i-coi na rourou **sē** *ika* CNJ POS-3S *i-coi* DEF taro-leaves CNJ fish	'and its *i-coi* is taro-leaves or fish.'

Note that *na* can be omitted in the second NP.

31.1.4 *Ia*

This conjunction has two functions. The first is to mark an opposing situation:

E ka-ya o koya ni dina, **ia** *au sega ni vaka-bau-t-a.*
3S say-3S PRP 3S SUB true CNJ 1S not SUB believe-TR-3S
'He says that it's true, but I don't believe it.' (*VV*)

The second is to introduce a topic:

Ia, *me da masu mada.* CNJ SUB 1PI pray INI	'Now, let us pray.' (VV)

31.2 SENTENCE MODIFIERS OF AFFIRMATION (AFF)[3]

Certain markers, whether they are sentence-final or sentence-internal, seem to modify whole sentences rather than individual words. They are also treated as verb phrase markers occurring after the head, referring to affirmation/negation (§18.15).

31.2.1 *Lī* 'isn't that so?'

For the following examples, Churchward (1941:54) suggested that "a negative or contrary answer would be the right one."

Sā dodonu **lī** *me da lako?* ASP right AFF SUB 1PI go	'Is it right that we should go?' (Churchward 1941:54)
Sā sega **lī** *ni dodonu?* ASP not AFF SUB right	'Is it not right?' (Churchward 1941:55)

E dina **lī** *ni ko ā naki-t-a   mo vaka-mate-i tamamu?*
3S true AFF SUB 2S PT intend-TR-3S SUB-2S CAU-die-TR father-2S
'Is it really true that you did mean to kill your father?'

A cava **lī** *ko ā sega ki-na ni tuku-n-a vei au?*
DEF what AFF 2S PT not ABL-2S SUB tell-TR-3S ABL 1S
'Why really, did you not tell me?'

E lasu **lī**? 3S lie AFF	'Is it really false?'
E sā sava oti **lī**? 3S ASP clean ASP AFF	'Has it really been washed?'

---

[3] Although these markers are also treated in §18l.15, their functions seem more oriented toward discourse.

31.2.2 Nē 'is it not?'

Churchward noted (1941:55) "that the implication of *ne* [*nē*] is the opposite of that of *li* [*lī*]."

*Qai bau savata   vakatotolo toka na noqu   isulu   **ne** [**nē**]?*
SEQ TEN wash-TR-3S MAN-fast CNT DEF POS-1S clothes AFF
'Do wash my clothes quickly, won't you? (Cammack 1962:66)

*O   na   lako **nē**?* 'You'll go, won't you? (Capell 1941:153)
2S FUT go   AFF

Cammack (1962:66) referred to *nē* as "quotative" as well, noting that it occurred in the set phrase *vakā oqō nē* 'to speak thus':

*E   ā   vakā   oqō   **nē**   na   kā   e   kaya   ko   Rusiate, "…"*
3S PT say-it DEM:1 AFF DEF thing 3S say PRP R
'Rusiate said something to this effect, " …"'

31.2.3 Ē Sentence-final affirmation

Cammack (1962:66) noted that "*E [ē]* is always final in a sentence. Its function is to request affirmation of the preceding assertion or command."

*O   na   lako tale   gā   i   Nausori, **ē**?*
2S FUT go ITR INT DIR N   AFF
'You're also going to Nausori, aren't you? (Cammack 1962:67)

31.3 SUMMARY OF OPERATIONS

In the preceding chapters, I have presented (implicitly) a broad syntactic outline for Fijian. Syntax is defined as the relationship among phrases. More specifically:

1. There are two main building blocks: VP and NP.
2. Two types of sentences, VP and (NP + NP), are basic sentences.
3. Every addition of a phrase (that is, an NP or another VP added to the basic phrase) fulfills the semantic function of narrowing (i.e., specifying) the reference.
4. Every different complex (and compound) sentence structure can be viewed as a different combination of VPs and NPs. "Different" here means:

    a. Different types of phrases and different combinations
    b. Different relationships between/among the phrases

Examples:
1. VP + VP
   Subordination
   Coordination

2. NP + VP stative
   Noun attribution
3. NP + VP active
   Relativization
4. NP + unmarked NP
   Subject, object, and possessive specification
5. VP + marked NP
   Ablative phrases: i.e., attribution

A more general statement about Fijian grammar is that certain grammatical and phonological units in Fijian have different functions than corresponding units in some other languages. For example, it is often phrases, not words, that are identified as to function.

SECTION V: PHONOLOGY

The language of these people is very different in sound from the Tonga language, and is much more harsh to pronounce; it is replete with very strong percussions on the tongue, and with a frequent rattling of the letter *r*.

An account of the Natives
of the Tonga Islands
Mariner 1827 (2):71

E DUA NA LALI. ©AJS

32 PHONOLOGICAL UNITS: A SUMMARY[1]

Since this grammar began by describing Fijian syntax and morphology, CH 1 presented a sketch of Fijian sounds and their relationship to orthography so that readers could "hear" example words and sentences in their minds as they read them. In addition to segmental phonemes, it also gave a summary description of two larger units—syllables and measures; unless we recognize these units, is impossible to know where the accents lie.

In this section, we describe in detail all these units, (and larger ones as well) as parts of a phonological hierarchy. We focus on the larger units, which have a DEMARCATIVE function (Martinet 1960:87, referred to in Hyman 1975:205)—that is, they provide the hearer with information about the peaks (if not always the borders) of grammatical units.[2] This is not to say that phonological and grammatical units are always isomorphic; §§39.3.1, 39.3.2, 39.3.3, and 39.3.5 show examples of common types of mismatches. But often one can find an approximate fit between the members of the pairs shown in table 32.1. (It begins with the measure, since there are no grammatical counterparts to segmental phonemes and syllables.)

TABLE 32.1: GRAMMATICAL CORRELATES TO PHONOLOGICAL UNITS

PHONOLOGICAL	GRAMMATICAL
measure	morpheme
phonological phrase	grammatical phrase
phonological sentence	grammatical sentence

32.1 PHONOLOGICAL UNITS AND THEIR CHARACTERISTICS

Fijian phonology is described here by defining five units in the phonological hierarchy and noting the relationship among them.[3] We begin with the smallest

---

[1] For this chapter, I found it more convenient to reverse the general organizational pattern of larger unit to smaller one.

[2] "Demarcate: to mark the limits of" (*Webster's new collegiate dictionary*, 8th ed.)

[3] Since language is linear in production, it might be possible to discuss phonology only in terms of longer and longer strings of the smallest perceptible units—the pho-

unit[4] and move to successively larger ones: the PHONEME, SYLLABLE, MEASURE, PHRASE, and SENTENCE.

Figure 32.1 shows the hierarchical relationships in the following sentence:

Kē cā, au tiko.   'If it's bad, I'm staying.

FIGURE 32.1: Hierarchical structure of a sample sentence.

phonemes	k ē	c ā	a u	t i k o
syllables	__	__	__	__ __ __
measures	__	__	__	_____
phrases	_____		_____	
sentence	_____			

Another way to view these units is to arrange them into two groups. The smaller units—phonemes, syllables, and measures—can be precisely defined as to their length and structure. The larger units—the phrase and the sentence—differ from the other units in two ways.

First, their length can be only loosely defined. A phrase *may* be limited by the structure of the grammatical phrase (which is its correlate) and by the speaker's breath span. Phonological sentences have fewer restrictions on length. For example, the breath span is no longer appropriate, since the speaker may breathe between phrases. Moreover, at least in theory, utterances of infinite length are possible: e.g., lists or house-that-Jack-built constructions.

Next, whereas the smaller units (phonemes and syllables) are purely phonological in their function,[5] the larger units are subtly bound to grammar and meaning. This property will become apparent in the following chapters, especially in the analysis of the complex relationship between phrases and sentences.

32.2 SEGMENTAL PHONEMES

Segmental phonemes are defined as minimum phonological units,[6] and are restricted to vowels and consonants. In the phonological hierarchy, they function as constituents of syllables. See the tables and descriptions in §1.1. The vowel system is treated in more detail in CH 33; consonants in CH 34.

---

nemes. But by doing so, one would be ignoring the evidence of higher levels in the phonological hierarchy.

[4] For some languages, it is also useful to deal with two more units: distinctive features and morae. Other linguists may not agree, but I don't find these concepts useful for describing Fijian. The mora comes closer to being useful, but if syllable weight is accounted for, the mora is not essential for the description.

[5] That is, they function only to make up larger units, and do not relate directly to grammar and meaning.

[6] See note 4.

32.3 SYLLABLES

A Fijian syllable consists of a vowel (the nucleus), which may be preceded by a consonant onset. This distribution is abbreviated as (C)V. Since consonants serve only as onsets, simple logic tells us that every consonant can appear in this position. The nucleus of the syllable can be SIMPLE (a vowel with little change of quality) or COMPLEX (a diphthong). Syllables can also be classified as SHORT or LONG.[7] See CH 33 for a more detailed discussion.

The function of syllables in the phonological hierarchy is to serve as constituents of MEASURES, the next larger unit.

32.4 MEASURES

A MEASURE is a stretch of speech that contains only one accented syllable. There are four main types. In the following notation, "V" represents a vowel or a diphthong. Although phonemic vowel length applies only to simple vowels, diphthongs are phonetically longer in certain positions and shorter in others. "C" represents a consonant, theoretically optional as an onset of any syllable in the measure. However, its omission between certain vowels would result in a diphthong or a long vowel, thus producing a different type of measure. Such details are discussed in §36.1, n. 1.

| 1. CVCV | *lako* | 2. CVCVCV | *vinaka* |
| 3. CV̄ | *vū, kau* | 4. CVCV̄ | *kilā, cakau* |

In forms consisting of more than one measure, raised periods separate the units, as in the following example: bata·batā 'cold'.

Other than in lists or examples that are typographically set off from the remainder of the text, a measure (or a series of measures) quoted as an example within a running text is marked by single vertical lines at the borders, which also indicate phrase boundaries.[8] An example is | bata·batā |.

The list above shows the form of measures. There are two main functions of measures. (1) to serve as building blocks for the next unit on the scale, the PHONOLOGICAL PHRASE. (2) to serve as an approximate guide to morphemes. See §36.7.

32.5 PHONOLOGICAL PHRASES

A phonological phrase consists of a measure or a series of measures, one of which is singled out as a PEAK. Phonetically, this peak is identified by a pitch change, a greater degree of stress, and a somewhat longer duration.[9]

---

[7] "Light" and "heavy" are alternate terms for "short" and "long."

[8] As discussed elsewhere, a measure in citation form is also a phonological phrase.

[9] Because of the nature of the morphemes in words, the peak measure in such a construction is usually the final measure. This situation has encouraged analyzing word accent in terms of primary accent (the penultimate syllable or final long syllable), secondary accent (the accented syllable on the preceding measure), and unaccented syllables (the remainder). The discussions in the following chapters show that such a pattern is a feature of phrases, not of words.

These phonetic features center on the accented syllable of the peak measure, shown below in boldface. As mentioned above, measure divisions are represented by raised periods. Since any phrase division also represents a measure division (at least in slow speech), phrase boundaries also show measure boundaries. An example above showed vertical lines marking phrase boundaries on a single measure which, as a citation form, constituted a phrase in itself. In the following example, they mark the boundaries of a longer phrase:

| kei·rau·lai·le**vu**ka | 'We (dual exclusive) went to Levuka.'

The demarcative function of a phonological phrase is to serve as an approximate guide to a grammatical phrase. In the phonological hierarchy, a phonological phrase serves as a constituent of a phonological sentence.

32.6 PHONOLOGICAL SENTENCES

A phonological sentence is an utterance that consists of a phrase or series of phrases, contains a TERMINAL, and is preceded and followed by pause.

For example, the following phonological sentence (whose borders are indicated by double vertical lines) consists of two phonological phrases (indicated here by space and boldface for the peak syllables):

Ni oti na sereki, keirau lai Levuka.
|| nioti·nase·**re**ki | kei·rau·lai·le**vu**ka ||
'After the term was over, we (dual exclusive) went to Levuka.'

The way this sentence is normally said, the hearer can recognize that the first portion contains a phrase peak. Since its end is not marked by a terminal but by "|", the hearer knows that more material follows.[10] The second phrase *is* marked with a terminal, signaling that the sentence ends with this phrase.

Although a sentence terminal is indicated by a combination of the phonetic ingredients of STRESS, DURATION, and PITCH CONTOUR, the principal ingredient is the pitch contour and its relationship to the register of the preceding material. Formally, there are two kinds of sentence terminals: those distinguished by PITCH FALL and by PITCH RISE. When necessary, a pitch fall is indicated by ↓, a rise by ↑ after the measure containing the peak syllable. But because terminals with pitch falls are much more common than those with rises, it is convenient to consider those unmarked,[11] and those with a rise, marked. The example sentence above ends with the unmarked variety.

At this state of our knowledge, the phonological hierarchy ends at the level of the sentence. The function of a phonological sentence as a constituent of a larger unit has not been investigated.

The following chapters treat these units in more detail.

---

[10] This phrase order is marked by the nonterminal contour after *sereki*. In normal phrase order, the subordinate VP would end the sentence.

[11] Following a suggestion by George W. Grace

33 VOWELS

Figure 33.1 shows the organization of the Fijian vowel system.

FIGURE 33.1: Hierarchical arrangement of the vowel system

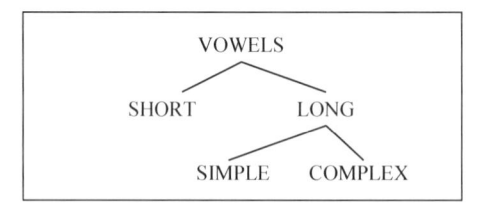

```
            VOWELS
           /      \
       SHORT      LONG
                  /    \
              SIMPLE   COMPLEX
```

Some types of vowels are limited in their occurrence in the measure. The following sections show examples of the different types in different positions in the measure.

33.1 SHORT VOWELS

In table 33:1, the five Fijian vowels, /i e a o u/, are arranged according to the phonetic features of tongue height, tongue advancement, and lip form.

TABLE 33.1: SHORT VOWELS

	front unrounded	central unrounded	back rounded
high	**i**		**u**
mid	**e**		**o**
low		**a**	

The mid front vowel /e/ is often heard as [ɛ], especially when short. Some phonetic studies (e.g., Scott 1948:738–39) have represented /o/ as [ɔ]; I hear it as closer to [o].

Short vowels can occur in both unaccented and accented syllables in the measure. In the following examples, the appropriate vowels are boldfaced:

ACCENTED SHORT VOWELS		UNACCENTED SHORT VOWELS	
b*a*le	'fall'	r*au*ta	'enough'
k*e*na	'its'	m*a*te	'dead'

dina	'true'	*moli*	'citrus'
dovu	'sugarcane'	*qalo*	'swim'
tuba	'outside'	*nomu*	'your'

As §32.4 and CH 36 show, a syllable whose vowel is short cannot constitute a measure by itself.

33.2 LONG VOWELS

Like a phoenix with repeated reincarnations, the interpretation of long vowels as sequences of the same vowel refuses to die. The following statement succinctly summarizes my own position: "If long vowels are phonemically in contrast with short vowels but fill the same structural position as is filled by single short vowels, the investigator may conclude that the long vowels represent single long vowel phonemes" (Pike 1947:138, quoted in Fox 2000:39).[1] For more detail, see §35.3 and subsections.

33.2.1 Simple long vowels

The following examples show contrasts for the five long vowels:

bā 'fence'
bē 'impudent'
bī 'ten turtles'
bō 'seize'
bū 'coconut at drinking stage'

Only one column is shown, since a long vowel cannot occur in an unaccented position in the measure. Nor can it occur in the penultimate syllable in a measure, putting Fijian in sharp contrast with most Polynesian languages. For example, Hawaiian allows such minimal pairs as:

kane	'skin disease'	*kāne*	'male'
'aina	'meal'	*'āina*	'land'[2]

Vowel- and diphthong-shortening patterns (discussed in §36.2 and following subsections) preclude any such contrasts for Fijian.

As a result, Fijian allows no vowel-length contrast without a change in accent as well. For example, in word-final position, the requirement that a long vowel must be accented produces different prosodic patterns in the following pair:

kíla 'wild' *kilá* 'know it'

---

[1] This statement of distribution is more accurate for Polynesian languages such as Hawaiian and Tongan, which allow long vowels in the penultimate position of a measure. Still, to look at the matter negatively, none of the double-vowel arguments are valid.

[2] Although I have not done a dictionary check, I get the impression that vowel-length contrast in this position does not carry a high functional load. In some cases, expected length has been lost: For example, based on Tongan *fo'ou* 'new', one would expect Hawaiian **hōu*. Instead, the form is *hou*.

Thus, this contrast is not minimal, since the prosodic pattern changes when a vowel is lengthened.

Nor can an accented syllable preceding a disyllable or a long syllable show a vowel-length contrast (the following forms are divided into measures):

    ˌmā·ˈcawa   'week'   maˈkawa 'old'

Thus, the relationship between vowel length and accent in Fijian suggests an interesting question: With minimal pairs for long and short vowels restricted, (at least within the category of content words), is vowel length "phonemic" in the same way that it is in Hawaiian?

There are a few minimal pairs without a change in accent, such as the following:

a	'the'	*ā*	(past tense marker)
se	(incomplete aspect marker)	*sē*	'flower'

However, the long syllables are accented in any position, whereas the short syllables would be accented only in certain combinations, such as:

    a tagane (ata·gane) 'the male'

Moreover, such contrasts are between function forms, or between function and content forms. Although one could propose the following minimal pair at the phrase level:

se totoka	'still beautiful'	seto·toka
sē totoka	'beautiful flower'	sē·totoka

the distinction would tend to disappear in casual speech, since the long vowel in the second phrase shortens. In other words,

    sē·totoka → seto·toka[3]

33.2 2 Complex long vowels (diphthongs)

33.2.2.1 Defining *diphthong*

The following vowel sequences are those that most observers hear as monosyllabic[4] in certain positions: any mid or low vowel followed by *i* or *u*, and also the sequence *iu*. In terms of prominence, the diphthongs are classified as FALLING, since the first element serves as the nucleus. The complete list of diphthongs is as follows: *ai, au, ei, eu, oi, ou,* and *iu*.[5]

---

[3] There might be a subtle difference in the accent level of the first syllable in each phrase, based on the different accent patterns in content and function forms (see §36.8, 39.3.5, and Schütz 1999),

[4] Thus, the concepts of syllable and diphthong are closely linked.

[5] The list omits *ae* and *ao*, which historically have undergone certain changes. However, *ae* appears in at least one borrowed word, and could be treated as a diphthong with limited occurrence. See §33.5.

To counter the objection that these sequences are called diphthongs because they are "just those most likely to be heard as monosyllabic by speakers of European languages" (Hockett 1990:292), I offer the following arguments:

1. In a number of informal experiments, Fijian speakers, asked to tap a rhythmic accompaniment to disyllables and trisyllables, interpreted such forms as *raica*, when spoken in casual style, as disyllables—that is, *rai + ca*.

2. The classification of Fijian diphthongs as falling diphthongs provides the main objective test: that is, whatever the position of these vowel sequences in an accent unit, the accent is on the first vowel, rather than the second. A long monosyllable, such as *rai* 'seen', provides no proof, since one could say that the *a* segment is accented because it is in penultimate position. However, if an added syllable moves *ai* to the left, the accent is still on *a*, in spite of its no longer being in penultimate position. Thus, we hear *ráica* rather than **raíca*. Again, in informal experiments, native speakers identified *a*, rather than *i*, as the accented vowel in such forms. For a more detailed argument and rebuttal of Hockett's position, see Schütz 2000.

3. Acoustic evidence also supports the existence of diphthongs in Fijian (King 1969:531):

> The pronunciation of native speakers, reinforced by spectrographic evidence, points to the existence in Fijian of diphthongs, i.e. sequences of two unlike vowels bearing one stress spread over both, in contrast to the same vowels occurring with a morpheme boundary between them. Figure 1 [spectrogram] shows the diphthong *ai* in *raica* 'see', the shift in formants from *a* to *i* being accompanied by none of the disturbance in harmonics (indicative of laryngealisation but not complete closure) which can be seen in Figure 2 [spectrogram] ... where the same vowels occur separated by a morpheme boundary in the phrase *na ika* 'the fish'.

4. The arguments above hinge mainly on form. But they lead to the main reason for considering certain vowel sequences as diphthongs: *They **function** as units, not as sequences.* To amplify on the example above, the sequence *ai* in penultimate position functions as the nucleus of a syllable. The opposite order, however—*ia*—never does so. For example, *diaka* 'hit him' is accented *diáka* and syllabified as *di-a-ka*.

In spite of this strong evidence, however, one cannot make a blanket statement about such vowel sequences. I suggest instead that they be considered POTENTIAL DIPHTHONGS, for two reasons.

The first, mentioned above in (2), is that in forms of the shape *rai* 'seen' or *tau* 'fall', the criteria on which to base the classification are only impressionistic. In other words, one might suggest that the accent falls on the first vowel because this is the position in which accent normally appears, making the accent pattern of such sequences such as *ai* and *au* no different from that of *ia* and *ua*.

The second is that across certain morpheme boundaries (illustrated by the example in the quotation above, *na ika* 'the fish'), diphthongization[6] is blocked, at least in more formal speech.[7]

To expand on the *diaka* example above: Sequences other than those in the list of diphthongs do not behave as units, but as separate vowels. In the following examples, it is the second of the two vowels that is accented:

luáca	'vomit on it'	*CuóCV	[no example]
buéla	(kind of shellfish)	*cióru*	'muddy'
Kiéta	(place name)	*Moála*	(island name)
Peáli	'Baal'		

The remaining sequence, *ui*, is more difficult to analyze, since it does not involve a change from a higher to a lower vowel, but instead (like its opposite number, *iu*), a change from a vowel of low sonority and high position to another of the same type. Still, forms with *ui* preceding an unaccented syllable sound like trisyllables, with the accent in the usual position:

kuíta 'octopus'

Phonetically, the sonority of the unaccented *u* is so slight that the effect is that of an on-glide:

[kwítə]

It is not interpreted as such within the phonological system, because there is no contrast between the following:

[kwítə]   and   [kuítə][8]

In short, there is nothing about the accentual behavior of such pairs to suggest that they are anything other than sequences.

In the same vein, Scott noted that the accent pattern in a sequence of two vowels was dependent on their order (1948:746):[9]

> When the second vowel is *a*, it fairly clearly does have the stress, the strong form of *a* being used: *lua* ['luə], *luaca* [lu'a·ðə]; *qia* ['ŋgiə], *qiata* [ŋgi'a·tə]. In other cases the impression received seems to depend, in part at least, on the inherent sonorities of the vowels involved; the first vowel in *ai* and *au*, even though it is the weakened variety of *a*, tends to dominate the *i* and *u*, as does *o* in *oi* and *ou*. *Raica* is usually heard as ['rəiðə], *taura* as ['təurə].

---

[6] Some phonologists prefer the term *resyllabification* over *diphthongization*. An earlier meaning of *diphthongization* confined the term to the process of a single vowel becoming a diphthong. I use the term differently: it is the process that allows two vowels to serve as the nucleus of a single syllable. The main reason that the term *diphthongization* is preferable is that this process has to precede resyllabification.

[7] These sequences, can, however, diphthongize in casual speech. See Tamata 1994.

[8] Since some *kw-* words from certain Western Fijian languages have been introduced into SF, there is now the potential for a contrast (see *VV*).

[9] Scott wrote phonetic forms in boldface; I have set such forms off with square brackets. In his notation, the centered period in the transcriptions indicates phonetic lengthening of an accented vowel.

33.3 VOWEL SEQUENCES ACROSS MORPHEME BOUNDARIES

The behavior of vowel sequences across morpheme boundaries depends largely on three conditions: (1) morpheme type; (2) the morpheme's position in the measure, and (3) speech style. In a more formal speech style, combining and realigning take place only with grammatical markers that consist of a light syllable and the following unaccented syllable of an uneven measure.

33.3.1 Accent determined by morpheme type

Certain types of morphemes, either in whole or in part, can combine in a way that diphthongs are formed across morpheme boundaries. For example, nouns that have been nominalized with *i-*, preceded by the definite article *na*, provide examples:

na i sulu	nai·sulu	'the sarong'
na i sele	nai·sele	'the knife'
na i sole	nai·sole	'the wrapper'
na i binibini	nai·bini·bini	'the heap'
na i seru	nai·seru	'the comb'

In the pattern shown here, the levels of accent on *na* and *i* contribute to diphthongization: the accented *na* and the unaccented *i* fulfill the conditions necessary for a falling diphthong. It should be noted, however, that the level of accent on *na*—a function form— is lower than that of the accented syllable in a content form. The best illustration in the list just above is nai·bini·bini. The last measure receives phrase accent (in citation form here). But the penultimate measure is still more strongly accented that the first one, which consists of function forms.

Vowel sequences formed by combining BASES that are ROOTS[10] do not resyllabify. For example, in

cina ika 'fishing by lamplight'

the *a* and the *i* do not form a diphthong, at least in more formal speech. Instead, the measure division is

cina·ika.

Other examples are

kere ibe	kere·ibe	'requesting mats'
kana uto	kana·uto	'eating breadfruit'
kana ika	kana·ika	'eating fish'

Similarly, the combination of like vowels through morphology does not produce a long vowel, except when two like vowels occur at the end of a basic phrase. Note the following:

| *vili ivi* | vili·ivi (not *vilīvi) | 'picking up *ivi*' |
| *na vei ivi* | navei·ivi (not *naveivi) | 'collection of *ivi*' |

---

[10] For definitions of base and root, with examples, see §39.2.1 and §39.2.2.

In most of these cases, the correct pronunciations are suggested by the conventional word boundaries: *na ura*, *na uca*, etc. However, it is not clear whether diphthongization and a diphthong result when reduplication produces a potential diphthong; e.g.:

*ur**ou**ro*   'square'
*ur**au**ra*   'paid in kind'

As with similar questions, the answer may depend on speech style.

From these examples, we can see that a vowel sequence described as a potential diphthong may behave differently between morphemes than it does within one morpheme.

33.3.2 Accent determined by position

When *na* precedes a noun that begins with an accented vowel, the diphthongization is blocked:

na ubi   'the cover'
na ivi   'the Tahitian chestnut'
na ibe   'the mat'

Ni 'of, related to' behaves similarly when followed by a morpheme beginning with *u-* (the only vowel with which *i*, as a peak, could combine to form a diphthong):

drau ni uluna   'his hair'

In this example, *ni* seems to attach prosodically with *drau* (with resultant shortening of *au*) rather than the following form. However, if the *ni* were preceded by a CVCV form, it would be accented, and there would be a stronger possibility that it could form a diphthong with the following u. Still, I have the impression that intonational features would separate the *i* and the *u* and block the diphthongization.

33.3.3 Accent determined by speech style

For a detailed description of a number of phonological changes in casual speech, not only at the segmental level, but the prosodic level as well, see Tamata 1994.

33.4 VOWEL ASSIMILATION

Because of their phonetic nature, vowels are especially subject to influence from their environment. Here we discuss three types of influence confined to the contiguous environment (that is, adjacent phonemes) or to simultaneously produced features (such as accent):

1. The phonetic manifestations of accent
2. The effect of adjacent vowels on each other (within a single syllable)
3. The effect of the position of consonants on the position of the vowel

33.4.1 The influence of accent on vowel quality and length

Since accent is a phonological term, it is necessary to describe its phonetic manifestations. We do so by treating five phonetic components of ACCENT: STRESS, LENGTH, PITCH, TENSION, and VOWEL POSITION. (Although Scott did not arrange his discussion of Fijian phonetics (1948) in this way, his observations form the basis for many of the following points.)

33.4.1.1 Stress

This feature can be defined as perceived amplitude—that is, how, in comparing two adjacent syllables, we hear one as louder than the other. Although different vowels and—to a certain extent—different consonants affect amplitude so that each syllable has its own specific loudness, a particular syllable will be louder in accented position than in unaccented position. The most satisfactory examples for such a contrast are sequences of otherwise identical syllables: /kaka/, /mimi/, /lolo/, etc. Even so, stress alone is difficult to isolate from the bundle that comprises accent.[11]

33.4.1.2 Length

Accented syllables are also longer than unaccented syllables, with a caveat similar to that above: that each consonant and each vowel has its own range of intrinsic length.[12] For example, syllables with /a/ are longer than those with /i/; syllables with /b/ are longer than those with /k/ (other factors being equal). However, in addition to this intrinsic length, syllables are longer when accented. Scott (1948) described vowels in the accented position as being "half long."[13] This length is discernible enough so that vowels in this position are sometimes mistakenly classed as phonologically long.[14]

33.4.1.3 Vowel position

The comparison of otherwise identical accented and unaccented syllables shows a regular relationship in vowel position. Accented vowels are nearer the periphery of the vowel chart (that is, low vowels lower, front vowels nearer the front, etc.) than unaccented vowels, which are—as in many other languages—somewhat centralized. /a/ is the vowel with the most noticeable change of posi-

---

[11] Any one of the components is difficult to isolate, because no one of them makes up the sole difference in a minimal pair. In other words, there are no utterances that differ solely because of stress or length or any of the other components, because they operate as a group.

[12] Not always discernible to the ear, but instrumentally measurable.

[13] I think he erred in trying to regularize vowel length or divide it into discrete units when phonetic, not phonological length, was involved. But such a problem is common in phonetics, when we are often forced to divide a continuum into discrete sections.

[14] The most prominent examples of such an interpretation are a number of entries in Capell 1941 that show length on penultimate vowels, which never occurs. An anecdotal example is that a native speaker of Fijian, transcribing some material for the FDP, regularly marked penultimate (and accented) vowels as long.

tion.[15] As he did with his label of "half-long," Scott tried to regularize this allophonic variation by writing an unaccented /a/ as [ə], but such symbolization suggests a precision that does not exist. In the strictest terms, one can only note that unaccented /a/ is more centralized (that is, in this case, higher) than accented /a/ and that it *may* occur as high as [ʌ].

§33.4.2 describes the possibility of even more variation in the position of /a/.

33.4.1.4 Tension

Tension refers to the relative muscular condition associated with the production of a sound. It is a phonetic feature that often accompanies stress; in fact, the two features may be inextricably bound.

33.4.1.5 Pitch

It is difficult to deal with pitch as a feature of accent separate from intonation, because all short utterances comprise a phrase in themselves, and the peak of a phrase is marked primarily by pitch. But the accented syllable doesn't always carry the highest pitch in the phrase. However, the following unaccented syllable is very likely to be lower in pitch, especially at the end of a phrase. See §38.1 and subsections.

33.4.2 Vowel assimilation in diphthongs

One way in which the syllabification has a phonetic effect (or—to look at the situation the other way round—one way to recognize that certain vowel sequences operate as one syllable) is the behavior of the vowel /a/ in its different functions. In the following example, since a/ and /i/ are separated by a consonant, /a/ is somewhat, but not extremely, influenced by the high vowel in the following syllable:[16]

    kati   'bite'

But a following /i/ or /u/ in the same syllable has a marked phonetic effect. Note Scott's transcription of /a/ before /i/ as [ə] in the quotation at the end of §33.2.1. As discussed above, in a syllable such as /ai/, the /a/ *can* assimilate far enough to the /i/ that it not only raises but fronts as well, and the diphthong approaches [ʌ] (see Scott 1948:739). Similarly, in /au/, the /a/ *can* approach /o/ so that the effect of the diphthong is [ow]. For example, I have heard the diphthongs in *kaukaua* 'strong' approach [ow]. As evidence that this assimilation is neither new nor unique to my own observations, note that Thomas Williams wrote *Lou* for *Lau* (*Somosomo Quarterly Letter* No. 4, June 1846).

It should be emphasized that phonetic raising and rounding are not either-or propositions, but a matter of degree.

---

[15] Possibly because speakers of English recognize a change in the height of /a/ more readily than, say, a change of /i/ or /u/ to a somewhat more central position.

[16] In Hawaiian, /a/ raises noticeably when followed by *i* or *u* in the same syllable or C*i* or C*u* in the same measure. Examples are *mai* 'hither' and *pali* 'precipice', in which /a/ is phonetically [ɔ] or [ʌ].

33.4.3 A note on different degrees of noncontrastive vowel length

There are several homophonous markers of the form *i*. When one of these occurs after an *-i* syllable within a phrase, the combination results in several potential types of phonetic vowel length.

Because of the structure of measures, the syllable preceding the *i* marker is unaccented unless long. The following examples represent different types of *i* + *i* combinations: "s" represents a short and unaccented vowel, "´" a short and accented vowel, and "–" a long and accented vowel.

E raici irau.	s + s	'He saw them (dual).'
E raici iratou.	s + ´	'He saw them (trial).'
na kolī i Mere	– + s	'M's dog'
na kolī i Marama	– + ´	'M's dog'

The variation between the spellings *kai Idia* and *Kai Dia* 'Indian' may reflect the uncertainty in representing a geminate sequence of unaccented vowels.

* * * * *

The vowel changes described above apply mainly to fairly formal speech. For a thorough treatment of vowel changes in casual speech, see Tamata 1994: 28–60. These include assimilation, vowel harmony, monophthongization, deletion, shortening, devoicing, and glide lowering and deletion.

33.5 VOWEL SEQUENCES *AO* AND *OE*

The sequence /ao/ has undergone changes[17] and is now rare in Fijian (except, perhaps, across morpheme boundaries, as in *na-i-ka-ono* 'sixth'; or across measure divisions: bā·ovi is an example of an *āo* sequence, but not within one measure). However, it now occurs in a few borrowings, but in these is treated as so unusual that it receives special pronunciation. For example, *paodi* 'pound' is trisyllabic, but the /a/ in the first syllable is not short and centralized as it would be in other trisyllables. After some deliberation, it was decided to spell the word *pāodi* in the dictionary to account for its irregular pronunciation.[18] In this instance, the macron indicates not so much the length of the vowel as its quality. Note that the form is not divided into two measures (according to the patterns discussed earlier), but is pronounced with only one accent. Thus, its pronunciation makes *pāodi* a misfit for our system ... but borrowed words often stretch the phonological system. Incidentally, it may be significant that there exists an alternate form *pauni* that better matches the prosodic pattern of indigenous words.

Oe has also re-entered the language through borrowings. E.g.:

boe, poe	'boy'	*boela*	'boil'

---

[17] Geraghty and Pawley 1977.

[18] *VV* has preserved this spelling.

On the basis of the accent pattern of the first example alone, it would be impossible to classify *oe*. However, *boela* is pronounced as two syllables, giving another potential diphthong with very limited distribution.

33.6 A RECENT ADDITION TO THE VOWEL INVENTORY

For the most part, the new sounds introduced in *VV* (through borrowings) are consonants (see CH 34). However, one vowel has been added:

Letter	Phonetic shape	Example	Gloss
è	[ɜ]	fès	first (rugby term)

34 CONSONANTS

In CH1, table 1.2, the consonant system was presented in tabular form. Now we discuss each consonant with respect to its phonetic manifestations, its distribution (if limited), and—in some cases—its phonological interpretation.

The chapter is divided into several parts: Indigenous consonants, "traditional" introduced consonants, consonants introduced from other Fijian languages, and consonants introduced by the staffs of the FDP and *VV*.[1]

34.1 INDIGENOUS CONSONANTS

These sounds are members of the consonant system of a theoretical construct: SF, without early additions from the Lauan languages and borrowings from Tongan and English, or later additions from Fijian languages further to the west, and—again—from English.

34.1.1 /t/ [t]. Voiceless apico-alveolar stop, unaspirated and lenis

Although the point of articulation for /t/ is primarily[2] apico-alveolar, the point and spread of contact change for different vowels. The syllable /ti/ especially is subject to a type of assimilation commonly called palatalization and less commonly, affrication.

The difference in position between the syllables /ta/[3] and /ti/ is marked enough to be observed. Conventional phonetic research (palatograms, x-ray photography, etc.) for other languages shows the different configurations of the tongue for different syllables. For example, for /ta/, the tongue touches a relatively small area of the roof of the mouth. However, for /ti/, the shape of the

---

[1] Admittedly, this division has little historical validity, especially with respect to what was obviously a long period of Lauan and Tongan influence on Bauan, the basis for Standard Fijian. However, it reflects the opinions of some early grammarians about what was and what was not Bauan.

[2] I use "primarily" here because there seems to be an insignificant variation on the continuum between apicodental and apicoalveolar, including the possibility of an articulation that covers both positions.

[3] I arbitrarily choose /-a/ syllables as a frame of reference for consonant position. Higher vowels automatically allow a larger area of tongue contact for consonants that involve the area from the upper rear portion of the incisors rearward.

tongue more nearly matches the shape of the roof of the mouth, and the apex itself is slightly but visibly thrust forward, with the area of contact for the articulator extending from the apex to the blade, and that of the point of articulation extending from the upper back dental area to the alveopalatal area.[4]

In Fijian, as in many other languages, this change in position of the syllable /ti/ is accompanied by a change in the manner of release. No longer is the release always "clear," as with the other /t-/ syllables, but it is made in such a way to permit friction. Such a release is called PALATALIZED (or FRICATIVIZED).[5] In addition, the quality of the fricative release is somewhat influenced by grooving of the tongue, which gives it a sibilant quality. As a matter of fact, it is as much this quality as the point of articulation that characterizes a palatalized consonant. The whole articulation (stop plus fricative) is classified as an AFFRICATE.[6]

It must be understood, however, that for native Fijian words, an affricate is not on a par with the other manners of articulation, for this manner is not distinctive. That is, it cannot serve as a feature to distinguish otherwise identical members of a pair that differ only in manner.[7] Although there are a number of words that differ only because one begins with a stop and the other with a nasal (e.g., *bē* 'irreverent' and *mē* 'goat') there are no such pairs for stop vs. affricate. Instead, there is a continuum of pronunciations between [ti] and [či], and the conditions that produce any particular point on this continuum seem complex (and as yet largely unstudied). However, the following factors seem related to the situation:

1. Palatalization in SF is rare in careful, precise speech, but the degree increases with speed and informality.

2. Because palatalization is common in many areas of Fiji, speakers from those areas often carry this pronunciation over to their pronunciation of SF, but perhaps to a lesser degree.

3. Although a modified [č] pronunciation is common for many words, for some it is unacceptable. For example, *tī* 'tea' seems clearly recognized as an English borrowing and not subject (at present) to the same processes as other words.

Borrowings, however, have produced minimal pairs for affricates ([č] and [nǰ]; see *j* and *z* below).

For a further discussion, see Tamata 1994:68–69.

---

[4] See the discussion of integrated syllables (§35.2) and Schütz 1978b, 2004 (called "natural syllables" in those works).

[5] *Palatalized* emphasizes the change of position; *fricativized*, the change of manner.

[6] The position of articulation is somewhat forward of that for the English pronunciation of the initial sound in *cheese*, and less aspirated.

[7] However, when borrowings are added to the data, the situation changes. See §34.2.3.

34.1.2 /k/ [k]. Voiceless dorso-velar stop, relatively unaspirated and lenis

Because the movement of the back part of the tongue is more restricted than that of the apex, the position of /k/ is more strongly influenced by the position required by the following vowel, especially /i/. In some Fijian languages other than SF (Schütz 1963:69), and in casual speech (Tamata 1994:70–74), /k/ fricativizes, especially in unaccented syllables.

34.1.3 /b/ [mb]. Voiced prenasalized bilabial stop

For all the prenasalized consonants (/b, d, q, dr/), the nasal onset is heard most clearly between vowels. At the beginning of an utterance, its duration is reduced, and in casual styles, eliminated.

34.1.4 /d/ [nd]. Voiced prenasalized apico-alveolar stop

The conditions that hold for the palatalization of /t/ hold for /d/ as well.

34.1.5 /q/ [ŋg]. Voiced prenasalized dorso-velar stop

34.1.6 /r/ [ř] ~ [ř̃]. Voiced apico-alveolar tap ~ trill

The environment for the tap-trill continuum seems to be fairly random, with the exception of a relationship to speed of speech. Slower speech, of course, makes a longer period available for the segment, and phonetic length in this instance means an increase in the number of taps.

34.1.7 /dr/ [nř] ~ [nř̃]. Voiced prenasalized apico-alveolar tap~trill

The consonant /dr/ presents special problems. First, it can be added to the set /b d q/, since it is preceded by a stretch of voicing perceived (by many observers) as [n]. Next, the [d] is heard "automatically" when [ř] is begun from closed position, rather than open. In other words, it is an excrescent sound, rather like the [t] in ENG *prince*. Writing the sound as a cluster is misleading, but (1) the spelling is well established, and (2) there is no appropriate letter available with which to write it.

34.1.8 /s/ [s]. Voiceless apico-alveolar grooved fricative

Scott (1948:740–41) noted the only prominent allophonic variation of /s/: an occasional pronunciation somewhat back of the apico-alveolar position, approaching [š]. I observed this variation of /s/ in other languages on Viti Levu, particularly before /i/ (Schütz 1962). However, this palatalization is never as prominent as that of /t/ before /i/. Moreover, taped data show that it varies from speaker to speaker. Unaccented /si/ and /su/ are often realized by [s:], especially in faster speech and in word-final position.

34.1.9 /v/ [ß]. Voiced bilabial slit fricative

Although in syllables with unrounded vowels the lips are not particularly protruded, neither is the spread position so pronounced nor the force of air so great that the consonant is fortis. See Scott 1948:740.

When in the final unaccented position in the accent measure, and especially when that measure ends an utterance, the syllable /vu/ is often a lengthened [ß:], with some devoicing of the consonant as well (see §35.2, §35.4.1).

34.1.10 /c/ [ð]. Voiced apico-dental fricative

The actual point of contract with the upper teeth can vary somewhat, so that the extent of protrusion of the tip varies. But the descriptive term "interdental" is not apt; the bottom teeth do not contribute to the articulation.

34.1.11 /m/ [m]. Voiced bilabial nasal

One /m-/ syllable, /mu/, patterns with /vu/ in its behavior. That is, in the position described for /vu/, /mu/ appears as [m:], sometimes with a residual protrusion of the lips representing the underlying /u/. See, for example, the *luvemu* example in Tamata 1994:76. See also §35.2, 35.4.1.

34.1.12 /n/ [n]. Voiced apicodental nasal

Based on palatograms, Scott (1948:740) described a marked difference in position for /n/ in the syllables /ni/ vs. /nu/: a front-back difference, with the nasals in the syllables /ne/, /na/, and /no/ occupying "intermediate positions."

34.1.13 /g/ [ŋ]. Voiced back-velar nasal

Scott (1948) reported that palatograms show assimilation similar to that for /k-/ and /q-/ syllables: a front-back relationship according to the position of the vowel.

34.1.14 /l/ [l]. Voiced apicoalveolar lateral

The quality of /l/ varies according to the different resonances produced by the position of the back of the tongue. In the syllable /li/, the back of the tongue is high; for /lo/, it is lower. In general, Fijian /l/ before low vowels is higher than English /l/ in a similar environment.

34.1.15 /w/ [w] High back rounded glide

Because /w/ has a limited distribution and some other anomalies, we now discuss it at length.

34.1.15.1 Problems with /w/

For a time at least, the Fijian alphabet did not include *w*, an omission that can most likely be traced to Tongan. Either Cargill was so accustomed to Tongan phonology that he "processed" what he heard from his first Fijian consultant, or the man himself, Mateinaniu, adopted a Tongan-like pronunciation because it was what outsiders expected. Even after he arrived in Fiji, Cargill continued writing *u* for what we now write as *w*: his journal mentions visits to the Lakeba village of "Uathiuathi" (*Waciwaci*).[8]

---

[8] In loanwords from English, TON interpreted an ENG *w-* as TON *u-*, as in *Uesiliana* 'Wesleyan'. The closest phonetic match to [w] occurs when the *u-* is followed by an accented vowel, as in the example just given.

Although Hale wrote *w* (and *y*) in his transcription of Fijian words, apparently he did not consider them to be essential elements of the alphabet (as he might have expressed the idea of a sound being "phonemic"—a concept unknown at the time). Or, in his words (1846:367): "The *y* and *w* are used instead of *i* and *u* when they begin a syllable, —as, *yava* for *iava*, *waluvu* for *ualuvu*."

There are certainly distributional limitations that, in part, support Hale's view. /w/ does not occur adjacent to the rounded vowels *u* and *o* (Scott 1948:741). However, in the earlier orthography at least, such sequences are permitted:

kaukauwa	'strong'	*quwava*	'guava'	*sowiri*	'spin'
drowa	'drawer'	*quwa*	'wipe'	*suwiti*	'sweet'
tauwelu	'towel'	*saluwaki*	'perfume'	*bowiri*[9]	'faint'

In *VV*, for some of these forms, spellings without *w* appear as the main entry, for others, alternate forms are given, and for still others, the *w* spellings do not appear at all. The crucial matter is not so much a phonetic one (e.g., the degree of lip rounding and constriction in this position), but a phonological one: in this position, /w/ is not contrastive.

The form *maniwa* 'manure' presents an interesting problem, for it would seem that a form like *maniua would come closer to the English model. In the hypothetical form, the sequence /iu/ would form a diphthong close to the one in the model. But is there really a contrast between /iua/ and /iwa/? Or is the difference indeterminate at present, reflecting a sound change from the first form to the second? Such a change would match others in the language, not so much in their forms, but in their function or goal: to eliminate syllables not of the shape CV.

34.1.16 /y/[10] [ɛ] ↔ [y][11]

Y is difficult to describe phonetically because of its range of manifestations, suggested by "↔." It is closer to the first symbol in the brackets above (a lower mid front unrounded glide) when it is in initial position, and closer to [y] between vowels. As for its distribution, we encounter some problems with *y*:

1. It occurs principally before /a/, except for a few questionable forms before /e/ (see the Fijian-English dictionary) and /o/ (as *toyovu*). *VV* includes four *ye-* entries and three *yo-* entries—one exclamation, three plants, and three borrowings.

---

[9] This word appears as *boiri* in *VV*.

[10] The italics and lack of slant lines here are deliberate—indications that the sound does not have phonemic status.

[11] Thanks to Andrew Pawley for his comments, which encouraged me to state my previous analysis in more decisive terms. However, he is not responsible for my possible misinterpretation of his position.

2. There seems to be no contrast between these sequences:

ia and *iya*
ea and *eya*

3. A number of forms vary (in spelling) between *ya-* and *a-*.

4. In English words with /a-/ or /æ-/ pronounced by a Fijian speaker, the vowel is often preceded by a mid-front unrounded glide.

5. The phonetic nature of the sound varies according to whether it is in word-initial or intervocalic position.

The main question regarding *y* is its status as a phoneme, a matter that has been debated for some time. Is it (1) a phoneme with a limited distribution, or (2) not a phoneme at all?

This analysis chooses (2), with this distributional statement: initial *y* is a feature of word-initial /a/, and medial *y* stems from [i]. The medial *y* is the result of [i] under two conditions: First, an /i/ syllable with no supporting consonant. Next, that syllable is unaccented.

Underlying this premise is an assumption that certain phonetic conditions result in /i/ taking such a form or being distributed in such a pattern that it becomes possible to interpret it as a consonant rather than as a vowel.

Support for this position comes, first, from the considerable number of *a-* entries in *VV* that refer to a *y-* form, and vice versa. Next, see the y and Ø as allomorphs of the thematic consonant, footnote to table 16.3

34.1.16.1 *Y*: Discussion

Y has been treated differently by several major Fijian grammarians.

Churchward 1941. In the main part of his grammar, Churchward's first comment about *y* (1941:9) was that it was pronounced "as in English" (which might be true intervocalicly but not initially). However, in the second part of his grammar, in which he discussed some topics in more detail, he wrote (p. 63):

> Note on Initial *Y*
>
> Fijian shows a tendency to develop a *y* before an initial *a* or *ā*. See *yādua* ... and *yatu*. Other examples are *yalewa* (woman) for the older form *alewa*, and the modern *yagilosi* for the introduced *agilosi* (angel). The fact that Fijian ... has so few words beginning with *a* or *ā*, and so many beginning with *ya* or *yā*, suggests that the initial *y* of many, if not most, of these words has been similarly developed.

Because Churchward was writing during a period in which the structuralist idea of phonemes was not widely known, we cannot expect him to have looked for minimal pairs.

Among grammarians familiar with the idea of phonemes, the following two quotations represent opposite points of view about *y*:

Milner 1972. Milner dealt with the topic very briefly (1972:4n): "One of the semivowels,[12] *y*, is *not* a unit of the phonological system, but it has been treated as such for the sake of convenience." However, he gave no supporting evidence for his position, nor did he point out the problems that this solution carries with it.

In the following excerpt from a review of Milner's grammar, the writers supported the opposite conclusion—that *y* was indeed a phoneme.

Biggs and Nayacakalou 1958. In a review of Milner 1956, Biggs and Nayacakalou wrote:

> [Milner] denies [y] a place in the phonetic system ... which can only be done if it is always predictable in terms of the other phonemes. Such pairs as *toa*, *totoya*; *kaa*, *kaya*; *tootaka*, *toyovu*; show that, in the author's phonemicisation this is not the case. Since [y] almost always occurs morpheme initially, it is tempting to regard it as a junctural phenomenon, an allophone of the juncture which must be introduced to account for the phonetic difference in the transition between vowels in such pairs as *rauta* [rauta], *vakauqeta* [vaka + ungeta]. But *toyovu* and a few dictionary words not known to the reviewers are single morphemes. It seems best therefore to include /y/ as a phoneme in its own right

The main problem with this point of view is that it proposes that *y* is an allophone of a putative unit—juncture.

For a more detailed discussion, see *TFL*, pp. 555–58.

To restate the solution at the beginning of the *y* section, we conclude that although the letter *y* is convenient for writing Fijian, it is not a phoneme in the underlying phonological system, but instead stems from two sources: (1) a glide that precedes an otherwise initial /a/; (2) a manifestation of an unaccented /i/ in certain positions.

34.2 "TRADITIONAL" INTRODUCED CONSONANTS

This set includes *p*, *f*, and *j* ([č] and [nj]), which may appear to be consonants borrowed from English, but which existed in Lau at the time Cargill and Cross began to translate the Bible into Fijian.

34.2.1 /p/ [p]. Voiceless bilabial stop, relatively unaspirated and lenis

Because of the Tongan influence in the eastern part of Fiji, it was long assumed that words with /p/ in that area were borrowed from Tongan. However, Geraghty (1983a:104) noted that for many forms, there is no evidence to suggest a Tongan source. Instead, the forms can be traced back to a Proto-Oceanic *p. No matter which of these two sources a particular word with *p* has, it is now an integral part of the Lauan system (see Schütz 1963).

---

[12] "Semivowel" is not a phonetic term. The correct term is "glide."

Since Cargill's "Feejeean" (the Lakeba language) included *p* in its inventory of sounds, he treated it no differently from the other voiceless stops. His manuscript dictionary (1839) of some five or six thousand entries also includes about a dozen *p-* words borrowed from English.

However, Hazlewood, basing his work on Bauan, viewed *p* as a sound found only in words introduced from other Fijian or foreign languages

The actual pronunciation of words spelled with *p* is complicated. For some words that seem to be confined largely to a Biblical context, [p] prevails. Examples are the words for *prophet* and *prophesy*. Many borrowings that are used more often in a secular context alternate between *p* and *v*: *peni ~ veni* 'pen' and *pusi ~ vusi* 'cat' are examples. And some early borrowings, such as *vinivō* 'dress' (from *pinafore*), have become assimilated to the extent that the English source seems to have been forgotten.

The present variation hinges on at least two criteria: the policies of speakers ranging from conservative to innovative, and the time elapsed since the words in question were borrowed. The complexity of the situation has left its mark on the language, for many *p* borrowings have alternate forms:

paipo / vaivo	'pipe'
paodi / paudi / vaoni / vaudi	'pound'
pasidia / vasidia	'passenger'
peleti / veleti	'plate'

Whereas Capell 1941 has six *p-*[13] entries, *VV* has 424, mainly from borrowings from English, Lau and other Fijian languages, Hindi, Tongan, Samoan, and Latin.

34.2.2 /f/ [f]. Voiceless labiodental slit fricative.

The status of *f* in Fijian is similar to that of *p*: it is phonemic in Lau (Schütz 1963:68, Geraghty 1983:98–120), present in many Tongan borrowings throughout eastern Fiji, and felt to be "foreign" in the standard language.

Hazlewood's reaction to this sound was similar to his treatment of *p* (see above). Since his time, words introduced from English have come to form a significant part of the vocabulary, and the status of sounds such as /f/ has to be reconsidered. For borrowings from English, the frequency of *f-* words is lower than that for *j-* or *p-*.[14]

Contrasting with two *f-* entries in Capell 1941, *VV* has 136, mainly borrowings from English, Tongan, Rotuman, Latin, and various eastern Fijian languages. About 25 of these have *v-* alternates listed: e.g., *falawa ~ valawa* 'flour'.

---

[13] Since I do not have access to a searchable version of *VV*, most of the statistics here on the occurrence of particular sounds in entries are confined to initial position.

[14] In Schütz 1978b, the counts are: *f-*: 15, *j-*: 23, *p-*: 70. One must remember, however, that the *j* in the earlier Fijian orthography stems from more than one English sound, and that the ratio of *f-* to *p-* words in English is roughly 1:2.

34.2.3 /j/ [č]. Voiceless alveo-palatal affricate

This sound, originally an allophone of /t/ before /i/, has achieved phonemic status in SF through borrowings, both from English and from other Fijian languages. An example of a minimal pair is *jaba* 'jumper' vs. *taba* 'arm, wing'. See §34.1.1.

Capell 1941 has no *j-* entries; *VV* has 138, mainly borrowings from ENG, TON, and languages from eastern Fiji.

It is significant that there are still a number of alternate forms that begin with *ji-* and *ti-*.

34.3 MORE RECENT INTRODUCTIONS FROM OTHER FIJIAN LANGUAGES

34.3.1 /z/ [nǰ]. Prenasalized voiced alveo-palatal affricate

Earlier forms of Fijian spelling did not distinguish between [č] and [nǰ], writing them both as *j*. The FDP filled a 150-year-old gap in the orthography by introducing *z* to represent [nǰ]. For example, following this convention, the word for 'ginger' is spelled *ziza*.

Since this symbol has only been a letter in the alphabet since the 1970s, one does not find it in Capell 1941. However, *VV* has 33 *z-* entries. An example of *z* in medial position: *jazi* 'chance'.

Although the sound itself—a palatalized form of /di/—exists in a number of Fijian languages, it is also used in borrowings from the following sources: English, Chinese, Lau, Hindi, and potential borrowings from Kadavu, Nadrogā, Navosa, Serua, et al.

34.3.2 /h/. Voiceless glottal fricative

The consonant *h* could also be considered a voiceless vowel, since its place of articulation varies according to the position of the following vowel.

Although most examples of *h* borrowings are from English, we have placed it in this category because it is phonemic in languages from the Nadrogā area, corresponding to SF *s*.

34.3.2.1 Discussion: *h*

Since the Fijian sound system was first analyzed (Davies 1825), the letter *h* has hovered on the periphery of the alphabet, sometimes included, usually excluded. Davies did not include it in his alphabet, but Cargill and Cross (1835) did. Moreover, they used it in the borrowed words *hevani* 'heaven' and *heli* 'hell'. As Cargill became more aware of the differences between the Lakeba language and Tongan, he included *h* as a member of the alphabet, but with special status (Cargill 1839):

> ... this letter does not occur in any word in the Feejeean language, but is inserted in the alphabet for the sake of those foreign words, which it may be necessary to introduce, as Hami, Ham.

The spelling leaf of 1840 contains *h*, complete with the syllabary *ha, he, hi, ho,* and *hu*.

From Hazlewood's time on, the letter was excluded, although as the missionaries grew more familiar with the languages to the west of the Bau-Rewa area, they realized that it did exist in Nadrogā. But in spite of its existence there, *h* has not generally been used for words borrowed into the language. Even the place name *Hawai'i* seems fixed as *Āwai*. Nor do any *h-* words appear in Hazlewood's or Capell's dictionary.

However, by the time that the FDP began combing through written materials, some examples from ENG could be included.

haya	'hire'	*haya-tak-a*	'hire it'	*hega*	'hanger'
hoki	'hockey'	*hula*	'hula'		

For some forms there are alternate spellings. For example, from a set of sixteen borrowings from English *h-*, the FDP found the following spellings:

oki / hoki	'hockey'	*afakasi / hafakasi*	'half-caste'
olo / holo	'hall'	*aleluya / haleluya*	'hallelujah'
ōsana / hōsana	'hosanna'	*ula / hula*	'hula'
ōtela / hōtela	'hotel'		

Adding considerably to this set, *VV* has 48 *h-* entries. Of these, 12 have alternate forms that begin with a vowel. Besides Fijian languages that include /h/ in their phonemic inventory, sources are borrowings from English, Hindi, Lau, Māori, and Tongan.

34.3.3 /ʔ/[15] *GATO* (GLOTTAL STOP)

Although not native to SF, the glottal stop is a significant feature of a number of other Fijian languages, particularly in the province of Rā and in parts of Vanua Levu. Thus, it was inevitable that some words from those languages should be borrowed into SF. See Tamata 2007.

VV has 42 entries beginning with ʔ-.[16]

34.3.4 /x/ Voiceless dorso-velar fricative

In a number of Fijian languages (see Schütz 1963 and the *VV* entry for *xā* for its distribution), *x* corresponds to *k*. In *VV* there are seven entries beginning with *x-*.

34.3.5 /xw/ Labialized voiceless dorso-velar fricative

This sound corresponds to *kw* in those languages that have a series of labialized velars. See Schütz 1963. The only entry in *VV* for the sound in initial position is *xwā*, which is the name of the letter. However, Bā *xwaxi* 'there by you' appears in the Introduction.

---

[15] Apparently because of font restrictions, *VV* uses an odd form of a question mark for this symbol.

[16] Because the glottal stop is not phonemic in SF, it does not precede otherwise initial vowels in borrowed words.

34.3.6 /kw/ Labialized voiceless dorso-velar stop

There are five entries for *kw-* in *VV*: four from Fijian languages other than SF, and one borrowing from ENG: *kwis* 'quiz'. In addition, *kwālevu* 'Tui Nadrogā' appears in the Introduction.

34.3.7 /qw/ Labialized voiced prenasalized dorso-velar stop

Of the six entries for *qw-* in *VV*, several are names of birds or fish from specific regions. In addition, *qwele* 'earth, dirt' appears in the Introduction.

34.3.6 /gw/ Labialized voiced dorso-velar nasal

VV has 13 entries for *gw-*, many of them plant or animal names, apparently indigenous to particular regions. In addition, *gwati* appears in the Introduction, but not as an entry.

34.4 MORE RECENT INTRODUCTIONS FROM OUTSIDE

As the previous sections demonstrate, both internal and external borrowings have affected the phonology of SF. As we will see in CH 35, some borrowings (perhaps not in SF (Standard Fijian) but in UF (Urban Fijian)[17] have even disrupted the CV syllable structure. In this section we discuss one radical change and a simple addition to the consonant inventory.

34.4.1 Voiced stops without a preceding nasal

VV includes the following innovation: borrowings /b/, /d/, and /q/ without the usual prenasalization.[18] Thus:

b (italicized) represents [b], not [mb]
d (italicized) represents [d], not [nd]
q (italicized) represents [g], not [ŋg]
z (italicized) represents [j], not [nǰ]

In the following examples, an italicized letter represents a voiced stop without a preceding nasal. To avoid confusion, Fijian forms in this list are not italicized.

*b*im	'beam'	*b*islamā	'Bislama'
*b*od*i*	'body-(building)'	*b*olpen	'ball pen'
*b*oeskaut	'boy scout'	*b*ā	'bar'
*b*a*b*ai	'bye-bye'	*q*rin	'green'
*z*ob[19]	'job'	fai*b*a	'fiber'
Fizi*b*at	'Fiji Hindi (Fiji bat)'	*z*īai	'G. I.'

---

[17] This is a tentative name for the type of Fijian that allows borrowings that do not conform to the usual phonological patterns of SF. However, because of the lack of sociolinguistic studies, it represents a hypothesis that has not yet been proved or disproved.

[18] An asymmetry in patterning is the lack of *dr*, which is phonetically [[nř]] ~ [nř̃]. However, it is rare in borrowings (*drili* 'drill' is an exception), and *VV*'s Introduction does not list a non-nasalized version of this sound among its new letters.

[19] This word appears in the Introduction but not as an entry.

This orthographical innovation is not ideal; especially in handwriting it would be difficult to make the letters in question visually distinctive, but perhaps underlining would suffice. In normal printed material, in an italicized context, if a word or letter needs to be highlighted, the usual convention is to use roman for the portion in question. In such a passage, what is now written as "b*im*" would be "b*im*." All in all, it is not a convenient convention for writers, editors, printers, and proofreaders.

34.5 NEW CONSONANTS BORROWED FROM ENGLISH

With each addition discussed above, the list of FIJ consonants—native, borrowed, and introduced—came more and more to resemble the list for ENG. Now, in terms of numbers, it has surpassed ENG: 32 vs. 24. Thus, this category is necessarily limited.

34.5.1 *sh* [š]

Note that the letters *s* and *h* already exist in written Fijian (SF and Nadrogā), but not as a cluster.[20] Here, *sh* is a combination of SF and Nadrogā. Examples are:

a|**sh**a	'usher'	ti|**sh**èt	't-shirt'	fla**sh**	'flush'
shot|hen	'shorthand'	**sh**eri	'sherry'		

34.6 ALTERNATE FORMS

Note that many entries have an alternate form that uses traditional consonants and follows the traditional syllable structure. The following list is only a sample.

*b*olpen ~ bolopeni	'ball pen'	Bositeni ~ Bostn	(a store)
bom ~ bomu	'bomb'	aitrozin ~ aitorojini	'hydrogen'
aisblok ~ aisibuloko	'ice block'	aiskirim ~ aisikirimu	'ice cream'
prentis ~ aperentisi	'apprentice'	asha ~ asa	'usher'
skuea ~ sukuea	'square'	sheri ~ seri	'sherry'
kwis ~ kuisi	'quiz'		

34.7 SOCIOLINGUISTIC CONTEXT

The existence of alternate forms such as those in §34.6 raises the important question of who is using the newly introduced consonants and in what contexts. Perhaps because changing traditional Fijian syllable structure seems more radical than introducing new consonants, this matter is discussed in the next chapter, Syllables (§35.5).

* * * * *

Table 34.2 summarizes the additions to the consonants that were used in writing up to the 1970s.

---

[20] *Sh* might be ambiguous if *-s* ended one syllable and *h-* began the next.

TABLE 34.2: RECENTLY INTRODUCED CONSONANTS[21]

	BL	LD	AD	AA	AP	DV	G
STOPS (vl)							ʔ
(lb)						kw	
- -
(vd)			*b* [b]	*d* [d]		*q* [g]	
(lb)						qw	
TRILLS/FLAPS							
FRICATIVES					sh	x	h
(lb)						xw	
(AFFRICATES)			- - -		*z* [j]		
NASALS	m		n			gw [ŋw]	

BL = bilabial   LD = labiodental   AD = apico-dental   AA = apico-alveolar
AP = alveo-palatal   DV = dorso-velar   G = glottal.
vl = voiceless   lb = labialized

---

[21] Cf. table 1.1, CH 1.

35 SYLLABLES

A syllable is the smallest rhythmic unit in the language; "rhythmic" means that it is characterized by a pulsation—a beat. Formally, it is composed of a vowel peak, which may be preceded by a consonant. Functionally, a syllable is a constituent of the next larger phonological unit—the measure.

Figure 35.1 is a rough representation of syllable peaks of different intensities. It reflects these variables: measure accent, phrase accent, and content form vs. grammatical marker.

FIGURE 35.1: SYLLABLE AND PHRASE PEAKS

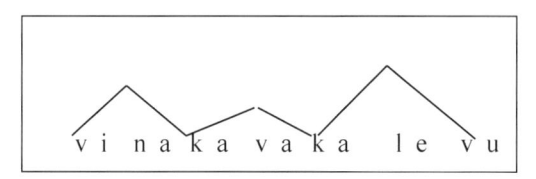

In figure 35.1, the highest peak represents the sentence and phrase peak, the peak of the measure |levu|, and the peak of the syllable /le/. Similarly, the other two peaks represent both measure and syllable peaks.[1]

35.1 TYPES OF SYLLABLES

Coincidentally, all of the syllables in figure 35.1 are of the type that is most frequent: CV (a consonant and a vowel).[2] But because a vowel alone can also

---

[1] This rough diagram represents peaks more clearly than boundaries. For example, it does not show clearly where the syllable divisions are, except at the beginning and the end of the phrase. These points are crucial, for they show that although phonetically each consonant in the middle of the phrase might serve as the border for two adjacent syllables, phonologically the consonant begins a syllable and a vowel ends it.

[2] Even a casual examination of a Fijian text or dictionary shows that CV is by far the favored syllable type. (The vowel can be short, long, or a diphthong.) Certain features in the language today, such as diphthongization, can be considered the result of moving toward more CV syllables. But still, V syllables do occur, and, as mentioned above, a more accurate symbolization of a syllable is (C)V. But to avoid the awkwardness of the

serve as a syllable, the canonical form of syllables must be symbolized as (C)V. In other words, a syllable consists of a consonant plus a vowel, or a vowel alone.

Syllables can be further classified according to the types of vowels or vowel sequences that can represent V in the formula (C)V. We can use the same classification as we used for vowels—a two-way classification into short vs. long, and simple vs. complex, shown in figure 35.2 (repeating figure 33.1).

FIGURE 35.2: HIERARCHICAL ARRANGEMENT OF PHONOLOGICAL UNITS

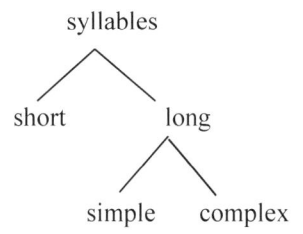

```
              syllables
              /       \
          short       long
                      /   \
                  simple   complex
```

The terms "short" and "long" here refer principally to duration, but there are other phonetic mechanisms at work as well, discussed in CH 33.

35.2 INTEGRATED SYLLABLES

Perceptual evidence for the existence of the syllable as a valid phonological unit involves the ability of Fijian speakers to recognize syllable peaks as pulsations or peaks of prominence in a stretch of speech and to count them. In fact, under certain conditions, these pulsations—or beats—take precedence over the requirement that a vowel peak be present in each syllable. For example, there are certain syllables, called integrated syllables here, that can be greatly altered in phonetic shape when they are not accented. An integrated syllable with a continuant as the onset (e.g. /si/, /mu/, /vu/) may be realized as a lengthened consonant: [s:], [m:], [ß:]. Those with other types of onsets may become totally voiceless: phonetically, /ti/ can be [ti̥] or [či̥]. Obviously, in these phonetic manifestations, one can no longer use the vowel peak as a criterion for syllabicity, because there is no such peak. But the beat goes on; [leß:] for /levu/ still has two syllables in slower speech, as does [nom:] for /nomu/.[3] This apparent discrepancy merely points out the difference between the phonetic and phonological definitions of the syllable.

The canonical form of the syllable seems paramount in what constitutes the "Fijian-ness" of the sound of the various indigenous languages in Fiji. So far as we know, Fijian languages vary considerably in their consonant systems, but not in canonical form of syllables or measures (at least for indigenous words and older borrowings; see §35.4 ff). Work on the phonological structure of phrases

---

parentheses in each representation, we omit them unless calling attention to initial vowels or vowel sequences across syllable boundaries.

[3] However, at some point further along the continuum from SF to very casual speech, the length of the consonant vanishes.

is not advanced enough to be conclusive. At any rate, note the "unfamiliar" consonants in [čū-ŋgwā-ŋgwā] (hyphens separate syllables)—the equivalent of SF *qase* 'old person' in a number of western languages. Because it retains a CV syllable structure, it is likely that it sounds "more Fijian" than a word that takes SF consonants and vowels and puts them in an unfamiliar order or in new combinations—discussed in §35.4.

35.3 TWO MAJOR INTERPRETATIONS OF FIJIAN SYLLABLES

Different trends in the interpretation of syllables in various Oceanic languages have had their effect on Fijian linguistics. For the most part, the trends are based on the interpretation of long syllables—those containing long vowels or diphthongs.

35.3.1 The phonetic syllable: An interpretation based on auditory impression

A major problem with the description of the Fijian syllable has been the potential of interpreting long vowels and certain vowel combinations as either one syllable or two. Opinions on this matter fall into two chronological groups: 1835–1941, and the period following. Although in Cargill's grammatical sketch (1839), he mentioned syllables only indirectly (indicating that two consonants do not occur together), his concept of syllable structure appeared a few years earlier in the primer that he and William Cross prepared before they left Tonga for Fiji. In this work, all monosyllables end in a vowel. However, we have no idea how he would have divided some longer forms, such as *andra* [*yadra* 'morning, awake'], into syllables.

Later grammarians (e.g., Hale, Hazlewood, and Churchward) extended Cargill's description to note that each syllable had to end in a vowel. Moreover, Hazlewood interpreted the prefix *vei-* as one syllable, thereby implicitly including diphthongs as possible syllable nuclei.

But in the same decade as the publication of Churchward's grammar (the 1940s), another point of view was developed—one we might call the phonological syllable.

35.3.2 The phonological syllable: An interpretation based on a possible underlying structure

Scott (1948) was the first to propose (implicitly) that Fijian syllables could be analyzed according to an underlying structure and that it was unnecessary to posit diphthongs or long vowels in order to describe the phonology. This is not to say that he denied the existence of diphthongs on a phonetic level. On the contrary—his discussion of diphthongs is detailed and accurate.[4] But after treating the phonetic nature of vowel sequences, he abandoned the concept of diphthongs and long vowels in favor of another interpretation: in a sequence of vowels (like or unlike), each comprises a separate syllable. His main argument rests

---

[4] For example, he noted the raising of /a/ when followed by /i/ or /u/.

on the functional similarity of CV̄ and CVV to CVCV in their composition of accent measures.

Milner also based his syllable on the underlying structure (1972:6):

> Length is a matter of syllables rather than vowels. That is to say, when a syllable ending with a certain vowel is followed by another syllable with the same vowel, but without a consonant, both syllables are pronounced as if they were one syllable with a long vowel ... Two degrees of length will be discussed and reference will be made to short and "long" vowels (or syllables) but the student should remember that a "long" vowel or syllable is actually produced by two identical short vowels and syllables.

Another treatment based on the one-syllable-per-vowel interpretation is Hockett's (1955:55):[5] "In Fijian there is a set of five vocoids, /i e a o u/, which occur only and always as peaks; and every peak consists of one or another of these five ... In Fijian, a sequence of two identical vocoids is structurally quite like a sequence of two different vocoids."[6]

Cammack (1962:27) carried on with the solution that had by now become orthodox: the distinction between phonetic and phonological syllables:

> Where two like vowels occur in succession (not separated by an onset) as in the second and third syllables of *ki.la.a*,[7] the second of the two constitutes a separate syllable by definition, but is phonetically merely a prolongation of the preceding vowel. The second and third syllables of *ki.la.a*, with unchanged vowel color, take the same length of time as the second and third syllables of *vi.na.ka*, where the final syllable includes an onset.[8]

35.3.3 Summary of the orthodox position

Most modern analysts have assumed that the Fijian syllable consists of a vowel alone or one with a preceding consonant. Such a description has certain advantages. First, with the kind of modified orthography exemplified by Cammack (1962)—that in which long vowels are written as geminate clusters—macrons are unnecessary. In addition, one small part of the description of accent is simplified: if *ā* is written as /aa/, its accent can be considered "regular" penultimate accent. Thus, if *wāwā* 'wait' is interpreted as four syllables, the two ac-

---

[5] At the time Hockett wrote this description, he had access only to Churchward's grammar and had never heard the language spoken. Later, he revised his opinion of Fijian phonology (p.c., 3/77).

[6] As I show later, this statement is disproved by vowel-shortening patterns of potential diphthongs and long vowels, which are not shared by other vowel sequences.

[7] In Cammack's notation, periods separate syllables.

[8] It is difficult to find the source of the idea that a long vowel is twice the duration of a short vowel, or equal in length to any other combination of two "syllables." As Condax's research (e.g., 1979) has shown, the perceptual and acoustic views of duration do not always match. Unfortunately, linguists continue to repeat the assertion either without any supporting evidence, or with acoustic measurements that compare the wrong elements.

cents can be described as penultimate and "on alternate preceding syllables", a phrase that often but erroneously (see Schütz 1978c) comprises the totality of the statement about accent in some grammars of Oceanic languages.

Next, a (C)V interpretation of the syllable simplifies the typology of measure types; it allowed Scott to set up only two types: those referred to in the present study as even and uneven (see the introduction to CH 36).

In principle, there seems to be nothing wrong with a phonological interpretation of the syllable. As a matter of fact, perhaps insisting on a universal phonetic definition kept many linguists from recognizing the syllable as a valid phonological unit.

Moreover, the interpretation of V̄ as VV is valid with respect to the historical development of some (but not all) long vowels.

But however satisfactory the simplistic phonological-syllable solution may be for accounting for the history of some long vowels, it is at great variance with one's[9] auditory impression of the number of syllables one hears. More important, it ignores a very important phonological feature—the shortening of long vowels and potential diphthongs in certain positions that allows us to say that both these long/complex vowels FUNCTION the same as short vowels when they occur in the accented position in disyllabic measures. It is becoming apparent from the study of vowel length in other languages (e.g., Stemberger 1984) that it is a phenomenon more closely associated with prosodic (that is, suprasegmental) than segmental features.

Parallel to interpreting V̄ as VV (and two syllables) is interpreting any sequence of two vowels, including potential diphthongs, as two syllables. As the discussion of diphthongs (§33.2.2.1) shows, this point of view ignores that different sequences function differently in terms of prosody. Therefore, although it may simplify the description, this is a false kind of simplification, since it obscures important facts about the language.

35.4 CHANGES TO THE TRADITIONAL SYLLABLE STRUCTURE

VV contains a number of new borrowings, mostly from English and Hindi,[10] and perhaps more from oral than written sources, that disturb the traditional (C)V SF syllable pattern. The patterns described below may be defining features for the hypothetical concept introduced earlier, Urban Fijian (UF).

---

[9] The argument here is rather difficult to prove; it depends, of course, on how we define the syllable. For example, if it depends primarily on duration, rather than on pulsation, syllable counting becomes much more difficult, and there might be little agreement among native speakers.

[10] I have singled out these two languages, rather than Fijian languages other than SF, Tongan, or Māori, because they have syllable structures quite different from (C)V. Even borrowings from Western Fijian languages with *kw*, *gw*, and other labialized consonants still adhere to the (C)V pattern, since those written clusters represent unit phonemes.

35.4.1 Syllable-final consonants

Note the alternation *fom ~ fomu* 'form'. The first spelling seems inconsistent, since SF, in all but the most formal style, reduces the final syllable /-mu/ to [mː], as in *nomu* [nomː] 'your'. It is unlikely that the spelling *nom would be recommended for the native form. Another example is *fès ~ fèsi*[11] 'first (rugby term)'. Similar to the deletion of /-u/ and the lengthening of the preceding /m/, a native word such as *masi* 'tapa' is often pronounced [masː]. Again, it is unlikely that it would be written *mas (see §35.2).

In the following list from *VV*, the syllable-final consonant is bolded. (Syllabic final consonant are treated in §35.4.3.) Where necessary, syllables are separated by "|".

*b*i**m**	beam	boeskau**t**	boy scout
*b*ol|pen	ball-point pen	bo**m**	bomb
Bos|tn	Boston	*b*ies|sī	BSc
ag|kl	uncle	aitrozi**n**	hydrogen
ais	ice	ais|kirim	ice cream
ākai**v**	archives	alam|klok	alarm clock
al|*b*am	album	pren|tis	apprentice
au**t**	out (sporting term)	pres|ap	press-up
*q*rin	green	zo**b**	job
sle**k**	slack	shot|hen	shorthand
kwi**s**	quiz	Fog|hun	Fong Hoon
fo**c**	fourth		

35.4.1.1 Resultant consonant combinations

One of the results of a nonfinal syllable ending with a consonant is a consonant combination (as opposed to a cluster; see §35.4.2). It is composed of consonants that are adjacent but belong to different syllables: the first as a syllable coda and the second as a syllable onset.

pren|tis	apprentice	*b*is|lamā	Bislama	an|ti	aunty
*b*ol|pen	ball pen	bies|sī	BSc		
ais|blok	ice block[12]	ais|kirim	ice cream[13]		
al|*b*am	album	elikop|ta	helicopter		

---

[11] Although the *VV* entries for these forms are spelled with *e*, according to the Introduction, it should be *è* (*e* with an accent grave).

[12] Shouldn't the *b* in this word be italicized—that is, pronounced without a preceding nasal?

[13] Note that the forms *kirimi* and *kirimu* 'cream' appear as entries. See the discussion of /-mu/ in §35.5.1.

35.4.2 Consonant clusters

Consonant clusters are sequences of consonants within one syllable. In the following examples, clusters are marked with boldface, and to avoid confusion, combinations (as in the previous section) are broken up with "|"

35.4.2.1 Syllable-initial clusters

As the following examples show, some common ENG initial clusters are reflected in some varieties of Fijian:

boe**sk**aut	boy scout	**pr**aima	primer
ai**tr**ozin	hydrogen	ais|**bl**ok	ice block
alam|**kl**ok	alarm clock	ase**bl**ī[14]	assembly
prem	pram	**pr**esap	press-up
qrin	green	**sk**uea	square
slek	slack	**tr**ektā	tractor

35.4.2.2 Syllable-final clusters

| fisi**ks** | physics | Alai**ns** | Alliance |
| fre**ns** | friends | | |

35.4.3 Syllabic consonants

The following examples show a syllable-final (and word-final) consonant that serves as the nucleus of a syllable. (A syllabic consonant must be a continuant.)

| Bos\|**tn** | Boston | ag\|**kl** | uncle |

35.5 SOCIOLINGUISTIC CONTEXT[15]

The changes to Fijian's syllable system described and exemplified in the previous section, alongside alternate words that conform to the unchanged CV syllable structure, raise important questions: Who uses the traditional forms and who uses the new ones? In what contexts is one type chosen over the other? In which media are the forms used? The answers to these questions involve the following oppositions or continua, among others:

1. Speech vs. writing
2. Regional dialectal
3. Generational: younger speakers vs. older speakers
4. Formal vs. informal speech
5. Innovative vs. conservative[16]
6. Urban vs. rural (also related to innovative vs. conservative)
7. Degree of control of English

It is obvious that some of these sets are interrelated. For example: regional and

---

[14] Note that whereas the components of /b/ ([mb]) belong to separate syllables in the English model, the unit is a syllable onset in the Fijian form.

[15] Note that this discussion expands §34.7.

[16] See §24.2 and subsections for discussions of *p* vs. *v*, *f* vs. *v*, et al.

urban/rural; generational and innovative/conservative; regional and control of English.

We now examine several of these points.

35.5.1 Speech vs. writing

With respect to spoken and written Fijian, Apolonia Tamata wrote (p.c., 10 January 2012):

> I don't think those new consonant forms will appear in written [material] as they only appear in speech, like *kreya* for *kereya*.

Her example illustrates the effect of consonant clusters on syllable structure. Moreover, they can affect the length of an utterance: here, as a result of a consonant cluster, a trisyllable (*kereya*) has been reduced to a disyllable (*kreya*).)

We are fortunate to have an excellent source of data that combines speech and writing. Seeking examples in context of several of the oppositions above, I searched through most of a recent work, the play *Lakovi* (Tamata and Thomas 2011), which appears in both written and DVD form (cf. #1 above). Moreover, it touches on some of the other oppositions, containing examples of different degrees of closeness to or distance from SF.

The most striking contrast stems from the organization of the work as a whole. The play opens and closes with formal, structured ceremonies—an introduction at the beginning, and supplements at the end, rather like bookends around the drama itself. In these more formal portions, although the spoken version contains some of the shortening features associated with rapid speech, the syllable structure in the printed version conforms to the traditional CV syllable structure of SF.

The dialog in the drama, however, is a different matter. The following examples and discussion show several types of variation (numbers correspond to the list just above; numbers in parentheses refer to page numbers in the printed version).

35.5.2 Regional and stylistic variation

Reflecting both these categories, I found *jiko* (pp. 10, 28) as a variation of SF *tiko* 'stay' and *seji* (33) for *seti*. Another kind of stylistic variation is the shortening of the prefix *vaka-*. For example, SF *vakacava* 'how?' appears in its longer form, but also as *vacava* (29).[17]

35.5.3 Generational differences and Urban Fijian

Another opposition is based on the relative ages of the characters. There is a distinct difference in the speech of the younger performers in Act I as opposed to several in Act II, who portray 'father', 'mother', 'aunt', 'grandfather' (as indicated in the *dramatis personae*).

---

[17] Apolonia Tamata confirmed (p.c., 27 May 2013) that the form may shorten not only to *vācava* but also to *vacava*.

The following words, all from Act I, illustrate the phonological changes taking place in younger, urban speech (page numbers are in parentheses).

(18)	*boefren*	'boyfriend'
	fren	'friend'
	gelfren	'girl friend'
	zob	'job'
	set	'okay, all right'
	borig	'boring'
(19)	*hausgel*	'house girl'
	skaip	'Skype'
(20)	*kompiuta*	'computer'
(22)	*stabi*	'stubby (beer bottle)'
(27)	*frens*	'friends (pl.)'
(30)	*Sa lus tiko*	
	e dua na skru.	'There's a screw loose.'[18]
(34)	*agkl*	'uncle'
(35)	*turis*	'tourists'
(33)	*seji*	*seti* (exclamation)[19]
(39)	*Krismas*	'Christmas'[20]
(40)	*Blekae*	'black eye'

35.5.4 Formal vs. informal

This category is well illustrated through the organization described above: the formal "bookends" around informal conversations, especially those among younger people (thus overlapping with #3).

35.5.5 Innovative vs. conservative

This category overlaps with all the preceding ones.

35.5.6 Urban vs. rural

Lakovi contains few overt clues to the regional backgrounds of the protagonists in the drama.[21]

35.5.7 Control of English

Another useful feature of *Lakovi* is that unassimilated English words are set off by quotation marks. For example, the following list contains just some of these words in a conversation between Kristin and Mela (pp. 33–37):

"bridesmaid"	"dress"	"straight"	"mother"
"take after my father"	"gold mine"	"Fijian side"	"Fijian style"
"husband"	"British Army"	"Excuse me. I may look"	

---

[18] Note this literal translation of an English idiom.
[19] Here, *j* represents [č], both a dialectal and a stylistic variation.
[20] Capell 1941 has *Siga ni Sucu*.
[21] See, however, pp. 33–35 for the origins of Kristin's family and her language.

This practice sets up a hierarchy of degrees of assimilation of loanwords into the language—i.e., English spelling and quotation marks, full assimilation to SF with CV structure, and finally, truncated forms with consonant clusters and syllable-final consonants.

But the situation may be more complex than it appears. Take *dress*, for example (p. 33). The context is that K is going to be a bridesmaid for a wedding and will be "dressed" *vakaViti*—'Fijian style'. But *vakaisulu* could have been used for 'dressed'. Does using *dress* suggest that as a loanword it might eventually replace *vakaisulu*? It is more likely that it serves as an identity badge to give us more sociolinguistic information about the character.

* * * * *

It is not necessarily discouraging that this last section asks more questions than it answers. On the contrary, it shows that Fijian sociolinguistics is a rich field for investigation, and that there is a wealth of data to be analyzed —from both expected and unexpected sources.

36 MEASURES AND ACCENT

CH 32 introduced the concept of the MEASURE: its form and its function in word building, especially with respect to combinations of different types of morphemes. In this chapter, we take a more detailed look at measures —their various shapes, the changes that can take place when they are combined, and the role of the concept in describing Fijian accent. Accent is not, of course, a unit in the phonological hierarchy. But because it is the principal defining feature of the measure, we treat the topics together.

Incidentally, using the term "accent" in this work as opposed to "stress" is deliberate. Years ago, Charles F. Hockett described the difference between the two terms as phonological versus phonetic. In other words, "accent" refers to a feature in the sound system of a language, and "stress" to one of its phonetic manifestations. This view is not noncontroversial, but it is a legitimate one, confirmed in Fox 2000:115:

> In the present book, "accent" is intended as the most neutral superordinate term, to refer to the linguistic phenomenon in which a particular element in the chain of speech is singled out in relation to surrounding elements, irrespective of the means by which this is achieved.

In CH 33 we commented on the phonetic components of accent. As in many other languages, accent in Fijian is an as-yet-unmeasured bundle of features: mainly amplitude, pitch, and length. Moreover, an accented syllable is less susceptible to changes in position conditioned by surrounding sounds.

As for pitch differences, the situation becomes more complicated: especially in disyllables as citation forms, an accented syllable is usually higher in pitch than the following unaccented syllable—at least with the intonation associated with statements. However, in longer words and phrases, often the syllable that precedes it, especially when the accented syllable is the peak of a phonological phrase, is slightly higher in pitch, even though lower in amplitude. For example, the word *vinaka* 'good' is often a phrase in itself. Although /na/ is the accented syllable, the preceding syllable /vi/, although lower in amplitude, is often higher in pitch, giving the whole phrase a downward stair-step pitch pattern.[1]

---

[1] This pattern can be confusing to speakers of some other languages, especially Japanese, in which pitch is the principal component of accent. See §38.1.1, footnote 5.

36.1 MEASURE TYPES

If we examine any common utterance in the language that contains only one accented syllable, we find that it falls into one of the four types shown in table 36.1. ((C) represents an optional consonant,[2] and V̄ can represent either a long vowel or a diphthong.)

TABLE 36.1: MEASURE TYPES

1. (C)V́(C)V	2. (C)V̄́	3. (C)V(C)V́(C)V	4. (C)V(C)V̄́
io 'yes'	*oi* (excl.)	*vinaka* 'good'	*e sō* 'some'
sega 'no'	*ō* (excl.)	*e sega* 'no'[3]	*e cā* 'it's bad'
bula 'hello'	*ā* (excl.)	*baleta* 'why'	*e vei* 'where?'
moce 'goodbye'	*ū* (excl.)		*o cei* 'who?'
talo 'pour'	*mai* 'come'		*i vei* 'where?'
lako 'go'			*segai* 'no'
kua 'don't'			
maca 'dry, empty''			
veka 'excrement'			

The formulae at the top of the table can be restated in prose: Fijian has the following measure types:

1. Two short syllables, with accent on the penultimate.   E.g., *búla*.
2. A long syllable (simple or complex), accented.   E.g., *tū́, mái*.
3. Three short syllables, with accent on the penultimate.   E.g., *vináka*.
4. A short syllable followed by an accented long one.   E.g., *oyā́, cakáu*.

We could also reorganize the list to group #1 and #2 together as bimoraic units (one long syllable or two short syllables), and then #3 and #4 as trimoraic units. Thus, their distinguishing characteristic is the absence or presence of the short onset syllable that appears in the second group. The first type we call EVEN; the second, UNEVEN. The significance of this distinction is that even measures are capable of accepting another short syllable at the beginning. For an uneven measure to do so, some realignment must take place. (See §39.3 for a more detailed discussion of the different behavior of these two types.)

---

[2] In this group, the second consonant is not always optional, as noted in §32.4. For example, deleting it from the disyllable *bula* 'hello' yields *bua* 'k.o. tree', another disyllable. But deleting the medial consonant in the disyllable *masu* 'pray' yields *mau* 'marry', a monosyllable. And if the vowels are identical, the result is a long vowel. Strictly speaking, each vowel pair should be listed separately, but for the sake of simplicity, this has not been done here.

[3] As this form and five others in the table show, a phrase, as well as a word, can consist of just one measure.

In the examples in table 36:1, each measure can be a separate utterance. Two conclusions follow:

1. Any stretch of speech shorter than these examples—i.e., a short syllable—cannot be an utterance on its own. Support for this statement lies in the lengthened citation forms of grammatical markers that consist of a short syllable. For example, when the ablative marker *i* is cited out of context, the syllable is lengthened, as in this example:

"Q: *O ā kaya "ī" sē "mai"*?   'Did you say "*ī*" or "*mai*"?'
A: *"Ī."*   '"*Ī*."'

Other examples of lengthened monosyllables in isolation are the names of the letters of the alphabet (the name for each letter is a long syllable: *ā*, *bā*, *cā*, etc.) and syllabic oral spelling[4] (*vī-nā-kā* for *vinaka* 'good').

2. Any stretch of speech longer than the examples above consists of more than one measure. These combinations show that accented and unaccented syllables do not occur randomly, but instead, in regular patterns. For example, sequences of two unaccented syllables or two accented syllables in succession (in boldface) occur only across measure boundaries (which are marked by raised periods):

ˌvia·to'toka	'want to be beautiful'
ˌbī· 'bī	'heavy'
ˌmā·'**ma**ca	'dry'

Such restrictions point to this conclusion: any form longer than the words or phrases in table 36:1 is made up of a series of measures.

In addition to the patterns of accented and unaccented syllables revealed by examining utterances for their measure structure, the concept throws a number of other phonological processes into sharper relief, or provides an explanation that is missing in other approaches. The following sections discuss some of these topics from the point of view of how certain elements function in measures..

36.2 DIPHTHONGIZATION AS A MEANS OF SHORTENING BASES

Whether or not certain vowel sequences, such as *ai*, *au*, and others, are diphthongs has long been debated. In this work, although the controversy is described, the answer is clear. For example, the sequence *ai* in *raica* 'see it' and *au* in *kauta* 'bring it' are diphthongs.[5] This interpretation is based on what many other analysts seem to ignore: **function**. In the penultimate position in a measure, the sequences *ai* and *au* function as a single unit. That they result, historically or otherwise, from an underlying sequence of two vowels is irrelevant.

---

[4] Syllabic oral spelling is sometimes used in place of letter-by-letter spelling. Syllable by syllable, the word *vinaka* is spelled /vī-nā-kā/; letter by letter, it is spelled /vā-ī-nā-ā-kā-ā/. Note that in both systems, each resultant syllable, or letter-name, must be lengthened so that it can be a measure in length.

[5] Except in some dialects, such as Lau, or in a slow, artificial pronunciation of SF.

Note the following two examples (hyphens separate syllables):

1. *ra-i-ca*   (uneven)   (From Lau or very slow SF)
2. *rai-ca*   (even)   (Normal SF pronunciation)

Form #1 is a trisyllable, classified as uneven. If a monosyllabic marker, such as *e* 'he/she' precedes it, the resultant form is four syllables long, and its measure alignment is as follows:

era·ica   two even measures

However, if *e* precedes #2, an even form, the resultant form is three syllables long—thus, one uneven measure: *eraica*.

This type of shortening is effected by simple realignment of measures. However, in #2 and the example just above, *ai* shortens because of its position in the measure. This type of shortening (see §36.3.2) and others are described in the next sections.

36.3 VOWEL AND DIPHTHONG SHORTENING

A prominent feature of Fijian phonology is the shortening of long vowels, both simple and complex (see CH 33), obligatorily in certain positions and optionally in others. The following sections describe this process.

36.3.1 Shortening of simple long vowels

Scott (1948:741n, 744) was apparently the first to report that long vowels do not occur in the penultimate syllable of a measure (or word, or phrase). So powerful is this restriction that when one of several morphological processes adds a short syllable to a word that consists of or ends with a long syllable, the long syllable regularly shortens to conform to measure structure.

The following examples show one form from each of the most common types:[6] (1) an inalienable noun followed by a short possessive suffix:

bū 'grandmother' + *qu* 'my' → *bu-qu*, not **bū-qu*

and (2) a verb followed by a one-syllable transitive suffix:

tā 'chop' + *y-a* (transitive, third person singular object)→ *ta-ya*, not **tāya*

(Forms such as *tā-taka* 'chop with it' suggest that the morpheme with the long vowel, not the short vowel, is the underlying one. Moreover, there are no content forms that consist of a short syllable alone.)

Other examples are:

bē 'irreverent'	*be-ca* 'act irreverently to him'
cā 'bad'	*ca-ta* 'hate her'
kō 'gargle'	*ko-ra* 'gargle (+throat)'
mū 'buttocks'	*mu-na* 'his/her buttocks'

In short (so to speak), any form that consists of one long syllable will shorten when a one-syllable suffix is added to it.

---

[6] See §36.6 for examples of other types.

36.3.2 Shortening of complex long vowels (diphthongs)

Just as simple long vowels shorten when they are followed by an unaccented syllable, so do the seven complex long vowels (diphthongs): *ai, au, ei, eu, ou, oi*, and *iu*.

The auditory impression of diphthong shortening has been verified by acoustic measurement. In her experiments, Iovanna D. Condax found different lengths of the sequence *au* in different positions in the word, which, in these examples, also corresponds to a measure (p.c., 3 February 1995):

All means are for 10 repetitions of the word embedded in a sentence.

1st sentence:

kau $\bar{X} = 97.00$
sd = 4.35

kauta $\bar{X} = 63.40$
sd = 4.43

2nd sentence:

kau $\bar{X} = 97.40$
sd = 7.18

kauta $\bar{X} = 56.60$
sd = 5.34

(sd = standard deviation)

For confirmation of diphthong shortening from another linguist (based, one assumes, on auditory impressions, not measurement), see Arms 1989:5. Using *raica* 'see it' as an example, he noted:

... [in *raica*] the *i* combines with the previous syllable to provide one short syllable *rai*. It is only in this context however that *rai* is short; in the forms *rai* 'see, seem', *rairai* 'seem' the *rai* combination is long and equivalent to two syllables[7] phonologically even though pronounced phonetically in a diphthongal way.

In the following examples, although length is not marked, each potential diphthong is shortened when followed by a short syllable that ends the measure:[8]

tau	'fall'	*tauca*	'fall on it'	*kou*	'call'	*kouva*	'call him'
rai	'see'	*raica*	'see it'	*boi*	'smell'	*boica*	'smell it'
ceu	'carved'	*ceuta*	'carve it'	*biu*	'left'	*biuta*	'leave it'
bei	'accuse'	*seila*	'cataract'	*kau*	'carried'	*kauta*	'carry it'

---

[7] In Arms's analysis, long vowels and diphthongs are treated as two syllables (i.e. moras).

[8] Note that neither the writing system (if long vowels are marked) nor a phonemic transcription shows this shortening. In an attempt to show it regularly, I marked long diphthongs in *TFL*. Unfortunately, this was overkill, since the potential shortening of a diphthong is predictable by its position in the measure.

Sequences with the opposite order (higher to lower vowel: *ua, ia, ue, ie, uo, io*) function not as one unit, but as two, and hence do not shorten (see §33.2.2; Schütz 2000). There is some disagreement about vowels at the same height—e.g., *iu* and *ui*. As mentioned in §33.5, *oe* and *eo* historically underwent changes and are now uncommon.

In fact, it is the shortening of potential diphthongs that serves as a defining feature for "diphthong," since in other than measure-penultimate position, there are no criteria for determining whether or not, for example, *ai* (as in *mai* 'hither') or *au* (as in *dau* 'expert') functions as a unit (see §33.2.2.1). This is the reason that elsewhere I referred to such sequences (out of context) as potential diphthongs. See §36.3.4.2.

It should be noted that unlike the contrast between short and long simple vowels, the shortening of diphthongs is not contrastive. In other words, there are no minimal pairs for short and long diphthongs.

36.3.3 Realignment of measures through vowel and diphthong shortening

The examples in the previous two sections show that long vowels and diphthongs shorten within a measure—and a word. The process can apply across word boundaries as well, realigning the measures. For example, a slow, precise pronunciation of the phrase:

Sā + vinaka   'It is good.'
ASP   good

produces the following sequence of measures:

sā·vinaka

But in faster (normal) speech, perhaps on the analogy of the vowel shortening that occurs in forms like *buqu* and *taya* (see §36.3.1), the unaccented onset syllable *vi* attaches to the preceding *sā*, with the result that *sā* shortens, forming the following measure division:

savi·naka

Still, the potential for length remains, and rather than write the morpheme *sā* (or any other long syllable that occurs in such a position) two different ways, we use the long syllable as a base form. In such positions, vowel length is more like a rheostat than an on-off switch, contrasting with the strict prohibition against long vowels in the penultimate syllable of a measure.

Since the phonological structure of *sā vinaka* can be indicated in two ways:

sā·vinaka   savi·naka

we are presented with an indeterminacy in the description. That is, to which measure does the syllable *vi* belong? One way to resolve (or perhaps avoid) this dilemma is to use the concept of INTERLUDES (Hockett 1958:86). Hockett used the term with respect to the occasional difficulty in deciding whether certain consonants or sequences of consonants (in English) belong to the preceding or following syllable. On this analogy, we could consider that since the measure division in such forms as those above is indeterminate, the syllable *vi* would not necessarily belong to one measure or the other, but would be an interlude.

On the other hand, since sā·vinaka is the form that appears in slow, careful speech, it may be more convenient to view that pattern as a base form, thus moving the *vi* problem to the area of casual speech. In other words, in some styles, *vi* belongs to the preceding measure; in other styles, to the following one.

36.3.4 The effects of vowel and diphthong shortening

Vowel shortening can affect more than just the measure in question. The following sections show some of the results of this process.

36.3.4.1 Reducing the number of syllables

It was noted in §36.2 that in careful (perhaps exaggerated), slow speech, *raica* 'see it' consists of three syllables. The processes of diphthongization (reducing the sequence *a* + *i* to a unit *ai*, which is then shortened) shortens a trisyllable to a disyllable.

36.3.4.2 Reducing the number of V syllables

A corollary to the preceding observation is that diphthongization decreases the number of syllables that consist of a vowel alone and increases the number that have the shape CV. An example is *kauta* 'carry it'. As mentioned earlier, in some varieties of Fijian, it is pronounced as three syllables, with the shape CV-V-CV. With diphthongization and shortening of the *au* sequence, the word now has two syllables, with the shape CV-CV.

It follows from the discussion of the measure that CV is favored over V as a syllable type: It is more common and more resistant to change.

The matters just discussed introduce a further complication: do we interpret a measure of the shape CVV as one or two syllables? In a sense, this kind of measure is indeterminate with respect to the number of syllables, but we can make some arbitrary decisions:

1. There seems to be little reason to call CV̄, as in *vā* 'four', two syllables (see the discussion in §35.4.3). Therefore, it can be considered one long syllable.

2. Because sequences classified as potential diphthongs are phonetically long in certain environments, and short in others, and because this pattern is the same as that for long vowels, we call sequences like *rai*, *kau*, and *tei*—when they constitute separate measures—long syllables, just like *bā* , *cā* , or *gā*.

3. Because vowel sequences other than potential diphthongs never shorten (i.e., never act as a unit), they are classified as disyllables. Examples are *via*, *kua*, and *bui*.

36.3.4.3 Reducing the number of measures

In Schütz 1983, I discussed the ways in which Fijian loanwords from English are accented to match the model most closely. Aside from dropping syllables, the principal means available is to lengthen a syllable to "attract the accent."

Thus, *Tēvita* (tē·vita) 'David' is the accepted form, rather than **Tevita* (one measure), since the latter has an accent pattern (*Tevíta*) rather unlike that of the model.

However, today one can hear *Tevíta*, as well as these other shortened forms:

bē·leti	→	beleti	'belt'
bī·kini	→	bikini	'beacon'
bō·nisi	→	bonisi	'bonus'

This pattern suggests that as the borrowed forms become more and more Fijian in the minds of the speakers, and the English models fade into the background, it becomes less important to match the accent pattern of the model. One might also suggest that such shortening is acceptable when no information is lost.

If this process applies to indigenous words as well, it might explain why there is an alternation between such forms as:

nō·daru ~ nodaru   'our (dual inclusive)'[9]

However, it should be noted that this shortening is not conditioned and is therefore irregular. That is, the long syllable is not followed by a short unaccented one to combine with, as in:

sā·vinaka → savi·naka

and there is no realignment of measures. Instead, a two-measure form (*nō·daru*) Is shortened to one measure (*nodaru*).

In a sense, the description of vowel shortening just above and in previous sections is only a beginning, and is limited to fairly formal speech. To see how the process continues, refer to Tamata 1994. For example (p. 13), she noted the shortening of mā·maca 'dry' through these stages: [mamáca] to [m:áca] and finally, [máca], showing a continuum of styles from formal speech to casual speech. With respect to length, the form morphs from two measures to one measure.

36.3.4.4 Movement toward CVCV—the optimum measure type

In the *sā vinaka* example above, we saw that a phrase consisting of two different types of measures—a long syllable followed by a trisyllable—changes into two disyllabic measures. We now discuss measures from the point of view of phrase-building. In the following discussion, the morphological type of particular forms plays an important role, but we are concerned here with the phonological effects of various combinations.

As a general principle that covers various phenomena at this phonological level, I suggest the following: certain types of measures seem to be favored over other types. One can draw such a conclusion after noting the behavior of particular shapes of morphemes when combined (as discussed above). For example:

---

[9] Also, as mentioned in §34.2.1, in some Fijian languages, the antepenultimate vowel varies in length.

1. When two morphemes with the shape CV and CVCVCV are combined in a phrase, two dissyllabic measures are automatically formed, since a measure cannot consist of a single short syllable.[10] Thus:

me + *balavu* → meba·lavu 'let it be long'

2. When two morphemes with the shape CV̄ and CVCVCV (or CVCV̄) are combined, the first syllable *can* shorten to combine with the following one, forming two measures of the type CVCV·CVCV or CVCV·CV̄. For example:

sā + *vinaka*	→	savi·naka	'It's good.'
sā + *kilā*	→	saki·lā	'She knows it.'
sē + *ni* + *kau*	→	seni·kau	'flower'

(As mentioned before, the long vowels may retain their length in slow, careful speech.)

36.3.4.4.1 The effect of diphthongization on the number of CVCV forms

Diphthongization significantly increases the number of CVCV forms[11] available. Looking again at the example from §36.2, we see that the trisyllable *ra-i-ca* is reduced to a disyllable *rai-ca*. When the process is applied to the total lexicon, the effect is significant. Note the simple statistics that follow:[12]

The phonemic inventory of moderately conservative[13] SF contains 20 consonants and 5 vowels.[14] Thus, 105 short syllables (CV) and 105 long syllables (CV̄) are possible ((20 x 5) + 5).[15] With respect to disyllables, CV̄ cannot appear in the accented position of a measure, but only after a short unaccented syllable. Disyllables consisting of no more than a single measure can have these shapes (accented syllables are in boldface):

| CVCV | **ma**ta 'eye' |
| CVCV̄ | ki**lā** 'know it' |

Including diphthongs in the equation adds another 7 vowel units that can appear in the accented position of a disyllable measure—either before or after a short unaccented syllable ("D" represents a diphthong):

---

[10] Note also that since the first morpheme is a short syllable, it is classed as a particle. Therefore, in terms of prosody, it can attach to following material, thus resulting in a mismatch between measures and morphemes (see §36.10). As stated elsewhere, only particles can cause a realignment of this type; bases retain their accent pattern (and measure division) in combination.

[11] For this discussion, CVCV excludes forms longer than one measure—i.e., two heavy syllables, such as *qāqā* or *rairai*.

[12] In most cases, C is optional; in §36.1, n. 2 we noted that for certain combination, eliminating C produced a diphthong, and the form was no longer disyllabic.)

[13] This variety of Fijian includes the older borrowed consonants *p, f, j*, and *z*, but neither newer consonants, syllable-final consonants, nor consonant clusters.

[14] In some positions, long vowels are prohibited. In others, they are allowed.

[15] The extra five syllables are those that consist of a vowel alone.

| CDCV | *kauta* 'carry it' |
| CVCD | *kilai* 'known' |

Thus, including adding diphthongs to the inventory of vowel units that can appear in the accented syllable of a disyllabic measure significantly increases the potential number of words of this shape.

36.4 THE RELATIVE STABILITY OF DIFFERENT MEASURE SHAPES

As the examples just above show, both roots (*sā*) and markers (*sē*) of the shape CV̄ can shorten. However, when they do so, they always retain their accent. In other words, neither *sā* nor *sē* (nor any other words in their respective classes) can be in an unaccented position.[16] This behavior leads one to suggest a hierarchy of stability (or preference) for measure types:

1. CVCV   stable in all environments[17]
2. CV̄   stable before accented syllables, unstable elsewhere
3. CVCVCV   stable only when not preceded by an element that can attract the first syllable, or followed by an unaccented syllable
4. CVCV̄   same as CVCVCV

These patterns indicate that a measure of the shape CVCV is the most stable, suggesting that it constitutes an "ideal" phonological shape at this level of the hierarchy. However, the word "ideal" should not be interpreted as evidence for a somewhat distorted view of Fijian prosody that proposes that words consist of a series of trochees, allowing the location of accented syllables to be predicted, and that words that do not fit into this pattern are exceptions. This topic will be discussed further in §36.8.2.

36.5 VOWEL SHORTENING ACROSS PHRASE BOUNDARIES

In slower, more careful speech, the syllable at the end of one phrase is not affected by the first syllable of the next phrase. Thus, so long as the speech style remains slow and precise, in the following sentence:

E cā na nodratou vanua.   'Their (trial) land was bad.'
|| e**cā** | **na**nodra·tou·vanua ||

the short syllable *na* does not cause the preceding long syllable *cā* to shorten. Or, to look at the situation the other way around, retaining vowel length in that position is one phonetic signal of a phrase boundary (pause and intonational features may be others).

---

[16] Except, perhaps, in very fast, casual speech.

[17] Both types 1 and 2, of course, will regularly pick up a preceding unaccented syllable if there is nothing else for that syllable to attach itself to. Moreover, for ideal stability, the consonant should be obligatory, not optional. Finally, as Tamata 1994 shows, statements about the stability of certain measure types have to be altered when casual speech is involved.

However, in faster speech, the barrier of the phrase boundary can disappear, resulting in a shortened syllable *ca*, and the possibility of a realigned measure:[18]

‖ ecana·nodra·tou·vanua ‖

Another example is:

Au kilā ni sā bula.   'I know she's well now.'
‖ au·kilā | nisā·bula ‖

In this example, the final vowel in *kilā*, as well as the potential diphthong *au*, can shorten:

‖ auki·lani·sā·bula ‖

Similarly, the long vowel in
e sō na tamata   'some people'
‖ esō | nata·mata ‖

usually shortens to form the following pattern:

| esona·tamata |

Here, the situation is somewhat different, since a construction with *e sō* is (so to speak) phonologically idiomatic—that is, the following NP (*na tamata*, in the example above) is seldom pronounced as a separate phonological phrase, except in very slow speech.

Taking the vowel-shortening rule a step further: under certain conditions, a long syllable can shorten if the following syllable is accented according to measure criteria, but unaccented according to the pattern of the phrase—that is, measures made up of particles are less accented.

For an example of the difference between the base form and the actual pronunciation, see the *VV* under *bā*. The base form for *bā ni ivalu* is:

bā·nii·valu

But it would normally be said not in three, but in two measures:

bani·ivalu[19]

---

[18] It is important to note that even if vowel shortening is not as fixed within a phrase as it is in the penultimate position of a word, it is significant that in neither case is there a contrast between the long and the short form. As mentioned in §33.2.1, unlike Hawaiian, Fijian does not contrast vowel length in the penultimate position of words. Nor does it have examples of such contrast within a phrase. In other words, the shortening of a syllable such as *tā* within *vakatākilā* 'reveal it' does not change the meaning of the form.

There is, however, a problem with so-called short *sa*—a dialectal or stylistic alternate of *se*. If *sa* occurs before a three-syllable word, this dilemma arises: either two constructions are ambiguous, or there is another phonological clue to keep them apart. Investigation so far seems to favor the second possibility: shortened *sā* seems to keep much of its vowel quality (low and central) when shortened; short *sa* is higher and further front. Obviously, this is a paradox in phonological terms.

[19] The *VV* entry for *banivalu* gives *baniivalu* as an alternate form.

36.6 THE EFFECT OF ONE-SYLLABLE SUFFIXES ON ACCENT

Section 36.3.1 showed the effect of a light suffix (i.e., particle) on a preceding long vowel or diphthong. Such suffixes are common; they include the following:

> the transitive suffix *-Ci*
> possessive suffixes (e.g., *-qu*, *-mu*, *-na*)

Less common are the "poetical" suffixes *-ri*, *-a*, and *-ya* (see §23.3) and perhaps those in such unexplained forms as *karakarawa*, in which the base form might be either *kara* or *karawa*.

When a particle is added to a form that ends in a long syllable, the syllable shortens, but it is still accented (e.g., *bū̃*, *bú-qu*). However, when added to a form that ends in a short syllable, such suffixes have the effect of what has been called "shifting the accent" one syllable to the right. However, it is more accurate to note that the position of the accent changes only with respect to the base form of the content word. In other words, it is the material under the prosodic umbrella that shifts. This type of suffixation is the only morphological process that results in an accentual mismatch between the base form and the derived form—e.g, *táma* 'father, *tamá-qu* 'my father'.

36.7 THE PHONEMIC STATUS OF ACCENT

The intricate relationship between vowel length and accent has long been a stumbling block for analyzing Fijian prosody. This section shows how the two phenomena are connected, but it also tries to treat each separately.

Even dealing with accent alone presents problems. Although Fijian has the *potential* of a contrast between two five-syllable words, with the same sequence of consonants and vowels but with different accent patterns (UNEVEN + EVEN versus EVEN + UNEVEN; see §36.1; §39.3.1), it does not seem to use it at the word level.

At the phrase level, however, one *can* find minimal pairs, the members of which differ only in measure division (and hence, accent patterning).[20] For example:

marama leka	'dwarfish lady'
mara maleka	'pleasant hollow, hole'
tabaka kala	'press on it at an angle'
taba kakala	'taking pictures of the *kakala* plant'
mocera rawa	?'possible to sleep on it'
moce rarawa	'sleep painfully'

Still, such pairs seem rare, suggesting that Fijian does not make much use of this potential contrast.

---

[20] The examples were either suggested or confirmed by Apolonia Tamata, a native speaker.

36.8 IS ACCENT PREDICTABLE?

To begin to discuss this question, first we return to the basic definition of accent: a system that emphasizes or otherwise sets apart a particular syllable in an utterance.

Next, we examine the reason for the emphasis. English uses accent (at one level) very much like segmental phonemes: as in *permít* vs. *pérmit*. However, such minimal pairs are uncommon. Japanese has more examples, such as the words for 'nose' and 'flower', which differ only in pitch accent.

Other languages use accent to delineate various units, giving clues to the hierarchy that evidently allows speakers to process what they hear more effectively than if it were a steady flow of units, delivered with the same intensity.

Finally, what does it mean when we say that the accent system of a particular language is predictable? Ideally it means that we can devise rules that state which syllables in a stretch of speech are accented, independent of word or morpheme division. For example, if a language regularly accents alternating syllables, or long vowels, or diphthongs (so long as they are explicitly defined) *irrespective of word or morpheme division*, this particular accent system is predictable.

Does Fijian function in this way? Only partially. The following sections show (1) why it is impossible to predict all aspects of Fijian accent, and (2) why certain aspects do seem predictable.

36.8.1 Rules based on syllable count

Fijian has not been immune to the "Polynesian accent myth": an often repeated but easily falsified proposal that word accent falls on long vowels, diphthongs, and the penultimate and alternate preceding syllables. Such rules are common in descriptions of Fijian. For example, the first of Anne King's rules (1969:532) states:

> Counting backwards within the word, assign stress to penultimate and alternate preceding vowels; i.e. to every even-numbered mora.[21]

A recent short description of Fijian word accent (Hayes 1995) also treats the topic in terms of moras, but expands the account in include syllables and foot structure. Based on the data and analysis in Schütz 1978b and in *TFL*, Hayes proposed this simple description to account for the majority of the data (p. 142):[22]

> a. If the final syllable is light, main stress falls on the penult.
> b. If the final syllable is heavy, main stress falls on the final syllable.
> c. Secondary stress falls on remaining heavy syllables, and on every other light syllable before another stress, counting from right to left.

---

[21] Because King's study was conducted under the direction of Bruce G. Biggs, the rule excludes long vowels and diphthongs, which Biggs treated as vowel sequences.

[22] Other than the point being discussed, I found Hayes's summary a careful and perceptive treatment of my data and analysis.

Do such rules work? They do indeed account for the accent in shorter forms:

ˈmata   'eye'   kiˈlā   'know it'

as well as in some longer forms of a certain shape:

ˌvakaˌtākiˈlā[23]   'reveal it'   ˌkataˈkata   'hot'

To account for words that do not conform to this rule—said to be certain loanwords from English—Hayes found it necessary to add a corollary. He noted (p. 144) that some "loanwords indicate that secondary stress can sometimes be assigned from left to right ..." For example:

ˌkonitaˈraki   'contract'   ˌparakaˈravu   'paragraph'

The first problem with this description is that it treats one accent pattern as the norm and others as exceptions. But perhaps this was because of the data the author used, especially those from Schütz 1978b, which describes the phonological patterning of English loanwords in Fijian. When I have used loanwords to illustrate Fijian prosodic behavior, it has been to show that the accent patterns in longer words cannot be described in terms of morpheme boundaries. Apparently, the disproportionate number of loanword examples overshadowed the many longer indigenous forms that do not follow an alternating-accent pattern, as §36.8.3.1 below shows.

36.8.2 The utility of loanwords as data

To describe Fijian accent without resorting to word or morpheme division, I used the data from a study of Fijian borrowings (Schütz 1978b, revised as 2004), with its appendix of nearly 800 words, transcribed from a professionally recorded tape and divided into measures. The most significant data are those words containing only short syllables, five or more, since long syllables (including diphthongs) are always accented, no matter what their position. Note the contrasting patterns in table 36.2. The words on the left follow the rule of alternating accent; those on the right do not. The numbers refer to the number of syllables in each measure; in each word, the penultimate syllable of the measure is accented.

TABLE 36.2: TWO ACCENTUAL PATTERNS

3 + 2		2 + 3	
sitili·wulu	'steel wool'	siti·vikiti	'certificate'
apeni·diki	'appendix'	esi·timeti	'estimate'
pirini·sese	'princess'	kiri·pilini	'crimplene'
palasi·tika	'plastic'	koni·feredi	'conference'
peresi·tedi	'president'	para·karavu	'paragraph'

---

[23] The first long vowel in this form retains its length only in a formal pronunciation. Vowel shortening is discussed in §36.2 and subsections. Also, the distinction between primary and secondary accent marked here is actually a feature of phrase accent (CH 37).

These examples show that for words consisting of short syllables alone, the rules do not work in words of two measures in length when a trimoraic measure appears in other than initial position. For example (from table 36.2), |apeni·diki| follows the "rules," |esi·timeti| does not.

Hayes (1995:144) tried to account for such forms as those on the right by calling them "exceptional." But aside from the inadvisability of using that term (which I call an "escape" word), how exceptional are such examples? The data from my study contain 31 words that consist of five short syllables. Of these, 11 fit into the 3 + 2 group, 20 into the 2 + 3 group. Thus, the borrowings with a so-called "exceptional" accent pattern outnumber those with a "regular" pattern.[24]

Is the 2 + 3 pattern confined to English loanwords? The next section shows that this pattern in common in indigenous words and phrases as well as in borrowings.

36.8.3 Accent patterns in indigenous words and phrases

As mentioned above, by using loanwords as illustrative data, I did not intend to imply that they were accented any differently than indigenous words. Instead (and I use italics here to emphasize the importance of this statement), these data were chosen to show that *all longer words, whether indigenous or borrowed, are combinations of even and uneven measures, in any order, irrespective of morpheme divisions.*[25] In other words, assimilated loanwords *illuminate* accent rules—not *contradict* them.

However, the data do show that even measures are probably more common than uneven ones. The following section suggests that this pattern may be due to the frequency of disyllabic morphemes in Fijian's vocabulary—a common feature in Oceanic languages.

36.8.3.1 Disyllables and trisyllables

The main reason that so many words have accent on the penultimate and alternate preceding syllables is that even roots are very common in Fijian (and Polynesian languages as well). When such roots are combined, the default rule proposed by Hayes works. That is, any word composed of a series of even roots[26] will show accent on the penultimate and alternating preceding syllables, in addition to that on a long vowel or a diphthong. For example:[27]

baka·baka	'older branches'	bala·bala	'tree fern'
bala·vatu	'k.o. fern'	bali·bali	'awkward'
rai·rai	'appearance'	qā·qā	'strong'

---

[24] I attach little significance to the ratio of nearly 2:1 between the two types. What is significant is that both patterns exist.

[25] Except, as mentioned elsewhere, for series of content forms.

[26] For our purposes here, we exclude even measures that consist of a long vowel or a diphthong.

[27] From here on, accent will not be marked, since it will be apparent from the measure divisions.

As table 36.2 shows, words beginning with an uneven measure, followed by any number of even measures, also fit the rule:

ikawa·kawa	'bridge'	yalewa·toto·lagi	'k.o. witch'
tamata·cā	'bad person'		

But although common, this is no means the only accent pattern in indigenous words, as the following examples show. Some are reduplicated forms, with either an unpredictable final element,[28] or partial rather than full reduplication. The following words (Capell 1941), with an uneven measure in final position, show the so-called exceptional pattern:

sava·savā	'clean'	buto·butō	'dark'
qula·qulau	'disorderly'	qiqo·qiqora	'thickset'

To emphasize that these are not isolated example, here is a sample of similar "exceptions."[29]

baka·niceva	'long clouds'	baka·nivudi	'k.o. tree'
bati·kaciwa	'k.o. bird'	bati·kasivi	'k.o. fish'
bati·nilovo	'edge of oven'	bati·nisavu	'cliff'

As additional evidence that this accent pattern is common, consider words formed by prefixing *vaka-* (causative) and suffixing a monosyllabic transitive marker and object. For example, note the following structure:

vaka- + verb stem + *-(C)a* [transitive marker and object]

When the verb stem is an even measure (which is often), the so-called exceptional pattern results. For example,

oti	'finish'	vaka·otia	'finish it'
yadra	'awake'	vaka·yadrata	'wake her'
dina	'true'	vaka·dinata	'believe it'
donu	'right'	vaka·donuya	'approve it'

Other common types of morphological or syntactic constructions will also produce a trimoraic measure in final position. For example:

1. A disyllabic possessive marker (*nona, kena, mena*, etc. + any three-syllable word)

kena·vinaka	'advantage'	nona·rarawa	'his sadness'
kena·balavu	'her height'	kena·kumala	'her sweet potato'

---

[28] For example, by comparing a number of morphological constructions, it seems clear that the root of the word for 'clean' is *sava*, and not *savā*.

[29] The initial consonant shows that this is only a small sample.

2. Phrases with *ni* 'of, for', with a dissyllable preceding and following:[30]

vale·nigunu	'bar'	vale·nisili	'bathroom'
mata·nisiga	'sun'	mata·nidalo	'taro stems'

These are only a few examples of the large number of indigenous forms created by these or similar morphological processes that would be considered "exceptional" by the alternating-accent rule cited above.

It should be added that Hayes's use of the concept of alternating syllables could be tied to the theme of the section in which his treatment of Fijian appears: moraic trochees. Acknowledging an alternate view (one that includes trimoraic units), he concluded that each approach handled the Fijian data, "though only moraic trochees would generalize to other languages."[31] Since this generalization is not important for the present grammar, I prefer the measure approach described in this chapter over one based on moraic trochees.

36.8.4 Does morphology play a role in determining measures?

The following short example shows why rules based on the morphological structure are inadequate. For some words, especially plant and animal names, the morphological structure is no longer obvious. For example, since Capell 1941 does not indicate accent, the following word:

kasacakula   sp. of moss

could be either kasa·cakula or kasaca·kula.[32]

Another example is:

talabusese   flee in all directions, of fish

Is it morphologically related to *tala* 'send', and accented as follows:

tala·busese

Or is it related to *sese* 'astray', with the following accent pattern:

talabu·sese

The answer must come not from rules but from a speaker who knows the words. *VV* writes it as **talábusese**, showing that the measure division is

talabu·sese

---

[30] The prosodic behavior of *ni* varies, according to speech style, speaker, and type of noun it follows. For example, following *yasa* 'side, place', *ni* is sometimes attached prosodically to the preceding disyllable, producing the measure *yasáni*·____. On 12 July 1979, a native speaker told me that such a pronunciation was common, but the citation form would be yása·ni____. See *TFL*, p. 479.

[31] I suggest that inadequate data and analyses for Hawaiian and Tongan led Hayes to classify them as "languages with Fijian-like stress." For these languages, an analysis based on even and uneven measures handles the data; one based on moraic trochees does not. See Schütz 2001 and 2010.

[32] The word does not appear in *VV*.

36.9 THE PREDICTABILITY OF ACCENT: SUMMARY

The preceding sections have shown that any rule that attempts to predict Fijian accent from written forms alone may account for part of the data, but never all of it.

In contrast to such an approach, the following statement (from a preliminary draft of a Fijian sketch grammar)[33] caught my eye because of its simplicity:

I write the stress where I hear it.

Of course, stating that one writes accent where one hears it is not only simple, but simplistic as well. For example, it does not tell us what kinds of syllables can and cannot occur in succession, or what happens when different types of forms are combined. In short, it doesn't *explain* the patterns of Fijian accent.

But it does start us on the right path. As a description of accent, it represents one end of the spectrum, with theoreticians' quixotic quest for all-inclusive rules at the other.

The problem with the rule-centered end of the spectrum is more serious, for many of the rules that have been proposed simply don't work. For example, Biggs (1978:700), in attempting to describe Māori accent, suggested rules that combined the now-familiar features of alternating syllables with another ingredient: morpheme boundaries:

… For Maori, the device we used to call plus-juncture, together with the concept of stress alternation, works fairly well, with the plus-junctures coming at plausible morpheme boundaries except in long loanwords from English.

We know now that the alternating-syllable rules don't work.[34] What about those that rely on "plausible morpheme boundaries"? Their main drawback is this: If rules are based on morphology, they are not directly related to phonology, which is concerned with what the hearer perceives.

Moreover, such rules do not apply to loanwords, which cannot be divided into morphemes. Finally, even in the native vocabulary, the morphemes in some words can no longer be identified.

It turns out, then, that neither principal component in this approach is adequate for predicting accent.

The reason that such rules fail is that the logic behind them is backwards. It ignores the main function of Fijian accent, which is not regular or contrastive, but demarcative (see CH 32). In other words, accent serves to help the hearer sort out strings of otherwise similar syllables into units that correspond—to some extent[35]—to morphemes and grammatical phrases. *It is accent that guides us to the morphology, not the other way around.*

---

[33] Hockett 1972:1–5. This of course is not the extent of Hockett's treatment of accent: he went on to propose a description similar to that of Hayes.

[34] See Schütz 1985b.

[35] Obviously, there is not a one-to-one correspondence. See CH 39 for the prosodic results of combining different types of morphemes.

This does not mean that measures and morphemes always share the same boundaries. The following section applies the methodology of a study of Hawaiian accent (Schütz 2010) to Fijian. It contrasts the matching of measure peaks and boundaries with those of morphemes, and measure boundaries with those of words.

36.10 THE RELATIONSHIP BETWEEN MEASURES AND MORPHEMES?

Now that the measure has been validated as a unit in the phonological hierarchy, a question arises: What is its function? As §36.7 showed, it could be contrastive. But Fijian doesn't seem to take advantage of this possibility. It is much more likely, then, that its function is demarcative. If so, what unit does it delineate? Because casual observation shows us that many measures correspond to morphemes or words, the following study was designed to examine the extent to which this actually happens.

36.10.1 The study

The data for this study come from Text No. 1, in Milner 1972:94 (with slight changes in the translations). I have divided it into measures and identified the different types. In this notation,

1. Measures are enclosed in brackets[36]
2. M = content morpheme
3. m = function morpheme (light syllable)
4. m̠ = function morpheme (heavy syllable or disyllable)
5. M̶ = part of a content morpheme that serves as a measure or part of a measure. Thus, M̶ + M̶ = M.
6. Hyphens separate morphemes (insofar as we can identify them) within a word.
7. Two spaces separate words.
8. The last line contains a translation.
9. A tentative notation for reduplication interprets a fully reduplicated form as MM, and a partially reduplicated form as either mM or m̠M, depending on the length of the first syllable.

The following sample shows the first ten phrases (or combinations of phrases) of the text.[37]

Na Cavu Drau

1 Dedē vakalailai,
[d e d ē] [v a k a -][l a i -][l a i]
M   m   M   M
After a while,

---

[36] Other works have separated measures with periods or raised periods. But here, because the notation is complicated, brackets make the divisions easier to see.

[37] Longer sentences were divided so that no sample was more than one line in length.

2 sā bāsika mai ko na wati i Manasa,
[sā] [bā][sika] [mai] [ko na] [watī]³⁸ [manasa]
m M̶ M̶ m m m M m M
Manasa's wife turned up,

3 sā mai tukuna sara vei keimami:
[sā] [mai] [tuku-na] [sara] [vei] [kei-][mami]
m̲ m̲ M m m̲ m̲ m̲ m̲
she said to us:

4 "Nī sā mai lako mo nī lai gunu tī."
[nī] [sā] [mai] [lako] [mo³⁹ nī] [lai] [gunu] [tī]
m̲ m̲ m̲ M m m̲ m̲ M M
"You come along and have breakfast (lit., drink tea)."

5 Keimami tukuna sara, "Sā vinaka!"
[kei-][mami] [tuku-na] [sara] [sā] [vinaka]⁴⁰
m m M m m̲ m̲ M
We replied, "All right."

6 "Da lako yani, dē ratou mate e na wāwā!"
[da lako] [yani] [dē] [ra-tou]⁴¹ [mate] [e na] [wā-][wā]
m M m̲ m̲ m m̲ M m m M M
"Let's go, lest they tire of waiting!"

7 Keimami sā lako sara yani,
[kei-][mami] [sā] [lako] [sara] [yani]
m m m̲ M m̲ m
We went at once,

8 keimami lai gunu tī .
[kei-][mami] [lai] [gunu] [tī
m̲ m m M M
we went to have our breakfast.

9 Keimami sā dabe sobu
[kei-][mami] [sā] [dabe] [sobu]
m̲ m m M m
We sat down

---

³⁸ As suggested by Apolonia Tamata and confirmed by David Dugucanavanua, the marker *i* combines with the preceding *-i* to form a long vowel. The resultant form is *watī*, with the accent shifting from *wa* to *tī*.

³⁹ *Mo* can also be analyzed as two morphemes: *me* + *o*.

⁴⁰ This sequence changes to [savi][naka] in normal speech.

⁴¹ In normal speech, *dē* shortens, resulting in [dera][tou].

10 e na loma ni vale ni kana.
[e na] [loma] [ni vale] [ni kana]
 m m   M   m M   m M
in the eating-house.

36.10.2 The results

Although only 10 phrases are shown above, the entire text sample consists of 55 sentences, many of which could be divided into phrases as in the sample above. Based on their morphological content, the measures exhibit a number of types. The following list shows these types and the number of instances of each:

M	86	m	152	mM	30	m̶M̶	17
M̶	26	mm	27	mm̲	25	mmm	3
Mm	24	M̶m̶	4	m̲M	1		

The results of the study are summarized as follows:

Out of a total of 396 measures:

> The accented syllable of a measure matches the accented syllable of a morpheme in 359 instances, or **90.6%**.
>
> The measure boundary matches a morpheme boundary (i.e., measures and morphemes coincide) in 228 instances, or **57.6%**.
>
> The measure boundary matches a word boundary in 177 instances, or **44.6%**.[42]

Thus, it is the peaks of the measures that are most significant for identifying morphemes.[43]

36.11 SUMMARY

This treatment of Fijian accent shows several of its essential characteristics:

1. Except for the accent that is obligatory on long vowels and on diphthongs, Fijian accent is predictable only at the measure level or on forms consisting of no more than four short syllables or a series of long vowels and/or diphthongs.

2. In order to describe the behavior of accent in longer forms, it is necessary to set up two basic types of units: even and uneven measures.

3. Different levels of accent cannot be described linearly, but are dependent on several phenomena in the language, such as phrase boundaries, discourse, the distinction between content and function morphemes, and types of function morphemes.

---

[42] The comparable percentages from the Hawaiian study (Schütz 2010) are 84%, 42%, and 31%.

[43] See also §39.3 and subsections for a more detailed account of the prosodic behavior of different combinations of morphemes.

37 PHONOLOGICAL PHRASES

The descriptions of a number of Oceanic languages, Fijian included, show that the analysts seem to have been unaware that every word said in isolation is a phonological phrase. (An exception is Biggs's explicit statement (1978:699). He wrote that in Māori, "... single words said alone are final phrases, and stressed accordingly ...")[1] This overlapping of units has usually led to proposing primary and secondary accent, whereas only one level is needed.

As described in §35.5, a phonological phrase consists of a measure or a series of measures, one of which is emphasized as a PEAK. Phonetically, this peak is identified by a pitch change, a greater degree of stress, and a somewhat longer duration. A phonological phrase is also defined by a TERMINAL.

In this chapter, we discuss more detailed characteristics of the phonological phrase, with respect to both its form and its function.

37.1 PHRASE PEAKS THAT INDICATE NORMAL PHRASE ACCENT

If there are no contextual reasons to do otherwise, a speaker emphasizes the last content[2] measure in a phonological phrase. In the following examples, the most prominent measure is marked by boldface type:

*evosa.vaka.**levu***   He talks a lot.   *edau.vodo.**gā***   She always rides.

To show that this assignment of accent is context-free, note the primary accent in the following three-measure loanwords:

*ala.pasi.**tā***	alabaster	*basi.kete.**polo***	basketball
*alu.mini.**umu***	aluminium	*cī.olo.**jī***	theology
*bani.masi.**tā***	bandmaster	*kē.misi.**tirī***	chemistry

In each, the last measure (of the phrase) is emphasized and perceived as primary accent, in spite of the varying placements of primary accent in the English originals.

To give a stylized representation of the phrase and its peak (in this case, also the sentence peak), we use the common expressing *vinaka vakalevu* 'thank you very much', repeating 35.1 (here, figure 37.1)[3]

---

[1] I would amend this statement, replacing "final phrases" to "phrase peaks."
[2] That is, a measure that consists of a content word/morpheme or part of such a form that contains the accented syllable of the base form.

FIGURE 37.1: PHRASE PEAK

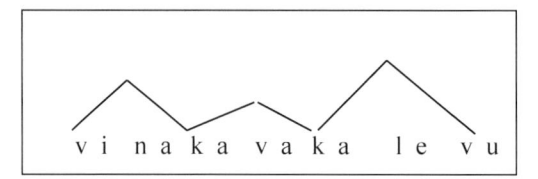

```
         /\      /\
    /\  /  \    /  \
   /  \/    \  /    \
  v i  n a k a  v a k a    l e    v u
```

Except in phrases containing only one content form, the peak is not fixed in one particular position, as shown in the following section.

37.2 PHRASE PEAKS THAT INDICATE CONTRAST

In some similar phrases, the location of the phrase peak (in boldface) hinges on the difference between content and function forms. The following example:

    ***La**ko mada!*   ::lako·mada↓::   'Please go!'

shows phrase accent not on the final measure, which consists of a function form, but on a content form preceding it.

Adding another marker also makes a semantic change, moving the peak to the element that adds meaning:

    *Lako mada **mai**!*   ::lako·mada·mai↓::[4]   'Please come here.'

Here, the peak of a phrase has the semantic function of focusing attention on the particular referent when more than one could be possible.

This feature—semantic function—is especially important in setting the phrase apart from the smaller phonological units, for here *meaning* must enter as a component of the unit. Thus, unlike the smaller units, a phrase of a particular kind has a particular grammatical function.

In order to illustrate this property, the phrases in question must be long enough to contain at least two items that can serve as peaks, for it is obvious that contrasting phrases could not be formed from a minimal construction such as:

    E levu.   'It is big.'

It is here that a complex relationship between phonology and grammar comes into play. Generally, phonological phrases that that are long enough to offer a choice of peaks are of particular grammatical types, for items that can serve as peaks are usually roots (see CH 39). For example, a common way to form a phrase with two roots is to link an attribute to a head. Attribution, in turn, is an extension of specification—a narrowing of the semantic range of a particular concept. Thus, in phrases containing an attribute, that attribute coincides

---

[3] Figure 37.1 is, of course, a rough representation. No instrumental measurement would give such an even picture, because each vowel and each consonant has its own level of prominence.

[4] As noted in §33.4.1.5 and CH 38, fn 5, the syllable preceding the peak may be higher in pitch.

with the peak measure, and it carries the line of discourse. For example (in the following phrases, terminals will not be marked; thus, the pitch arrow follows the peak measure):

E vosa vaka-levu.   'He talks a lot.'
:evosa·vaka·**levu**↓:

In this phrase, the peak is on the root *levu*, for it is the attribute that serves semantically as the most important segment. In a different context, however, another root could serve as the peak. For example, we could construct a conversation, the gist of which is (in English):

He talks a lot.
Did you say he eats a lot?
No, he *talks* a lot.

In this situation, the attribute would no longer carry the thread of discourse, and the phonological form of the phrase would be:

:e**vo**sa↓·vaka·levu: 'He *talks* a lot.'

For another example, we take the phrase

:e vodo **gā**:   'He always rides.'

Gā behaves like an attribute; that is, in a noncontrasting situation, the phrase peak is on the measure that coincides with *gā*. In a contrastive situation, however, the peak could coincide with a different morpheme. In the following examples, I have attempted to convey some of the intonational information of the English gloss by using italics for the accented word:

(*E sega ni taubale tiko*)   ('He's not walking;')
:edau·**vo**do↓·gā: 'He always *rides*.'

Finally, one can show contrast between "sometimes" and "always." Note the following:

(*O koya e taubale e na sō na gauna?*)   ('Does he walk some of the time?')
(*Sega.*) :**edau** ↓·vodo·gā: ('No), he *always* rides.'

37.3 PHRASE TERMINALS

Terminals are defined mainly in terms of pitch. To deal with pitch change in greater detail, we divide pitch into three components: direction of change (rise vs. fall), relative height, and interval. But we take the position here that these details are not an integral part of the phrase until it serves some function in the sentence. Therefore, the phrase peak is like a chameleon, taking on different "colorations"—that is, phonetic detail—in different situations.

Because the accented measure can fall anywhere in the phrase, it does not regularly indicate the boundaries of a phrase. Nor does any other auditorily perceptible sign consistently mark these boundaries, unless the phrase happens to begin or end a sentence, or comprise the whole sentence itself. (An exception to this observation is a fronted phrase; see §38.5.2.) Note the following example:

::e**ma**su↓·laka·ena·vei·ma**ta**ka↓::   'He prays for it every morning.'

Although two peaks are clearly indicated, a boundary is not. In particular, we do not know whether the phonological phrase boundary occurs after the measures |emasu|, |laka|, or |vei|.[5] In the absence of real marking, we can use a loosely-defined aid for establishing some kinds of phonological boundaries: potential pause. In slower speech, there may be pause between the phrases, as follows:

::e**ma**su↓·laka: :ena·vei·ma**ta**ka↓::

In addition to strictly phonological criteria, we can use grammatical clues, not as proof, but as suggestions. Thus, we have to take into account the boundaries of the grammatical phrases, which, in turn, makes it necessary to use meaning. By doing so, we match the boundaries of the phonological phrases to those of the grammatical phrases.[6] We also use two traditional criteria for immediate constituent analysis: substitutability and freedom of occurrence—ways to determine just what constitutes a putative construction. In this construction, although certainly not in all, the second phrase happens to be moveable; it can also occur at the beginning of the sentence.

37.4 DISCUSSION: PHONOLOGICAL PHRASES AS CONTRASTIVE UNITS

Milner wrote (1972:13):

> It is not possible in Fijian (as it is in English) to emphasize a word by using more energy to articulate it than would be used if it was not emphasized. (In English this feature is often indicated by underlining a word or printing it in italics: I *did* tell you, he *gave* it to me, etc.)

This observation is valid for many examples, since the emphasis signaled in English by accent is often signaled in Fijian by markers of emphasis, such as *gā*. Such markers also regularly take phrase accent (as part of the thread of discourse), and moreover, often occur at the end of a grammatical phrase, which usually coincides with the phonological phrase, and which is also the default position for phrase accent.

However, contrastive accent *is* possible. This is how I reached the conclusions described in §37.2. To test Milner's assertion, I asked Fijian consultants to read the same sentence in different contexts. In the first example, read with no context explained, the boldfaced measure shows the normal position for phrase accent:

*evosa.vaka.**levu***   He talks a lot.

To emphasize that it was *talking*, and not some other activity, that was abundant, the reading was changed to:

---

[5] The pitch rises again on *vei*, which indicates that it belongs to the second phrase.

[6] Is this procedure so unusual? For some languages, such as English, the borders between certain kinds of syllables cannot be fixed phonologically. Yet, we can agree that the units are present. And segmentation of sounds is often a phonological, rather than a strictly phonetic, matter.

e vosa.vaka.levu	He talks a lot.

Similarly, to emphasize *riding*, as opposed to some other activity:

edau.vodo.gā	She always rides.

was changed to:

*edau.**vodo**.gā*	She always rides.

And to emphasize the habitual nature of the action (marked by *dau*), the sentence was changed to:

*e**dau**.vodo.gā*	She always rides.

Thus, "primary" accent may move from one position in the phrase to another for the purpose of highlighting an item, and its placement cannot be predicted by a rule that counts syllables.

It is easy enough to understand why the contrastive function of accent has not been noted, for Fijian has several other ways to indicate the "focus" in discourse. The first, as mentioned above, is to use modifying markers, such as *gā* (limiter), *tale* (iteration), *qai* (sequential), and *wale* (limiter), to emphasize situational contrast. The second is to front certain types of phrases, which can show the importance of the themes therein. Perhaps contrastive accent is used less in Fijian than in English. But as the examples show, it does occur.[7]

---

[7] It is also possible that English patterns have been overlaid onto Fijian intonation.

38 PHONOLOGICAL SENTENCES

In CH 32, the phonological sentence was sketched with broad strokes. In this chapter, we examine the distinguishing features of that unit in more detail. These features come under the general term INTONATION—that is, the phonological system that uses the phonetic features of pitch, stress, and duration[1] to indicate phenomena that are not distinguished by the orthography.[2]

38.1 PHONETIC DETAILS

In this discussion of the phonetics of sentence intonation, we begin with sentences that consist of just one phrase. Such sentences can be divided into three portions, each of which is characterized by a particular pitch pattern.[3]

38.1.1 Portion 1

The first portion of most sentences is characterized by a pitch that can be considered NEUTRAL, meaning that the starting pitch of a sentence seems to have no contrastive function. It is not *significantly* high, mid, low, or any other relative pitch. This pitch level generally extends over "introductory material" (any markers that begin a sentence) or over unaccented portions of bases. For example, in the following sentence, the measure |ena| (*e na*) comprises portion 1.

::*ena·qai·lako*↓:: (*E na qai lako.*)   'Then she'll go.'

There is a reason for the qualifiers "most" and "generally" in the paragraph above: some sentences contain no such introductory material. For example, in a sentence that consists of only one even measure (that is, a disyllable or one long syllable), there is no introductory material over which portion 1 can extend:

::*lako*↓::   'Go!'
::*mai*↓::   'Come here!'

Longer sentences that begin with the same kind of material also avoid portion 1. Thus, the following sentence contains no material at the beginning that is appropriate for the neutral pitch:

---

[1] As part of intonation, duration figures as a phonetic component of accent, operating as a system separate from vowel length.

[2] Except in a general way by punctuation, italics, or underlines.

[3] Languages use pitch in a contrastive, not absolute, fashion.

::*lako·mada·**mai**↓*::   'Please come here.'

Similarly, some morphemes that are clearly grammatical markers but phonological bases (see §39.2.1 and §39.2.2) are ambiguous in their behavior. Examples are subjects, such as *eratou*, *erau*, or *au*, and the aspect marker *sā*. Phrases that begin with such forms seem to have the option of omitting this neutral initial pitch level.

However, there are some markers that regularly take the neutral pitch: e.g., *e* (third person singular) and *e* (ablative). Combinations of these markers and others—such as *e na* 'in the' and *i na* 'to the'—also take the neutral pitch, even though each forms a measure in itself:

    ena   'in the'   *ina*   'to the'

As a result, the occurrence and extent of portion 1 is fairly predictable on the basis of the type of material that begins a sentence.

The following list shows examples of sentences beginning with and without a pitch rise on the first measure, depending on the grammatical classification of the material within that measure (M 16Z).[4]

MEASURE DIVISION	MORPHEME DIVISION	GLOSS
RISE ON FIRST MEASURE		
1 navei·kā[5]	na vei-kā	everything
2 nanodra·tou	na no-dratou	their (trial)
3 edua·nabilo	e dua na bilo	a bowl
4 ekata·kata	e kata-kata	it's hot
5 etolu·nanodra	e tolu na no-dra	they (pl.) have three
6 nanō·drau	na nō-drau	their (dual)
7 evitu	e vitu	there are seven
8 elai·lai	e lai-lai	it's small
RISE NOT ON FIRST MEASURE		
9 nona·bulu·balavu	no-na bulu-balavu	its being buried long
10 eto·tolo·sara	e totolo sara	it's fast indeed
11 ema·kawa·sara	e makawa sara	it's very old
12 era·tou·sā·cina·ika	eratou sā cina ika	they (trial) were fishing

---

[4] To achieve a degree of unity, and also to insure that the examples can be checked if necessary, I have taken many of the examples for the description of intonation from a set of records made to accompany Milner 1972. Copies of these records, along with a transcription, are on file at the Center for Language & Technology, University of Hawai'i at Mānoa. I am grateful to G. B. Milner for giving me the records.

[5] This seems the place for an anecdote about the effect of one's native language on his/her perception of another language. Note that on the second syllable, *vei*, the pitch glides to a higher level than that on the following syllable, *kā*, which has phrase accent. Some years ago I was using Fijian in a field methods class I was conducting. One student, a speaker of Japanese, which has pitch accent, refused to believe that *vei* was not the principal accented syllable in the phrase. See also CH 36, fn 1.

13 era·sā·laki·qoli	era sā laki qoli	they (pl.) went fishing
14 erau·tiko	erau tiko	they (dual) stayed
15 sā·bata·batā	sā bata-batā	it's cold
16 evi·naka	e vinaka	it's good

In numbers (1–8), the accented syllable of each of the opening measures is composed of all or part of a morpheme that attracts the higher pitch. Most of them are roots, or the accented part of a root. In numbers (1, 2, 6), the rise is not on a root, but on the type of marker that often receives accent as if it were a root. In numbers (9–16), the opposite situation holds: the accented syllable of the opening measure is all or part of a marker, an item that does not attract phrase accent. An example (in 10, 11, 16) is *e* (third person singular).

Numbers (2, 9) present a problem: although *nodratou* 'their (trial)' and *nona* 'his, her, its' belong to the same morpheme category (mentioned in the preceding paragraph), they behave differently in this sample. I suggest that (9) would also be acceptable with an intonation pattern that omits portion 1.

38.1.2 Portion 2

In the second portion of the sentence, there is a change to the mid level, and the pitch stays at this *general* level until the end. Here, there may be a higher pitch to emphasize the fall in the final portion.

The placement of this rise is dependent on the shape of the peak measure. If it is of the even variety—that is, of the shape CVCV or CV̄—the slight rise will occur on the last syllable of the measure preceding the peak measure. For example:

::nawaqa·**levu**↓::	'the big canoe'
::nawaqa·**levu**↑::	'the big canoe?'

In each of these examples, the syllable /qa/, even though unaccented, may take the highest pitch in the sentence, signaling the phrase peak that follows.

A rough analogue of the pitch patterns is as follows:

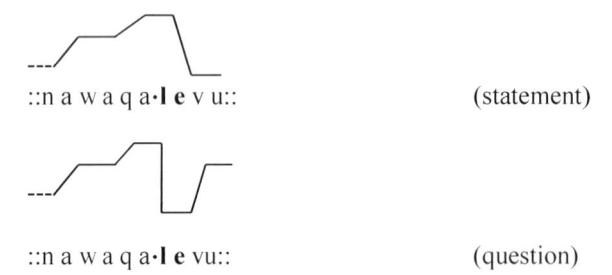

::n a w a q a·**l e** v u::	(statement)
::n a w a q a·**l e** vu::	(question)

If the peak measure is uneven—that is, of the shape CVCVCV, CVCD, or CVCV̄—the first, unaccented syllable in the measure that can take the higher pitch. Note that it is still the syllable that precedes the peak syllable:

::nawaqa·**to**tolo::	'the fast canoe'
::nawaqao**qō**::	'this canoe'

Thus, in these examples, the syllables /to/ and /o/, respectively, contain the higher pitch that highlights the fall. Again, note that they immediately precede the peak syllable.

38.1.3 Portion 3. The terminal

This part of the sentence contains the most important intonational information, for the behavior of the pitch at the sentence peak determines the function of the sentence. There are two major types of peaks: those with FALLING intonation, and those with RISING. As indicated in §32.6, falling intonation is considered basic, or UNMARKED, and rising intonation, MARKED. Thus, the first and largest part of our discussion concerns peaks with falling intonation.

Sentences whose peaks have rising intonation are generally questions (without a question morpheme), members of a series (except for the final item), and adverbial clauses that never serve as independent sentences except as answers to questions.

38.2 MATCH BETWEEN INTONATION PORTIONS AND MEASURES

It would be descriptively convenient if the borders between intonation portions matched those between measures, but they don't. Note the following example (brackets separate portions):

    Portion 1   2   3
        [na] [vei] [**va**le]   'the (distributive) houses'
        navei·vale

This phrase contains three intonation segments, but only two measures.

In short, the occurrence of uneven measures or utterances shorter than three measures results in a mismatch between intonation portions borders and measure borders.

38.3 INTONATIONAL SEGMENTATION OF SHORTER SENTENCES

As mentioned above, when the material preceding the accented syllable of the peak measure becomes shorter and shorter, the first two portions of the phrase become more and more restricted. The following examples show what happens to a phrase as material is deleted from the beginning portions.

    ::ena·sega·ni**la**ko↓::   'She won't go.'
     1   2   3

This sentence shows the full range of pitch levels. (The numbers beneath the notation mark the beginnings of the intonation portions.) Portion 1 includes the first measure; portion 2 includes the next measure and the pick-up syllable (/ni/) of the final measure; and portion 3 includes the remaining two syllables.

In the next example:

    ::kua·ni**la**ko↓::   'Don't go!'
     2   3

there are no markers to carry the low pitch, so the phrase begins with portion 2. The domain of portion 3 is the same as that in the first example.

In the next example:

::mo**la**ko↓::   'you might go'
   2 3

the phrase begins directly on a high pitch that intensifies the fall.

Finally, in an even shorter phrase:

::**la**ko↓::   'Go!'
  3

with no material preceding the accented syllable of the peak measure, the contrast between high and low has to be established in a different way. There are two possibilities. The first is a fall on the syllable /la/ itself; the second is a high-low pattern for the two syllables /la/ and /ko/. In either case, the phrase consists of only portion 3.

38.4 STEP VS. GLIDE

Even though an underlying pitch pattern may be described as high-low, there are two quite different phonetic manifestations of such a pattern, depending on the nature of the syllables involved. When a pitch change occurs across syllables, the second of which begins with a voiceless consonant, the phonetic effect is that of a step—since pitch stops when voicing stops. The opposite situation—a pitch change over a sequence of voiced syllables, or especially one long syllable or a diphthong—produces the effect of a phonetic glide.

Thus, the phonetic effects, with respect to pitch, of the following phrases are strikingly different:

1   ::ekata•**ka**ta↓::   It's hot.
2   ::sā•**drō**↓::   He's fled.

In the first, because the fall is on the syllable /ka/, by the time the voicing begins, the level is already fairly low. Thus, the phonetic effect is nearly that of steps—that is, different levels.

In the second, voicing is continuous after the first consonant. Therefore, pitch changes take the form of glides.

It seems more economical to regard the step pattern as the basic one, with glides then the result of assimilation of one pitch to another through voiced segments.

In statistical terms, however, there is a predominance of glides over steps. First, on a succession of V syllables or on a long syllable or diphthong, a pitch change is always manifested as a glide. Next, even with intervening consonants, the ratio of voiceless to voiced consonants is 7:13. However, one would have to take into account the frequency count of consonants to arrive at an accurate ratio of glides to steps.

Thus, because of the phonetic complexities of step vs. glide, and the contrastive, not absolute, use of pitch, I have tried to avoid showing intonation either by an analogue of pitch and accent, or by a system showing arbitrary levels.

Instead, with the notation used above, in combination with some knowledge about the grammatical classification of morphemes, we can reconstruct a rough model of the intonation. By these means, we may be able to escape the constrictions of a detailed transcription and come closer to understanding how hearers use what they know about the language.

38.5 FORMAL AND FUNCTIONAL CLASSIFICATION

A phonological sentence is composed of one obligatory phrase, which is (by definition) marked by a terminal. Other phrases may precede it; they are classified as nonterminal phrases.

38.5.1 Terminal phrases

The category of terminal phrases is divided into two formal types: those whose terminals are characterized by a pitch fall, and those characterized by a pitch rise.

38.5.1.1 Falling phrases

Phrases characterized by a pitch fall are (in a sense) unmarked. They indicate actual or potential sentences that express (in a broad semantic sense) some degree of completion or assertion. The exception to this general description is a phrase that contains such question words as *cava* 'what', *cei* 'who', *naica* 'when', et al.

38.5.1.1.1 Special characteristics of questions with question words

Even though questions with *cava* 'what?' and other question words have a falling intonation, they are marked in another way: by a raised register preceding the pitch fall. Thus, the intonation sets them apart from statements.

38.5.1.2 Rising phrases

Sentences that serve as questions ("yes–no" type, excluding the type just mentioned) are marked by a pitch rise on the peak. Such sentences differ from those already discussed in that the location of the peak is fixed on the last measure in the phrase. Thus, contrastive intonation seems rather limited with questions of this type.

The question intonation is also characterized by a raised register throughout. The register of all three segments is raised. In segment 2, the last syllable is raised to emphasize the low pitch on the next syllable—the peak syllable of the final phrase. The final syllable is high again.

As with the falling intonation, rising pitch takes the form of a glide when it occurs on a long syllable or throughout a stretch of voiced sounds.

Other than a higher register throughout the sentence, the intonational shape of questions is similar in most respects to that of statements, except (of course) for the contour of the peak measure. There is one major difference, however, in the pattern of this particular intonation: when questions are composed of more than one phrase, the behavior of all the phrases is affected by the question intonation. For example, in the following sentences:

::edua·tale:nanona·ose↑::⁶   'Does he have another horse?'
::sā·**rau**ta:nakemu·ma**drai**↑::   'Do you have enough bread?'

(each of which consists of a VP + specified NP), the first phrase, after the initial rise, continues on a near monotone. Thus, phonetically, the accent on the peak is distinguished more by increased stress than by pitch change. The pattern is similar on the following sentence, even though the grammatical classification of the phrases is different (VP + LOC):

::oā·**rai**ci·koya:ena·**noa**↑::   'Did you see him yesterday?'

In other respects, the placement of the individual segments of the pitch contours is similar to that on statements. The following examples are discussed individually so that the reader can observe the patterns. (Phrase and measure divisions are shown; conventional word divisions are retained for easier reading (examples from 12Z).)

1   ::e **yali**↑::   'Is it lost?'

This sentence consists of one phrase, and one measure as well. Since such brevity does not provide much space for the usual pitch changes, the pattern must be truncated. Thus, there is a rise on /e/, because a high point must be established to emphasize the following low point. Moreover, because the material preceding the peak is so short, the syllable /ya/ cannot be low itself, but must fall to a low point. The significant contour, then, is the contrast between the pitches on /ya/ and /li/. One could propose an underlying pitch structure of: neutral to high on /e/, low on /ya/, and high on /li/. Because all the elements in the sentence are voiced, and because of the short distance between the beginning and the peak, the pitch changes take the form of glides, rather than steps.

2   ::sā·**lako**↑::   'Has she gone?'

This sentence consists of one phrase, but two measures, thus providing more space for the pitch pattern. The first measure allows the pitch to rise from neutral to a point we call high+ —that is, the optional higher pitch (discussed earlier) that helps underline the significant contour of the peak. The peak itself it low; the "significant contour" is the jump to high on the last syllable.

3   ::e vi·**naka**↑::   'Is it all right?'

In this sentence, there is now enough material for the pitch pattern to manifest itself without being condensed in any way. The syllable /e/ is neutral, /vi/ has high+, /na/ is low, and /ka/ is high. Note that the highest pitch in the sentence is on /vi/, which is an unaccented syllable.

---

⁶ In these examples, "↑" represents a pattern more complicated than just a rise. Instead, the significant portion of the pattern is this: a "raised register throughout" (mentioned above), a slight pitch fall on the peak syllable, and a slight rise on any remaining material. If the peak syllable is final (and therefore with a nucleus of a long vowel or a diphthong, these changes occur on the nucleus itself.

4 ::e **mo**ce:na **go**ne↑::   'Is the child asleep?'

This sentence provides an example of the phenomenon discussed earlier: the monotonic[7] nature of longer material preceding the sentence peak. Here, /e/ is neutral, and the pitch rises on the syllable /mo/ and stays at that general level until high+ is established before the sentence peak. Thus, there is no significant pitch difference between /mo/ and /ce/, and the phrase peak (and measure accent as well) is manifested by stronger stress.

38.5.1.2.1 Vocatives

Unmarked vocatives (that is, without *i*) occur at the end of a sentence and comprise a separate intonational phrase. They are characterized by a pitch rise:

::sā·**mo**ce:**go**ne↑::   'Goodbye, child.' (14Z:30)
::nī·bula:**jo**ne↑::   'Hello, Jone.'

However, the rise may be short; in these examples, the peak syllable of the vocative may be at the same level as that of the preceding syllable—roughly, mid.

38.5.2 Nonterminal phrases

A nonterminal phrase is a phrase with a pitch fall, but one slight enough to be recognized as nonterminal. Many of them could serve as independent sentences themselves, but they are followed by optional material, such as a specifying NP or a modifying NP. In the following sentences, the nonterminal nature of the first phrase is marked by a fall to mid on the last syllable (underlined).

[VP]   [specifying NP]
[sā mat<u>e</u>]   [na vonu]   'The turtle is dead.' (11Z)
 ASP dead   DEF turtle

Others are not grammatically independent, but are subordinate VPs, time phrases, or specifying NPs that are fronted in the sentence. For example:

[subordinate VP]   [VP]
[ni oti   na bos<u>e</u>]   [era sā suka]   'When the meeting was
 SUB finished DEF meeting   3P ASP disperse   finished, they dispersed.'

[time phrase]   [VP]
[e na vula oq<u>ō</u>]   [e sā lesu mai]   'This month she returned.'
 ABL DEF month DEM:1   3S ASP return DIR

[fronted specifying NP] [VP]
[o Pit<u>a</u>]   [na no-qu i-tau] 'As for P, he's my friend.'
 PRP Pita   DEF POS-1S friend

---

[7] David Arms (10/84) suggested that this stretch is not necessarily monotonic, sometimes having a gradual descent. I mean here that any slight pitch change that may occur is not significant.

[NP]	[NP]	
[*oqō*]	[*na me-qu dovu*]	'This is my sugarcane.'
DEM:1	DEF POS-1X sugarcane	

38.5.2.1 Series intonation

Phrases that serve as items in a series are also marked by a nonterminal intonation, but different from that just described. Here, the direction of the pitch change is rising. The characteristic feature of the series intonation is a slightly raised final syllable. Within the following short phrases, the pitch level begins at a neutral pitch, rises to mid on the first accented syllable, remains at that height, and climbs to high on the final syllable.

na oko·**to**pa↑	'October'
na no·**ve**ba↑	'November'
natī·**se**ba↓	'December'

39 LINKS BETWEEN GRAMMAR AND PHONOLOGY

It was mentioned earlier that in the 1840s, the missionary-linguists in Fiji used the *Quarterlies* as a medium for discussing questions about grammar and translation. With the orthography fixed by the late '30s, one might expect to find all major spelling problems solved by this time. But a problem that has persisted until this day is word division. The following comments and questions (*Somosomo Quarterly*, 24 June 1846) illustrate the missionaries' concern about how to write certain combinations of morphemes.

> Concerning *vei* ... [with verbs] it is perhaps generally agreed, that it ought to be united to the verb. But how ought we to work it when it has the other sense?
>
> Is there any reason for this distinction between *ena* and *e na*? We cannot think of one.[1]
>
> Ought not *dau*, when used intensively, always to be united with the word which it precedes?
>
> We call your attention to the following plan for securing uniformity in writing the following pronouns: ... *koi rau, ko iratou, ko ira.*

The most publicized and persistent disagreement over word boundaries involves nouns formed with the instrumental marker *i* (see §24.1 for a morphological description). We now look at this construction more carefully, seeking the cause of the controversy. Discussing *i*, Hale (1846:368) stated that "although ... it belongs to the word which follows it, it is nevertheless affixed in pronunciation to that which precedes." His successors[2] had varying interpretations. For example, the word (or phrase) that translates 'the knife', consisting of the morphemes *na* (definite article), *i* (instrumental), and *sele* 'cut', has been written as:

> *nai sele*   *na isele*   *na i sele*

In short, every potential word division has been used (except no division at all).

Even today, people disagree about how to write such constructions. To understand why, one must look at the conflict between phonological units and morphological units.

---

[1] There is no difference in pronunciation: each is pronounced as one measure.
[2] E.g., Hazlewood 1872 [1850], Codrington 1885:146, Hocart 1910, and Ray 1910.

Hale's comments about the dilemma explain the problem clearly if we rephrase them in more current terminology. When he said that *i* "belongs to the word which follows it," he must have meant that it is allied in meaning and function to the following noun. Thus, with respect to morphology, the hierarchical structure of the phrase above is:

(*na* (*i sele*))

His description "affixed in pronunciation to that which precedes" can be rephrased as follows: with respect to pronunciation, the *a* and the *i* form a unit, *ai* (see §33.2.2 and following subsections),[3] which occurs in one measure. Thus, the prosodic structure of the phrase is:

nai·sele

Na i-sele, then, is a concise example of a mismatch between morphological units and phonological units.

Other examples show that the affiliation of *i* can become more complicated as the phrase grows. In other words, it does not always join with the preceding vowel. For example, if the possessive modifier *nona* is added to *na i-sele*, the prosodic structure is as follows:

nanona·isele

Here, since *i* cannot form a diphthong with the preceding unaccented *a* (all diphthongs are accented), it is prosodically affixed to *sele*, and the two morphemes occur in the same measure. In fact, on the basis of such variability, the definite article was once interpreted as having two forms—*na* and *nai*—and was written that way for a fairly long period.[4]

39.1 THE RELATIONSHIP OF ACCENT TO MORPHOLOGY-SYNTAX[5]

For Fijian, as for many other Austronesian languages, statements about the placement and different levels of accent have often been confusing and contradictory. The following statements, some of which are conflicting, are typical of what one can find, in various descriptions:

1. All words have penultimate accent.
2. Each word has only one accented syllable.
3. There are also secondary accents elsewhere in the word.
4. Content forms have a stronger accent than do function words.

In the following sections, we examine Fijian accent from this position: how different forms behave prosodically in different combinations.

---

[3] Strictly speaking, *ai* here is a potential diphthong, since it doesn't occur in measure-penultimate position.

[4] In case some readers might recognize this argument and the supporting examples from another work, they will find the original analysis in *TFL*:273–74.

[5] See the study in CH 36.

39.2 FORMAL AND FUNCTIONAL CLASSIFICATION OF MORPHEMES

Because many grammatical markers consist of one short syllable (and therefore cannot serve as an independent measure), such morphemes must be allied with other morphemes, or parts of morphemes, in order to constitute a measure. So that we may understand this process, we classify morphemes according to two criteria: **form** and **function**.

39.2.1 Classification according to form (phonological)

The significant units in this classification are the measure and the syllable. Since a short syllable alone cannot serve as a measure, we can set up the following division:

BASE: a form that can serve as a measure (i.e., a heavy syllable or disyllable)
PARTICLE: a form that cannot serve as a measure (i.e., a light syllable)

The following morphemes are bases:

vavi	'baked'	*dalo*	'taro'
qai	(sequential)	*kece*	(inclusion)

And the following morphemes are particles:

na	(definite article)	*e*	(third person singular subject)
i	(directional ablative)	*-qu*	(first person singular possessive)

39.2.2 Classification according to function (grammatical)

This classification has been used in the description of the VP and the NP. Morphemes that serve as content forms are called ROOTS; those that serve as grammatical forms are called MARKERS.

ROOT: a morpheme that functions as the head of a phrase
MARKER: a morpheme that functions in the periphery of a phrase

The following morphemes are roots:

tiko	'stay'	*kau*	'wood'
vinaka	'good'	*tū*	'stand'

And the following morphemes are markers:

na	(definite article)	*e*	(third person singular subject)
i	(directional ablative)	*-qu*	(first person singular possessive)
qai	(sequential)	*tiko*	(continuative)
kece	(inclusion)	*sā*	(aspect)

If we examine the examples, we can see that the two systems of classification are not equivalent. There are two relationships that produce overlapping:

1. Every root must have the form of a base. That is, in order to serve as the head of a phrase, a form must be at least one measure in length.

2. A particle always functions as a marker, not as the head of a phrase. That is, a form such as *na* (definite article), *e* (third person singular subject), or *-qu* 'my' serves in the periphery of a phrase, not as the head.

The examples also show that some bases have dual functions: for example, *tiko* appears in both lists. However, another view of such words is that they represent two morphemes of the same shape: one that serves as a root, and the other as a marker.

39.3 COMBINING FORMS

In §36.1, we introduced the distinction between even and uneven measures. We now demonstrate the significance of this division by examining how the two types behave differently when morphemes are combined into words and phrases. The major possible combinations are:[6]

1. Particle + base
2. Base + particle
3. Base + particle + base
4. Base + base
5. Particle + particle
6. Particle + base + particle

The following sections treat each of these types.

39.3.1 Particle + base

This combination of forms produces different prosodic effects, depending on whether the base is even or uneven. As stated above, an even base will accept a particle as an onset syllable, so that the resultant form is still one measure in length.

se + levu	→	se**le**vu 'there's still a lot'
na + vū	→	na**vū** 'the origin'
na + bai	→	na**bai** 'the fence'

If we examine the resultant measures, we see that each has an ideal accent pattern with respect to morpheme classification: one of the syllables of the base is accented, and the particle is unaccented.

When a particle combines with an uneven base, the base fills the measure to the utmost, and the particle cannot be assimilated. Thus, a new measure is formed—one that consists of the particle plus the onset syllable of the base:

me + kilā	→	**me**ki·**lā** 'that he might know it'
i + Levuka	→	**i**le·**vu**ka 'to Levuka'
se + totoka	→	**se**to·**to**ka 'it's still beautiful'
e + balavu	→	**e**ba·**la**vu 'it's long'

In each of these constructions, the nature of the constituents has produced a measure that is less than ideal: one whose form forces a particle to be accented. As a result, although each of these measures occupies a place in the rhythm of the phrase, and although there is still a contrast between accented and unaccented syllables, the overall level of energy is less than that on an "ideal" measure.

---

[6] Note that #3 and #6 are layered constructions.

Using the first example above, the phonetic effect could be transcribed as follows:[7]

[mèkilá]

39.3.2 Base + particle

There are fewer examples of this construction than those of the preceding type, since particles that follow a base are largely confined to the following types:

Inalienable possessive suffixes; e.g., *-qu, -mu, -na*
Monosyllabic transitive suffixes + *a*: e.g., *-ca, -ka*
Stative suffixes; e.g., *-a, -wa*
Syllables added to lines in *meke*; e.g., *-ri*

Examples of the first two categories abound both in the lexicon and in discourse. Members of the second two categories are fewer in number.

The following forms show particles attached to even bases:

mata + -qu	→	ma**ta**qu	'my eye'
kaba + -ta	→	ka**ba**ta	'climb it'
savasava + -a	→	sa**va**·savā	'clean'
koro + -ri	→	ko**ro**ri	'village' (syllable added to balance meter)
kau + -ta	→	**kau**ta	'carry it'
bū + -qu	→	**bu**qu	'my grandmother'

The last example shows the shortening of a long vowel in measure-penultimate position (**būqu→buqu*). (The syllable *kau* in *kauta* also shortens, but this is not reflected in the orthography.)

The following example shows an uneven base followed by a particle:[8]

daliga + -na	→	da**li**·ga**na**

All the examples except *kauta* and *buqu* illustrate the so-called "accent shift," in which the accent moves from the accented syllable of the base form. The accent in *kauta* and *buqu*—whose base forms consist of one long syllable—cannot shift, since there is no preceding syllable to receive it.

39.3.3 Base + particle + base

Although this combination might be considered a variation of either type 1 or type 2, we treat it separately for the following reasons.

First, although a construction such as

na lewe ni koro   'the inhabitants of the village'

may look like a simple combination of two phrases, it forms one phonological phrase and has the following hierarchical grammatical structure:

---

[7] Since a word in citation form is also a phonological phrase, the syllable /lā/, as its peak, receives a stronger accent, intensifying its measure accent. Moreover, perhaps the first syllable would have a tertiary (rather than secondary) accent, since I assume that the accent pattern would be slightly different from that of a base + base: e.g., *vale levu*.

[8] I have not yet found any examples of CVCV̄ + CV within this category.

(na (lewe (ni koro)))

Thus, *lewe ni koro* operates grammatically as a unit.

Next, there is some variation as to the prosodic behavior of the two linking markers that commonly occur as the particle in this construction—*i* and *ni*. Note the following constructions and their measure groupings. We first treat *i*:

tama + i + keirau	→ ta**mai**·**kei**·rau	'our (dual exclusive) father'
tina + i + Saikiusa	→ ti**nai**·**sai**ki·usa	'S's mother'

In these examples, the *i* is attached prosodically to the preceding word, in each case forming a diphthong with /a/. Note that the accent of the base form (*táma* and *tína*) shifts to the following newly formed diphthong. Note also that these two forms belong to the semantic category of inalienable and partitive. Thus, forms such as *tamána* 'her father' and *tináqu* 'my mother', with a similar accent shift, are common.

When *i* is used as an alternate to *nei* (which marks alienable, neutral possession), it does not attach prosodically to the first base, but to the second:

kato + i + Mere	→ **ka**to·**i**me**re**	'M's box'
i-sulu + i + Bale	→ **i**su**lu**·**i**ba**le**	'B's clothes'

However, it should be noted that *kato* and *i-sulu* do not belong to the same semantic category as *tama* and *tina*, and thus do not occur with light suffixes such as *-na* and *-qu*. Thus, an accent shift would be unusual.

39.3.4 Base + base

When two bases are combined, they generally keep the measure grouping they had as separate bases. With even bases, there is no option for realignment:

kā + vou → **kā**·**vou** 'new thing'

No other measure grouping is possible.

But the combination of even base + uneven base, or two uneven bases, would theoretically offer an option for realignment. For example, one might suppose that combining

vale + balavu 'long house'

would allow two potential groupings:

vale·**ba**la**vu** and *****va**le**ba**·**la**vu

However, only the first option—the one that preserves the accent pattern of the individual bases—is possible.

Similarly, although combining two uneven bases, such as

vanua + totoka 'beautiful land'

offers the theoretical possibility of three disyllables:

*****va**nu·**a**to·**to**ka

in addition to two trisyllables:

va**nu**a·to**to**ka

only the latter form exists—again, the one that preserves the accent pattern of the base forms.

The reason for the qualifier "generally" in the first paragraph of this section is that one type of change can take place when two bases are combined: the shortening of a long syllable. Thus, even though

    kā + *balavu*   'long thing'

consists of two roots, the form *can* realign to this measure grouping:

    kaba·lavu

Note, however, that the accented syllables of the base form and the resultant form are the same. This phenomenon is discussed more fully in §36.1.5.

39.3.5 Particle + particle

Within a phrase, the combinatorial possibilities of particles before a base[9] can produce sequences of particles that make up measures in themselves. For example (particles are boldfaced):

ki + ***na*** + *vale*	→	kina·vale	'to the house'
me + ***ra*** + *lako*	→	mera·lako	'that they might go'
na + ***i*** + sele	→	nai·sele	'the knife'

In each of these examples, the first measure is made up of particles, the first of which must be accented. But as in previous examples in which a particle was accented, the degree of prominence given to such a measure is less than that given to a measure in which the accent syllable belongs to a base. Thus, the phonetic manifestations of the forms above, with respect to accent, are:

    [kìnavále]   [mèraláko]   [nàiséle]

It is also possible to have three particles preceding a base, producing the following measure structure:

    e + *na* + *i* + *sele*   →   ena·isele   'with the knife'

In fast (normal) speech, it is often difficult to recognize any of the syllables in such measures as |kina| and |enai| above as accented. Perhaps for this reason, as an argument against my analysis of Fijian measure structure, Arms (1987: 116) maintained that sequences of three unaccented syllables are possible, thereby refuting the idea of a limited number of measure types. In the following examples (ibid.), given in conventional spelling, the underlined portions show what Arms interpreted as sequences of three unaccented syllables:

---

[9] There seem to be no combinations of particles after a base. (Although the underlying form of a -*Ca* suffix is *Ci* + *a*, this combination does not occur in surface forms.) Except for those particles discussed as type 2, all the markers that occur after a root are bases.

na táma i tinána	the father of his mother
è na yasána imatáu	on its right side
è na ikatólu ni síga	on the third day

In each example, the underlined portion corresponds to a combination of final unaccented syllable of a measure, a one-syllable function form, or the first unaccented syllable of a trimoraic measure (not necessarily in that order).

Admittedly, a disagreement on this matter is based partially on different perceptions.[10] However, Arms's analysis seems to operate on a phonetic level only, ignoring that a measure composed of a particle and another unaccented syllable has a lower level of accent than one that corresponds wholly to a content morpheme. Thus, in the following notation (showing measure structure of the examples above):

natama•iti•nana

ena•yasana•ima•tau

ena•ika•tolu•nisiga

the underlined measures are less prominent than ones composed entirely of content morphemes. Still, each forms a measure. As confirmation, note that Tamata (1994:30), a native speaker of Fijian, marked the accent in a similar construction as follows:[11]

sega ni kilā 'not know it' séga•níki•lá

Although the syllables *ni* + *ki* are exactly the same in type as those underlined in the examples above, Tamata treated them as comprising a measure on their own, with the appropriate accent pattern.

Thus, even though a measure that is composed of sequences of syllables that, for morphological reasons, has a low level of prominence, it still occupies a place in the metrical structure of the phrase, especially when spoken in a more formal style.

39.3.6 Particle + base + particle

This pattern is included mainly to make the list of possible combinations symmetrical. An example is

o + *tina* + *qu*   'my mother' (as a proper noun)   oti•naqu

This is a layered phrase, with the structure (*o* (*tina-qu*)). Because the first measure, |oti|, is a combination of function morphemes, it has a lower level of accent than |tina-qu|, giving the impression of a secondary accent on *o*.

It is also possible to include these three types of morphemes in a one-measure form. For example, combining *o* + *bū* 'grandmother' + *-qu* produces:

---

[10] As an example of differing perceptions, another linguist marked a phrase similar to the second and third example above in this way: *e na vále* 'in the house'—that is, with an unaccented preposition *e*.

[11] I have changed Tamata's phonetic symbols back to the conventional ones, but have kept her measure divisions.

|obuqu| 'my grandmother'

39.3.7 Summary

The main point of this section is that even when markers that are particles are placed in the accented position of a measure, that level of accent is less than that in a measure in which the accented syllable is part of a base. On the other hand, markers that are bases are accented as if they were roots. For example (markers are boldfaced):

*Sā **qai** lako.*   **sā**·**qai**·lako   'And then she went.'

Here, each of the three measures is a base, but as for function, there are two different categories represented. The measure |lako| corresponds to a root; |sā| and |qai| each to a marker. As a more extreme example:

Au sā bau dau tadra sara toka gā.   **Au**·**sā**·**bau**·**dau**·tadra·**sara**·**toka**·**gā**
'I always dream.' (*FR3*:45)

As in the previous example, each measure corresponds to a base. However, with respect to function (morphology), only the measure |tadra| corresponds to a root; each of the others corresponds to a marker.

39.4 THE EFFECT OF COMPLEMENTARY OR OPPOSING TENDENCIES

So far, two prosodic tendencies or pressures have been noted:

1. Long vowels regularly shorten before CV at the end of a phonological phrase; they *tend* to shorten before CV in other positions.
2. There is a tendency to avoid accenting a particle whenever possible.

Because of the first tendency, we find the following alternate pronunciations:

$$s\bar{e} + ni + kau \quad \begin{matrix} s\bar{e}\cdot nikau \\ seni\cdot kau \end{matrix} \quad \text{'flower'}$$

This alternation presents no particular problem, since neither alternative puts the particle *ni* in the accented position.

However, *bā + ni + vuaka* 'pig pen' is different. Here, of the two alternatives:

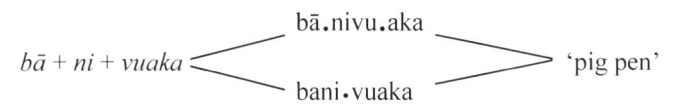

$$b\bar{a} + ni + vuaka \quad \begin{matrix} b\bar{a}\cdot nivu\cdot aka \\ bani\cdot vuaka \end{matrix} \quad \text{'pig pen'}$$

the second is preferable, since it puts the particle *ni* in an unaccented position. Moreover, the utterance is prosodically shorter—two measures rather than three (see §36.2.4.3). Thus, the tendency for *bā* to shorten before an unaccented short syllable is reinforced.

40 INTONATION AND ITS GRAMMATICAL CORRELATES

This chapter discusses the relationship between intonation and the grammatical organization of sentences. Sentences are classified according to the grammatical function of the individual phrases. The peak of each phrase is indicated by boldface type; phrase boundaries are marked by "|"; sentence boundaries by "||"; and measure boundaries that do not coincide with phrase or sentence boundaries by "·". Since the distinction between questions and statements is not important here, sentence terminals are not marked with upward or downward arrows;

The reasons for the present notation have already been discussed. In order to give the reader a better idea of the phonetic manifestations of these rather abstract representations, I have interspersed discussions of intonation, especially with regard to the assimilation that occurs when phrases are put together.

A disclaimer: The methodology in this chapter is experimental, and sometimes decisions were made on impressionistic grounds.

40.1 SENTENCES CONSISTING OF TWO PHRASES

Although formed from different grammatical elements, all the sentences in this section can be characterized as follows: in a very broad sense they consist of HEAD + ATTRIBUTE. But here, "attribute" refers to a part of the sentence that is somehow subordinate to the principal one. Another way to express the relationship between the two parts is to label the construction ENDOCENTRIC (Hockett 1958:184–85): that is, a construction that centers on a head within the construction itself.

A. VP + specified subject
|| sā **ma**te | navo**nu** ||[1]   'The turtle is dead.' (11Z)[2]

---

[1] The placement of the sentence peak on many of the examples is a feature of the recording from which they are taken. Since the recording consists of lists of sentences out of context, many of them have the option of having their peak on a different phrase—in a particular context.

|| e**du**a | nabilo·niya·qona·**le**vu || '(There's) a large bowl of kava' (16Z)
|| e**vi**tu | nakato·**le**levu || '(There are) seven large boxes' (16Z-14)

As a preliminary to discussing intonation, we need to note the grammatical character of the sentences above. In each of them, the first phrase is capable of serving as a sentence by itself. The grammatical function of the second phrase is to specify the subject of the first phrase. The intonational behavior of such sentences is different from that of some other types.

In the examples above, and all those in this category, the phrases have pitch falls. However, the interval of the first fall is relatively short; this characteristic identifies it as a nonterminal phrase. By this particular intonation, the hearer is informed that another phrase follows. The second phrase contains the terminal, which is identified as such by the long interval of the pitch fall.

Another phonetic characteristic shared by all the examples in this section is DOWNDRIFT. This term means that the pitch register often falls slightly with successive phrases.

B. Noun + stative

|| na**wa**qa | to**to**lo || 'the fast canoe'

Examples such as this—that is, treating a modified noun as two phrases—are rare, and dependent on the speaker's speed and style. Since this particular example comes from a set of short sentences, most of which fall under pattern A, the intonation might be the result of unconscious analogy. This construction is usually subsumed under one phonological phrase, particularly so when it is part of a larger construction. At any rate, the existence of such a pattern is an interesting parallel to the grammatical analysis of this construction in §28.3.1.

C. Possessive NP + specified possessor

|| nanō·drau·kā·**ni**qito | na**go**ne ||[3]   'the two children's play-gear' (16Z-9)
|| nona·bula·**ba**lavu | na**qa**se || 'the old person's long life' (16Z-11)
|| nanodra·tou·gunu·ya**qo**na | na**qa**se || 'the old persons' (trial) kava drinking (17Z-5)

The intonational pattern of these sentences is identical to that of the preceding sentences.

D. VP + locative phrase

|| era·sā·laki·qoli·**vo**nu | mai·ca**kau** ||[4]   'They (plural) went turtle fishing on the reef (16Z-12)
|| kara.tou.sā.**mo**ce | ena.vale.o**qō** || 'And they (trial) slept in this house.' (16Z-20)

---

[2] The numbers and letters refer to Milner's index of sentences recorded on 12-inch disks at 78 rpm, which are nearly inaccessible now because of changes in technology.

[3] In each of the examples marked, a long vowel has the option of shortening before a following unaccented short syllable. Thus, the notation |kā·niqito|, for example, indicates an underlying form.

[4] See the previous note. Before an unaccented vowel, *mai* has the option of shortening in faster speech. The measure division would then be |maica·kau|.

|| era·sā·laki·**su**va | mai·nanodra·vei·**ko**ro ||[5]   'They (plural) went to Suva from their villages.' (17Z-6)

E. [VP + specified subject] +time phrase||
|| edua·nacagi·bata·ba**tā** | ena·bogi·**le**vu || 'There was a cold wind in the middle of the night (17Z-4)
|| evitu·navale·**le**vu | maina·**ko**ro ||[6]   'There are seven large (main) houses in the village.' (17Z-16)

In these two sentences, the first phonological phrase is a combination of two grammatical phrases, or, in the style represented by example B, three phrases. They show how phonological phrases can coalesce when part of a longer sentence.

|| e**ti**ko [|] edua·nawaqa·niviti·**le**vu | maila·**ke**ba ||[7]   'There's a large Fijian canoe at Lakeba.'

In this sentence, the fall on *tiko* is slight enough that one might consider all the material through *levu* to be one phonological phrase. Another view is that there are degrees of phrase boundaries, with one major boundary always separating longer utterances into two units. With respect to layers of phrases, even the second potential phrase:

| edua·nawaqa·niviti·**le**vu |

could consist of two phonological phrases if it constituted a sentence on its own:

|| **ed**ua | nawaqa·niviti·**le**vu || 'There's one large Fijian canoe.'

F. :Fronted NP or subordinate VP: :VP:

The characteristic feature of this pattern is that the fall on the peak is slight enough to distinguish it from a phrase that could stand alone as a complete phonological sentence. There is also a pause between the phrases, and the second begins as a complete sentence would begin.

|| o**me**re | esega·nitiko·o**qō** || 'As for Mary, she's not here now.'
|| nioti·**na**kana | era·**su**ka || 'After eating, they dispersed.'

From these examples, one might draw the conclusion that there are a number of ways that a particular stretch of material could be divided into phonological phrases. This is not to say that there are no rules, for there are of course many constructions that cannot possibly contain two phonological phrases. But this much is apparent: the levels of grammatical structure of sentences provide a number of points at which a phrase division is *possible*.

---

[5] See the previous note. In faster speech, |mai·nanodra| has the option of shortening to |maina·nodra|.

[6] Note the measure division in *mai na koro* 'in the village'. On the recording, *mai* has been shortened, combining with *na* to form a measure. Cf. the two previous notes.

[7] In this sentence, as in the previous one, *mai* has shortened before an unaccented syllable, forming the measure |maila|.

40.1.1 Embedding of phonological phrases

The last examples above show that as phrases are combined into sentences, two (or more) phonological phrases can be combined, or EMBEDDED, into one. Note the following pairs of examples:

		sā·**ya**li	nanodra·tū**ra**ga			'Their (plural) chief is gone.'
		sā·yali·nanodra·tūraga	mai·**na**koro			'Their (plural) chief is gone from the village.' (20Z-5)
		erau·sā·**mo**ce·tiko	na**go**ne			'The (dual) children were asleep.'
		erau·sā·moce·tiko·nagone	ena·dua·navale·**la**ca			'The (dual) children were asleep in the sail house.'
		e**ta**ro·tiko	na**go**ne			'The child asks questions.'
		etaro·tiko·nagone	ka**sau**ma	naqase·ni**vu**li			'The child asks questions, and the teacher answers them.'

In such phonological sentences as the last, certain phrase boundaries are not always firmly fixed. It would be possible to combine the two last phrases, so that the whole sentence would consist of two similar parts:

|| etaro·tiko·na**go**ne | kasauma·naqase·ni**vu**li ||

However, the conjunction *ka* is always preceded by a phrase boundary.

40.2 PHONOLOGICAL SENTENCES CONSISTING OF MORE THAN TWO PHRASES

The following examples show sentences that consist of more than two phrases. In general, the phonetic details pertinent to the preceding set hold: each phrase is characterized by a pitch fall, but both nonterminal and terminal falls are distinguished. Also, the pitch register generally falls throughout the sentence. (In each example, the sentence is given first with conventional word divisions.)

E totolo sara na nodra vosa na gone ni Viti.
|| eto·tolo·**sa**ra || nanodra·**vo**sa || nagone·ni**vi**ti || 'Fijians' speech is fast.' (16Z-2)

E vinaka na cagi ka ra sā laki qoli na cauravou e na mataka lailai.
|| evi·naka·na**ca**gi || kara·sā·laki·**qo**li || nacaura·**vou** || ena·mataka·lai·**lai** ||
'The wind was good, and the youths went fishing early in the morning.' (16Z-19)

The second sentence shows an example of embedding: the first phrase, which, alone and spoken slowly, would be:

E vinaka na cagi.   'The wind was good.'
|| evi·**na**ka || na**ca**gi ||

It is likely that the second and third phrases could also be embedded:
ka ra sā laki qoli na cauravou
|| kara·sā·laki·qoli·nacaura·**vou** ||

40.2.1 Hierarchical structure

Because these sentences consist of more than two phrases, there are two possibilities of structure: a purely sequential arrangement, or a hierarchical one. The strong marking of certain borders (such as that preceding the conjunction *ka*, as opposed to the tendency of others to disappear when two phrases are combined, suggests that the arrangement is hierarchical. For the following examples, I have tried, from the nature of the borders, to construct tentative hierarchical models.

1. *Eratou lewe lima na gone lalai, ka ratou sā moce e na vale oqō.*
'There were five children who slept in this house.' (16Z-20)

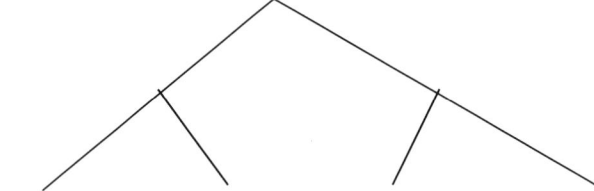

|| era·tou·lewe·**lima** || nagone·la**lai** || kara·tou·sā·**moce** || ena·vale·**oqō** ||[8]

In this example, the major boundary (before *ka*) is strongly marked (by a pitch fall of a greater interval on the peak of the preceding phrase, and by pause), and the secondary boundaries are weakly marked.

2. *E lailai sara ka sā cā na nodratou ibe.*
their (trial) mats were very small and bad (16Z-21)

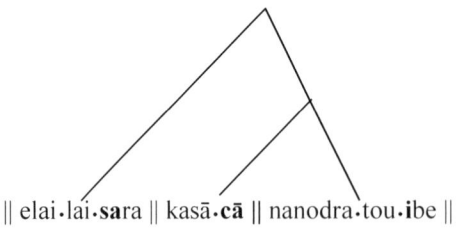

|| elai·lai·**sa**ra || kasā·**cā** || nanodra·tou·**ibe** ||

I suggest this phrase structure on the basis of the pause before *ka*, in spite of its being contrary to the grammatical structure.[9] It would be interesting to examine other examples of such possible conflict between the phonological structure and the grammatical structure.

---

[8] Could the length of the second phrase influence whether it can be embedded in the first? For example, the following intonation doesn't sound right:

||era·tou·lewe·**lima**||na**gone**||kara·tou ... (etc.)

In the same way, the former example doesn't sound right if the second phrase is shortened:

:eto·tolo·**sa**ra||na**vo**sa||nagone·ni**vi**ti:

[9] The last phrase has the same relationship to each of the preceding VPs: it specifies the subject.

3. *E tiko na buka kei na wai mai na vale ni kuro.*
'There's firewood and water in the kitchen.' (16Z-22)

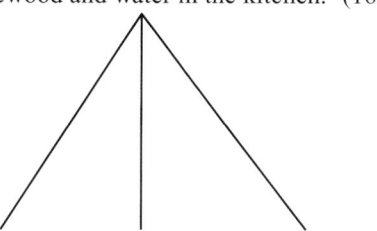

|| etiko·na**bu**ka || kei·na**wai** || mai·navale·ni**ku**ro||[10]

The structure above appears because of the way the reader read the sentence, but the even division among three units sounds rather strange (see the conclusion to this chapter). The following diagram suggests another grouping for the phrases, one that sounds more natural.

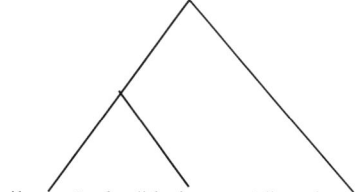

|| etiko·na**bu**ka || kei·na**wai** || mai·navale·ni**ku**ro ||

4. *O Bau, e dua na nodra koro tūraga na gone ni Viti.*
"As for Bau, it is the Fijians' chiefly village.' (16Z-23)

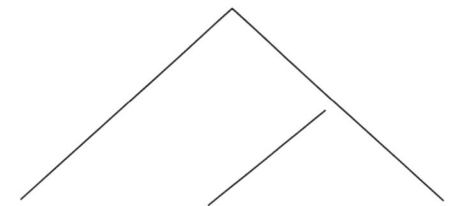

|| o**bau** || edua·nanodra·koro·tū·**ra**ga || nagone·ni**vi**ti ||

The fronted phrase *o Bau* functions as a TOPICALIZED phrase. Note, incidentally, that this order lessens the chance for ambiguity, for there are two items to specify—the subject and the possessor, both third person singular. AS (5/81) confirmed that the order above is preferred to the following:

*E dua na nodra koro tūraga na gone ni Viti o Bau.

---

[10] This sentence contains two examples of long syllables followed by short unaccented syllables: *kei na* and *mai na*. As in the examples discussed in note 3 and following notes, in normal speech, the long syllables shorten, and the measures are realigned accordingly: |keina·wai| and |maina·vale|.

5. *Erau lewe rua na tagane ka ratou lewe lima na yalewa e na vale e rua oqō.*
'There are two men and five women in this house.' (17Z-12)

|| erau·lewe·rua·nata·**ga**ne·kara·tou·lewe·lima·naya·**le**wa·ena·**va**le·erua·oqō ||

(Incidentally, note the number of mismatches between measures and morphemes in this sentence, reflected here fairly accurately by conventional word division. See §36.10.)

The phrasing of this sentence seems to defy immediate constituent analysis. Could the latter part of the sentence have been divided into phrases because of limitations of the breath stream? I would have expected the following:

*|| ena·vale·erua·oqō ||

6. *E vinaka sara na nodratou ibe vou na marama qase.*
'The old women's new mats are very good.' (17Z-13)

Grammatically, this sentence shows a succession of items to be specified. First, the subject *e* is specified by the following phrase, and that phrase contains *nodratou*, which is, in turn, specified by the next phrase. In grammatical terms, I should expect the following hierarchical structure:

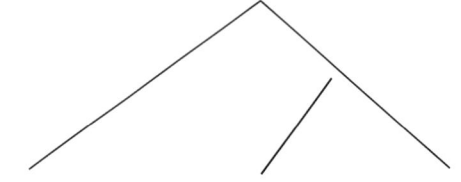

|| evi·naka·**sa**ra || nanodra·tou·ibe·**vou** || nama·rama·**qa**se ||

7. *Era gunu tī e na veimataka na tūraga ni Viti ka ra gunu yaqona e na veibogi.*
'Fijian chiefs drink tea every morning and drink kava every night.' (17Z-18)

In this sentence, the principal division is before the *ka*. The phonological hierarchy of the whole sentence is as follows:

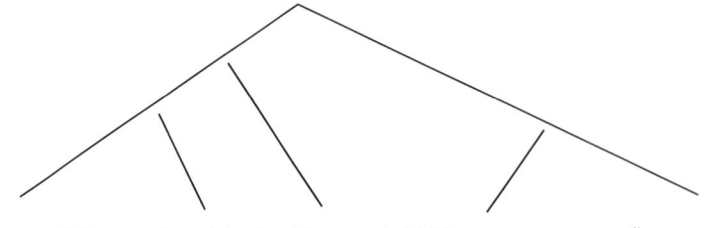

|| era·gunu·**tī** || ena·vei·ma**ta**ka || natū·raga·ni**vi**ti || kara·gunu·ya**qo**na || ena·vei·**bo**gi ||

This judgment is rather subjective, but its very subjectivity is suggestive. It is not surprising to find the first two phrases loosely bound, for the second phrase (grammatically, a time phrase) is not fixed in that position; the following is also possible:

|| ena·vei·ma**ta**ka || era·gunu·**tī** || natū·raga·ni**vi**ti || ...

8. *E vinaka na cagi ka katakata na siga.*
'The wind is good and the day is hot.' (17Z-19)

This sentence has a straightforward, symmetrical structure:

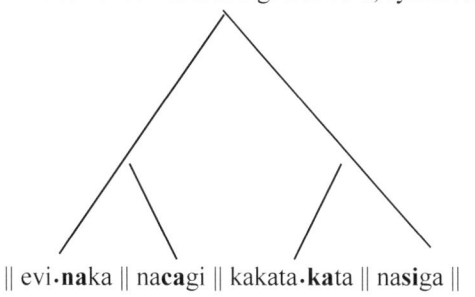

|| evi·**na**ka || na**ca**gi || kakata·**ka**ta || na**si**ga ||

In each of the subdivisions, the division between the two phrases was not distinctly marked. In less formal speech, it is likely that the whole sentence would consist of not four, but two phonological phrases.

|| evi·**na**ka·na**ca**gi || kakata·**ka**ta·na**si**ga ||

9. *E na mataka, era sā laki qoli na tagane kei na yalewa ka ratou sā laki cina ika na cauravou e na vei bogi.*
'In the morning, the men and the women go fishing, and the young men go torch fishing every night.' (17Z-20)

|| ena·**ma**taka || era·sā·laki·**qo**li || nata·**ga**ne || kei·naya·**le**wa || kara·tou·sā·laki·cina·**i**ka || nacaura·**vou**·ena·vei·**bo**gi ||

It is difficult to establish a hierarchical structure from the reading on the recording. The speaker may have paused for breath—which is not surprising, for probably only a singer with good breath control and an ability to plan ahead would have read the sentence at its deliberate speed on one breath. I expected the main pause to occur before *ka*, but instead, it occurred before the *kei* phrase. I should add that the first phrase belongs to a different type when it is in that position, similar to the phrase *o Bau* in (4), since it is a non-final. One might also consider that the first phrase has been fronted (making the order "marked"), for in a different order, each of the phrases can be a final (with, of course, assimilation at the borders):

|| era·sā·laki·**qo**li || ena·**ma**taka||nata·**ga**ne || kei·naya·**le**wa || kara·tou·sā·laki·cina·**i**ka || nacaura·**vou** || ena·vei·**bo**gi ||

With this reordering, each phrase end is a potential sentence end. Thus, by examining various orders, one can find the "natural" or "unmarked" order of phrases within the sentence.

40.3 SUMMARY

From these few examples, two patterns emerge. First, for these sentences of medium length, there is a tendency to group the material into two main intonational units (note that we have no name for this putative and rather indistinct phonological unit). There is support for this hypothesis: some speakers divide even very short stretches of speech into two phrases: for example, the construction noun + stative (see section B).

Second, although the hypothesis is as yet ill-formed, there may be a general preferred length of phrases. Items that are too short to fit this general length seem to be discouraged if there is a way to avoid them (excepting, perhaps, vocatives and other short material that comprise a separate phrase). This tendency may explain why some speakers add modifying markers, such as *gā* (limiter) to some phrases, even though the situation doesn't seem to call for it. I have heard this explanation: "It sounds too light without it."

Thus, there may be opposing tendencies that account for the problem with sentence (3). The first: to divide the intonation into two parts, and the second: to avoid ill-balanced units within the sentence.

Finally, some of the mismatches between phonological and grammatical phrases may reflect a tendency to shorten that extends over several layers of the phonological hierarchy: i.e., shortening of vowels, measures, and phrases.

41 THE LAST WORD

As I put the finishing touches on this work, the lineage of Fijian grammars reaches back over 170 years into the past. Of these grammars, only the first—David Cargill's—is original, and even then, it is not entirely so. In his study of Fijian, Cargill was able to draw on his training in the European grammatical tradition, his knowledge of several languages, and his familiarity with Tongan grammar.

Cargill's work, although little-known now, spawned a succession of studies that eventually made Fijian one of the best-studied of the Oceanic language family. As a matter of fact, Robert H. Codrington, in his classic *The Melanesian languages* (1885:7), apologized for leaving Fiji out of his survey with this sentence (which nearly defies parsing):

> ... But the language of Fiji, so much the most important of all, is so well known as not to need what it would be a presumption on the part of one not practically acquainted with it to offer.

With such a long history and a variety of studies that include unpublished manuscripts, published grammars (both descriptive and pedagogical), published and manuscript dictionaries, and many articles that view some feature of Fijian grammar or phonology through the lens of contemporary theories, why write another grammar? (Or, perhaps more accurately, why revise one that has already been published?) One practical reason is that *TFL* has been out of print for years, and it is hard to find it on the Internet. Moreover, for the few used copies available, some prices asked are unreasonable.[1] If one searches the Internet for "Fijian grammar," most hits refer to three works in particular: the first a slim volume of 94 pages, the second a combination of a grammar and a primer, and the third a grammar not of SF but of a closely related Fijian language.

Indirectly, the topic of the Internet leads us to the title. I chose the earlier one, *The Fijian language* (*TFL*), because including the introductory chapters on the history of work on the language, and the extensive appendix of twenty annotated pre-missionary word lists that enclosed the main body of the work seemed to call for a title that suggested more than just "grammar." Now that these parts

---

[1] A check in January 2012, showed prices over US$900 for a used copy.

have been deleted and will appear as a separate publication,[2] perhaps the new title will be more visible in searches.

Still, the present grammar is more than an abridged and renamed version of the previous one. In the next sections, I discuss the features that are new, along with some that are old but have somehow remained outside the range of vision of linguists who have since written about Fijian. Finally, I discuss some of the criticisms in reviews and other works—accepting some points and refuting others.

41.1 NEW FEATURES

Several topics that did not appear in *TFL* have been added to this edition.

1. A study of the relationship between accent measures and morphemes (§36.7), based on a similar study for Hawaiian (Schütz 2010) adds weight to my argument that the role of accent in Fijian is demarcative,[3] and that any effort to write linear rules cannot succeed, particularly as they proceed awkwardly leftward or rightward, depending on the data. The study concludes that accent guides the hearer to meaning, not the other way around.

2. Discussions of recent loanwords illustrate added phonemes and altered syllable types (CH 34, 35). With the publication of *VV*, such examples are now readily accessible. However, because the dictionary does not include much sociolinguistic data beyond identifying words from Fijian languages other than SF, the treatment here is open-ended, pointing the way to potential research on which domains allow, or do not allow, the new loanwords containing what appear to be non-Fijian sounds and combinations of sounds.

3. An embryonic sociolinguistic study grew out of the play *Lakovi*, which exists in both printed and DVD form. It allowed me to view and hear different speech styles in context, while also providing such information as approximate ages and kinship relationships among the speakers. See §35.5.

41.2 FEATURES THAT ARE NOT NEW, BUT NEED TO BE EMPHASIZED

> *Tū na inima ka luvu na waqa.* 'The bailer is here, but the canoe sinks.' This idiom was explained by Anare K. Raiwalui (1954:38–39, #123) as follows: "... trying everything but the right way, when the solution is right before our eyes, but which we do not discover ..."

This *ivosavosa* 'idiom' seems an appropriate introduction to a discussion of certain topics that I consider important, but which have been ignored in recent works that touch on some aspect of Fijian grammar.

41.2.1 Phonology

Some topics, treated in *TFL*, are examples of important features of Fijian, and some other Oceanic languages, that still, after nearly thirty years, have not been

---

[2] Tentatively titled *Early studies of Fijian*.
[3] See CH 32 and §36.10 ff.

handled adequately in most other works on these languages. A few examples are:

    Prosodic analysis based on measures. See my various articles on Fijian, in addition to those on Tongan, Māori, Samoan, and Hawaiian, from Schütz 1976 to the present work.[4]

    Reorganization of morphological material dependent on measure sequences (§36.7).

    Vowel and diphthong shortening (§36.2.4 *et seq.*).

    The patterning of accented and unaccented syllables (§36.1). This topic includes combinations of light syllables, not "without accent," but which comprise measures with a lower level of accent (§36.1, §39.3.5).

    A hierarchical view of prosody (CH 40).

    Links between phonology and grammar (CH 39).

41.2.2. Subjects, objects, and transitivity

Classifying "pronominal" elements in the VP as subject and object allows us to reinterpret the NPs that occur outside the VP and give more information about these items. This analysis eliminates the need for terms such as "split subject," "subject pronouns," and "agreement markers." Specification also accounts for NPs in possessive constructions as well. Above all, the concept shows that context is essential for grammatical analysis, demonstrating that analyzing sentences out of context skews one's picture of the grammar. See CH 26.

Because so many secondhand linguists[5] have ignored this analysis, they are unaware that interpreting Fijian as a VOS (Verb-Object-Subject) language is a house built on the shifting sands of elicited sentences or those taken out of context. In a recent example (a 2012 *Oceanic Linguistics* article), Fijian is grouped among VOS languages. Although a number of linguists have used this approach, here are some examples from just a few sources.[6]

One study claimed that the word order in Fijian is the same as it is in Polynesian languages—that is, verb-initial. Leaving out third-person subjects for the time being, note the obvious structural difference between the following HAW and FIJ sentences:

    HAW: *Hele au.*   'I'm going.'   FIJ: *Au lako.*   'I'm going.'
         go   1s   1s go

Clearly, HAW is a verb-initial language and FIJ isn't.

---

[4] A fuller set of references can be found on the website of the Department of Linguistics, University of Hawai'i at Mānoa.

[5] I have coined this term (similar to "armchair linguist/anthropologist" of some years ago) to refer to linguists who use written data from other works without investigating the context or making an effort to hear the language spoken. The term can be altered slightly to be more specific, e.g., secondhand phonologists, secondhand grammarians, and others.

[6] Scholarship and politeness are at odds here: I have tried to paraphrase the pertinent selections so that the names of the writers are not obvious.

With such evidence at hand, why has the verb-initial label survived? Perhaps analysts feel that subjects and objects have to be NPs. Otherwise, it is difficult to understand how they could ignore the large number of sentences whose subjects are in first or second person and do not have to be further specified.

Sentences with third person subjects operate differently: as noted several paragraphs above, somewhere in the discourse, almost always at the beginning, the subject needs to be specified. Unfortunately, many sample sentences in grammars are taken out of context. This often leads to the conclusion that NPs specifying subjects and objects are obligatory.

Other linguists have written about "the order of the nominals after the verb." The definite article before *nominals* in that phrase gives the impression that NPs following the verb are obligatory; as earlier discussions in this grammar should have made clear, they are optional and determined by context. This statement would be closer to being accurate if the phrase *if any* were inserted after *nominals*. Still, when those NPs do occur, the one that specifies the object *usually* precedes the one that specifies the subject.

It is not surprising to find that the example sentence given in this argument has this form:[7]

[Subject verb TR marker object]	[NP]	[NP]
Era gunu- v- a	na yaqona	na tūraga
'The chiefs drink the kava.'	(kava)	(chief)

In other words, the example has the form of a typical elicited sentence, not one appearing in normal discourse. If the context had already been established, the sentence would have this form:

Era gunuva. 'They drink it.'

Another article uses the phrase "pronominal agreement markers," which prompts these questions:

What is agreeing with what?

What is marking what?

Do VPs with the subject and object in first or second person have only pronominal agreement markers and no subjects or objects?

What do "preverbal subject markers" mark if there are no specifying NPs in the sentence?

At the time of writing, the situation has not changed much. A recent article on Fijian transitivity (Aranovich 2013) contains such statements as the following:

... Particles like *au* ... or *e* ... specify the person and number of the subject ... these person/number markers are analyzed as agreement markers, not as subjects, since they can co-occur with an overt subject ... (p. 467)

Obviously, the questions just above apply to this analysis as well.

---

[7] I have substituted a sentence of the same form for the example given in the source.

Here are some additional problems:

1. The article suggests that it is a new idea that pronouns and proper nouns are part of the verb phrase (p. 471).

2. It uses the well-worn phrase "incorporated objects" (pp. 478 ff.), apparently not realizing that in a construction such as *gunu yaqona* 'kava drinking', *yaqona* is not an object, but a modifier (Milner 1972:26), and that the construction has a discourse function of focusing on the **activity** rather than the **entity**. In other words, the construction is intransitive, not transitive. This is only one of many examples that lead to this conclusion: context seems to play little or no role in any part of the analysis.

3. It credits a 1998 article for the idea that a NP specifying an object [my terminology here] is **appositional**, ignoring the same proposal—and term—in Schütz and Nawadra 1972 (see *TFL* 403). This view eventually led to my analyzing so-called pronominal elements in the VP as subjects and objects and NPs as specified subjects and objects, added if the hearer (or reader) does not have this information.[8]

In conclusion: as with so many similar studies, the article cited approaches the matter from the wrong direction.

41.2.3 Specificity

The idea that specification operates as a grammatical category began as the linguistic equivalent of a flashing red light: different forms with the same translation. As explained in CH 26, the following two sentences were both translated as 'The pig was trapped' (Biggs 1974:425):

E tobo na vuaka.
E tobo-ki na vuaka.

When TRN (p.c.) explained the subtle difference in meaning between the two sentences, it became clear that neither sentence is specific about the actor. However, whereas in the first, the actor is completely out of the picture, he/she/it is suggested in the second. This subtle difference led to the discovery that instead of the binary opposition of intransitive vs. transitive in SF senten-ces, there are four degrees of specificity about the actor and the goal.

In the present edition of the grammar, the original table (*TFL*, table 30.5) showing seventeen different combinations of specificity has been enlarged to twenty-two (table 26.5).

As the chapter on specificity explains, this system is not confined to transitivity, but extends to other grammatical topics as well.

---

[8] On a different level, I find it discouraging that this study, based on at least a short period in the field and on many published sources, should ignore vowel length in the examples in which it occurs.

41.2.4 Verb classification

Previous descriptions of verb classification have been either minimal (e.g., confined to the opposition between transitive vs. intransitive) or tied to particular affixes. In this work, although such affixes are listed and described, classifying verbs according to two dimensions—Active (A) vs. Stative (S), and One-referent (1) vs. Two-referent (2)—allows us for the first time to describe verb derivation in an organized, symmetrical way.

The class of A1 (i.e., an active verb without semantic or formal reference to a goal), has been disputed in some other treatments. To counter this argument, I have checked the examples here with the entries in *VV*.[9] However, as mentioned earlier in this work and in *TFL*, not all speakers interpret and use certain words (e.g., *gādē* 'stroll') as A1.

41.2.5 Verb derivation

Another argument for the A1 class, missed by critics, is a class of A1 verbs produced by derivation. For these verbs, a prefix deletes the goal (see §13.4).

The discussion of verb derivation and its relationship to the four-part system of verb classification is unmatched in any other study. Instead of noting the effects of certain affixes (as alluded to in the previous section), this treatment begins with the 2 x 2 system named just above, and notes the types of changes that *can* be made. Examples are A2 → S2; S2 + *-Ca* → A2; S2 + reduplication → A2, *et al.*

41.2.6 *Na*: Definite N marker

The prevailing view in the writings on Fijian grammar preceding *TFL* was that *na* was a common marker or a "determiner." For example, Pawley wrote (1977):

> ... *na* does no more than indicate that the noun is common, the definiteness being marked by the person-marker."[10]

I countered this view in an article (Schütz 1982) and in *TFL*, in which the discussion of the complex areas of **definite**, **indefinite**, and **general** extends from pp. 323–35[11] and the analysis relies heavily on discourse data.

Although earlier, Arms (1974:61–62) had called *na* a marker of common nouns (as opposed to proper nouns), marking an absence of indefiniteness, in his review of *TFL* (1987:113) he changed his position, writing: "Schütz makes an excellent case for treating the article *na* as truly a 'definite article.'"

---

[9] As a result, I have deleted some examples that appeared in *TFL*. In *VV*'s treatment, generally one of the part-of-speech designations for words such as those listed here is "*v*"—in contrast to "*vt*," which shows that the word can enter into transitive constructions.

[10] Pawley may have changed his opinion since then. Later (1986:108) he glossed *na* as "ART—specific common noun marker."

[11] For reasons mentioned in the Introduction, this long discussion has been deleted in the present edition.

Other grammarians apparently did not read either the section or the review very carefully. Dixon (1988:114–15) wrote:

> The common article *a ~ na* is used with common nouns ...
> The common article is basically unmarked for definiteness (See Arms 1974:61–[6]3); it can often be translated by the definite article *the* in English and sometimes by the indefinite article *a(n)* ... A rough rule is this: if *a* or *an* in English can be replaced by *one* (as in *I own a pig*), it can be translated by *e dua a* NOUN; otherwise, just use the Fijian common article *a* (e.g. *I'm a schoolteacher*).

Aside from the circularity of the first phrase, the vagueness and invalidity of the claim that *a ~ na* is "basically unmarked for definiteness," and the absence of any evidence that discourse data were used in the investigation of the function of *na*, what stands out in this treatment is the anachronistic translation analysis.

41.3 HOW SUGGESTIONS FROM REVIEWS ARE TREATED

When writers revise a work, comprehensive reviews of the first edition provide them with an opportunity to improve, correct, and expand. I have tried to treat each constructive criticism from two major review articles (Siegel 1987, Arms 1987) one by one, either accepting it or rejecting it. After all, it is the writer's choice.

The suggestions most readily accepted are those that pointed out omissions from my list of grammatical markers.[12] Another valid criticism (Arms, 115) concerned my misguided decision to mark diphthongs as long where they did not shorten. While writing *TFL*, I changed my mind several times and finally settled on the wrong choice. Correcting that error was one of the first changes to this edition.

A different kind of change, not widely suggested by reviewers, was to eliminate the long historical introduction and the pre-missionary word lists. I did this not because the historical section was "anecdotal" or the lists "of very limited pertinence to the core of the work" (Arms 1987:102), but because the book was too long. I still consider these topics to be important, as they are for the study of any language.[13] Originally, these parts of the grammar were aimed at Fijian teachers,[14] as is the proposed publication of these excised sections.

Those criticisms that have been rejected concern differences in our points of view. Some examples are:

---

[12] As noted in the pertinent sections, I found the treatment in Arms 1986 extremely useful. I have tried to expand the lists that appear in *TFL*, but make no claim that they are now complete.

[13] For example, Siegel wrote (1987:122): "These materials are invaluable not only for historians, but also for sociolinguists studying language contact and pidginization, as I have found in my own work ..."

[14] Four of the lists comprised part of the materials written for the first Fijian Language Workshop (Schütz 1978d). After hearing the lectures and seeing the material, Tevita R. Nawadra said, "I knew more about the War of the Roses than I did about the history of my own language."

1. Choice of topics. Why did I choose to describe one grammatical category in detail rather than another? For example, I chose transitivity over possession because I found the topic more complicated and my treatment more controversial/interesting. In other words, there was more to say about it, and I thought it was important to show how my view differed from those of others. In contrast, I found possession less interesting in that my treatment added little to the views of others, except (1) for an important refinement of the "control" aspect of alienable vs. inalienable possession (see §30.1.2), and (2) the idea that NPs could specify certain possessive markers in addition to subjects and objects, thus including possession in the realm of specification.

2. Phonological differences of opinion. For the most part, I ignored any criticisms of my basing the treatment of phonology solidly on the concept of the measure; it was clear that some critics did not understand the system. In particular, I found statements that there could be a series of more than two unaccented syllables in succession[15] to be mistaken. See Schütz 1987:126.

3. Interpretation of the grammatical subject. In his review of *TFL*, Arms (1987:103) suggested that my analysis of specification "does not mean that noun phrases cannot also be subjects." I reject this idea; in my treatment, the only subjects are the person-number markers that occur before the verb. My use of the term "specified subject" (perhaps a misleading term) does not imply that any NP is a subject.

Arms also maintained (p. 104) that "the 'optional' noun phrase may not be so optional at all." This is his supporting example sentence, with emphasis added:

Eratou sā liu i Nadi **na marama** '**The women** have gone ahead to Nadi.'

His point was that within a "particular discourse … *na marama* would be a necessary part of the utterance if 'the women' were being introduced into the conversation for the first time …" However, this approach mixes discourse requirements with sentence structure. *Eratou* is still the subject, and *na marama* is still an NP that specifies the subject.

4. Omission of certain elements in casual style. Trying to deal with different speech styles in one work is a type of mixing of levels. My view is that one begins with a fairly formal style of the language, and then proceeds to other levels. For some topics, I have mentioned changes due to "fast speech," but for the most part have left this style for others to describe. For a pioneering example of such a treatment, see Tamata 1994.

5. Lack of an extended text. Several reviewers of *TFL* expressed their disappointment that no texts were included. My original plans included not texts *per se*, but a chapter on discourse analysis. As I wrote in Schütz 1987:127, it was to be called

"Beyond the sentence." As it turned out, however, it was beyond *me*. Discourse is a

---

[15] Even two successive unaccented syllables have to belong to separate measures.

complex topic, the methodology is not well defined, and it would have added years to the completion of the grammar. So I opted for publication over perfection.

Including an extended text (without discourse analysis) can be valuable (e.g., that in Dixon 1988). However, this practice is more useful for a language/dialect in which little written material exists than for a language with a body of literature. SF belongs in the latter category because of the amount of printed material available, including Fijian-language newspapers. In the Introduction, the reader can find ten sources for example sentences, and within the body of the grammar, a majority of the example sentences are identified so that with the help of a library that specializes in Pacific material, the reader can find the context.

For topics in which a larger context is immediately necessary in order to understand, say, a particular function word, more examples are given. See, for example, the treatments of *qai* (sequential marker, §5.4.1), preverbal *mai* (directional, §5.14.1), or *dui* (individuality, §5.9.1).

41.4 SUMMARY

It should be obvious that this grammar is primarily descriptive. Whether it fits into any theoretical framework, past or present, may be of interest to some of its readers, but not to me. For this reason, I found the following quotation satisfying:

> [Douglas] Oliver[16] evidenced little interest in the theoretical issues of anthropology. He thought theories have a limited shelf life and that they come and go with time. In both print and conversation he emphasized the importance of solid description. He valued straightforward language and had little or no tolerance for the use of jargon ... (Kiste 2011:14).

As examples of linguistic approaches with "a limited shelf life," consider tagmemics, stratificational grammar, and lexicase. Realizing that works written in any of these frameworks are now nearly unreadable, I opted for a more neutral approach, using mainly traditional grammatical terms and avoiding jargon when possible.

The approaches listed above are from the past; there would have been no pressure to use them. As for current models, I have no doubt that most—perhaps all—of them will also eventually become passé.

To conclude this work, I return to the topic of how to deal with criticism, using two examples that tell us more about what was included, and what was not, in one of the major works in the lineage of Fijian grammars. The following passage (*TFL*:125) was deleted from its logical place in the current work. However, here, in its slightly altered form, its message can be instructive.

Churchward's published grammar (1941) did not include one of the author's major insights into the language, as revealed in correspondence about his project. In early 1937, Churchward gave two copies of his draft to the Acting Secretary for Native Affairs in Fiji, asking for criticism. The Secretary sent one

---

[16] Oliver was a well-known figure in Pacific anthropology, especially for his work on Tahitian history and culture.

copy to the Rev. Fr. J. Neyret, who was compiling a Fijian-English dictionary at the time.

Much of Neyret's criticism (1937) seems to reflect an entirely semantic approach to parts of speech, a stance inappropriate for Fijian. For example, consider Churchward's suggestion that verbs and adjectives are related, to which Neyret responded (Churchward 1938):

> I deny the parity between *savasava* [*savasavā* 'clean'] and *cici* ['run'].[17] The fact that *cici* must take the particle *sa* [*sā*], like all the Fijian verbs, does not prove that *savasava* is a verb in the sentence *Sa savasava na gone* ['the child is clean'].[18] *Cici* means the action of running. Whereas *savasava* means only the quality of being clean.
>
> "Quod gratis asseritur gratis negatur." [That which is freely asserted is just as freely negated.]

Contrary to Neyret's assertions, the words in question are both verbs: a stative (S1) and an active (A2). But at another level, they do differ, in that statives can modify nouns, whereas actives almost never do.

Unfortunately, Churchward accepted this "correction" and adopted a more traditional division of verbs and adjectives into separate parts of speech. It remained for Milner to make the (implicit) connection between adjectives and verbs—at least at one level.

However, Churchward did not yield all his territory. As he wrote to Neyret (29/1/38): "… whenever I have found that what I wrote is correct, criticisms notwithstanding, I am leaving things as they were." Such is the case with his analysis of *sega* 'not' as a verb (1941:25). Neyret questioned this analysis, ignoring the syntactic properties of *sega*, and writing:

> "Sega" is really a Verb? "Gratis asseritur".
> Why is it not a Negative Adverb?

But Churchward maintained his position. And perhaps following his model, later grammarians, studying a number of Oceanic languages, have also noted that negatives behave not as adverbs, but as verbs.

How does this story relate to the present grammar? Some of the criticisms of the ideas expressed in *TFL* simply involve different points of view. In such cases, I can only state that I believe my views more accurately reflect the way the language works. Thus, to repeat Churchward's terse rejoinder,

"… criticisms notwithstanding, I am leaving things as they were."

---

[17] To mark forms and glosses, I have used current linguistic conventions. Unless Churchward's original draft still exists, we do not know how he phrased his idea or what examples he gave.

[18] Neyret's use of *must* is inaccurate: *sā*, an aspect marker, *may* occur before the verb, but is not required to. Treating it as an obligatory particle obscures its meaning and function, and reflects a practice common in the mid-nineteenth century when the Bible was being translated into Fijian.

REFERENCES

A fuller account and acknowledgments appear in *TFL*, pp. 623–72. In the references to that edition of the grammar, I tried to include every work that I could find—major or minor—connected with Fijian grammar. With one exception, the references here are only those that appear in the body of *FRG*.

The exception is that I have included the linguistic writings of Tevita R. Nawadra—at least the ones I have a record of. It is a small effort to honor his memory.

Conventions

a. Names. If an author signed a work with last name and initials, I have tried to supply the first name (enclosed in brackets). The purpose of this information is to make it easier to find an item in card catalogues, whether traditional or electronic.

b. Contrary to usual practice for the references at the end of a book, page numbers are supplied for many of the books and monographs, including small roman numerals to indicate front matter and back matter. The conventions used, however, are somewhat simpler than those used by cataloguers.

c. Where possible, call numbers for manuscript material are included as part of the main entry.

Explanation of minimal annotation. Square brackets contain two main types of information:

a. Bracketed material written as part of the reference contains (1) information about the location of unpublished material and rare published material, and (2) miscellaneous information about publication, such as reprints and new editions.

b. Bracketed material written separately after a reference is sketch annotation. It accompanies items whose titles do not give an indication of their relationship to Fijian grammar or the history of grammatical scholarship.

Text material

Material *in* the Fijian language has not been included, except for that which discusses the grammar or that which has been used for examples in the grammar. A list of Fijian language material used as examples in the text can be found in the front matter under "5. Text and source abbreviations."

Anderson, William. 1776–77. *A journal of a voyage made in His Majestys Sloop Resolution.* In Beaglehole 1955–74 (III, pt. 2):721–986. [See p. 959.]

Aranovich, Raúl. 2013. Transitivity and polysynthesis in Fijian. *Language* 89(3):465–500.

Arms, David G. 1973. Whence the Fijian transitive endings? *Papers of the First International Conference on Comparative Austronesian Linguistics, 1974. Oceanic Linguistics* 12:503–58.

———. 1974. Transitivity in Standard Fijian. University of Michigan PhD dissertation. xii, 278 *ll*.

———. 1978. Fijian "sā" and "se" aspect. *Second International Conference on Austronesian Linguistics: Proceedings*, ed. by S[tephen] A. Wurm and Lois Carrington, 691–716. Fascicle 2: Eastern Austronesian. Canberra: Australian National University.

———. 1984. Surface order in the Standard Fijian verb phrase. Paper presented at the Fourth International Conference on Austronesian Linguistics, Suva, Fiji. 28 pp. Revised Feb. 1985.

———. 1985. Revised version of Arms 1984.

———. 1986. Published version of Arms 1984. *FOCAL I: Papers from the Fourth International Conference on Austronesian Linguistics*, ed. by Paul Geraghty, Lois Carrington, and S[tephen] A. Wurm, 199–230. Canberra: Pacific Linguistics, C-93.

———. 1987. Review of Schütz 1985a. *Te Reo* 30:123–27. [See Schütz 1987 for reply.]

———. 1989. Problems in Fijian orthography. *VICAL 1, Oceanic Languages. Papers from the Fifth International Conference on Austronesian Linguistics*, Auckland, New Zealand, January 1988, ed. by Ray Harlow and Robin Hooper, 1–31. Auckland: Linguistic Society of New Zealand.

Beauclerc, G[eorge] A. F. W. 1908–10. The Fijian language. *Transactions of the Fijian Society*, 65–69.

Biggs, Bruce G. 1974. Some problems of Polynesian grammar. *Journal of the Polynesian Society* 83(4):401–26. [Pp. 424–25: discussion of verb classes in Fijian.]

———. 1975. Correspondence concerning "Some problems of Polynesian grammar." *Journal of the Polynesian Society* 84(4):493. [Correction to text of 1974 article, with further argumentation.]

———. 1978. The history of Polynesian phonology. *Second International Conference on Austronesian Linguistics: Proceedings*, ed. by S[tephen] A. Wurm and Lois Carrington, 691–716. Fascicle 2: Eastern Austronesian. Canberra: Australian National University.

———, and Rusiate R. Nayacakalou. 1958. Review of Milner 1956. *Journal of the Polynesian Society* 67(1):80–83.

Buse, J[asper] E. 1963. The structure of the Rarotongan verbal piece. *Bulletin of the School of Oriental (and African) Studies* 26(1):152–69.

Cammack, Floyd M. 1962. Bauan grammar. Cornell University PhD dissertation. 219 *ll*.

Capell, A[rthur]. 1941. *A new Fijian dictionary.* Sydney: Australasian Medical Publishing Co. x, 464 pp. [Actual date of completion: October 1942. 2nd ed. (1957), Glasgow: Wilson Guthrie. 3rd ed. (1968), Suva: Government Printer. First reprint (1973), Suva: Government Printer. vii, 407 pp. Second reprint (1984).]

Cargill, David. 1839. A grammar of the Feejeean language, Lakemba, 7th March 1839. 171 pp. ML MS. B 562. [Published as Schütz and Geraghty 1980.]

——, and William Cross. 1835. *A vosa vaka Viji i manda* [First book in Fijian]. Tongataboo [Tongatapu]: Wesleyan) Mission Press. 4 pp. [British and Foreign Bible Society, London.]

Chafe, Wallace. 1970. *Meaning and the structure of language.* Chicago: University of Chicago Press. 360 pp.

Churchward, C[lerk] Maxwell. 1938. Correspondence concerning *A new Fijian grammar.* Fiji Archives N44/85.

——. 1941. *A new Fijian grammar.* Sydney: Australasian Medical Publishing Company. 94 pp. [Subsequent printings, Suva: Government Printer.]

——. 1959. *Tongan dictionary.* London: Oxford University Press. xiv, 836 pp.

Clark, Ross. 1973. Transitivity and case in Eastern Oceanic languages. *Papers of the First International Conference on Comparative Austronesian Linguistics. Oceanic Linguistics* 12(1,2):559–605.

——. 1977. Eastern Oceanic transitive suffixes and the genesis of rules. Paper read to the Austronesian Symposium, Linguistic Society of America Summer Institute, University of Hawai'i at Mānoa, 18–20 August. Typescript. 26 *ll*.

Codrington, R[obert] H. 1885. *The Melanesian languages.* Oxford: Clarendon Press. viii, 572 pp. [P. 10: minimized the idea of Polynesian influence on Fijian.]

Condax, Iovanna D. 1979. Syllable durations and phonological groups. *Journal of the Acoustical Society of America* 66 (S1), S50 (A).

Crystal, David. 1980. *A first dictionary of linguistics and phonetics.* Boulder: Westview Press. 390 pp.

Davies, John. 1825. *Sa alphabeta na vosa faka Fiji.* Burder's Point (Tahiti): London Missionary Society Press. 8 pp.

De Ricci, J[ames] H. 1875. *Fiji: Our new province in the South Seas.* London: Edward Stanford. viii, 332 pp.

Dixon, R.M.W. 1988. *A grammar of Boumaa Fijian*. Chicago: University of Chicago Press. xx, 375pp.

Dumont d'Urville, Jules S. C. 1834. *Voyage de découvertes de l'*Astrolabe *exécuté par ordre du Roi pendant les années 1826–1827–1828–1829.* Paris: Ministère de la Marine. 6 pts. in 15 v. [V. 2 of Pt. 6 (on philology), pp. 137–42: Fijian word list, collected by Joseph P. Gaimard.]

Foley, William A. 1976. Comparative syntax in Austronesian. University of California, Berkeley PhD dissertation. 241 *ll*. [Pp. 47, 54–62, 155–86: treatment of Fijian grammar.]

Forbes, Litton. 1875. *Two years in Fiji*. London: Longmans, Green and Co. xii, 340 pp.

Fox, Anthony. 2000. *Prosodic features and prosodic structure: The phonology of suprasegmentals*. Oxford and New York: Oxford University Press. [See p. 39 for Kenneth Pike's (1947) criteria for deciding between long vowels and geminate vowels, and p. 115 for the distinction between stress and accent, which happens to match the approach used in the present grammar.]

Geraghty, Paul. 1973. Constraints on bi-syllabic morphemes. Unpublished paper.

———. 1976. Fijian prepositions. *Journal of the Polynesian Society* 85(4):507–20.

———. 1977. The development of the pronoun system of Bauan Fijian. Paper read to the Austronesian Symposium, Linguistic Society of America Summer Institute, University of Hawai'i at Mānoa, 18–20 August. Typescript, 31 *ll*.

———. 1979. Topics in Fijian language history. University of Hawai'i at Mānoa PhD dissertation. xx, 398 *ll*. Published as Geraghty 1983.

———. 1982. Na vosa vakaViti raraba kei na kena i volavolai. Na lewa e so ni I Volavosa VakaViti [Standard Fijian and its spelling. Some rules from the Fijian Dictionary Project]. Typescript, 9 *ll*. Suva, Fijian Dictionary Project.

———. 1983. *The history of the Fijian languages*. Oceanic Linguistics Special Publication no. 19. Honolulu: University of Hawai'i Press. 483 pp. [Published version of Geraghty 1979.]

———. 1984. Language policy in Fiji and Rotuma. In Milner, Arms, and Geraghty 1984:32–84.

Geraghty, Paul, and Andrew Pawley. 1977. Fijian reflexes of Proto-Central Pacific *ae and *ao. Mimeographed, 20 *ll*. [Preliminary version of Geraghty and Pawley 1981.]

Geraghty, Paul, and Andrew Pawley. 1981. The relative chronology of some innovations in the Fijian languages. *Studies in Pacific languages & cultures in honour of Bruce Biggs*, ed. By K[enneth] Hollyman and Andrew Pawley,

159-78. Auckland: Linguistic Society of New Zealand. [Published version of Geraghty and Pawley 1977.]

Hale, Horatio [Emmons]. 1846. A grammar and vocabulary of the Vitian language. In *Ethnology and philology, United States Exploring Expedition 1838–42*, vol. 6, 365–424. Philadelphia: Lea and Blanchard. (Unofficial issue; reprinted 1968. Ridgewood, N.J.: The Gregg Press.)

Hayes, Bruce. 1995. *Metrical stress theory: Principles and case studies*. Chicago and London: University of Chicago Press. xv, 455 pp.

Hazlewood, David. 1841–50. Journal. 3 vols. ML Methodist Church, Dept. of Overseas Missions. Book 132.

———. 1850. *A compendious grammar of the Feejeean language* ... Vewa [Viwa]: Wesleyan Mission Press. 72 pp. [According to Wood 1978:91, the dictionary was finished in March 1851. Because it was sent to the printer in sections, it is likely that 1850 is the date of the printing of the first section of the dictionary. It follows, then, that the printing of the grammar was completed even later. The dictionary and grammar were bound together in the 1872 edition, edited by James Calvert. London: Sampson Low, Marston & Co. 1914 edition: London: Waterlow & Sons. Reprint of the 1872 edition: New York: AMS Press (1979).]

———. 1872. See Hazlewood 1850.

———. 1914. See Hazlewood 1850. [This is the version I have used as a reference; page numbers in citations follow this edition.]

Hockett, Charles F. 1955. *A manual of phonology*. Memoir 11 of the IJAL. v, 246 pp. [P. 95: interpretation of Fijian consonant system discussed. Other Fijian references on pp. 55, 86, 92, 95, 99, 124, 125.]

———. 1958. *A course in modern linguistics*. New York: Macmillan. xi, 621 pp. [Fijian references on pp. 193, 230ff, 234, 284ff, 288ff, 311ff, 469ff.]

———. 1972. An outline of Fijian (preliminary version). Typescript. 90 *ll*.

———. 1990. Review of *Pacific Island languages: Essays in honour of G. B. Milner*, ed. by Jeremy H. C. S. Davidson. *Oceanic Linguistics* 31(2):287–96.

Hornell, James. 1927. String figures from Fiji and Western Polynesia. *Bull. Bishop Mus.* 39. ii, 88 pp.

Hyman, Larry M. 1975. *Phonology: Theory and analysis*. New York: Holt, Rinehart & Winston. xiii, 268 pp.

King, Anne. 1969. A note on stress in Fijian. *Journal of the Polynesian Society* 78(4):531–32.

Kiste, Robert C. 2011. *Douglas Oliver, February 10, 1913–October 30, 2009. A biographical memoir.* Washington D.C.: National Academy of Sciences.

Krupa, Viktor. 1966. The phonemic structure of bi-vocalic morphemic forms in Oceanic languages. *Journal of the Polynesian Society* 75(4):458–97.

Lehmann, Christian. 1982. Directions for interlinear morphemic translations. *Folia Linguistica* 16:199–224.

Lynch, John D. 1973. Verbal aspects of possession in Melanesian languages. *Papers of the First International Conference on Comparative Austronesian Linguistics, 1974. Oceanic Linguistics* 12(1,2):69–102.

Lyons, John. 1966. Toward a "notional" theory of the "parts of speech." *Journal of Linguistics* 2:209–36.

——. 1968. *Introduction to theoretical linguistics*. Cambridge: University Press. x, 519 pp.

Mariner, William. 1827. An account of the natives of the Tonga Islands. Compiled by John Martin. 2 vols. London: Constable. [Vol. 2, p. 76: a brief comment on Fijian.]

Martinet, André. 1960/64. *Elements of general linguistics*. (Originally in French. Paris: Librairie Armand Colin.) Translated by Elisabeth Palmer. Chicago: University of Chicago Press. 205 pp.

Milner, G[eorge] B. 1956. *Fijian grammar*. Suva: Government Press. vii, 150 pp. [2nd. ed., 1967; 3rd. ed., 1972, 195 pp. An index was added to the 3rd edition. Moreover, some page numbers in the text differ from those in the 1956 edition. Citations in the present work are from the 1972 edition.]

——. 1966. *Samoan dictionary*. London: Oxford University Press. xlvi, 465 pp.

——. 1972. See Milner 1956.

——. 1982. Consonant and vowel harmony in Fijian verbal suffixes. Paper for a Festschrift for Eugénie Henderson. Typescript. 27 *ll*. [Preliminary version of Milner 1985, which has a different title.]

——. 1985. On prosodic relations between Fijian bases and verbal suffixes. *South-East Asian linguistics: Essays in honour of Eugénie J. A. Henderson*, ed. by J. H. C. S. Davidson, 59–87. London: School of Oriental and African Studies. [Published version of Milner 1982.]

——. 1998. Draft version of Fijian-English dictionary.[The introduction, some 60 typescript pp., contains some idiosyncratic ideas about Fijian grammar and what a dictionary should contain (or omit), especially with respect to borrowings from English. So far as I know, the work has not been published or made available on-line.]

——, and Tevita R. Nawadra. 1981. Cutting words in Fijian. *Studies in Pacific languages & cultures in honour of Bruce Biggs*, ed. by K[enneth] Hollyman and Andrew Pawley, 179–96. Auckland: Linguistic Society of New Zealand.

——; D[avid] G. Arms; and P[aul] Geraghty. 1984. *Duivosavosa / Fiji's languages: Their use and their future*. Fiji Museum Bulletin No. 8. 84 pp.

Moore, William J. 1906. A practical course to facilitate the study of the Fijian language. By a Marist Brother. Suva: Alport Barker.

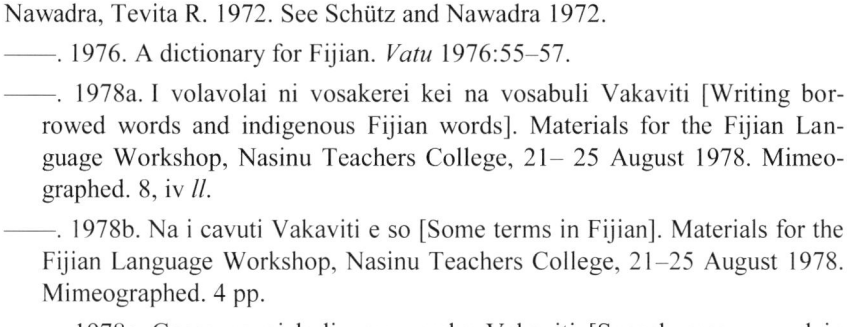

Nawadra, Tevita R. 1972. See Schütz and Nawadra 1972.

——. 1976. A dictionary for Fijian. *Vatu* 1976:55–57.

——. 1978a. I volavolai ni vosakerei kei na vosabuli Vakaviti [Writing borrowed words and indigenous Fijian words]. Materials for the Fijian Language Workshop, Nasinu Teachers College, 21– 25 August 1978. Mimeographed. 8, iv *ll*.

——. 1978b. Na i cavuti Vakaviti e so [Some terms in Fijian]. Materials for the Fijian Language Workshop, Nasinu Teachers College, 21–25 August 1978. Mimeographed. 4 pp.

——. 1978c. Gacagaca ni buli vosa raraba Vakaviti [Speech organs used in Standard Fijian]. Materials for the Fijian Language Workshop, Nasinu Teachers College, 21–25 August 1978. Mimeographed. 2 *ll*.

——. 1979. A monolingual Fijian dictionary. Paper read to the Australian and New Zealand Association for the Advancement of Science, 49th Congress. University of Auckland, New Zealand, 22–26 January. 9, v l.

——. 1981. Na we ni nomu i kuita, au sa mai beci au tu kina [It is because of the weals of your whip that I despise myself]. *Sinnet: A Fiji Literary Quarterly* 2(3):23–29. [A discussion of the effects of past language policy in Fiji.]

——. 1981. See Milner and Nawadra 1981.

——. 1982. Na vosa vakaViti vakaBau [Bauan Fijian]. Typescript, 3 *ll*.

——. 1984. Na buli ni ivolavosa vakaViti [The form of the Fijian dictionary]. Paper presented at the Fourth International Conference on Austronesian Linguistics, Suva, Fiji. 5 + 3 pp.

——. n.d. Na veika vakaturi me i dusidusi ni i volavolai ni vosa Vakaviti [Proposed guide to Fijian spelling]. Typescript. 12 *ll*.

Naylor, Paz Buenaventura, ed. 1980. *Austronesian studies. Papers from the Second Eastern Conference on Austronesian Languages*. Ann Arbor, Michigan Papers on South and Southeast Asia, no. 15. Center for South and South-east Asian Studies, The University of Michigan. 314 pp.

Neyret, Jean-Marie. 1937. Letter to Secretary for Native Affairs, and critique of draft of Churchward's Fijian grammar. From Cawaci (Ovalau), 11 Dec. 17 *ll*. Fiji Archives (Ref.: Fijian Affairs Board, File No. N44/85).

Palmer, Bill, and Dunstan Brown. 2007. Heads in Oceanic indirect possession. *Oceanic Linguistics* 46(1):199–209.

Parke, Aubrey L. 1981. Clause structure of Fijian. Australian National University MA thesis.

Pawley, Andrew K. 1972. On the internal relationships of Eastern Oceanic languages. *Studies in Oceanic culture history,* vol. 3, ed. by R[oger] C. Green and M[arion] Kelly. Honolulu, Bishop Mus. *Pacific Anthropological Records* 13:1–142.

———. 1973a. Fijian *y*. Lecture notes for Ling. 770, University of Hawai'i at Mānoa, fall semester. Typescript, 5 *ll*.

———. 1973b. Some problems in Proto-Oceanic grammar. *Papers of the First International Conference on Comparative Austronesian Linguistics. Oceanic Linguistics* 12(1,2):103–88.

———. 1986. A reanalysis of Fijian transitive constructions. *Te Reo* 29:81–112.

Pike, Kenneth L. 1947. *Phonemics: A technique for reducing languages to writing*. Ann Arbor: University of Michigan Press. xx, 254 pp.

Priscillien, (Brother). 1950. *Fijian as it should be spoken. A practical course to facilitate the study of the Fijian language.* By a Marist Brother. Sydney: O'Loughlin Brothers. 144 pp. [The cover reads: *Fijian as spoken. Compiled by the Marist Brothers*. A revised edition of Moore 1906.]

Pukui, Mary Kawena, and Samuel H. Elbert. 1986. *Hawaiian dictionary.* Honolulu: University of Hawai'i Press. xxvi, 572 pp.

Raiwalui, Anare K. 1954. *Na i vosavosa Vakaviti e so: A collection of Fijian idioms.* Melbourne: Oxford University Press. Published in association with the South Pacific Commission Literature Bureau. xvi, 51 pp.

Sapir, Edward. 1921. *Language: An introduction to the study of speech*. New York: Harcourt, Brace.

Schütz, Albert J. 1962. A dialect survey of Viti Levu. Cornell University PhD dissertation. v, 531 *ll*.

———. 1963. A phonemic typology of Fijian dialects. *Oceanic Linguistics* 2(2):62–79.

———. 1969. *Nguna grammar*. Oceanic Linguistics Special Publication No. 5. Honolulu: University of Hawai'i Press. 88 pp.

———. 1972a. *The languages of Fiji*. Oxford: Clarendon Press.

———. 1972b. *Say it in Fijian.* Sydney: Pacific Publications Pty. 54 pp. Revised editions 2003 and in preparation.

———. 1975. At a loss for words: the problem of word classes for Fijian. *Oceanic Linguistics* 14(2):100–118.

———, ed. 1978a. *Fijian language studies: Borrowing and pidginization. Bulletin of the Fiji Museum*, no. 4. vi, 98 p.

———. 1978b. English loanwords in Fijian. In Schütz 1978a:1–50.

———. 1978c. Accent in two Oceanic languages. *Anthropological Linguistics* 20(4):141–49.

———. 1978d. Fijian grammar for teachers: Materials used at the first Fijian workshop, Nasinu Teachers' College, August, 1978. 95 pp, 28 cm. Published as Schütz 1979.

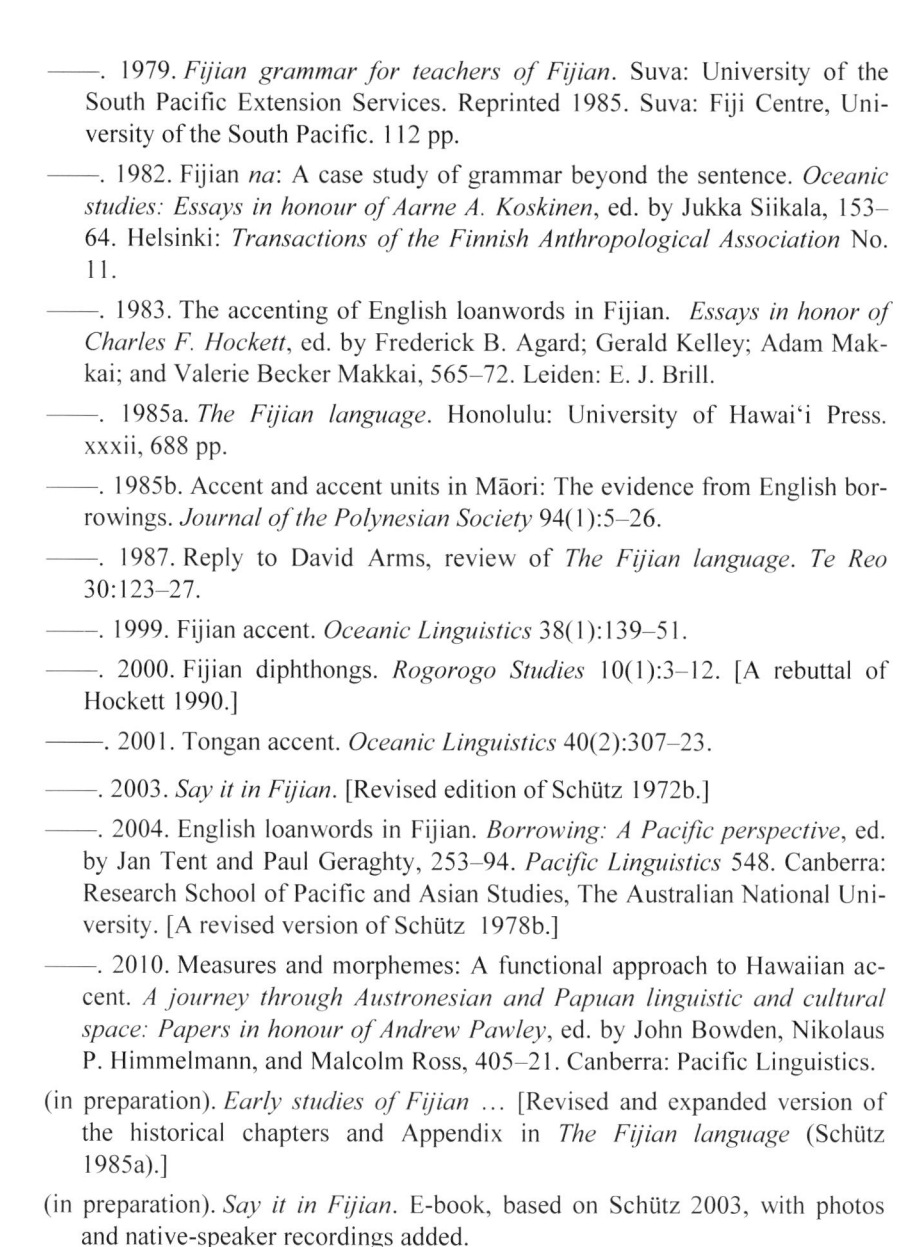

———. 1979. *Fijian grammar for teachers of Fijian*. Suva: University of the South Pacific Extension Services. Reprinted 1985. Suva: Fiji Centre, University of the South Pacific. 112 pp.

———. 1982. Fijian *na*: A case study of grammar beyond the sentence. *Oceanic studies: Essays in honour of Aarne A. Koskinen*, ed. by Jukka Siikala, 153–64. Helsinki: *Transactions of the Finnish Anthropological Association* No. 11.

———. 1983. The accenting of English loanwords in Fijian. *Essays in honor of Charles F. Hockett*, ed. by Frederick B. Agard; Gerald Kelley; Adam Makkai; and Valerie Becker Makkai, 565–72. Leiden: E. J. Brill.

———. 1985a. *The Fijian language*. Honolulu: University of Hawai'i Press. xxxii, 688 pp.

———. 1985b. Accent and accent units in Māori: The evidence from English borrowings. *Journal of the Polynesian Society* 94(1):5–26.

———. 1987. Reply to David Arms, review of *The Fijian language*. *Te Reo* 30:123–27.

———. 1999. Fijian accent. *Oceanic Linguistics* 38(1):139–51.

———. 2000. Fijian diphthongs. *Rogorogo Studies* 10(1):3–12. [A rebuttal of Hockett 1990.]

———. 2001. Tongan accent. *Oceanic Linguistics* 40(2):307–23.

———. 2003. *Say it in Fijian*. [Revised edition of Schütz 1972b.]

———. 2004. English loanwords in Fijian. *Borrowing: A Pacific perspective*, ed. by Jan Tent and Paul Geraghty, 253–94. *Pacific Linguistics* 548. Canberra: Research School of Pacific and Asian Studies, The Australian National University. [A revised version of Schütz 1978b.]

———. 2010. Measures and morphemes: A functional approach to Hawaiian accent. *A journey through Austronesian and Papuan linguistic and cultural space: Papers in honour of Andrew Pawley*, ed. by John Bowden, Nikolaus P. Himmelmann, and Malcolm Ross, 405–21. Canberra: Pacific Linguistics.

(in preparation). *Early studies of Fijian* … [Revised and expanded version of the historical chapters and Appendix in *The Fijian language* (Schütz 1985a).]

(in preparation). *Say it in Fijian*. E-book, based on Schütz 2003, with photos and native-speaker recordings added.

———, and Paul Geraghty, eds. 1980. *Fijian language studies II: David Cargill's Fijian grammar. Bulletin of the Fiji Museum*, no. 6. xxxii, 51 pp.

———, and Rusiate T. Komaitai. 1971. *Spoken Fijian*. Honolulu: University of Hawai'i Press. 257 pp. 2nd ed., 1979.

———, and Tevita R. Nawadra. 1972. A refutation of the notion "passive" in Fijian. *Oceanic Linguistics* 11(2):88–109.

Scott, N[orman] C. 1948. A study in the phonetics of Fijian. *Bulletin of the School of Oriental (and African) Studies* 12:737–52.

Siegel, Jeff. 1987. Review of *The Fijian language* (Schütz 1985a). *Oceanic Linguistics* 26(1,2):114–23.

Somosomo Quarterly. 24 June 1846. Mitchell Library MS. C 342.

Spelling Leaf Primer. 1840. ML P 390.07/7. [The alphabet, a few simple words and sentences, also illustrating type sizes.]

Spooner, Thomas, and George Melville. 1955. *Brother John: The life of the Rev. John Hobbs.* Auckland, *Wesley Historical Society (N.Z. branch) Proceedings* 13(2–4). 54 pp.

Stemberger, Joseph Paul. 1984. Length as a suprasegmental. *Language* 60(4): 895–913.

Tamata, Apolonia. 1994. Phonological changes in Standard Fijian casual speech. University of Hawai'i at Mānoa MA thesis.

———. 2003. The Fijian transitive ending – *(C)aki/a* in loan words. *Journal of Asian and African Studies* 65:207–27.

———. 2007. The glottal stop in Nasarowaqa Fijian and other Oceanic languages. University of the South Pacific PhD dissertation.

———, and Larry Thomas. 2011. *Lakovi*. Suva: iTaukei Trust Fund Board.

Tippet, A. R. 1953–54. An interesting aspect of sound movement and decay in the Fijian language. *Oceania* 24(3): 229–33. [Discussion of reduplication.]

iVolavosa vakaViti. [Fijian dictionary]. 2005. Suva: Tabana ni Vosa kei na iTovo Vakaviti. xvii, 996 pp.

Waterhouse, Joseph. 1866. *The king and people of Fiji: Containing a life of Thakombau; with notices of the Fijian, their manners, customs, and superstitions, previous to the great religious reformation in 1854.* Edited by George Stringer Rowe. London: Wesleyan Conference Office. xii, 435 pp. [P. 348–50: discussion of the language, including the author's thesis that Fijian languages can be divided into two distinct groups: aborigines and immigrants.]

Williams, Thomas. 1858. *Fiji and the Fijians: The Islands and their inhabitants.* Vol. 1, edited by George Stringer Rowe. London: Alexander Heylin.

———, and James Calvert. 1870. *Fiji and the Fijians, and missionary labours among the cannibals*, 3rd ed. London: Hodder and Stoughton.

Wolff, John U. 1980. Verbal morphology and verbal sentences in PAN. *Austronesian studies. Papers from the Second Eastern Conference on Austronesian Languages*, ed. by Paz Buenaventura Naylor, 153–67. [Pp. 155–60: proposed a focus system for Fijian.]

Wood, A. Harold. 1978. *Overseas missions of the Australian Methodist Church, vol. II, Fiji*. Melbourne: Aldersgate Press. viii, 410 pp.

INDEX

A

a: phonetic description, 4–5, 336; rising, before high vowels, 344
-a ('poetical suffix'): 233
a vs. *na*: 208–9
ā (past tense): 41–42
A1 verbs: definition, 92; examples, 92–93; through goal-deleting prefix, 110–11
A2 verbs: definition, 94–95; examples, 94–95. See CH 16.
ablative markers: examples, 21. See CH 21.
ablative NPs, 212–16; functions, 216–24; discussion, 223–24
accent: 5–6, 370; degree of predictability, 5–6, 382–88; determined by measure type, 341–42; determined by position, 342; determined by speech style, 342; vs. stress, 370; in disyllables and trisyllables, 384–86; influence on vowel quality and length, 343; loanwords as data, 383–84; patterns in native words and phrases, 384–86; phonemic status, 381; phonetic components, 370; relationship to morphology-syntax, 406; rules based on syllable count, 382–83; summary, 390
accompaniment, definition: 189
action/state, definition: 250
active, definition: 11–12
active to stative: A2 to S2, 104–5; S2 +-C-*a* to A2, 105–6
actor: 91; definition, 189, 250
addressee (2nd person): 29
adverbs: 271–75
affirmation, markers of: 186
aforementioned (*gona*): 180
aimless action, function of reduplication: 121
alienable possession: 304; definition and discussion, 306, 308–9; vs. inalienable, 306–7: variables, 320

alphabet: history, 6–8; table, 4
ambiguity, in ablative phrases: 215–16; avoiding, function of reduplication, 122
Anderson, William, samples of Fijian: 3
ao, rarity of vowel sequence: 345–46
appearance (VP, *rairai*): 55
Arms 1974: 36, 78, 106, 109, 110, 113, 122, 127, 200, 428
Arms 1978: 44
Arms 1984: 166
Arms 1986: 40, 46, 47, 50, 55
Arms 1987: 28, 411, 429, 430
Arms 1989: 374
articles, examples: 21. See CH 20.
artificial, created (V affix, *-tā-*): 79–80
aspect: contrast (past, *sā*), 42–43; contrast (future, *se*), 43–44
attributive possessive: see CH 30, 227
ayā, alternate of *oyā*: 243

B

b: reason for choosing, 7; phonetic description, 6, 349
baci (VP, iteration): 46–47
bagi (VP, expectation): 180
base: definition, 407; use of term in Milner 1972, 23n
basic sentences, 10
bau (VP, limitation): 48–49, 170–71
beka (VP, initiation): 179; (NP, moderative, dubitative): 230
Biggs 1974: 250–51, 427
Biggs 1975: test for actives, 86n
Biggs 1978: 387, 391
Biggs and Nayacakalou 1958: criticism of Milner 1972; part-of-speech treatment, 23; on *y*, 353
borrowed consonants, alternate forms: 358
borrowed words, reduplication in: 128
Bua, use of *era*: 30
bulu (VP, limitation): 170–71

Buse 1963: separating NP and VP, 23n

C

c: reason for choosing, 7; phonetic description, 6, 350
-(C)*a* (stative suffix): 80–81
cake (VP, 'upward' direction): 166–67
Cammack 1961: 32, 37
Cammack 1962: 36, 126, 186, 262, 324, 329, 363
Capell 1941: 22n, 48, 51, 78–79, 109, 110, 113, 125, 128, 145, 156n, 158, 168, 172n, 180, 186, 272, 310, 312, 329, 343n, 354, 355
Cargill, David: 7
Cargill 1839: 76, 112, 208, 303, 354, 355, 362, 423; use of *ko*, 32
Cargill and Cross 1835: 355
causative: 57–62
cause: definition, 189; indicated by *ni* phrases, 290–91
cava 'what?': 196
cei 'who?': 196
Chafe 1970: 99
Churchward 1938: 431–32
Churchward 1941: 35, 36, 37–38, 67, 81, 112, 113, 116, 127–28, 147, 149, 158, 160, 168, 177, 179, 186, 208, 225, 233, 234, 246, 261, 297, 306, 310, 317, 321, 322, 323, 324, 326, 327, 328, 329, 431; on *y*, 352; *sega* as a verb, 432
Churchward 1959: 66
cluster: 7
Codrington 1883: 303
Codrington 1885: 405n, 423
collections/groups, indicating: function of reduplication: 118–19
comitative NPs: 224–25
comment, definition: 10, 10n
common noun, definition: 192
common/definite article (*na*): 199–201
completion (VP, *tini*): 51–52
completive aspect (VP, *oti*): 169
compound verb: definition, 129; formal classification, 130–31; semantics, 131–32
compounds, reduplication of: 126
concomitant: 168–69
Condax, Iovanna, study of diphthong shortening: 374–75
Condax 1979: 363
consonants: table, 4; combinations, 365; indigenous, 347–53; introduced—traditional, 353–55; recent borrowings from English, 358; introductions, 353–58; syllable-final, 365; syllabic, 366
consonant changes: sociolinguistic context, 358; table, 359; formal vs. informal, 368; generational differences, 367–68; innovative vs. conservative, 368; regional and stylistic, 367; urban vs. rural, 368
consonant clusters: 366; syllable-final, 366; syllable-initial, 366
content word (root): 16, 19–21
continuative aspect: 176–79. See *tiko, tū, koto, nō, toka, voli*.
continuing motion (VP, *sau-*): 80
contractions of ablative markers: 221–23
coordination: 326–28
Cross, William: 7
Crystal 1980: 212
(C)V syllable shape: 5
CVCV, optimum measure type: 377–78

D

d: reason for choosing, 7; phonetic description, 6, 349
dau (VP, habitual): 47, 50; order changes, 47
Davies 1825: 355
dē (VP, 'lest'): 301–2; adversative vs. subjunctive, 301–2; morphophonemic changes, 302

definiteness: 199–201; with possessives, 319–20
deictic locative nouns: 242–46; to mark time, 243–44; optional *o*, 245–46
demonstratives referring to time: 243–44
derivation, types: 104–7
derived adverbs (*vaka-* + root): 273–75; deictic locatives, 273; *vaka* + nouns, 274; numerals, 274; statives, 273–75; verb + ablative NP, 275; verb + noun, 275; verb + subordinate VP, 275
derived forms, reduplication of: 124–26
derived nominalization: *i-* nouns, 235–39
desiderative (*via-* + V): 74–76
diphthong: list and definition: 5; definition, 338–40
diphthongization: as means of shortening bases, 372–75; effect on number of CVCV forms, 378–79; potential, definition, 339–40
direct goal, definition: 189
direction markers: 166–68, 182–86
directional NPs: 218–20
directionals (VP): preverbal *mai*, 52–53; *lai*$_1$, 54; *lai*$_2$, 54–55
discontinuous, dispersive function of reduplication: 120
distributive counter (*yā-*): 81
Dixon 1988: 96, 429, 431
dr: 7; phonetic description, 349
duadua (VP, 'alone', inclusion): 172
dual number: 29
dubitative, moderative (*beka*): VP, 179; NP, 230
dui (individuality): VP, 49–50; NP, 233
Duponceau, Peter, "phonology of language": 3

E

e, phonetic description: 336
e (locative): 216–17

ē (VP, sentence-final affirmation): 186
early studies of Fijian: 6–8
elliptical sentence, definition: 10–11
emission/projection verbs: 99
endocentric: 414
era, used in Bua and Lakeba: 30
even measures: 371, 381, 408
excess marker (VP, *rui*): 50
exclamations: 11
exclusive pronouns: 28, 29
existential verbs: definition, 12, 82–84; *tiko*, 83; *tū*, 83; *e* + numeral, 83–84; less common, 83
expectation marker (VP, *bagi*): 180
expressed level of specificity: 253–54
extreme, marker (VP, *rui*): 50

F

f: 7; phonetic description and history, 354
FDP (Fijian Dictionary Project): xxvii, xxix, xxxi, 87, 96, 347, 355, 356
Feejee (spelling): 8
Fejee (spelling): 8
Fijian, first written samples: 3
first person (subject): 29
Foley 1976: 99
Foreigner Talk: 3n
form: 11, 14–17
forming S1 verbs, function of reduplication: 117
Fox 2000: 337, 370
full sentence: definition, 10
function, criterion for part of speech: 20–21
function word (marker): 16
future tense marker (*na*): 42

G

g: reason for choosing: 7; phonetic description, 6, 350
gā (marker of limitation): VP, 181–82; NP, 231
generalization, discourse requirements, 204–5

genitive, Fijian: 261
Geraghty 1973: 122
Geraghty 1976: 178n, 216, 218, 220n, 223
Geraghty 1977: 20n, 28n, 32, 33, 165, 293n
Geraghty 1979: 238–39, 293n
Geraghty 1983: 20n, 26n, 37, 43n, 100n, 123n, 195, 240, 308, 310, 320n, 321, 322
Geraghty 1983a: 258, 353
Geraghty 1984: 224
Geraghty and Pawley 1977: 345n
glide: 353; lack of in Fijian vowel codas, 5
goal: 91; definition, 250
gona (VP, 'aforementioned'): 180, 228
grammatical correlates to phonological units: 332
grammatical idioms: 289
gw: phonetic description and discussion, 357

H

h: phonetic description, history, and discussion, 355–56
habitual marker (VP, *dau*): 47
Hale 1846: 34, 120, 351, 405
Halliday, M. A. K.: 99n
Hayes 1995: 382–84
Hazlewood, David: 9; on compound verbs, 132
Hazlewood [1850] 1872: 32, 35, 57n, 67, 76, 112, 113, 118, 208, 258, 261, 354, 405n
Hobbs, John: 7
Hocart 1910: 405n
Hocart 1917: 36
Hockett 1955: 363
Hockett 1958: 10n, 324, 375, 414; common vs. proper as gender, 192n; privileges of occurrence, 82n
Hockett 1972: 387n
Hockett 1990: 339
Hornell 1927: 73

Hyman 1975: 332
hyphens, use of: 10n

I

i: phonetic description, 4–5, 336
i (possessive marker): 317; with possessive classifiers, 317–18
i (proper object marker): 198, 226
i (vocative): 226–27
i/ki (directional): 218–19
i- nouns: another source?, 238–39; derived nominalization, 235–39; reduplication, 236; from derived verbs, 236–37; semantic view, 237–38
identfying sentences: definition, 13; definite and indefinite, 13
implicit level of specificity: 252
impression prefix (VP, *viavia-*): 76
inalienable possession: 304; definition, 306–7; types, 307
inclusion, markers (*kece, taucoko*): VP, 171–72; NP, 229–30
inclusive pronouns: 28, 29
indefinite constructions: 202–3
indefinite identifying constructions: in Milner's part-of-speech argument, 23
indicative: 32, 33n
indirect goal, definition: 189
individuality marker, VP, (*dui, yā*): 49, 50; NP, (*dui*): 233
infinitive form in Latin: 24
initiation (VP, *tei*): 48; (*beka, mada, bagi*): 179–80
instrument, definition: 189
integral noun: definition, 191; modification, 279
intensifier marker (NP, *sara*), 230; (VP, *soti/sō/sara*), 172–73
interlinear glosses, 10n
interludes: 375–76
intonation in S of two phrases: 414–17
intonation, guide to grammatical structure, meaning: 18

intonation portions: relationship to measures, 399
intonational features, phrase order: 17
Italianate (vowels): 6
iteration markers, VP: *baci*, 46–47; *tale, tale gā*, 174; NP, 230

J

j: 7–8; phonetic description and history, 355
judgment verbs: 100–101

K

k, phonetic description: 349
ka (coordination): 326–27
ka, linking numerals: 327
ka mani, linking numerals: 327
ka ni ('because'): meaning and use, 293, 327
kaya (*kei + a*): 225
kē: 296–97; marking two phrases, 297; morphophonemic changes, 298
kē-₁ (possessive prefix): 310
kē-₂ (possessive prefix): 308
kei (comitative): 224–25
kei (possessive): 318
kece (inclusion): VP, 171; NP, 229
kevakā ('if'): 298, 298n
ki: see *i*, 218–19
kin terms, as inalienable possessives: 306–7
ki-na: 221–22
ki vei vs. *mai vei*: 221
King 1969: 339, 382, 382n
Kiste 2011: 431
ko: in Lau-Vanua Levu area, 32
ko ~ o: 32
koto, VP (continuative aspect): 178
koto nō (VP, continuative aspect): 177–78
Krupa 1966: 122
kw: phonetic description and discussion, 357

L

l: phonetic description, 350

lā (VP, 'only'): 182
lai (VP, directional): 53–55
laivi (VP ,'utterly'), direction: 168
Lakovi (title of play): 367–69; 424
Latin, infinitive form: 24
length, as component of accent: 343
lī (VP, negation): 186
limitation, VP (*wale, bau, bulu*), 170–71; (*gā, lā*), 180–81; NP (*gā*), 231
limits (VP, *tekivū, tini*): 51–52
location 1, definition: 189
location 2, definition: 189
locative NP as comment: 217–18
locatives: 216–18
long vowel: simple, 337–38; complex (diphthong), 338–40
Lynch 1973: 307
Lyons 1966: 37n
Lyons 1968: 10n, 29, 99n, 201n, 218, 286, 286n, 306, 318, 319n
Lyth, Richard B.: on reduplication, 118

M

m, phonetic description: 350
ma- (stative prefix): 78–79
mada (VP, initiation): 179–80
mada gā (VP, 'just'): 182
mai (VP, motion toward): 52–53, 182–84; (NP), ablative vs. postverbal, 220; locative phrases, 216–17; *mai vei* vs. *ki vei*: 221
mani (VP, sequence): 46
mani, linking numerals: 327
marker (function word): 15, 16, 407; definition, 19–20, 407; reduplication of, 126–28
Martinet 1960: 332
Mateinaniu: 350
material/contents phrases: 215
me: 294–96; morphophonemic changes, 296
mē- (possessive prefix): 309–10
me phrases: 294–96
me vakā ('such as'): 296
meaning: 11

means or instrument: 214–15
measure: 6, 57n, 370–90; even, uneven, 371; formal types, 334, 371; relative stability, 379; table, 371–72
measures and morphemes: 386; relationship, 388–90; details of study, 388; summary of study, 390
mei (possessive): 317
metaphorical space or time phrases: 215
Methodist missionaries: 7
Milner 1966: 66
Milner 1971: 239n
Milner 1972 [1956]: 28n, 33, 35–36, 40n, 44, 67, 69, 76, 79, 81, 116n, 165, 166n, 174, 178, 199n, 208, 221n, 234, 243n, 246, 260, 261, 297n, 308, 309, 324, 327, 363, 388, 394; on *y*, 353; roots and markers, 23
Milner 1982: 122–23, 135
Milner 1985: 135
Milner 1986: 166n
miscellaneous verbs: 101–2
moderative, dubitative (*beka*): 230
Moore 1906: 113
morpheme classification: gray areas, 21–22; by form, 407; by function, 407–8; formal and functional classification, 407–8
morphemes: combining forms, 408–13; morphology: base+base, 410 – 11; base+particle, 409; base+ particle+base, 409–10; particle+ base, 408–9; particle+ base+ particle, 412–13; particle+particle, 411–12
motion: verbs: 98
mu: realization as [m:], 350, 361, 365

N

n, phonetic description: 350
na (common/definite article): 199–210; vs. *a*, 208-10; optional omission before possessives, 209
na (VP, future): 42
naica 'when?': 401

nē (VP, affirmation): 186
negation: marker, 186; with *ni* phrases, 289
negative (V prefix, *tawa-*): 76
nei (possessive): 318
Neyret, Fr J.: 432
ng: Tongan spelling, 7
Nguna: verbal prepositions, 22
ni (possessive): 311–17
ni: semantic narrowing, 311–12; word-building, 316–17
ni + subjects, table: 293
ni phrases: indicating cause, 290–91; intonation, 293–94; layering, 289, 312–14; meaning of, 291–92; morphophonemic changes, 292–93; nominalization, 315–16; outside attribution, 316; that modify, 289–92
nō (VP, continuative aspect): 178
nō- (possessive prefix): 310; morphophonemic changes, 310
nominalization: derived, 235–39; direct, 239–41
nominative (subject): 34–39
nominative absolute: Hale's view, 34–35
noun and NP classification: 191–94
noun modification: semantic range, 276–77; +*i* + stative of extent, 280; by active verb, 281; by *dau* + active verb, 282; by *i* + stative, 279; by nouns, 278, 284–85; by S2 + N, 280–81; by series of modifiers, 281; by stative, 279, 280; by verb or VP, 278–83; by VP, 282–83; formal types, 278
nouns, proper: see PROPER NOUNS
nouns: semantic and grammatical mismatches, 195; taking *na*, *o*, or both, 209–10
noun vs. verb: in part-of-speech classification: 23–26
NP: basic, definition, 195–96; semantic functions, 189; sentences, 16–17; primary: definition, 193; secondary: definition, 211; speci-

fying both the subject and the object, 256–57; specifying the object, 256
nucleus, vowel: 5
number: 28–29
numerals, forming: 327

O

o: phonetic description, 336
o, ko: in Bau-Rewa area, 32; optional in demonstratives, 245–46
o (proper article): 197–99
object: 15, 91, 163–65; definition, 250; 1st & 2nd person, proper noun, 164; 3rd person, 164; person-number markers & names, 163–64; table, 163; underlying *i* marker, 164–65
object specification: 256; with *ni*, 287–88
oe, rarity of vowel sequence: 345–46
offglide: 5; 338–41; 350–53
Old High Fijian: 165n
Oliver, Douglas: 431
one-syllable suffixes: effect on accent, 381
operations: 247–330; summary, 329–30
origin (VP, *tekivū*): 51
(o)qō: 242–46
(o)qori: 242–46
oti (VP, completive aspect): 169
(o)yā: 242–46; vs. *koyā*, 246

P

p: phonetic description, history, 353–54
palatalization: 8; 355
Palmer and Brown 2007: 323
Parke 1981: 166n
particle: definition, 407; Milner 1972 use in part-of-speech classification, 23n
partitive function of reduplication: 121
partitive noun, definition: 191; 304; modification, 279–80
part-of-speech classification: 19–20
passive: 95, 104–5, 308
passive prefixes (*ta-, ca-*, et al.): 112–14
past tense marker (*ā*): 41–42
Pawley 1972: 66, 261
Pawley 1973a: 36
Pawley 1973b: 200n
Pawley 1977: 428, 428n
Pawley 1986: 38; 428
person: 28–29; definition, 29
personal locatives: in NP+NP construction, 244–45; used as locative phrases, 242–43
personal names, types: 193
personal suffixes, table: 305
person-number forms: as subjects: 28–39; table: 28; objects: 163–65; table: 163
person-number markers: in possession, 307–8; reduplication of, 128; in secondary NPs, specifying NPs, 262–64
phonological hierarchy: five units of, table: 332; discussion: 332–35
phonological phrases: 334–35, 391–95; as contrastive units, 394–95; embedding, 417
phonological sentences: falling phrases, 401; phonetic details, 396–99; terminal phrases, 335n 401; hierarchical structure, 417–22; non-terminal phrases, 403–4; question words, 401; rising phrases, 401–3; S = two+ phrases, 417–22; series intonation, 404; vocatives, 403
phonological units: correlates to grammatical units, 332; hierarchy, 361
phrase order, intonational features: 17–18
phrase peaks: in normal phrase accent, 391–92; indicating contrast, 392–93
phrase terminals: 393–94
Pike 1947: 337

pitch: as component of accent, 344; in an accented syllable, 370
place names: 192–93; common nouns used to indicate location, 192–93
plural (in subjects and objects): 29
poetical suffixes (-*ri*, -*a*, -*ya*): 233
possession, 303–25; specification with NPs, 260–62; forms, 304–6; specification, effects of "translationese," 261; suffixes, 304; syntactic patterns, 305–6; possessive classifier prefixes, 304, 309–10; phrasal modifiers, 310–18; possessor and possessed, relationship: 306; table, 318; as nouns, 322–23; reduplication, 323; as gender, 324–25; semantic and formal mismatches, 322; semantics, 318–19; specification and variation, 323–24
potential (*rawa*): 169–70
predicate: 15
prefixes, samples: 21
prefixes that delete the actor: 107–10
pretense, aimlessness: function of reduplication, 119
primary NP, definition: 193–94
Priscillien 1950: 257
process verbs: 99
proper accusative NPs: 226
proper article (*o*): 197–98
proper noun: definition, 192–93; as part of VP, 197–99; special use, 199; as objects, 254–55
proper object marker (*i*): 198
proper pronouns: specifying subjects, 198–99, specifying objects, 199; table, 199
proximity VP marker (*vakarau*): 50–51
Pukui and Elbert 1986: 66

Q

q: reasons for choosing, 7; phonetic description, 6, 349
qai (VP, sequence): 45–46
qō: See *(o)qō*
qori: See *(o)qori*
questions (yes–no): 401–3
question words, intonation: 401
qw, phonetic description and discussion: 357

R

r, phonetic description: 349
rairai (VP, appearance): 55
Raiwalui 1954: 424
Rarotongan, in Buse 1963: 23n
rawa (VP, potential): 169–70
Ray 1910: 405n
readiness VP marker (*vakarau*): 50–51
realignment of measures, through vowel and diphthong shortening: 375–76
reason construction, definition: 189; 138–40
reciprocal (*vei-*): 67–69; spacial, distance, 70; types of verbs, 68–69; mutual (stative): kin terms, 69–70
reduplication: grammatical & semantic functions, 115, 116–22; misc. changes, 121–22; noun roots, 234; partial, with *vaka-*, *-tā-*, 119–20; restrictions, 123–24; to modify verbs, 120; providing contrasting forms, 111
referent: definition, 91, 250; human or non-human?, 30–31
reflexive: Hale's view, 35
repetition, frequency, or prolongation: functions of reduplication, 116
respect: forms of, 30; address, 174–75
resyllabification, definition: 340n.
-*ri* (poetical suffix): 233
root (content word): 16; definition, 19, 407
rui (VP, extreme): 50

S

s: phonetic description, 349; palatalization, 349;
S1 verbs: definition: 94; examples, 94; from S2 verbs, through reduplication, 121
S2 verbs: definition and examples, 95–96; used actively through reduplication, 117
sa- (stative prefix): 80
sā (VP, aspect): 42–43
saka (VP, respectful address): 174–75
sara (intensifier): VP, 172–73; NP, 230
sau- (continuing motion): VP, 80
Schütz 1963: 349, 353, 356
Schütz 1969: 22
Schütz 1972: 6n, 324
Schütz 1975: 22, 195n
Schütz 1976: 425
Schütz 1978b: 312, 348n, 354n, 382, 383
Schütz 1978c: 364
Schütz 1978d: 429n
Schütz 1983: 376–77
Schütz 1985b: 387n
Schütz 1987: 430–31
Schütz 1999: 338n
Schütz 2000: 339, 375
Schütz 2001: 386n
Schütz 2004: 312, 348n
Schütz 2010: 386n, 388, 390n, 424
Schütz and Nawadra 1972: 34n, 88, 113, 306n, 427
Scott 1948: 336, 340, 343, 344, 349, 351, 362, 373
se (VP, aspect): 43–44
sē ('or'): 298–300; morphophonemic changes, 301; phrases, question words in, 300–301
secondary NP, definition: 194
semantic attribution, types: 276–77
semantic changes through reduplication: 121–22
semantic terms in specification, 249–50

semivowel, incorrectness of term: 353n
sentence intonation: step vs. glide, 400–401
sentence modifiers: 328–29
sentence types, based on form: 14–17
sequence (*mani*, marked): 46; (*qai*, unmarked): 45
serial verb: 131–32
sh [š]: phonetic description and discussion, 358
shortening: complex long vowels (diphthongs), 374–75; simple long vowels, 373
shorter sentences: intonational segmentation, 399–400
/si/: phonetic manifestations, 349
Siegel 1987: 429n
signaled level of specificity, 252–53
singular number: 29
skills, verbs referring to: 101
sō: see *soti/sō*
sobu ('downward'): VP, 167
soti/sō (intensifier): VP, 172; NP, 229–30
space, phrases referring to: 212–14
speaker (1st person): 29
specification: 249–70; definition, 249; outside the VP, added NP (specified level), 255–62; in secondary NPs, 262–64 how many referents?, 264; multiple, 264–65; possessed forms: limitations, 260–61; discussion of possessed forms, 261–62; examples of different levels, 265–69; within the VP, 250–55; hierarchy, 251; levels, 252–54; summary, 269–70
specified level of specificity, 255–62
spoken-about (3rd person): 29
spoken-to (2nd person): 29
Spooner and Melville 1955:7
state of mind: verbs showing, 99–100
stative: definition, 12
stative prefix: *sa-*, 80; *lau-*, 77–78; *ma-*, 78–79

stative suffix (-C*a*): 80–81
stative to active: S2+-C-*a* to A2, 105–6; S2+modifier to A2, 106–7; S2+reduplication to A2, 106; *vei*+S2 to A2, 107; S1 to A2, 107
statives, distinctions among: 109–10
Stemberger 1984: 364
stress, component of accent: 343
stress vs. accent: 370
/su/: phonetic manifestations, 349
subjects: 15, 28–39, 91; definition, 16, 28, 250; traditional analysis, 34–36, 38; Churchward's view, 35; reanalysis, 36–38; present view, 38–39; changes in order of markers, 40–41; table, 28; morphological analysis, 32; morphophonemic changes, 32–33; phonological variation, 33–34; subject and object NP specification: ambiguity, 257–59; summary, 259–60; subject raising: specification with *ni* phrases, 286–87, 288–89
subordinate VP: 286; *ni* phrases that specify, 286–87
suffixes: examples, 21
syllable: constituents, 334; 360–66; integrated, 361–62; types, 360–61; shape, 5; phonetic, 362; phonological, 362–63; summary, 363–64
syllable nucleus: complex, 334; simple, 334
syllable structure: changes, 364–66
syllable system: sociolinguistic context, 366–69; changes: speech vs. writing, 367
syllable-final consonants: 365

T

t: phonetic description, palatalization, 347–48
-*tā*- (V, artificial, created): 79–80
tabu- (V prefix, negative): 77
tale (VP, iteration): 174

tale, tale gā, iteration: VP, 181; NP, 230
Tamata 1994: 342, 348, 349, 350, 377, 412, 430
Tamata 2007: 356
Tamata, A. and L. Thomas 2011: 367–69
tani (VP, direction, 'away, different'): 167–68
taucoko (inclusion, 'all'): VP, 171–72; NP, 229
tawa- (V prefix, negative): 76
tei (VP, iteration): 48
tekivū (VP, origin): 51
tense markers, past and future: 41–42
tension, as component of accent: 344
tentative VP marker (*bau*): 48–49
text analysis: definiteness, indefiniteness, & generality, 206–8
TFL (*The Fijian language*): 6n, 96, 323, 382, 386n, 406n, 423, 424, 427, 431, 432; reviews, 429–31
theme, definition: 249
third person (spoken-about): 29
Thomas, L., and A. Tamata 2011: 367–69
tiko (VP, continuative aspect): 175–76
/ti/, phonetic manifestations: 347–48
time, demonstratives used as time words: 243–44
time and space phrases: 213–14
tini (VP, completion): 51–52
Tippett 1953–54: 124n
toka (VP, continuative aspect): 176–77
Tongan *g, ng*: 7, 7n
Tongan influence on consonants: 353–56
Tongan *u*-: 350n
topic, definition: 10
transitive, close vs. remote: 191
transitivity, 133–62; formal manifestations (specificity): 251–52
trial number: 29
tū (VP, continuative aspect): 176

U

u: phonetic description, 336
uneven measures: 371, 381, 408–13
Urban Fijian: 357, 364, 367–68; generational differences: 367–68; related to control of English: 368

V

v: phonetic description, 349–50
vā- See *vaka*-
vaka-: causative, 57–62; frequentative, distributive, extensive, 62–63; discussion, 66; grammatical ambituity, 65–66; manner, time, 63–64; possessing, characterized by, 65; pretend, game, 65, 119–20; conditions for *vā*- alternate, 56
vakarau (VP, proximity): 50–51
valency: 85, 92, 97, 104
vata (VP, concomitant): 168–69
vei- (V prefix): reciprocal, mutual (active) 67–69; general, formalized V forms, 71–73; verbs of motion, 71–72
vei (NP, locative and directional): 220–21
vei- (N prefix, collective, distributive): 232–33
verb classification: active vs. stative, 85–86; criteria, 82; functional criterion, 86; problems, 86–90; semantic criteria, 85–86
verb modification: + stative, 271–75; derived (*vaka*-), 273–75; to modify noun, function of reduplication, 118
verbs: A1, 92–94; A2, 94–95; one-referent, 92–94; S1, 94; S2, 95–96; two-referent, 94–96
via- (desiderative V prefix): 74–76
viavia- (impression V prefix): 76
vocative (i_3), N marker: 226–27
voiced stops without prenasalization: 357–58
voli (V, continuative aspect): 178
vowel: short, 336–37; long, 337–40

vowel: English equivalents, 5; table, 4
vowel and diphthong shortening: 373–79; across phrase boundaries, 379–80; effects, 376–79; reducing number of measures, 376–77; reducing number of syllables, 376; reducing number of V syllables, 376
vowel assimilation: 342–45; in diphthongs, 344
vowel inventory, recent addition through borrowing: 346
vowel position as component of accent: 343–44
vowel sequences across morpheme boundaries, 341
VP markers, order change: 44
VP sentences: components, 16; definition, 15–16
/vu/, phonetic manifestations: 349–50
vuā: 222–23
VV (*Na ivolavosa vakaViti*), 22, 78, 96, 171, 226, 315n, 351, 352, 354, 355, 356, 357, 364, 365, 380n, 386, 424

W

w: phonetic description, 350; further details, 350–51; interpretation, 350–51
wale (VP, limitation): 170
wale gā (VP marker): 181–82; NP marker: 228–29
word, difficulty defining: 19

X

x: phonetic description and discussion, 356
xw: phonetic description and discussion, 356

Y

y: distribution and status, 351–53; interpretation, 351–53; phonetic description, 351

-*ya* (poetical suffix): 233
yā- (distributive counter): 50, 81
yani (VP marker, direction): 184–86

Z

z: phonetic description and history, 355

ʔ

ʔ: description and discussion, 356

Printed in Germany
by Amazon Distribution
GmbH, Leipzig